TABLE OF CONTENTS

INTRODUCTION

Welcome to sociology and welcome to this book. Sociology is about you and the society you live in. As such it is important and exciting. And it can also be fun. This book is full of entertaining and amusing cartoons illustrating key points. It is also full of interesting photographs and case studies reflecting issues of the day – Donald Trump laying down the law on how women should behave, a transgender community in India, and a little boy pushing a baby doll in a toy pram.

The book has been specially written for AQA sociology and contains a chapter on how to do well in the exam. But there's a lot more to sociology than passing exams. If we've done our job properly, sociology will open your eyes to all sorts of new ideas. It will help you to see the world and yourself from a variety of different perspectives. It will encourage you to question everything you're told and to criticise politicians of every political party. We hope you'll enjoy the book and do well in the exam.

How to use this book

The book contains a number of features to help you to understand and enjoy sociology and to develop your skills for examination success. They include the following.

Key terms and summary boxes

Each chapter is divided into parts and units. Each unit ends with a key terms box which defines the key terms used in the unit, and a summary box which recaps the main points covered in the unit. The summary boxes provide short and straightforward outlines. They are ideal for revision.

Key terms

Culture The learned, shared behaviour of members of society.

Norm A guide to appropriate behaviour for particular people in particular situations.

Value A belief that something is important and worthwhile, right or wrong.

Social solidarity Social unity, social cohesion, sticking together.

Status A position in society.

Role A set of norms which defines appropriate behaviour for a particular status.

Socialisation The process by which culture is learned.

Primary socialisation The earliest and probably the most important part of socialisation.

Instinct Behaviour directed by genes.

Social control The methods designed to ensure that members of society conform to approved ways of behaving.

Summary

1. Norms provide order in society. They make social life predictable and comprehensible.

2. Shared values produce social solidarity and social cohesion.

3. Statuses and roles define who a person is and orders their behaviour.

4. Socialisation is essential for individuals to learn the culture of their society.

Cartoons, photographs and activities

The book contains many specially drawn cartoons. Cartoons are fun. They are also important. They provide entertaining and memorable snapshots of key ideas. They can add clarity and understanding at a glance.

There are lots of carefully selected photographs in the book. Photographs bring the real world into sociology. They show the relevance of sociology to today's society.

Each cartoon and photograph is accompanied by an activity – one or more questions which ask you to think about and comment on the picture with reference to the preceding text. These activities give you the opportunity to apply what you've just learned.

Collins

HARALAMBOS & HOLBORN
AQA A-LEVEL SOCIOLOGY
Themes and Perspectives
YEAR 1 AND AS

Michael Haralambos
Martin Holborn
Pauline Wilson

Contributing authors:
Judith Copeland
thew Wilkin

William Collins' dream of knowledge for all began with the publication of his first book in 1819.

A self-educated mill worker, he not only enriched millions of lives, but also founded a flourishing publishing house. Today, staying true to this spirit, Collins books are packed with inspiration, innovation and practical expertise. They place you at the centre of a world of possibility and give you exactly what you need to explore it.

Collins. Freedom to teach.

Published by Collins

An imprint of HarperCollins*Publishers*
The News Building
1 London Bridge Street
London
SE1 9GF

Browse the complete Collins catalogue at
www.collins.co.uk

10 9 8 7 6 5 4 3 2 1

ISBN 978-0-00-824277-0

British Library Cataloguing in Publication Data

A catalogue record for this publication is available from the British Library.

Authors: Michael Haralambos, Martin Holborn and Pauline Wilson
Contributing authors: Judith Copeland and Matthew Wilkin
Commissioning editor: Cathy Martin
In-house project editor: Isabelle Sinclair
Development editor: Hetty Marx
Copyeditor: Lucy Hyde
Proofreader: Rosalind Horton
Text permissions researcher: Rachel Thorne
Image permissions researcher: Jane Taylor
Cover designer: Julie Martin
Cover photo: © weedezign/Shutterstock.com
Typesetter: Jouve India Private Limited
Production controller: Tina Paul
Printed and bound by: Grafica Veneta SpA in Italy

MIX
Paper from
responsible sources
FSC C007454

This book is produced from independently certified FSC paper to ensure responsible forest management.

For more information visit:
www.harpercollins.co.uk/green

In 2016 the government announced that all schools were to become academies by 2022. In the face of considerable opposition, they abandoned these plans.

What support do the Education Policy Institute's findings provide for this demonstration?

ONE OF THESE MEN WILL FILL MY QUOTA. I'LL CHOOSE THE FRIENDLY LOOKING ONE.

Selecting people for a quota sample.

With some reference to the picture, suggest why quota sampling is unlikely to produce a sample which is representative of the research population.

Contemporary issues

Contemporary issues are another type of activity. They ask you to apply sociological ideas to issues of the day. This shows the relevance of sociology to you and the society you live in. For example, do we live in a fair and just society? Is there equality of opportunity? Does everybody have an equal chance to succeed in the education system? These are fundamental questions which we hope will stay with you long after your A-level exams.

Contemporary issues: Recent rises in the birth rate

Short-term trends are not always in line with this longer-term trend. As noted earlier, birth rates have increased in recent years such that in 2010 the total fertility rate was the highest since 1973 (ONS, 2013). The Office for National Statistics attributed this to the following factors:

- A rise in the fertility rate among women in their 20s with more women currently in their 20s having children.
- Women born in the 1960s and 1970s who had postponed having children doing so in middle age (sometimes with the help of new reproductive technologies).

'Taking back control' of borders with respect to immigration from the EU was one of the important issues in the campaign.

Then and now

This is a feature which revisits ground-breaking sociological studies from the last fifty years. Usually written by the original authors, Then and now features assess the significance of these classic studies to today's society. They also give you an insight into how sociologists think and carry out their research.

Then and now: Paul Willis — *Learning to Labour* (1977)

"My Research Question has always been as much to do with the 'How' of it as with the 'Why' of it. Hence the subtitle of my book: *How Working-Class Kids get Working-Class Jobs*. When I did the research in the 1970s, there were many ideas about why working-class students so often 'failed' in education, ideas which were usually very insulting of them. But there were very few ideas concerning the 'how'. I wanted to fill this gap with a detailed account of their 'lived culture', the meanings they gave to the context in which they lived, how they came to accept a future of manual labour, how it seemed natural to them.

Exam practice

Each chapter ends with exam-practice questions for AS and A-level. In the final chapter, these questions are explored in detail with examiner guidance and sample answers at Grade A and Grade C.

ACKNOWLEDGEMENTS

With many thanks to the following sociologists for contributing a 'Then and now' feature:

› Professor Rebecca Dobash, University of Manchester
› Professor Russell Dobash, University of Manchester
› Professor Becky Francis, University College London
› Professor Valerie Hey, University of Sussex
› Professor Carol Smart, University of Manchester
› Professor Paul Willis, Beijing Normal University (retired).

Special thanks also to Matt Timson for the excellent cartoons.

With many thanks to the following sociology teachers for reviewing chapters of the book:

Wilhelmenia Etoga Ngono, Brighton, Hove and Sussex Sixth Form College, Brighton; Emily Painter, Cadbury Sixth Form College, Birmingham; Matthew Wilkin, Bellerby's College, Brighton; Zoe Parkinson, Preston College, Preston; Amy Scott, Newcastle Sixth Form College, Newcastle; Heather Green, Batley Girls' High School, Batley; Judith Copeland, Derby College, Derby; Sumita Gupta, The Barclay School, Stevenage; Chris Deakin, Banbury Academy, Banbury; Paul Sullivan, British School of Brussels, Belgium; Charlotte Belmore, Saint Benedict Catholic Voluntary Academy, Derby.

1 INTRODUCING SOCIOLOGY

Chapter contents

Sociology is the study of people in groups. Think of the groups you are a part of. You probably belong to a family and a friendship group. You are a member of an ethnic majority or an ethnic minority group. You are a member of a social class group and you belong to a national group. And you, and everybody else, are a member of global society.

Think how your membership of these groups has influenced your life. What has your family taught you? What have your friends done for you? How has your ethnicity affected your outlook on life? How has your social class shaped the way you behave? Has your nationality influenced your view of the world? And what effect might being a member of a global society have on your future?

Sociologists study all these groups and more. They ask how does group membership influence behaviour, shape experience, and construct a view of life?

This chapter introduces some of the main sociological theories which claim to explain how society works and how human beings behave.

PART 1 CULTURE AND SOCIETY

Different societies have different ways of living, different ways of behaving and different views of the way the world works – they have different cultures. A **society** consists of a group of people who share the same culture, who live in the same area and who feel part of that group.

This part looks at **culture** – the learned, shared behaviour of members of society. It asks: What is culture? How do we learn culture? How do we share it? How does culture shape our behaviour? How does culture influence our identity? These are fundamental questions. Without culture, human society would not exist.

Culture

Most of the time we take our culture for granted. We are not aware of how much of our behaviour is learned and how much of it is shared with other members of our society. The following picture illustrates these points.

Activity

It takes meetings such as this to reveal how much of our behaviour is shaped by culture and how much is taken for granted.

1. Why do the two men feel uncomfortable about their conversation?

2. How might this affect their relationship?

The picture shows a man from the USA with his back to the wall. He has retreated backwards down a hall 40 feet long. He is talking to a man from Brazil who has pursued him all the way down the hall. For the American man, the Brazilian comes too close to him for a normal conversation. And for the Brazilian man, the American is too far away. Each of them is trying to establish the normal conversation distance defined by their culture (Hall, 1973).

Culture, norms and values

Culture is the learned, shared behaviour of members of society which is passed on from generation to generation. It consists of ways of behaving which are seen as normal. It is the way of life of a particular society.

Norms are an important part of culture. A **norm** defines appropriate and acceptable behaviour for particular people in particular situations. For example, there are norms of dress which state the type of clothing appropriate for each gender (male and female), age group and social situation – for the workplace, party, wedding or funeral.

As part of culture, norms are learned and shared and vary from society to society. This can be seen clearly by comparing the traditional norms of eating amongst the Bedouin of North Africa with those in the West. The Bedouin, which translates as 'desert people', eat with the fingers of their right hand from a shared tray of food while sitting on the ground. People eat from the section of the tray directly in front of them. It is bad manners to lick your fingers then continue eating. Men and women eat separately. Men are served first.

Norms provide order in society. Imagine a situation in which 'anything goes'. The result is likely to be confusion and disorder. Norms help to make social life predictable and comprehensible. If there were no norms stating how people should express pleasure or irritation, warmth or hostility, it would be difficult to understand how others felt, to predict their behaviour and respond in appropriate ways.

Values are much less specific than norms. They are general guides for behaviour. A **value** is a belief that something is important and worthwhile. A value states what is right and wrong. Values are translated into behaviour by a range of norms. Take the value placed on human life in our society. It is reflected in a thousand and one aspects of normative behaviour

Activity

Bedouin men in Egypt

1. How might this example differ from Western norms of eating?

2. How might a man from Western society feel if he joined them for a meal?

from highway regulations, to ways of settling an argument, to rules for the preservation of food. In each case the norms are designed to protect human life.

Some sociologists see shared values as essential for the wellbeing of society. They argue that shared values produce **social solidarity** – the cohesion and unity necessary for society to run smoothly. Without shared values people would be pulling in different directions. The result might be disruption and conflict.

Like norms, values vary from society to society. This can be seen from a comparison of some of the traditional values of the Cheyenne, a Native American tribe who lived on the Great Plains of the USA, with the values of today's Western society.

The Cheyenne believe that wealth, in the form of horses and weapons, is not to be hoarded by the owner. Instead it is to be given away. Generosity is highly regarded and people who accumulate wealth and keep it for themselves are looked down upon. A person who gives does not expect an equal amount in return. The greatest gift they can receive is prestige and respect for their generous action.

Bravery on the battlefield is one of the main ways a man can achieve high standing in the eyes of the tribe. Killing an enemy, however, does not rank as highly as a number of other deeds. Touching or striking an enemy with the hand or a weapon, rescuing a wounded comrade, or charging the enemy alone while the rest of the war party looks on are amongst the highest deeds of bravery.

Status and role

Every society has a number of positions or **statuses** which people occupy. For instance, in Western society a person would usually have an occupational status, for example as a doctor or a bricklayer, and a family status, for example as a sister and/or a mother. Each status is accompanied by a **role** – a set of norms which outline appropriate and expected behaviour for a particular status.

Statuses and roles allow us to order our behaviour and predict the behaviour of others. For example, the statuses and roles of doctor and patient spell out their behaviour and direct their relationship.

Statuses and roles are culturally defined and vary from society to society. Take the example of gender statuses. In Western societies most people recognise only two gender statuses – male and female. Some other cultures identify three or more gender statuses. For example, some Native American tribes traditionally recognised a third gender – a 'two-spirit' person who is doubly blessed with the spirit of a man and a woman. The picture on page 4 shows We'wha, a two-spirited person from the Zuñi tribe of New Mexico (Williams, 1991).

Socialisation and social control

Socialisation is the process by which people learn the culture of their society. The most important part of this process probably takes place during a person's early years. Known as **primary socialisation** it usually takes place within the family. By responding to the approval and disapproval of family members and copying their example, the child learns the language and many of the basic behaviour patterns of their society.

Secondary socialisation is the socialisation received in later life. In **peer groups** – groups whose members share similar circumstances and are often the same age – children play games and learn that social life is based on rules and norms of behaviour. At school they learn lessons for life and more specialised aspects of culture such as maths and science (see the next chapter). The mass media and social media can provide role models and ways of communicating which continue into later life. And in their adult occupations young people soon learn the rules of the game and the tricks of the trade.

Without socialisation, an individual would bear little resemblance to a human being defined as normal by the standards of their society. This can be seen from the example of Ssabunnya who spent part of his early life with a troupe of colobus monkeys, as described in the activity on page 5.

3

Contemporary issues: How many genders?

In 2011, Australian passports changed to three gender options – male, female and indeterminate. According to the Australian government this was to remove discrimination against transgender people and intersex people – those born with a sexual anatomy which does not fit the standard definitions of male and female. This was an important step for travellers at airports who are questioned or detained because their appearance does not seem to fit their gender status. The option of a third gender follows similar decisions in Nepal, Pakistan and Bangladesh.

In 2014, the Hijras, India's transgender minority, finally achieved full legal recognition as a third gender. This means for the first time there are quotas of government jobs and college places for Hijras (*The Guardian*, 16.04.2014).

We'wha (1849–1896), a 'two-spirit' person

Members of the Hijra community in India.

In the UK Maria Miller, who chairs the Women and Equalities Committee, says that passports and driving licences should be gender neutral – they should not mention gender (*The Guardian*, 02.01.2016).

Questions

1. Should we legally recognise additional genders?

2. If so, why and how many more genders? If not, why not?

3. Two-spirit people were highly respected. Why do you think this was?

Culture and instinct

To what extent is the behaviour of living creatures directed by instinct and to what extent is it directed by learning?

The behaviour of some creatures is based on instinct – it is directed by their genes. Bees provide an example. The closer we get to human beings, the less important instincts are for directing behaviour and the more important learning becomes. For example,

studies of Japanese macaque monkeys show how they can learn brand new behaviours, for instance how to swim.

Sociologists see learned behaviour as the key to understanding human society. Culture – norms and values – is seen as directing human behaviour. And socialisation is seen as vital for learning culture. The importance of learned behaviour can be seen from the experience of John Ssabunnya outlined in the following activity.

Activity – An unusual socialisation

Walking through a Ugandan forest, a woman spotted a group of monkeys. To her astonishment, she realised that one member of the group was a small boy. Local villagers 'rescued' the boy and identified him as John Ssabunnya who had been abandoned as a two-year old.

For the past three years, John had lived with a troupe of colobus monkeys. He had learned to communicate with them – with chatters, shrieks, facial expressions and body language. He shared their diet of fruit, nuts and berries, he became skilled at climbing trees and, like those who adopted him, he walked on all fours. He was terrified of his 'rescuers' and fought to remain with his family of monkeys.

John was washed and clothed – much to his disgust – and taken to an orphanage. He gradually learned to behave like a human being. Slowly but surely, he began to sing, laugh, talk, play, dress and walk like children of his age.

Today, John is a member of the Pearl of Africa Choir which has successfully toured the United Kingdom.

John, aged 14.

Based on an article in BBC News online, 06.10.1999

Questions

1. How does the example of John Ssabunnya indicate that human behaviour is learned rather than based on instinct?

2. Culture is not fixed, it can and does change. How does John's experience support this statement?

Social control

Socialisation is closely linked to **social control** – the ways in which people's behaviour is kept in line with the norms and values of society. Every society has various methods for ensuring that its members conform with – act in terms of – the accepted and approved ways of behaving. For example, in many traditional hunting societies such as the Inuit, the hunter has a moral duty to share his kill with other members of the community. If he does not, he is ostracised – shunned by and cut off from the group. Without some form of social control, it is difficult to see how the socialisation process could be effective and how standardised and predicable behaviour could be maintained. And without such behaviour human society could not operate.

In every society the family is a major agency of social control. Children are born helpless – they are totally dependent on adults. This gives parents enormous power both to teach and enforce what they teach. They are able to apply a battery of positive and negative sanctions – rewards and punishments – to ensure conformity. These range from words and expressions of approval and disapproval through to physical violence.

In every area of social life there is a variety of mechanisms of social control – for example, the promise of promotion or the threat of dismissal in the workplace, and the encouraging smile or disapproving glance within a circle of friends. In many societies certain aspects of behaviour are defined as crimes. Officials are appointed to deal with such behaviour and apply punishment to those who have broken the law. However, most mechanisms of social control are much more subtle than the heavy hand of the law. For example, religion is a major instrument of social control in many societies. Religious beliefs often encourage people to conform to accepted ways of behaving. They may offer rewards such as an afterlife of everlasting happiness for those who follow the straight and narrow and punishments such as eternal damnation for those who do not.

5

Culture and identity

A society's culture provides individuals with a major part of their identity — it tells them who they are and where they've come from. Take this culture away and they are left in a vacuum, they are lost. In recent years, many Aboriginal Australians and Native Americans have attempted to recapture their traditional cultures, restore a sense of who they are and where they've come from, and to socialise their children to recognise their cultural heritage and identity. This looking back and moving forwards can be seen in the activity below.

Colonial powers sometimes attempt to destroy the cultures of those they conquer in the belief that this will produce willing and obedient citizens. Separating children from their parents, removing them from their way of life, banning them from using their language, from following their norms of dress, from practising their religion, and from performing their music are seen as ways of destroying existing identities and creating new ones.

Activity – Cultural identities

The Stolen Generations

Australia's Aboriginal people have the world's oldest living culture, a culture that has existed for at least 60,000 years. From the 19th century through to the 1970s, Australian governments have attempted to systematically eradicate Aboriginal culture.

From 1910 to 1970 some 20,000 to 50,000 Aboriginal children, depending on the estimate, were forcibly removed from their parents and placed in 'care homes', 'schools', missions or with White foster families. In many of these institutions their possessions were taken away, they were officially referred to by a number, forbidden to speak their own language and locked in at midnight. Those who broke the rules or tried to escape were severely punished – beaten or placed in solitary confinement. Boys were usually trained as agricultural labourers and girls as domestic servants. In order to make them into Australian 'citizens' they were cut off from their families, language, art, music, customs, ceremonies and their cultural identity.

And reports indicate that in the 21st century the numbers of Aboriginal children placed into 'care' by welfare officials is greater than for any similar time period in the 20th century.

Based on Human Rights and Equal Opportunities Commission, 1997; Pilger, 2014; Behrendt, 2016.

'Killing the Indian in him'

During the late 19th and first half of the 20th century, the United States government attempted to transform Native Americans into 'American citizens'. Part of this policy involved transporting children to White-run boarding schools often hundreds of miles from their homes. The intention, in the words of Captain Richard H. Pratt who founded the Carlisle Indian School in 1879, was to 'kill the Indian in him and save the man'.

At these schools, children were stripped of all outward appearances that linked them to their Native American past. Their clothing was taken away from them, their long hair was cut, and they were dressed in uniforms and Victorian costumes. They were banned from speaking their tribal languages. Their own people were depicted as 'evil', 'heathenish', and 'savage'. Most lost self-esteem and turned against, or came to doubt, their own identity. The memories of Sun Elk, a Taos Pueblo, were typical.

'We all wore White man's clothes and ate White man's food and went to White man's churches and spoke White man's talk. And so after a while we also began to say Indians were bad. We laughed at our own people and their blankets and cooking pots and sacred societies and dances.' Some tried to resist. Lone Wolf, a Blackfoot, describes his experiences.

'If we thought that the days were bad, the nights were much worse. This was the time when real loneliness set in. Many boys ran away but most of them were caught and brought back by the police. We were told never to talk Indian and if we were caught, we got a strapping with a leather belt.'

Based on Josephy Jr, 1984 and 1995.

Questions

1. Many people have condemned the Australian and American governments for the way they have treated the original populations. What are your views?

2. Why do you think the governments acted as they did?

Sioux Native American boys as they entered Carlisle Indian School in 1883.

The same boys three years later.

Key terms

Culture The learned, shared behaviour of members of society.

Norm A guide to appropriate behaviour for particular people in particular situations.

Value A belief that something is important and worthwhile, right or wrong.

Social solidarity Social unity, social cohesion, sticking together.

Status A position in society.

Role A set of norms which defines appropriate behaviour for a particular status.

Socialisation The process by which culture is learned.

Primary socialisation The earliest and probably the most important part of socialisation.

Secondary socialisation The socialisation received in later life.

Peer group A group in which members share similar circumstances.

Instinct Behaviour directed by genes.

Social control The methods designed to ensure that members of society conform to approved ways of behaving.

Summary

1. Norms provide order in society. They make social life predictable and comprehensible.

2. Shared values produce social solidarity and social cohesion.

3. Statuses and roles define who a person is and orders their behaviour.

4. Socialisation is essential for individuals to learn the culture of their society.

5. Social control encourages people to act in terms of society's norms and values.

6. Culture provides individuals with a sense of identity.

7

PART 2 SOCIAL GROUPS AND SOCIAL INEQUALITY

This chapter began by defining sociology as the study of people in social groups. This part looks briefly at three of the most important groups in Western society – social class, ethnic groups and gender groups. A theme running through sociological studies of these groups is inequality. For example, research has shown that the higher your social class position the more likely your chances of educational success, of obtaining a high status, well-paid job, and of living a long and healthy life.

Studies of the inequalities which divide social groups raise important questions. Do we live in a fair and just society? Should steps be taken to reduce social inequality?

Social class

Social class is a system of social inequality containing various levels in which people are grouped in terms of income and wealth, power and prestige. Occupation is often used as the main measure of people's class position. Table 1.1 shows the Office for National Statistics Socio-economic Classification (NS-SEC) developed from sociological classifications. It shows a five class version of the class system in the UK (Office for National Statistics, 2005).

Table 1.1 The NS-SEC class system

Class 1 Managerial and professional occupations – business executives, lawyers, doctors
Class 2 Intermediate occupations – clerical workers, secretaries
Class 3 Small employers and self-employed – shopkeepers, taxi drivers
Class 4 Lower supervisory and technical occupations – plumbers, train drivers
Class 5 Semi-routine and routine occupations – hairdressers, cleaners, labourers

Sociologists sometimes identify an 'upper class' which is not included in the Office for National Statistics classification. This is because it is very small – around 1 per cent of the population – and it is difficult to classify in terms occupation. For example, it includes the aristocracy who sometimes own vast areas of land and enormous amounts of property. For instance, the Duke of Northumberland owns over 100,000 acres of land and the Duke of Westminster's property and land was valued at £9 billion in 2016 (*Independent*, 12.08.2016).

Sociologists focus on the middle class and the working class. The middle class refers to class 1 and 2 and part of class 3 and the working class to the other part of class 3 plus classes 4 and 5.

Social class inequalities

The social class structure tends to shape people's experiences and influence their behaviour. The lower people are in the class system the more likely their experiences are to be negative. For example, the more likely they are to suffer from physical and mental illness, to live in sub-standard housing, to be a victim of crime, to be unemployed, to be unable to afford a holiday, to lack educational qualifications and to have a relatively short life expectancy. Here are some instances of class inequalities.

Income and wealth Income refers to money from wages, investments and rent, wealth refers to ownership of land, buildings, stocks and shares. In the financial year ending 2016, the average income of the richest fifth of UK households before taxes and benefits was £85,000. This was over 12 times greater than the poorest fifth who had an average income of £7,000 (Office for National Statistics, 10.01.2017). In terms of wealth, the top 1 per cent own about 20 per cent of household wealth, the top 5 per cent around 40 per cent and the top 10 per cent over 50 per cent (Institute for Fiscal Studies, 19.04.2016).

Life expectancy Figure 1 shows that life expectancy closely follows the social class gradient. Those in Class 1, professionals such as accountants and lawyers, can expect to live longer than those in Class 2 and so on down steadily to Class 5 which includes 'unskilled' workers such as labourers and cleaners.

Class 3 is divided into 3N skilled non-manual and 3M skilled manual.

Health As the figures on life expectancy suggest, the richer you are, the better your health is likely to be.

Figure 1.1: Life expectancy at birth for men and women by social class, 2002–2005 in England and Wales

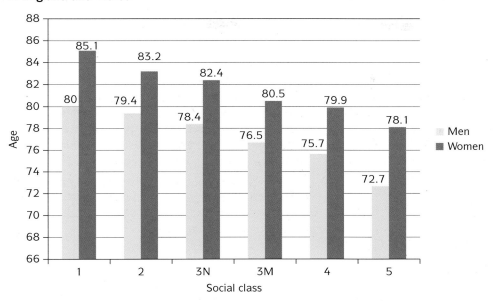

Source: Office for National Statistics

There is a social class gradient in health. The lower a person is in the class system, the more likely they are to suffer from a variety of illnesses and, as they grow older, the more rapidly their hand grip tends to weaken and their memory declines (Marmot, 2015).

Education As the following chapter shows, social class is the most significant factor affecting educational attainment. Performance at every level of the educational system reflects social class position. In Key Stage tests, GCSEs, A-levels, university entrance and degree level, the higher a person's class position, the more likely they are to do well.

Social class inequalities The distribution of many of the things which people value – a long and healthy life, a decent house and educational success – mirror the distribution of income and wealth and reflect the class system. Clearly class has a significant influence on people's lives, but it does not determine them. For example, many people from Class 5 go to university, but members of this class are least likely to do so.

Ethnic groups

An **ethnic group** is a group within society who are seen by themselves and/or by others as culturally distinct, as having their own **subculture** – certain distinctive norms and values – and who have a common origin. They often have their own group identity. They may see themselves as White, Chinese, Pakistani, and so on.

Membership of an ethnic group may influence people's lives. For example, in terms of educational attainment at GCSE, the top two ethnic groups are Chinese and Indian and the bottom two are White British and Black Caribbean. Possible reasons for these differences are examined in Chapter 2 Education.

Members of ethnic groups may experience negative discrimination and disadvantages due to their ethnicity. For example, a study by the Institute for Social & Economic Research shows that ethnic minority British graduates are at a disadvantage in the labour market (Zwysen and Longhi, 2016). Compared to White graduates they are significantly less likely to be employed six months after graduation. And students who are unemployed after graduation can expect to earn 20 per cent to 25 per cent less in later life than those who find jobs soon after leaving university.

Gender groups

Gender groups refer to female and male groups. There are significant differences between these two groups. For example, at every level of the educational system from GCSE to degree level, girls and women outperform boys and men. However, this success is not transferred to the job market. Women do not have equal access to higher level jobs and the gender pay gap in favour of men, though narrowing, still exists. It appears that part of this inequality in the job market is due to discrimination against women.

Gender, jobs and pay At the close of 2015, women made up only 29 per cent of British MPs, 25 per cent of all judges and less than 9 per cent of boardroom business executives. In 2014, only four women, Beyoncé, Taylor Swift, Pink and Rihanna made it into the top 20 in the music charts. Among the top 100 films of 2014, only 11.2 per cent of the writers and 18.9 per cent of the producers were women (*The Guardian*, 30.12.2015).

In 2016, women's average hourly wages were 18 per cent less than those of men, down from 23 per cent in 2003 and 28 per cent in 1993 (Allen, 2016). According to the World Economic Forum, more than a third of the **gender pay gap** is due to gender discrimination (Annese, 2016). In this respect, women are paid less simply because they are women.

Social groups and social inequality

This part has indicated the importance of social groups to the lives of their members. It has shown that each of the groups discussed above is divided by significant inequalities. Those who make up social classes, ethnic and gender groups are far from equal. This information is essential for judgements about what should be done to bring about a fair and just society.

Key terms

Social class A system of social inequality in which people are grouped in terms of income, wealth, power and prestige.

Subculture The distinctive norms and values of a group which shares many of the aspects of the mainstream culture.

Ethnic group A group who are seen by themselves and/or by others as having a distinctive subculture and who often have their own group identity.

Gender group A group composed of males or females.

Gender pay gap The gap in the average wage of men and women.

Summary

1. The higher a person's class position the more likely they are to have positive experiences.

2. Members of minority ethnic groups tend to experience negative discrimination and disadvantage.

3. Women do not have equal access to higher level jobs. Their average pay is below that of men.

PART 3 SOCIOLOGICAL THEORIES

This part provides a brief introduction to four sociological theories – functionalism, Marxism, symbolic interactionism, and feminism. A theory is a set of ideas which claims to explain something. A sociological theory claims to explain how society works.

Functionalism

Emile Durkheim The French sociologist Emile Durkheim (1858–1917), one of the founders of modern sociology, is often seen as the first functionalist. His main focus was an analysis of the **functions** of the various parts of society – that is the contribution the parts make to society as a whole.

Durkheim argued that the main function of society's parts is to provide 'the essential similarities which collective life demands'. These similarities provide the basis for cooperation, order and social unity.

They include shared moral beliefs and shared norms and values. Without these essential similarities self-interest would be 'the only ruling force' and each individual would find themselves 'in a state of war with every other'. To prevent this, Durkheim argues, 'society has to present in the individual' – society's morality, norms and values must be part of the individual's consciousness.

The major function of society's parts is to instil, to implant, these essential similarities. Thus, the family socialises children in terms of society's norms and values. And the education system continues this process. This provides a 'collective conscience' – shared moral beliefs – and shared norms and values which are necessary for cooperation and order.

Talcott Parsons Functionalism was developed by the American sociologist Talcott Parsons (1902–1979). Like Durkheim, Parsons began with the question of how social order was possible. His answer was **value consensus**, an agreement of members of society about values – what is desirable, worthwhile and worth striving for. Values define right and wrong, they support social norms, they provide the basis for social control. Value consensus is therefore essential for order in society.

Activity

1. How do parents teach norms and values?

2. How can religion reinforce value consensus?

A vital function of the parts of society is to transmit – pass on – and reinforce – back up – shared values. The family is therefore a vital social institution as it transmits value consensus to each generation. The education system performs a similar function. And, in Parsons' view, 'the values of society are rooted in religion'. Religious beliefs often reflect and reinforce society's values with the authority of supernatural power.

Functionalists see society as a system of interconnected parts. In Western society, these parts include the family and the educational, legal and political systems. Each part is seen to contribute to the maintenance and wellbeing of the social system as a whole.

Functionalism became the dominant theoretical perspective in sociology during the 1940s and 1950s, particularly in the USA. From the mid-1960s onwards its popularity steadily declined, due partly to damaging criticism, partly to competing theories which appeared to provide superior explanations, and partly to changes in fashion.

Marxism

Marxist theory became increasingly influential in sociology during the 1970s. Marxism takes its name from its founder, the German-born philosopher, economist and sociologist, Karl Marx (1818–1883). The following account is a simplified version of Marxist theory. It must also be seen as one interpretation of that theory. Marx's extensive writings have been variously interpreted and, since his death, several schools of Marxism have developed.

Ruling and subject classes Marxist theory begins with the simple observation that in order to survive, humans must produce food and material objects. In doing so, they enter into social relationships with other people – the **relations of production**. Production also includes a component known as the **means of production**. These are the things used in the production of goods and services. In today's society, they include raw materials, tools and machinery, factory and office buildings, land and mines.

Marx maintained that, with the possible exception of the societies of prehistory, the relations of production in all societies consisted of two main classes – a **ruling class** and a **subject class**. The ruling class own the means of production and the subject class produce the goods and services. Marx believed that the ruling class oppressed and exploited the subject class – they used the subject class for their own gain.

11

According to Marx, in industrial society the means of production are owned by a rich and powerful capitalist ruling class. The workers – the subject class – produce the goods but their wages are only a part of the value of those goods. Some of the value is taken away in the form of profits by the capitalist ruling class. Marx saw this as exploitation. Marx called the ruling class in capitalist society the bourgeoisie and the subject class the proletariat. (Capitalism is an economic system in which businesses are privately owned – by capitalists – and run, using wage labour, for the purpose of profit.)

Infrastructure and superstructure Taken together, the relations of production and the means of production form the economic base, the **infrastructure**, of society. Marx believed that the infrastructure largely shapes the rest of society, the **superstructure**. This means that the economic relationships between the ruling and subject class will be reflected in the superstructure. For example, the state will support the ruling class passing laws to legalise the private ownership of industry and the right of owners to take any profits which might be made. Other parts of the superstructure will also reinforce the position of the ruling class. The education system will produce the kind of workers that capitalism requires. And religion, which Marx called the opium of the people, will produce false happiness and delusions of pleasure. In doing so, it will ease the pain of exploitation and this will keep the subject class in their place.

Ruling class ideology As part of the superstructure, Marx saw the beliefs and values of society as justifying and reinforcing ruling class power. For Marx, ideology is a false view of reality. **Ruling class ideology** is a set of beliefs which present a false and distorted view of society. In doing so, it disguises the true nature of class society and conceals the exploitation on which it is based. In Marx's words, it produces a **false class consciousness** – a false picture of their class position.

The revolution Marx believed that the workers would eventually see society as it really was. They would overthrow capitalism and replace it with communism – an equal society in which the forces of production were communally owned (owned by all the people). Eventually, after communism replaced capitalism, there would be no need for the state. The state would 'wither away' and people would govern themselves.

Key terms

Theory A set of ideas which claims to explain something.

Function The contribution a part of society makes to society as a whole.

Value consensus An agreement about values.

Ruling class The class who own the forces of production.

Subject class The class who are exploited by the ruling class.

Relations of production The relationships people enter into to produce food and material objects.

Means of production The things used to produce goods and services, for example raw materials.

Infrastructure The economic base of society.

Superstructure The rest of society which is largely shaped by the infrastructure.

Ruling class ideology A set of beliefs which present a false picture of society and justify the position of the ruling class.

False class consciousness The false picture of class society which conceals the exploitation on which it is based.

Summary

1. Functionalism sees society as a system of interconnected parts.

2. The function of the parts is the contribution they make to the wellbeing of society.

3. Durkheim argues that their main function is to provide the 'essential similarities' needed for order and unity in society.

4. Talcott Parsons argues their main function is to provide value consensus.

5. Marx argues that societies are based on the exploitation by a ruling class of a subject class.

6. This exploitation is disguised by ruling class ideology.

7. Marx argues that the economic relationships in the infrastructure are reflected in the superstructure.

Symbolic interactionism

Functionalism and Marxism tend to look at society as a whole. Symbolic interactionism usually looks at small groups and the interaction between members of those groups.

Meanings

This section introduces **symbolic interactionism**, one of the sociological theories which focuses on the meanings people use to direct their actions. Meanings, in terms of this theory, refer to the way people see, interpret, define and make sense of the social world.

Symbolic interactionism asks how meanings are constructed and where they come. It looks at the way meanings direct action – for example, how people act towards others if they see them as friendly or hostile, happy or sad.

People and situations can be given many different meanings. Look at the picture of the bandaged figure. It illustrates some of the many ways that people can make sense of her or his situation. And the way they interpret the bandaged figure can affect the way they behave towards her or him.

Activity

'The invisible person'.

Suggest reasons why individuals might interpret the person's appearance in different ways.

The American philosopher George Herbert Mead (1863–1931) is one of the founders of symbolic interactionism. According to Mead, human beings interact – act with each other – in terms of meanings. Symbolic interactionists tend to focus on small-scale interaction situations rather than society as a whole.

Key ideas

Definition of the situation This refers to the meanings people give to situations. People define situations in particular ways and act in terms of their definitions. Picture the following situation. A man is lying on the pavement, apparently unconscious. On another occasion, the same man is in the same position with an empty whisky bottle beside him. Why might people respond differently to the two situations?

People respond in terms of the meanings they give to situations. In the first instance, they will probably see the man as ill, feel sympathetic, try to revive him and maybe call an ambulance. In the second situation, they may define him as drunk, show little or no sympathy, and walk on by. The two situations are likely to be defined differently. As a result, the response is likely to be different.

Role-taking involves putting yourself in the position of others and interpreting their actions. For instance, if you observe someone smiling, laughing, waving a hand or shaking a fist you put yourself in their place in order to interpret their meaning and intention. A similar gesture can be interpreted in different ways. For example, shaking a fist can be seen as indicating hostility or a bit of fun.

Self-concept and looking-glass self A person's self-concept is their view of themselves. Role-taking helps to develop a self-concept. It allows people to observe themselves from the standpoint of others. A person's picture of self comes in part from their perception of the way others see them. This is known as their looking-glass self. It's as though others are holding up a mirror to you.

Self-fulfilling prophecy A person's looking-glass self can produce a self-fulfilling prophecy – a prediction that comes to pass. They tend to act in terms of the way they believe others see them.

Performance According to the Canadian sociologist Erving Goffman (1922–1982) social interaction has many similarities with acting in a play. He sees social interaction as a series of 'theatrical

13

Activity

Seeing herself as others respond to her.

How might this thought result in a self-fulfilling prophecy?

---

performances' – we present ourselves to an audience in an attempt to give a believable performance, use suitable props, and adopt appropriate mannerisms. In these respects, we are like actors in a play.

Activity

The props of the courtroom.

1. What might the props in this picture 'say' to an audience?

2. What props might you use for a) an interview b) a party c) spectating at a Premier League football match?

Props are the clothes and objects used in stage performances. Goffman applies the term to social interaction in real life. Props can help to make a performance believable by setting a tone, giving an impression, and defining a situation. Clothing provides an example – for instance, uniforms immediately indicate the part a person is playing – as a nurse, police person, soldier and so on.

Impression management refers to creating and managing the impression of self given to others. For impression management to work requires an effective performance and appropriate props.

Symbolic interactionism looks at the meanings developed and applied in interaction situations. It focuses on small-scale interactions rather than society as a whole. It sees people constructing meaning rather than responding to the social system.

Feminism

In 1974, *The Sociology of Housework* by the British sociologist and feminist Ann Oakley was published. She saw women's traditional domestic roles as limiting and oppressive. Her male colleagues were puzzled that she chose to study something so 'insignificant' at a time when no self-respecting male sociologist would even consider studying housework. Despite some resistance and ridicule Oakley opened the door to feminism in sociology.

Feminists brought women into mainstream sociology. They catalogued the inequalities between women and men, provided explanations for them and suggested routes to equality. There are three main feminist perspectives in sociology – radical feminism, Marxist feminism and liberal feminism.

Radical feminism Radical feminists see society as based on **patriarchy** – male dominance, rule by men. They see male dominance extending to every part of society and culture – from the job market to the home, from beliefs and values to day-to-day behaviour. In order to end the subordination and oppression of women, every aspect of life must be questioned from, in Sylvia Walby's (1990) words, 'who does the housework, or who interrupts whom in conversation'. Radical feminists see sweeping and fundamental changes in society as essential to end patriarchy, to end in Elizabeth Stanko's words 'men's physical and sexual intimidation and violence' and to bring about a society based on gender equality.

Marxist feminism Where radical feminists blame men for women's oppression, Marxist feminists blame the capitalist system. They see women's labour as essential to capitalism. First, as mothers, women provide and socialise new generations of workers at no cost to the capitalists. Second, as housewives, they provide domestic services and support for male workers, again at no costs to capitalists. Third, they provide a reserve army of labour which can be called upon when needed by capitalist employers – for example, if there is a shortage of workers in a time of rapid economic expansion. Since women's work is seen as secondary to that of men, they can be paid less and channelled into and out of low-status and part-time work as required. Women's position is justified and reinforced by ideologies praising their role as a loving mother and a caring and selfless wife. Marxist feminists argue that the first and most important step to end women's exploitation and oppression is the destruction of the capitalist system.

Liberal feminism Liberal feminists demand equal rights for women. They believe that this can be largely achieved by laws providing equal opportunities and banning gender discrimination, and by changes in attitudes. In the UK, the Equal Pay Act (1970) and the Sex Discrimination Act (1975) went some way to meeting their demands. Liberal feminists look for reform to the existing system to produce gender equality unlike radical feminists and Marxist feminists who look for revolutionary change.

Contemporary issues: Donald Trump and women's rights

Reproductive rights

President Donald Trump has surrounded himself with men who are opposed to abortion. The picture shows him, with cabinet members and advisers in attendance, signing the Global Gag Rule on 23 January, 2017. This rule withdraws American government funding from any international organisation which even discusses abortion with women and girls overseas. Trump states he is 'totally against abortion' except in cases of rape, incest and when the mother's life is in danger. His vice-president, Mike Pence (on the left of the picture) vowed to consign the ruling which allows American women to have an abortion 'to the ash heap of history where it belongs' (quoted in Boland, 2017).

Trump has promised to repeal the Affordable Care Act, also known as Obamacare, which provides around $1.4 billion of contraceptive funding to American women each year. This would result in many women being unable to afford effective contraception (Boland, 2017; Fenton, 2017).

The Women's March

This was a worldwide protest by women (and some men) against Donald Trump's policies. Estimates place the number of demonstrators at 5 million globally and 500 000 for the Women's March on Washington. One of the main messages was 'Women's rights are human rights' which must be advanced and defended. This can be seen from the statements on placards and posters carried by the demonstrators:

- KEEP YOUR POLICIES OFF MY BODY
- ABORT PATRIARCHY, REPRODUCE DIGNITY
- KEEP ABORTION LEGAL
- WE WILL FIGHT TO PROTECT REPRODUCTIVE RIGHTS OUR MOTHERS WON
- TRUMP DEMEANS WOMEN
- MY BODY MY CHOICE
- GIRLS JUST WANT TO HAVE FUN-DAMENTAL RIGHTS
- DOWN WITH MISOGYNIST TRUMP

(Taken from pictures on Google Images.)

Questions

1. Trump is wealthy and male. Those who suffer most from his policies will be poor and female. Discuss.

2. Trump, his cabinet and his advisers are examples of patriarchy. Discuss.

Key terms

Symbolic interactionism A theory which argues that people interact in terms of meanings.

Definition of the situation Defining and giving meaning to situations.

Role-taking Putting yourself in the position of another person.

Self-concept A person's view of themselves.

Looking-glass self A person's perception of the way others see them.

Self-fulfilling prophecy A prediction that comes to pass simply because it has been made.

Performance The way people act in front of an audience.

Props The clothes and objects used in performances.

Impression management Managing the impression of self given to others.

Patriarchy Male dominance of society.

Summary

1. Theories focusing on meanings see human beings interpreting, defining and making sense of the social world.

2. Symbolic interactionism examines the meanings developed and applied in interaction situations.

3. Radical feminists see women's oppression based on patriarchy.

4. Marxist feminists see women's oppression based on capitalism.

5. Liberal feminists look to legal reforms within the existing system as the way to produce gender equality.

PART 4 VIEWS OF SOCIETY

This part looks at some of the ways sociologists have pictured the past 250 years. The term **modernity** has been used to describe this stage of the development of society. More recently, some sociologists argue that the West has entered a **postmodern era**, a period after modernity. Other sociologists refer to this period as **late modernity**, **second modernity** or **liquid modernity**, seeing it as an extension of the modern era.

Modernity

According to Lee and Newby (1983), modernity involved four major transformations of society:

1. **Industrialism** The industrial revolution which started in the late 18th century, transformed Britain, and later other societies, from mainly agricultural to mainly manufacturing economies.

2. **Capitalism** Closely connected with industrialism was the development of capitalism – privately owned businesses run for profit in a market economy employing wage labour. New classes emerged – a class of business owners and a working class of wage labourers.

3. **Urbanism** A large population movement from rural to urban areas accompanied the development of industry. In Britain in 1750, before the industrial revolution, only two cities had populations of over 50,000 – London and Edinburgh. By 1851, 29 British cities had a population of more than 50,000 with people increasingly concentrated in the centres of capitalist industry.

4. **Democracy** The overthrow of the monarchy in France by the revolution of 1789 and the American War of Independence (1775–1783) indicated that people were increasingly demanding a say in the way they were governed. This led to the development of political parties and democratic systems of government.

Modernity also involves a new ethos – new perspectives, new outlooks on life. These include beliefs in the possibility of human progress; in rational planning to achieve objectives; in the superiority of reason over emotion, faith and tradition; in the ability of technology and science to solve human problems and of industry to improve living standards; in the right and capability of humans to shape their own lives.

Postmodernity

Some sociologists believe that we have now entered a postmodern era which involves fundamental changes in outlook and circumstances. Here are some of the changes they suggest.

Loss of faith in science and technology People are losing faith in the ability of science and technology to solve problems. For example, they are increasingly aware of the damaging effects of pollution, the threat of global warming, the dangers of nuclear power and nuclear war. All point to science and technology gone wrong. They have become more sceptical of the benefits of rational thought and planning. For example, many people doubt whether rational bureaucratic organisations such as the National Health Service can meet human needs. And they have lost faith in politics and in grand theories which claim to provide answers to human problems. As a result, more people are turning to spirituality, alternative medicine and a variety of therapies.

A diversity of images and values Postmodern society is dominated by new information and communication technologies which bring the world into our homes and into our consciousness. Computer generated images, websites, social media, computer games, and terrestrial, satellite and cable TV bombard us with sounds, symbols and images from across the globe. They expose us to an increasingly diverse range of ideas and values, many of which have little connection with our present or past lives. This can cut us off from our past, make our present seem rootless and unstable, and our future unpredictable.

This myriad of diverse images and values is constantly changing. New lifestyles come and go, new styles of music and fashion and new types of foods and drink are regularly appearing. Everything appears fluid – nothing seems permanent and solid. The mainstream culture of modern society is replaced by the fleeting, unstable, fragmented culture of postmodern society.

Postmodern identities In modern societies, people's identities were usually drawn from their class, gender as male or female, occupation and ethnic group. In postmodern society, people have more opportunity to construct their own identities and more options to choose from. For example, a woman can be heterosexual, bisexual, lesbian or transgender, a business executive and a mother, she can be British, a Sikh and a member of Greenpeace.

With all the choices on offer, it is fairly easy for people to change their identities, or to have several identities which they put on and take off depending on their social situation. As a result, postmodern identities are more unstable and fragile. They offer choice, but they don't always provide a firm and lasting foundation.

Late modernity

Some sociologists reject the idea of a postmodern society. They argue that society has entered a later stage of modernity rather than a brand new era. The British sociologist Anthony Giddens (1991, 2009) takes this view, arguing that we are now living in **late modernity**.

Giddens sees late modernity as a 'world of rapid change'. It is like 'a juggernaut, a runaway engine of enormous power which we can drive to some extent but which also threatens to rush out of our control'. The ride can be exhilarating but never entirely secure as it is 'fraught with risk' and uncertainty. We recognise the risks of living in late modernity – financial crises, climate change, nuclear catastrophes. We question the trust we are expected to place in the agencies who deal with such matters, in people we don't know or never meet.

The second modernity

The German sociologist Ulrich Beck (1992, 2009, and with Elisabeth Beck-Gernsheim 2001) believes we have moved into a new phase of modernity. He calls this phase **second modernity**. It is characterised by risk, uncertainty and **individualisation**.

Risk and uncertainty characterise personal relationships and the job market. The job market is increasingly unstable with job changes, short-term contracts and retraining more frequent. And personal relationships are more fragile with rising divorce and separation rates.

Risk is magnified by the process of **globalisation** – the increasing interconnection of parts of the world. This can be seen from the global nature of financial crises, terrorism, nuclear accidents, depletion of fish stocks and deforestation, all of which cross national boundaries.

Beck and Beck-Gernsheim see individualisation as a key characteristic of the second modernity. In their words, 'Individualisation is becoming the social structure of second modern society itself'. People

17

are increasingly seeing themselves as individuals rather than members of social groups. This reduces the control of traditional roles and social structures over their behaviour. As a result, people have greater freedom to select and construct their own identities and design their own lifestyles. For example, they have greater freedom to choose and design their relationships – to marry, to cohabit, to divorce, to live in a heterosexual or a gay or lesbian relationship, and so on.

Activity

How does this person reflect risk, uncertainty and individualisation?

Liquid modernity

Born in Poland, Zygmunt Bauman (1925–2017) was Professor of Sociology at the Universities of Leeds and Warsaw. He calls the latest stage of modernism **liquid modernity**. It is fluid, flowing and flexible. 'Change is *the only* permanence and uncertainty *the only* certainty' (Bauman, 2012).

Modern society has moved from 'solid' to 'liquid'. Change is constant. In Bauman's (2007) words, 'social forms … decompose and melt faster than the time it takes to cast them'. As a result, uncertainty is constant. This generates anxiety, insecurity and fear.

Like other social commentators, Zygmunt Bauman sees individualisation as central to 21st century Western society. He sees the bonds between couples in liquid modernity as fragile. There is a conflict between the desire for individual freedom and the need for security. This means that the bonds have to be 'loosely tied, so that they can be untied again, with little delay' should relationships prove unsatisfactory. The result is 'semi-detached couples' in 'top pocket relationships' – people can pull their partner out of their pocket when required. 'Liquid love' is frail, insecure and often temporary.

Individualisation is a mixed blessing. It gives freedom to create identities. But it can place blame for failure on individuals. Especially for the poor and powerless, the loss of a job or a partner can result in self-blame and 'broken, loveless and prospectless lives' (Bauman, 2012).

Activity

How can individualisation and 'liquid love' add to the uncertainty and insecurity of liquid modern society?

Activity – What use is sociology?

The sociological imagination

The American sociologist C. Wright Mills (1916–1962) coined the term 'the sociological imagination'. He defined it as 'the vivid awareness of the relationship between personal experience and the wider society'. It is the ability to connect 'personal troubles to public issues'.

Mills gives the example of unemployment to illustrate the connection between the personal and the public, between the individual and the wider society. If only a small number of people are unemployed then their personal troubles probably lie in 'their character, their skills and their immediate opportunities'. However, if 10 per cent of the workforce is unemployed, then personal troubles are also public issues and we must look to 'the economic and political institutions of society' for their solution.

Think of the personal problems associated with living in poverty, the experience of racism, and life with a physical disability. Assuming these problems are widespread, how can they be reduced? For Mills, the solution lies in applying the sociological imagination, seeing personal problems as public issues and making changes to the wider society – for example, reducing inequality, passing laws against racism and improving facilities for disabled people.

For Mills, 'It is the political task of the social scientist – as of any liberal educator – continually to translate personal troubles into public issues, and public issues into the terms of their human meaning… It is his task to display this kind of sociological imagination.'

(Source: C. Wright Mills, *The sociological imagination, 1959*)

Questions

1. According to C. Wright Mills, what is the 'political task of the social scientist'?

2. Apart from the examples mentioned above, suggest other personal troubles which are also public issues.

3. The AQA Sociology course focuses on topics such as Education and Family, things that you have some experience of. How might this help you to develop your sociological imagination?

Key terms

Modernity A term often used to describe the period from the industrial revolution to the present day.

Postmodern A term used by some sociologists for what they see as a new period after modernity, from the late 20th century onwards.

Late modernity, second modernity, liquid modernity Terms used by sociologists to describe the period from the late 20th century onwards which they see as a late phase of the modern era.

Individualisation An increasing emphasis on the individual rather than the group.

Globalisation The increasing interconnection of parts of the world.

Summary

1. Modernity involves industrialism, capitalism, urbanism and democracy.

2. Postmodernism involves a lack of faith in science and technology and a diversity of values and identities.

3. Late modernity involves rapid change, risk and uncertainty.

4. The second modernity is characterised by risk, uncertainty and individualisation.

5. Liquid modernity involves constant change which generates anxiety, insecurity and fear.

2 EDUCATION

Chapter contents

You've spent most of your life at school. Some sociologists would see this as a worthwhile experience. You've learned to read and write and you're now doing academic subjects at A-level. And you are preparing for life in the wider society.

Other sociologists take a more negative view. They see education as benefiting the rich and powerful rather than all members of society. They see education as preparing you to accept life in an unequal society. And they say you are largely unaware of what education is doing to you and the rest of society.

This chapter looks at the positive and negative views of education and assesses the evidence for and against these positions. It moves on to government education policies which have shaped your experience at school. Why are you tested and examined over and over again? Why is the government so keen on every school becoming an academy? Why are they pouring money – our money – into free schools?

A main focus of this chapter is social class, ethnicity and gender. Why do those at the top of the class system tend to get the best exam results and go to the highest ranking universities? Why do different ethnic groups have different levels of educational attainment? And why are girls outperforming boys at every level of the educational system?

What goes on in schools and classrooms forms another focus of this chapter. What are the pros and cons of placing many of you into sets for different subjects? How might the friendship groups you belong to affect your exam results and your education in general?

Finally, what should education be about? Passing exams? Assessing ability? Learning skills? Thinking critically? Dealing with global issues such as human rights, global warming and widening inequality? Answers to these and other important questions are suggested throughout this chapter.

PART 1 EDUCATION AND SOCIETY

Contents

This part looks at the role of education in society. It asks does education contribute to the wellbeing of society as a whole? Or does it mainly serve the interests of the rich and powerful? Does the education system provide equality of opportunity for all members of society? Or does it favour those at the top of the class system?

This part also looks at education in global society. Is there a global system of education? Do countries across the world have similar ideas about the purpose of education? Are organisations developing to meet global educational requirements?

Next, the question of a possible business takeover of education is raised. Private companies are increasingly servicing a global educational market. And countries across the world are seeing education as the key to success in a fiercely competitive global market. Will education simply become a means to economic ends?

This part closes with a look at two perspectives which have influenced the development of education – social democracy and neoliberalism. Neoliberalism/new right with its emphasis on competition, the market and economic growth, is steadily becoming the driving force in global education. But should there be more to education than servicing the economy?

2.1.1 Functionalist perspectives

The sociological theory of functionalism was introduced and evaluated in Chapter 1. Here is a brief recap. Functionalists see society as a system made up of interrelated parts. The parts work together to maintain society as a whole. The job of the sociologist is to examine the function of each part – that is, how it contributes to the maintenance of the social system.

Functionalists argue that certain things are essential for the maintenance of society. These include a shared culture, in particular shared norms – accepted ways of behaving – and shared values – beliefs about what is right and desirable. Given the importance they attach to these factors, functionalists focus on how the parts of society contribute to the production of shared norms and values.

Two related questions have guided functionalist research into education:

▶ What are the functions of education for society as a whole?

▶ What are the functional relationships between education and other parts of the social system?

As with functionalist analysis in general, the functionalist view of education tends to focus on the positive contributions education makes to the maintenance of the social system. This unit looks at three of the main functionalist theories of education.

Emile Durkheim – education and social solidarity

The French sociologist Emile Durkheim (1858–1917) saw the major function of education as the transmission, the passing on, of society's norms and values. He maintained:

> *Society can survive only if there exists among its members a sufficient degree of homogeneity (sameness). Education perpetuates and reinforces this homogeneity by fixing in the child from the beginning the essential similarities which collective life demands.*   Durkheim, 1961

Without these 'essential similarities', cooperation, social unity, and therefore social life itself would be impossible. A vital task for all societies is the welding of a mass of individuals into a united whole – in other words, the creation of **social solidarity**. This involves a commitment to society, a sense of belonging, and a feeling that the social unit is more important than the individual. Durkheim (1961) argued: 'To become attached to society, the child must feel in it something that is real, alive and powerful, which dominates the person and to which he also owes the best part of himself.'

Activity

School children take the Pledge of Allegiance to the American flag. The USA has ge degree by immigrants. Education has helped to provide a common language, shared values and a national identity.

How might this picture illustrate Durkheim's view that schools develop social solidarity?

Education, and in particular the teaching of history, provides this link between the individual and society. If the history of their society is brought alive to children, they will come to see that they are part of something larger than themselves: they will develop a sense of commitment to the social group.

Education and social rules

Durkheim saw the school as society in miniature, a model of the social system. In school, the child must interact with other members of the school community in terms of a fixed set of rules. This experience prepares them for interacting with members of society as a whole in terms of society's rules.

Durkheim stated:

It is by respecting the school rules that the child learns to respect rules in general, that he develops the habit of self-control and restraint simply because he should control and restrain himself. It is a first initiation into the austerity of duty. Serious life has now begun. Durkheim, 1961

Education and the division of labour

Durkheim argued that education teaches the skills needed for future occupations. Industrial society has a **specialised division of labour** – people have specialised jobs which require specific skills and knowledge. For example, the skills and knowledge required by plumbers, electricians, teachers

and doctors are very different. In preindustrial societies there were fewer specialised occupations. Occupational skills were often passed from parents to children. According to Durkheim, the specialised division of labour in industrial societies relies increasingly on the educational system to provide the skills and knowledge required by the workforce.

Evaluation of Durkheim

Durkheim provided the basis for functionalist views of education. However, there are a number of criticisms of his work:

1. Durkheim assumes societies have a shared culture that can be passed on by the education system. Some sociologists now see countries such as Britain as multicultural – as having a variety of cultures. As a result, there is not a single culture for schools to pass on. However, it can be argued that in a multicultural society *some* shared norms and values are essential for society to hold together – for example, a common language and a shared belief in tolerance and freedom of speech.

2. Marxists argue that the education system serves the interests of the ruling class rather than of society as a whole (see pp. 26–34).

3. Some researchers argue that schools emphasise individual competition through the exam system, rather than encouraging working together, cooperation and social solidarity (Hargreaves, 1982).

4. Despite these criticisms, Durkheim laid the foundation for functionalist theories of education.

Talcott Parsons – education and universalistic values

The American sociologist Talcott Parsons (1951) outlined what has become the main functionalist view of education. Parsons argued that, after **primary socialisation** within the family, the school takes over as the main socialising agency. It acts as a bridge between the family and society as a whole, preparing children for their adult role. This is known as **secondary socialisation**.

Within the family, the child is judged and treated largely in terms of **particularistic** standards. Parents treat the child as their particular child rather than judging them in terms of standards or yardsticks that can be applied to every individual. For example, my daughter has her own particular sense of humour. However, in the wider society the individual is treated and judged in terms of **universalistic** standards, which are applied to all members, regardless of their kinship ties.

Within the family, the child's status is **ascribed,** it is fixed at birth. For example, she is a daughter and, in some cases, a sister. However, in advanced industrial society, status in adult life is largely **achieved** – for example, individuals achieve their occupational status. Thus the child must move from the particularistic standards and ascribed status of the family to the universalistic standards and achieved status of adult society.

The school prepares young people for this transition. It establishes universalistic standards in terms of which all students achieve their status. Their conduct is assessed against the yardstick of the school rules; their achievement is measured by performance in examinations. The same standards are applied to all students regardless of ascribed characteristics such as gender, ethnicity or class of origin. Schools operate on **meritocratic** principles: status is achieved on the basis of merit – ability and motivation.

Like Durkheim, Parsons argued that the school represents society in miniature. Modern industrial society is increasingly based on achievement rather than ascription, on universalistic rather than particularistic standards, on meritocratic principles that apply to all its members. By reflecting the operation of society as a whole, the school prepares young people for their adult roles.

Activity

Taking exams.

How does this picture illustrate 1) achievement as individuals and 2) judgement by universalistic standards?

Education and value consensus

As part of the process of secondary socialisation, schools socialise young people into the basic values of society. Parsons, like many functionalists, maintained that **value consensus** – an agreement about the main values – is essential for society to operate effectively. According to Parsons, schools in American society instil two major values:

1. The value of achievement.
2. The value of equality of opportunity.

By encouraging students to strive for high levels of academic attainment, and by rewarding those who succeed, schools develop the value of achievement. By placing individuals in the same situation in the classroom and so allowing them to compete on equal terms in examinations, schools develop the value of equality of opportunity.

These values have important functions in society as a whole. Advanced industrial society requires a highly motivated, achievement-orientated workforce. This necessitates differential reward for differential achievement, a principle that has been established in schools. Both the winners (the high achievers) and the losers (the low achievers) will see the system as just and fair, since their status or position is achieved in a situation where all have an equal chance. Again, the principles of the school mirror those that operate in the wider society.

Education and selection

Finally, Parsons saw the educational system as an important mechanism for the selection of individuals for their future role in society. In his words, it 'functions to allocate these human resources within the role-structure of adult society'. Thus schools, by testing and evaluating students, match their talents, skills and capacities to the jobs for which they are best suited. The school is therefore seen as the major mechanism for **role allocation**.

Evaluation of Parsons

Like Durkheim, Parsons fails to give adequate consideration to the possibility that the values transmitted by the educational system may be those which benefit a ruling minority rather than society as a whole. His view that schools operate on meritocratic principles is open to question – a point that will be examined in detail in later sections.

Support for Parsons comes from the view that the increasing cultural diversity and difference in today's societies requires the transmission of at least some shared norms and values. And in this respect schools have an important role to play (Green, 1997).

Contemporary issues: Shared values

Religion and schools – the UK and France

In the UK, the government funds faith schools – schools which are linked to one particular religion. Faith schools are free to teach their own religion in religious studies lessons. In 2015, there were 6,817 state-funded faith schools in England – 37 per cent of primary schools and 19 per cent of secondary schools. Most were either Church of England or Roman Catholic. In 2014 in England, there were 47 Jewish, 23 Muslim, 10 Sikh and 4 Hindu schools (Long and Bolton, 2015).

In France, the teaching of religion in state-funded schools is banned, as is the wearing of 'conspicuous religious symbols' such as Christian crosses, Muslim headscarves, Sikh turbans and Jewish caps. According to the French education minister, pupils must be 'protected from all forms of religious proselytising' (attempts to convert them) that might prevent their freedom of thought.

Shared values in the UK and France

In recent years there has been a growing concern in some societies about what some see as a decline in shared values. They see an increasingly multicultural society in which cultural differences are replacing shared values. This concern can be seen in the UK and France where there are growing demands for schools to promote national values. In an article in the *Mail on Sunday* (15 June, 2014) the then prime minister David Cameron stated that 'British values should be promoted in every school and to every child in our country'.

In France, partly in response to terrorist attacks in Paris, the education minister Najat Vallaud-Belkacem met teaching unions, parents and students to find the best way of re-establishing shared values. In particular, she was concerned with promoting in schools what she saw as the French values of democracy and coexistence (freedom and living together peacefully). Her hope was to unite what appeared to be an increasingly divided society (Grey, 2015).

Questions

1. What effect might a variety of faith schools have on shared values and social solidarity?

2. Can education successfully promote shared values in a multicultural society?

A Roman Catholic school.

An Islamic school.

Kingsley Davis and Wilbert E. Moore — education and role allocation

Like Parsons, Davis and Moore (1967, first published 1945) saw education as a means of role allocation, but they linked the educational system more directly with the system of **social stratification** – in Western society, the class system. Davis and Moore see social stratification as a mechanism for ensuring that the most talented and able members of society are allocated to those positions that are functionally most important for society. High rewards, which act as incentives, are attached to those positions. This means, in theory, that everybody will compete for them and the most talented will win through.

The education system is an important part of this process. In Davis's words, it is the 'proving ground for ability and hence the selective agency for placing people in different statuses according to their capacities'. Thus the education system sifts, sorts and grades individuals in terms of their talents and abilities. It rewards the most talented with high qualifications, which in turn provide entry to those occupations that are functionally most important to society.

Evaluation of Davis and Moore

There are a number of criticisms of Davis and Moore's theory:

1. The relationship between academic credentials and occupational reward is not particularly close. For example, income is only weakly linked to educational attainment.

2. There is considerable doubt about the claim that the educational system grades people in terms of ability. In particular, it has been argued that intelligence has little effect upon educational attainment.

3. There is widespread evidence to suggest that social stratification largely prevents the educational system from efficiently grading individuals in terms of ability.

These points will be considered throughout the rest of the chapter.

Key terms

Social solidarity Social unity.

Primary socialisation Socialisation in the early years, usually in the family.

Secondary socialisation The next stage of socialisation in later years, mainly in school.

Specialised division of labour A labour force with a large number of specialised occupations.

Ascribed status Status or position in society fixed by birth.

Achieved status Status or position in society based on achievement.

Meritocracy A system in which a person's position is based on merit – for example, talent and hard work.

Particularistic standards Standards which apply to particular people.

Universalistic standards Standards which apply to everybody.

Value consensus An agreement about the main values of society.

Equality of opportunity A system in which every person has an equal chance of success.

Role allocation A system of allocating people to roles which best suit their aptitudes and capabilities.

Social stratification A system of social inequality such as the class system.

Summary

1. Emile Durkheim argues that education:

   » transmits society's norms and values and creates 'essential similarities'

   » produces social solidarity

   » prepares young people to act in terms of society's rules

   » teaches the skills and knowledge needed for occupational roles.

2. Talcott Parsons states that schools socialise young people for adult roles by:

   » judging them in terms of universalistic rather than particularistic standards

   » transmitting society's values and creating value consensus

   » developing an achievement-oriented workforce

   » allocating young people to positions in adult society for which they are best suited.

3. Davis and Moore argue that education works with the stratification system to grade and select young people so that the most able are allocated to the most important jobs in society.

4. Functionalist theories have been criticised for assuming that education always makes positive contributions to society as a whole and that it benefits all members of society.

2.1.2 Marxist perspectives

This unit begins with three Marxist theories of the role of education in society. There are several varieties of Marxist theory. They largely share the following ideas which are outlined in more detail in Chapter 1.

In capitalist industrial society there are two main social classes – the ruling class (the bourgeoisie) and the subject class (the proletariat). The powerful ruling class own the means of production – the factories and the raw materials – and the capital (money) to invest in the production of goods and services. The relatively powerless subject class produce the goods and services and sell their labour in return for wages. However, the value of their wages is considerably less than the profits taken by the ruling capitalists. In this respect, the subject class are exploited.

The economic base of society – the infrastructure – largely shapes the rest of society – the superstructure. The economic relationships between the two classes, the relations of production, are reflected in the superstructure which represents the interests of the ruling class. Beliefs and values form a **ruling class ideology** which produces a **false class consciousness** – a distorted and false picture of society which blinds the subject class to their exploitation and justifies and legitimates (makes right and legal) the position of the ruling class.

Louis Althusser – the reproduction of labour power

Louis Althusser (1972), a French philosopher, presents a general framework for the analysis of education from a Marxist perspective. As a part of the superstructure, the educational system is ultimately shaped by the infrastructure. It will therefore reflect the relations of production and serve the interests of the capitalist ruling class. For the ruling class to survive and prosper, the 'reproduction of labour power is essential'. Generations of workers must be reproduced to create the profits on which capitalism depends.

Althusser argues that the reproduction of labour power involves two processes. First, the reproduction of the skills necessary for an efficient labour force. Second, the reproduction of ruling class ideology and the socialisation of workers in terms of it. These processes combine to reproduce a technically efficient and submissive and obedient workforce. The role of education in capitalist society is the reproduction of such a workforce.

Althusser argues that no class can hold power for any length of time simply by the use of force. Ideological control provides a far more efficient means of maintaining ruling class power. If members of the subject class accept their position as normal, natural and inevitable, and fail to realise the true nature of their situation, then they will be unlikely to challenge ruling class dominance. Physical force is an inefficient means of control compared to winning over hearts and minds. The maintenance of class rule largely depends on the reproduction of ruling class ideology. Thus Althusser argues that 'the reproduction of labour power requires not only a reproduction of its skills, but also, at the same time, a reproduction of its submission to the ruling ideology'.

The subject class is kept in its place by a number of **Ideological State Apparatuses** which include the mass media, the law, religion and education. Ideological State Apparatuses transmit ruling class ideology which creates a false class consciousness – a false and distorted picture which makes society seem reasonable and which disguises the exploitation of the subject class and justifies the position of the ruling class. In pre-capitalist society Althusser sees the church as the main Ideological State Apparatus. In capitalist society it has largely been replaced by the educational system.

Althusser identifies another means of keeping the subject class in its place. He calls it the **Repressive State Apparatus**. It includes the army, the police and the prison system, which are ultimately based on force. However, he sees it as much more obvious and far less effective than the Ideological State Apparatuses.

Evaluation of Althusser

As Althusser himself admits, he has presented only a very general framework for an analysis of education in capitalist society. He provides very little evidence to support his views. Althusser has been criticised

Activity

An early picture of capitalist society from a Marxist viewpoint.

1. Identify an Ideological State Apparatus and a Repressive State Apparatus in this picture.

2. From a Marxist point of view, how might religion 'fool you' and keep you in your place?

for picturing members of society as 'cultural dopes', passively accepting their position in society and failing to question the dominant ideology. There is no indication of any opposition to the ruling class and 'no sense of the politics of ideological struggle' (Elliott, 2009).

Samuel Bowles and Herbert Gintis – *Schooling in Capitalist America*

Like Althusser, the Marxist economists Bowles and Gintis (1976) see the role of education in capitalist society as the reproduction of labour power. The education system does this by 'the forms of consciousness, interpersonal behaviour and personality it fosters and reinforces in students'. This is a **hidden curriculum**, a curriculum apart from the actual subjects taught, a curriculum that students and teachers are largely unaware of.

Bowles and Gintis's theory is known as a **correspondence theory**. They see 'a close correspondence between the social relationships in the workplace and the social relationships of the education system'. This correspondence produces the hardworking, obedient and motivated workforce required by capitalism. It does this in the following ways.

Submission to authority

In a study based on a sample of 237 members of the senior year in a New York high school, Bowles, Gintis and Meyer examined the relationship between grades and personality traits. They found that low grades are related to creativity, aggressiveness and independence and conclude that such traits are penalised by the school. They found a number of characteristics which they argue indicate 'subordinacy and discipline' associated with high grades and conclude that such characteristics are rewarded by the school. These characteristics include perseverance, consistency, dependability and punctuality. By encouraging certain personality characteristics and discouraging others, schools help to produce the obedient and subservient workers capitalism requires.

Schools are organised on a hierarchical principle of authority and control. Teachers give orders, students obey. Students have little control over the subjects they study or how they study them. This prepares them for relationships within the workplace where they will be required to accept the authority of supervisors and managers. Bowles and Gintis argue that social relationships in schools mirror 'the hierarchical division of labour in the workplace'.

External rewards

Because students have little control over their work, they get little direct (intrinsic) satisfaction from it. They have little opportunity to express themselves and find self-fulfilment at school. They are motivated by external (extrinsic) rewards – the possibility of examination success and the promise of employment it offers.

Responding to external rewards is mirrored in the world of work. Workers are motivated by wages rather than work itself. Lack of personal involvement and fulfilment in school reflects **alienation** from work in later life – a feeling of being cut off from and unable to find satisfaction from work.

Activity

The external rewards of education – celebrating examination success.

How does this picture illustrate Bowles and Gintis's view of 'external rewards' and education?

Legitimating inequality

For capitalism to operate efficiently, the inequalities it produces must be seen as legitimate and just. Bowles and Gintis argue that, 'It is essential that the individual accept, and indeed, come to see as natural, those undemocratic and unequal aspects of the workaday world'. They suggest that a large part of the justification for and acceptance of the inequalities of capitalist society is provided by the educational system.

Education legitimates inequality by creating the belief that schools provide the opportunity for fair and open competition whereby talents and abilities are developed, graded and certificated. The educational system is thus seen as a meritocracy. Those with the highest qualifications deserve them – they have earned them on merit. The same belief is then applied to the economic system. It is assumed that those with the highest qualifications receive the highest rewards in the world of work. In this way, the educational system justifies inequalities in the economic system.

Bowles and Gintis reject the view that rewards in the educational and economic system are based on merit. They argue that educational and occupational attainment are related to family background rather than talent. Thus the children of the wealthy and powerful tend to obtain high qualifications and highly rewarded jobs irrespective of their ability. It is this the educational system disguises with its myth of meritocracy. In this way education provides 'the legitimation of pre-existing economic disparities'.

Then and now: Samuel Bowles and Herbert Gintis — *Schooling in Capitalist America* (1976)

Looking back on *Schooling in Capitalist America* published in 1976, Samuel Bowles and Herbert Gintis recall their hope that education would provide a more equal society with greater freedom and opportunity for all. Both then and now they feel distressed 'at how woefully the US educational system is failing these objectives'.

Assessing their findings from 1976, Bowles and Gintis state that the main findings 'have remained plausible and their validity has even been strengthened over the past quarter century'. In terms of the evidence which they used, Bowles and Gintis state, 'We are now reasonably certain we had the facts straight'. Since then numerous studies have provided similar evidence. For example, recent research indicates that employers see attitudes such as conscientiousness, perseverance and industriousness as key factors when hiring and promoting workers. And these are the very attitudes transmitted and rewarded by schools.

Critics have argued that Bowles and Gintis have pictured students as passively accepting the values promoted by schools rather than questioning or resisting them. To some extent Bowles and Gintis accept this criticism. Schools do reflect the demands of a capitalist economy. But they also reflect the principles of a democratic political system, such as freedom of speech, which can contradict these demands. By mirroring these contradictions, schools also reflect the conflicts they produce. As a result, schools can produce docile and obedient workers but they can also produce 'misfits and rebels'.

Looking to the future Bowles and Gintis see schools continuing to express the conflicts and hopes of an unequal society. They hope that schools will 'be both testing grounds and battlegrounds for building a society that extends its freedoms and material benefits to everyone'.

(Quotations from 'Schooling in Capitalist America Revisited', Bowles and Gintis, 2002)

Evaluation of Bowles and Gintis

According to David L. Swartz (2003), *Schooling in Capitalist America* is undoubtedly one of the classics in the sociology of education 'having had a major impact on education theory and research'. As a result, it has had both widespread support and criticism.

The main criticism is that the argument is too deterministic – it sees education as determined by the economy. As such, it ignores the possible effects of other aspects of society. And it gives too much emphasis to capitalism. For example, Karabel and Halsey (1977) maintain that education in communist Cuba placed 'heavy reliance on grades and exams as sources of student motivation' and teaching is based on a 'generally authoritarian and teacher-centred method of instruction'.

Critics have also argued that Bowles and Gintis largely ignored resistance in schools and in the wider society to the type of education they describe. Numerous studies show that many students have scant regard for school rules and little respect for the authority of teachers as the following section shows. And, as Henry Giroux (1984) argues, schools can be seen as **sites of ideological struggle** – clashes based on conflicting views within and between various groups such as teachers, school managers, parents, students, school inspectors, school governors, local authorities and the ministry of education.

Key terms

Ruling class ideology A system of ideas which justifies the position of the ruling class (the bourgeoisie).

False class consciousness A false picture of society which disguises the exploitation of the subject class (the proletariat).

Ideological State Apparatuses Institutions, including the education system, which transmit ruling class ideology.

Repressive State Apparatuses Institutions, such as the army and the police, which keep the subject class in its place.

Hidden curriculum A curriculum apart from the subjects taught that is hidden from teachers and students.

Correspondence theory A theory that states that there is a similarity between two things.

Alienation Cut off from, unable to find satisfaction from.

Sites of ideological struggle Places where there are conflicts based on different beliefs and values.

Summary

1. According to Althusser, education, as part of the Ideological State Apparatuses, transmits ruling class ideology.

2. Critics say that Althusser:

   » provides only a general framework with little evidence to support his views

   » treats people as 'cultural dopes' who passively accept ruling class ideology.

3. According to Bowles and Gintis, education in capitalist society reproduces labour power. It does this by:

   » rewarding discipline

   » legitimating inequality and disguising exploitation by promoting the myth of a meritocracy.

4. Critics argue that Bowles and Gintis:

   » give a deterministic view seeing education shaped by the economy

   » ignore resistance to and conflict within the education system.

Paul Willis – *Learning to Labour*

In an important study titled *Learning to Labour: How Working Class Kids get Working-Class Jobs,* Paul Willis (1977) developed a distinctive, neo-Marxist (new Marxist) approach to education. Willis studied a Midlands school in England in the 1970s. He used a variety of methods – 'observation and participant observation in class, around the school and during leisure activities, regular recorded group discussions, informal interviews and diaries'. Willis did not just rely on analysis of the relationship between education and the economy. He also tried to understand the experience of schooling from the perspective of the students and how they saw the present and the future. He soon found that schools were not as successful as Bowles and Gintis supposed in producing docile and conformist workers.

The counter-school culture

The school Willis studied was situated on a working-class housing estate in a mainly industrial small town. The main focus of his study was a group of 12 working-class boys whom he observed over their last 18 months at school, and their first few months at work. The 12 students formed a friendship group with a distinctive attitude to school. The 'lads', as they called themselves, had their own **counter-school culture**, which was opposed to the values promoted by the school.

This counter-school culture had the following features. The lads felt superior both to teachers, and to conformist students whom they referred to as 'ear 'oles'. The lads attached little or no value to the academic work of the school and had no interest in gaining qualifications. They resented the school trying to take control – they constantly tried to win 'symbolic and physical space from the institution and its rules'.

While avoiding work, the lads kept themselves entertained with 'irreverent marauding misbehaviour'.

'Having a laff' was a high priority. Willis described some of the behaviour that resulted:

> *During films in the hall they tie the projector leads into impossible knots, make animal figures or obscene shapes on the screen with their fingers, and gratuitously dig and jab the backs of the 'ear 'oles' in front of them.* Willis, 1977

To the lads, the school equalled boredom, while the outside world offered possibilities for excitement. Smoking cigarettes, drinking alcohol, part-time jobs and going out at night were ways in which they tried to identify with the adult, male world.

Activity – The lads' view of life

Extract from a poem written by one of the lads in an English lesson:

> On a night we go out on the street
> Troubling other people,
> I suppose we're anti-social,
> But we enjoy it.
> The older generation
> They don't like our hair,
> Or the clothes we wear
> They seem to love running us down,
> I don't know what I would do if I didn't have the gang.

In what ways does this poem reflect the lads' view of life?

According to Willis, the lads were eager to leave school at the earliest possible moment, and they looked forward to their first full-time jobs. While the ear 'oles took notice of career lessons and were concerned about the types of job they would eventually get, the lads were content to go on to any job, so long as it was a male, manual job. Such jobs were considered 'real work', in contrast to the office jobs which the ear 'oles were heading for.

The education system appears to be failing to produce the kind of workers some see as ideal for capitalism. The lads neither accepted authority nor were they obedient and docile. Yet despite this, Willis argues that the lads were well prepared for the work that they would do. It was their very rejection of school that made them suitable for male, unskilled or semi-skilled manual work.

Working-class masculinity The lads saw themselves and their future work as tough, hard and manly. Manual work was masculine, mental work was 'sissy' – effeminate. The lads' construction of masculinity was both offensive and defensive. It gave power to their

resistance, superiority over those the school defined as successful and self-respect where teachers saw them as failures.

Shop-floor culture and counter-school culture

When Willis followed the lads into their first jobs in factories, he found strong similarities between **shop-floor culture** (shop floor is the factory floor) and the counter-school culture. There was the same lack of respect for authority, the same emphasis on masculinity, and the same belief in the worth of manual labour. Having a 'laff' was equally important in both cultures, and on the shop floor, as in the school, the maximum possible freedom was sought. The lads and their new workmates tried to control the pace at which they worked, and to win some time and space in which they were free from the boredom and tedium of work.

According to Willis, both the counter-school culture and the shop-floor culture are ways of coping with tedium and oppression. Life is made more tolerable by having a 'laff' and winning a little space from the supervisor, the manager or the teacher. In both settings, though, the challenges to authority never go too far. The lads and workers hope to gain a little freedom, but they do not challenge the institution head-on. They know that they must do a certain amount of work in the factory or risk dismissal, and they realise that the state can enforce school attendance if it is determined to do so.

Willis concludes that the lads are not persuaded to act as they do by the school, nor are they forced to seek manual labour. Instead, they actively create their own subculture, which leads them to look for manual jobs. They learn about the culture of the shop floor from fathers, elder brothers and other men in the local community. They are attracted to this masculine, adult world. They see the school and its values as irrelevant to their chosen work.

Capitalism and the counter-school culture

Willis claims that in some ways the lads see through the capitalist system, but in other ways they contribute to their own exploitation. He calls their insights into the workings of capitalism **penetrations**.

According to Willis, the lads recognise that 'the possibility of real upward mobility is so remote as to be meaningless', that any qualifications they might get will be unlikely to affect their job choices, and that investing time, emotion and energy into school work is hardly worth the effort. The counter-school culture 'knows' that meritocracy is an illusion and that the majority of working-class lads will remain at the bottom of the class system.

Despite these 'partial penetrations' into the nature of capitalism, the lads prepare themselves for manual work at school. The counter-school culture directs them into low-skill employment. And the lads condemn themselves to 'a precise insertion into a system of exploitation and oppression for working-class people'.

Evaluation of Willis

According to Madeleine Arnot (2004), *Learning to Labour* by Paul Willis 'has greater, not less, relevance in the current school climate'. First, schools are

increasingly exam-driven, competitive and pressured. Second, the deindustrialisation of Western society and the disappearance of the majority of manual jobs have led to growing uncertainty about occupational futures. These factors might make working-class masculinity and resistance to schools even more relevant today.

Willis provides a framework to study and understand the relationship between class, gender, schooling and the economy. He looks at the construction of meaning. He shows how the lads' definition of the situation has a logic and sense in terms of their class situation and culture, their gender, the priorities of the school and the employment and economic context of the time. As Liz Gordon (1984), states, Willis 'has provided the model on which most subsequent cultural studies investigation within education has been based'. Nevertheless, Willis has his critics:

- ❯ They suggest Willis's sample is inadequate as a basis for generalising about working-class education. Willis focused on only 12 students, all of them male, who were by no means typical of the students at the school he studied, never mind of working-class students in the population as a whole.

- ❯ They accuse Willis of largely ignoring the existence of a variety of subcultures within the school. They point out that many students came somewhere in between the extremes of being totally conformist and being totally committed to the counter-school culture.

- ❯ They question the relevance of Willis's study in today's increasingly de-industrialised society where manual jobs are rapidly disappearing.

In terms of this last criticism, Willis continues to provide a reference point and a benchmark for later research. This can be seen from the title of Michael Ward's (2015) study, *From Labouring to Learning: Working-Class Masculinities, Education and De-industrialisation*. This study of working-class young men in South Wales shows that in several respects working-class culture has remained the same despite the disappearance of many traditional working-class jobs – see p.105.

Then and now: Paul Willis — *Learning to Labour* (1977)

"My Research Question has always been as much to do with the 'How' of it as with the 'Why' of it. Hence the subtitle of my book: *How Working-Class Kids get Working-Class Jobs.* When I did the research in the 1970s, there were many ideas about why working-class students so often 'failed' in education, ideas which were usually very insulting of them. But there were very few ideas concerning the 'how'. I wanted to fill this gap with a detailed account of their 'lived culture', the meanings they gave to the context in which they lived, how they came to accept a future of manual labour, how it seemed natural to them.

To do this I chose ethnography as my research method — studying behaviour in the situation in which it occurs and discovering the meanings used to make sense of the present and future. This type of research requires a specific focus — in this case a focus on class and gender in order to understand the experience of 'the lads'.

I believe that this approach is essential for an in-depth understanding of the 'meanings world', the 'social grammar' and the 'structure of feeling' of a social group. For this reason, I think that my approach continues to be highly, perhaps even more, relevant to understand today's working class and what is going on both in and out of school. It is very pleasing to me to have opened up a new approach which can be applied to the study of any social group.

I have been criticised for having an 'old fashioned view' of class, a view that has been outdated by economic change and de-industrialisation. There often seems to be an assumption that that class has largely disappeared and is no longer relevant. This greatly overstates things. The working class is undoubtedly being re-formed and fractured in complex ways but certainly not abolished. Some working-class students proceed to still available industrial, construction and maintenance jobs, following more or less traditional patterns. Some find intermittent and insecure work. Some are 'parked' for long periods of time in colleges or on government schemes. Others move to non-manual and 'mental work' while retaining many aspects of working-class culture. These experiences demand ethnographic attention with a focus on the 'how'.

My main hope for the continuing contribution of my book is to remind scholars and researchers that the 'how' question should always be included and to show respect for the 'lived culture' of those under study. Find that creative 'cultural production' which always lives no matter how deeply buried in the belly of the beast of social reproduction! Despite everything, that is always a source of optimism and hope."

Key terms

Counter-school culture A rejection of the norms and values of the school and their replacement with anti-school norms and values.

Shop-floor culture The culture of low-skill workers which has similarities to the counter-school culture.

Penetrations Insights into the false pictures presented by ruling class ideology.

Summary

1. According to Willis, the lads developed their own counter-school culture. This involved:

   » having a 'laff'
   » misbehaving and rejecting authority
   » doing as little work as possible
   » getting involved in the male, adult world outside school.

2. The similarity between counter-school culture and shop-floor culture prepared the lads to accept and cope with low-skill, manual work.

3. Critics argue that:

   » Willis's sample is too small to generalise from
   » he ignored other student subcultures
   » his study is no longer relevant because of economic change
   » despite these criticisms, his work has been very influential and provided a model for later research.

Glenn Rikowski – education, capitalism and globalisation

Glenn Rikowski (2002, 2005) argues that the development of educational systems can be best understood within a Marxist framework. Marx claimed that as capitalism developed, social services such as education and heath would become increasingly capitalised. This means they would be **privatised** – privately owned rather than state owned. In this way, education becomes like any other **commodity** – a product to be bought and sold in the market with the aim of making a profit. Rikowski (2005) argues that 'educational services operating within markets' are 'being transformed into commodities'.

Marx claimed that a constant expansion of the market is necessary for the development of capitalism. As a result, there is a built-in tendency for capitalists to create a world market. This can be seen today from the rapid expansion of multinational companies. Rikowski (2002) argues that today's **globalisation** is 'essentially capitalist globalisation'. He sees education as part of this process. Education is becoming a global commodity. And the driving force behind global educational institutions is the generation of profit.

These developments reflect the logic of capitalism. But, although there are considerable pressures within the system to move capitalism in this direction, the process is not inevitable.

The business takeover of schools

Although there is a long way to go, Rikowski claims that the beginnings of 'the business takeover of schools' are well established:

> More and more of the school's requirements are subcontracted to private industry – for example, school dinners and cleaning.

> The aim of private industry is first and foremost to make a profit.

> As a result, educational activities are steadily being transformed into commodities.

> If this process continues then private corporations may one day take over the entire education system. Then education will become primarily a profit-making activity rather than educating young people as an end in itself.

Rikowski points to various aspects of the education policy of the Labour government of the time to support his claims. These policies largely continue today. They include:

> increasing links between schools and business, particularly business sponsorship of academies

> the marketisation of schools, with schools competing in the marketplace for customers; additional funds are provided for increasing numbers of students

> schools operating increasingly as commercial enterprises – 'selling' their product and becoming successful or failing as a result of consumer demand for their services.

Rikowski argues that if the processes outlined above continue unchecked, then education may well become privatised and will be run 'primarily for the benefit of shareholders' – those who own educational businesses.

Globalisation and education

A world market in educational services would be extremely profitable. According to Rikowski (2002), the World Trade Organization and the World Bank are supporting global educational businesses as a way to increase productivity and economic growth, especially for developing nations. And this is being welcomed by many governments who see education as the key to success in an increasingly competitive global economy.

The UK company Nord Anglia Education is a forerunner in the trend that Rikowski anticipates. According to its website, Nord Anglia operates '42 International schools located in 15 countries across China, Europe, the Middle East, North America and Southeast Asia' with 32 000 students aged 2 to 18. It has a 'global campus' and offers a 'global education' (Nord Anglia Education, 2016).

Universities are increasingly operating in a similar way to business institutions. For example, departments of education in UK universities generate large amounts of income by acting as consultants for developing school systems in countries such as Chile, Poland and Romania.

Universities are also establishing campuses in various countries. For example, Middlesex University has international branch campuses in Dubai, Malta and Mauritius. And the University of Nottingham has **branch campuses** in Malaysia and China.

Rikowski sees a global trend in which 'educational services will be progressively commercialised, privatised and capitalised'.

Activity

The Middlesex University branch campus in Dubai was opened in 2005. By 2016 it had over 2500 students of more than 90 different nationalities.

How do this picture and the caption indicate the increasing globalisation of education?

Opposition to global capitalism

Despite the above arguments, Rikowski is optimistic about the possibility of opposing the influence of global capitalism in education. He argues that teachers and lecturers may well prevent the smooth flow of labour production – the production of students suited for the workforce required by capitalism. Many educators are concerned with social justice, social equality and human rights, principles which are opposed to education as a commodity. According to Rikowski, teachers and lecturers are in a uniquely strong position to challenge global capitalism with teaching based on these principles.

Evaluation of Rikowski

Over the last 30 years, Marxist sociology has become unfashionable. Rikowski has given a new lease of life to Marxist perspectives on education. As he admits, he is looking at the beginnings of a possible trend. Is the capitalisation and globalisation of education the agenda for the future?

Rikowski's critics accept that schools are increasingly run on business lines, that they are exposed to market forces, that some educational services are subcontracted to the private sector, and that there is a growing market for the export of educational services. However, this is a long way from saying that education is becoming a global commodity, controlled by global capitalism for the primary purpose of generating ever-increasing profit.

Critics argue that governments control education and will do so for the foreseeable future. Schools for

profit are unlikely to appear as part of present or future educational policy in the UK (Hatcher, 2005).

Despite these criticisms, recent evidence provides some support for Rikowski's concerns about the possible future of education (see pp. 40–42).

Key terms

Commodity Something that can be bought and sold

Privatise Move from state ownership to private ownership.

Globalisation An increasing connection between parts of the world. In this case, a process where goods and services become steadily worldwide.

Branch campus A campus which is a branch of the main university.

Summary

1. According to Rikowski:

   > the business takeover of schools has begun but the completion of this process is not inevitable

   > the globalisation of educational services is increasing

   > many governments welcome educational businesses. They see education as the key to success in an increasingly competitive global economy.

2. Critics argue that Rikowski may have overstated the case for education becoming a global commodity.

2.1.3 Social reproduction

This unit looks at the views of Pierre Bourdieu on the role of education in society. Pierre Bourdieu (1930–2002) is regarded by many as one of the most important sociologists of the late 20th century. He saw the main role of education as social reproduction – the reproduction of social inequality from one generation to the next, in particular, the reproduction of the power and privileges of the 'dominant classes'.

Capitals

Bourdieu (2016) refers to the main resources which determine people's position in society as **capital**. He identifies four forms of capital – economic capital, social capital, symbolic capital and cultural capital. In general, the greater the amount of capital an individual or group possesses, the higher their position in the class system. Each form of capital can contribute to success in the educational system, with cultural capital being the most important.

Economic capital refers to financial resources such as income and wealth. It can be used to further educational success by investing in private education, buying a house in the catchment area of a top state school and providing personal tutors.

Social capital refers to the network of family, friends and acquaintances. Social contacts can be seen as a resource. They may provide advice on the best schools and universities, the top jobs and appropriate training.

Symbolic capital refers to honour, prestige and reputation. Symbolic capital is high in the nobility and those who have received titles and awards such as knighthoods and OBEs. Families with high symbolic capital can raise the expectations and boost the confidence of their children.

Cultural capital refers to manners, tastes, interests and language. It includes so-called 'high culture' such as classical music, ballet, opera and visual art. Cultural capital is the culture of the 'dominant classes'. According to Bourdieu, it is a resource because the more cultural capital an individual has, the more likely they are to succeed in the educational system and enjoy the rewards that this can bring.

Conversions The various capitals can reinforce and increase each other. Their interaction can, in Bourdieu's term, lead to **conversion**. For example, the rich tend to mix with the rich, which may increase their social capital. Similarly, the ability to pay for private education may also increase their social capital. For instance, in 2016, over 53 per cent of the UK Cabinet were educated in fee-paying schools compared with 7 per cent of the general population (*The Guardian*, News Data Blog, 2016). Valuable social contacts may result from friendships made at private schools.

Cultural capital and education

Bourdieu (1974, 2016) claims that the possession of cultural capital is the key to high educational attainment. Cultural capital is concentrated in the 'dominant classes'. Bourdieu also claims that educational success depends mainly on the culture learned during a child's early years. In his words. 'The scholastic yield from educational action depends on

the cultural capital previously invested by the family' (Bourdieu, 2016).

Children of the 'dominant classes' therefore have a head start when they begin school and this advantage continues throughout their educational career.

Social reproduction

Bourdieu argues that cultural capital and the educational qualifications it produces are essential to social reproduction – to perpetuating social inequality from generation to generation and maintaining the power of the 'dominant classes'.

In addition, educational success legitimates social reproduction – makes it appear just, right and deserved. The so-called talent and ability which are seen to produce educational success are basically 'the investment of cultural capital'.

This process is hidden and, as such, is safeguarded. In Bourdieu's (2016) words, 'the continuous transmission [of cultural capital] within the family escapes observation and control'. And this helps to maintain social reproduction. The 'invisibility' of cultural capital largely prevents any criticism and challenge to the advantages it brings.

Evaluation of Bourdieu

Bourdieu's views have been extremely influential. They have stimulated a large body of research. Bourdieu has provided a framework for the study of education which has been used by a number of prominent British sociologists (see pp. 81–88). And his ideas have formed the basis for recent studies of class cultures (Bennett *et al.*, 2009) and the British class structure (Savage, 2015).

Bourdieu's views have brought both praise and criticism. His critics claim that he has presented an overly rigid picture of a society which constrains behaviour and structures action. There appears little room for creativity or resistance. People are presented as creatures of the social system (Elliott, 2009).

Marxists argue that Bourdieu neglects the economy and places too much emphasis on cultural capital and not enough on economic oppression.

Critics also argue that Bourdieu's description of cultural capital lacks precision and detail. And that he has failed to spell out how cultural capital is converted into educational qualifications (Sullivan, 2001). These criticisms are examined in the unit on social class and educational attainment (pp. 66–93).

Contemporary issues: High in capitals

David Cameron

The former prime minister David Cameron is descended from King William IV. He was born into a wealthy family. His father was a stockbroker and his mother was a justice of the peace. He attended a high-status private preparatory school, went to fee-paying Eton College (annual fees over £35 000 in 2016), then on to Oxford University. There, he joined the Bullingdon Club, home of the rich and famous and his contemporary Boris Johnson. On the day of his job interview at Conservative Central Office, it is reported that a man from Buckingham Palace called to put in a good word for him.

Questions

1. Use Bourdieu's idea of capitals to explain David Cameron's rise to prime minister.

2. Do you think that the influence of capitals on educational attainment results in a fair system?

Contemporary issues: Private education

Eton College, seen as one of the top private schools.

Eddie Redmayne, a former student of Eton College, receiving an Oscar.

Expensive schools, top jobs

About 7 per cent of UK students attend private schools. Yet the percentage of these students who go on to the top universities and top jobs is far higher. For example, 32 per cent of MPs were privately educated and 26 per cent went on to Oxbridge (Oxford and Cambridge universities). 74 per cent of top judges went to private schools and the same percentage went to Oxbridge. In journalism, 51 per cent of leading journalists were privately educated and 54 per cent went to Oxbridge. And in film, 67 per cent of British winners of the main Oscars went to private schools (Kirby, 2016).

Private schools are expensive. Putting a child through a 14-year private education in the UK averages £286 000. Why pay this large amount? A survey of 250 parents suggests that it's 'worth it', 'I or a member of my family went there', 'the small class sizes' and 'the connections my children will get' (BBC News online, 15.07.2015).

Research by Durham University Centre for Evaluation and Monitoring indicates that attending a private school in England is the equivalent of two years of extra schooling by the age of 16. At GCSE, private schools have higher average scores in all subjects (Ndaji, Little and Coe, 2016). But, according to the Sutton Trust, a leading organisation for educational research, it's not just exam results that lead to career success. According to Sir Peter Lampl (2016), Chairman of the Sutton Trust, privately educated students often have higher aspirations, greater social skills, more confidence and greater access to professional networks.

Charitable status

Most private schools are registered charities. Here are two views about this (*The Guardian,* 29.11.2014).

Carole Cadwalladr (*Observer* journalist) 'We shouldn't be subsidising Britain's private schools to the tune of £700 million a year. We might as well subsidise five-star hotels. They're both the preserve of a small privileged elite, the difference being that five-star hotels don't shore up a centuries-old system of institutionalised inequality. Because private schools underpin everything that is most wrong, most iniquitous, most stiflingly, claustrophobically unjust and undemocratic and unmodern about Britain today.'

Charlotte Vere (acting general secretary of the Independent Schools Council which represents over half of private schools) 'The financial benefits of being a charity are few – for example, charities, unlike businesses, can't reclaim VAT ... So what of the public benefit of fee-paying independent schools? ... First, there are 40 000 children from low-income families on bursaries (grants) in independent schools. This public benefit alone amounts to £300 million. Second, the schools ... save the taxpayer £3 billion by educating children outside the state system.'

Questions

1. How might Bourdieu see the role of private education in society?

2. Should private education have charitable status?

Key terms

Social reproduction The reproduction of social inequality from one generation to the next.

Economic capital Financial resources.

Social capital A social network that can be used as a resource.

Symbolic capital Honour, prestige and reputation.

Cultural capital The manners, tastes, interests and language of the 'dominant classes'.

Conversion The process by which one form of capital reinforces another.

Summary

1. According to Bourdieu:

   - the 'dominant classes' have the highest amount of capital

   - the more cultural capital an individual has, the greater their chance of educational success

   - this gives the children of the 'dominant classes' a head start when they begin school.

2. Critics state that:

   - Bourdieu's description of cultural capital lacks precision and detail

   - Marxists argue that he ignores the power of the economy to shape the education system.

2.1.4 Social democratic perspectives

The social democratic perspective is a political ideology that has had a major influence on the development of Western democracies. It has also influenced sociological thinking. This can be seen in the sociology of education.

From a social democratic perspective, the state should represent the interests of the population as a whole. This requires a democratic system in which adult members of society elect those who govern them. Democracy is seen as the best way to ensure equal rights – for example, every citizen is equal under the law – and to ensure equal opportunity – every member of society has an equal chance of becoming successful.

In some respects, social democratic views are similar to functionalism. Both see education as a means towards equality of opportunity, and both see education as essential for economic growth. However, many social democrats argue that inequalities in society can (1) prevent equality of educational opportunity, and (2) reduce the effectiveness of education in promoting economic growth.

Social democratic views have had an important influence on the sociology of education, particularly during the 1960s. And they continue to influence government educational policy in the UK.

Equality of opportunity

Social democrats such as the British sociologist A.H. Halsey argue that the inequalities produced by a free market economy prevent equality of opportunity. Those who succeed in the educational system tend to be the sons and daughters of the middle and upper classes, and those who fail are disproportionately from working-class backgrounds. The class system appears to stand in the way of equal opportunity.

Social democrats believe in a **meritocracy** – a society in which a person's status is achieved on the basis of merit, on their talent and motivation. For a meritocracy to operate effectively, equality of opportunity is essential. Could reforming the educational system provide equality of educational opportunity?

In the 1960s, around two-thirds of students from middle and upper class backgrounds attended grammar schools at age 11, compared with only a quarter of students from working-class backgrounds. A grammar school education was the route to further and higher education and to high-status, well-paid jobs. Most young people went to secondary modern schools. They were mainly from working-class backgrounds and they were usually seen as educational failures. Clearly, selection at age 11 favoured middle and upper class children and did not provide equality of educational opportunity. (This system of secondary education is examined in detail later in the chapter, pp. 44–45).

From a social democratic perspective, this system was both unfair and inefficient. It was unfair because it discriminated against working-class students. It was inefficient because it did not develop their talents. This 'wastage of talent' failed to produce the highly educated workforce required by a modern industrial economy.

During the 1960s and 1970s, many social democrats argued that a change in the system of secondary education would promote equality of opportunity. Some saw the comprehensive system as the answer – one type of schooling for all. Selection at age 11 would stop and young people from all social classes would receive the same type of education in the same type of schools (except for those in private schools).

Economic growth

According to social democrats, education has a major role to play in economic growth. Halsey *et al.* stated that:

> *Education is a crucial type of investment for the exploitation of modern technology. In advanced industrial societies it is inevitable that the education system should come into a closer relationship with the economy … as the proportion of the labour force engaged in manual work declines and the demand for white-collar, professional and managerial workers rises.* Halsey *et al.*, 1961

Equality of educational opportunity would make society more meritocratic. It would provide everyone with the opportunity to develop their potential and so maximise their contribution to the economy. In doing so, they would make greater contributions to economic growth which would bring prosperity to all.

Evaluation of social democratic theory

Equality of opportunity According to social democratic theory, there are two ways of moving towards equality of opportunity – either by changing the education system in order to provide all students with an equal chance to succeed, or changing the class system by reducing the inequalities which divide society. Despite attempts by various governments to address these issues, there has been little change in class differences in educational attainment from the 1940s to the present day.

Social democratic theory has been criticised for placing too much importance on changing the education system as a means of reducing inequality of educational opportunity. Over the past 60 years, changes in primary, secondary, further and higher education do not appear to have significantly reduced class differences in educational attainment. It appears, in the words of the British sociologist Basil Bernstein (1971), that 'education cannot compensate for society'. In other words, education cannot make up for inequalities in the wider society.

Many social democrats now argue that only a reduction in social inequality in society as a whole can reduce inequality in educational opportunity. However, the evidence does not hold out much hope for such a reduction. Inequality has grown steadily in the UK over the past 30 years according to a report by the Organisation for Economic Cooperation and Development (OECD) (Cingano, 2014).

Economic growth Does education promote economic growth as social democratic theory claims? Critics make the following points.

First, the school curriculum often fails to meet the requirements of employers. It is not designed to provide the skills needed for economic growth.

Second, more education does not necessarily lead to more growth in the economy. Alison Woolf (2002) analysed educational expenditure and economic growth in a number of countries. She found that, 'among the most successful economies, there is in fact no clear link between growth and spending on education'. In Switzerland, for example, expenditure on education is relatively low, but in terms of per capita income Switzerland is one of the richest countries in the world. Among less developed countries, Egypt massively expanded its education spending between 1980 and 1995, but failed to improve its economic position relative to other countries.

Third, according to the OECD, the level of economic growth depends on the extent of inequality. Countries with the lowest level of inequality have the highest growth rates. The OECD report argues that an increase in the income of the poor would reduce inequality and boost growth. And the way to do this is 'to promote equality of opportunity in access to, and quality of, education' and 'promoting employment for disadvantaged groups' (Cingano, 2014).

All governments see more education for more people as vital for economic growth in an increasingly competitive global economy. As competition intensifies, growth is seen to be increasingly dependent on the development of scientific knowledge, technological innovation, and a more highly skilled workforce. And education is seen as crucial for these developments (Lauder *et al.*, 2006).

Summary

1. Social democratic perspectives:

   > support equality of opportunity in education and in the wider society

   > state that social class prevents equality of educational opportunity

   > some argue that changes in the education system can reduce inequality of opportunity in schools

   > others argue that only a reduction of social class inequality in the wider society can reduce inequality of opportunity in education.

2. Social democratic perspectives state that education promotes economic growth. Critics argue that:

   > the school curriculum is not designed to provide the skills needed for growth

   > there is not a clear link between spending on education and economic growth

   > although education has a part to play, it is a reduction in inequality in society that leads to economic growth.

2.1.5 Neoliberal/new right perspectives

Neoliberalism, also known as new right, is a political and economic ideology rather than a sociological theory. It has become a global perspective, guiding the economic policies of governments across the world.

Neoliberalism is about competition in national and global markets. It sees competition as the key to efficiency and economic growth. Competition only works in a free market, a market free from government regulations and restrictions.

Competition offers choice to consumers. Choice is only available when companies compete to provide goods and services. There is no choice when the state has a monopoly. State owned monopolies such as the provision of health and education should be privatised – sold to private investors.

Competition between private companies in a free market will bring choice, efficiency, economic growth and improvements in the quality of goods and services.

There is increasing evidence that neoliberalism is shaping government educational policy as Part 2 Educational Policy in the UK shows. And, as we have already seen, there has been a growth in global education companies whose primary concern is profit and who view education as a commodity.

Education and the market

From a neoliberal perspective, education is central to economic growth. Raising standards in education will raise living standards and promote growth.

Marketisation According to neoliberalism, **marketisation** is the key to raising standards in education. Schools, colleges and universities must compete for customers in a free and open market. Parents and students should have the freedom to select the educational institutions of their choice. This will improve standards as parents will choose to send their children to the most successful schools and students will apply to the top universities. This will give educational institutions an incentive to raise their standards in order to attract students. In a market system, public money will follow the choices made by parents and children. This will give successful institutions the funds to expand and failing institutions an incentive to improve or face closure.

For an educational market to work efficiently, information on the standards achieved by schools must be widely available. Without this, parents, students and politicians cannot make informed decisions. Testing regimes must be put in place to provide information on which to base choice. Students must be regularly assessed and the results published. Schools can then be directly compared and ranked in 'league tables'. Measuring school performance is essential for informed choice and for raising standards.

In order to compete in the market, educational institutions must behave like businesses. Not only should students be continually assessed, but so also should teachers and educational institutions. Teachers are assessed in terms of the test results of their students. Ofsted, a UK government inspection organisation, assesses schools and colleges. The guiding concept is **performativity** – a focus on performance and its measurement. In Stephen J. Ball's words, this leads to 'audits, inspections, appraisals, self-reviews, quality assurance, research assessment and output indicators'. It directs teaching and research towards areas 'which are likely to have a positive impact on measurable performance' (Ball, 2012).

Activity

A rally in Texas in support of the right to choose schools. In a number of states in the USA the School Choice Program provides students with the opportunity to attend a school other than their neighbourhood school.

Why do you think the parents and students are demonstrating for the right to choose schools?

Privatisation

From a neoliberal perspective, part of the process of acting like a business and entering the market is **privatisation**. This means private sector participation in education. Privatisation is seen as a means of making schools, colleges and universities more efficient and raising standards.

Privatisation of education takes a number of forms. It includes obtaining income through deals with private companies, for example vending machines in schools selling products such as Cadbury's chocolate and promotions such as Walker's crisps' scheme to collect vouchers for school equipment. This entry of private companies into schools is called **cola-isation** in the USA (Ball, 2007).

Another aspect of privatisation is the subcontracting of services to private companies. This includes cleaning, school dinners, and counselling and management services. The private sector is often seen as a more efficient means of provision.

Private companies have become increasingly involved in education itself. They now offer services such as testing and tutoring. And there has been a rapid growth in 'schools for profit' – private schools run as business enterprises. For example, in the USA, Charter Schools is a private company operating schools. And information is provided to investors to manage their 'education investment portfolios'. There is now a growing and highly profitable education industry (Robertson, 2007).

Neoliberalism, globalisation and education

Neoliberal perspectives have become global. Education is seen as the key to success in an increasingly competitive global market. It provides the skills needed to compete and the scientific knowledge and new technology to stay in the race. These beliefs have become universal. They are an 'educational gospel', an 'article of faith' which states that educational growth will lead to 'social and individual salvation' (Grubb and Lazerson, 2006).

With this emphasis on education and the economy, schools and colleges have increasingly focused on **vocationalism** – training and preparation for occupations. According to Brown and Lauder (2006), 'Schools, colleges, universities, think-tanks, design centres and research laboratories are now on the front line in the search for competitive advantage'.

In *Global Education Inc.*, Stephen J. Ball (2012) looks at the growth of 'global education policy' based on neoliberal ideology. He argues that global organisations such as the World Bank and the World Trade Organization, international businesses and think-tanks are increasingly involved in 'producing and disseminating global educational policies'.

Activity

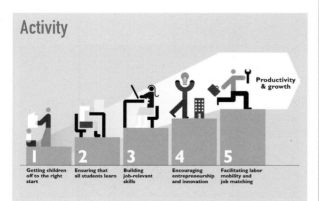

The World Bank's STEP framework for productivity and economic growth. The World Bank encourages countries to see education as a means of developing the skills needed for economic growth.

How does the World Bank's STEP framework illustrate their view that education is vital and should be directed to economic growth?

Ball points to the development of **multinational education businesses** (MNEBs) which sell educational policies and practices based on neoliberal principles. For example, Cambridge Education, a UK-based MNEB, works with nation states such as Thailand and cities such as St Petersburg, Florida and New York City, providing consultancy, training, management services, professional development and a range of assessment materials. According to Ball, 'There is clearly now something we can call "global education policy" – a generic (overall) set of concepts, language and practices that is recognisable in various forms and is for sale!' For more on the globalisation of education see pp. 58–66.

Evaluation of neoliberal perspectives on education

Educational markets are unfair Do parents have an equal choice in the educational market? Some parents have more knowledge and understanding of the education system and more money. They are in a better position to manipulate educational markets to get the most out of them. For example, middle-class parents will be more likely to get their children into the schools with the best reputations, or they will be able to afford to pay for them to attend successful private schools. In some areas, for some parents, choice is not available – there is no alternative to the local comprehensive.

Raising standards Will competition and choice raise standards? A detailed study of evidence from the USA indicates the following. Based on findings of 25 separate studies, the evidence suggests that competition and choice do produce small improvements in student achievement (Levin and Belfield, 2006). However, these 'modest' improvements are well below the levels expected by supporters of market approaches.

Will this modest improvement be spread evenly across the student population, or will some gain more than others? Evidence from the USA suggests that market approaches will lead to greater social inequalities – in particular, the children of higher-income parents will gain most, leading to a wider attainment gap between rich and poor (Levin and Belfield, 2006).

Neoliberal ideas have been widely applied in New Zealand. In some low-achieving schools, student numbers did decline as expected with competition and freedom of choice. But this was mainly because middle-class students moved to schools with higher reputations, leaving their working-class counterparts behind in inferior schools (Lauder *et al*., 1999).

Selection by schools In an open market, consumer choice may sometimes result in provider choice. In terms of education, this may lead to schools (the providers) choosing students, rather than parents (the consumers) choosing schools. For example, the most successful schools may not have enough places for all the students who wish to attend. This means that schools must select (Ranson, 1996).

Given their desire to remain at the top of the league table, there is pressure on these schools to select those they see as the most able students. Such students are usually seen as those from middle-class backgrounds. This process is sometimes known as **creaming.**

Education as a means to an end Some critics believe that the marketisation of education leads to a narrow view of education as a means to an end. For example, Stewart Ranson (1996) argues that markets are based upon the assumption that each individual will pursue an 'instrumental rationality'

in which their sole concern will be to maximise their own self-interest. Ranson believes that when individuals act in this way it is because the market encourages them to do so. It undermines values that stress the importance of selflessness and cooperation with others.

Frank Coffield and Bill Williamson (2011) claim that schools have been turned into 'exam factories'. Exam results have become a measure of success for students, teachers and schools. Teachers 'teach to the test' and students are 'mark hungry and obsessed by exams'.

According to Hugh Lauder *et al*. (2006), the view that 'education is a servant of the economy' is flawed. This view of education is 'blind to the fundamental problems of the age' – to global warming, ageing societies, inequality and environmental issues. And what about creativity, critical thinking, questioning and self-awareness? And exploring knowledge for its own sake and developing the potential of each student? There is little room for these concerns in neoliberal education policy.

Contemporary issues: Neoliberalism and schools

Exam factories

Critics of neoliberalism make the following points. Today, educational policy is framed by a

concern to promote international competitiveness and economic growth in a globalised economy. Governments routinely boast that educational standards have risen. Here standards are narrowly defined as increasing test scores. The intense pressures applied by governments to increase test scores have turned many schools into exam factories, where teaching to the test, gaining qualifications, and developing learning techniques to pass exams are now what matters.

The main driving force for educational change in England has become fear – fear of poor exam results, fear of poor inspection grades, fear of sliding down the national league tables, and fear of public humiliation and closure. The impact on students has been to make them mark hungry, obsessed with exams, and physically and emotionally stressed (adapted from Coffield and Williamson, 2011).

Question

Do you agree with the above arguments? Give reasons for your answer.

Key terms

Marketisation The process where organisations compete in the market.

Performativity How well an individual or organisation performs.

Privatisation A process where 1) services are subcontracted to private companies, 2) where private companies compete with public organisations which previously held a monopoly of the services.

Cola-isation The entry of private companies promoting their goods into schools and colleges.

Multinational education businesses Private education companies which have branches in two or more countries.

Creaming Selecting students who appear most likely to succeed for entry to educational institutions.

Summary

1. Neoliberalism sees competition in the market as the way to improve standards in education. This would involve:

   » consumer choice
   » measuring school performance
   » privatisation.

2. Neoliberal perspectives are now global:

   » education is seen as essential for providing the skills needed in an increasingly competitive global market
   » multinational educational businesses are rapidly growing to meet this demand.

3. Critics of neoliberalism argue that:

   » educational markets are unfair
   » competition only leads to 'modest' improvements
   » the supposedly 'best' schools select students by 'creaming'
   » there is more to education than servicing the economy.

PART 2 EDUCATIONAL POLICY IN THE UK

Contents

This part looks at government educational policy in the UK from 1945 to the present. It begins with a brief introduction to the development of state education from 1870 to 1945. It then examines the influence of social democratic and neoliberal/new right perspectives on government policy. It looks at the main developments in policy from the introduction of grammar and secondary modern schools to their replacement by comprehensives, to the move to academies and the expansion of higher education.

The growing influence of neoliberal policies is critically examined. Should parents and students have a choice of schools? Should schools compete with each other? Should league tables be used to assess schools? Are schools turning into exam factories?

More recent concerns are examined. Should grammar schools be reinstated? Are academies the answer to many of the problems faced by schools? Does education contribute to social mobility?

2.2.1 Educational policy, 1945–1979

This unit begins with a brief summary of state education from its beginnings in 1870. It moves on to look at educational policy in the UK from 1945 to 1979. It pays particular attention to the influence of two major perspectives – social democracy and neoliberalism – on government policy.

Social democracy provided the framework for educational policy from 1945 to 1979. The social democratic perspective was outlined earlier in this chapter (see pp. 37–39). The main points are summarised below:

> Society should be based on justice and fairness.

> This means that everyone should have an equal chance to succeed – there should be equality of opportunity for all.

> Society should be meritocratic. People's position should be based on merit – on talent and hard work.

> Education has an important part to play in a meritocracy. It should provide all young people with an equal chance to develop their talents.

> This will lead to a better-educated and more highly skilled workforce. This, in turn, will lead to greater productivity and economic growth.

> As a result, living standards will rise.

State education from 1870

In Britain free compulsory state education conducted in formal institutions by full-time professionals began in 1870. By 1880, attendance was made compulsory up to the age of 10. With the Fisher Education Act of 1918 the state became responsible for secondary education, and attendance was made compulsory up to the age of 14. The school-leaving age was raised to 15 in 1947, to 16 in 1972, 17 in 2013 and 18 in 2015.

For most of the 20th century and during the 21st century, increasing numbers of people continued in education after the compulsory period of attendance, or returned to education later in life. In 1900, only 1.2 per cent of 18-year-olds entered full-time further or higher education; by 1938 the figure had reached 5.8 per cent.

There was rapid growth of post-compulsory education in the 1950s, 1960s and early 1970s. New universities were built, polytechnics were established, and the Open University gave adults fresh educational opportunities. Young people of school-leaving age were encouraged to stay on in school sixth forms, or to attend college. By 2014, 71.5 per cent of 16- to 18-year-olds in England were participating in some form of education or training (DfE, 25 June 2015).

The growth in higher education slowed down in the late 1970s and early 1980s, but rapid growth resumed in the late 1980s and early 1990s. Most existing universities expanded, as did the polytechnics, which were given university status in 1992. The number of higher education students in the UK increased from just over one million in 1990/91 to 2.26 million in 2014/15 (HESA, 2016).

The tripartite system

The 1944 Education Act was strongly influenced by social democratic principles. It aimed to provide equality of opportunity for all young people. The school leaving age was raised to 15 and the **tripartite** (three part) system of secondary education was introduced. This system consisted of three types of school – **grammar schools** for academic students, **secondary technical schools** for those with an aptitude for technical subjects such as engineering, and **secondary modern schools** focusing on subjects such as woodwork, metalwork, cookery and needlework for students seen to be best suited to practical tasks and manual jobs.

The tripartite system was introduced to provide separate but equal schools for students seen to have different abilities and aptitudes. Each type of school was to have **parity of esteem** – equal status – with similar funding, and buildings, equipment and staffing of similar quality. Students took an exam, the 11-plus, to discover which type of school they were best suited for.

Criticisms of the tripartite system

1. Grammar schools, attended by around 20 per cent of young people, were seen as the most prestigious type of secondary school. They specialised in academic subjects that led to high-status, well-paid jobs. Secondary modern schools, attended by most young people (around 75 per cent), were seen as low-status institutions. Parity of esteem did not exist.

2. The system wasted talent. Many secondary modern students were not allowed to take O-level exams

(similar to GCSEs), which meant their education finished at the age of 15. They were denied the opportunity to progress further. This prevented many from realising their potential and from making a full contribution to the economy.

3. One of the main aims of the 1944 Education Act was to increase the opportunities of working-class students. Yet the social class divide remained. For example, two-thirds of boys from middle-class backgrounds went to grammar schools but only a quarter of working-class boys (Halsey *et al.*, 1980).

The comprehensive system

By the 1960s, it was clear to many that the tripartite system was wasting talent. The education and skills needed for economic growth were not being provided. Nor was the equality of educational opportunity which the 1944 Act looked forward to. The comprehensive system offered a possible solution. It would provide a single form of state secondary education for all. There would be one type of school – the comprehensive school – for students of all backgrounds and all abilities who would be offered the same opportunities to obtain qualifications and training.

Supporters of comprehensive education believed that it would reduce social class differences in educational attainment. But, despite an improvement in the educational qualifications of all school leavers, class differences in educational attainment remained largely unchanged as discussed in Part 3 *Class and educational attainment*.

A more equal society

It appeared that social class prevented equality of educational opportunity. In other words, class inequality led to inequality of educational opportunity. Some social democrats argued that the only way to move towards equal opportunity was to reduce social inequality in society as a whole. One way to do this was to target resources on the most disadvantaged.

This was the thinking behind **Educational Priority Areas** in the late 1960s. Additional resources were provided for low-income areas in England, in the hope of raising standards. The emphasis was on pre-school and primary education. Although it was difficult to evaluate the results, the available evidence suggests that Educational Priority Areas produced little change (Midwinter, 1975).

Key terms

Tripartite system A three-part system of secondary education.

Grammar schools Secondary schools seen as suitable for academic students.

Secondary technical schools Schools seen as suitable for students with an aptitude for technical subjects.

Secondary modern schools Schools seen as suitable for students best suited to practical tasks.

Parity of esteem Equal status.

Educational Priority Areas Low-income areas given additional resources for education.

Summary

1. The tripartite system was designed to provide equal opportunities for all young people.

2. It consisted of three types of schools for students seen to have different aptitudes and talents.

3. The three types of schools did not have parity of esteem. The system wasted talent. Working-class students were concentrated in secondary moderns, the lowest status schools.

4. Comprehensive schools were intended to provide a single type of state secondary school for all students.

5. Despite improvements in educational qualifications for all in the comprehensive system, social class differences in attainment remained.

6. Educational Priority Areas appeared to produce little change.

2.2.2 Conservative educational policy, 1979–1997

Neoliberal/new right policies (see Chapter 2, Part 1, pp. 45–49) became increasingly influential during the Conservative governments from 1979 to 1997. These policies are briefly summarised below:

❯ Education should be mainly concerned with promoting economic growth through improving the skills of the workforce.

❯ The best way to achieve this is to encourage competition in the educational marketplace. The introduction of market forces will make schools more efficient and raise standards.

❯ Competition will only work if parents have a real choice between schools. They will select the most successful schools for their children. The greater the competition, the greater the incentive for schools to improve. Unsuccessful schools will either have to raise their standards or face the possibility of closure.

❯ Parents must have a means of assessing the quality of schools. This is provided by government inspections and a rigorous system of testing students. The results of these inspections and tests must be made available to parents so that they can make an informed choice.

The 1988 Education Reform Act

The Education Reform Act of 1988 was the most far-reaching legislation since the 1944 Education Act. It introduced the following measures:

1. **Grant maintained schools** State schools were allowed to opt out of local authority control if a sufficient number of parents voted to support this move. Known as grant maintained schools, they were funded directly by central government. The idea was to free schools to specialise in particular subjects or particular types of students. This, it was hoped, would offer diversity and real choice for parents, and encourage schools to compete in the educational marketplace.

2. **City technology colleges** Diversity, choice and competition were to be extended by the introduction of city technology colleges. Financed by central government and private industry, they would focus on maths, science and technology. They were to be built mainly in inner-city areas, for 11- to 18-year-old students, and they were to compete with existing schools. In the 1990s, the Conservatives introduced two further types of schools – schools specialising in either languages or technology. They were called colleges to indicate their prestige and importance. By 1996, there were 1100 grant maintained schools, accounting for one in five of all secondary students. There were 15 city technology colleges, 30 language colleges and 151 new technology colleges (Chitty, 2002).

3. **Open enrolment** Parents were given the right to send their children to the school of their choice. This would encourage schools to compete and improve their results.

4. **Formula funding** Under this new system of funding, the financing of schools was largely based on the number of enrolments. This was intended to reward successful schools that attracted large numbers of students, while giving less successful schools an incentive to improve.

5. **National Curriculum** For the first time, the government told teachers in England and Wales what to teach, and provided tests – Key Stage tests for students at age 7, 11 and 14 – in order to assess parts of the National Curriculum. These tests were also used to assess teachers and schools.

6. **League tables** The testing and assessment process introduced by the 1988 Education Act was developed during the 1990s. In 1992, state secondary schools in England and Wales were required to publish their Key Stage, GCSE and A-level results. In 1997, primary schools were required to publish their Key Stage results. Local and national league tables of schools were based on these results. They were intended to provide parents with the information they needed to make an informed choice of school, and to intensify competition between schools by encouraging them to improve their position in the league.

In 1993, the Office for Standards in Education (Ofsted) was set up to inspect schools in England and Wales. All schools were to be inspected every four years and a report published on the quality of teaching and the standard achieved. Ofsted reports provided further information for the assessment of schools.

Activity

How does this picture illustrate the aims of Conservative educational policy?

Vocational education and training

Conservative governments from 1979 to 1997 aimed to develop a vocational education and training system to meet the needs of industry. Until the 1970s, **vocational training** – training for work – was seen as the responsibility of employers. This view began to change in the 1970s with the rapid rise in youth unemployment. Many argued that this rise was largely due to schools failing to teach appropriate work skills to young people. As a result, industry faced a skills shortage. A number of measures were designed to solve this problem. They included the following:

1. **National Vocational Qualifications (NVQs)** In 1986, the National Council for Vocational Qualifications was set up to introduce standardised vocational qualifications for particular occupations. By 1990, around 170 NVQs had been established.

2. **General National Vocational Qualifications (GNVQs)** More general vocational qualifications covering wider areas – for example, leisure and tourism and health and social care – were available from 1995. They were intended to provide a vocational alternative to traditional academic qualifications such as GCSEs and A-levels.

3. **Modern apprenticeships** From 1995, these programmes combined training at work with part-time attendance at college, with the aim of achieving an NVQ qualification at Level 3 (equivalent to A-level).

4. **The new vocationalism** This term was used to describe new vocational training initiatives introduced in the 1970s and aimed initially at unemployed young people. Started by the Labour government in the early 1970s, they were developed by the Conservatives. For example, the **Youth Training Scheme (YTS)** was a training scheme for school leavers, combining work experience with education.

Evaluating educational policy, 1979–1997

This section examines sociological studies that have attempted to evaluate the changes in educational policy from 1979 to 1997. These studies were conducted when the Conservatives were in power. However, in some respects, they are also relevant for evaluating Labour policies after 1997, since Labour retained many of the competitive, market-based reforms introduced by the Conservatives.

The marketisation of schools

Between 1991 and 1994, Stephen J. Ball, Richard Bowe and Sharon Gewirtz conducted a study of 15 schools in three neighbouring local educational authorities (LEAs) (Ball *et al.*, 1994; Gewirtz *et al.*, 1995).

They visited the schools, attended meetings, examined documents and interviewed a sample of teachers.

They also interviewed about 150 parents who had children in primary schools and who were at the point of making the choice about the secondary schools their children should attend. The study attempted to discover the effects that parental choice and the encouragement of competition between schools were having on school performance.

The effects on schools

The study found that most schools were 'paying a lot more attention to what parents want for their children's education. Or more precisely what schools think that parents want'. However, it was not the case that schools were equally keen to attract all students. The publication of league tables meant that schools were increasingly keen to attract academically able students who would boost the school's league table performance and thus improve its reputation. According to Ball *et al.* (1994), 'There is a shift of emphasis from student needs to student performance, from what the school can do for the students to what the students can do for the school'.

This emphasis had encouraged some schools to direct more resources to children who were likely to be successful in examinations and tests. In some cases, it had led to students being seen as commodities by the school.

As schools have concentrated on the more able students, they have paid less attention to those with Special Educational Needs (SENs). Indeed, Ball *et al.* argue, 'some of the money and energy previously devoted to educational endeavours like SEN work are now focused on marketing activities'. In an effort to attract students, some schools were publishing glossy brochures and some brought in public relations firms. Staff were expected to devote more time and energy to marketing activities such as open evenings.

Sharon Gewirtz *et al.* (1995) saw a move towards market values with 'commercial rather than educational principles' becoming increasingly dominant. Schools were competing rather than cooperating. A concern with league tables influenced

47

what went on in the classroom and the allocation of resources.

The educational market and parental choice

Gewirtz *et al.* found that the amount of choice involved in selecting a school was limited both by the availability of schools and by the ability of parents to judge and choose between them. And in this respect, parents were not equal. Three broad groups were distinguished in terms of their ability effectively to choose between schools:

1. **Privileged/skilled choosers** are strongly motivated to choose a school for their children and they have the necessary skills to do so. They have the ability to understand the nature of different schools and to evaluate the claims made by schools in their publicity material. They are likely to devote considerable time and energy to finding out about different schools and their admission criteria. Privileged/skilled choosers often have the money to make a range of choices that will assist their children's education. These choices may include moving house or paying for private education. Privileged/skilled choosers are usually middle class.

2. **Semi-skilled choosers** 'have strong inclination but limited capacity to engage with the market' (Gewirtz *et al.*, 1995). They are just as concerned to get the best possible education for their children but they do not have the same level of skill as their privileged/skilled counterparts. They tend to lack the 'experiences or inside knowledge of the school system and the social contacts and cultural skills to choose "effectively"'.

3. **Disconnected choosers** are not inclined to get very involved with the educational market. They are concerned about their children's welfare and education but they usually only consider a smaller number of options, and frequently just the two closest schools to where they live. They tend to believe there is little difference between schools, and put more emphasis on the happiness of their child than on the academic reputation of the school. The result is that disconnected choosers are more likely to send their children to the local school where their friends are going, rather than have them travel further afield to a supposedly better school. Disconnected choosers are likely to be working class.

These differences result in certain groups being more likely to benefit from the educational market than others. Generally, the higher a person's social class, the more likely they are to benefit from the best state schooling (or to be able to choose private schooling). The market leads to a hierarchy of schools and, even without selection by academic ability, this can lead to a growing division between predominantly middle-class and working-class schools.

Conclusion

Stephen J. Ball *et al.* (1994) conclude that the encouragement of parental choice, the publication of exam results in league tables, open enrolment, formula funding, and other policies designed to make education more market-orientated, have all served to make education less egalitarian. Those whose children are already advantaged in the system seem to be gaining even more benefits, while those who are already disadvantaged are losing further ground.

At the same time schools are becoming more concerned with attracting the gifted and the advantaged than with helping the disadvantaged. According to Ball *et al.*'s research: 'we are likely to end up with a more socially differentiated and divisive system of education. In any market there are winners and losers. In this market we may all end up losing out!' (For more discussion of this research, see Part 3.)

Youth training schemes

The various youth training schemes introduced in the 1970s and 1980s were seen by governments as a way of improving work skills and reducing rising unemployment. These schemes were strongly attacked by some critics. For example, Dan Finn (1987) argued that the main reason that many young people were unemployed was not a lack of appropriate work skills. Instead, it was simply a lack of jobs. Finn claimed that youth training schemes were developed to:

» keep young unemployed people 'off the streets' in order to reduce the risk of crime and social unrest

» provide employers with a source of cheap labour at a time of declining profits

» reduce the embarrassingly high unemployment statistics – those on training schemes were not included in these statistics.

Key terms

Marketisation of schools The introduction of market principles such as competition into the education system.

Grant maintained schools Schools funded directly by the government and allowed to opt out of local authority control.

City technology colleges Funded directly by central government and private industry. Specialised in maths, science and technology.

Open enrolment Parents have the right to send their children to the school of their choice.

Formula funding Schools are financed mainly on the basis of the number of students enrolled in the school.

National curriculum A curriculum which instructed all state schools what to teach.

League tables The ranking of schools in terms of their test and exam results.

Vocational education and training An education and training system designed to teach work skills to meet the needs of industry.

Summary

1. The Conservative governments from 1979 to 1997 were strongly influenced by neoliberal policies. They saw the marketisation of schools as a means of raising standards which they believed would contribute to economic growth.

2. Open enrolment and league tables are examples of marketisation. They were seen as ways of increasing competition and raising standards.

3. Critics argue that the marketisation of education favoured the middle class, 'the advantaged', at the expense of the working class, 'the disadvantaged'. This can be seen in parents' skill differences in selecting schools for their children.

2.2.3 Labour educational policy, 1997–2010

Coming to power in 1997, Tony Blair, leader of the Labour Party, announced that his priorities were 'Education, Education, Education'. This section looks at how Labour translated these priorities into policy and practice.

Labour's educational policy was influenced by both social democratic and neoliberal perspectives. This unit begins by outlining legislation reflecting social democratic concerns with equality of educational opportunity.

The influence of social democratic perspectives

A number of Labour policies were influenced by social democratic perspectives. They include the following.

Education Action Zones (EAZs)

Education Action Zones were set up in 1998 to raise the motivation and attainment levels of underachieving students in 'deprived', low-income, inner-city areas. By 2003, there were 73 EAZs in England. They were funded by central government with additional funding from business. An Action Forum, made up of parents and representatives from local schools and businesses and from local and national government, ran each zone.

An Ofsted report on EAZs praised some initiatives, such as homework clubs and breakfast clubs. The report found some improvement in standards at Key Stage 1 but no change at Key Stage 3 or GCSE results at Key Stage 4 (McKnight *et al.*, 2005).

Excellence in Cities (EiC)

The **Excellence in Cities** programme steadily replaced EAZs. It targeted local education authorities in disadvantaged inner-city areas. Like EAZs, it aimed to improve attainment levels of students from low-income backgrounds. The main initiatives of EiC were special programmes for gifted students, city learning centres with IT facilities, learning mentors and low-cost leasing for home computers (Tomlinson, 2005). Various reports evaluating the EiC programme produced mixed results. In general, however, they indicated only limited success (McKnight *et al.*, 2005). The EiC programme was ended in 2006.

Sure Start

This programme targeted the under-fives and their families living in the most deprived areas of England. It aimed to improve their health, education and employment prospects. **Sure Start** is based on the idea that early intervention – for example, home visits and play centres run by professionals – will have long-term positive results. Started in 1999, by 2010 there were 3631 Sure Start children's centres (DfE, November 2010).

A major evaluation of Sure Start programmes examined over 7000 families in 150 Sure Start areas and compared them with families in similarly disadvantaged areas without Sure Start. Mothers in the Sure Start areas reported a more stimulating home environment for their children. And their children had better physical health. However, by the end of Labour's time in office the benefits of Sure Start appeared 'modest' (DfE, November 2010).

Academies

Academies were originally designed to replace 'failing' comprehensive schools in low-income, inner-city areas. They aimed to drive up educational standards. Academies were sponsored by individuals, businesses, religious faiths, charities, and by city education authorities. Sponsors contributed up to £2 million and appointed the majority of governors who ran the school. Central government contributed around £25 million for each academy. The first three academies were opened in 2002, there were 46 by 2006, and 203 in 2010.

Academies have considerable freedom. They are independent from the local authority, they choose their own head teacher and they develop their own curriculum. National curriculum teaching is required only in the core subjects. Part of the idea behind academies is that the freedom they provide will lead to new strategies to combat underachievement.

The day-to-day running of academies is in the hands of the head teacher. They are overseen by charitable trusts known as **academy trusts**. The trusts provide advice, expertise, policy and direction. They are not owned by the state but they cannot run schools for profit.

Studies of how well academies were doing produced mixed results. Most researchers argued that it was too early to judge their performance (Machin and Vernoit, 2010). Where there were improvements, for example in GCSE results, some claim that this was mainly due to academies taking fewer students with special educational needs and behaviour problems. For a full evaluation of academies see pp. 58–60.

Further and higher education (FE and HE)

Labour aimed to widen access to further and higher education – in particular, to increase the number and proportion of working-class students in FE and HE.

Further education The proportion of 16- to 18-year-olds in England in education and training grew steadily under Labour, from 56.4 per cent in 1997 to 68.6 per cent in 2010 (DfE, 28.6.2012). However, participation varied by social class. For

example, in England and Wales in 2004, 85 per cent of 16-year-olds from the higher professional class were in full-time education, compared to 57 per cent from the working class (DfES, 24.02.2005).

The **Education Maintenance Allowance (EMA)** was introduced in 2004 in an attempt to reduce the class gap in FE. EMA was a weekly cash allowance payable to 16- to 19-year-olds from low-income families who remained in education. Pilot studies found that staying-on rates increased by around 6 per cent with EMA (McKnight *et al.*, 2005).

Higher education (HE) There has been a rapid increase in student numbers in higher education in the UK. Under Labour the numbers increased from 2 million in 1997/8 to 2.5 million in 2009/10. The Labour government aimed to have 50 per cent of 17- to 30-year-olds in higher education by 2010. The percentage for England for 2010/11 was 47 per cent (HESA, 2012).

Despite increasing numbers of students from all social classes, the class gap in HE participants has been steadily widening. For example, in Britain in 2001, 79 per cent of young people from professional backgrounds were in HE, compared with 55 per cent in 1991 – a gain of 24 percentage points. At the other end of the scale, 15 per cent of young people from unskilled manual backgrounds were in HE in 2001, compared with 6 per cent in 1991, a gain of only 9 percentage points. This indicates that those at the top of the class system have gained far more from the expansion of places in higher education (Galindo-Rueda *et al.*, 2004).

Labour introduced **tuition fees** for higher education starting from September 1998. They did so in order to pay for expanding student numbers, to improve facilities and raise standards, and to allow universities to compete successfully with increasing global competition.

In England, students were required to pay £1,000 a year in tuition fees. Tuition was free to students from low-income families. The student grant was abolished and replaced by student loans. In 2004, **variable tuition fees** were introduced – fees which varied from one university to another. Universities were allowed to charge up to £3,000 a year. Scotland, Wales and Northern Ireland had their own arrangements for tuition.

Despite Labour's aim to close the class gap in higher education, there is some evidence to suggest that at first tuition fees and loans reduced participation by students from low-income backgrounds (see *Unit 2.2.3 Labour educational policy, 1997–2010*). But the widening gap may simply be a continuation of a long-term trend – a trend that was well under way before Labour's election in 1997 (Galindo-Rueda *et al.*, 2004). However, during the later years of Labour's administration, the class gap in higher education slowly narrowed. The evidence for this is examined in Part 3 on social class and educational attainment.

The influence of neoliberal perspectives

Specialist schools

Labour continued the Conservative policy of **specialist schools**. They rejected the idea of the 'one-size-fits-all' comprehensive. Rather than a single type of school for everyone, schools should specialise in particular subject areas. This would provide diversity and choice within the educational marketplace, it would increase competition and it would raise standards. According to former Secretary of State for Education, Estelle Morris, 'Specialist schools and Colleges will have a key contribution to make in raising standards and delivering excellence in schools' (quoted in Chitty, 2002).

In 1997, Labour inherited 196 specialist schools from the Conservatives. Ten years later, there were over 2500 specialist schools – over 75 per cent of all secondary schools in England (Tomlinson, 2005; www.standards.dfes.gov.uk/specialistschools).

Evaluation of specialist schools

In 2005, the House of Commons Select Committee on Education and Skills published a report on a two-year investigation into secondary education. Here is a summary of its main findings (Select Committee on Education and Skills, 2005):

> **Specialist schools and standards** The government claimed that the specialist school policy would raise standards. Although standards have risen in many specialist schools, it is not clear why they have risen. Is it the specialism? An Ofsted report found that schools often achieve better results in subjects outside their specialist area. Improvement might be due to additional government funding during a specialist school's first four years.

> **Social class and specialist schools** Specialist schools tend to have a higher middle-class intake than non-specialist schools. This may account for their better results.

> **Admissions policy and selection** Evidence indicates 'a troubling slide away from parents choosing schools for their children and towards schools choosing the students they wish to admit'. This is due to a shortage of places in schools which parents choose. Research suggests that some schools will select those they see as the most able students in order to boost their results – and these tend to be middle-class students.

Responding to this criticism, the government published new rules for admissions in 2006, in order to make the process fairer – for example, by banning interviews with parents and/or students (Taylor, 2006).

Various methods have been suggested for dealing with oversubscribed schools. One suggestion is a lottery system whereby students are randomly selected. Another suggestion is that, to ensure a range of ability, children take an admission test. They are then placed in ability bands on the basis of the test results, and a number of children are selected from each band (Shepherd, 2007).

Activity

Bags of cultural capital! '*There is a shift of emphasis from student needs to student performance: from what the school can do for the students to what the students can do for the school*' (Ball et al., 1994).

How does the picture illustrate this quote?

Assessment and targets

Labour largely welcomed the testing and assessment regime developed by the Conservatives. Students, teachers and schools were rigorously assessed with Key Stage tests, GCSE and A-level examinations, Ofsted inspections, and a range of other measures such as truancy rates. These assessments were published and schools ranked in league tables.

In addition, performance targets were set for Key Stage tests. The thinking behind assessment and performance targets included the following:

» Measurements of performance are essential if parents are to make an informed choice of school.

» They will encourage schools to compete – for example, to improve their position in school league tables and to increase student numbers.

» This will raise standards by providing incentives to improve test and exam results.

» Performance targets will improve standards by providing clear targets to aim for and by rewarding success.

School league tables

Since 1992, secondary schools have been required to publish their GCSE and A-level results. At first, league tables were based on examination results. They showed, for example, the percentage of students obtaining at least five grades A*–C at GCSE. Later, additional measures were included – for example, **value added** and **most improved**. The **value added** score measures the difference schools have made between the ages of 11 and 16 – for example, how much a school has improved a student's attainment over the five years of secondary education. '**Most improved**' looks at the improvements in GCSE results in particular schools over time.

Evaluation of league tables League tables have been strongly criticised. Critics argue that they fail to provide an accurate measure of school performance. GCSE results may say more about the social background of students than the performance of the school. In general, the higher the proportion of middle-class students, the better the school's GCSE results. The value added measure goes some way to meet this criticism but it does not take the social background of students into account.

In 2006, social factors were included for the first time. This measure indicates what students might be expected to achieve given their social background. Schools whose students exceed this expectation will do well in this league table. Results using this measure show that many schools in low-income, 'deprived' areas are doing far better than either the exam results or the value added measures indicate (Crace, 2006).

Despite the introduction of alternative league tables, the original measure – exam results – remains the basis for many parents' judgement of schools. As a result, this will encourage schools to recruit 'able' middle-class students and avoid those with special needs and excluded children. Also, the priority given to exam results will encourage teachers to 'teach to the test' – to teach students how to pass exams rather than improving understanding and learning (Thrupp and Hursh, 2006).

The educational triage In a study entitled *Rationing Education* David Gillborn and Deborah Youdell (2000) looked at some of the effects on teaching of league tables and the marketisation of schools. Their detailed research over a two-year period was based on interviews and observations in two London secondary schools. They found that teachers divided students into three groups in terms of their predicted performance at GCSE. The first group consisted of students who were expected to attain an A to C grade with little difficulty. The second group were seen as 'borderline cases' – students on the border of grades C and B. The third group were seen as 'hopeless cases' – students with little or no hope of reaching a grade C or above. Gillborn and Youdell call this three-part grouping the **educational triage**.

Gillborn and Youdell found that teachers 'rationed' their teaching for each group in the triage. Their main focus was the second group – the 'borderline cases'. They were given the most experienced teachers, additional teaching, close attention to their progress, and further resources such as new textbooks – all aimed at boosting their GCSE grades.

The main measure for judging secondary school performance was the proportion of students obtaining five or more GCSEs with grades A* to C. The aim of the educational triage was to maximise this proportion. The most effective way of doing this was seen as additional resources of time, effort and money directed at the borderline cases. And the main reason for doing this was to improve the school's position in the league table.

This focus on borderline cases discriminated against the first and third triage. It was particularly harmful to the third triage, those in the lower sets who arguably needed the most help. In the schools studied by Gillborn and Youdell these were mainly working class and Black-Caribbean students. Teachers often recognised this as the following quote from John Dunford, general secretary of the Secondary Heads Association indicates. 'Schools are forced by league tables to put a disproportionate amount of resources into the C/D borderlines which they would prefer to use evenly to raise the performance of all pupils' (quoted in *The Guardian*, 19 March, 2002).

The educational triage

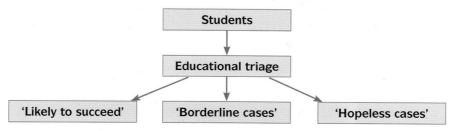

Vocational education and training

In 2005, Labour leader Tony Blair stated: 'We have to secure Britain's future in a world driven by globalisation. We have to change and modernise ... to equip everyone for this changing world'. He saw the way to do this was to raise standards in education.

In many ways, Labour's education policy was driven by neoliberal ideas which see the main role of education as providing the skills and knowledge required by the workforce in an increasingly competitive global society. According to Sally Tomlinson (2005), 'education was subordinated to the economy'. In this sense, all education was vocational education. From Labour's point of view, the education system must 'respond to a competitive global economy by improving the skills and qualifications of young people' (Tomlinson, 2005).

Vocational qualifications

GNVQs (General National Vocational Qualifications) were introduced by the Conservatives in 1995 as vocational alternatives to GCSE and A-level. They covered broad vocational areas such as health and social care, business and finance, and leisure and tourism.

In 2001, Labour rebranded GNVQs as **vocational GCSEs** and **vocational A-levels** in an attempt to raise their status so that they would be seen as equivalent to academic qualifications. Critics saw this as a cosmetic exercise, seeing most vocational qualifications as primarily a route into lower-paid, lower-status jobs. Traditionally, it has been students from working-class backgrounds who have been channelled into vocational courses (Tomlinson, 2005).

Evaluation of Labour's policies

As previous sections have shown, both social democratic and neoliberal perspectives influenced Labour's educational policies. From Labour's

point of view, policies based on these two perspectives are complementary rather than contradictory. For example, raising standards through competition and choice will also increase the opportunities of those from disadvantaged backgrounds, thereby reducing inequality of opportunity. In the process, the skills of the workforce will be raised, so improving the UK's ability to compete in a competitive global economy. However, many critics have questioned both the effectiveness and compatibility of Labour's policies.

Sally Tomlinson: *Education in a Post-Welfare Society*

Tomlinson believes that Labour narrowed education to an economic function. The party became preoccupied with raising standards in order for the UK to compete effectively in an increasingly global market. In Tomlinson's words:

> In an effort to keep the UK economy competitive, education and training are elevated to key positions; 'raising standards', 'learning to compete' and getting education 'right' become major policy objectives.   Tomlinson, 2005

According to Tomlinson, Labour saw the application of market principles to schools as the main way to raise standards. Competition and choice would drive up standards in an educational market. However, this almost compulsive preoccupation with 'standards' had a down side.

First, it favoured the middle classes. The success of some schools in the educational market meant they were oversubscribed. As a result, they were able to select their own customers. The pressure to remain market leaders and maintain their position in the league table led them to select those they saw as most able. In practice, this meant mainly middle-class students.

In a market system, schools are judged largely on results. With league tables based on Key Stage

53

tests, GCSE and A-level results, there is considerable pressure on teachers to teach to the tests. The priority has increasingly become 'examination techniques, rote learning and revision'. This, combined with the view of education as being primarily about 'jobs, business, enterprise and competition', may be a threat to the well-being of society. Tomlinson (2005) concludes:

Critiques of the narrowing of education to economic ends want to reclaim education as a humanising, liberalising, democratising force, directed, as the UN (1948) Universal Declaration of Human Rights put it, to 'the full development of the human personality and a strengthening of respect for human rights and fundamental freedoms'.

Paul Trowler: social and educational inequalities

In *Education Policy*, Paul Trowler (2003) saw initiatives such as Excellence in Cities, directed at low-income, inner-city areas, as a positive move. However, he warned about seeing such initiatives as the answer to significantly reducing inequality of educational opportunity.

Like many sociologists, Trowler argues that changes in the educational system cannot compensate for social inequality in the wider society. As long as social inequality exists, it will be reflected in educational attainment. It follows that a significant reduction in inequality of educational opportunity requires a significant reduction in social inequality in society as a whole. Trowler (2003) concludes:

Although Labour has learned a lot about educational policy, it continues to have unrealistic expectations of what education can do and has a similarly unrealistic expectation of how far deep-rooted social inequalities can be successfully reduced through the educative process.

Key terms

Education Action Zones (EAZs) A programme to raise the attainment of students in low-income, inner-city areas.

Excellence in Cities A programme which replaced EAZs with similar aims.

Sure Start A programme to improve the health and education of the under-fives and their families in the most deprived areas of England.

Academies Under Labour, academies were designed to replace 'failing' schools and drive up standards.

Academy trusts Charitable trusts which provide the overall policy and direction for academies.

Vocational GCSEs and vocational A-levels New exams introduced in the hope of raising the status of vocational courses to the same level as academic qualifications.

Education Maintenance Allowance (EMA) A cash allowance payable to students aged 16–19 from low-income families in further education.

Tuition fees Fees that most students in England are required to pay for a university education.

Specialist schools Secondary schools specialising in particular subject areas.

New Deal for Young People A programme designed to reduce youth unemployment.

Educational triage The division of students into three groups in terms of their expected GCSE grades.

Summary

1. Labour's educational policy was influenced by both social democratic and neoliberal perspectives.

2. Education Action Zones, Excellence in Cities and Sure Start aimed to improve educational performance in low-income areas. These programmes had only limited success.

3. Academies replaced 'failing' secondary schools. Researchers argued that it was too early to judge their performance.

4. Labour aimed to close the class gap in further education (FE) and higher education (HE). The Education Maintenance Allowance increased the numbers of students in FE from low-income families. In HE the class gap grew during the early years of Labour's time in office, then slowly narrowed in the later years.

5. Labour introduced further specialist schools to provide diversity and choice in the educational market. In general, specialist schools improved exam results but this may simply be due to an increase in middle-class students in these schools.

6. Labour continued the assessment of schools and the league tables introduced by the Conservatives, seeing them as a way of raising standards.

7. Labour saw the main role of education as providing the skills and knowledge required in an increasingly competitive global society.

8. The focus on the economy has been seen as narrowing the content of education. What about human rights, democracy and the common good?

9. Critics argue that Labour's focus on competition and choice favoured the middle class.

10. Many sociologists argue that programmes such as Excellence in Cities cannot significantly reduce inequality of educational opportunity. This requires a major reduction of social inequality in the wider society.

11. The educational triage has been seen to discriminate against those expected to get high grades and low grades at GCSE.

2.2.4 Coalition educational policy, 2010–2015

In May 2010, the Conservative–Liberal Democrat Coalition government came to power. The Conservatives were the dominant party in numerical terms and their views are more strongly represented in Coalition educational policy.

Coalition policy is based on the following views about what makes outstanding schools:

1. **Independence** – the freedom for head teachers and staff to develop teaching strategies and styles best suited to their particular students.

2. **Accountability** to parents rather than to local and national government bureaucracies.

3. **Competition** between schools will drive up standards. Successful schools will expand and failing schools will go to the wall.

4. **Diversity and choice** – real choice requires diversity – a range of different schools to choose from. These views are strongly influenced by neoliberal ideas.

Academies

Under Labour, academies were designed to replace underperforming secondary schools in low-income,

disadvantaged areas. The Coalition's policy for academies was much more ambitious. Labour's concern with disadvantaged children remains, but now all schools, both primary and secondary, outstanding and average, in high and low-income areas, can apply to convert to an academy. The then education secretary, Michael Gove, outlined the thinking behind this policy:

When a school becomes an academy, there's only one focus – the children. And the question that everyone asks is: How can we ensure, working with the additional freedoms and resources that we have, that we focus on raising attainment for the very poorest? The Guardian, 10.04.2012

There are now two types of academy: **sponsored academies**, which are instructed to become academies by the Department for Education because they were 'failing', and **converter academies**, which choose to become academies. When the coalition government came to power in May 2010 there were 203 academies. By April 2012, there were 1176, of which 464 were primary schools. Most of these were converter academies.

Why have so many schools converted in such a short period of time? A survey of 478 academies suggested that money was a major reason: 78 per cent said they converted partly because they believed they would be better off; 39 per cent said this was their main reason (*The Schools' Network*, 2012).

Evaluation of the new academies

The debate about the performance of academies continues. The Department for Education (22 June, 2012) claimed that the improvement in GCSE results for academies from 2010 to 2011 was twice that of non-academies. However, a comparison of academies and non-academies in disadvantaged areas – a comparison of like with like – shows no difference in their levels of improvement from 2010 to 2011 (Stewart, 2012). But it is probably still too early to judge the effectiveness of the academies programme. A full evaluation of academies is provided on pp. 58–60.

Free schools

Whereas academies were developed from Labour policies, **free schools** were a new departure. Rather than replacing existing schools, they form new ones. The first free schools opened in 2011. According to the Coalition, the aim of free schools is to increase diversity, so adding to parental choice, and to increase competition, in order to drive up standards. This will be achieved by giving teachers the freedom to design teaching styles to meet local needs and by giving parents the opportunity to choose suitable schools based on knowledge of their children. In the then education secretary Michael Gove's words, free schools will provide 'a greater opportunity for children to learn and develop in the way that's best for them'. Although free schools are seen to benefit all children, additional funding is provided for free schools in disadvantaged areas.

According to the Department for Education, free schools are non-profit-making, state-funded schools. They are independent from local authorities but subject to Ofsted inspection. They do not have to follow the National Curriculum as long as they teach English, maths and science. Teachers do not have to have teaching qualifications. Free schools are to be set up in response to what local people want and need. This will lead to a variety of schools rather than 'one size fits all'. A range of groups can set up free schools. These include teachers, charities, academy sponsors, universities, independent schools, community and faith groups, parents and businesses. Between 2010 and 2015 over 400 free schools were approved for opening by the Coalition.

The above description of free schools is taken from information provided by the Department for Education. It will therefore tend to be positive. However, a number of criticisms have been raised.

Evaluation of free schools

1. There is no evidence that free schools have improved standards. According to Ofsted in its 2015 report, 'We have inspected 158 free schools and inspection outcomes are broadly in line with those for all schools' (Ofsted, 2015). However, it's early days for free schools.

2. In some areas, free schools are competing against good neighbouring schools where there is already a surplus of school places or sufficient places to meet local needs. According to the National Audit Office, this can lead 'to a drop in funding for existing schools and can have a negative effect on pupils in these schools' (National Audit Office, 2013).

3. Free schools receive a much higher level of state funding – in 2013–14, £7761 per pupil compared with £4767 for local authority schools (National Union of Teachers, 2016).

4. A study by the Institute of Education supports the Coalition's claim that free schools would start up in disadvantaged areas as well as middle-class areas. However, the study also supports critics' concerns that schools might become socially selective – choosing pupils likely to succeed. Free schools in disadvantaged areas had a lower proportion of pupils with free school meals than the average for the area (Green *et al.*, 2014).

5. The first set of GCSE results from free schools which had educated students throughout their secondary school careers were produced in 2016. The results were mixed – some were excellent, some were poor (Vaughan, 2016).

Further and higher education

The proportion of 16 to 18-year-olds in full-time education in England fell slightly from 70.6 per cent in 2010 to 70.5 per cent in 2011. This was the first time it had fallen since 2001 (DfE, 21 February, 2013). This decline coincided with the removal of the Education Maintenance Allowance (EMA), which was designed to encourage students from low-income families to continue their education. EMA was worth £560 million a year. The allowance that replaced it in England, the 16 to 19 Bursary Fund, was worth

Activity

*Student protest against the abolition of the EMA. Jan Moir commented in the **Daily Mail** on this protest, 'Stop whingeing you spoilt little brats – and get a paper round… Doesn't it seem outrageous that struggling pensioners, plus you and me, should be helping to bankroll what is essentially state-funded pocket money?'. **Daily Mail**, 21.01.2011.*

What do you think about this comment from Jan Moir?

£180 million. According to the Department for Education, financial support was now targeted at students 'who need it most'. Critics argued that the reduction in the allowance had led to the decline in FE student numbers (BBC News online, 13.10.2011). Alan Milburn, the Coalition's adviser for social mobility and poverty, described the abolition of EMA as 'a very bad mistake'. He stated that EMA had 'significantly increased staying on rates and attainment' and its replacement had considerably reduced the number of students eligible for support (Wintour, 2012).

Tuition fees

The Coalition government raised the limit on tuition fees for the 2012/13 academic year. From September 2012, universities were allowed to charge fees of up to £9000 a year, nearly three times the previous limit. The Coalition's reasons for this rise were similar to the Labour government's – rapidly growing student numbers and an increasingly competitive global education market.

The Independent Commission on Fees was set up in 2011 to measure the impact of the increase in fees. It found that there was a fall in university applications in 2011 but in 2012 there were more applications than ever before and they continued to rise.

Applications from students from low-income families also grew. But there was a steady fall in part-time and mature students applying, many of whom came from less well-off backgrounds. According to the commission, 'the new fees were a major contributing factor'.

In its final report in 2015, the Commission concludes that 'while the number of students applying to university has not been significantly affected by the new fee regime, there is a continuing and concerning gap between the recruitment of students from less advantaged and more advantaged backgrounds, in favour of the latter' (Independent Commission on Fees, 2015).

The pupil premium and the social mobility strategy

Social democratic concerns about equal opportunities continued to influence education policy. This can be seen from the **pupil premium**, which was introduced by the Coalition in 2011. This was an additional payment to schools based on the number of free school meals students enrolled. According to the

then Deputy Prime Minister Nick Clegg, it aims 'to equip every school to support students from the most disadvantaged backgrounds to help us build a more socially mobile Britain' (Clegg, 2012).

The idea was welcomed. However, a survey of over 2000 head teachers conducted by the National Association of Head Teachers indicated doubts about the effectiveness of the pupil premium. Over 30 per cent of head teachers said the additional money merely made up for cuts elsewhere, and over 50 per cent said it did not even do that. However, 15 per cent felt it would make a difference (Paton, 2012).

The pupil premium forms part of the Coalition's **social mobility strategy** launched in 2011 (HM Government, 2011). Social mobility is the movement from one social class to another. This strategy aims to make Britain a 'fairer and more open society'. It recognises that 'The income and social class of parents continue to have a huge bearing on a child's chances'. It aims to increase the chances of upward social mobility for students from low-income families.

In 2012, the Coalition established the Social Mobility and Child Poverty Commission, now called the Social Mobility Commission. The Commission 'monitors the progress of government and others in improving social mobility and reducing child poverty in the United Kingdom' (Gov.UK-social-mobility-commission, 2016).

Key terms

Sponsored academies Underperforming schools instructed by the Department for Education to become an academy. Run by sponsors – individuals or organisations.

Converter academies Schools which accept an invitation from the Department for Education to 'convert' to an academy. Usually high performing schools.

Free schools Non-profit making, state-funded schools set up by a variety of groups and approved by the Department for Education.

Independent Commission on Fees An independent organisation set up in 2011 to measure the impact of the increase in university fees.

Student premium An additional payment to schools based on the number of their students with free school meals. Intended to raise the attainment of students from low-income families.

Social mobility Movement from one social class to another.

Social mobility strategy A government strategy to measure the effect of social class on social mobility and to improve the chances of upward mobility for students from low-income families.

Summary

1. The Coalition expanded Labour's academy programme adding to the number of sponsored academies and introducing converter academies.

2. The Coalition opened the first free schools seeing them as increasing diversity and parental choice and improving standards.

3. Ofsted found no evidence that free schools improved standards. Critics argued that they sometimes added school places where none were needed, that they received higher funding at the expense of other schools, and that they sometimes selected pupils more likely to succeed.

4. The Independent Commission on Fees found that the rise in tuition fees did not appear to affect the overall number of students applying to university.

5. The student premium was often used to make up for the cuts in funding to schools rather than being directed to students from low-income families.

6. The social mobility strategy aims to make Britain a fairer and more open society.

2.2.5 Conservative educational policy from 2015

This unit starts with the first major evaluation of academies. It then looks at the possible effects of globalisation on educational policy. It considers new ways of measuring school performance – Progress 8 and the English Baccalaureate. It moves on to outline Prime Minister Theresa May's education policy, in particular her controversial view that grammar schools should be reinstated and the fierce opposition that this view aroused. The unit closes with the following questions. Can education, as the government believes:

❯ provide a meritocratic society

❯ increase social mobility?

Academies

The Conservatives continued the rapid growth of academies under the Coalition. In 2016, 2075 out of the 3381 secondary schools had become academies and 2,440 out of the 16 766 primary schools (BBC News online, 07.05.2016).

There was also a rapid growth of **academy chains** – a number of academies which join together, sharing policy and expertise. Sometimes they form a fairly loose group, sometimes a fairly tight group governed by a **multi-academy trust**.

At one point, the Conservatives decided to make it compulsory for all schools to become academies. In the face of considerable opposition from schools and even members of their own party, they dropped this demand. Despite this, they stated 'Our ambition remains for all schools to become academies with more schools joining multi-academy trusts. Our evidence shows this is the best way to bring about sustained improvement.'

Evaluating academies

Timo Hannay (2016) conducted an important study evaluating converter and sponsored secondary academies based on their GCSE results.

Converter academies 792 secondary schools converted to academies in 2010 and 2011. Before conversion most were rated 'good' or 'outstanding' by Ofsted (Office for Standards in Education). Their GCSE results for 2015 were compared with those of 'similar' local authority (LA) secondary schools. (Local authority schools receive funding and oversight from local education authorities. Academies receive their funding directly from central government and are independent from local authorities.)

In 2015, 68.1 per cent of converter academy students gained five 'good' GCSEs (A*–C grades, including English and Maths). This compares with 66.1 per cent of pupils in 'similar LA schools'. Most of this difference can be explained by prior attainment and economic factors. Students in the converter academies had higher attainment levels before starting secondary school and were less likely to have free school meals. Timo Hannay (2016) concludes that, 'The shift to academy status doesn't seem to have made much difference to the academic performance of these schools'.

Sponsored academies Hannay's evaluation of sponsored academies looks at a sample of 188 schools which became sponsored academies in

Contemporary issues: Living the academy high life

A joint study by Channel 4's *Dispatches* and the *Observer* newspaper raised concerns about the way some leaders of multi-academy trusts rewarded themselves. Here are some of their findings (Channel 4, 25.07.2016; *Guardian*, 24.07.2016).

The chief executives of over half of the largest 50 academy chains paid themselves more than the prime minister (more than £143 000). They stayed in luxury hotels, ate in top restaurants, travelled first-class, received private health care, drove top of the range cars and enjoyed 'soaring salaries'. And all this was paid for by the taxpayer.

Financial transactions with companies and individuals with close links to the directors of academy chains 'have multiplied'. For example, one trust paid £700 000 for services to a company owned by its chief executive. And another trust awarded a £123 000 two-year contract to the chairman's daughter for clerking services. Of the 100 trusts surveyed, around half gave contracts worth over £9 million to the trusts' directors or their relatives.

More than £14 billion of public money goes directly to academy trusts. Margaret Hodge, the former chairperson of the Commons Public Accounts Committee said, 'This money is supposed to be there for the education of our children. The governance system is inadequate. There ought to be proper oversight so these things don't happen'.

The Local Government Association claims that money earmarked for education is too often 'disappearing into the back pockets of those in charge'. They argue that local councils 'should monitor academy cash' and that the Education Secretary should restore local oversight of all school finances in order to provide 'democratic accountability so that parents and communities can be confident their children aren't missing out' (BBC News online, 26.08.2016).

Questions

1. Should academy directors award their own pay, expenses and other rewards?

2. Do you agree with Margaret Hodge and the Local Government Association? Give reasons for your answer.

2010–2012 compared to 'similar LA schools'. In terms of this comparison, sponsored academies do 'almost as well' as similar LA schools judging by GCSE results. But most of these academies started life as badly performing, 'failing' schools. If we look at the amount of improvement from their start as sponsored academies until 2015, then it is *always* better than that of similar LA schools, particularly for low-attaining and disadvantaged students.

Hannay concludes that while converter academies 'seem to have very little impact on the academic performance of successful schools', the move to sponsored academies 'does seem to be an effective way to improve the performance of struggling schools'.

Multi-academy trusts

Around two-thirds of academies work with others in academy chains governed by multi-academy trusts. The Education Policy Institute compared the performance of multi-academy trusts and local authority schools. Two indicators were used to measure their performance: 1) how well the school improved over time and 2) its overall performance

Activity

In 2016 the government announced that all schools were to become academies by 2022. In the face of considerable opposition, they abandoned these plans.

What support do the Education Policy Institute's findings provide for this demonstration?

taking into account the starting point of its pupils. The results showed that multi-academy trusts 'make up a disproportionate number of the lowest performing school groups'. Multi-academy trusts are not the be all and end all – some are good and others are poor. If the government forced all schools to become academies, then some of the best local authority schools might end up in low performing multi-academy trusts. The report concludes: 'The government should not pursue full academisation as a policy. Instead, the objective should be for pupils to be in a good school, regardless of whether that is a high performing multi-academy trust or local authority school' (Andrews, 2016).

Globalisation and educational policy

From the Labour Party in 1997 to the Conservative Party from 2015 onwards, educational policy has been increasingly based on global perspectives. Education has been seen as the key to success in a highly competitive global market. Labour prime minister Tony Blair stated 'Education is our best economic policy'. It follows from this view that international competition extends to educational achievement. Nick Clegg, deputy prime minister in the Coalition government, stated that education 'will define our economic growth and our country's future. The truth is, at the moment, we are standing still while others race past … The only way we can catch up, and have the world-class schools our children deserve, is by learning the lessons of other countries success'. Former Conservative prime minister David Cameron commenting on the UK's position in the global educational league tables asks, 'If they're soaring through the world rankings in Estonia, why can't we? If they're making huge strides in science and maths in India, what's to stop us?' (Speech in Norwich, 09.09.2011.)

Global educational league tables

A number of organisations produce international comparisons of educational attainment. One of the most important is PISA – Programme for International Student Assessment – provided by the Organisation for Economic Cooperation and Development based in Paris. It ranks over 70 countries every three years using tests for maths, science and reading given to samples of 15-year-olds. Results published in 2016 show that Asian countries tend to dominate the rankings – for example, with 7 in the top 10 for maths, with the UK in 27th place (BBC News online, 09.12.2016).

Global educational league tables are taken very seriously. The 2015 Conservative Manifesto stated that their aim was 'to make Britain the best place in the world to study maths, science and engineering, measured by improved performance in the PISA league tables'. Low rankings can result in changes in educational policy. This happened in Wales after the 2016 PISA results. And when Scotland's position in the rankings went down compared to the previous survey, the Scottish Education Secretary said 'The results underline the case for radical reform of Scotland's education system' (BBC News online, 06.12.2016).

Evaluation How seriously should the global league tables be taken? Not very seriously according to Harry Torrance (2006) who has assessed the main providers. Each uses different tests, different samples and different age groups so their results cannot be directly compared. In addition, Torrance states, 'The core of the studies – the basic test results and rankings – are almost meaningless since they could be used to argue virtually any case that one wanted to present'. Dylan Wiliam illustrates this point with the following example. Singapore and Finland are two of the most successful countries in the rankings. Singapore groups its students by ability. Should lower ranking countries do the same to improve their position? Not necessarily – Finland does not group students by ability. Wiliam concludes that 'little will be learned' from global educational league tables (Wiliam, 2016).

Progress 8 – Measuring secondary school performance

Progress 8 is a measure of secondary school performance which was introduced in 2016. It aims to measure the progress that students have made from the end of primary school to the end of secondary school. Before Progress 8, secondary schools were ranked in terms of the proportion of students achieving grades A* to C in five or more GCSE subjects including maths and English.

Progress 8 predicts students' GCSE results on the basis of their Key Stage 2 results at the end of primary school. The predicted GCSE grade for each student is based on the average GCSE grade of all students nationally who had a similar score at Key Stage 2.

GCSE results are given a numerical grade from 1 to 9 with the top grade of 9. Every increase a student achieves over their predicted grades will add additional points to a school's performance table.

Progress 8 – a positive evaluation Before Progress 8, secondary schools tended to focus on students seen as borderline C to D grade GCSE candidates. Schools saw that the most effective way to improve their position in the league tables was to concentrate resources on these students in order to raise their attainment. This was at the expense of those expected to achieve high grades and those who were seen as having no hope of attaining a grade C or above (see pp. 52–53 and p. 93 on the educational triage).

With Progress 8 literally every student counts. They can all add points to the school's performance tables. Rebecca Allen, director of the Education Datalab research unit says 'I think it's a fantastic improvement. It incentivises schools to offer a good curriculum and lets them focus on all students, from the top to the bottom' (quoted in Adams, 2016). However, Rebecca Allen also sees a downside to Progress 8.

Progress 8 – a negative evaluation Progress 8 takes no account of the fact that some schools are located in disadvantaged areas with many of their students coming from low-income families. Is it reasonable to judge these schools on the same basis as schools nationally which have a larger proportion of students from higher-income families?

Research by Rebecca Allen (2015) looked at 7000 students who were in the top 10 per cent nationally at the end of primary school but whose GCSE results in 2014 placed them well outside the top 25 per cent. They included over 1550 students from low-income homes. This research indicated that coming from a poor family more than doubled their chances of missing out on the top GCSE grades.

Should schools be blamed for their underachievement or is it mainly due to poverty? Research indicates that a low-income background is the main reason for their underachievement. A study based on official statistics by Robert Cassen and Geeta Kingdon (2007) concluded that only about 6 per cent of the low achievement of students receiving free school meals is due to attending 'worse quality schools'.

Critics of Programme 8 argue that it is unreasonable to judge schools in disadvantaged areas on the basis of national student performance. In the words of one critic, 'It is grossly unfair to blame teachers for underachievement caused by economic injustice. And this is precisely what Progress 8 does' (Reclaiming Schools, 21.01.2017).

What should be done? According to Rebecca Allen, 'Progress 8 compares pupil performance with a national picture, rather than matching schools with similar intakes' (quoted in Adams, 2016). Schools in disadvantaged areas should be compared with similar schools. Predicted GCSE grades should be based on students from these schools who had similar scores at Key Stage 2, not students nationally. Allowance would then be made for the effects of poverty on students' progress.

EBacc – The English Baccalaureate

In 2010 the Coalition government introduced a 'core curriculum' for secondary schools, known as the English Baccalaureate – EBacc for short. It recommended that students take GCSEs in five subjects – English, maths, a science, history or geography and a modern language. In 2015, the Conservative government made EBacc compulsory stating that students who start secondary school in 2015 will take EBacc at GCSE in 2020.

The government made EBacc compulsory because they saw it as providing 'a rigorous academic education' and 'a broad and balanced curriculum' (Richardson, 2016). This would equip all students for a progression to further study and work. In addition, there was growing concern about the decline of GCSE entries in science subjects, modern languages and history. Since its introduction in 2010, the proportion of students in state schools entered for EBacc rose from 22 per cent to 39 per cent in 2015.

EBacc was also a performance measure for schools alongside Progress 8. In the Department for Education's term, it was a new 'headline accountability measure'. Schools would be assessed on the proportion of students entered for EBacc subjects at GCSE and the grades they achieved.

Evaluation The main criticism of EBacc was that it would leave less room for vocational subjects such as design and technology and creative subjects such as music and art. However, over the five years from 2011 to 2016, the number of entries for arts subjects rose (Adams, 2017).

Rebecca Allen and Dave Thompson (2016) assessed the effects of EBacc by comparing students from EBacc schools who took their GCSEs in 2012/13 with students who took their GCSEs three years earlier. They found that, overall, students benefited from the changes, in particular with improved results in English and maths. As the government predicted, those who gained most were students from low-income backgrounds. However, head teachers had a number of concerns. They felt that EBacc was not suitable for every student. They also felt that specialist teacher shortages meant that providing

EBacc for 90 per cent of students by 2020 – the government plan – would not be possible.

Theresa May's education policy

A meritocracy

In 2016, Theresa May replaced David Cameron as Conservative prime minister. This is how she described her education policy.

> *I want Britain to be the world's greatest meritocracy, where advantage is based on merit not privilege, talent not circumstance, hard work not background … A society where everyone has a fair chance to go as far as their talent and hard work will allow.*   *Daily Mail,* 10.09.2016

She wants to give everybody an equal chance to succeed, in particular those in the lower levels of the class system. She says that her priorities are those of 'ordinary working-class people'. She sees in today's educational system a 'manifest unfairness'. In her words:

> *At the moment, opportunity is too often the preserve of the wealthy or a quirk of circumstance. Those who can afford to can move near a good school, pay to go private or fund the extra tuition their child needs to succeed … I want to correct this manifest unfairness … to deliver a good school place that caters for every child … that caters for their individual talents and needs.*   *Daily Mail,* 10.09.2016

Theresa May has a vision of a fair and just society in which people achieve their position on the basis of merit. She claims that the result would be a high level of social mobility. In particular, working-class people will have the opportunity to move upwards in the class system to a level which matches their talent and ability and their motivation and hard work.

Selective schools

Theresa May sees **selective schools** as one of the main ways to create a meritocratic society and to promote upward social mobility. In particular, she has advocated the return of grammar schools based on selection by ability. Traditionally, grammar schools were, and the remaining ones still are, largely populated by the children of the middle classes. The new grammar schools she proposes would take a fixed proportion of pupils from low-income, working-class families. And they would often be located in disadvantaged areas.

Today, there are 163 grammar schools in England. Middle-class parents often pay for private tutors to teach their children the skills needed to pass the 11-plus admission tests. Now, new tests will be devised which are 'tutor-proof' – no amount of tutoring will improve the chances of passing them. The tests will measure 'natural ability' rather than tutor-taught skills. A child's future education will no longer be decided at age 11. Entry to grammar schools will be provided at ages 11, 14 and 16.

In addition to grammar schools, all secondary schools will be able to select pupils on the basis of ability, if the school wishes and if there is a demand for this kind of selection in the area. Those who don't go to grammar schools will have a variety of schools to choose from – academies, free schools and faith schools. Diversity and choice will provide an appropriate education to suit the abilities and skills of all children.

Critics of selective schools

Theresa May's plans for an education system based on selection by ability have been strongly criticised. Ofsted's former chief inspector of schools Michael Wilshaw describes the idea that poor children would benefit from a return to grammar schools as 'tosh' and 'nonsense' (BBC News online, 05.06.2016). Like many critics he argues that selection on the basis of presumed ability will simply mirror, maintain and in some respects widen social class inequalities and reduce upward social mobility. The middle classes will use their money and know-how of the education system to keep their children in grammar schools.

Support for this view is provided by today's grammar schools which are largely populated by middle-class children. In parts of the country where there are both selective grammars and non-selective state schools, only 2.7 per cent of pupils in grammar schools receive free school meals compared to 18 per cent in non-selective state schools. Nearly 13 per cent of the pupils in today's grammar schools went to fee-paying preparatory schools and many more received intensive private tutoring to prepare for the 11-plus (Sutton Trust, 2013).

The idea of 'tutor proof' 11-plus admission tests has been dismissed. The Centre for Evaluation and Monitoring at Durham University attempted to produce one. Children who took this test did worse than those who had taken the standard tests. Critics claim there can be no such thing as a 'tutor-proof test' (Millar, 2016).

Critics also claim that children from poor backgrounds who fail to get into grammar schools will be dumped into 'sink schools'. The expansion of grammar schools will create the equivalent of secondary moderns for three quarters of the school population. And these students may well be defined, and see themselves, as failures as in the days of the tripartite system. Alan Milburn, the chair of the government's Social Mobility Commission said that selective education risks creating an 'us and them' divide in the school system. As a result, 'It will be a social mobility disaster' (*The Guardian*, 08.09.16).

No more grammar schools?

In June 2017 the Conservative government called a general election. They lost their overall parliamentary majority. As a result, they put aside a number of controversial issues in their manifesto. The Queen's Speech on 21 June 2017 outlined their planned legislation for the next two years. There was no mention of grammar schools. The plans were for 'every child to go to a good or outstanding school' and that 'all options' remained open for new schools (BBC News online, 21.06.2017). It appears that the possibility for new grammar schools remains.

Social mobility and education

Is education the answer? Governments over the past 60 years have seen education as the main way of providing equal opportunity, creating a meritocratic society and increasing upward social mobility. The education system has steadily expanded with growing numbers of all social classes improving their educational qualifications.

However, Alan Milburn, chair of the Social Mobility Commission, has serious doubts about the promise of education. 'I was brought up to believe that if you stuck in at school you'd get on in life. Unfortunately, there's pretty compelling data to suggest that may no longer be the case' (*The Guardian,* 12.03.2016). In other words, hard work and educational success may not be the route to upward mobility and top jobs.

The golden age of social mobility Professor John Goldthorpe has spent most of his life studying social class and social mobility in the UK. He compares the situation today with 'the golden age of social mobility' in the 1950s and 1960s. Then upward mobility – moving to a higher class than that of your parent/s – was greater than downward mobility. Why? Because there was simply 'more room at the top' due to a rapid expansion of managerial and professional jobs.

Now, according to Goldthorpe (2016), 'A situation is emerging that is quite new in modern British history. Young people entering the labour market today face far less mobility prospects than did their parents – or their grandparents'.

What can education do? Changes in the educational system appear to have little effect on social mobility. Despite the expansion of education, class differences in educational attainment remain largely unchanged. In Goldthorpe's words this is due to:

> *Parents in more advantaged class positions will respond to any expansion or reform of the educational system by using superior resources – economic, cultural and social – to help their children retain a competitive edge in the system and, in turn, the labour market.*

Directions for government policy What does this suggest for government policy? First, if everybody is to have an equal chance of social mobility – of moving up, down, or staying the same – then everybody should have an equal chance in the educational system. This can only happen if people have equal resources. Government policy should therefore aim to reduce inequality in society.

Second, if the aim is to change the pattern of social mobility and return to a 'golden age', where upward mobility is the main form of mobility, then the government should aim to create more jobs at the top. In Goldthorpe's (2016) words, this means 'policies aimed at raising our presently poor level of investment in research and development, at creating a modernised and environmentally friendly infrastructure, and at the progressive upgrading of the quality of all social and other public services'.

In today's society, neither of the above – more jobs at the top or reducing inequality – seems likely. The fastest growing jobs in the first 10 years of this century were educational assistants and care assistants. And there was a decline in professional occupations (Reay, 2013). And in recent years the gap between rich and poor has steadily widened.

Diane Reay (2013) draws the following conclusions about government policy on social mobility. She argues that all the 'fuss' about social mobility makes it appear that governments care about social inequality. But all this does is divert attention from the widening gap between top and bottom and disguise the 'gaping wound' caused by the growing extremes of income and wealth. In Reay's words:

Welcome to the twenty-first century version of the rat race in which social mobility operates as a very inadequate sticking plaster over the gaping wound social inequalities have become in the 2010s. Social mobility, rather than the ailments it is supposed to cure, has become the main focus of attention, a politically driven distraction that diverts our attention from the real problems that need to be addressed. Governmental insistence on its commitment to social mobility and equal opportunities clearly distracts attention from larger systematic processes that are making hierarchies steeper and opportunities more restricted.

Contemporary issues: A divided society?

Theresa May on grammar schools

We know that grammar schools are hugely popular with parents. We know they are good for the pupils that attend them. Indeed, the attainment gap between rich and poor pupils is reduced to almost zero for children who attend them.

They provide a stretching education for the most academically able, regardless of their background, and they deliver outstanding results. In a true meritocracy, we should not be apologetic about stretching the most academically able to the very highest levels of attainment.

We will ensure that these schools contribute meaningfully to raising the outcomes of all pupils in every part of the system. In practice, this could mean taking a proportion of pupils from lower income areas.

There will be no return to secondary moderns. Far from a binary (two part) system, we are supporting the most diverse school system we have ever had in this country.

Adapted from *New Statesman*, 09.09.2016

'Failing' the 11 plus

Michael Morpurgo is an award-winning children's author. Unlike his success in later life, he 'failed' the 11-plus. This is what it meant to him.

Failure is the worst thing you can do to a child, it crushes their confidence. I condemned

myself because of this failure, you were named and shamed. You knew you had disappointed everyone. It hurt to feel stupid. At home there was silent disapproval and disappointment of the worst kind. My early blithe confidence had been shattered. All school work and all tests became fearful to me. When asked to read aloud or recite a poem I stuttered.

Adapted from *The Guardian*, 13.09.2016.

John Prescott is a former Labour Deputy Prime Minister. He too 'failed' the 11-plus and, as a result, he and his girlfriend separated.

We parted because I wasn't good enough to pass a test. She'd managed to pass the 11-plus. I did not. I sent her a love letter pledging my undying love. She sent it back correcting my spelling and grammar mistakes.

It didn't stop there. My dad Bert promised me and my brother Ray a bicycle if we got to grammar school. Ray got a bike. I got a 20-mile bus trip to my secondary modern.

You might say so what. It didn't stop me going on to become an MP and deputy prime minister. But I did both in spite of failing the 11-plus, not because of it.

Mirror online, 10.09.2016

Letters to Theresa May

Where grammars are created other schools become secondary moderns.

Letter from nine secondary state school head teachers in North Somerset, BBC News online 21.01.2017

It is impossible to have grammar schools without secondary modern schools or their equivalent.

Letter from almost all secondary state school head teachers in Surrey, BBC News online, 08.11.2016

Questions

1. Do we need grammar schools to stretch the 'most academically able'?

2. Will the return of grammar schools result in a divided society?

Activity

No jobs at the top!

They've got the qualifications but are the jobs there? This is the problem for upward social mobility. Discuss.

Key terms

Academy chains A number of academies which join together to share policy and expertise.

Multi-academy trust A charitable organisation which governs academy chains.

Global educational league tables Rankings based on international comparisons of educational attainment.

PISA Programme for International Student Assessment.

Progress 8 A measure of school performance based on the progress students have made from the end of primary school to GCSE.

EBacc The English Baccalaureate. A GCSE programme of five core subjects for all students. Also used to measure school performance.

Selective schools Schools which select their pupils — for example, grammar schools who select on the basis of 'ability'.

Tutor-proof tests Tests in which results cannot be improved by tutors.

Summary

1. There has been a rapid growth of academies and academy chains under the Conservatives.

2. Based on GCSE results, moving to a converter academy doesn't seem to have much effect on a school's performance.

3. Becoming a sponsored academy appears to improve the performance of 'failing' schools, especially for disadvantaged students.

4. The performance of multi-academy trusts is varied – some are good, others are poor.

5. Education policy in the UK is increasingly based on global perspectives.

6. Progress 8 has been seen as a fairer test of school performance as it directly involves all students. Critics argue that it does not take the effect of poverty on students' progress into account.

7. Judging from GCSE results, EBacc has improved grades, particularly for students from low-income families.

8. Theresa May looks forward to a meritocratic society with a high level of social mobility. There will be equal opportunity for all. She sees the return of grammar schools with entry based on selection by ability as one of the main ways of achieving this.

9. The new grammar schools will take a fixed proportion of pupils from disadvantaged areas. Admission tests will be 'tutor proof'.

10. Theresa May's critics argue that:

     - Selection by so-called 'ability' will increase class inequality and reduce social mobility.

     - It is not possible to construct tutor-proof tests.

     - New grammar schools will result in a modern version of secondary modern schools for the majority of pupils.

11. The high level of upward social mobility in the 1950s and 1960s was due to the expansion of professional and managerial jobs. There was more room at the top.

12. The only way to provide equality of opportunity is to reduce social inequality. And the main way to increase upward social mobility is to increase top jobs. At present, there is no sign of either occurring.

PART 3 CLASS AND EDUCATIONAL ATTAINMENT

Contents

Differential educational attainment refers to the fact that different groups – for example, different class, ethnic and gender groups – have different levels of educational attainment. This part looks at evidence and explanations for class differences in educational attainment.

Research shows that the higher a person's social class, the higher their educational attainment is likely to be. The children of parents in higher social classes are more likely to attain high grades in Key Stage tests and at GCSE; they are more likely to stay on in post-compulsory education and to take and pass A-level examinations; and they are more likely to gain university entrance.

These class differences were a feature of British education throughout the 20th century and they have continued to the present day. Whether there has been any reduction in class differences in educational attainment is debatable. There is some evidence that may indicate a reduction in recent years. However, the gap in educational attainment between the top and bottom classes remains significant.

This part begins by looking at the evidence for class differences in educational attainment and critically assessing the available statistics. It then examines subcultural explanations for class differences in attainment. More recent explanations based on Pierre Bourdieu's ideas of cultural, social and economic capital are looked at. The final unit investigates how students' class position affects how they are treated in the classroom and how this might affect their educational attainment.

This part raises important questions. To what extent does class affect educational attainment? What can be done to provide equality of educational opportunity? Can it be done by schools and teachers? Or is the answer to reduce inequality in the wider society?

2.3.1 Measuring class attainment

This unit looks at the ways of measuring social class differences in educational attainment. Measurements are based mainly on class differences in examination results at GCSE and A-level and entry into university. Measurements are complicated by the fact that different definitions of social class have been used over the years plus different measures of GCSE attainment. Despite this, one thing is clear – class differences in educational attainment are significant and show no signs of disappearing. For an introduction to social class see pp. 8–10.

Social class

Social class is the main form of **social stratification** in Western societies. Social stratification is a system of social inequality in which people are grouped, one group above another. Social class refers to groups who are divided in terms of income, wealth, power and status or prestige. The essence of class is economic inequalities.

Two different classifications of social class have been used to measure class differences in educational attainment – SEG (Socio-Economic Group) and NS-SEC (National Statistics Socio-Economic Classification) which replaced SEG in official surveys. Both classifications use occupation as an indicator of people's class position though there are differences in the way they assign occupations to each social class. As a result, evidence based on each of the two classifications cannot be directly compared. Neither version of the class system specifically identifies the wealthy upper class, many of whose members go to private rather than state schools.

Here is a summary of the NS-SEC classification. It contains five social classes with examples of the occupations in each class. Class 1 has the highest levels of income, wealth, power and occupational status. These levels steadily reduce through each class with Class 5 having the lowest levels.

NS-SEC social class

- **Class 1** Managerial and professional occupations – business executives, lawyers, doctors

- **Class 2** Intermediate occupations – clerical workers, secretaries

- **Class 3** Small employers and self-employed – shopkeepers, taxi drivers

- **Class 4** Lower supervisory and technical occupations – train drivers, plumbers

- **Class 5** Semi-routine and routine occupations – hairdressers, cleaners, labourers

The five classes are often divided into the middle class and the working class. Using the NS-SEC classification, the middle class consists of Classes 1 and 2 and part of Class 3 and the working class consists of the second part of Class 3 plus Classes 4 and 5.

Since 2011, the Department for Education has not produced data on social class differences at GCSE and A-level. Instead, it has compared the educational attainment of two groups – those who receive free school meals and those who do not. As outlined shortly, this measure is an inadequate substitute for social class.

Class attainment at GCSE

Table 2.3.1 shows the percentage of 16-year-olds from each social class who attained five or more GCSE grades A*–C from 1988 to 1997. The SEG classification of class is used for these years. Table 2.3.2 updates these statistics to 2006, using the NS-SEC classification of class. Data for 1999, 2001 and 2003 are for 16-year-olds in England and Wales, while figures for 2006 are for England only.

Both tables show that the higher the class position, the greater the percentage of students attaining five or more GCSE grades A*–C. For example, in 2003, 76 per cent of students from higher professional backgrounds attained these grades, compared to only 33 per cent from routine backgrounds.

Table 2.3.1 Attainment of five or more GCSE grades A*–C, by social class, 1988–97 England and Wales (percentages)

Parental occupation (SEG)	1988	1990	1991	1993	1995	1997	Percentage point gain 1988–97
Managerial/professional	52	58	60	66	68	69	+17
Other non-manual	42	49	51	58	58	60	+18
Skilled manual	21	27	29	36	36	40	+19
Semi-skilled manual	16	20	23	26	29	32	+16
Unskilled manual	12	15	16	16	24	20	+8

Source: DfES (24.02.2005).

Table 2.3.2 Attainment of five or more GCSE grades A*–C, by social class, England and Wales, 1999–2003, and England, 2006 (percentages)

Parental occupation (NS-SEC)	1999	2001	2003	Percentage point gain 1999–2003	2006
Higher professional	75	77	76	+1	81
Lower professional	62	64	65	+3	73
Intermediate	49	51	53	+4	59
Lower supervisory	34	34	41	+7	46
Routine	26	31	33	+7	42

Source: Adapted from DfES (24.02.2005); DCSF (26.06.2008).

The figures in the 'Percentage point gain' column show the increase in percentage points for each class (in Table 2.3.2, figures for percentage point gain in 2006 are not included as the figures for this year are for England only). For example, in 2003, 76 per cent of students from higher professional backgrounds attained five or more GCSE grades A*–C, compared with 75 per cent in 1999. This is a gain of 1 percentage point.

The percentage point gain figures for 1999 to 2003 suggest that the class gap is narrowing. The greatest gains are now at the bottom of the class system. The routine class gained 7 percentage points, compared with a gain of 1 by the higher professional class. However, although the gap between top and bottom has narrowed, it still remains wide.

Free school meals and GCSE results

The Department for Education no longer publishes data on social class and educational attainment. Instead, it uses a comparison of students who receive free school meals and those who do not in order to measure the effect of social inequality. Free school meals (FSM) are available to children whose parents receive one or more of a range of benefits – for example, Income Support. FSM data give some indication of the **attainment gap** between those in the lower levels of the class structure and those above them. However, this is only a rough measure as it does not give the various levels of inequality provided by classifications of social class.

To make matters worse, FSM is also a poor measure of disadvantage. It does not include a large number of children from low-income families.

It is estimated that around 1.4 million (21 per cent) of children aged 4–15 in state schools in England are entitled to receive FSM. Yet only 1.2 million (18 per cent) claim FSM. Therefore around 200 000 are entitled to but not claiming FSM (Iniesta-Martinez and Evans, 2012).

The children of parents receiving Working Tax Credit are not eligible for FSM. It is estimated that around 700 000 children from these low-income families should be defined, like FSM children, as disadvantaged (Garrod, 2016). Not only is FSM a

Table 2.3.3 Attainment gap at GCSE between non-FSM and FSM students, England – first measure 5 or more grades A*–C

2005/06	2006/07	2007/08	2008/09	2009/10	2010/11	2011/12	2012/13
28.0	27.2	26.7	24.0	20.3	18.4	16.5	16.0

Source: Adapted from DfE (16.12. 2010, 23. 01.2014).

Table 2.3.4 Attainment gap at GCSE between non-FSM and FSM students, England – second measure 5 or more grades A*–C including English and mathematics

2005/06	2006/07	2007/08	2008/09	2009/10	2010/11	2011/12	2012/13	2013/14	2014/15
28.1	28.0	27.9	27.7	27.6	27.4	26.3	26.7	27.0	27.8

Source: Adapted from DfE (16.12.2010, 23.01.2014).

poor substitute for social class, it is also an inadequate measure of disadvantage.

Table 2.3.3 shows the attainment gap between non-FSM students and **FSM students** who receive 5 or more grades A*–C at GCSE or equivalent exams. For example, in 2012/13, 85.3 per cent of non-FSM students obtained these grades compared with 69.3 per cent of FSM students. The attainment gap is 85.3 minus 69.3, which is 16 percentage points. Between 2005/06 and 2012/13 the gap reduced from 28.0 to 16.0 percentage points. This may indicate a continuation of the closing of the class attainment gap indicated in Table 2.3.2.

Table 2.3.4 provides a different measure of GCSE attainment. It continues to use 5 or more GCSEs grades A*–C, but this time the GCSEs must include English and mathematics. This gives a rather different picture from Table 2.3.3. As Table 2.3.4 shows, it indicates little change in the attainment gap between non-FSM and FSM students.

Measuring class differences in educational attainment

Measuring class differences in attainment at GCSE is complicated for the following reasons:

1. Different classifications of social class are used.

2. More recent statistics simply compare two measures of social inequality – those receiving free school meals and the rest of the student population.

3. Different measures of GCSE attainment are used.

4. Sometimes the figures are for England and Wales, at other times just for England.

Activity

The statistics on class differences on educational attainment cannot be directly compared. However, they indicate that there is some reduction in class differences in attainment at GCSE. But they also indicate that a significant gap in attainment between the classes remains.

Look at Tables 2.3.1, 2.3.2, 2.3.3 and 2.3.4 and provide evidence to assess these statements.

Class attainment at A-level

Table 2.3.5 shows the percentage of 18-year-olds from each social class in England and Wales who attained one or more A/AS-levels or equivalent qualifications from 2002 to 2006. Figures for 2009 are for England only. The percentage point gain figures indicate a narrowing of class differences, with the greatest gains being made in the middle and lower levels of the class system. However, the gap between top and bottom remains large (41 percentage points in 2006).

Table 2.3.6 shows attainment of two or more A/AS-levels or equivalent qualifications by the age of 19 for non-FSM and FSM students. Both groups improved their attainment between 2005 and 2011. However, there has only been a small reduction in the percentage point gap between them (26.4 in 2005; 24.5 in 2015).

Activity

Look at Tables 2.3.5 and 2.3.6. What evidence do they provide which reflects the trends shown in the tables for GCSE results?

Table 2.3.5 Attainment of one or more A/AS-levels or equivalent qualifications, by social class, England and Wales, 2002–6, and England, 2009 (percentages)

Parental occupation (NS-SEC)	2002	2004	2006	Percentage point gain 2002–6	2009
Higher professional	57	63	57	0	70
Lower professional	42	46	45	+ 3	62
Intermediate	24	32	33	+ 9	47
Lower supervisory	18	16	23	+ 5	35
Routine	11	16	16	+ 5	28

Source: Adapted from DfES (20.02.2003, 25.11.2004, 28.11.2006); DfE (22.07.2010).

Table 2.3.6 Attainment of two or more A/AS-levels or equivalent qualifications, non-FSM and FSM students, England, 2005–15 (percentages)

	2005	2006	2007	2008	2009	2010	2011	2012	2013	2014	2015
Non-FSM students	46.3	47.2	48.4	49.7	51.4	53.9	56.7	58.3	59.6	60.5	60.9
FSM students	19.9	21.0	22.8	24.6	26.9	29.7	32.0	34.1	35.3	35.7	36.4
Percentage point gap	26.4	26.3	25.6	25.1	24.6	24.2	24.7	24.2	24.3	24.8	24.5

Source: Adapted from DfE (07.04. 2016).

Participation in higher education

Table 2.3.7 shows the percentage of people in Britain aged under 21 from each SEG social class who entered undergraduate courses at university from 1991 to 2001. The figures on the right in the 'Percentage point gain' column show that the greatest gainers were those from the professional class, with a gain of 24 percentage points, followed by the intermediate class with a gain of 14 points. In 1991 there was a gap of 49 percentage points between the top and bottom classes. By 2001, this had grown to 64. Clearly it was those at the top who gained most from the expansion of higher education places during these years. (The Age Participation Index from which these figures are drawn was discontinued in 2001.)

The percentage point gain of those at the top from 1991 to 2001 is extremely large. It does not reflect the figures for GCSE which indicate a reduction in the percentage point gap between the classes. However, more recent figures in Table 2.3.8 suggest that compared to other classes the increase in the percentage point gain of the top class has largely ended.

Table 2.3.8 shows the percentage of 19-year-olds in England and Wales from each NS-SEC class who entered undergraduate courses in 2003, 2005 and 2007. Figures for 2010 are for England only. The figures for 2003 to 2007 show a gain for all social classes. However, the percentage point gap between top and bottom classes increased from 38 to 39 percentage points.

Table 2.3.7 Participation rates in higher education, by social class, UK, 1991–2001 (percentages)

Parental occupation (SEG)	1991	1992	1993	1994	1995	1996	1997	1998	1999	2000	2001	Percentage point gain 1991–2001
Professional	55	71	73	78	79	82	79	82	73	76	79	+ 24
Intermediate	36	39	42	45	45	47	48	45	45	48	50	+ 14
Skilled non-manual	22	27	29	31	31	32	31	29	30	33	33	+ 11
Skilled manual	11	15	17	18	18	18	19	18	18	19	21	+ 10
Partly skilled	12	14	16	17	17	17	18	17	17	19	18	+ 6
Unskilled	6	9	11	11	12	13	14	13	13	14	15	+ 9

Source: Adapted from Age Participation Index, DfES, 2003.

Table 2.3.8 Nineteen-year-olds in higher education, by social class, England and Wales, 2003–2007, and England, 2010 (percentages)

Parental occupation (NS-SEC)	2003	2005	2007	Percentage point gain 2003–7	2010
Higher professional	52	59	57	+ 5	60
Lower professional	40	45	46	+ 6	53
Intermediate	26	32	34	+ 8	37
Lower supervisory	17	16	25	+ 8	27
Routine	14	19	18	+ 4	22

Source: Adapted from various Youth Cohort Studies.

Table 2.3.9 Participation rates in higher education, non-FSM and FSM students, state-funded schools, England, 2009/2010 to 2013/2014 (percentages)

	2009/10	2010/11	2011/12	2012/13	2013/14
Non-FSM students	36	38	39	40	39
FSM students	18	20	21	23	22
Percentage point gap	18	18	18	17	17

Source: Adapted from DfE (03.08.2016).

In recent years the non-FSM/FSM distinction has been used to measure class difference in participation in higher education. Table 2.3.9 uses this measure. It indicates an increase in the percentage of both groups going on to university and a small reduction in the percentage point gap between them.

Activity

Compare Table 2.3.8 with Table 2.3.7. What does this comparison indicate about the trend in class differences in entry into higher education?

Conclusion

It is difficult to draw firm conclusions about the extent of, and changes in, class differences in educational attainment. This is mainly due to differences in the way class is defined. Two measures of class inequality have been used:

1. Socio-Economic Group (SEG)

2. National Statistics Socio-Economic Classification (NS-SEC)

In addition, class as a measure of social inequality has been replaced in recent years by non-FSM and FSM.

The use of three different measures of social inequality means the results based on each cannot be directly compared. In addition, non-FSM and FSM is a very rough measure. It does not provide the detailed evidence of social class divisions.

Added to the above difficulties is the problem of what qualifications are being measured. This can be seen from the two main ways of measuring GCSE qualifications – whether or not English and maths are included. And this gives two very different results for the attainment gap between non-FSM and FSM students.

However, despite the above difficulties, most of the available evidence suggests the following conclusions:

» In general, the higher a person's class position the higher their educational attainment.

» All social classes are increasing their attainment levels and their participation in higher education.

» There is some evidence to suggest that the attainment gap between classes has narrowed.

» Whatever measures are used, the attainment gap between top and bottom remains wide and shows no signs of disappearing in the foreseeable future.

Contemporary issues: Unequal universities, unequal access

Universities are ranked – judged to be better and worse, higher status and lower status. In general, the higher your class position, the higher the status of the university you enter. At the top are Oxford and Cambridge (Oxbridge), next come the Russell Group (which includes Oxbridge) made up of 24 universities from major cities such as London, Manchester, Cardiff, Edinburgh and Belfast.

Oxford University. The odds of an FSM student going to Oxbridge are nearly 2,000 to one against. The odds for a privately educated student from a fee-paying school/college are 20 to one (Social Mobility and Child Poverty Commission, 2013).

Question

According to the Social Mobility & Child Poverty Commission (2013) 'There is a long way to go before access to higher education can be said to be truly classless'. How does the above evidence support this statement?

Manchester University. 5 per cent of FSM students went to a Russell Group university in 2013/14 compared with 12 per cent of non-FSM students. (DfE, 03.08.2016).

Key terms

Differential educational attainment The different attainment levels of different groups – for example, class, gender and ethnic groups.

Social stratification A system of social inequality in which people are grouped at different levels.

Social class The system of social stratification in Western society in which people are divided in terms of income, wealth, power and prestige.

Attainment gap The percentage point gap in educational attainment between different social groups.

FSM students Those receiving free school meals.

Summary

1. The higher a person's social class the more likely they are to have high educational attainment.

2. Social class and social inequality have been measured by parental occupation and whether or not a student receives FSM.

3. Since different indicators of class and social inequality and different indicators of attainment have been used, the results cannot be directly compared.

4. FSM is a poor substitute for social class and an inadequate measure of disadvantage.

5. Members of all social classes are increasing their attainment levels and there is some evidence that the attainment gap between classes is narrowing.

6. Despite this, the gap between top and bottom remains wide and shows no sign of disappearing in the foreseeable future.

2.3.2 Social class subcultures and cultural deprivation

This unit examines the view that differences in class subcultures account for class differences in educational attainment. It states that the relatively low attainment of working-class students is due mainly to working-class subculture. This leads to government policies which aim to compensate for the supposedly negative effects of working-class subcultures on educational attainment.

This view is sometimes known as **cultural deprivation theory**. It states that the subculture of low-income groups is deprived of factors which are necessary for high educational attainment. The so-called culturally-deprived child is pictured as lacking the language and reasoning skills needed for intellectual tasks, and as deficient in important attitudes and values required for educational success. Cultural deprivation theory has been strongly criticised.

This unit closes with an alternative view – that class differences in attainment are more the result of class differences in material factors – income and wealth and the things that money can buy – than differences in subcultures.

Class subcultures and educational attainment

It has been argued that the **subculture** – the distinctive **norms** and **values** – of social classes affect performance in the educational system. Norms are guides to appropriate behaviour in particular situations. Values are beliefs that something is important and worthwhile. A subculture is the distinctive norms and values of a particular group in society. While sharing the culture of mainstream society, they also have some of their own norms and values, their own subculture.

The view that social class subcultures affect educational attainment was first spelled out in detail by the American sociologist Herbert H. Hyman (1967) in an article entitled 'The value systems of different classes'. He argued that the value system of the lower classes creates 'a self-imposed barrier to an improved position'.

Using a wide range of data from opinion polls and surveys conducted by sociologists, Hyman outlined what he saw as differences between working-class and middle-class value systems:

1. Members of the working class place a lower value on education.

2. They place a lower value on achieving high occupational status.

3. Compared to their middle-class counterparts, members of the working class believe there is less opportunity for personal advancement.

The values Hyman outlined did not characterise all members of the working class – a sizeable minority did not share them. In general, however, he concluded that motivation to achieve, whether in school or outside it, is generally lower for members of the working class.

Attitudes and orientations

The British sociologist Barry Sugarman (1970) argued that middle- and working-class subcultures contain different attitudes and orientations, which may account for class differences in educational attainment. In particular, he claims that working-class subculture emphasises fatalism, immediate gratification, present-time orientation and collectivism.

1. **Fatalism** involves an acceptance of the situation rather than efforts to improve it. As such it will not encourage high achievement in the classroom.

2. **Immediate gratification and present time orientation** emphasise the enjoyment of pleasures of the moment rather than sacrifice for future reward. This will tend to discourage sustained effort with its promise of examination success. It will also tend to encourage early school-leaving for the more immediate rewards of a wage packet, adult status and freedom from the disciplines of school.

3. **Collectivism** involves loyalty to the group rather than the emphasis on individual achievement that the school system demands.

Sugarman therefore concluded that the subculture of students from working-class backgrounds places them at a disadvantage in the educational system.

Class subcultures – problems of method

There are a number of criticisms of the concept of social class subculture and the methods used to establish its existence:

1. So-called working-class subculture may simply be a response in terms of mainstream culture to the circumstances of working-class life. Thus, members of the working class may be realistic rather than fatalistic – they might defer gratification if they had the resources to defer, and they might be future-oriented if the opportunities for successful future planning were available.

From this point of view, members of the working class share the same norms and values as any other members of society. Their behaviour is not directed by a distinctive subculture. It is simply their situation that prevents them from expressing society's norms and values in the same way as members of the middle class.

2. The content of working-class subculture is sometimes derived from interviews and questionnaires. Hyman's and Sugarman's data were largely obtained from these sources. However, what people say in response to interviews or questionnaires may not provide an accurate indication of how they behave in other situations. In addition, people in interviews tend to give answers that they think the interviewer wants.

3. In a criticism of American studies, R.H. Turner (discussed in Colquhoun, 1976) notes that social class differences reported from interviews and questionnaire data are often slight. Sociologists tend to ignore similarities between classes and emphasise the differences. Sometimes this is because differences tend to support their views – in this case that they help to explain class differences in educational attainment.

J.W.B. Douglas – *The Home and the School*

J.W.B. Douglas and his associates (Douglas, 1964; Douglas *et al*. 1970) conducted an influential longitudinal study (that is, a study of the same group over time). They followed the educational careers of 5362 British children born in the first week of March 1946, through primary and secondary school up to the age of 16 in 1962.

Douglas divided the students into groups in terms of their ability, which was measured by a battery of tests, including IQ tests. He also divided the students into four social class groupings, and found significant variations in educational attainment between students of similar ability but from different social classes. He also found that length of stay in the educational system was related to social class. Within the 'high ability' group, 50 per cent of the students from the lower working-class left secondary school in their fifth year, compared with 33 per cent from the upper working class, 22 per cent from the lower-middle class and 10 per cent from the upper-middle class.

Parental interest in education Douglas related educational attainment to a variety of factors, including the student's health, the size of their family, and the quality of the school. The single most important factor appeared to be the degree of parents' interest in their children's education. In general, middle-class parents expressed a greater interest, as indicated by more frequent visits to the school to discuss their children's progress. They were more likely to want their children to stay on at school beyond the minimum leaving age and to encourage them to do so. Douglas found that parental interest and encouragement became increasingly important as a spur to high attainment as the children grew older.

Douglas also attached importance to the child's early years, since, in many cases, performance during the first years of schooling is reflected throughout the secondary school. He suggested that, during primary socialisation, middle-class children receive greater attention and stimulus from their parents. Middle-class parents were likely to encourage their children to do their best in a wide variety of activities. This formed a basis for high achievement in the educational system.

Leon Feinstein – parental support

Leon Feinstein (2003) conducted more recent research on the factors affecting success in education. He used data from the National Child Development Study (which followed the development of all children born in one week in March 1958) and the British Cohort Study (which conducted similar research on a group of children born in 1970).

Like Douglas, Feinstein claimed that the main factor influencing educational attainment was the degree of parental interest and support. He saw class differences in parental support accounting for class differences in educational attainment. Parental support was measured by teachers' assessments of how much interest parents showed in their children's education.

Evaluation

The studies discussed above appear to give strong support to the view that class subcultures influence educational attainment, particularly through differences in parental encouragement of children at school. However, these studies should be viewed with some caution.

A number of arguments have been advanced to suggest that working-class parents are not necessarily less interested in their children's education just because they go to their children's schools less frequently than their middle-class counterparts. Tessa Blackstone and Jo Mortimore (1994) make the following points:

1. Working-class parents may have less time to attend school because of the demands of their jobs. Manual jobs typically involve longer and less regular hours than non-manual jobs.

2. Working-class parents may be very interested in their children's education but they are put off going to the school because of the way teachers interact with them. Blackstone and Mortimore (1994) argue that it is possible that 'working-class parents feel ill at ease or the subject of criticism when they visit school. Teachers represent authority and parents who have had unhappy experiences at school or with authority figures may be reluctant to meet them'.

3. The data used by both Douglas and Feinstein may not actually measure parental interest in education, but teachers' perceptions of their interest. It is possible that teachers perceive middle-class parents as more interested than working-class parents because of the way they interact with teachers when they attend school.

Gillian Evans – parents, class and education

Gillian Evans gives a somewhat different picture of the relationship between parents, class and education in *Educational Failure and Working Class White Children in Britain* (2007). As an anthropologist, Evans was trained to immerse herself in a community and to see life through their eyes. She spent 18 months conducting fieldwork on a working-class council estate in Bermondsey in southeast London. And, at the same time, she was a middle-class mother living on the estate.

Evans spent part of her time visiting parents in their homes. She found that most parents placed a high value on education and encouraged their children to do well. In her words: 'The majority of working-class parents want, more than anything, for their children to do well at school because they know only too well that it will lead to a better livelihood in the future' (Evans, 2007).

According to Evans, it is not the value placed on education that accounts for class differences in attainment but, instead, class differences in socialisation. She argues that middle-class mothers, particularly those who are more highly educated, incorporate **formal-learning-type skills** 'in an informal, playful way, into the caring relationship with the child at home'. Such skills include counting, shape and colour recognition and speaking and writing. Middle-class children often enjoy these tasks as they are part of the loving relationship with their mother, and they can be fun. As a result, by the age of two, the children of 'well-educated' mothers are likely to do particularly well in preschool formal learning tasks.

For working-class mothers, caring and formal learning tasks tend not to go together – 'formal learning plays little part in the way that caring relationships are established in the home'. Formal learning is seen as what happens at school. As a result, working-class children are less prepared for school. Middle-class children have a head start, which tends to stay with them throughout their educational careers – careers that are largely based on formal learning skills.

Gillian Evans does not make judgements about better or worse. She is at pains to point out that her argument does not mean that social relationships in working-class families are second-rate and deprive children of something valuable. Instead, she sees the relationships as different from those of middle-class families rather than substandard. In other words, she rejects the idea of cultural deprivation theory.

Basil Bernstein – speech patterns

The English sociologist Basil Bernstein suggested that class differences in speech patterns are related to educational attainment.

Since speech is an important medium of communication and learning, attainment levels in schools may be related to differences in speech patterns. Bernstein (1961, 1970, 1972) identified two forms of speech pattern that he termed the **elaborated code** and the **restricted code**. In general, he argued that members of the working class are limited to the use of restricted codes, whereas members of the middle class use both codes.

Restricted codes are a kind of shorthand speech. Those conversing in terms of the code have so much in common that there is no need to make meanings explicit in speech. Married couples often use restricted codes, since their shared experience and understandings make it unnecessary to spell out their meanings and intentions in detail.

Bernstein stated that restricted codes are characterised by 'short, grammatically simple, often unfinished sentences'. There is limited use of adjectives and adjectival clauses, and of adverbs and adverbial clauses. Meaning and intention are conveyed more by gesture, voice intonation and the context in which the communication takes place.

Restricted codes tend to operate in terms of **particularistic meanings**, and as such are tied to specific contexts. Since so much is taken for granted and relatively little is made explicit, restricted codes are largely limited to dealing with objects, events and relationships that are familiar to those communicating. Thus the meanings conveyed by the code are limited to a particular social group: they are bound to a particular social context and are not readily available to outsiders.

In contrast, an elaborated code explicitly verbalises many of the meanings that are taken for granted in a restricted code. It fills in the detail, spells out the relationships and provides the explanations omitted by restricted codes. As such, its meanings tend to be **universalistic**: they are not tied to a particular context. The listener need not be plugged in to the experience and understanding of the speaker, since the meanings are spelled out verbally.

Speech patterns and educational attainment

Bernstein used class differences in speech codes to account in part for differences in educational attainment:

1. Education in schools is conducted in terms of an elaborated code. Bernstein stated: 'The school is necessarily concerned with the transmission and development of universalistic orders of meaning'. This places working-class children at a disadvantage because they tend to be limited to the restricted code.

2. The restricted code, by its very nature, reduces the chances of working-class students successfully acquiring some of the skills demanded by the educational system.

Bernstein did not dismiss working-class speech patterns as inadequate or substandard – he described them as having 'warmth and vitality' and 'simplicity and directness'. However, particularly in his earlier writings, he did imply that, in certain respects, they are inferior to an elaborated code. He suggested that an elaborated code is superior for explicitly differentiating and distinguishing objects and events, for analysing relationships between them, for logically and rationally developing an argument, for making generalisations and for handling higher-level concepts. Since such skills and operations form an important part of formal education, limitation to a restricted code may provide a partial explanation for the relatively low attainment of working-class students.

Evaluation of Bernstein

Bernstein's ideas have been strongly criticised for the following reasons:

▶ He lumps together all manual workers into the working class and all non-manual workers into the

Activity – Transformation to an elaborated code

The pictures illustrate part of a series of interviews used to assess the language skills of African-American boys. They were asked to describe a toy plane. In the first interview, the boy gives short answers followed by long silences. In the second interview, where he is joined by his best friend and given a packet of crisps, he gives a detailed description of the plane (Labov, 1973).

Questions

1. Suggest reasons for the boy's different responses in the two interviews.

2. How might this be used to question Bernstein's findings?

middle class. This ignores the various levels within these classes.

» He provides little actual evidence of the existence and the use of the restricted and elaborated codes.

» Much of his evidence is drawn from interviews with children. The context of an interview and the appearance, gender, age and ethnicity of the interviewer can affect the results.

» Although he does not actually state that working-class speech patterns are substandard, Bernstein appears to imply this. Critics argue that he has created the myth that middle-class speech patterns are superior (Rosen, 1974).

Cultural deprivation theory — evaluation

The picture presented by cultural deprivation theory of working-class subculture is not an attractive one. It was portrayed as substandard, inadequate and deficient.

Cultural deprivation theory was developed mainly by White American middle-class psychologists in the 1960s, partly in an attempt to explain the low educational attainment of African-American students. The following description of the supposed culturally-deprived child by Charlotte K. Brooks gives some idea of where they were coming from.

He is essentially the child who has been isolated from those rich experiences that should be his. This isolation has been brought about by poverty, by meagreness of intellectual resources in his home and surroundings, by the incapacity, illiteracy or indifference of his elders or of the entire community. He may have come to school without ever having heard his mother singing him the traditional lullabies, and with no knowledge of nursery rhymes, fairy stories, or the folklore of his country...He probably knows nothing of poetry, painting or even of indoor plumbing.

Fieldman, 1976

This description probably says more about Charlotte K. Brooks's middle-class upbringing and her ignorance of working-class and ethnic subcultures than it does about the child she is attempting to describe.

From this portrayal, the theory of cultural deprivation was developed. The theory has been criticised for placing the blame for educational failure on the children and their family, their neighbourhood and the subculture of their social group. Nell Keddie (1973) calls this theory 'the myth of cultural deprivation'.

She argues that it is this myth which largely accounts for educational failure. The myth informs and directs interaction in schools, 'teachers' ways of assessing and typifying students and the ways in which teachers and students give meanings to educational situations'. As a result, children from low-income working class and ethnic backgrounds are seen 'as less "educable" than other children'. Keddie argues that 'The perception of working-class subcultures as deficient seems to arise from the ignorance of those who belong to what they perceive as the dominant cultural tradition'.

Compensatory education and positive discrimination

From the viewpoint of cultural deprivation theory, equality of educational opportunity could only become a reality by compensating for the deprivations and deficiencies of low-income groups. Only then would low-income students have an equal chance to seize the opportunities provided for all members of society.

From this kind of reasoning developed the idea of **positive discrimination** in favour of culturally deprived children — they must be given a helping hand to compete on equal terms with other children. This took the form of **compensatory education** — additional educational provision for the culturally deprived. Since, according to many educational psychologists, most of the damage was done during primary socialisation, when a substandard culture was internalised in an environment largely devoid of 'richness' and stimulation, compensatory education should concentrate on the pre-school years.

This thinking lay behind many of the programmes instituted by the Office of Economic Opportunity during President Johnson's 'war on poverty' in the USA (from the 1960s to the early 1970s). Billions of dollars were poured into **Operation Head Start**, a massive programme of pre-school education, beginning in Harlem in New York City and extended to low-income areas across America. This and similar programmes aimed to provide **planned enrichment** — a stimulating educational environment in which to instil achievement motivation and lay the foundation for effective learning in the school system.

The results were very disappointing. In a large-scale evaluation of Operation Head Start, the Westinghouse Corporation concluded that it produced no long-term beneficial results. Despite such gloomy conclusions, there is still support for compensatory education. Some argue that it has failed because the programmes

77

developed have been inappropriate, or because the scale of the operation had been insufficient.

Educational Priority Areas, Education Action Zones and Excellence in Cities

In Britain, compensatory education began in the late 1960s with the government allocating extra resources for school building in low-income areas and supplements to the salaries of teachers working in those areas.

Four areas – parts of Liverpool and Birmingham, Conisbrough and Denaby in the then West Riding of Yorkshire, and Deptford in southeast London – were designated **Educational Priority Areas** (EPAs). Programmes of compensatory education were introduced in the EPAs. These were based mainly on preschool education and additional measures in primary schools to raise literacy standards. Although it is difficult to evaluate the results, reports from the EPAs were generally disappointing.

A.H. Halsey, who directed the EPA projects, argued that positive discrimination in England has yet to be given a fair trial. It has operated on a shoestring compared to American programmes – for example, in 1973 only one-fifth of 1 per cent of the total education budget was spent on compensatory education. Writing in 1977, Halsey stated: 'Positive discrimination is about resources. The principle stands and is most urgently in need of application'.

More recent examples of compensatory education include Education Action Zones (EAZs) and Excellence in Cities (EiC). These programmes directed resources to low-income, inner-city areas in an attempt to raise educational attainment. Available evidence indicates at best they produced only small improvements.

Evaluation of compensatory education

Critics of cultural deprivation theory have seen it as a smokescreen that disguises the real factors preventing equality of educational opportunity. By placing the blame for failure on the child and his or her background, it diverts attention from the deficiencies of the educational system. William Labov (1973) argued that Operation Head Start was 'designed to repair the child rather than the school; to the extent it is based upon this inverted logic, it is bound to fail'.

Sharon Gewirtz (2001) sees EAZs as being firmly based upon the idea of cultural deprivation. She says they involve a 'massive programme of resourcing and re-education which has as its ultimate aim the eradication of cultural difference by transforming working-class parents into middle-class parents'.

Geoff Whitty (2002) criticises EAZs for being based on a cultural deprivation model – the working class are seen as lacking the necessary culture to succeed in education. Rather than the working class having to change to fit in with education, it is education that should change and place a higher value on working-class culture.

Whitty argues that EAZs are likely to have only limited success in raising achievement because they involve quite a modest redistribution of resources to poor areas. They are therefore unlikely to do much to compensate for the inequalities in the wider society which lead to low attainment in deprived areas in the first place.

Any positive effects of EAZs and the EiC programme that replaced them may become more evident in the long term, but so far there is little evidence they will make a major impact on educational disadvantage.

Material deprivation and educational attainment

So far, explanations for class differences in educational attainment have focused on culture – for example, class subcultures and so-called cultural deprivation. But class is also about material factors – in particular, differences in income and wealth. Many sociologists argue that material factors play an important part in determining levels of educational attainment. In particular, they see **material deprivation** – a lack of material resources – as a major factor accounting for the relatively low attainment of those in the lower levels of the class system.

Cognitive development

Parental income makes an important difference to educational attainment. In particular, students receiving free school meals have lower attainment at GCSE and A-level and are less likely to go on to university. Research by Jane Waldfogel and Elizabeth Washbrook (2010) looked at the relationship between low income and cognitive development. They assessed the cognitive ability of five-year-old children from the Millennium Cohort Survey, a longitudinal study of 12 644 children from birth onwards.

Cognitive ability was based on the results of three tests. The researchers divided the children into five groups based on parental income. They compared the test results of the lowest income group – the bottom 20 per cent with income below the official poverty line – with the results of the middle-income group – the middle 20 per cent. There was a significant score gap between the lowest and the middle groups. The largest gap, 11.1 months, was on the Naming Vocabulary Test in which children were shown pictures of objects and asked to name them. This test indicated that the cognitive development of children in poverty when they started school was nearly a year behind that of middle-income children. This gap was reduced to nine months for children who spoke only English at home. But the gap remains important since it is likely to be reflected in the attainment gap throughout the children's educational career.

The researchers then attempted to identity factors which might help to explain the income-related cognitive development gap. In terms of material factors, lack of a home computer and a car were the most apparent. For example, 62 per cent of the poorest group had no access to the internet compared to 17 per cent of the middle group. Lack of an annual holiday was a distinguishing factor. 57 per cent of the poorest group could not afford one compared to 15 per cent of the middle group. In terms of health, lower birth weight and poorer health generally appeared to make a 'modest contribution' to lowering cognitive development. Factors which seemed to make a positive contribution to cognitive development were parents reading to children and family trips to places of interest.

Private tuition and extra-curricular activities

Private tutors provide students, at a cost, with direct help with their school work. A survey commissioned by the Sutton Trust in 2014 showed that 23 per cent of young people received private tuition. There was a 12 percentage point gap between the highest and the lowest income families (Sutton Trust, 04.09.2014).

Research indicates that **extra-curricular activities** – organised activities outside school – can have a positive effect on educational attainment. A survey conducted by the Office for National Statistics showed that 35 per cent of households in the top fifth income group had paid for their children to attend extra-curricular activities such as classes in sport, dance, drama and music. This compares with only 9 per cent in the lowest fifth income group (Sutton Trust, 04.09.2014).

Schools in disadvantaged areas

Ofsted, the official schools assessment body, reports that, in general, the higher the level of deprivation in an area the lower the quality of schools. Ruth Lupton (2004) studied schools in deprived low-income areas. She gives the following description. Teachers had serious pupil welfare issues to worry about. Compared to better off areas, pupils tended to be 'anxious, traumatised, unhappy, jealous, angry or vulnerable'. They were more likely to disrupt lessons and truant from school. Teachers had difficulty maintaining high expectations as they were often disappointed. They were careful to select inexpensive school trips because parents often lacked the money to pay for them.

A study by Cambridge University based on a sample of 2500 teachers in England found that those teaching in poorer areas tended to be inexperienced and less effective. Research by the Sutton Trust found that good teaching was particularly important for students from low-income families. Over a school year with a very effective teacher they gained one and a half years of learning, compared with six months with an ineffective teacher (Weale, 2016). However, according to one estimate, only 14 per cent of variation in students' performance is accounted for by the quality of the school (Hirsch, 2007).

Barriers to learning

In a study of the effects of poverty on schooling, Theresa Smith and Michael Noble (1995) list some of the 'barriers to learning' that can result from low income. These include:

» insufficient funds to pay for school uniforms, school trips, transport to and from school, classroom materials and, in some cases, school textbooks. This can lead to children being isolated, bullied and stigmatised. As a result, they may fall behind in their schoolwork

» children from low-income families are more likely to suffer from ill health, which can affect their attendance and performance at school

» low income reduces the likelihood of a desk, educational toys, books and space to do homework, and a comfortable well-heated home

» the marketisation of schools, which is likely to increase the division between successful, well-resourced schools in affluent areas, and under-subscribed, poorly resourced schools in poor areas. This will 'reduce rather than increase opportunities for children from poor families, by concentrating socially disadvantaged children in a limited number of increasingly unpopular schools' (Smith and Noble, 1995).

Conclusion

This unit has looked at some of the factors which may account for class differences in educational attainment. Its focus has been outside the school in the wider society rather than what happens in the classroom. It has examined social class subcultures and material differences between social classes. Some sociologists argue that a combination of these factors explains class differences in educational attainment.

The following unit examines class differences in attainment in terms of Pierre Bourdieu's theory of social reproduction – the reproduction of social inequality from generation to generation. Bourdieu's ideas of cultural capital, social capital and economic capital bring together both cultural and material factors and factors external and internal to the school. (See pp. 34–35 for an introduction to Bourdieu's theory.)

Key terms

Norms Guides to appropriate behaviour in particular situations.

Values Beliefs that something is important and worthwhile

Subculture The distinctive norms and values of a particular group in society.

Fatalism Accepting a situation rather than making efforts to improve it.

Immediate gratification Focusing on pleasures of the moment rather than putting them off for future reward.

Present-time orientation A focus on the present rather than the future.

Collectivism Emphasis on the group rather than the individual.

Formal-learning-type skills The kind of skills used in formal learning such as counting, speaking and writing.

Restricted code A kind of shorthand speech in which meanings are not spelled out.

Particularistic meanings Meanings which are tied to a particular social context and not readily available to outsiders.

Elaborated code Speech in which meanings are made explicit, spelled out.

Universalistic meanings Meanings which are not tied to a particular context or situation.

Cultural deprivation theory The idea that certain groups are deprived of or deficient in things seen as necessary for high educational attainment.

Positive discrimination Discriminating in favour of a particular group.

Compensatory education Making up for or compensating for the supposed deficiencies of so-called culturally deprived groups.

Operation Head Start A programme of pre-school compensatory education in the USA.

Educational Priority Areas Programmes of compensatory education in parts of England.

Material deprivation A lack of material resources.

Summary

1. Some researchers see differences in class subcultures as the main reason for class differences in educational attainment.

2. Class differences in parental interest in children's education have been seen as a reason for class differences in attainment.

3. Basil Bernstein argued that class differences in speech patterns contribute to class differences in attainment.

4. Gillian Evans argues that most working-class parents place a high value on education. The attainment gap between the middle and working classes is mainly due to differences in children's primary socialisation.

5. Cultural deprivation theory states that the reason for the relatively low attainment of working-class children is due to the lack of the skills, attitudes and values required for high educational attainment.

6. Cultural deprivation theory has been criticised for blaming the child and their background rather than the school for educational failure.

7. Compensatory education aims to compensate for the supposed deficiencies of children from low-income families and give them a head start in school.

8. Some researchers argue that material factors, in particular poverty, can place 'barriers to learning'.

2.3.3 Cultural, social and economic capital and differential attainment

As outlined in Part 1, the French sociologist Pierre Bourdieu saw the main role of education in society as social reproduction – the reproduction of social inequality from one generation to the next – in particular, the reproduction of the wealth, power and privilege of the 'dominant classes'.

This unit examines how Bourdieu's ideas of cultural, social and economic capital have been used to explain class differences in educational attainment. The unit starts with Bourdieu's application of his own theory. It moves on to look at how British sociologists have developed his ideas.

This unit raises a very difficult question. Will equality of opportunity ever be possible when those at the top have an armoury of cultural, social and economic capital to keep themselves up there?

Pierre Bourdieu

Bourdieu (1971, 1974) argues that the education system is based on the culture of the dominant classes. They have the power to 'impose meanings and to impose them as legitimate'. They are able to define their own culture as 'worthy of being sought and possessed', and to establish it as the basis for knowledge in the educational system.

However, there is no way of showing that their culture is any better or worse than other subcultures in society. The high value placed on dominant culture in society as a whole simply stems from the ability of the powerful to impose their definition of reality on others. This is very different from cultural deprivation theory which states that the subculture of those in the lower levels of the class system is substandard and deficient compared to the subcultures of those above them in the system.

Cultural capital

Bourdieu refers to possession of the dominant culture as **cultural capital** because, via the educational system, it can be translated into wealth, power and status. Cultural capital is not evenly distributed throughout the class system, and this largely accounts for class differences in educational attainment. Students with upper-class and to a lesser extent middle-class backgrounds have a built-in advantage because they have been socialised into the dominant culture.

Bourdieu claims, 'the success of all school education depends fundamentally on the education previously accomplished in the earliest years of life'. Education in school merely builds on this basis – it does not start from scratch but assumes prior skills and prior knowledge. Children from the dominant classes have internalised these skills and knowledge during their pre-school years. Their success is based on 'the cultural capital previously invested by the family' (Bourdieu, 2016). They possess the key to unlock the messages transmitted in the classroom. In Bourdieu's words, they 'possess the code of the message'.

The educational attainment of social groups is therefore directly related to the amount of cultural capital they possess. Thus upper and middle-class students have higher success rates than working-class students because they have more of the dominant culture and therefore more cultural capital.

Bourdieu is somewhat vague when he attempts to pinpoint the skills and knowledge required for educational success. He places particular emphasis on style, on form rather than content, and he suggests that the way in which students present their work and themselves counts for more than the actual scholastic content of their work. He argues that, in awarding grades, teachers are strongly influenced by 'the intangible nuances of manners and style'. The closer students' style is to that of the dominant classes, the more likely they are to succeed.

The emphasis on style discriminates against working-class students in two ways:

1. Because their style departs from that of the dominant culture, their work is devalued and penalised.

2. They are unable to grasp the range of meanings that are embedded in the 'grammar, accent, tone, delivery' of the teachers. Since teachers use 'bourgeois parlance' as opposed to 'common parlance', working-class students have an in-built barrier to learning in schools.

Habitus, class and education

Bourdieu used the concept of habitus to develop his ideas. Habitus refers to the values, attitudes, dispositions and expectations held by particular groups. It defines everyday ways of doing things – in Bourdieu's words, 'ways of walking or blowing your nose, ways of eating or talking'. It constructs ways of seeing the world and states what is reasonable, appropriate, and to be expected. As a result, habitus generates 'thoughts, perceptions, expressions and actions'. Habitus is learned from an early age within the family. It is a major part of primary socialisation. It varies from class to class.

Bourdieu argues that the habitus of the dominant classes provides them with an advantage in the educational system. As a result of their habitus, parents and children are likely to have a positive attitude towards education. This attitude is based on 'a system of dispositions towards the school understood as a propensity (tendency) to consent to the investment in time, effort and money necessary to conserve and increase cultural capital' (Bourdieu, 1977). This means they will have an inclination to do what is required to succeed in education – from parents investing money in private tutors and fee-paying schools, to children seeing education as important and working hard to pass exams and gain admission to a top university.

This dominant class habitus will be recognised by teachers as a readiness for school knowledge. Teachers will take the view that they and the students are working towards the same goal. As a result, teachers will tend to favour the children of the dominant classes.

Activity

A successful start.

How does the teacher recognise his dominant class habitus and 'readiness for school knowledge'?

By comparison, the habitus of the working class tends to have a more negative attitude towards education. It has lower expectations of success and sometimes rejects the values of school. It may encourage resistance to the school and a 'negative withdrawal which upsets teachers'. And this may lead to low attainment by some working-class students.

Taste, class and education

In *Distinction: A Social Critique of the Judgement of Taste* (1984), Bourdieu discusses the development and importance of taste.

Using survey data as evidence, Bourdieu claims that people's tastes – for example, tastes in art, films, music and food – are related to their upbringing, their class, and their educational attainment.

The tastes of the dominant classes, which Bourdieu refers to as 'legitimate taste', tend to have the highest prestige. They include so-called 'high culture' – classical music, opera, ballet, theatre, fine art and 'good' literature. A study of class in Britain (Savage *et al.*, 2015) found that these tastes were often seen as 'respectable and worthy', that they went 'hand-in-hand with a sense of entitlement and authority', that they gave a sense of 'self-assurance and self-confidence'. Students with these tastes and qualities tended to be 'better placed to understand their school curriculum' and to get 'better qualifications'.

Legitimate taste on its own does not guarantee educational success or a well-paid job, but it certainly helps. For example, it helps you get into the most prestigious schools and universities. It also shapes teachers' perceptions of their students. Unconsciously, teachers recognise different tastes and the types of behaviour typical of different classes. They value and reward legitimate taste more than middlebrow taste, and, in turn, middlebrow taste is valued more than popular taste. Such tastes may not even be part of the formal curriculum but they play an important role in giving those from higher-class backgrounds more chance of success. In Bourdieu's (1984) words, 'In awarding grades teachers are strongly influenced by the intangible nuances (subtle shades of meaning) of manners and style'.

The social function of elimination

Bourdieu claims that a major role of the educational system is the social function of **elimination** (Bourdieu, 1974; Bourdieu and Passeron, 1977). This involves the elimination of members of the working class from higher levels of education. It is accomplished in two ways:

1. Examination failure

2. Self-elimination

Due to their lack of cultural capital, working-class students are more likely to fail examinations, which prevents them from entering higher education. However, their decision to vacate the system of their own accord accounts for a higher proportion of elimination. Bourdieu regards this decision as 'reasonable' and 'realistic'. Working-class students know what is in store for them. They know that the dice are loaded against them. Their attitudes towards education are shaped by 'objective conditions', and these attitudes will continue 'as long as real chances of success are slim'. And these attitudes form part of working-class habitus. According to Bourdieu (1977), it is 'the negative predispositions towards school which result in the self-elimination of most children from the most culturally unfavoured classes who are deprived of cultural capital'.

Conclusions

The arguments outlined in this unit lead Bourdieu to conclude that the major role of education in society is the contribution it makes to **social reproduction** – the reproduction of the inequalities of wealth, income, power and privilege between social classes. Social inequality is reproduced in the educational system and as a result it is legitimated. The privileged position of the dominant classes is justified by educational success; the underprivileged position of the lower classes is legitimated by educational failure.

The educational system is particularly effective in maintaining the power of the dominant classes, since it presents itself as a neutral body based on meritocratic principles providing equal opportunity for all. And unlike economic capital, 'the transmission of cultural capital is heavily disguised or even invisible'. As such it 'escapes observation and control'. Bourdieu (2016) concludes that, in practice, education is essentially concerned with 'the reproduction of the established order'.

Alice Sullivan – a test of Bourdieu's theory

Alice Sullivan (2001, 2002) conducted a questionnaire survey of 465 16-year-old students in four English schools in order to test Bourdieu's theory of class

differences in educational attainment. She used the occupation of the parent to determine the class of the children – where there were two parents she chose the one with the highest status job. And she used educational qualifications to measure the parent's cultural capital.

A number of measures of students' cultural capital were used. Students were asked about the books they read, the television programmes they watched, the music they listened to, whether they played a musical instrument, and their attendance at art galleries, theatres and concerts. Tests of vocabulary and knowledge were also given in order to test Bourdieu's idea of the 'development of skills'.

The research then examined which of these factors, if any, are linked with educational performance in GCSEs. Sullivan found that students were more likely to be successful if they read more complex fiction and watched TV programmes such as arts, science and current affairs documentaries, and more sophisticated drama. Watching programmes such as soap operas and game shows did not improve GCSE performance. Attendance at cultural events and involvement in music had no significant effect, suggesting that these should not be considered important aspects of cultural capital. Students who read widely and watched more intellectual and 'highbrow' television developed wider vocabularies and greater knowledge and this was reflected in higher GCSE grades.

Sullivan found that students' cultural capital was strongly correlated with parental cultural capital (i.e. their parents' educational qualifications), which in turn was closely linked to their social class. Graduate parents in higher professions had children with the most cultural capital and who were most successful in exams.

On the surface, this research provides strong support for Bourdieu. However, Sullivan also found that there were significant differences in educational attainment between middle-class and working-class children even after the effects of cultural capital had been taken into account. This led her to conclude that Bourdieu's theory could only account for part of the class differences in attainment. She says:

Parents' social class retains a large and significant direct effect on GCSE attainment, controlling for the cultural capital variables. Therefore, it seems that cultural capital is one mechanism through which higher-class families ensure educational advantage for their children, but it leaves most of the social class differential in attainment unexplained. Other mechanisms, such as class differentials in material resources and educational aspirations, must account for the remaining differentials in educational attainment. Sullivan, 2001

Sullivan's conclusion suggests that cultural capital, *and* parental interest in education, *and* parents' economic situation all contribute to class inequality in educational attainment.

Evaluation of Bourdieu

The evaluation of Bourdieu's views of the role of education in society outlined in Part 1 also applies to this section.

1. Bourdieu has been criticised, particularly by Marxists, for what they see as his downplaying of certain material factors, in particular, economic exploitation and oppression.

2. Critics argue that he places too much emphasis on the structure of society shaping people's behaviour rather than looking at how individuals can change and transform society. For example, they argue that habitus is presented as determining behaviour rather than giving opportunities for individuals to direct their own actions. As Alice Sullivan (2002) puts it, 'Bourdieu's theory has no place not only for individual agency, but even for individual consciousness'.

3. Concepts such as cultural capital and habitus have been criticised as vague, lacking in precision and detail and difficult to operationalise – put into a form which can be measured.

4. Alice Sullivan's test of Bourdieu's theory suggests that cultural capital explains only a part of educational attainment.

5. Despite the above criticisms, Bourdieu's work has been extremely influential. It has informed many studies in many countries. And, as the following sections show, concepts such as cultural, social and economic capital and habitus have inspired and directed many important research projects.

Activity

A family high in cultural, social, economic and symbolic capital.

1. Give evidence from the picture to support the above description of this family.

2. Briefly suggest how these capitals might help their children's education.

Diane Reay — mothers and class work

In an important study entitled *Class Work: Mothers' Involvement in Their Children's Primary Schooling*, Diane Reay (1998) states that, 'It is mothers who are making cultural capital work for their children'. Her research is based on interviews with the mothers of 33 children at two London primary schools.

All the mothers are actively involved in their children's education. The working-class mothers worked just as hard as the middle-class mothers. But it was not simply hard work that counted. In addition, it was the amount of cultural capital available. And the middle-class mothers had most.

Middle-class mothers had higher educational qualifications and more information about how the educational system operated. They used this cultural capital to good effect – helping children with their homework, bolstering their confidence and sorting out problems with their teachers. Where the middle-class mothers had the confidence and self-assurance to make demands on teachers, the working-class mothers talked in terms of 'plucking up courage' and 'making myself go and see the teacher'. Where middle-class mothers knew what the school expected from their children and how to help them, working-class mothers felt they lacked the knowledge and ability to help their children.

Middle-class mothers not only have more cultural capital, they also have more economic capital – more money. Over half the middle-class mothers had cleaners, au pairs or both. This gave them more time to support their children. Working-class mothers could not afford help with domestic work. Nor could they afford private tuition which many middle-class mothers provided for their children.

According to Diane Reay, it is mothers who have the main influence on their children's education. Their effectiveness depends on the amount of cultural and economic capital at their disposal. And this depends on their social class.

Class, capitals, and choosing schools

Studies of class differences in choosing schools conducted by Stephen J. Ball, Sharon Gewirtz and Richard Bowe show the importance of cultural, social and economic capital. As a result of their greater capitals, middle-class parents were in a better position than working-class parents to assess available schools for their children. And they had a wider choice of schools. They had more knowledge, contacts, time and money to help them make decisions (Ball *et al.*, 1994). (See p. 48.)

Middle-class parents were more likely to have the economic capital to widen their choice of schools – money to pay for coaching for entrance exams into grammar schools or private schools, fees for private schools, the expense of moving house to the catchment area of a successful school, the costs of transportation to more distant schools.

With their greater cultural capital, middle-class parents were better able to judge the quality of schools, analyse the league tables and gather information from teachers on open days.

Added to the above is the greater likelihood of middle-class parents having more social capital – a wider and more informative network of relatives, friends and acquaintances who can be called upon to provide advice and information on the choice of schools. In *Class Strategies and the Education Market: The Middle-Classes and Social Advantage*, Stephen J. Ball (2003) states that, 'Middle-class parents have 'enough capitals in the right currency to ensure a high probability of success for their children'. The following quotations from middle-class mothers about choosing schools for their children show how they use their social capital (Ball, 2003).

You talk to other people who've got children there who come from Riversway, how they are coping. You spend a lot of time talking outside the school gates to people you know in the same situation, that's how you discover things really. (Mrs Grafton)

We spoke to teachers in the schools, spoke to other parents, and spoke to my friends who are scattered across the borough about where their children went and what they thought about it. (Mrs Gosling)

Class, capitals and higher education

Using Bourdieu's ideas as a framework for their research, Diane Reay, Miriam David and Stephen Ball (2005) looked at the influence of social class on university choices. Their sample was based on students from six schools and colleges in and around London – an 11–18 comprehensive, a comprehensive sixth-form consortium, two FE colleges and two private schools. They gave a questionnaire to 502 students, ran focus groups and conducted 120 in-depth interviews.

Habitus

The researchers found Bourdieu's concept of habitus (see pp. 81–82) particularly useful. **Habitus** refers to the dispositions, tastes and expectations of the social groups to which individuals belong – for example, their family, school and social class.

Bourdieu (1973) states that 'the habitus acquired in the family is at the basis of the structuring of school experiences'. This habitus is strongly influenced by the family's position in the class structure. It defines a person's identity – who they are, where they belong and what is appropriate for them.

The habitus acquired in the family has an important influence on higher education choices. For example, many of the privileged middle-class students at the two private schools came from families where university attendance was taken for granted, and where elite universities were seen as appropriate for 'people like them'. These views were usually confirmed by the habitus of the fee-paying schools they attended. Progression to elite universities was seen as normal and natural for their kind of students.

Privately educated, middle-class students often had detailed knowledge of premier division universities, which they had acquired from both family and school. In addition, they had a 'confidence, certainty and

sense of entitlement', which led many to choose the top universities. By comparison, many working-class students lacked this knowledge and confidence. They tended to see elite universities such as Oxford and Cambridge as 'not for the likes of them'. They had insufficient cultural capital to avoid 'feelings of risk, fear, shame and guilt', which resulted from their perception of a greater likelihood of academic and social failure should they attend an elite university. For many, this led to a 'process of self-exclusion' – by not applying, they barred themselves from the top universities.

Stratification in higher education

As noted in earlier sections, there has been a rapid expansion of higher education places over the past 30 years (see Part 2). As a result, increasing numbers from all social classes are attending universities and gaining degrees. However, the more widespread a qualification becomes, the more it is devalued (Bourdieu, 1993). One way of preventing this is to stratify universities and the degrees they award – for example, by defining degrees as high status if they are obtained from a high-status university.

Reay *et al.*'s research shows that the privately educated, middle-class students were most likely to attend elite universities such as Oxford and Cambridge. Middle-class students from state schools tended to choose the middle-ranking, 'old', pre-1992 redbrick universities such as Manchester and Liverpool (Russell Group universities).

Working-class students were more likely to choose the 'new', less prestigious, post-1992 universities that make up the lowest rank of the university hierarchy. As a result, there is a match between the rank of universities and the class background of students.

Mobilising capitals in higher education

In an article entitled 'Higher education, social class and the mobilisation of capitals: recognising and playing the game', Ann-Marie Bathmaker, Nicola Ingram and Richard Waller (2013) develop an important argument. A major concern has been to end class differences in educational attainment, to ensure that people from all social classes have equal access to higher education, and that class does not affect the level of the degree they attain. In recent years, the higher education 'game' has been changing. Going to university is not just about getting a degree. Increasingly, it is also about building personal capitals in order to succeed in the labour market. And, in this respect, middle-class students have a decided advantage. As a result, 'University does not become a social leveller, but rather it becomes another site for the middle classes to compound and exploit their advantages'.

Bathmaker *et al.'s* research is based on a longitudinal study — a study of the same group over time — of undergraduates at Bristol's two universities. The sample consists of 41 middle-class and 40 working-class students. Previous research has indicated that getting a degree is no longer enough. In order to improve their future economic and social position, students must build on existing capitals and generate new forms of capital while at university. Those who are best at 'playing this game' start university with the most cultural, social and **economic capital**. And they are likely to be from middle-class rather than working-class backgrounds.

Adding value

How do students add value to their degrees and produce the right capitals to succeed in the labour market? First, work experience, in particular internships — temporary positions involving on-the-job training, paid or unpaid, lasting between a week and 12 months and maybe leading to full-time employment. Middle-class students were more likely to have the social capital to obtain suitable internships. For example, Nathan who wanted to work in finance said, 'I'm sure my networking helped. My dad put me in touch with a family member in an investment bank in London'. Middle-class students were also more likely to have the economic capital to afford unpaid internships in the UK and abroad. 23 middle-class students secured internships compared to 10 working-class students.

Other ways of increasing capitals at university were less direct. These were extra-curricular activities not related to academic studies. Examples included joining university clubs and societies, becoming committee members and accepting positions such as president and vice-president. Some students recognised that these activities would look good on their CVs (short accounts of a person's education and work experience usually sent with a job application). Middle-class students were more likely to get involved in extra-curricular activities and to see their relevance for obtaining employment.

As the title of Bathmaker *et al.'s* research indicates, middle-class university students were more likely to 'recognise and play the game'. They were more likely to 'exploit the advantages they had already acquired through privileged backgrounds'. In conclusion, 'The middle classes are not only dealt the better cards in a high-stakes game, but they have internalised the knowledge, through economic and cultural advantages of when and how to play them'.

Contemporary issues: Internships

Protesting about unpaid internships in the fashion industry.

The Association of Graduate Recruiters (2016) surveyed over 200 employers who offered internships. Compared to 2015, there was a 13 per cent increase in internships and students were securing them earlier in their degree course. 45 per cent of the previous years' interns were employed full-time by the same company. Banks, engineering companies and accountants hired the most interns.

In 2014 during London Fashion Week, students from King's College London protested against the use of unpaid internships in the fashion industry. In the words of one student, 'Unpaid internships have a massive impact when it comes to access to certain careers, particularly for people from low socio-economic backgrounds' (*The Guardian*, 14.02.2014). According to the Sutton Trust (12.11.2014), 31 per cent of graduate interns report working for no pay.

Questions

1. What 'capitals' are often put to use in order to gain internships?

2. How are internships obtained?

3. How useful are they?

The concepts of capitals and habitus — evaluation

The concepts of cultural, social and economic capital and the idea of habitus have directed a range of research projects on social class and educational attainment. They have been extremely useful in throwing new light on the importance of:

» Socialisation within the family.

» Choosing schools and universities.

» Building on existing advantages at university.

» Class attainment and the wider society.

The concepts of capitals and habitus have shown the connection between money, social contacts, ways of thinking, and attitudes and expectations. As a result of the ideas of capitals and habitus, researchers have asked new questions and provided new answers. These ideas have brought together cultural and material factors and factors both internal and external to schools and the education system.

Key terms

Social reproduction The reproduction of social inequality from one generation to the next.

Cultural capital The culture of the 'dominant classes' which can be translated into wealth, income, power and prestige.

Social capital A social network that can be used as a resource.

Economic capital Financial resources – income and wealth.

Habitus The dispositions, expectations, attitudes and values held by particular groups.

Elimination The elimination of members of the working class from higher levels of education.

Mobilising capitals Using capitals to advance your position. Building on existing advantages.

Summary

1. According to Bourdieu, educational success is mainly based on cultural capital.

2. In general, the higher a person's position in the class system, the more cultural capital they possess.

3. Dominant class habitus includes attitudes and expectations which provide a significant advantage in the educational system.

4. Students from the lower levels of the class system tend to eliminate themselves from the higher levels of the educational system.

5. Sullivan's test of Bourdieu's theory suggests that cultural capital explains only a part of educational attainment.

6. Reay's research indicates that middle-class mothers' cultural and economic capital gives their children an advantage in education.

7. The greater capitals of the middle and upper classes give them an advantage in choosing schools.

8. The habitus of the dominant classes leads them to select the highest ranking universities.

9. At university, students with the highest level of capitals are most likely to mobilise them to further their chances in the job market.

10. The concepts of capitals and habitus have directed important research projects.

2.3.4 Social class in the classroom

Explanations of class differences in attainment examined in previous sections have been largely based on factors outside the school. They look at the wider society and argue that an individual's position in the social structure has an important effect on their educational attainment. Structural explanations, in this case explanations based on the class structure, see behaviour as shaped by external factors over which the individual has little control. Their behaviour is seen as largely determined by the directives of class subcultures, by material factors, and by cultural, social and economic capitals.

This unit looks at small-scale interaction situations in the classroom. It examines teachers' perceptions of students' social class and how this might affect their placement in ability groups – for example, the tendency for working-class students to be placed in lower sets and streams. This, in turn, might affect how students see themselves and their attainment. This unit asks, does interaction in the classroom reinforce factors in the wider society which result in class differences in educational attainment?

Interactionist perspectives

This section looks at social class and educational attainment from an interactionist perspective. The focus is narrowed from the wider society to the classroom. Attention is directed to small-scale interaction situations and the meanings which develop and guide action within those situations.

Interactionists argue that a person's **self-concept**, their view of themselves, develops from interaction with others. Interaction in the classroom, with teachers and students, helps to shape a person's self-concept; and their self-concept can have a significant effect on their educational attainment. (For an introduction to interactionism/symbolic interactionism see pp. 13–14.)

The way students are classified as 'high attainers' and 'likely to succeed' and 'low attainers' and 'unlikely to succeed' is often influenced by students' social class. Middle-class students tend to be classified as 'high attainers' and working-class students as 'low attainers'. This will affect teachers' expectations of students' attainment.

In this respect, students have been labelled. A **label** defines how others see a person and how they behave towards them. It can also influence how a person sees themselves and how they behave in response to the label.

Labelling and social class

In a study of an American kindergarten, Ray C. Rist (1970) found that as early as the eighth day of school the children were permanently seated at three separate tables. Table 1 was reserved for 'fast

learners', tables 2 and 3 for the 'less able'. According to Rist, it was not ability that determined where each child sat, but the degree to which they conformed to the teacher's own middle-class standards. For example, the teacher appeared to take account of whether the children had neat and clean appearances, and whether they were known to come from an educated family with one or both parents in middle-class occupations. In other words, the kindergarten teacher was evaluating and labelling students on the basis of her perception of their social class, not on their abilities.

The **labelling** of students can have important effects on their progress in education. Aaron V. Cicourel and John I. Kitsuse (1963) conducted a study of the decisions of counsellors in an American high school. The counsellors played a significant part in the students' educational careers since they largely decided which students should be placed on courses designed for preparation for college entry. Although the counsellors claimed to use grades and the results of IQ tests as the basis for classifying students in terms of achievement, Cicourel and Kitsuse found significant differences between these measures and the ways in which students were classified.

They found that the students' social class was an important influence on the way they were evaluated. Even when students from different social backgrounds had similar academic records, counsellors were more likely to perceive those from middle- and upper-middle-class origins as natural 'college prospects', and place them on higher-level courses.

The self-fulfilling prophecy theory

Labelling theory argues that once a label is attached to a person there is a tendency for them to see themselves in terms of the label and act accordingly. And there is a tendency for others to see them in terms of the label and act towards them on this basis. This may result in a **self-fulfilling prophecy**.

The self-fulfilling prophecy theory argues that predictions made by teachers about the future success or failure of students will tend to come true. The teacher defines the student in a particular way, such as clever or not so clever. Based on this definition, the teacher makes predictions or prophecies about the behaviour of the student – for example, that they will get high or low grades.

The teacher's interaction with students will be influenced by their definition of the students. They may, for example, expect higher quality work from

Activity

Teachers responding to the information they've been given by the researchers.

A teacher's expectations.

How do these pictures illustrate the idea of labelling and the self-fulfilling prophecy?

and give greater encouragement to those they have defined as 'bright' students. The students' self-concepts will tend to be shaped by the teacher's definition. Their actions will, in part, be a reflection of what the teacher expects from them. In this way the prophecy is fulfilled – the predictions made by the teacher have come to pass. Thus the student's attainment level is to some degree a result of interaction between the student and the teacher.

There have been a number of attempts to test the validity of the self-fulfilling prophecy theory. The most famous one was conducted by Robert Rosenthal and Leonora Jacobson (1968) in an elementary school in California. They selected a random sample of 20 per cent of the student population and informed the teachers that these children could be expected to show rapid intellectual growth. They tested all students for IQ at the beginning of the experiment. After one year the children were re-tested and, in general, the sample population showed greater gains in IQ. In addition, report cards indicated that teachers believed that this group had made greater advances in reading skills.

Although Rosenthal and Jacobson did not observe interaction in the classroom, they claimed that 'teachers' expectations can significantly affect their students' performance'. They suggested that teachers had communicated their belief that the chosen 20 per cent had greater potential and that the children

responded by improving their performance. Rosenthal and Jacobson speculated that the teachers' manner, facial expressions, posture, degree of friendliness and encouragement conveyed this impression which, in turn, produced a self-fulfilling prophecy.

Evaluation of labelling and the self-fulfilling prophecy

Despite seeming reasonable, the self-fulfilling prophecy theory has been criticised. One area of criticism concerns the evidence. Rosenthal and Jacobson have been strongly attacked for the methods they used in their study. In particular, it has been suggested that the IQ tests they used were of dubious quality and were improperly administered.

In almost all the research based on labelling and the self-fulfilling prophecy, the actual process, which is supposed to have led to changes in self-concept and behaviour, has not been directly observed. For example, Rosenthal and Jacobson only speculated on how the changes in the children's performance came about. They were not in the classroom to observe how changes in the teachers' attitudes might have led to changes in the students' behaviour (Rist, 2016).

There is evidence that students sometimes reject negative labels. In a study of a group of Black girls in a London comprehensive school, Margaret Fuller (1984) found that the girls resented the negative stereotypes associated with being both female and Black. They felt that many people expected them to fail, but, far from living up to these expectations, they tried to prove them wrong. The girls devoted themselves to school work in order to try to ensure their success.

This suggests that labels can have a variety of effects. They may produce a self-fulfilling prophecy. They may be rejected and result in the opposite behaviour to that implied by the label.

Ability grouping

In many schools, students are placed in **ability groups** – groups based on their perceived ability. There are several types of ability grouping. These include the following:

> **Streaming:** Students are placed in a class on the basis of their overall ability. They remain in that class for most subjects.

> **Banding:** This is a less rigid form of streaming. Each band contains two or more classes, which may be regrouped for different subjects.

> **Setting:** Students are placed in classes on the basis of their attainment in particular subjects. For example, they may be in set 1 for English and set 3 for maths.

> **Mixed ability:** Students are randomly or intentionally mixed in terms of their perceived ability (Ireson and Hallam, 2001).

Is the selection of students for ability groups affected by their social class? Does ability grouping affect students' attainment? The following study answers 'yes' to both these questions.

'Psychological prisons'

Jo Boaler (2005) conducted a study of students aged 13 to 16 in mathematics classes in two schools. The two groups were similar in terms of social class and previous attainment. In School A, students were taught in mixed ability classes until a few months before their GCSEs. In School B, students were placed in eight sets for maths at the age of 13. Middle-class students tended to be placed in higher sets, working-class students in lower sets. In School A there were no significant social class differences in exam results. And the results were significantly higher than those of School B. However, in School B most of the higher grades were attained by middle-class students, most of the lower grades by working-class students.

Eight years after their GCSEs, Boaler interviewed 10 former students from each school. Those from School

A who had been taught in mixed ability groups gave positive reports of their school experience saying that 'teachers had regarded everyone as a high achiever'. All the students from School B were keenly aware of their ability group experience. Those from Set 1 were happy with their placement, those from Set 2 on down were not. In the words of one young man from School B:

The lower sets are like a psychological prison… It just breaks all their ambition, particularly working-class kids… That's why I dislike the set system so much because I think it almost formally labels kids as stupid.

Boaler concludes that ability grouping in sets, rather than promoting high achievement for all 'reproduces social class inequalities'.

Streaming in primary schools

Streaming by ability in primary schools appears to increase the gap between higher and lower attaining pupils. It also widens social class differences because those from low-income families tend to be placed in lower streams, those from better-off homes in higher streams. Evidence for this comes from a study of 2544 Year 2 pupils (aged six and seven) born in the UK in 2000–2001 who took part in the Millennium Cohort Study – a longitudinal study (Centre for Longitudinal Studies, 2014).

One in six children in English primary schools were placed in streams – where pupils are taught in the same class and grouped by ability across several subjects. Compared to children in mixed-ability teaching groups, pupils in the top streams did better in reading and maths, those in the bottom streams did 'significantly worse'. The study found that working-class pupils were 'disproportionately placed in lower streams' and that streaming, particularly when it begins at a very early age, is likely to increase the gap between top and bottom and between social classes.

How does streaming do this? 'Grouping children by ability changes teachers' expectations. This impacts on what is taught to different groups, how it is taught and the unspoken messages given to pupils' (Hallam and Parsons, 2014).

Student voices

In an article entitled, 'The zombie stalking English schools: social class and educational inequality', Diane Reay (2006) looks at 'some of the ways in which class is lived in classrooms'. The article is based on discussions with groups of students and interviews with individual students in two secondary schools. In one school, students in the bottom sets were all working class, those in the top sets mainly middle class. This positioned 'working-class pupils as inadequate learners with inadequate cultural backgrounds, looked down on for their "stupidity"'. In the words of two of the boys:

> Kenny: *Some teachers are a bit snobby, sort of. And some teachers act as if the child is stupid. It's because teachers have got a posh accent. Like they talk without 'innits' and 'mans', like they talk proper English. And they say, 'That isn't the way you talk' – like putting you down. Like I think telling you a different way is sort of good, but I think the way they do it isn't good because they correct you and make you look stupid.*
>
> Martin: *Those teachers look down on you.*
>
> Kenny: *Yeah, like they think you're dumb… we don't expect them to treat us like their own children. We're not. But we are still kids. I'd say to them, You've got kids. You treat them with love but you don't need to love us. All you need to do is treat us like humans.*

The working-class boys in the lower sets wondered whether there was any point in working hard. They felt educationally worthless, disrespected and undervalued.

The second school was based on mixed ability groups. Despite this, the working-class students' feelings of opposition and alienation were 'just as raw and tangible'. The quotations below from working-class girls voice their feelings about a teacher's preference for middle-class pupils.

> Sharmaine: *Sometimes we feel left out.*
>
> Sarah: *Because you know, teachers are not meant to have favourites.*
>
> Sharmaine: *You can have, but you can't show it, you know. That's unfair to the other people.*
>
> Sarah: *Because there's a whole class there and you want to pick that particular person, and you are nice to that one, and the rest you don't care about.*
>
> Alex: *But everyone has to be the same.*
>
> Sharmaine: *He needs to treat everyone equal.*

In Diane Reay's words, 'Evident in the girls' account is a strong sense of being marginalised from positive learning experiences'.

Activity

A zombie in the classroom.

Why does Diane Reay title her article 'The zombie stalking English schools'?

In conclusion, Reay states: 'Social class remains the one educational problem that comes back to haunt English education again and again and again: the area of educational inequality on which education policy has had virtually no impact'. (For further material on ability and mixed-ability teaching groups see pp. 127–130.)

Counter–school culture/anti–school culture

Counter-school cultures, also known as **anti-school cultures**, are subcultures which reject the norms and values of the school. They are usually found amongst students in lower sets. Students in lower sets tend to be working class. Counter-school cultures have a negative effect on students' progress and reduce their chances of gaining qualifications.

Paul Willis's study of working-class 'lads' provides an illustration of a counter-school culture (see pp. 29–32). The 'lads' saw no value in academic work and had no interest in gaining qualifications. They misbehaved, disrupted lessons and focused their attention on 'having a laff'.

In his study of a West Midlands' comprehensive school, Maírtín Mac an Ghail (1994) identified a group he called the 'Macho Lads' – working-class boys in the lowest sets. The teachers saw them as low-ability, non-academic troublemakers. Their main priority was policing rather than teaching the Macho Lads who, in turn, saw the teachers as hostile and controlling.

Defined as troublemakers and as underachievers with little or no chance of academic success, the Macho Lads reacted by developing an anti-school culture. They saw school work as meaningless and those who conformed to school rules as 'dickhead achievers'. Their main concerns were 'acting tough', 'looking after your mates', and 'having a laugh'. They refused to accept the teachers' authority. In the words of one boy, 'schools are for keeping you down and bossing you around'. Stuck in the bottom sets, they saw the teachers as 'just looking down on us'.

As with 'the lads' in Paul Willis's research, the anti-school culture developed by the working-class Macho Lads gave them little chance of gaining qualifications. (See pp. 120–124 for further coverage of counter-school/anti-school cultures.)

The educational triage

The idea of an **educational triage** was first examined on pp. 52–53. To briefly recap, the educational triage is a three-part division of GCSE students. The first part is made up of students expected to achieve 5 or more GCSEs, grades A* to C. These students tended to be middle class. The second part consists of 'borderline cases', students judged to be on the borders of C and D grades. The third part is made up of 'hopeless cases', students seen as having little or no hope of obtaining 5 or more GCSEs grades A* to C. These students tended to be working class.

Research by David Gillborn and Deborah Youdell (2000) in two London secondary schools indicates that teachers focus on the 'borderline cases' in order to improve their school's GCSE results and its position in the league tables. This group received additional teaching provided by the most experienced teachers. This is at the expense of the other two groups. The first group is expected to obtain 5 or more GCSE grades A* to C grades without additional help. And as 'hopeless cases' there's little point in providing additional resources for the third group. Arguably, this third, largely working-class, group needs the most help. From this point of view, it suffers most from the educational triage.

Conclusion

This unit has shown that what happens inside schools often reinforces class inequalities in the wider society. The inequalities of social class outside school produces social class differences in educational attainment. Rather than reducing these differences, what happens in the classroom may well increase them and widen the gap between top and bottom. Many of the points examined in this unit are developed in Part 6 *Relationships and Processes in Schools* (see p. 118), which takes a further look at student subcultures and teachers' perceptions of students.

Key terms

Interactionism A sociological theory which examines interaction – the action between members of small social groups.

Self-concept An individual's picture or view of themselves.

Label A definition of a person placed on them by others.

Self-fulfilling prophecy A tendency for the way people are labelled to shape their actions.

Ability groups Groups in which students are placed on the basis of their perceived ability.

Counter-school culture/anti-school culture Student subcultures which reject the norms and values of the school.

Educational triage The division of students into three groups in terms of their expected GCSE grades.

Summary

1. The interactionist perspective indicates:

   ‣ how students' self-concept might be shaped in the classroom

   ‣ how students are sometimes labelled

   ‣ how labelling might lead to a self-fulfilling prophecy.

2. Students might reject negative labels.

3. In many schools students are placed in ability groups based on their perceived ability.

4. There is a tendency for middle-class students to be placed in higher ability groups and working-class students in lower groups even when their grades are similar.

5. Placement in ability groups is likely to widen the attainment gap between the higher and lower groups and, as a result, to reproduce social class differences in educational attainment.

6. Students in lower groups tend to feel educationally worthless, disrespected and undervalued.

7. Counter-school/anti-school cultures are usually found in lower sets consisting of mainly working-class students. They reduce their chances of gaining qualifications.

8. By focusing time and effort on borderline cases, the educational triage discriminates against the first, largely middle-class, group and particularly against the third, mainly working-class, group.

PART 4 GENDER AND EDUCATION

Contents

In the UK today, girls and young women are outperforming their male counterparts at every level of the educational system – from primary school to university. This is a dramatic change that has happened during the last 30 years and is reflected worldwide. Across cultures and continents, from the USA to Japan, from Mexico to New Zealand, from Portugal to South Korea, girls have reversed the picture that would have been expected 30 years ago.

In the 1970s the focus of research was on girls' 'underachievement'. Since the 1990s it has been 'underachieving boys' who have been the focus of gender research in education.

It is important to place the 'gender effect' in perspective. Class has over five times the effect on educational attainment that gender has. And ethnicity has twice the effect (Gillborn and Mirza, 2000). But, as the following unit shows, the effect of gender on educational attainment is still significant.

This part begins with statistical evidence which shows girls outperforming boys at every level of the educational system. It then looks at possible reasons for girls' so-called 'educational underachievement' in the 1970s and 80s. It moves on to possible reasons for the rapid rise in girls' educational attainment from the 1990s onwards. Gender differences in subject choice in school and university are then examined. Possible reasons for boys' so-called 'educational underachievement' are given along with some evidence that changes in the job market may be leading to an increase in boys' attainment. However, the question remains: Will boys ever catch up with girls?

2.4.1 Gender and attainment – the evidence

Research over the past 60 years shows that girls have always outperformed boys in primary school tests. The same applied to the 11-plus (as noted on pp. 44–45). However, girls' scores in the 11-plus were 'adjusted' in order to ensure that equal numbers of girls and boys obtained grammar school places (Tomlinson, 2005). This shameful procedure was kept quiet.

This unit examines gender differences over time in test and exam results from Key Stage 2 tests to A-level. It then moves on to gender differences in university entrance and level of degree.

Key Stage 2 assessments

Table 2.4.1 shows the results of Key Stage 2 tests in reading, writing and mathematics. It gives the percentages of boys and girls in Year 6 (10–11 year olds) reaching the expected standard. Girls consistently outperform boys. The gender gap in percentage points

Table 2.4.1 Key Stage 2 assessments. Boys and girls reaching the expected standard. England, 2012–2016 (percentages)

Year	Boys	Girls	Gender gap (percentage points)
2012	71	79	8
2013	72	79	7
2014	75	82	7
2015	77	83	6
2016	50	57	7

Source: DfE (10.12.2015; 01.09.2016).

remains much the same from 2012–2016. However, the percentage reaching the expected standard in 2016 was significantly lower because of 'new and more challenging tests' (DfE, 01.09.2016).

GCSE

Before the introduction of the GCSE examination, the gender gap at age 16 was either slightly in favour of girls or non-existent (Machin and McNally, 2006).

Table 2.4.2 shows the percentage of boys and girls attaining five or more GCSE grades A* to C from 1990 to 2012. The gender gap steadily widened from 7.6

Table 2.4.2 Male and female students attaining five or more GCSE grades A*−C, England, 1990–2016 (percentages)

Year	Males	Females	Gender difference (percentage points)
1990	30.8	38.4	7.6
1994	39.1	47.8	8.7
1998	41.3	51.5	10.2
2002	46.4	57.0	10.6
2006	52.6	62.2	9.6
2010	65.4	72.6	7.2
2012	65.4	73.3	7.9
2014	64.3	73.1	8.8
2016	62.4	71.3	8.9

Source: Adapted from various DfE publications and various issues of *The Guardian*.

percentage points in 1990 to 10.6 in 2002. After that it narrowed to 7.2 in 2010, and then rose to 8.9 in 2016.

A-level

Table 2.4.3 shows the percentage of male and female students in England attaining two or more A-levels or equivalent qualifications from 2002/3 to 2010/11.

Table 2.4.3 Male and female students attaining two or more A-levels or equivalent qualifications, England, 2002/2003–2010/11 (percentages)

Year	Males	Females	Gender difference (percentage points)
2002/3	87.9	91.2	3.3
2004/5	90.6	93.0	2.4
2006/7	94.0	96.1	2.1
2008/9	94.1	96.0	1.9
2009/10	93.9	95.6	1.7
2010/11	93.9	94.2	0.3

Source: Adapted from DfES (18.01.2006); DCSF (14 .01.2009); DfE (26.01.2012).

Table 2.4.4 Average point score for male and female A-level students, England, 2010–2015

	2010	2011	2012	2013	2014	2015
Male	209.7 (C)	211.8 (C)	211.2 (C)	212.6 (C)	212.6 (C)	213.1 (C)
Female	216.2 (C+)	217.8 (C+)	217.5 (C+)	218.1 (C+)	217.9 (C+)	218.4 (C+)

Source: Adapted from DfE (21.01.2016).

It shows the gender gap steadily closing from 3.3 percentage points in 2002/3 to 0.3 in 2010/11.

The Department for Education now produces statistics on A-level attainment in the form of point scores. Grade C is 210 points and a grade B is 240 points. Table 2.4.4 shows the average A-level point score for males and females from 2010 to 2015. It indicates that males averaged grade C, females grade C+ (C plus). Despite being behind overall, boys are slightly ahead in the top grades. In 2016, 8.5 per cent of boys and 7.7 per cent of girls were awarded an A* (*The Guardian*, 18.08.2016).

Higher education

Figure 2.4.1 shows that the number of men and women in higher education (HE) in the UK has grown rapidly over

Figure 2.4.1 Male and female students in higher education, UK, 1970/1971–2014/2015

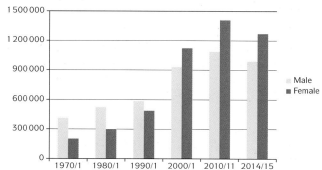

Source: *Social Trends*, 2007, 2011; HESA (Higher Education Statistics Agency) (2016).

the past 45 years. The rate of growth has been much faster for women. In 1970/1971 women made up 33 per cent of HE students. By 2014/2015 they made up 56 per cent, outnumbering men by over 281 000.

Figure 2.4.1 indicates that the number of students in higher education in 2010/11 is greater than the 2014/15. This is simply due to a change in the way higher education students are classified. For example, a number of nursing courses were reclassified and this reduced the number of higher education students.

Table 2.4.5 Men and women attaining first class and upper second class degrees, UK, 1994/1995–2014/2015 (percentages)

Date	Men	Women	Gender gap (percentage points)
1994/5	44	51	7
2004/5	55	62	7
2009/10	60	65	5
2014/15	69	74	5

Source: HESA (Higher Education Statistics Agency) (2016) www.hesa.ac.uk.

Interpreting the statistics

The picture often presented by the media is of girls racing ahead and boys trailing behind, of achieving girls and failing boys. This makes good headlines but the picture is more complex as the following summary indicates.

Summary

1. In general, both males and females have improved their performance over the past 45 years.

2. As shown later in this unit, only some working-class boys could be described as 'underachieving'.

3. On balance, however, girls and young women are outperforming boys and young men at every level of the educational system.

2.4.2 Explaining girls' 'underachievement' — the 1970s and 1980s

In the 1970s and 1980s, the main focus of gender research in education was girls' 'underachievement'. Although the gender gap at 16 was either non-existent or slightly in favour of girls, at A-level and degree level boys were outperforming girls. This unit looks briefly at explanations for this gender difference. In one respect, these explanations are now redundant, with girls outperforming boys at every level of the educational system. However, some of the explanations may still be relevant — they may point to factors which, even today, are preventing girls from reaching their full potential.

Early socialisation

As Fiona Norman and her colleagues (1988) point out, before children start school, gender socialisation has already begun. From the types of play that girls and boys are encouraged to engage in and the types of toys they are given, different sets of aptitudes and attitudes may be developed.

The educational aspirations of girls may be influenced through playing with dolls and other toys that reinforce the stereotype of women as 'carers'. Boys tend to be encouraged to be more active than girls, and this may be reflected in their attitudes in classrooms. Furthermore, boys are more likely to be given constructional toys that can help develop scientific and mathematical concepts. The media, through magazines, books, computer games, television and advertising, can further reinforce stereotypes of males and females.

One possible consequence of early gender stereotyping is that girls may come to attach less value to education than boys. Research conducted by Sue Sharpe (1976) into a group of mainly working-class girls in London schools in the early 1970s found that the girls had a set of priorities that were unlikely to encourage them to attach great importance to education. She found that their concerns were 'love, marriage, husbands, children, jobs, and careers, more or less in that order'. Sharpe argued that, if girls tended to see their future largely in terms of marriage rather than work, then they might have little incentive to try to achieve high educational standards.

In the 1990s, Sharpe repeated her research and found that girls' priorities had changed. Now jobs/careers were their chief concern for the future (Sharpe, 1994). This change may help to explain why the educational attainment of girls at school is now higher than that of boys.

Socialisation in school

Many sociologists have claimed there is bias against girls in the educational system. Research by Glenys

Lobban (1974) found evidence of gender bias in some educational reading schemes. From a study of 179 stories in six reading schemes, Lobban found that only 35 stories had heroines, compared to 71 that had heroes. Girls and women were almost exclusively portrayed in traditional domestic roles and it was nearly always men and boys who took the lead in non-domestic tasks. In at least three of the schemes, females took the lead in only three activities in which both genders were involved: hopping, shopping with parents, and skipping. Males took the lead in seven joint activities: exploring, climbing trees, building things, looking after pets, sailing boats, flying kites and washing cars.

Lobban's research was conducted in the 1970s, but more recent research has also found evidence of gender stereotyping. In 1992, Lesley Best and her students examined a sample of 132 books for preschool-age children in an attempt to discover whether gender bias in children's books had decreased.

They found that little had changed. In 132 books, 792 male and 356 female characters were portrayed. There were 94 male heroes but just 44 heroines. Some 75 per cent of the female characters featured in the books were portrayed in family situations, compared to just 15 per cent of the male characters. And men were shown in 69 different occupations, but women in only 18.

Activity

The cover of one of the books in the Ladybird Reading Scheme.

How does the cover of this book, published in the 1960s, reflect traditional gender stereotypes?

Behaviour in the classroom

The active and dominant males in the reading schemes may be reflected in the behaviour of boys and girls in the classroom. From their own classroom observations and from their analysis of other studies, Barbara G. Licht and Carol S. Dweck (1987) reached the following conclusions about gender differences in young children's self-confidence.

They found that girls lacked confidence in their ability to carry out intellectual tasks successfully. Despite the superior performance of young girls compared to boys in primary schools, it was the girls who generally expected to encounter most difficulty when learning new things.

According to Licht and Dweck, boys are able to shrug off failures by attributing them to a lack of effort on their part, or unfair assessment by teachers. Girls, on the other hand, constantly underestimate their ability, fail to attach significance to their successes, and lose confidence when they fail.

Michelle Stanworth — gender differences in further education

Michelle Stanworth (1983) examined A-level classes in a further education college. She interviewed teachers and students from seven different classes in the humanities department. Her findings suggested that in the sixth form a number of the attitudes displayed by teachers would impede the educational progress of girls.

Teachers found it much more difficult to remember the girls in their classes. Without exception, all the students whom teachers said it was difficult to name and recall were girls. Quiet boys were remembered, but quiet girls seemed to blend into the background and made little impression on their teachers.

Stanworth found that teachers held stereotypical views of what their female students would be doing in the future. Only one girl was seen as having the potential to enter a professional occupation. Interestingly, she was the most assertive of the girls in the classroom but her academic performance was not particularly good. One teacher described the most academically successful girl as likely to become a 'personal assistant for someone rather important'. Even for this girl, marriage was suggested as one of the most significant aspects of her future life. And male teachers mentioned nothing other than marriage as the future for two-thirds of the female students.

When asked which students were given the most attention by teachers, the students themselves named boys two and a half times as often as girls, although girls outnumbered boys by nearly two to one in the classes studied. The students reported that boys were four times more likely to join in classroom discussions, twice as likely to seek help from the teacher, and twice as likely to be asked questions.

Furthermore, girls were consistently likely to underestimate their ability, while boys overestimated theirs. Students were asked to rank themselves in terms of ability in each class. In 19 of the 24 cases in which teachers and students disagreed about the ranking, all of the girls placed themselves lower than the teachers' estimates, and all but one boy placed themselves higher.

Stanworth claimed that classroom interaction disadvantaged girls. Teachers had an important role in this, but students themselves also 'played an active part in the regeneration of a gender hierarchy, in which boys are the indisputably dominant partners'.

Stanworth's work was based on interviews and not direct classroom observation. It therefore gives some indication of what teachers and students perceive to be happening in classrooms, but does not actually establish, for example, that teachers give more attention to boys (Randall, 1987). However, later research supports the claim that boys tend to dominate classrooms.

Becky Francis — girls and achievement

In *Boys, Girls and Achievement*, Becky Francis (2000) reviews studies on gender in the classroom, and describes her own research in this area. She says:

> *Almost two decades on, research shows that girls' educational achievement has improved despite the continuing male dominance of the classroom, curriculum content (for example, history's focus on the lives of men) and greater demands on teacher time.*　Francis, 2000

Francis conducted her own research in three London secondary schools in 1998–9. The schools had different levels of overall achievement and were located in different areas, but all had a majority of working-class students. She observed four different classes of 14- to 16-year-olds in each school, visiting each class three times. Half the classes were in English and half in maths. In addition to classroom observations, she interviewed a sample of students.

Like earlier researchers, Francis found evidence that classrooms were gendered and boys tended to dominate. She found that 'boys tend to monopolise space in the classroom and playground, and girls tend to draw less attention to themselves than do boys'. In 8 of the 12 classes boys were considerably noisier than girls. A number of the teachers, though not all, treated male and female students differently.

There were a number of incidents where boys were disciplined more harshly or more frequently than girls. Francis says that sometimes this might have reflected the greater noisiness of boys. Girls who were not paying attention tended to talk quietly rather than disrupt the classroom with more obvious, noisy behaviour.

Francis found evidence that girls were still getting less attention than boys and that schools remained largely male-dominated. However, in some classes there was little evidence that boys and girls were treated significantly differently. Furthermore, Francis did find that some things had changed. For example, she found that students no longer took for granted the belief that girls were less academically able than boys.

Summary

The following reasons have been given for girls' supposed 'underachievement' in the 1970s and 1980s:

1. Early gender socialisation at home — for example, girls' and boys' toys.

2. Socialisation at school — for example, gender stereotypes in reading schemes.

3. Girls' lack of confidence and underestimating their ability.

4. Teachers' focusing on boys and seeing girls as less academically able.

5. Boys dominating lessons.

6. Marriage, motherhood and domesticity seen as girls' future priorities.

2.4.3 Explaining girls' 'achievement'

Over the past 30 years, the improvement in the educational attainment of girls and young women has been dramatic and unprecedented. Yet relatively little has been written to explain it. Instead, the focus has been on the so-called 'underachievement' of boys. According to Becky Francis and Christine Skelton (2005), 'this reveals the marginalisation of girls, how their school performance is seen as peripheral to that of boys, how they do not count'. This unit looks at some of the explanations for the rise in girls' educational attainment.

Changing attitudes and expectations

As noted earlier, Sue Sharpe's (1976) study of working-class schoolgirls in the early 1970s showed that their main priorities for the future were 'love, marriage, husbands and children'. When she repeated this study in the 1990s, she found significant changes. Now, the girls' main concerns were 'job, career and being able to support themselves' (Sharpe, 1994). They were more confident, assertive and ambitious. They saw education as the main route to a good job and financial independence.

In the 1970s, over 80 per cent of girls wanted to get married; by the 1990s this had dropped to 45 per cent. The girls were increasingly wary of marriage. With the rapidly rising divorce rate throughout the 1980s and 1990s, they had seen adult relationships breaking up around them. They had also seen women standing on their own two feet rather than depending on financial support from a man. Paid employment and financial independence were now major concerns.

Although many of the girls in the 1990s expected to work in 'women's jobs' such as primary school teaching, nursing, beautician work and clerical work, they were more likely than girls in the 1970s to consider 'men's jobs' such as car mechanics and firefighters, and to look forward to professional careers such as being a doctor or a lawyer. Given their hopes and concerns, educational success was more important to the 1990s girls than their 1970s counterparts.

The changing attitudes and expectations of girls were reflected both by their parents and by their schools. A number of studies, particularly those of girls from middle-class families, indicate that parents increasingly expect exam success, and in some cases make their daughters feel that they could 'never be good enough' (Francis and Skelton, 2005).

A study entitled *Education and the Middle Class* (Power *et al*., 2003) showed that girls were often 'driven ... by the ambitions of their school' to maintain or improve its position in the league tables. This was particularly apparent in all-girls private schools where it was assumed that every student would aim to

continue to A-level and university. As one girl put it, 'It was just one track and that was that'.

The women's movement and feminism

Many of the rights that feminists and the women's movement fought for in the 1960s and 1970s have now been translated into law – for example, the Equal Pay Act (1970) and the Sex Discrimination Act. The ideals on which those rights are based have been increasingly taken for granted. Although today's young women may not see themselves as feminists, they expect equal opportunity in education and in the labour market. According to Mitsos and Browne (1998), the women's movement has provided both incentives and direction for young women in education. In their view, the 'women's movement and feminism have achieved considerable success in improving the rights and raising the expectations and self-esteem of women'.

Changes in the labour market

The decline in heavy industry, the growth in service sector work, and the increasing employment of 'flexible' part-time workers and workers on fixed-term contracts have all expanded employment opportunities for women. The employment rate for working-age women in the UK rose from 53 per cent in 1971 to 70 per cent in 2016. The same period saw a drop in the male rate from 92 per cent to 79 per cent (Labour Market Statistics, ONS, 2016). Jobs in the service industries – which have a higher proportion of women employees – increased by 21.5 percentage points between 1979 and 2010, while jobs in manufacturing – where men have traditionally been employed – fell by 17.2 percentage points over the same period (*Social Trends*, 2011).

The growth in employment opportunities, along with the rise in young women's occupational ambitions, has increased their incentives to gain educational qualifications. Studies of both primary and secondary school students show that many girls are now looking forward to jobs that require degree level qualifications (Francis and Skelton, 2005).

Individualisation and the risk society

Ulrich Beck (1992) argued that we are moving from modernity into 'the second modernity (see pp. 17–18). His views have been used to help explain the dramatic change in women's educational achievements.

According to Beck, today's society is characterised by **risk** and **uncertainty** and by a process of individualisation. For example, with the rising divorce rate, marriage is increasingly associated with risk and uncertainty. Employment is becoming increasingly unstable. There are fewer 'jobs for life'; people are changing jobs more often, retraining, improving and/or learning new skills. As a result, the job market and career paths become less predictable.

A process of individualisation accompanies risk and uncertainty. People are increasingly thrown back on themselves as individuals – they are more and more responsible for their own fate, their own security, their own future. People are becoming more self-sufficient and self-reliant. Beck sees women at the forefront of the individualised self – they are 'setting the pace for change'. He argues that this is due to changes in women's family life, education, occupations and laws on gender equality.

In this increasingly insecure, individualised society, individuals must equip themselves for self-reliance and self-sufficiency. Financial independence is seen as one of the main ways of doing this, and education is seen as one of the main routes to well-paid jobs that can provide financial independence.

However, education is not simply a means to financial security. Sociologists who picture a second modernity generally agree that there is an increasing emphasis on the construction of self and on the creation of identity. Studies of girls in primary and secondary schools illustrate this emphasis. According to Francis and Skelton (2005), 'The majority appear to see their chosen career as reflecting their identity, as a vehicle for future fulfilment, rather than as simply a stopgap before marriage'.

Activity

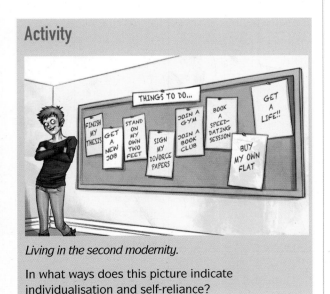

Living in the second modernity.

In what ways does this picture indicate individualisation and self-reliance?

Key term

Individualisation An emphasis on the individual, on self-construction, self-reliance and self-sufficiency.

Summary

The following reasons have been given for girls' educational achievement:

1. Changing attitudes and expectations. Now girls' main concerns were jobs and being able to support themselves.

2. The women's movement and feminism raising women's expectations and self-esteem.

3. Changes in the labour market – more job opportunities for women.

4. Changes in society – individualisation, risk and uncertainty leading to an emphasis on self-reliance and self-sufficiency.

2.4.4 Gender and subject choice

This unit looks at gender differences in subject choice at GCSE, A-level and university, and the explanations put forward for these differences. Gender differences in subject choice matter as they may well place women at a disadvantage in the labour market in terms of job status and pay.

Despite significant changes in girls' educational attainment, there are still important gender differences in subject choice. At GCSE, these differences are fairly small. They are wider at A-level and university. Table 2.4.6 shows the three most popular subjects for females and males at A-level in 2016 and the percentage of entrants by gender taking each subject. For example, English is the most popular female subject

Table 2.4.6 Three most popular subjects at A-level by gender in 2016, England (percentages)

Female	Male
1. English 72.9 per cent	1. Mathematics 61.3 per cent
2. Psychology 76.3 per cent	2. Physics 78.4 per cent
3. Biology 61.1 per cent	3. Chemistry 50.1 per cent

Source: Adapted from Earlham Sociology, 2017.

and 72.9 per cent of those taking it in 2016 were female. Art and design, sociology and religious studies were in the female 10 most popular subjects at A-level but not in the male top 10. Physics, economics and business studies were in the male top 10 but not in the female.

At university, men dominate in science and engineering and outnumber women in computer science and economics. Women are much more likely to take nursing courses (9:1), and outnumber men in psychology, social work, education, and design (*The Guardian*, 03.05.2016).

Gender differences in subject choice may well disadvantage women in the labour market. The subjects they tend to choose may lead to lower status and lower paid occupations than those chosen by men.

Explaining gender differences in subject choice

A variety of reasons have been suggested for gender differences in subject choice. They include the following.

Socialisation There are gender differences in the way children are socialised, for instance in the toys parents choose for boys and girls. This may affect gender identity and in turn, subject choice. For example, boys tend to be given and to play with construction toys, which may influence their choice of engineering in later life.

Gender identity Gender stereotypes and social norms define what is typical, normal and appropriate behaviour for males and females. They can produce gender identities which encourage the acceptance of traditional gender roles. Breaching these roles and venturing into new gender areas may produce guilt and uncertainty. As a result, there may be pressure to select subjects which fit and seem appropriate for gender identities (Favara, 2012).

Gender identities may also be shaped by gender discrimination in the labour market and perceptions of 'men's jobs' and 'women's jobs'. Again, this may influence subject choice.

Learning styles It has been argued that there are **gendered learning styles** and, as a result, some subjects are more suitable for boys and others for girls. Rationality, objectivity, abstract 'facts' and memorisation of rules are seen as fitting male learning styles and subjects such as science and maths. Female learning styles are seen to be based more on subjectivity, emotion and real situations. As a result, they are more suited to English, the arts and humanities (discussed in Francis and Skelton, 2005).

Teacher expectations Research from the 1980s indicated that teachers and careers officers tended to steer girls and boys towards gender-stereotypical subject choices. However, later research suggested that these directives were less apparent (Francis and Skelton, 2005).

WISE – Women into Science and Education

WISE is a campaign for gender balance in science, technology and engineering from the classroom to the boardroom. Its aim is summarised in the following quote.

WISE enables and energises people in business, industry and education to increase the participation, contribution and success of women in science, technology, engineering and mathematics (STEM). WISE members inspire girls to choose maths, physics and computing. WISE members attract, retain, develop and progress female talent in their companies.

To promote these aims WISE works with businesses such as Sky and Siemens, educational institutions such as the Royal Academy of Engineering, organisations such as the NHS, and schools and colleges across the UK to encourage more girls to retain STEM subjects post 16. Membership of WISE has grown rapidly in recent years as has the number of women in STEM (science, technology, engineering and mathematics) occupations – 'over 860 000 in 2017 and our goal of 1 million women in STEM by 2020 within reach'.

Contemporary issues: Gendered toys

A mother and son in a toy shop

I saw the looks you gave me and my three-year-old son today. I saw the way you watched him pick out the pink dolls pram and push it round the shop with pure joy. I saw the way you came over frowning at a child simply enjoying a toy. I listened as you tried to belittle my son for his choice of toy.

'Oh, you don't want that, it's just for girls, not boys. It's all pink and girly. There's cars and dinosaurs over there, why would you want that girly thing.'

I was about to have a go at you but my boy got there first and answered you so much better than I could've: 'Cos I like it'.

(Rheann MacLaren, 2016)

Let Toys Be Toys

Let Toys Be Toys is an organisation which campaigns to stop manufacturers and retailers from promoting some toys and books as only suitable for girls and others for boys. Their 2012 survey showed that 50 per cent of shops used signs for 'Boys' toys' and 'Girls' toys'. Their 2016 survey showed that these signs had 'pretty much disappeared'. However, their research gave a different picture for toy manufacturers whose packaging, ads and catalogues were still based on stereotypes. Girls were twice as likely to be shown with household toys and five times as likely to be shown with toys for caring such as dolls. Boys were twice as likely to be pictured playing with construction toys and 16 times more likely to be playing with guns and soldiers (Let Toys Be Toys, 2016).

Similar findings come from research by the Institution for Engineering and Technology. They found that 31 per cent of toys with a science, technology, engineering and maths focus were listed for boys and only 11 per cent for girls on toy retailers' websites.

Questions

1. Grown-ups are responsible for gendered toys. What do you think?

2. What effect might gendered toys have on gender subject choices at school and university?

Key term

Gendered learning styles The idea that males and females have different styles of learning.

Summary

1. There are still important differences in gender subject choice.

2. The following reasons have been suggested for these differences:

   › Gender differences in early socialisation.

   › Different gender identities – selecting subjects which social norms define as gender appropriate.

   › Different gendered learning styles which result in some subjects being more suitable for girls, others for boys.

2.4.5 Explaining boys' 'underachievement'

This unit begins by questioning the view that boys are underachieving. It continues with a look at various explanations for boys' supposed underachievement.

These include their construction of masculinity – in particular 'laddism' and the idea that it's uncool to work hard at schoolwork. The unit closes with a study which provides evidence that suggests that deindustrialisation and the decline of traditional manual jobs has led to working-class boys placing a higher value on education and going on to further and sometimes higher education.

A moral panic

'We are talking about boys. They cannot read, write their own names or speak properly. They are physically and socially clumsy. Increasingly they cannot even do boys' stuff like maths and science.' This quote comes from the editorial of a respected newspaper, *The Observer* (05.01.1998). It reflects the growing concern about so-called 'underachieving', 'underperforming' or 'failing' boys. That same year, the Labour government produced 'a coordinated plan of action to tackle the underachievement of boys'. Eight years later, Labour chancellor Gordon Brown was warning of the prospect of 'a wasted generation of boys' (*The Guardian*, 13.10.2006). Some commentators suggested that this concern had reached the level of a **moral panic** among British newspapers and politicians (Francis and Skelton, 2005).

Are boys underachieving?

In the 1970s and 1980s, concern about the 'gender effect' was focused on girls' 'underachievement'. By the 1990s this concern was reversed. Now it was boys 'underachieving'. But were they?

In general, the educational attainment of boys and young men has steadily improved over the past 50 years. This does not indicate underachievement. However, certain boys are underachieving – a higher proportion of working-class boys are doing badly compared with other social groups. But the same can be said for working-class girls. However, White working-class boys from low-income families who receive free school meals are the lowest performing group in terms of ethnicity, class and gender.

What has changed is the overall rate of improvement for boys and girls. As the statistics outlined earlier show, girls' educational performance over the last 30 years has improved at a faster rate than boys', resulting in a significant widening of the gender gap. And this applies to boys and girls from all social classes. Whether this should be seen as 'boys' underachievement' is a matter of opinion.

There have been many attempts to explain boys' failure to keep pace with girls. Some of these will now be examined. They are based on the assumption that boys are underachieving and that something should be done to raise their educational attainment. In particular, reasons for the low attainment of White working-class boys will be discussed.

Constructions of masculinity

The school is a major setting for the construction of masculinity. Recent research argues that the form of masculinity constructed in the classroom contributes to the underachievement of male students. Earlier research had made a similar argument with reference to the anti-school subculture developed by some working-class boys, particularly those placed in lower ability groups. However, studies now indicate that 'laddish' behaviours have spread to most boys – both working-class and middle-class – and to some extent to girls (Jackson, 2006).

In a study entitled *Lads and Ladettes in School: Gender and a fear of failure* (2006), Carolyn Jackson examined 'laddish behaviour' among 13- to 14-year-old (Year 9) boys and girls. Her research was based on interviews with 203 students in eight schools and questionnaire data from 800 students in six schools.

Laddish behaviour is based on the idea that it is 'uncool' to work and that appearing 'cool' is necessary to be popular. This aspect of laddishness was accepted by the vast majority of boys and girls, whatever their social class background.

Boys' laddish behaviour was constructed within a framework of **hegemonic masculinity** – the dominant and pervasive view of masculinity. It was based on heterosexuality, toughness, and competitiveness. It was expressed in acting 'hard', being one of the lads, disrupting lessons, having a laugh and being demanding and assertive. Academic work was defined as effeminate and uncool.

Students are faced with a dilemma. They want to do well academically, yet they also want to appear cool and to be popular. But if they are seen to work hard, they are a 'geek', a 'nerd' or a 'swot' – terms of derision. The solution is to appear to reject schoolwork, do the requisite amount of messing around, but work secretly, usually at home. This favours middle-class boys who have the resources at home to do their homework quickly and efficiently – the space, privacy, a desk and a computer. They are better able to balance being popular and academically successful (Jackson, 2006).

If laddish behaviour is holding boys back, then its development should parallel the widening of the gender gap in attainment. Some researchers argue that this is the case. The following are some suggested explanations for the development of laddish behaviours. They point to changes in the wider society which have occurred at the same time as the widening gender gap in educational attainment.

Pressure to succeed and fear of failure

A number of sociologists have seen competitive individualism and individual responsibility as major themes in today's society. This promotes fears of academic failure and directs responsibility for failure to the individual. Laddish behaviour can be seen as a response to this. The argument that it is uncool to work can be used as an excuse for poor academic performance.

The marketisation of schools has placed further pressure on students. Schools compete in the educational market, striving to raise standards and climb league tables. The importance of examination success is increasingly emphasised and students are under growing pressure to achieve high grades. Laddish behaviour can be seen as a defensive strategy to reduce the fear of poor academic performance or to excuse the reality of failure (Jackson, 2006).

Changes in the labour market

Over the past 30 years there has been a rapid decline in unskilled and semi-skilled manual jobs. These 'macho' manual jobs reflected traditional male working-class identities. Their disappearance has left these identities uncertain and threatened. The new jobs in the service sector, such as care work, call centre and office work, require what have traditionally been seen as feminine skills and sensitivities. Working-class boys may have responded to these threats to their traditional identities by turning to

laddish behaviour to restore their sense of masculinity (Jackson, 2006).

Reaction to political correctness

Becky Francis (1999) suggests that the rise of 'laddish' behaviour in the 1990s can be seen as a backlash against 'political correctness'. She argues that: 'This led to a defiant resurgence of traditional "laddish" values in the media, typified by the men's magazine *Loaded* and the popular sit-com *Men Behaving Badly*'.

Educational aspirations and attitudes

Research by Tina Rampino and Mark Taylor (2013, 2015) based on self-completion questionnaires given to 13–15 year olds produced the following findings. Girls were more likely than boys to see education in a positive light, to want to continue in school after age 16 and go on to university. These gender differences remained whatever their parents' income and education.

Boys' educational aspirations and attitudes tended to become less positive from the ages of 12 and 13 whereas those of girls stayed the same or improved as they grew older. Unlike boys, girls were more aware of economic downturns when it was harder to get a job. They were more likely to see education as important for employment.

Conclusion

Boys' 'underachievement' became a major concern. Large amounts of time and money were spent on a range of government initiatives aimed at raising boys' educational attainment. By 2005, the Department for Education and Skills website listed 54 academic books and articles on raising boys' achievement plus reports from the four year Raising Boys' Achievement Project.

Some critics have argued that the whole question of equality of educational opportunity has been reduced to gender and focused on boys. This has diverted attention from class, ethnicity and girls (Francis and Skelton, 2005). According to Stephen J. Ball (2013), 'To a great extent the problem of boys' underachievement is a working-class one, and one for those from some minority ethnic groups, but this is often lost sight of in both the media and policy initiatives'.

From labouring to learning

From Labouring to Learning: Working-Class Masculinities, Education and De-industrialisation by Michael R.M. Ward (2015) examines a group of young working-class men in a de-industrialised community in the South Wales Valleys. Like most young people in the UK today, they continued their education after 16 in order to gain qualifications and because there were few other options open to them.

Manual jobs in the local area had all but gone – in particular, the coal mines had closed down. This challenged the traditional working-class culture of masculinity – the emphasis on physical labour, toughness and having a laugh. Unlike the lads in Willis's research, they had no available manual jobs in which to express this form of masculinity.

Michael Ward spent two and a half years following the educational and social lives of 32 young men. His research was based on participant observation, semi-structured and unstructured interviews, and conversations with individuals and groups. He identified two main groups in his study – the Boiz and the Geeks.

The Boiz At school and in further education the Boiz continued to enact the more traditional form of working-class masculinity. They tended to take 'male' subjects such as physical education, motor vehicle studies and A-levels in maths, science, electronics and business studies. In class they were boisterous, disruptive, joking and having a laugh. Despite this behaviour, four members of the Boiz (one third of the group) went on to university.

In their leisure, the Boiz followed traditional activities of young, working-class men – sport – rugby and football, drinking large amounts of alcohol, sexual conquests and fast cars. They looked down on the Geeks as they called them. They saw the Geeks as effeminate and socially inadequate, bullied them and 'took the piss' out of them.

The Geeks Compared to the Boiz, the Geeks were studious, quiet and well-behaved. They followed school rules and wore school uniform. They were determined to achieve, they got high grades and nearly all went to university. They took a mixture of A-levels – maths, science, English, history and media studies.

Outside school the Geeks read books and comics, wrote poetry and played computer games. At times they followed traditional working-class leisure pursuits. However, they looked forward to escaping from their working-class community and taking up middle-class occupations.

Continuity and change Both groups adapted to de-industrialisation in different ways. The Boiz continued with traditional working-class masculinity in terms of their identities and behaviour apart from recognising the need to continue to further education and, for a third of them, to go to university.

The Geeks made greater changes. Their masculinity was now based on educational success and a desire for a new way of life outside the working-class community in which they were raised.

Evaluation of *From Labouring to Learning* This study moves away from the so-called 'crisis in masculinity'. It suggests that, at least to some extent, traditional working-class masculinity can co-exist with educational success. In this respect, the 'lads' and 'ear 'oles' of Willis's 1970s study have adapted fairly well to become the 'Boiz' and the 'Geeks' of the 2010s.

Contemporary issues: Will girls' educational achievements lead to gender equality?

Will girls' achievements in education be reflected in the job market? Will their success smash through the glass ceiling? Will it lead to a closure of the gender pay gap? And will it translate to an equal division of labour in the home?

One argument states that patience is the answer. These changes will come in time. Another argument states that a lot more than patience is required. What might schools do to promote gender equality?

> First, fight sexism, make girls and boys aware of the existence of patriarchal ideology and misogyny and the possibility of a patriarchal hidden curriculum. Here's what happened to one girl who set up a feminist society in a grammar

school. '[There was] a massive backlash from the boys. ... They took to Twitter and started a campaign of abuse against me. I was called a "feminist bitch"' (*The Guardian*, 20.06.2013).

》 Girls are often abused and bullied online by boys from their own school. The girl who set up the feminist society states that there is 'a whole new battleground opening up online where boys can attack, humiliate, belittle us and do everything in their power to destroy our confidence before we even leave school'. Schools should treat online abuse in much the same way as they do bullying in the playground.

》 Schools should discourage gender-based subject choices and make girls more aware of the highly paid, high status jobs in science and technology.

》 There should be an end to the preoccupation with 'underachieving boys' and the assumption that girls don't need much help when nearly 40 per cent fail to get 5 GCSEs *A–C.

》 In an article entitled '*Teach girls to disrupt, subvert and challenge authority*', Kevin Stannard (2013) argues that schools should not just praise girls who conform, they should encourage them to question and debate, to reject gender stereotypes, to challenge authority, and recognise the value of disruption 'since experts say that disruption is a proven path to success'.

Mike Younger (2014) suggests that these are some of the contributions schools might make to further gender equality.

Source: Part of the material in this activity is based on an article by Mike Younger (2014).

Questions

1. Which of the views below do you agree with? Give reasons for your answer:

   a) Have patience! That's all that's needed to translate girls' educational success into gender equality in the job market and the home.
   b) Every major advance in feminism comes with a concerted struggle. It's no different today.

2. Schools should also focus on changing boys' attitudes, even those who favour gender equality. Discuss.

Key terms

Moral panic A widespread panic that something is morally wrong.

Hegemonic masculinity The dominant and pervasive view of masculinity.

Summary

1. The concern about boys' supposed 'underachievement' became a moral panic.

2. The spread of 'laddish behaviour' as an expression of masculinity has been seen as a major reason for boys' 'underachievement'.

3. The following reasons have been suggested for the spread of laddish behaviour:

   》 as a defensive strategy resulting from pressure to succeed and fear of failure

   》 changes in the labour market threatening traditional male, working-class identities

   》 as a reaction to political correctness.

4. Boys are less likely than girls to see education in a positive light.

5. Michael Ward's *From Labouring to Learning* argues that the traditional working-class culture of masculinity does not necessarily prevent educational achievement.

PART 5 ETHNICITY AND EDUCATION

Contents

There are significant differences in the educational attainment of different ethnic groups. This part starts with statistical evidence of the differences in attainment. It moves on to various factors which may affect ethnic attainment and looks at the relationship between ethnicity, class and gender.

Ethnic group subcultures are then examined with particular reference to cultural capital.

The focus then moves to particular ethnic groups. The low attainment and, more recently, improved attainment of Black-Caribbean boys is examined along with competing explanations – racism or Black subculture. The 'myth of underachievement' of Black girls is then outlined. The final unit looks at British Asian students, in particular Muslim boys. The unit closes with an explanation for the high aspirations of British Asian students.

This part raises some interesting questions. For example, why are British Chinese the highest attaining ethnic group? And why are White British the lowest attaining ethnic group of students entitled to free school meals?

2.5.1 Ethnicity and educational attainment

An **ethnic group** is a group within society who are seen by themselves and/or by others as culturally distinct – as having their own norms and values. They often have their own identity. They may, for example, see themselves as White, Chinese, Pakistani and so on. This unit looks at the educational attainment of ethnic groups. All groups have improved their attainment over time, some more than others.

GCSE and ethnicity

Table 2.5.1 shows that Chinese and Indian students have the highest attainment at GCSE level from 2004–13. They consistently exceed the White British average. All groups have increased their attainment during these years with Bangladeshi students making the greatest gains. Black African students have overtaken White British students. And Black Caribbean and Pakistani students have significantly reduced the gap with White British students, though gaps remain.

Table 2.5.1 Percentage of students attaining 5 or more GCSEs A*–C (including English and maths) by ethnic group, 2004–13 (England)

Ethnic group	2004	2005	2006	2007	2008	2009	2010	2011	2012	2013
White British	41.6	42.9	44.3	46.1	48.4	50.9	55.0	58.2	58.9	60.5
Indian	54.5	57.4	59.1	62.0	65.1	67.0	71.3	74.4	74.4	75.7
Pakistani	31.3	32.5	34.6	37.3	40.0	42.9	49.1	52.6	54.4	55.5
Bangladeshi	32.5	34.5	39.0	41.4	45.0	48.3	53.7	59.7	62.2	64.0
Black Caribbean	23.2	27.1	29.5	33.2	36.4	39.4	43.5	48.6	49.8	53.3
Black African	31.3	35.0	37.5	40.8	43.9	48.4	52.8	57.9	58.0	61.2
Chinese	63.9	68.8	65.8	70.7	69.9	71.6	75.1	78.5	76.4	78.1

Source: Adapted from S. Strand, 2015.

GCSE, ethnicity and free school meals

Table 2.5.2 shows GCSE results for free school meal (FSM) students. FSM students from all ethnic groups have improved their performance at GCSE from 2004 to 2013. However, by 2013, all ethnic minority groups in Table 2.5.2 had a higher attainment than White British students. Assuming FSM gives some indication of working-class attainment, then it appears that having a working-class background affects White British attainment to a greater extent than other ethnic groups.

This can be seen from a comparison of Tables 2.5.1 and 2.5.2. For example, Table 2.5.1 shows that in 2013, 60.5 per cent of White British students attained 5 or more GCSEs A*–C. Table 2.5.2 shows that in 2013 only 32.3 per cent of White British FSM students obtained this result. For Chinese students the figures are 78.1 per cent for all students and 76.8 per cent for FSM students. For White British students, coming from a low-income group appears to make a significant difference. For Chinese students, a low- income background does not seem to make a significant difference to GCSE results.

Table 2.5.2 Percentage of students entitled to free school meals attaining 5 or more GCSEs A*–C (including English and maths) by ethnic group, 2004–13 (England)

Ethnic group	2004	2005	2006	2007	2008	2009	2010	2011	2012	2013
White British	14.1	14.7	16.0	17.4	19.1	21.5	25.3	28.8	30.5	32.3
Indian	35.3	37.4	39.5	41.9	45.9	48.0	55.0	57.0	57.9	61.5
Pakistani	22.5	24.1	27.1	29.5	32.3	34.2	40.6	42.9	46.5	46.8
Bangladeshi	29.3	30.5	35.3	36.4	41.7	43.0	50.3	56.2	58.6	59.2
Black Caribbean	13.9	18.8	19.5	24.2	26.2	29.5	33.1	37.8	40.2	42.2
Black African	19.1	22.4	25.5	29.2	32.1	35.6	42.1	47.2	48.4	51.4
Chinese	55.4	58.6	53.8	60.7	63.1	70.8	68.4	73.5	68.2	76.8

Source: Adapted from S. Strand, 2015.

Activity

What are the main trends shown in Tables 2.5.1 and 2.5.2?

Higher education and ethnicity

Table 2.5.3 shows that ethnic minority students are more likely to go to university than White British students. As with GCSE results, Chinese and Indian students are the most successful.

Comparing students who took their GCSEs in 2003 and 2008, university entrance has risen by 5 per cent. Going to university has risen most rapidly for those from low-income backgrounds. Despite this, those from the highest socio-economic group are the most likely to go to university. And girls are around 8 percentage points more likely to go than boys (Institute for Fiscal Studies, 2015).

Table 2.5.3 Percentage of students taking their GCSEs in England in 2003 and 2008 who go on to university in the UK at age 18 or 19 by ethnicity (England)

Ethnic group	2003	2008
White British	28.2	32.6
Black African	40.9	56.6
Black Caribbean	26.6	37.4
Indian	64.1	67.4
Pakistani	37.0	44.7
Bangladeshi	34.5	48.8
Chinese	66.1	75.7

Source: Adapted from Institute for Fiscal Studies, 2015.

Ethnicity, income, material deprivation and educational attainment

This section looks at possible connections between ethnicity, income, material deprivation and educational attainment.

Free school meals are an indication of **material deprivation** – of a lack of material resources. Free school meals are provided for students from low-income families. Low income can mean insufficient funds to pay for school uniforms, school trips, transport to and from school and basic materials for homework such as stationery, rulers and pens. Low income can result in low quality housing, overcrowding and poorly heated homes. It reduces the likelihood of a computer with internet access at home, a desk, educational toys, books and space to do homework. Low income can also result in a poor diet and ill health which can affect attendance and performance at school. (See pp. 78–79 for further information on material deprivation.)

Material deprivation can play an important part in educational attainment. This is suggested by the relatively low attainment of FSM students. A comparison of Tables 2.5.1 and 2.5.2 indicates that in many cases FSM students from low-income households perform less well than students from higher-income families. However, the performance of different ethnic groups does not appear to be affected in the same way by low income.

Further evidence to support this view is provided by Table 2.5.4 which compares the GCSE results and the median (average) income of five ethnic groups.

(Household income figures are combined for Black Caribbean and Black African so these ethnic groups are not included in this table.)

Table 2.5.4 Percentage of students attaining 5 or more GCSEs A*–C, England, 2013 (column 1). Median household income UK 2012–13 (column 2)

Chinese	78.1%	£395
Indian	75.7%	£435
Bangladeshi	64.0%	£284
White British	60.5%	£455
Pakistani	55.5%	£287

Source: Adapted from Strand, 2015; Gov:UK, 09.02.2015.

The top two groups in terms of GCSE results – Chinese and Indian – have relatively high average incomes but the White British group who are number 1 in terms of income are number 4 in terms of GCSE results. And, the Bangladeshi group who have the lowest average income are number 3 in terms of GCSE results. Again we see that to some extent income appears to affect ethnic groups' educational attainment in different ways. Clearly other factors are involved in ethnic group attainment. They will be examined throughout the rest of this chapter.

Key terms

Ethnic group A group in society who are seen by themselves and/or by others to have their own subculture – their own norms and values. Ethnic group members often share a group identity and a sense of belonging.

Material deprivation A lack of material resources.

Summary

1. There are wide ethnic differences in attainment at GCSE.

2. Chinese and Indian students have the highest attainment, Pakistani and Black Caribbean the lowest.

3. In terms of free school meal students, Chinese have the highest attainment at GCSE, White British the lowest.

4. In terms of university admission, Chinese students have the highest percentage, White British the lowest.

5. Income and material deprivation appear to affect the educational attainment of ethnic groups. But, to some extent, they affect different groups' performances in different ways.

2.5.2 Factors affecting ethnic educational attainment

In an article entitled 'Ethnicity, gender, social class and achievement gaps at age 16', Steve Strand (2015) uses a longitudinal study of 15 000 students in England to analyse the differences in attainment between various ethnic groups. He found that the attainment gap associated with social class was twice as large as the biggest ethnic gap and six times as large as the gender gap. However, he found that class, ethnicity and gender were not sufficient to explain differences in attainment. The following student and school factors also needed to be taken into account.

Parental factors

Parental attitudes and behaviour were 'significantly associated with attainment'. Parents' expectations that students would continue their education after age 16 were particularly important as were providing a computer for their children and a private tutor. In general, ethnic minority parents were more likely than White British parents to have positive attitudes and behaviour towards education.

Student factors

Strand divides student factors into 'resilience factors' which encourage high attainment and 'risk factors' which reduce attainment levels.

Resilience factors These include a strong academic self-concept, a positive attitude towards school, planning for the future, hoping to continue education after age 16 and completing homework every evening. Ethnic minority groups were likely to have higher levels of resilience factors than White British students.

Risk factors These include special educational needs, having been excluded from school (high for Black Caribbean students), extended absence from school (high for Pakistani students), truancy, involvement with police, welfare and/or social services. Overall, risk factors were most likely to be found in White British groups.

School factors

In general, the quality of the school appeared to have only a moderate effect on educational attainment except in the case of Black Caribbean students where factors such as teachers' expectations might make a difference.

Class, ethnicity and gender

Social class As noted earlier, social class differences are a major factor affecting educational attainment. The attainment of White British students was affected by class to a greater extent than other ethnic groups.

Ethnicity There is evidence that ethnic subcultures influence educational attainment. This can be seen from the following section on Chinese students.

Gender White working-class girls had the lowest attainment of ethnic group girls. However, they did better than White working-class boys. The gender gap in favour of girls was particularly high for Black Caribbean and Bangladeshi students.

Recent immigration

Strand suggests that recent immigration may be a factor in explaining the relatively high performance of low-income minority ethnic groups compared to low-income White working-class students.

More recent groups... often see education as a way out of the poverty they have come from. By contrast, if you've been in a White working-class family for three generations, with high unemployment, you don't necessarily believe that education is going to change that. Strand, 2008

Ethnic group subcultures

To some extent ethnic groups have their own subcultures – distinctive norms and values. As the following study suggests, these subcultures may well influence educational attainment.

As the statistics in the previous unit show, British Chinese students have the highest grades at GCSE, the highest grades of those entitled to free school meals and the highest percentage of students going to university. Louise Archer and Becky Francis (2007) conducted semi-structured interviews with 80 14- to 16-year-old British Chinese students, 30 Chinese parents and 30 teachers from London schools with Chinese students. Parents from all social classes placed a very high value on education, as did their children. Working-class parents with little formal education were 'passionately committed to providing their children with the opportunities they had lacked'. Both middle- and working-class parents saw university as 'a must'. And all 80 students interviewed said they wanted to go to university.

Parents invested considerable time, energy and money in their children. They monitored their children's progress and often hired home tutors and arranged supplementary schooling. Education was a 'family project'. A family's standing in the community was partly related to the educational performance of their children. And children appreciated their parents' high expectations, encouragement and support. These findings applied to both middle- and working-class families.

To some extent, the high value placed on education is due to Chinese subculture. In this respect, the high attainment of Chinese students may be partly the result of their subculture.

Cultural capital

Bourdieu's idea of cultural capital may help to explain the educational attainment of some ethnic minority students. For example, Chinese and Indians have the largest proportion of middle-class members and the highest attainment. Their high attainment may result from having the largest amount of cultural capital. But what about Bangladeshis and Pakistanis who are doing much better than their class position would suggest? In view of their relatively high proportion of low-income members, these groups should not, in theory, have the cultural capital to produce their level of attainment

(see Table 2.5.2). The same applies to the FSM Chinese students, who should not, in theory, have the cultural capital to reach their high attainment at GCSE. Tariq Modood (2004) gives the following possible explanations for this.

Many members of minority ethnic groups may have more cultural capital than would be expected from their present class position. This may be because their jobs after migrating to the UK were lower in pay and prestige than their previous jobs. This might be due to the time taken to find suitable jobs after arrival in the UK or to discrimination in the labour market.

A number of things may result from this:

1. A reservoir of cultural capital that derives from earlier occupations.

2. A powerful desire on the part of migrants to improve their position and the prospects for their children.

3. A high value placed on education as a means for doing this.

4. This value is passed on to their children.

Contemporary issues: Ethnicity, private tuition and homework

Research based on 19 000 11-year-olds born in 2000 and 2001 showed that 48 per cent of Chinese pupils had help from private tutors compared to 20 per cent of White pupils. 25 per cent of Chinese pupils spent five hours or more a week on homework compared to 7 per cent of White pupils (Nuffield Foundation, 2015).

Question

To what extent may ethnic differences in the use of private tutors be reflected in GCSE results?

Private tutor with a young Chinese pupil.

Key terms

Resilience factors Things which encourage high attainment, for example, completing homework every evening.

Risk factors Things which reduce attainment, for example, extended absence from school.

Summary

Ethnic differences in educational attainment are affected by:

> social class

> gender

> - parental attitudes and expectations
> - a student's resilience and risk factors
> - length of stay in the country
> - ethnic subcultures
> - amount of cultural capital.

2.5.3 Black–Caribbean students

In the 1980s and 1990s, the main focus of research on ethnicity and education was Black-Caribbean male 'underachievement'. As the following sections indicate, there were two main explanations. The first places the blame on racism in schools. The second sees underachievement as a result of Black subculture.

To some extent the focus has changed to Black 'achievement'. First, the success of Black girls is examined. Second, reasons for the steady improvement in Black attainment are suggested.

David Gillborn and Deborah Youdell – Racism in the classroom

Gillborn and Youdell (2000, 2001) studied two London comprehensive schools over a two-year period, using lesson observation, analysis of documents, and interviews with students and teachers. The study was based on students in Key Stage 4 (14–16) with a particular focus on GCSEs.

This was a time of increasing concern with examination success, league tables and the marketisation of schools. As a result, 'some students are sacrificed to the more important goal of raising attainment in the league table statistics'. The students 'sacrificed' tended to be working class and Black Caribbean. These students were seen as 'less able', and placed in lower sets. Students in higher sets had the most experienced teachers and were given more teacher time, support and effort. Students in lower sets were 'systematically neglected'.

Gillborn and Youdell found that 'widespread inequalities of opportunity are endured by Black children'. Teachers had an expectation that 'Black students will generally present disciplinary problems, and they therefore tended to feel that "control and punishment" had to be given higher priority than "academic concerns"'.

Most Black students felt they were disadvantaged by their treatment in schools. By and large, they expected to be blamed for disciplinary problems and they expected that teachers would underestimate their future achievements. In these circumstances it was hardly surprising that they ended up doing, on average, less well than the White students attending the same schools.

Gillborn and Youdell see teachers' perceptions of and behaviour towards Black Caribbean pupils as racist. However, most teachers are unaware of this. In fact, 'many teachers are passionately committed to challenging the very inequalities that they participate in reinforcing'. Their racism takes the form of **institutional racism** – part of the taken-for-granted operation and assumptions of institutions – in this case schools.

Tony Sewell – Black masculinities and schooling

Tony Sewell, a Black-Caribbean researcher, questions the view that Black underachievement is based on racism in schools. In an article entitled 'Racism is not the problem' (2008) he states, 'The idea that teachers are directly or indirectly holding back Black pupils is questionable. More likely, it is to do with the inability or unwillingness of these students to break away from an anti-education peer group that loves the street rather than the classroom'. Sewell's research (1997) is based on a study of Black-Caribbean boys in a boys-only 11–16 comprehensive school.

Street culture and Black masculinity

A high proportion of Black-Caribbean boys are raised in lone-parent families, usually headed by women. In 2001, lone parents headed 57 per cent of Black-Caribbean families with dependent children, compared with 25 per cent of white families (*Social Trends*, 2006). As a result, many boys lack the positive male role model and the discipline that can be provided by a father figure. According to Sewell, this makes them more vulnerable to peer group pressure.

Some young men are drawn into gangs that emphasise an aggressive, macho form of masculinity. Members demand respect, reject authority figures such as teachers and police, and focus on up-to-the-minute street fashion and music. This form of Black masculinity is reflected and reinforced by the media, with gangsta rap and hip-hop fashions and news reports emphasising Black street crime and gun culture.

According to Sewell, this subculture of Black masculinity provides a 'comfort zone' for many Black-Caribbean young men. Acceptance and support from the peer group compensate for their sense of rejection by their fathers and by a society and education system that they often experience as racist.

In schools, this version of Black masculinity can lead to opposition to the authority of teachers, a rejection of academic achievement, and a definition of hard work as effeminate. However, Sewell's research indicated that *only* a minority (18 per cent) of Black-Caribbean boys adopted this approach.

Black masculinities in school

Sewell identified four main groups of Black students in the comprehensive he studied:

Conformists This was the largest group, making up 41 per cent of the sample. They saw education as the route to success and conformed to the norms and values of the school.

Innovators This group (35 per cent) also saw education as important but they rejected the process of schooling and the demands they saw it making on their identity and behaviour. Although anti-school, they attempted to keep out of trouble.

Retreatists Students in this category (6 per cent) were loners and kept themselves to themselves. Many had special educational needs.

Rebels This group (18 per cent) rejected both the norms and values of the school and the importance of education. Many saw educational qualifications as worthless since racism would disqualify them from high-status, well-paid jobs. The rebels reacted aggressively to what they saw as racism in school. They were confrontational and challenging, adopting a macho masculinity and demanding respect.

Evaluation

Tony Sewell has been attacked for what his critics see as blaming Black Caribbeans for their underachievement. They argue that, in the process, Sewell has diverted attention from what they see as the real cause of Black underachievement – a racist society, a racist education system and economic deprivation.

Supporters of Sewell reject this criticism. They argue that he is attempting to describe and explain rather

Activity

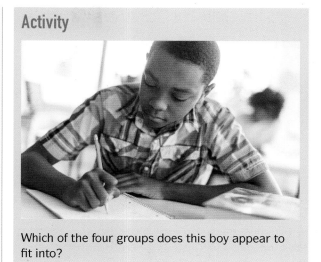

Which of the four groups does this boy appear to fit into?

than allocate blame. Sewell provides a possible explanation for the decline in the attainment of many Black-Caribbean boys during secondary education. In addition, his research rejects the stereotype of the young aggressive black male personified by the Rebels by showing that they formed only a relatively small minority (18 per cent) of the Black-Caribbean boys in the school he studied.

Heidi Safia Mirza – Young, Female and Black

In *Young, Female and Black*, Heidi Mirza (1992) describes the results of a study of 198 young women and men, including 62 Black women aged 15–19 who were the main focus of the study. They all attended two comprehensive schools in south London.

The myth of underachievement Mirza argues that there is a 'myth of underachievement' for Black women. The girls in her sample did better in exams than Black boys and White students in the school, and Mirza believes that in general the educational achievements of Black women are underestimated.

Mirza also challenges the labelling theory of educational underachievement. Although there was evidence of racism from some teachers, she denies this had the effect of undermining the self-esteem of the Black girls. When asked whom they most admired, 48 per cent of the Black girls named themselves and over half named somebody who was Black.

Overall, Mirza found that the Black girls in her study had positive self-esteem, were concerned with academic success and were prepared to work hard.

Black–Caribbean achievement

More recent research has focused on the reasons for Black-Caribbean educational success rather than failure. This may be partly due to a recognition that their attainment has steadily increased over the past 20 years.

Ian Law, Sarah Finney, Sarah Jane Swann – schooling and aspirations

In a study of 15-year-old Black-Caribbean and Black-African male students in three Northern England schools, Law, Finney and Swann (2014) look at how they succeed despite the odds against them. They were often placed in low sets and taught by inexperienced staff with low expectations of their attainment. To some extent they experienced a negative impact from 'gang and "gangsta" culture and racial stereotyping'. They tended to feel that their work was undervalued and their behaviour was unfairly responded to. Yet despite all this, they saw racism in school as of minor importance.

The key finding of this research was 'there was no clear or strong link between being young, Black and male and having low educational or career aspirations'. Across *all* ethnic groups, 70 per cent intended to continue their education after GCSEs. Many Black students had a positive self-concept, a strong sense of self-reliance and a belief in hard work and the value of educational achievement. Many hoped to go to university and obtain professional jobs as architects, accountants and engineers. They often had strong support from their parents. And they largely insulated themselves from barriers and constraints they experienced in school and in the wider society.

An ethnocentric curriculum

Ethnocentric refers to the belief that your own ethnic group or culture is superior to others. **Ethnocentrism** focuses on and prioritises a particular ethnic or cultural group to the exclusion of others. The UK school curriculum has been described as ethnocentric. Critics argue that White British culture and ethnicity are presented as superior and dominate the curriculum while ethnic minority cultures are largely excluded, for example from history, literature, art and music.

A study based on interviews with 84 African-Caribbean students provided evidence to support this view (Tikly *et al.*, 2006). It found that, 'A significant number of African-Caribbean pupils noted their invisibility in the curriculum and were exasperated by the White European focus'. And, when Black history was included, 'many pupils reported their frustration with the tendency to focus on slavery'. As one Year 11 pupil put it, 'It's always slavery … it's like they don't know about the good things. Whereas for us, yeah, slavery is only a small part of our history. But it's the baddest.'

Tikly *et al.* argue that Black-Caribbean students have a need for 'curriculum inclusion' so they don't feel marginalised and excluded. They suggest that this can be done by including Black-Caribbean history, culture and experience across the curriculum.

While a feeling of inclusion is desirable, it is not clear how it might affect attainment. The highest attaining students are of Chinese and Indian heritage yet they too are largely absent from the curriculum.

Ethnic minority education – government policy

According to Andrew Pilkington (2003), from the 1960s onwards governments lacked a 'clearly formulated, coherent policy' on ethnic minority education. Stephen J. Ball (2013) takes a similar view. He sees government policies as stops and starts, often as a response to moments of 'race crisis', such as urban riots. Governments have lacked clear direction and concerted action, and have focused on 'taskforces, policy groups, websites and conferences' rather than legislation.

In the 1960s and 70s governments did little. They expected 'immigrants' to **assimilate** – become part of the general population and lose their distinctive subcultures. When this did not happen, governments looked to **integration** based on diversity and respect for differences. This would be helped by **multicultural education** for all members of society – a school curriculum which included the history, perspectives and beliefs of people from different ethnic backgrounds. Multicultural education was seen as a way to reduce prejudice and discrimination against ethnic minorities by promoting respect for different cultures (Walters, 2012).

In the 1980s, the government recognised that some minority groups were underachieving

Contemporary issues: Ethnocentrism

A draft of the 2013 national curriculum for Key Stage 1 and 2 History caused controversy by its focus on British history and by excluding figures such as Mary Seacole from its content. (Mary Seacole was later reinstated.)

Protest In 2013, the Black and Asian Studies Association protested against the then secretary for education Michael Gove's proposed new history curriculum which they saw as ethnocentric. One of their placards read, 'Do NOT deprive young students the opportunity to find out who they are and where they come from'.

History teaching History teacher Katherine Edwards described the place of ethnic minorities in the history curriculum as follows: 'Black and Asian

people are excluded completely from the primary history curriculum and ... they only feature as slaves in the secondary curriculum until the arrival of the Windrush Generation [Black-Caribbean immigrants in the 1950s]. British Asians only appear as refugees from East Africa. This obscures the long and important history of people of African and Asian origin' (Edwards, 2013).

Questions

1. Do you agree with the statement about young students on the protestor's placard?

2. Judging by Katherine Edwards' description of the history curriculum, would you see it as ethnocentric? Give reasons for your answer.

---

in education. In 1981, the Rampton Report stated that racism was one of the reasons for Black-Caribbean underachievement. However, no direct policy was developed to deal with racism in schools.

From the 1990s onwards, government policy focused on raising the attainment of underachieving ethnic minority groups. In 2003, the Department for Education and Skills started Aiming High: African-Caribbean Achievement Project. It was based on 30 schools and aimed to raise the attainment of Black-Caribbean students. Interviews with students found that, 'An overwhelming majority of both high and low achieving African Caribbean pupils indicated that they were aware of the lower academic expectations that some teachers of them'. The project passed their findings on to teachers and encouraged them to change their expectations and styles of teaching in the hope of raising attainment. An evaluation of Aiming High found some evidence of improvement but Black-Caribbean boys remained the lowest achieving group at Key Stages 3 and 4 (Tickly *et al.*, 2008).

More recently, governments have looked to schools for examples of 'good practice'. The Ethnic Minority Achievement Programme published newsletters online to 'disseminate successful strategies to raise attainment' (Department for Children, Schools and Families, 2009). Programmes developed by schools, for example in teaching English and working with parents, were outlined and presented as good practice to be used to raise the attainment of ethnic minorities.

Key terms

Institutional racism Racial prejudice and discrimination which form part of the taken-for-granted assumptions and operations of institutions.

Ethnocentrism A belief that your own ethnic group or culture is superior to others.

Assimilate Become part of, and develop the culture of, the wider community.

Integrate As used in this unit, to become part of the wider community while retaining a distinctive subculture.

Multicultural education Teaching based on a curriculum which includes the history and perspectives of the various ethnic groups in society.

Summary

1. According to Gillborn and Youdell, the relatively low attainment of Black Caribbeans is due to institutional racism.

2. According to Tony Sewell, it is mainly due to Black street culture and Black perceptions and performance of their masculinity.

3. The Black girls in Heidi Mirza's study achieved higher standards than Black boys and White students in their school.

4. Law *et al.*'s recent study of Black students showed that most had a strong belief in

hard work and education and hoped to go to university.

5. There is evidence to indicate that the UK school curriculum is ethnocentric.

6. Government policy for ethnic minority education since the 1960s has been seen as lacking direction and coherence.

7. In the 1960s and 70s, governments looked first to assimilation, then to integration and multicultural education as the direction for ethnic minority education.

8. In the 1980s, governments recognised racism in schools but failed to develop an effective policy to deal with it.

9. From the 1990s, governments focused on raising the attainment of underachieving ethnic minorities.

2.5.4 British Asian students

This unit begins with a summary of an important study of Muslim boys of Pakistani and Bangladeshi heritage. It examines their religious and gender identities, the value they place on education as a means of getting a well-paid job, and their positive view of the family as a source of love and security. This is followed by a second study which looks at how the parents and grandparents of British Asians place a high value on education, see it as a route to upward social mobility and encourage their children and grandchildren to work hard and go on to university.

Louise Archer – Muslim boys and education

In *Race, Masculinity and Schooling: Muslim Boys and Education* (2003), Louise Archer examined how Muslim boys saw themselves, their schooling and their future. Her sample consisted of 31 Muslim boys aged 14–15 and her data came from discussion groups led by three interviewers/discussion leaders – two British women of Pakistani heritage and Archer herself, a White British middle-class woman. The boys were mainly of Pakistani and Bangladeshi heritage. Archer's main aim was to see how the boys 'constructed and negotiated their masculine identities'.

Muslim and Black identities

In the discussion groups, all the boys identified themselves first and foremost as Muslim. They saw this as a positive masculine identity. They were proud of belonging to a local and global Muslim brotherhood. They saw this as a strong masculine identity as opposed to the traditional stereotype of a 'weak', 'passive' Asian masculinity.

Although most of the boys were born in England, they did not feel they belonged in England, nor in the countries of origin of their parents or grandparents – mainly Pakistan and Bangladesh. Although they saw themselves as Muslim, many of the boys were not particularly religious in terms of their behaviour – for example, most did not attend the mosque on Friday.

When constructing their identities, the boys drew partly on Black-Caribbean and African-American styles of masculinity. They sometimes referred to themselves as 'Black' in comparison to the 'White' majority. However, the boys' Black identity was ambiguous – Black 'gangsta' forms of masculinity were drawn on rather than forming the basis for their identities.

Gendered identities

The boys' gender identity as male was constructed in relation to girls. They were aware of boys' supposed 'underachievement' and girls' superior exam performance and they complained that teachers unfairly favoured girls. They responded to this with laddish remarks, seeing 'messing around' and 'having a laugh' as typical of a desirable macho masculinity. This response probably reflected their class position as well as their gender – most of the boys came from working-class families.

The boys saw part of their gender identity as deriving from their Asian Muslim subculture. Men are the breadwinners – they have freedom and autonomy, power and control. Women are primarily concerned with domestic matters as housewives and mothers – as such, they are subservient. It is a man's duty to make sure that women's behaviour is appropriate – for example, that their appearance and clothing are respectable. The boys admitted that in certain respects gender roles were unfair but believed that this was part of their religious/cultural tradition and therefore they should abide by it.

However, the boys recognised that the gender relations outlined above were not reflected in their everyday experiences. Muslim girls often refused to do as they were expected – from the boys' point of view they were often 'out of control'.

Education and the breadwinner identity

The boys saw themselves as future breadwinners and saw education as a means towards successfully performing this role. They held a strong belief in the value of education for 'getting ahead' and obtaining a well-paid job. Most of the boys expressed an interest in continuing their education beyond GCSE and were encouraged by their parents to do so.

Despite this view of education, some of the boys felt that the value of qualifications was reduced by racism. They believed that this made it more difficult for them to translate qualifications into appropriate occupations. Because of this, some saw falling back on family businesses – for example, restaurants – which did not require qualifications, as an alternative route.

The boys described their family lives in 'overwhelmingly positive terms' – home was a source of warmth, love and security. They saw adult Muslim masculinity as involving a breadwinner providing for his family, caring for his parents in their old age, and supporting relatives locally and 'back home' in Bangladesh or Pakistan. Successfully performing this role was a 'source of pride and a symbol of masculinity', and education was seen as a means to this end.

Evaluation

This is an important study because it illustrates that identities are fluid and complex, they derive from different sources, they change according to the social context and they are always in the process of construction and reconstruction. For example, the boys 'shifted across and between' Muslim, Black, Asian, Bangladeshi/Pakistani, English and British identities, selecting one or more depending on the situation, context or topic of conversation. And the boys' ethnicity, religion, class, gender and experiences of family life influenced their identity. Their attitudes towards and experience of education must be seen in terms of this fluid and complex social context.

Archer's insistence on the importance of social context may indicate a weakness in her research method. The data came from small discussion groups led by two British Pakistani women and one middle-class White British woman. Each boy had an audience, consisting of other boys in the group and one of these women. Each boy's projection of

Activity

A White-British woman leading a discussion with 14–15-year-old Pakistani and Bangladeshi boys. How might the gender and ethnicity of the researcher influence the responses of the students?

particular identities will reflect his perception of the audience. Archer recognises this. However, it may place limitations on her data – for example, what would the boys say in the presence of their father, mother, sister, brother, male friends, female friends and so on? Wider sources of data drawn from different contexts would provide a fuller picture.

Themina Basit – British Asians and educational capital

Themina Basit (2013) studied a group of 36 Indian and Pakistani students – Hindus, Sikhs and Muslims – and their parents and grandparents. The students were age 15–16 from a West Midlands town. Their grandparents were working class as were some of their parents, the others were middle class. The research was based on individual interviews and focus groups.

Whatever their ethnicity, religion, age or social class, 'It was strikingly clear that education was seen as capital that would transform the lives of the younger generation'. Parents and grandparents impressed on young people the importance of a good education and how it would lead to a well-paid job and a high standard of living. According to Basit, 'Migrants and their children always have aspirations of upward social mobility. This is a key attribute of peoples who leave their country of origin in search of a better life for themselves and their future generations'.

Students, both girls and boys, accepted the advice of their elders as the following quotations indicate:

❱ 'I think it's good that they're encouraging me.'

❱ 'My parents are always telling me education is good.'

117

❯ 'I'd like to go to Birmingham University to become a doctor.'

❯ 'My parents are working hard for us to do our best in the future and go to university.'

Summary

1. The boys in Archer's study saw themselves first and foremost as Muslims.

2. In terms of their gender identity they felt males should have power over women.

3. They saw themselves as future breadwinners taking pride in caring for their family and parents.

4. They had a strong belief in the value of education and hoped to continue beyond their GCSEs.

5. However, some felt that racism might reduce their chances in the job market.

6. The data came from discussion groups led by two British Pakistani women and one middle-class White British woman. Their gender and ethnicity might influence the results.

7. Themina Basit's research showed that British Asian families impressed the value of education on young people.

8. As migrants, they had high hopes for upward social mobility and a better life.

PART 6 RELATIONSHIPS AND PROCESSES IN SCHOOLS

Contents

This part focuses on what goes on in schools. It introduces the concept of the hidden curriculum – the attitudes and ideas transmitted by schools which are not part of the official school curriculum and of which teachers and students are largely unaware. Examples include the transmission of ruling class ideology, of neoliberal ideology, of society's core values and of patriarchal ideology.

Various male and female student subcultures are then examined along with their possible effects on educational attainment. Teachers' views of students' class, ethnicity and gender are investigated in terms of how they might affect their assessment of students' ability, their expectations of how students will behave, and how these might affect students' attainment.

The final unit returns to the question of ability groups and how they affect students' identity, friendship groups and educational attainment. The unit closes with a global survey of research on setting and possible solutions to its negative effects. Should ability groups be replaced by mixed ability teaching groups? Would this change result in greater equality of educational opportunity?

2.6.1 The hidden curriculum

The **formal school curriculum** consists of the stated knowledge and skills which students are expected to acquire. The **hidden curriculum** is the messages schools transmit to pupils without directly teaching them or spelling them out. It consists of ideas, beliefs, norms and values which are often taken for granted and transmitted as part of the normal routines and procedures of school life. It includes the unwritten and often unstated rules and regulations which guide and direct everyday school behaviour (Ballantine and Spade, 2001).

A Marxist view of the hidden curriculum

As outlined earlier, Marxists argue that the main job of schools is social reproduction – producing the next generation of workers schooled to accept their roles in capitalist society.

For Bowles and Gintis (1976), this is done primarily through the hidden curriculum. They claim that schools produce subordinate, well-disciplined workers who will submit to control from above and take orders rather than question them. Schools do this by rewarding conformity, obedience, hard work and punctuality, and by penalising creativity, originality and independence.

Schools are seen to transmit ruling class ideology – a false picture of society, which justifies social inequality and the capitalist system (see pp. 11–12 and 26–32).

A radical view of the hidden curriculum

This section looks at the views of Henry A. Giroux (2011), a radical thinker who argues that there is a hidden curriculum in American, and increasingly global education, based on neoliberal ideology (see pp. 39–42). In Giroux's view, 'Neoliberal ideology emphasises winning at all costs, even if it means a ruthless competitiveness, an almost rabid individualism and a market driven rationality!' As noted earlier, government education policy is at least partly based on neoliberal views – schools compete in an educational market place and aim to be top of the educational league tables. And the job of schools is mainly to promote economic growth in an increasingly competitive global market.

How is this translated into the classroom? According to Giroux, 'Students are educated to acquire market-oriented skills in order to compete favourably in the global economy'. They are taught to compete as individuals in an examination-based system, to climb the educational ladder and prepare themselves to succeed in a competitive labour market.

What should replace this hidden curriculum? In Giroux's view:

- 'knowledge and power should always be subject to debate, held accountable and critically engaged'
- students should be taught to think critically
- students should be taught to be citizens of the world. This means that they should have 'duties and responsibilities to others' in a global society.

This is not possible as long as schools are based on neoliberal thinking which 'strips education of its public values, critical content and civil responsibilities'.

The hidden curriculum – a functionalist view

As outlined earlier, functionalists see the transmission of society's core values as one of the main functions of the education system. This can be seen as part of the hidden curriculum. It is hidden in the sense that teachers and pupils are often unaware of the process.

Talcott Parsons (1951, 1961) provides an example using the value of individual achievement, one of the major values in Western industrial society. In schools, young people are required to achieve as individuals. They take exams on their own, not as a member of a team. Their individual achievements are carefully graded and assessed. High achievement is rewarded with praise, high status, good grades and valuable qualifications. In this way, young people are encouraged to value individual achievement. And this prepares them to achieve as individuals in the wider society.

The hidden curriculum – a feminist view

From a feminist view, schools transmit **patriarchal ideology** – the idea that male dominance in society is reasonable and acceptable. Schools still fail to provide a gender neutral curriculum. For example, women are often absent from history textbooks, both in their individual achievements and contributions to society and in terms of issues which are particularly relevant to their gender. In the classroom, girls still tend to take a back seat compared to more boisterous and demanding boys. In government policy, boys' 'underachievement' compared to girls' educational attainment became a matter of serious concern – even a 'moral panic'. When the reverse was the case, government policy showed little concern to improve girls' educational attainment.

Subject choices, particularly at A-level and university are still influenced by gender. Male students tend to choose subjects such as physics, chemistry, engineering and business studies which are more likely to lead to highly paid jobs. Gender divisions are also present in vocational courses such as childcare, hairdressing and beauty care which are largely taught and taken by women and which usually lead to low paid jobs.

In *A Feminist Manifesto for Education*, Miriam David (2016) argues that schools must ensure that 'women

119

and girls are afforded dignity and respect in all aspects of their lives'. Schools must address issues of 'sexual abuse and harassment, bullying, rape and violence'. 59 per cent of girls and young women surveyed for Girlguiding UK said they had faced some form of sexual harassment at school or college. Failure to recognise and prioritise this can be seen as part of a hidden curriculum which ignores female suffering and abuse.

Conclusion

The idea of a hidden curriculum is useful. Clearly, there's a lot more being taught and learned in schools than the formal curriculum of English, maths, science, and so on. And clearly much of this is 'hidden' – teachers and learners are often unaware of what's going on.

The content of the hidden curriculum is open to interpretation. Have the functionalists got it right? Have the Marxists got it right? This partly depends on your own values and how you see capitalist society.

Key terms

Formal school curriculum The stated knowledge and skills which students are expected to acquire.

Hidden curriculum The messages schools transmit which are not part of the standard taught curriculum and which are largely hidden from staff and students.

Patriarchal ideology The idea that male dominance in society is reasonable and acceptable.

Summary

Views of the hidden curriculum include:

» Marxist – the transmission of ruling class ideology

» Radical – the transmission of neoliberal ideology

» Functionalist – the transmission of societies' core values

» Feminist – the transmission of patriarchal ideology.

2.6.2 Pupil identities and subcultures

This unit begins by looking at the idea of **intersectionality** – how different factors intersect,

overlap and combine to affect people's experiences and behaviour, in this case students' identities and subcultures.

The unit looks at the influence of class, ethnicity and gender on the formation of student subcultures. It examines how subcultures shape students' identity, shape how they see education, shape their progress through school and their exam results. Student subcultures also affect the way teachers see students and the sets they place them in.

Intersectionality

The final part of this chapter revisits some of the areas already covered. Only this time it looks at them in terms of the idea of intersectionality. This theory examines how different factors intersect or overlap to form people's identities and their experiences. For example, it looks at how the interaction of class, ethnicity and gender shape their lives and interconnect to form their identities.

Intersectionality states that social factors such as class, ethnicity and gender do not act independently or separately. Instead they are interconnected, they intersect.

This unit looks at pupil or student subcultures – the distinctive norms and values developed by young people in schools and colleges – and the relationship of the subcultures to their identities – how they see themselves.

Working-class male subcultures

The 'lads'

The 'lads' in Paul Willis's *Learning to Labour: How Working-Class Kids get Working-Class Jobs* (1977) developed an anti-school or counter-school subculture which rejected the norms and values of the school (see pp. 29–32). They saw school as a waste of time. They didn't need academic qualifications for the jobs they intended to get – unskilled and semi-skilled manual labour. They despised those who conformed to the school's values seeing them as 'sissies'. They misbehaved in the classroom and spent their time messing around and having a 'laff'.

The anti-school subculture of the 'lads' reflected the traditional working-class culture they'd learned from their fathers, elder brothers and other men in the community. And it reflected the shop-floor culture of the jobs they were heading for. The 'lads' saw manual

Activity – The Macho Lads

Darren: It's the teachers that make the rules. It's them that decide that it's either them or us. So you are often put into a situation with teachers where you have to defend yourself. Sometimes it's direct in the classroom. But it's mainly the head cases that would hit a teacher. Most of the time it's all the little things.

Interviewer: Like what?

Gilroy: Acting tough by truanting, coming late to lessons, not doing homework, acting cool by not answering teachers, pretending you didn't hear them; that gets them mad. Lots of different things.

Noel: Teachers are always suspicious of us. Just like the cops, trying to set you up.

Source: Adapted from Mac an Ghaill, 1994.

Questions

1. How does the boys' behaviour indicate an anti-school subculture?

2. Suggest intersected factors which might explain the boys' behaviour.

---

work as manly and tough and the 'mental work' of the school as effeminate. Their anti-school subculture was an expression of the masculinity they admired, their class and gender, their expectations of the jobs they planned to get and the subculture they brought to school with them. These factors intersected to form their identity and their anti-school subculture.

The Macho Lads

Paul Willis's study of the 'lads' was conducted in the 1970s. A study conducted in the early 1990s by Maírtín Mac an Ghaill (1994) in a West Midlands comprehensive identified an anti-school working-class male group he called the Macho Lads (see pp. 92–93). They were similar to Willis's 'lads'.

The Macho Lads saw the school as representing 'hostile authority' and making 'meaningless work demands' on them. They were placed in the bottom two sets for all their subjects. They were seen as academic failures and treated as such by their teachers. Like Willis's lads, they rejected the school's values and the teachers' authority. Their concerns were acting tough, having a laugh, looking after their mates and looking smart. They saw school work as unsuitable for 'real men'. The teachers viewed them with suspicion and policed their

behaviour, banning certain clothes and hairstyles, and making constant demands – 'Sit up straight', 'Look at me when I'm talking to you' and 'Walk properly down the corridor'.

The Boiz

Michael R.M. Ward (2015) conducted a study from 2008 to 2010 entitled *From Labouring to Learning: Working-Class Masculinities, Education and De-industrialisation* (see p.105). Ward identified a group he called 'The Boiz' who, in some respects, were similar to 'the lads' and the 'Macho Lads'.

The Boiz lived in a former coal mining community in the South Wales valleys. In school and college they often displayed anti-school attitudes – having a laugh, messing around and disrupting lessons with boisterous behaviour. They walked with a 'macho swagger' and poked fun at and bullied 'The Geeks' who obeyed school rules. They texted and listened to music in class and replaced school uniforms with colourful tracksuits.

The Boiz grew up in a working-class community and their behaviour, to some extent, reflected traditional working-class culture. However, unlike 'the lads' they had few, if any working-class jobs to go to. The coal mines had shut down and there had been a significant decline in manual industrial labour in the area. The Boiz recognised this. As a result, they saw little option other than continuing their education after 16. They did not reject or despise academic qualifications. In fact, four out of the 12 Boiz studied went on to university.

Positive male working-class school subcultures

Academic Achievers and New Enterprisers Apart from the Macho Lads, Mac an Ghaill identified two other working-class male groups in the comprehensive school he studied – the Academic Achievers and the New Enterprisers. Each group had their own definition of masculine identity and their own subculture. According to Mac an Ghaill, all three groups developed their subcultures in response to the following intersectional factors.

> The way students were organised into sets.

> The curriculum they followed.

> The teacher-student relations which resulted from the above.

> The students' position within the working class.

> The changes in the labour market, for example the rapid decline in unskilled and semi-skilled manual jobs.

Academic Achievers They saw hard work and educational qualifications as the route to success. They looked forward to upward social mobility and a professional career. They were highly regarded by teachers and expected to do well. The Academic Achievers were in the top sets, and received preferential treatment in terms of timetabling, books and experienced teachers. They tended to come from the upper levels of the working class.

New Enterprisers They saw the school curriculum in a positive light and chose vocational subjects like technology and business studies. They saw their future in the high-skilled sector of the labour market.

The Geeks Michael Ward identified another working-class school subculture – 'The Geeks' – in his study of young men in South Wales. The Geeks tended to reject traditional male working-class culture. They achieved top grades and 'gained teachers' support and favour'. They were well-behaved, studious, followed school rules and wore school uniforms. They looked forward to middle-class occupations and 'escaping' from the Welsh valleys. Nearly all the group went to university.

Some of the Geeks had parents in working-class jobs. Others had parents who had experience of higher education and were employed in professional jobs as surveyors and teachers. To some extent, the Geeks' positive outlook on education was probably influenced by their parents.

Female school subcultures

Rebel girls

Alexandra Allan (2010) conducted a two-year study of 25 middle-class, 11–12-year-old girls in a single-sex, high achieving school. Some of the girls were seen by teachers as 'underachievers'. They were seen by many of the other girls as 'rebels', 'bad girls' and 'misbehavers'. The rebels played practical jokes, they were known for their humour and their view that it was uncool to work.

The Rebels saw themselves as different. Although they were middle class, they saw themselves as 'common', as 'lacking the right know-how to compete'. They defined most of the other girls as 'posh' – wealthy, overly confident, haughty and 'stuck up'. In the words of one rebel, 'They have been to private schools which means they are taught better because you pay for the privilege. You can tell they are different because they are just so confident'.

The Rebels downplayed the importance of academic achievement and weren't impressed with those who achieved – 'they are not really that clever, their parents had used their money to make them clever'. This view can be seen as a defence mechanism, as 'self-worth protection by those defined as underachievers'.

But, despite all this, the Rebels achieved well on a national scale, but not in a high-achieving school. Yet they saw themselves as 'common', as below most of the girls in social class terms and as lacking in cultural and economic capital.

Asian girls

Farzana Shain (2010) studied 44 Asian girls, age 13–16, mostly from Pakistani backgrounds. The girls attended eight schools in economically deprived areas of Greater Manchester and Staffordshire. Shain identifies four main groups:

1. **The Gang Girls** opposed the culture of the schools which they saw as White and racist. This led to an emphasis on Asian subculture and a withdrawal from the other students.

2. **The Survivors** conformed to the values of the school in order to achieve academic success despite their experience of racism and sexism.

3. **The Rebels** So-called by the teachers, the rebels were critical of what they saw as unequal gender relations in their home community and of the subculture of the Gang Girls.

4. **The Faith Girls** gave priority to religion but were well integrated with other ethnic groups and followed a survival strategy in order to achieve academic success.

In an article entitled 'Refusing to integrate: asian girls, achievement and the experience of schooling', Farzana Shain (2010) focuses on the subculture of the Gang Girls. She argues that setting by ability is 'a critical factor in friendship patterns which were central to the girls' academic and social experiences throughout schooling'. The Gang Girls were defined by the teachers as 'underachievers' and placed in lower sets.

Like most Asian girls they experienced racist abuse being called 'Paki' and 'black bitch' and 'terrorist' and 'suicide bomber'. They fought back insulting those who insulted them. They responded to racist abuse and relegation to lower sets by forming an all-Asian female subculture. They wore traditional dress which they 'fiercely defended' as a 'visible marker of Asian identities'. They rejected what they saw as the White, racist culture of the school and excluded from their group Asian students who appeared to mix in friendship with White students.

Teachers saw the Gang Girls as troublemakers. Confined to lower sets and regarded as failures, the Gang Girls 'gradually withdrew from learning'.

Girls and boys

In *Lads and Ladettes in School: Gender and a Fear of Failure*, Carolyn Jackson (2006) argues that a student subculture has developed which crosses class and gender boundaries. This is a subculture based on 'laddish behaviour'.

Jackson studied 13–14-year-olds in eight schools in the north of England. 203 pupils and 30 teachers were interviewed and 800 pupils completed questionnaires. She argues that a laddish subculture was developed by both girls and boys in all social classes as a response to two things – pressures to succeed and a desire to be popular.

Pressures to succeed Neoliberalism has led to the marketisation of schools, competition between schools, league tables based on test and examination results and a culture of 'competitive individualism'. In Jackson's words, 'these factors come together to create climates in which a fear of academic failure is commonplace'. This places considerable pressure on students to achieve.

Popularity Being popular and having friends are very important to most pupils. Laddish behaviour is seen as a precondition of popularity for both girls and boys. It includes being loud and disruptive, having a laugh with your mates, being mildly aggressive and answering back. Central to laddish behaviour is being cool. It is not cool to work hard. Labels such as 'swot' and 'geek' are terms of abuse. Publicly avoiding school work and appearing not to care about academic success is cool.

Being cool is not just about popularity. Jackson argues that it is also 'a defensive strategy that is prompted by a fear of academic failure'. Failing exams can be explained by a rejection of academic work – by being cool. This avoids explaining failure by negative factors such as 'stupidity'. In this way being cool protects self-worth and cushions self-esteem.

Conclusion and evaluation

This unit has looked at some of the many examples of pupil subcultures. It has shown how the idea of intersectionality is a useful approach to understanding how students' identities and subcultures are formed by a number of interconnected factors. These factors include class, ethnicity and gender, the pressure to succeed and the fear of failure, the placing of pupils into ability groups, the changing labour market and the influence of neoliberalism on the educational system.

Key term

Intersectionality A theory which examines how different factors intersect and combine to form people's identities and experiences.

Summary

1. The 'lads' developed an anti-school subculture which reflected working-class culture and shop-floor culture.

2. The Macho Lads developed a similar anti-school culture.

3. The Boiz were similar in some respects to the 'lads' and The Macho Lads but, in the absence of manual jobs, they had little alternative to continuing their education after 16.

4. Positive working-class school subcultures increasingly developed with de-industrialisation.

5. The middle-class Rebel Girls who were seen as underachievers downplayed the importance of education to protect their self-worth.

6. The Asian Gang Girls rejected the culture of their school which they saw as White and racist.

7. A subculture of laddish behaviour was developed by both girls and boys as a result of pressure to succeed, fear of failure, a desire to protect their self-esteem and a desire to be popular.

8. Many factors intersect to make up students' identities and school subcultures. These include class, gender, ethnicity, ability groups and the changing labour market.

2.6.3 Teachers and students

This unit looks at how teachers relate to students – how they see them and how they expect them to behave. It examines teachers' perceptions of students' social class, ethnicity and gender and how these factors affect teacher-student relationships and how students are assessed and placed into groups on the basis of their presumed ability and expected examination performance.

Teachers' perceptions of social class

Class and the ideal pupil An early study of teachers' perceptions of social class was conducted by the American sociologist Howard Becker. He interviewed 60 teachers from Chicago high schools and found they tended to share an image of the 'ideal pupil'.

Teachers perceived middle-class pupils as closest to this ideal, and pupils from the lower working class as furthest from it. Those in the lowest class grouping were seen as less able, lacking motivation and difficult to control. As a result, teachers felt the best they could do was 'just try to get some basic things over to them'. (Becker, 1970).

Teachers were unaware that the social class background of pupils influenced their assessments. Nor did they realise that perceptions of class also influenced the level of work they felt appropriate for pupils.

Class and 'ability' David Gillborn and Deborah Youdell (2001) conducted research in two London secondary schools from 1995 to 1997. They discovered that teachers had a 'common sense understanding of ability'. Using this as a yardstick, they allocated pupils to different sets.

Working-class pupils were more likely to be seen as disruptive, as lacking in motivation and lacking in parental support. As a result, they 'face a particular problem in convincing teachers that they have "ability"'. And because of this, they are more likely to be placed on lower level sets.

As a result of making a link between so-called 'ability' and social class, teachers systematically discriminated against working-class pupils.

Cultural capital and habitus According to Pierre Bourdieu (1984) teachers recognise the high levels of cultural capital possessed by students from the 'dominant classes'. As a result, they see them as having the skills, attitudes and ambitions to succeed. Teachers also recognise the habitus of these students and believe it encourages a positive view of education.

Class and teacher-pupil relationships Generally, teachers prefer to teach pupils they see as able and highly motivated. They place these students in higher sets and respond more favourably towards them. As a result, teacher-pupil relationships tend to be positive.

Conversely, teachers' views of students who have been defined as less able and placed in lower sets tend to be less favourable. These students may respond with resentment and hostility. And this can result in discipline problems and negative relationships between teachers and pupils.

This can be seen from teachers' views of the Macho Lads in Mac an Ghaill's (1994) study of a West Midlands comprehensive. The Macho Lads were working-class boys in the lowest sets. The teachers saw them as low ability, non-academic troublemakers. Their main priority was policing the Macho Lads who, in turn, saw the teachers as controlling and hostile.

Activity – Teaching top and bottom sets

Teacher A: You don't find any behaviour problems with the top set – they've got the intelligence.

Teacher B: When you get your next year's timetable and you see that it is a top or bottom set then you get certain images. If you get a top set you tend to think that their behaviour will be better. You tend to think with a bottom set you will get more discipline problems. I look forward to teaching my top-set third year but dread my bottom-set third year. With the bottom group I go in with a stony face but I know that with the top set if I say fun's over they will stop. But if I give a bottom set rope they'll take advantage of you.

Source: Abraham, 1995.

Questions

1. What effects might the teachers' views have on the students' behaviour and attainment?

2. Why does the teacher in the picture have her colleague's sympathy?

Teachers' perceptions of ethnicity

Teachers tend to view different ethnic groups in different ways. This can affect their expectations of each group and the way they teach them. And this, in turn, can affect the behaviour and attainment of different ethnic groups.

Black-Caribbean boys

Racism From their research in London secondary schools Gillborn and Youdell (2001) found that teachers tended to see Black-Caribbean boys, whatever their social class, as less able and more disruptive than White boys. They were more likely to place Black boys in lower sets and give priority to 'control and punishment'. Gillborn and Youdell saw their behaviour as racist (see p. 112).

Types of teachers Tony Sewell's (1997) study of a boys' 11–16 comprehensive school suggested that Black-Caribbean boys were singled out for punishment. For example, they made up 32 per cent of the student population but comprised 85 per cent of those excluded.

Relationships with teachers were often strained and difficult. According to Sewell, teachers were sometimes frightened by the physical size and aggression of some of the more assertive pupils. There was a tendency to lump all Black-Caribbean

boys together. Those who conformed to the school's values and those who rebelled against them were often judged and treated in terms of the same negative stereotypes (see p. 90).

Sewell divided the teachers into three groups in terms of their relationships with Black-Caribbean pupils:

1. **Supportive teachers** About 10 per cent of staff. They did their best to support and guide pupils and usually established good relationships.

2. **Irritated teachers** About 60 per cent of staff. Although they could be supportive, they felt firmer discipline was needed. They blamed the boys' street culture for many of the school's problems.

3. **Antagonistic teachers** Around 30 per cent who were either openly racist or objected to Black-Caribbean street culture – for example, hairstyles and 'bopping' (a stylised walk). As the term 'antagonistic teacher' suggests, their relationships with Black-Caribbean pupils were strained and sometimes hostile.

Black-Caribbean girls

A study by Heidi Mirza (1992) of two south London comprehensives focused on 62 young Black women, aged 15–19. Mirza identifies five types of teacher in terms of their relationships with and attitudes towards Black students.

1. **Overt racists** A small minority who the girls avoided where possible.

2. **The Christians** Tried to be 'colour blind', claiming to see no difference between ethnic groups and the White majority, and refusing to see racism as a problem. They sometimes expected too little from the girls and gave them glowing reports for average achievement.

3. **The crusaders** Anti-racists who tried to make their lessons relevant to Black students. Because they knew little about their students, lessons tended to be confusing and irrelevant.

4. **Liberal chauvinists** Like the crusaders, they were well-meaning, but tended to underestimate their students' ability.

5. **Black teachers** A small group who showed no favouritism and were liked and respected. The girls found their help and advice extremely valuable.

In general, the young women in Mirza's research were ambitious, hard-working and determined to succeed. They rejected the negative views of their blackness, the low expectations of their potential, and the patronising and unhelpful 'help'. They tended to keep their distance and maintain a cool relationship with their teachers.

South-Asian students

Primary pupils Paul Connolly's (1998) study of a multi-ethnic, inner-city primary school gives the following picture of the relationship between South Asian five and six-year-olds and their teachers. The children were seen as obedient, hard-working and conformist. Teachers expected them to produce high-quality work.

Girls were seen as models of good behaviour. When the boys did misbehave, this was seen as 'silly' rather than a challenge to the teachers' authority. As a result, they were not punished as much as Black-Caribbean boys. Boys were often praised for good work, while girls tended to be left alone – teachers felt they didn't need the same help and encouragement.

Gang Girls Teachers saw the Asian Gang Girls in Farzana Shain's (2010) research as troublemakers. They objected to assertive girls in gangs partly because this challenged their stereotypical perception of Asian 'passive femininity'. This negative view of the girls and their placement in bottom sets convinced teachers they were low achievers. As a result, the girls gradually withdrew from learning. As one girl put it, 'I'm not interested. I don't want to do anything. I just like coming to school to meet my friends'.

Teachers' perceptions of gender

Gender expectations Teachers' perceptions of pupils are often based on gender. For example, what is acceptable behaviour for one gender may not be acceptable for the other. Diane Reay's (2001) study of seven-year-olds in a London primary school noted that teachers in the staffroom sometimes referred to girls who misbehaved as 'little cows' and 'scheming little madams'. Their behaviour was seen as inappropriate for girls. However, boys who behaved in a similar way were simply seen as 'mucking about'. Girls who misbehaved were sometimes seen as having a problem but, in the case of boys, misbehaviour was usually dismissed as 'high spirits'.

Perceptions of ability A number of studies have indicated that teachers tend to see boys as naturally talented but lazy. By comparison, girls achievements are seen as a result of hard work rather than ability as such. This may help to explain why boys often over-estimate their ability while girls under-estimate theirs (Francis and Skelton, 2005).

Activity – Attending to boys

Alison to an interviewer: 'If a boy and a girl put their hand up at the same time, they'd always talk to the boy. They never have time for the girls'. (Abraham, 1995)

Question

What does this picture suggest about gendered attention?

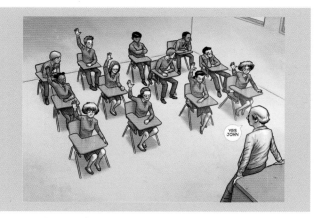

Attending to boys In *Invisible Women: The Schooling Scandal*, Dale Spender (1982) recorded lessons given by herself and other teachers. Boys received over 60 per cent of teachers' time – 62 per cent in her case even though she tried to divide her time equally between boys and girls. Compared with boys, girls were 'invisible'. They tended to blend into the background, a strategy encouraged by the fact that boys often poked fun at girls' contributions to lessons. And teachers usually allowed boys to get away with insulting comments to girls.

Michelle Stanworth's (1983) study of A-level students and teachers in a college of further education reflects this focus on boys (see pp. 97–98). Stanworth found that teachers gave more time and attention to boys, were more likely to know boys' names, and expressed more concern and interest in them.

Summary

1. Teachers tend to have a picture of an 'ideal pupil'. She/he is middle class.

2. They are likely to see middle-class students as more able and to place them in higher sets.

3. Teachers have tended to see Black-Caribbean boys as less able and more disruptive than White boys. This view has been seen as racist.

4. Black-Caribbean girls reject the low expectations that some teachers have of their potential. Many are ambitious and hard working.

5. Teachers saw Gang Girls as troublemakers. They challenged the teachers' stereotype of passive Asian femininity.

6. Teachers' perceptions of students were often based on gender.

7. Teachers' tended to see aspects of girls' behaviour as misbehaviour while similar behaviour from boys was simply seen as 'high spirits'.

8. Teachers often gave boys more time and attention.

2.6.4 Teaching groups

This unit looks at how pupils are allocated to teaching groups, and how this shapes what they are taught and the examinations they take. It looks at the case for and against ability groups and mixed ability groups. It asks whether students are advantaged or disadvantaged by the type of group they are placed in. And it looks at a global survey on the effects of ability groups (see also pp. 91–92).

Types of teaching groups

There are two main types of teaching groups – **ability groups** and **mixed-ability groups**:

Ability groups These are groups of pupils who are seen to have similar abilities. **Setting** and **streaming** are two ways of dividing students into ability groups. Setting allocates pupils to subject groups – a pupil could be set 1 for English and set 3 for maths. Streaming places pupils in the same ability group for all subjects – for example, a pupil is placed in class 3 and taught at that level for all subjects.

Mixed-ability groups In these groups, pupils are randomly placed or intentionally mixed in terms of their perceived ability.

Setting is the most common form of ability grouping in schools in England and Wales. It becomes increasingly common as pupils approach GCSE. Streaming was typical of primary schools in the 1940s and 1950s. It began to die out with the decline of the 11-plus exam. Mixed-ability teaching throughout pupils' school careers is found in only a small number of schools.

Ability groups versus mixed ability groups

Supporters of ability groups make the following points.

Different abilities – different teaching Young people have different abilities. This means they need to be taught:

› at different speeds

› in different ways

› at different levels.

The most efficient way of doing this is to create teaching groups of pupils with similar abilities.

Different abilities – different tasks There's no point in giving the same tasks to pupils of different ability. For example, only some can cope with higher level maths.

Different abilities – different exams Because pupils have different abilities, they need different exams at different levels – for example, GCSE at higher and foundation levels.

Mixed-ability groups

Supporters of mixed-ability groups make the following points.

Social benefits Mixed-ability groups encourage cooperation and friendly relationships between students. For the wider society, they reduce class differences and class conflict.

Ability is not fixed In practice, most pupils remain in the same set. This assumes that their ability is fixed – that it won't change. However, there is considerable evidence which suggests that ability – as measured by tests – is not fixed.

Setting affects attainment The set in which a pupil is placed can affect their attainment. For example, it can raise attainment in the top set and lower attainment in the bottom set. This is unfair – all pupils should have an equal chance (see pp. 91–92).

Setting discriminates Those allocated to lower sets or streams tend to be from working-class or minority ethnic backgrounds. This can prevent them from obtaining the knowledge required for a high grade in examinations – for example, at GCSE level. In contrast, a disproportionate number of White, middle-class pupils are placed in the upper sets. Ability groups discriminate in favour of the White middle-classes and against those from working-class and minority ethnic backgrounds.

Behaviour rather than ability Perceptions of behaviour have been used as a basis for allocating pupils to ability groups. For example, there is evidence that Black-Caribbean pupils have been placed in examination sets which were below their measured ability because their behaviour was seen as unsuitable for higher sets (see p. 112).

Setting and examination results

Comparing schools with different types of ability groups

In an article entitled 'Ability grouping in the secondary school: Effects at Key Stage 4', Judith Ireson, Susan Hallam and Clare Hurley (2001) attempted to measure the possible effects of setting on GCSE results. Their sample consisted of 45 mixed comprehensives in England, representing three types of ability grouping:

> **Mixed ability schools** – mostly mixed ability classes in all subjects, with setting in no more than two subjects in Year 9.

> **Partially set schools** – setting in no more than two subjects in Year 7, increasing to a maximum of four subjects in Year 9.

> **Set schools** –setting in at least four subjects from Year 7.

Their main findings were that 'For mathematics, science and English, the amount of setting a student experiences from Year 7 to Year 11 does not have an effect on GCSE attainment'. This conclusion is based on a comparison of schools with different amounts of setting. A different picture is provided by looking at the possible effects of setting within individual schools. This is shown by the following research.

The effects of setting within individual schools

If we compare two schools with similar GCSE results, one with sets and one with mixed ability groups, then it might appear that setting makes no difference to exam results. But setting might have the following effect. Those in the top sets will do better and those in the bottom sets will do worse due to setting. So, the overall GCSE results for the two schools will be similar. But, in this case, setting has had an important effect on particular pupils' GCSE results. There is evidence to support this possibility.

Advantages and disadvantages of different sets

Advantages of top sets In his study of a West Midlands comprehensive, Mac an Ghaill (1994) outlines the advantages of being in the top sets. The teachers' main concern was the needs of students in the top sets. These students had permanent teaching locations in a school with a shortage of classrooms and were given priority for using specialist classrooms such as science laboratories. They were provided with the most experienced teachers and received preferential treatment in terms of timetabling, equipment and books. They were given first pick of the option choices in Year 9. Teachers respected students in the top sets and had high expectations of their academic progress and examination success. And students were aware of these positive views of their prospects. Similar pictures of the advantages of top sets are given by other studies – for example, Michael Ward's (2015) research in South Wales schools.

Disadvantages of bottom sets Students in the bottom sets were seen as having low ability and as unlikely to succeed. They were aware of this view of their ability and prospects. They were provided with less experienced teachers who were often not keen on teaching them. Even when they were being prepared for the same exams as those in higher sets, they were taught to a lower level. The information they were given was tailored to their assumed ability.

Effects of sets on identity and progress

The ideas of labelling and the self-fulfilling prophecy were outlined on pp. 89–91. To briefly recap, if someone is labelled as a certain type of person – for example, as a high or low achiever – others will tend to see and behave towards them in terms of the label. The result might be a self-fulfilling prophecy. Those who have been labelled might see themselves in terms of the label and act accordingly. So, students defined as bright might see themselves as such, which will increase their confidence which, in turn, will improve their academic performance.

However, labelling can produce the opposite effect. As noted earlier, Black girls in a London comprehensive felt that they were expected to fail. Far from living up to these expectations, they did their best to prove them wrong, worked hard and got good results (Fuller, 1984), (see pp. 90–91).

There is evidence that placement in low sets can have negative results. Looking back on his experience of low sets, a young man states, 'The lower sets are like a psychological prison… It just breaks all ambition' (Boaler, 2005). And, as one of the Gang Girls in Farzana Shain's (2010) study found, being confined to bottom sets and regarded as a failure led her to dismiss school as a place of learning.

Setting – a global survey

Adam Gamoran (2010) conducted a survey of research on setting in a range of countries from the UK and the USA to Germany, Belgium, South Africa, Japan and Australia. The results of this large body of research all point in the same direction:

1. Those in high sets gain, those in low sets lose.

2. In terms of the overall exam results of the school, 'the gains of the high achievers are offset by the losses of the low achievers'.

3. Over the course of schooling, the attainment gap between students assigned to high and low sets grows steadily wider.

4. Since middle-class students tend to be placed in high sets and working-class students in low sets, setting tends to reinforce social inequality in the wider society.

Possible solutions How might the negative effects of setting be reduced or removed? Based on his survey, Adam Gamoran finds two possibilities.

First, academic standards in the lower sets should be raised and combined with specific rewards for high performance such as entry to further education and access to jobs. Second, mixed-ability classes should have specially designed supplementary instruction available for students who are having difficulty. Both approaches have been tried with varying degrees of success.

Key terms

Ability groups Groups in which students are placed on the basis of their perceived ability.

Mixed-ability groups Groups in which students are randomly placed or intentionally mixed in terms of their perceived ability.

Setting Placing students in ability groups for particular subjects.

Streaming Placing students in ability groups for all subjects. The whole class becomes an ability group.

Summary

1. Students in the top sets have a number of advantages. These include more experienced teachers with high expectations of their exam performance.

2. Students in the lower sets have a number of disadvantages. These include less experienced teachers with low expectations of their exam performance.

3. Teachers' expectations might lead to a self-fulfilling prophecy.

4. Comparing schools with different amounts of setting suggests that setting has no effect on exam results.

5. However, this might be due to the gains of those in the top sets cancelling out the losses of those in the bottom sets. In other words, setting does affect attainment.

6. Research in a number of countries shows that:

   ❯ The attainment gap between those in the top sets and those in the bottom sets steadily widens throughout schooling.

   ❯ Setting reinforces social inequality since middle-class students tend to be placed in the higher sets and working-class students in the lower sets.

EXAM PRACTICE QUESTIONS

AS-LEVEL PAPER 1
EDUCATION

| 0 1 | Define the term 'ethnocentric curriculum'. | [2 marks] |

| 0 2 | Using **one** example briefly explain how material factors can result in social class differences in educational achievement. | [2 marks] |

| 0 3 | Outline **three** reasons why students may join anti-school subcultures. | [6 marks] |

| 0 4 | Outline and explain **two** reasons for boys' underachievement. | [10 marks] |

| 0 5 | Read **Item A** below and answer the question that follows. |

Item A

Functionalist sociologists would suggest the education system of societies such as Britain benefits everyone and helps society to run smoothly. Not only does education teach shared values, but it also helps to train the workforce and allows employers to select the people with the most appropriate skills for the most appropriate jobs. These views are, however, questioned by many sociologists who do not support functionalism, including feminists and Marxists.

Applying material from **Item A** and your own knowledge, evaluate the view that the education system is functional for society as a whole. [20 marks]

A-LEVEL PAPER 1
EDUCATION

0 1　Outline **two** factors within school that may influence social class differences in academic achievement.　**[4 marks]**

0 2　Outline **three** ways in which the introduction of league tables has had an impact on schools.　**[6 marks]**

0 3　Read **Item A** below and answer the question that follows.

Item A

In recent years, the A-level subjects with the highest proportions of female students were English, biology and psychology, whereas those with highest proportions of male students were mathematics, physics and chemistry. When explaining these differences, some sociologists emphasise the image and nature of different subjects, the way they are taught, and the learning style associated with particular subjects. Others emphasise factors outside school such as gender differences in the way children are socialised.

Applying material from **Item A**, analyse **two** reasons for gender differences in subject choice. **[10 marks]**

0 4　Read **Item B** below and answer the question that follows.

Item B

There are significant ethnic differences in educational achievement in Britain. British Chinese students are the highest attaining at GCSE with pupils of Indian ethnicity doing next best. White British students do less well than Bangladeshi and Black African students but better than Pakistani and Black Caribbean students. However, White British pupils are the lowest attaining ethnic group amongst pupils entitled to free school meals. Some sociologists see cultural differences between ethnic groups as the main factor explaining these differences in achievement.

Applying material from **Item B** and elsewhere, evaluate the view that ethnic differences in educational achievement are mainly the result of cultural factors.　**[30 marks]**

3 RESEARCH METHODS

Chapter contents

You've heard them on the news, you've read them in the papers, you've seen them on TV – facts and figures telling you what's happening, keeping you informed, and claiming to reflect reality. But do any of these facts and figures come anywhere near the truth?

What do we really know? How do we find out what's true? We could observe something that's happening. Then find evidence that supports our observation and confirms what we see. But we tend not to look for evidence which might contradict what we think we see. We could rely on common sense. But today's common sense may well be tomorrow's nonsense. We could

listen to experts. But they often disagree amongst themselves. So how do we decide what to believe?

We are bombarded with so-called facts online, on TV, on radio, in newspapers and magazines, in academic books and journals. Plus, we are presented with 'fake news' whose producers know they are providing us with false information. But those who are exposed to fake news on social media sometimes believe it to be true.

This all sounds pretty negative. But this chapter offers something more positive. It looks at research methods, the methods used to gather information and find out what may or may not be true. These methods are not perfect. But at least they show us how information is produced. And we can recognise their strengths and weaknesses. This helps us to form judgements about the quality of the information that each method produces.

This chapter looks at the methods sociologists use to find out about social life. These methods range from observations of people's behaviour to questionnaires and interviews. They include interpreting and analysing information from pictures and paintings to websites, television broadcasts and autobiographies. The chapter assesses the strengths and weaknesses of each method and the practical issues involved in using them. It also examines the theories which influence the choice of methods for research.

PART 1 STARTING RESEARCH

Contents

This part looks at things to consider when starting research. Put yourself in the position of a researcher. What topic would you choose to research? Does it really interest you? Is it worth doing? What about the practical issues? Have you got the time and money to conduct the research? What kind of information do you want and what are the best methods for collecting it? Is the way you plan to conduct the research ethical – is it morally the right way to treat those who take part in your research? These are some of the questions that this part answers.

3.1.1 Designing a research project

This unit looks at various aspects of starting research. It examines different types of information produced by and used in research projects. It looks at choosing a topic to research, selecting appropriate research methods, and thinking about practical issues such as the amount of money needed to conduct the research. It also looks at two main approaches to research in sociology which affect the choice of data and the selection of methods.

Types of data

Primary and secondary data

One of the first questions sociologists ask when starting their research is 'What kind of data do I want?' **Data** are the information produced by and used in a research project. There are two main types of data – **primary data** and **secondary data**. Often researchers use both types.

Primary data refers to information which was not present before the research began. It is generated by the researcher during the actual process of research. It includes data produced by questionnaires, interviews and observations.

Secondary data refers to information which already exists. It includes data from historical records, official statistics, government reports, diaries, autobiographies, novels, newspapers, films and recorded music.

Quantitative and qualitative data

A second question sociologists ask when starting research is 'What form do I want the data in?' There are two forms of data – **quantitative data** and **qualitative data**. Researchers often use both forms.

Quantitative data This is data in the form of numbers. Examples include statistics on crime, unemployment, marriage and divorce. Quantitative data are particularly useful for measuring the strength of possible relationships between various factors, for example, age and internet use, and ethnicity and educational attainment.

Qualitative data refers to all types of data that are not in the form of numbers. It includes:

> descriptive data from observations, for example, a description of behaviour in a pub

> quotes from interviews, for example, views on marriage

> written sources, for example, diaries, novels and autobiographies

> pictures, for example, photographs, paintings and posters

> films and recorded music.

Qualitative data can often provide a richer and more in-depth picture of social life than the numbers provided by quantitative data. Many sociologists combine quantitative and qualitative data in their research.

Validity and reliability

A third question sociologists often ask when starting research is 'How good will my data be?' Ideally, they want data which are valid and reliable.

Validity Data are valid if they present a true and accurate description or measurement. For example, official statistics on crime are valid if they provide an accurate measurement of the extent of crime. Statistics on police recorded crime have often been used to

Activity – Types of data

Collecting qualitative data by observing the match from the crowd.

Collecting qualitative data from a discussion between fans after a football match. The researcher is listening and watching and will take notes on what she heard and saw as soon as the discussion is over.

Quantitative data. Score 3–1				
Possession		Pass success	Shots at goal	Yellow penalty cards
Winner	56%	82%	16	1	1
Loser	44%	74%	11	3	0

Questions

1. Using the above information, briefly outline the difference between quantitative and qualitative data.

2. How might a combination of both types of data provide a fuller picture than either one?

measure the extent of crime in England and Wales. This is not a valid measure for two main reasons. First, there are many crimes not reported to the police which are therefore not recorded. Second, research by Her Majesty's Inspectorate of Constabulary (2014) indicates that around 800 000 crimes (19 per cent of all recorded crime) reported to the police each year were not recorded. Clearly, police recorded crime does not provide valid data on the extent of crime.

Data are valid if the methods and procedures used to gather the data measure what they are supposed to measure and/or accurately describe what they are intended to describe.

Reliability Data are reliable when different researchers using the same methods obtain the same results. For example, if a number of researchers use the same procedures to measure attendance rates at the same school and they all get the same results, then the data would be reliable. However, this does not mean the data are valid. For example, the researchers may have used class registers to measure attendance and the registers may not have been filled in accurately. As a result, they were not measuring what they were designed to measure and the data they produced would not be valid.

Activity

Yakima Native-American children were given an intelligence test consisting of placing variously shaped wooden blocks into appropriately shaped holes. The children had no problem with the test but they were all given low scores because they failed to finish in the required time. Unlike Western culture, Yakima culture did not place a high priority on speed (Klineberg, 1971).

1. Why are the test results reliable?

2. Why are the test results not valid?

The research process

Designing a research project, conducting the research, and analysing the results involve a number of decisions. These include choosing a topic, selecting appropriate research methods, and deciding whether the research is morally right.

Choosing a topic

Choosing a topic for research is influenced by a range of factors. Some of these will now be briefly examined.

Values and interests of the researcher Researchers are likely to study something they consider to be important. And what they see as important is influenced by their values – their beliefs about right and wrong, good and bad. For example, a sociologist who believes strongly in equality of opportunity may study the relationship between social class and educational attainment, since there is evidence that class inequality prevents equality of educational opportunity. Similarly, a sociologist who believes in gender equality may study the position of women at work and compare their job status, workloads and rewards with those of men.

Researchers sometimes choose a research topic because it reflects their hobbies and interests. For example, they might be really involved with music and decide to do research on music festivals. Or, they might like a particular type of music such as rap and examine whether it reflects the concerns of young African Americans.

Issues of the day Major concerns in society are sometimes reflected in sociological research. Today, issues such as human rights, globalisation, the increasing gap between rich and poor, obesity, an ageing population, immigration and radicalisation are concerns both in society and research projects.

Funding Choosing a research project is also influenced by a number of practical issues. For example, is it affordable? Most research projects conducted by professional sociologists require funding. Research funds are available from various sources – charitable foundations such as the Joseph Rowntree Foundation and the Runnymede Trust, government organisations such as the Economic and Social Research Council (ESRC), and business organisations.

Each funding body has its own priorities. For example, industrial organisations will tend to fund projects dealing with their particular concerns, such as solutions to stress in the workplace. The Joseph Rowntree Foundation 'makes grants available to individuals and projects seeking the creation of a peaceful world, political equality and social justice'. The choice of research project is sometimes shaped by the priorities of the funding body.

Access to and availability of data It makes little sense to choose a research topic where there is little or no data available and/or little chance of producing it. Ease of access to people and places varies. For example, there is little chance of conducting a systematic study of secret service organisations such as MI5 and MI6.

Access to public places is relatively easy. People can usually be observed without too much trouble in streets, shopping malls, pubs, clubs, museums, art galleries, concerts and music festivals. However, permission is needed to research in places such as schools and hospitals. It is difficult to gain access to and conduct research with certain groups – criminal gangs are an obvious example.

Theoretical position Choosing a research topic is also influenced by the theoretical position of the sociologist. Every theoretical position sees certain aspects of society as particularly important. For example, Marxism sees the class system as the foundation of capitalist society. As a result, Marxists tend to focus on topics such as class inequality, class conflict and class identity. And feminist sociologists will tend to focus on gender issues, in particular gender inequality.

Choosing research methods – practical issues

Having selected a topic, the researcher must then choose appropriate methods to collect data. The choice of methods depends on a number of factors. Some of these factors will be introduced briefly here and examined in more detail later. There are a number of practical issues involved in the study of research methods. They include the following.

Money Research costs money. Sociologists may have a grant to pay for their research. However, they must choose methods which match the money they have available. For example, if they were doing a survey of parents and children about school dinners, then the money available might not cover lengthy interviews but it might be enough for a brief questionnaire survey.

Time Different research methods can take different amounts of time. For example, participant observation, a method in which the researcher joins the group they are studying, sometimes takes more than a year. A researcher's time is limited. This might involve deciding to conduct a number of interviews rather than a lengthy participant observation study.

People being studied Some methods are more suitable than others for studying certain groups of people. Think about studying a teenage gang whose members are hostile to outsiders, particularly those they see as representing authority. Asking gang members for interviews or presenting them with questionnaires is unlikely to produce the required data. However, joining in their activities and gaining their trust can allow the researcher to obtain information by observing their behaviour. This method has been used successfully by a number of sociologists.

Safety When choosing methods, researchers must be aware of possible emotional and physical dangers to themselves. Michael Haralambos's research on African-American music in Chicago was based on participant observation – observing by joining those he was studying. It was stressful and, at times, dangerous. He was threatened with a gun on more than one occasion. But he needed to use participant observation as he was in and out of bars, dancehalls, clubs and concerts, watching and listening (Haralambos,1994), In this case the end – good data – in his view justified the risk.

Characteristics of the researcher Researchers have a number of characteristics which may affect their choice of research methods. For example, they have a certain age, gender, ethnicity and class which must be considered when selecting methods for different types of research. This can be seen from Julia O'Connell Davidson's study of prostitution shown in the pictures. She chose participant observation and acted as a receptionist in a brothel. In this case, gender was an important consideration for her choice of method. In her words, 'My identity as a woman affected the data I collected'. Both clients and workers were more likely to talk freely and feel at ease with a woman rather than a man (O'Connell Davidson and Layder, 1994).

Ethics Today there are ethical guidelines for research – guidelines for the right and wrong ways to conduct research. For example, people should be made aware that they are participating in research, be able to decide whether or not to take part, and be protected from physical and psychological harm. These guidelines will affect the choice of method and the design of the research. The unit on ethics gives an example of a notorious experiment which did not follow the above guidelines (see p. 141).

Activity

Here are three topics for research.

❭ The relationship between gender and choice of TV programmes.

❭ The relationship between ethnicity and tastes in music.

❭ The relationship between social class and diet.

1. Select one of these topics for research and say why you chose it.

2. What will you need to think about when choosing a method for your research?

Activity

Julia O'Connell Davidson (on the right) acting as a receptionist in the brothel.

How did gender influence Julia O'Connell Davidson's choice of research method? Refer to the pictures in your answer.

Generalisation and representativeness

When planning their research, sociologists need to decide whether they want to **generalise** from results of their research. Generalising means making a statement about all on the basis of some. In terms of research, making a statement about the group that has been studied and applying that statement to members of the same group in the wider society. For example, making a statement about the attitudes of all women aged 20 to 30 in the UK based on the attitudes of some women aged 20 to 30 in the UK.

To make a generalisation from their research, sociologists must try to make sure that their research participants are **representative** of the group in the wider society. In terms of the above example, researchers will try to make sure that the women aged 20 to 30 in their study are similar to the women aged 20 to 30 as a whole. For instance, if all the women in their study had children, were not in paid employment, had university degrees and were of Chinese heritage, then they would not represent women aged 20 to 30 in the UK. As a result, they would not provide a basis for generalisation of all women of that age group in the UK.

If a sociologist aims to generalise from their research participants, then they must try to select a **sample** which is representative of the group as a whole. There are various ways of doing this, which will be examined later in this chapter (see pp. 160–164).

Pilot studies

Before starting the main research, some sociologists conduct a **pilot study**. This is a small-scale study to check on the suitability of the methods to be used in the main research. Pilot studies often use a small sample of the main group to be studied. Members of this sample will not, however, take part in the final research. Here are some of the uses of a pilot study:

1. If interviews or questionnaires are to be used, the questions can be tried out to make sure they are understood by and make sense to the research participants.

2. This is particularly important for self-completion questionnaires where the researcher is not present to explain any difficulties or clear up any confusion. This preliminary test might reveal that instructions for completing the questionnaire and the wording of questions need clarifying.

3. An in-depth interview may be useful for constructing the questionnaire for the main research. It may identify the concerns and priorities of the participants, which should be included in the questionnaire.

Objectivity

Most sociologists try to be **objective** when conducting their research. This means that they try to prevent their values, political views, religious beliefs and prejudices from influencing their research. Many researchers believe that an objective, value-free sociology is not possible. They argue that values affect the whole research process from the choice of topic to the collection and interpretation of data to the final conclusions.

The American sociologist Howard Becker (1970) argues that it is impossible to conduct research 'uncontaminated by personal and political sympathies'. His sympathies are with the 'underdog' – the poor and the powerless. Karl Marx's (1880–1883) sympathies are there for all to see – he saw capitalism as an evil and exploitative system. And today David Harvey (2014) shares Marx's vision and values. They direct his research and the questions he asks. Harvey's values are clear from his following statement, 'We need revolutionary politics to replace capitalism with a just and fair society'.

Activity

Marx's view of capitalist society.

1. How does this picture illustrate Marx's political views, his sympathies and his values?

2. Today, some sociologists share Marx's views. How might this influence their research?

Does this mean that sociologists should give up the pursuit of objectivity? The short answer is no! Sociologists accept that complete objectivity is impossible but this does not mean giving up on trying to be objective. Clifford Geertz (1973) makes the case brilliantly for the pursuit of objectivity.

I have never been impressed by the argument that, as complete objectivity is impossible, one might as well let one's sentiments run loose. That is like saying that as a perfectly aseptic (germ free) environment is impossible, one might as well conduct surgery in a sewer.

Choosing methods – theoretical approaches

A number of sociologists have suggested that there are two main research traditions or approaches in sociology – **positivism** and **interpretivism**. They are based on different views of human behaviour and sometimes lead to the use of different research methods. Here is a brief introduction to these approaches.

Positivism

Auguste Comte (1798–1857), one of the founders of sociology, believed it was possible to create a 'science of society' based on the methods and assumptions of the natural sciences such as physics and chemistry. He called his approach positivism. Positivism states that human behaviour can be measured and quantified just like matter in the natural sciences. In this way it can be shown whether behaviour is the result of cause and effect relationships.

Positivist sociology favours quantitative data. It attempts to measure behaviour by presenting it in the form of numbers. This makes it possible to use statistical tests to measure the strength of relationships between two or more factors. A **correlation** – a statistical link – may indicate a causal relationship, that one factor causes another. However, correlation does not necessarily indicate causation, that is to say it does not mean that one thing necessarily causes another.

Some research methods are more likely than others to produce quantitative data. It is fairly easy to translate the answers to a questionnaire and responses to certain types of interviews into numbers. As a result, positivists are likely to prefer these research methods. And they tend to prefer secondary data in a numerical form – for example, official statistics such as unemployment and crime statistics.

Positivists aim to make **generalisations** about human behaviour. As discussed earlier, a generalisation is a statement made about a whole group based on findings from a relatively small number of members of that group. To do this they need to study a sample of people who are **representative** of that group – a sample which has the same characteristics as the larger group. So if the study is based on middle-class, African-Caribbean women aged 20–30 the sample should have these characteristics. If the sample is representative, then data from the sample are more likely to reflect the group in society as a whole.

Interpretivism

Some sociologists argue that understanding human behaviour involves seeing the world through the eyes of those being studied. People give meaning to their own actions and to the actions of others, they define situations in certain ways and act accordingly. To understand their behaviour, it is essential to discover the meanings and definitions which guide their actions. This approach is sometimes called interpretivism – the researcher's job is to interpret meanings and definitions of the situation.

Interpretivists reject the view that the methods and assumptions of the natural sciences are applicable to the study of human beings. Matter simply reacts to external stimuli such as temperature and pressure. Human beings act in terms of meanings which they use to direct their behaviour. The job of the sociologist is to discover these meanings.

Interpretivists tend to favour particular research methods. Many see participant observation as one of the best ways to discover meanings. It provides researchers with the opportunity to observe people in their normal, everyday situations, to see life as it is lived. Interpretivists also favour in-depth, unstructured interviews which allow **research participants** to express their own view of the world and define situations in their own way. Interpretivists see these methods as more likely to provide qualitative data which they believe is richer and more meaningful than quantitative data. In terms of secondary data, they prefer personal documents such as diaries and autobiographies in which people express their meanings and feelings in their own way.

Evaluation Dividing sociology into positivism and interpretivism has been criticised by some researchers. According to Ray Pawson (1989) instead of two approaches there is a whole range of different approaches, different views and different assumptions.

Increasingly, sociologists are using **mixed methods** approaches – mixing quantitative and qualitative methods, for example participant observation and questionnaires, on a single research project. This can be seen as providing the benefits of two or more methods. For example, it could result in producing both quantitative and qualitative data to give a fuller picture.

Key terms

Data Information used in and/or produced by a research project.

Primary data New data produced by the researcher during the research process.

Secondary data Data that already exist which may be used by the researcher.

Quantitative data Numerical data – data in the form of numbers.

Qualitative data All data that are not in the form of numbers.

Validity Data are valid if they represent a true and accurate description or measurement.

Reliability Data are reliable when different researchers using the same methods obtain the same results.

Research participants Those who take part in research projects and are studied by researchers.

Representative group A smaller group which has the same characteristics as a larger group.

Sample A selection of research participants from the larger group to be studied.

Representative sample A sample which is typical of the group in the wider society.

Generalisation A statement based on a relatively small group which is then applied to a larger group.

Pilot study A small-scale study to check on the suitability of the methods used in the main study.

Positivism An approach partly based on the methods used in the natural sciences. It favours quantitative data.

Interpretivism An approach focusing on meanings which are seen to direct human action. It favours qualitative data.

Mixed methods Using two or more methods in the same research project.

Summary

1. Sociologists identify different types of data – primary and secondary data and quantitative and qualitative data.

2. The choice of research topic may be influenced by the:
    » Values of the researcher
    » Issues of the day
    » Priorities of the funding provider
    » Availability of the data
    » Theoretical position of the researcher.

3. The choice of research methods may be influenced by the:
    » Money available
    » Time available
    » People being studied
    » Safety of the project
    » Characteristics of the researcher.

4. To make generalisations, sociologists try to make sure that their sample is representative of the group in the wider society.

5. Most researchers believe that a completely objective sociology is not possible. However, most do their best to be objective.

6. Some sociologists see two main research traditions or approaches in sociology – positivism and interpretivism. Each favours particular research methods and types of data.

3.1.2 Research ethics

Ethical considerations can have an important influence on the research process. Ethics are moral principles – beliefs about what is right and wrong. In terms of research, ethics are the moral principles which guide research. Sociological associations in many countries have a set of ethical guidelines for conducting research. Sociology departments in universities usually have an ethics committee to ensure that research conducted by members of the department is in line with these guidelines.

Ethical guidelines

Here are some of the ethical guidelines which sociologists usually follow when conducting their research.

Informed consent Many researchers argue that those they are studying should be given the opportunity to agree to or to refuse to participate in research. This decision should be 'informed' – information must be made available on which to base a decision to participate or not. Researchers should therefore provide information about the aims of the research, what the conduct of the research involves, and the purposes to which the research findings will be put.

Deception Ethical guidelines often state that research participants should not be deceived. Deception can take various forms. Information may be withheld from participants or they may be given false information. They may be unaware they are participating in a research study. They may be misled about the purpose of the study and the events that may take place during the research.

Activity – Research ethics

The American psychologist Stanley Milgram (1963) conducted an experiment to see how far people would obey commands which they felt were wrong and would harm others. The research participants were told that the experiment was a 'scientific study' of the effect of punishment – electric shocks – on learning. Unknown to the participants, the shocks were not real.

The man on the left of the picture is a participant, the man in centre and the man in the side room on the right are both actors. The man on the right is pretending to be in extreme pain. Milgram describes the response of one of the participants. 'At one point he pushed his fist into his forehead and muttered: "Oh God, let's stop it". And yet he continued to respond to every word of the experimenter, and obeyed to the end.'

Milgram defends his experiment in the following way. First, he argues that the importance of his findings justifies the methods he used. In his words, 'If this experiment serves to jar people out of their complacency, it will have served its end. If an anonymous experimenter can successfully command adults to subdue a 50-year-old man and force on him painful electric shocks against his protests, one can

only wonder what government, with its vastly greater authority and prestige, can command of its subjects.'

Milgram admits that in some cases there was psychological harm but claims this was only short term. He hired a psychiatrist to interview the participants one year after the experiment. There appeared to be no long-term harm.

Milgram's experiment was deception from beginning to end. He justifies this by saying, 'I had to deceive them for the experiment to work'. Over 80 per cent of the participants saw deception as necessary and therefore acceptable.

Did the participants have the right to withdraw from the experiment? Only after four commands to continue, the final command being, 'You have no other choice. You must go on'.

Questions

1. It is very unlikely that ethics committees in university departments would allow Milgram's experiments to be conducted today. Why not?

2. Do you think his experiment was justified? Give reasons for your answer.

Clearly, participants cannot give informed consent if they are deceived. Is deception ever justifiable? Some researchers argue that deception is justified if there is no other way of gathering data.

Privacy Researchers generally agree that participants' privacy should be respected. The problem here is that most research intrudes into people's lives. It has been argued that if participants consent to take part in research, then they accept this. However, they may be unaware of the extent of the intrusion. With hindsight, they may see it as an invasion of privacy.

Certain research methods, which are generally considered ethical, may result in an invasion of privacy. Take the case of an informal, unstructured interview – it often develops into a friendly chat between researcher and participant. In this relaxed atmosphere, participants may reveal all sorts of personal and private matters which they may later regret.

Confidentiality It is generally agreed that the identity of research participants should be kept secret. According to the British Sociological Association's *Statement of Ethical Practice* (1996), confidentiality must be honoured 'unless there are clear and overriding reasons to do otherwise'. It has been argued that when people in powerful positions misuse their power, then there may be a case for naming names (Homan, 1991).

Protection from harm There is general agreement that research participants should be protected from both physical and psychological harm. This includes any harmful effects of participating in the actual research process and any harmful consequences of the research. For example, publication of research findings may harm those who have been studied. Particular care should be taken to protect members of vulnerable groups, for example victims of domestic violence.

Exceptions Some argue that in certain instances ethical guidelines should not be followed. For example, in a study of child abuse deception might be judged to be acceptable if it helps to bring the abusers to justice.

Key terms

Ethics Moral principles stating what is right and wrong.

Ethical guidelines for research The rights and wrongs of conducting research provided by social science organisations and university departments.

Summary

1. Research ethics state that research participants:

   - should be given sufficient information for informed consent to take part in research
   - should not be deceived
   - should have their privacy respected
   - should have their identity kept secret
   - should be protected from harm.

2. There are occasions when these guidelines might not be followed – for example when research participants are harming others.

PART 2 OBSERVATION

Contents

One of the aims of sociological research is to find out how people behave in their normal, everyday settings – at work, in their leisure time, with their friends and family. One way is to ask them to fill out a questionnaire or agree to an interview.

Another way is to observe them in their everyday settings. The sociologist may join the group they are observing. This is known as **participant observation**. They may join the group for a drink in the pub or a chat on the street corner. They may tell the group that that they are observing their behaviour. This is known as **overt observation** – open observation. Or they may decide not to tell them. This is known as **covert observation** – hidden observation.

People can be observed without directly joining them. This is known as **non-participant observation**. Examples include observing people at a music festival, at a sporting event, in a playground, in a café. Again this type of observation may be overt – open, or covert – hidden.

Observation has its advantages and disadvantages. For example, it allows sociologists to directly observe people's behaviour rather than relying on them to describe their own behaviour. However, if people know they are being observed they may not act normally. This part describes and evaluates the different types of observation.

3.2.1 Participant observation

Participant observation has been used in a variety of settings. It was used by John Howard Griffin (1960) a White journalist who dyed his skin black in order to discover what it was like to live as a Black man in the southern states of America in the late 1950s. It was used by the anthropologist Bronislaw Malinowski (1922) who spent many years studying the Trobriand Islanders of New Guinea. It was used by the sociologist Erving Goffman (1968) when he adopted the role of assistant to the athletics director in order to study the experience of patients in a mental hospital in Washington D.C. And it was used by Richard Giulianotti (1995) in his study of two groups of Scottish football hooligans.

This unit looks at participant observation. It asks how do researchers gain entry into a group of people. Should they tell those they are observing what they are really doing? How should they conduct their research in order to get the best results? How does participant observation online work?

Ethnography

Participant observation is one of the main research methods used in **ethnography**. Ethnography is the study of the way of life of a group of people – their culture and the structure of their society. Often researchers attempt to 'walk a mile in their shoes' – to see the world from their perspective, discover their meanings and appreciate their experiences. Many argue that participant observation is the most effective method for doing this.

Participant observation gives researchers the opportunity to observe people in their normal settings as opposed to the more artificial contexts of the laboratory or the interview. It allows researchers to see what people do as opposed to what they say they do.

Participant observation has produced a number of classic ethnographies – William F. Whyte's (1955) account of an Italian-American gang in Boston, Massachusetts and Sudhir Venkatesh's (2009) study of the Black Kings, an African-American gang who sold crack cocaine in Chicago.

Gaining entry

Participant observation cannot work unless the researcher gains entry into the group and acceptance from its members. Gaining entry means that the group allows the researcher to join them. Gaining acceptance means that to some degree members of the group come to trust the researcher. This can be difficult. Many groups don't want to be studied, especially those whose activities are seen as criminal by the wider society. However, as the following examples indicate, it is often possible to enter even closed groups.

For his research in the USA into casual sex between men in public toilets – the 'tearoom trade' – Laud Humphreys (1970) acted as a lookout. By performing this role, he gained the trust of those he observed without having to directly join their activities.

On other occasions, researchers have to participate more directly in order to gain entry. Dick Hobbs (1994) wanted to research the relationship between criminals and detectives in the East End of London. He was coaching a local soccer team when he discovered that Simon, a detective, was the father of one of the players. He developed a friendship with Simon who provided him with introductions and vouched for him (said he was OK). Hobbs also drank in The Pump, a local pub that was frequented by several detectives. These contacts enabled him to gain entry into the world of the detectives – he joined their conversations and observed their activities.

Sometimes researchers are forced into even greater participation to gain entry. Leon Festinger (1956) found that the only way to observe a small religious sect was to pretend to be a believer and become a member of the sect.

Covert and overt research The above methods of gaining entry involve hiding the identity and purpose of the researcher. This is known as covert or hidden research. Covert research has certain advantages. If the group sees the observer as 'one of them' they will be more likely to behave normally and reveal information they may not give to an outsider. For example, Jason Ditton (1977) got a part-time job in a bakery to investigate 'fiddling' by the salesmen. He kept his real purpose a secret. As a result, the salesmen told him how they stole bread and overcharged customers and how they saw these activities as 'perks of the job' rather than crimes. Many sociologists regard covert research as unethical – morally wrong. For example, it does not give those being observed the opportunity to consent to participating in the research.

Overt research (open research) has its own problems of entry and acceptance as illustrated in the picture of Sudhir Venkatesh's first day with the Black Kings in Chicago. Some of the gang saw him as a possible threat – hence the knife and gun. Some saw him as a harmless source of amusement. One gang member saw him as a spy from a rival Mexican gang. The gang leader J.T. gave Sudhir his support which provided entry and eventual acceptance into the world of the Black Kings.

One of the advantages of overt participation observation is that it can lead to the development of key informants who go out of their way to assist in the research. A **key informant** is a member of the group being studied who has a special relationship with the researcher, provides important information and often acts as a sponsor, telling the rest of the group that the researcher can be trusted. J.T., the leader of the Black Kings, was a key informant for Sudhir Venkatesh. In Sudhir's words, 'I felt a strange kind of intimacy with J.T., unlike the bond I'd felt even with good friends'.

Looking and listening Participant observation involves looking and listening. The general rule is to stand back and try to avoid influencing people's behaviour. Since the aim is to observe people in their normal setting, the researcher must not disturb that setting. Blending into the background is usually recommended, though this is not always possible. For example, a participant observer in a classroom can stand out like a sore thumb. This may result in an artificial and untypical lesson which can reduce the validity of the observations. But it's surprising how soon the researcher becomes 'invisible' and taken for granted. In his study of a secondary school, Walford (1993), found that it took four weeks of observation before any students misbehaved. However, the situation changed rapidly after this time and Walford was soon watching 'mock wrestling' and chairs flying around the classroom!

Key informants As noted earlier, key informants can be extremely valuable. But the relationship between a researcher and a key informant may have drawbacks. In his participant observation study of the Italian-American gang in Boston, William Whyte had a special relationship with Doc, the gang leader. In Whyte's words, 'Doc became in a very real sense a collaborator in the research'. However, this close relationship may cause problems if it changes the informant's behaviour. In Doc's words, 'Now, when I do something, I have to think what Bill Whyte would want to know about it and how I can explain it. Before, I used

Activity

Sudhir's first meeting with the Black Kings.

Suggest reasons for Sudhir's initial rejection by the gang.

to do things by instinct'. And it might also change the researcher's behaviour as the picture below indicates.

Activity

Doc on the left, William Whyte on the right.

What problems for Whytes' research are indicated in the picture?

Insights and knowledge Participant observation can provide insights and knowledge which may not be available from other research methods. Looking back on his research, Sudhir Venkatesh (2009) says, 'I was an outsider looking at life from the inside… I had no experience whatsoever in an urban ghetto'. Sudhir was a young, middle-class university student. He was entering the unknown. His only hope of gaining an insight into this new world was, in his words, 'to hang out with the people'. Participant observation gave him the opportunity. Looking back on his research in Boston, William Whyte (1955) recalled a similar learning experience. Like Sudhir, he was discovering things that he had previously known nothing about. In his words, 'As I sat and listened, I learned the answers to questions that I would not have had the sense to ask if I had been getting my information solely on an interviewing basis'.

Meanings and context Participant observation is a favourite method of those who want qualitative data. Spending possibly years observing a fairly small group of people means that the researcher can really get to know them. This provides a real opportunity to discover the meanings which direct their behaviour, construct their view of the world and make sense of their experiences.

By comparison, other research methods such as questionnaires and interviews provide one-off, snapshot answers. They are unlikely to present a full picture. Participant observation provides opportunities to observe people's behaviour in different contexts, in different circumstances and with different audiences. And the same people can express very different meanings in different contexts as the following study illustrates.

Elliot Liebow (1967) spent one and a half years as a participant observer studying African-American men in Washington D.C. The men were either on welfare or in low-paid jobs. Their income was insufficient to support a family. Most had failed marriages. Failure as a husband is explained by being a man. Boasting about 'many flaws' helps to restore self-respect. However, on another occasion in a different context, very different and contradictory meanings are expressed, as shown in the pictures. People often live with contradictory views. Participant observation provides opportunities to observe these contradictions which are unlikely to be revealed by other research methods such as interviews and questionnaires.

'Going native' The personal involvement which participant observation demands can reduce objectivity, and prevent an impartial view. This can affect the validity of research observations. An observer can identify so strongly with a group that the behaviour of its members is invariably seen in a positive light. In rare cases, this identification is carried to its extreme – observers 'go native', join the group and never return to their former lives.

Time, money and personal cost Participant observation can be a long and expensive process. It can require dedication, stamina and courage. Researchers are often cut off from the normal supports of family and friends, sometimes living a double life in an alien setting. And participant observation can be dangerous. For example, Richard Giulianotti (1995) was told by one of the football hooligans he studied that 'during my first contact with the gang, some had held the view that I should only depart in a body bag'. However, given the quality of information that participant observation can produce, some might see these risks as acceptable.

Validity and reliability Supporters of participant observation see it as the best method for obtaining valid data – for providing a true picture of the meanings which guide behaviour.

However, participant observation is often seen as an unreliable method. It is therefore unlikely that different researchers will produce the same results.

145

Activity

Observations from Elliot Liebow's research in Washington D.C.

1. Why is it important to see meanings in context?

2. Why is participant observation an excellent method to discover meanings?

There are various reasons for this. Participant observation is usually seen as unsystematic – there are no fixed procedures, things happen and the observer tags along. Data are rarely quantified – put into numbers. Participant observation relies heavily on the personal qualities of the researcher. To some degree, these qualities will affect how well they get on with those they observe, what they see and how they interpret it.

Generalisation Sample sizes in participant observation studies are small. The researchers can't be everywhere observing large numbers of people. In view of the small numbers, it is not possible to generalise from the findings of participant observation – to apply them to a larger group. However, these findings can be used to question or support generalisations from larger studies. Or they can produce fresh insights which can then be investigated on a larger scale.

Participating online

Virtual worlds such as *Second Life*, *World of Warcraft* and *Dreamscape* and online games such as *Gravity*, *Battlefield 1* and *Sparta: War of Empires* are leisure activities for millions of people. Participant observation is a key method for studying virtual worlds and online games and those who play them.

Probably the best way to learn the rules and conventions of online games is to directly participate – that is to play

the game. And online communication with other players is sometimes essential for playing the game.

Online and physical world communities Some participants in online games and virtual worlds form virtual communities. Some members of these communities meet in the physical world. Understanding the importance of community is necessary for understanding the significance of virtual worlds for some participants. They may 'live' part of their lives in such communities as the title of one world, *Second Life*, suggests.

Sometimes researchers and research participants meet face-to-face. Attending a meeting in the physical world provided further valuable insights for T.L. Taylor's research. Taylor met 30 people who played the game she was studying. This led to a discussion of her avatar (her online virtual person) who had a female head and a male body. The discussion covered the main themes of her research – embodiment, identity and performance (Taylor, 2002; Boellstorff *et al.*, 2012).

Involvement How far to get involved is a difficult question for participant observers. As a general rule, they tend to stay in the background so as not to influence the behaviour of those they observe.

Celia Pearce (2006, 2009) studied an online game called *Buggy Polo*. She tried not to influence the players and stayed on the sidelines. They told her she

Activity

T.L. Taylor's avatar and her physical world discussion with virtual world participants.

Why was participant observation useful for T.L. Taylor's research on virtual worlds?

was too detached. She got more involved and in doing so gained the trust and respect of the other players. In this case participating more directly was necessary for Pearce's research.

Ethnography and Virtual Worlds: A Handbook of Method by Tom Boellstorff, Bonnie Nardi, Celia Pearce and T.L. Taylor (2012) is an excellent book on participant observation in virtual worlds. They saw participant observation as 'the heart and soul of our work'. They found that 'when studying virtual worlds, good participant observation means play and research in parallel' and that 'greater involvement in play activities gave a deeper understanding'.

Positivism and interpretivism

Positivism From a positivist viewpoint, participant observation has its uses. It provides information which can be used to construct relevant and meaningful questions for questionnaires. This will improve the quality of the questions and of the quantitative data they produce.

However, as an end in itself, a participant observation study is not seen as particularly useful by positivists. It produces little if any quantifiable data. The numbers observed are small – too small to provide a representative sample which can form a basis for generalisations. And the method is not reliable –

different researchers are unlikely to produce the same observations.

Interpretivism As noted earlier, participant observation gives the researcher an opportunity to capture the 'insider's view' – to see the world from the point of view of those being observed. Interpretivists are concerned with the meanings and definitions which direct action. Often these meanings and definitions are taken for granted – people are not aware of them. Observing their behaviour provides an opportunity for the researcher to interpret these taken-for-granted meanings. As a result, interpretivists tend to favour participant observation as a method for collecting data. In addition, the qualitative data produced by participant observation are often seen to have a richness and depth not usually available from other research methods.

Ethics and participant observation

Covert participant observation is usually seen as the most ethically unsound form of observation. The following example looks at one of the most infamous cases.

Laud Humphreys (1970) studied casual sex between men in public toilets in the USA. This was known as the 'tearoom trade' in gay slang. Humphreys acted as a 'watchqueen' warning of the approach of strangers and

147

the police. He kept his identity as a researcher secret. A year later, Humphreys interviewed 50 of the men he had observed. The interviews were conducted in their homes. Humphreys changed his appearance – his hairstyle and his clothes – and pretended that he was doing a survey on health. He tracked down their names and addresses from the licence plate numbers on their cars. He interviewed them about their jobs, sexual orientation and marriages – most of the men were married to women.

Humphreys has been accused of totally ignoring a number of key ethical guidelines. He kept his identity as a researcher secret and falsely presented himself – firstly as a 'watchqueen', and secondly, as a health researcher. He gave the participants no chance to consent to the research or refuse to participate. He invaded their privacy.

Activity

At the time of Humphreys' research, sex between men was illegal in most US states. Had the police got hold of his data the men might have lost their jobs, their family lives might have been ruined and they may even have been arrested and imprisoned. Humphreys justified his research by saying that secrecy, deception and invasion of privacy were necessary to conduct the research. He claimed that the data were invaluable for destroying a number of harmful myths by showing that gays were *not* a threat to society, that 'straight people' were *not* drawn into gay sex and that extensive police surveillance was *not* necessary. He claims that his research showed that his participants were not 'dangerous deviants' as portrayed by the stereotype of the time. In fact, many of them were so-called 'respectable' married men.

1. Does Humphreys' defence of his research justify covert participant observation?

2. Can you think of any circumstances in which covert participant observation is justified?

Overt participant observation Participant observers can spend years 'in the field' conducting their research. During this time, they will probably make mistakes and be unaware that they had not followed ethical guidelines. This happened in Sudhir Venkatesh's study of the Black Kings in Chicago.

As part of his research Venkatesh asked hustlers (petty criminals) in the neighbourhood where they got their money. A few days later he saw several of the hustlers. One of them said, 'You realise you can't trust nobody'. J.T., the leader of the Black Kings took a share of the hustlers' income for 'protection'. He started 'taxing'

them for income they hadn't reported, based on information he received from Venkatesh. The hustlers were furious and refused to speak to Venkatesh again.

Although he had betrayed their trust and said the information was confidential, Venkatesh hadn't realised the consequences of telling J.T. Spending a year or more with a group of people and becoming a part of their lives, researchers are likely to occasionally make mistakes, upset people unintentionally and be unaware they are breaking ethical guidelines.

Online participant observation Researchers who observe and participate in virtual worlds are very aware of ethical issues. In *Ethnography and Virtual Worlds* (2002) Tom Boellstorff, Bonnie Nard, Celia Pearce and T.L. Taylor spell out the ethics for online participant observation. Researchers must 'take good care' of participants, they must realise that 'avatars are under the agency of real people with feelings and rights'. They must be honest and open, and give participants the information for informed consent. For example, T.L. Taylor attached the phrase 'Avatar Research' to her avatar and directed participants to a website which included a consent form to participate and an explanation about the research. Emphasis was given to protecting informants' identity and privacy while at the same time making sure that, '...we work to create the fairest and most accurate portrayal of informants' lifeworlds'.

Advantages and disadvantages of participant observation

Advantages

- Gives researchers the opportunity to observe people in their normal, everyday situations and in a variety of contexts.

- Offers the chance to discover the meanings which direct behaviour, meanings which participants often take for granted.

- Provides insights which might not be available using other research methods.

- Seen by many researchers as one of the best methods for obtaining valid data.

- A key method for studying virtual worlds, online games and those who play them.

- A source of rich and in-depth qualitative data.

Disadvantages

- Sometimes difficult to gain entrance to and acceptance by the group.

- Might be costly, time consuming, stressful and even dangerous.

- Observation may prevent the participants from behaving normally.

- Small numbers of participants. Not enough to generalise from.

- Unlikely to produce quantitative data.

- Sometimes seen as an unreliable method with little chance of replication.

- The researcher may become too involved, lose objectivity and, in extreme cases, go native.

Key terms

Ethnography The study of the way of life of a group of people in order to see their world from their perspective.

Covert research Hidden research where the researcher's true identity and the purpose of the research is hidden from participants.

Overt research Open research where the researcher's true identity and the purpose of the research is revealed to participants.

Key informant A member of the group being studied who provides important information and often sponsors the researcher.

Going native The researcher actually becomes a part of the group they are studying and does not return to their previous life.

Summary

1. Participant observation involves the researcher joining those they wish to study.

2. It can be overt (open) or covert (hidden). Covert participant observation is usually regarded as unethical.

3. Participant observation is based mainly on looking and listening and, where possible, standing back to avoid influencing participants' behaviour.

4. Positivists tend not to favour participant observation as it produces little if any quantitative data, the samples are too small for generalisation and the method is not seen as reliable.

5. Interpretivists favour participant observation, seeing it as an excellent method for discovering meanings and for providing rich and valid data.

3.2.2 Non-participant observation

The researcher need not participate to observe people's behaviour. A non-participant observer is a bit like a birdwatcher in a hide, observing behaviour without joining in. For example, a researcher may observe children's behaviour in a school playground from an upstairs room in the school or they may stand back and observe the audience at a music festival. This unit looks at **non-participant observation**.

Types of non-participant observation

There are two main types of non-participant observation – structured and unstructured observation. **Structured observation**, sometimes known as **systematic observation**, uses an **observation schedule** which tells the observer exactly what to look for and how to record it. Completing an observation schedule is a bit like ticking pre-set boxes on a questionnaire.

Unstructured observation, as its name suggests, does not use an observation schedule systematically to record specified aspects of behaviour. Instead, it simply describes the behaviour as seen by the researcher.

Observing car driving behaviour

Here is an example of structured non-participant observation. Paul Piff conducted a study in California to test the hypothesis (the prediction) that wealthy, upper-class people were more selfish and uncaring than people lower down the social scale. Part of the study was based on driving behaviour. It was assumed that the make and age of cars reflected the driver's wealth and status in society (Piff *et al.*, 2012).

The first study was a non-participation observation of 274 drivers at a busy 4-way intersection (crossroads) with stop signs on all sides. The drivers did not know they were being observed. The observers were not aware of the hypothesis being tested. They were placed out of drivers' direct line of vision. They were asked to record the make, age and physical appearance of the vehicle, the gender of the driver and whether he or she cut in front of other vehicles at the intersection. The California Vehicle Code states that vehicles approaching an intersection should yield right-of-way to any other vehicle which had already arrived at the intersection.

Activity

4-way intersection.

Pedestrian crossing.

1. In what ways does this research support Piff's hypothesis?

2. Can you think of any problems with Piff's research?

The second study looked at the behaviour of 154 drivers as they approached a pedestrian crossing on a busy road. Again, the drivers did not know they were being observed. The observers were unaware of the hypothesis and placed themselves out of the drivers' direct line of vision. As in the first study, they were asked to record the make, age and appearance of the car and the gender of the driver. This time, they were asked to record whether or not the driver gave right-of-way to a pedestrian waiting at the crossing – the pedestrian was part of the research team. The Californian Vehicle Code states that a driver must give right-of-way to a pedestrian waiting to cross the road at a marked crossing.

The observations showed that the more expensive and newer the cars, the more likely drivers were to cut off other vehicles rather than wait their turn at 4-way intersections, and the less likely they were to stop for people at pedestrian crossings. Paul Piff concluded that the observations provided support for his hypothesis that wealthy, upper-class people were more selfish and uncaring than those lower down the social scale (Piff *et al.*, 2012).

Positivism and interpretivism

Positivism Positivists would prefer structured non-participant observation because the results are easier to quantify and the strict instructions of the observation schedule would make this method more reliable.

Interpretivism Interpretivists would prefer the qualitative data provided by unstructured non-participant observation and the fact that there is no observation schedule imposing the researcher's rules and definitions on the descriptions of the behaviour observed.

Ethics and non–participant observation

Non-participant observation is often covert – people are not aware they are being observed. As a result, informed consent is not available. However, there are many cases where obtaining consent is just not practical – for instance, observing a crowd at a football match or watching drivers in moving cars, as in Paul Piff's research outlined earlier. Examples such as these do not necessarily break ethical guidelines.

Advantages and disadvantages of non–participant observation

Advantages

» Since people are often unaware that they are being observed, the researcher is unlikely to affect their behaviour.

» If an observation schedule is used, the data are usually quantifiable and the method reliable, with different observers producing similar results.

Disadvantages

» Non-participant observers are unlikely to get to know those they observe or to see them in various contexts. This reduces the chances of discovering the meanings which direct behaviour.

» As a result, researchers are more likely to impose their meanings and their interpretations on the behaviour of those they observe.

Key terms

Non-participant observation Observation in which the researcher does not join those they are observing.

Structured/systematic observation Observation which follows specific instructions.

Unstructured observation A description of behaviour as seen by the researcher.

Observation schedule Instructions which tell the observer what to look for and how to record it.

Summary

1. There are two main types of non-participant observation – structured observation and non-structured observation.

2. Structured observation uses an observation schedule and produces quantifiable data.

3. Non-structured observation provides a description of the behaviour observed.

PART 3 INTERVIEWS

Interviews are one of the main research methods used by sociologists. They usually involve two people – the interviewer and the interviewee or participant. They can take place in a variety of contexts – the interviewer's office, the participant's home or place of work, on the telephone or online. They can be personal and face-to-face or, at the other extreme, online by email where those involved never speak to or see each other.

In one type of interview the questions are pre-set and the interviewer reads them out. Participants are given little chance to develop their answers. They usually respond with one word, one phrase or one sentence, then the interviewer moves on to the next question. At the other extreme interviews are more like conversations. Participants are allowed to answer in their own time and in their own way. They are encouraged to develop their answers and take the interview into areas they choose.

This part looks at various types of interviews. It examines the kinds of data each type produces. It assesses the advantages and disadvantages of each type.

Structured interviews

Structured interviews are simply questionnaires – lists of questions – which are read to the participant by the interviewer. The same questions are read in the same order to all participants. The questions are usually simple and straightforward. For example, 'How old are you?' 'What is your occupation?' 'Which party did you vote for in the last general election?'

The questions are usually designed to produce short answers which do not require development or explanation.

Advantages of structured interviews

Quantifiable data It is relatively easy to quantify – put into numbers – the responses to structured interviews. For example, 52 per cent stated that they voted to leave the European Union. Questions can be structured to provide yes/no answers or choices between a set of alternatives. For example, 'How often do you attend a place of worship? Once a week. Once a month. Once a year. Never.' Again, the responses are easy to quantify. For example, 12 per cent stated once a month.

151

Comparable data Structured interviews are more likely to produce data which can be directly compared. All participants are asked exactly the same questions so their answers are not affected by possible differences in the wording of questions. As a result, structured interviews are more reliable than other types of interview. Different researchers are likely to get the same results from the same participants as they are asking the same questions.

Time and money Structured interviews are usually faster and cost less than other types of interview.

Less bias Compared to other types of interview, practically all the interviewer has to do is read out the questions and record the answers. Because of this there is less chance of **interviewer bias** – of the participant's answers being influenced by the interviewer – for example, by the interviewer's age, gender, ethnicity and manner.

Disadvantages of structured interviews

Limited responses Limitations are often placed on participants' responses as in pre-set yes/no answers and choosing between given alternatives. Participants have little or no opportunity to discuss or qualify their answers.

Interviewers' priorities Interviewers have set the questions based on their priorities and concerns. In this respect they have imposed on the participant what they see as important. Participants have no opportunity to introduce or develop issues which reflect their concerns.

Semi-structured interviews

Each semi-structured interview usually has the same set of questions which are read out to the participant. In this respect semi-structured interviews have some of the advantages of the structured interviews. In addition, a semi-structured interview allows the interviewer to 'probe' – to jog participants' memories and to ask them to develop, clarify, spell out and give examples of particular points. This can add depth and detail to the answers.

However, this gain is accompanied by a loss of standardisation and comparability. Although the basic questions are pre-set, probes are not, which results in non-standard interviews. This means that each interview is somewhat different. As a result, the data are not directly comparable since, to some extent, participants are responding to different questions.

Unstructured interviews

Unstructured interviews are more like a conversation. They are more informal, open-ended, flexible and free-flowing. Some questions may be pre-set as researchers usually have certain topics they wish to cover. The setting tends to be more informal and the atmosphere often more relaxed – for example, fireside armchairs and a cup of coffee.

Advantages of unstructured interviews

Participant direction An unstructured interview offers greater opportunity for participants to take control, to define priorities and to direct the interview into areas which they see as interesting and significant. In this way, they have a greater chance to express their own viewpoints. And this can lead to new and important insights for the researcher.

Meanings Many researchers see unstructured interviews as particularly suitable for discovering meanings. They give participants the opportunity to express how they feel about a range of issues. Meanings are complex. A skilled interviewer can help and encourage participants to spell out this complexity. For example, what does religion mean to the participant? The pre-set questions in a structured interview are unlikely to capture the shades of meaning associated with religion.

Validity and depth If participants see the freedom of an unstructured interview as a means of expressing themselves in their own way they are more likely to open up and say what they really mean. They are therefore more likely to provide valid data and richer and more colourful data.

Sensitive groups Members of sensitive groups are less likely to provide information for researchers. They might be suspicious of outsiders, hostile towards them, afraid of them or simply uncomfortable in their presence. An unstructured interview can diminish these feelings as it provides an opportunity for understanding and trust to develop between interviewer and participant. This can be seen from the following example. Postal questionnaires were used in London to find out why people did not apply for welfare benefits to which they were entitled. The response rate was very low, due partly to fear and suspicion, a reaction often found amongst the frail and the elderly. Research indicated that a one-to-one unstructured interview was the most effective way of gaining information, in large part because interviewers were able to put participants' minds at rest (Fielding, 1993).

Sensitive topics Unstructured interviews are also seen as particularly suitable for sensitive topics. Respondents may be more likely to discuss sensitive and painful experiences if they feel that the interviewer is sympathetic and understanding. Unstructured interviews provide the opportunity for developing this kind of relationship. Joan Smith's (1998) study about the family background of homeless young people produced detailed and in-depth information using unstructured interviews.

Disadvantages of unstructured interviews

Interviewer bias Unstructured interviews are interaction situations in which a relationship develops between the interviewer and participant. This relationship can affect the development of the interview. In particular, it can lead to **interviewer bias**. This is the effect the interviewer has on the participant's responses. To some extent, this bias is unavoidable. Interviewers are people with social characteristics – they have a nationality, ethnicity, gender, social class and so on. They also have particular personalities – they may be shy or outgoing, caring or uncaring, aggressive or unaggressive.

These social and psychological characteristics will be perceived in certain ways by participants and will have some effect on their responses.

A number of studies have examined the effect of the social characteristics of interviewers. J. Allen Williams Jr (1971) claims that the greater the status difference between interviewer and participant, the less likely participants are to express their true feelings. He found that African Americans in the 1960s were more likely to say they approved of civil rights demonstrations if the interviewer was Black rather than White.

Social desirability effect In general, people like to present themselves in a favourable light. This can result in participants emphasising socially desirable aspects of their behaviour and attitudes in the presence of interviewers. For example, a survey based on interviews found that 35 per cent of Episcopalians in the USA said that they had been to church in the last seven days. Yet figures from the churches showed that only 16 per cent actually did so. Participants tended to exaggerate the frequency of their church attendance in order to appear upright and respectable in the eyes of the interviewer (Bruce, 1995).

Activity

In a study of business organisations, Martin Parker (2000) found that different participants saw him in different ways.

1. How did each participant see Martin Parker and how might this affect their answers?

2. How might Martin's age and dress affect the participants' responses?

The social desirability effect can reduce the validity of interview data, particularly in unstructured interviews where participants have a relatively close relationship with the interviewer.

Comparability Unstructured interviews can develop in all sorts of directions. As a result, data from one interview to the next can vary considerably. This makes comparisons between data from different interviews difficult. It also means that generalisations should be treated with caution.

The interview process

Interviewers are often trained in how to conduct effective interviews and how to avoid pitfalls.

Non-directive interviewing The standard advice is to be **non-directive**, to avoid leading respondents and to allow them to express themselves in their own way. The idea is to minimise interviewer bias. It is important to establish **rapport** – a friendly and understanding relationship – while at the same time appearing sensible and businesslike. Interviewers should not be too familiar. They must maintain a certain distance or respondents will be unduly influenced. Probing – digging a little deeper with further questions – is allowed, in order to get participants to clarify or develop their answers, but it must be used with care as it can easily result in leading questions – questions which direct the participant to a certain answer (Fielding, 1993).

Active approaches Non-directive interviewing can result in an artificial situation which makes respondents feel uneasy. Some sociologists have found that non-directive approaches can be frustrating for both parties. Platt (1976) notes that participants 'would have liked guidance on what I regarded as relevant, but I was anxious not to mould the data to my preconceptions by giving them any. This produced a few tortured interviews in which an unhappy participant spoke at length on aspects of the research which it was probably clear were not of interest to me.'

There is some evidence that more direct and aggressive interviewing techniques can produce more valid data. In particular, participants might respond by putting social desirability aside and giving more honest answers. Howard Becker (1971) used this approach with some success in his interviews with Chicago schoolteachers. He found that many of the teachers were prejudiced against working-class and ethnic minority pupils, information they would

not normally volunteer. However, by adopting an aggressive approach Becker states, 'I coerced many interviewees into being considerably more frank than they had originally intended'.

Listening Advice about how to conduct an interview is usually about asking questions. However, Edwards and Holland (2013) make the following points with particular reference to unstructured interviewing.

It's not just about asking questions. The participant is central. Listening to the participant 'is a crucial skill'. You must be 'attuned, alert and attentive to what the interviewee is telling you or not even telling you'. This is the key. 'It is the foundation of being able to respond to what the interviewee is saying, and being able to probe and follow up their answers to your questions effectively and sensitively.'

Focus groups

Focus groups are a way of collecting data from a group of people. They are sometimes called group interviews. However, they are usually more like discussions. Group members are asked to talk amongst themselves. They are guided by a **moderator** who asks them to focus on particular topics. Focus groups usually have between four and 10 members.

Activity

Five focus groups each made up of four boys or men of similar ages were asked to discuss body image, diet and exercise. According to the researchers, they were more likely to disclose sensitive, personal feelings in a small group of people like themselves rather than in a one-to-one interview situation (Grogan and Richards, 2002).

How might the similarities of the focus group members help them to disclose sensitive and personal feelings?

Often focus group members have certain things in common – for example, similarities of age, gender, experience or expertise. These similarities can encourage discussion and interest and minimise the intervention of the moderator (Morgan, 2006).

Group interaction The main characteristic of a focus group is that it involves interaction between the participants. Compared to a one-to-one interview, this can produce different kinds of data. Participants in a focus group discuss and debate, agree and disagree. This encourages group members to really think about their views. Focus groups can also show how people make sense of things collectively and develop a shared viewpoint.

Sensitive topics Some researchers argue that focus groups are not suitable for sensitive topics as participants might find the discussion too personal and embarrassing. However, this did not stop an effective discussion on body image between the young men in the picture. And focus groups have been successfully used to study sensitive topics such as homelessness and sexual abuse of young women. In such cases, focus groups can provide social support and empowerment for vulnerable participants with shared experiences (Edwards and Holland, 2013).

Despite these advantages, focus groups have their limitations. These include the following:

> Researchers have less control than in standard interviews.

> Despite trying to minimise their intervention, the moderator has to sometimes get involved so things run smoothly – for example, to prevent one member of the group from dominating the discussion.

> It is not clear to what extent agreement on particular views reflects group pressure rather than the actual beliefs of all participants.

> The extent to which social desirability affects the views expressed in the group context is not always clear.

Email interviews

This section looks at email interviews in which the questions and answers are typed. Lucy Gibson (2010) gives the following description of her study based on email interviews with 55 music fans, aged 30 plus. Although lacking the spontaneity of face-to-face interviews, her research produced 'rich and complex accounts [of participants'] music experiences and memories'. The interviewees really enjoyed writing their own accounts. The pace was slow and interviews could stretch over months. However, it gave the participants time to think about their responses and 'construct complex and carefully crafted stories' at times of their own choosing.

In practical terms, it reduced Lucy Gibson's travel time and costs to zero. Email interviews produced ready-made interview transcripts which saved considerable time transcribing audio recordings.

Advantages of email interviews

Compared to face-to-face interviews, email interviews have a number of advantages:

> **Relaxed setting** Participants may feel more relaxed in their own home and without the interviewer being present, especially if they are shy and lacking in confidence.

> **Considered answers** Participants can respond in their own time, consider their answers and not feel the need to reply immediately.

> **Impaired speech** Online interviews are particularly suitable for people with speech impediments. For example, Nicole Ison (2009) found email interviews useful in her study of young people with cerebral palsy, some of whom had speech impediments.

> **Sensitive issues** Some people find it easier to communicate in the privacy of their home in a written form about sensitive issues. For example, Shani Orgad (2005) in her book *Storytelling Online: Talking Breast Cancer on the Internet* found email interviews produced rich qualitative data.

> **Heartfelt statements** At times email interviews can produce heartfelt confessions and deep emotional outpourings which might not be expressed in face-to-face interviews.

> **Time and money** Email interviews are cost effective and efficient. There is no need for transcription (transferring it into a written form) as in a recorded verbal interview. Several interviews can be running at the same time. As with the participant, the researcher can communicate when it's convenient for them. Distance is no object. The interviews can be global.

155

Disadvantages of email interviews

Lack of immediacy Email interviews lack the immediacy of a face-to-face interview. The to-and-fro of social interaction can lead to a rapidly developing, unconsidered conversation which may produce new and fresh data.

Samples Email interviews are unlikely to be based on a cross-section of the population being investigated as low-income groups are less likely to have access to a computer.

Body language Body language and facial expressions are not available in text-based interviews. And emotions can be more difficult to convey without verbal communication.

Online focus groups

Online focus groups have some of the advantages of email interviews. However, they have an immediacy which email interviews lack as several participants and one or more moderators are online at the same time. This can be seen from the following activity.

The picture below shows an online focus group using conferencing software. The participants – young mothers and expectant mothers – are typing their contributions to the discussion in their own homes. The topic is parenting. The right-hand picture shows one of the moderators. Kerry (on screen) is a participant, Hen and Clare are moderators. As mothers with young children themselves, Hen and Clare found they could relate to the focus group and build rapport (O'Connor and Madge, 2001).

Positivism and interpretivism

Positivism In terms of the interviews they prefer, positivists and interpretivists are on opposite ends of the spectrum. Positivists prefer structured interviews. The responses they provide are easy to quantify, especially questions which require yes/no answers and choices between pre-set alternatives. Positivists see structured interviews as more reliable as every participant is asked exactly the same questions.

Interpretivism In contrast, interpretivists prefer unstructured interviews, in particular in-depth interviews which are designed to discover meanings. They give participants the freedom to express themselves in their own way. The qualitative data produced are seen as more likely to be valid than the data produced by structured interviews.

Activity – An online focus group

Question

Suggest reasons for the thoughts of the focus group participants.

Ethics and interviews

Openness and honesty are key ethical guidelines. The interviewer should state who they are, what the research is about and what they intend to do with the data. This is essential for informed consent (Allmark *et al.*, 2009).

Even when informed consent is given, participants cannot be sure where the interview is going. This is especially true of unstructured interviews which sometimes go into unanticipated areas. Participants should be told that they can end the interview at any time. This is particularly important when the interview covers sensitive areas such as bereavement or domestic violence. Ethical guidelines state that participants should be protected from emotional harm. At signs of stress and discomfort, the interviewer should ask if they wish to continue.

Ethical guidelines state that privacy and confidentiality are essential. It must be made clear to participants that their privacy will be protected, that they will remain anonymous, and that all information they provide will be confidential. This can raise problems. If, for example, the interviewee states that they intend to commit a crime, should this be reported to the police? This is a difficult decision for the interviewer.

As part of their training, interviewers are advised not to take sides. However, some feminist interviewers reject the idea of a 'neutral interviewer'. They argue that women should be interviewed by women, that the interviewer should express sympathy and understanding based on shared experience and, where possible, be on the same side as the interviewee.

Focus groups raise particular ethical problems. The moderator should make sure that all participants have a chance to be heard. They should, if possible, make sure that all questions are suitable for a group setting and won't be embarrassing or hurtful. Focus groups raise particular problems for confidentiality and privacy. Everything that is said is shared. The moderator can request, but not ensure, that identities and what is said remain within the group.

Applying the standard ethical guidelines to online interviews has particular problems. For example, privacy and confidentiality cannot be guaranteed in cyberspace. Alan Bryman (2012) reaches the following conclusion. The 'venues' he refers to include personal email sites, online chat rooms, message boards, blogs and discussion groups where the public and the private are sometimes blurred. 'The more the venue is acknowledged to be public, the less obligation there is on the researcher to protect anonymity of individuals using the venue, or to seek their informed consent.'

Advantages and disadvantages of interviews

Structured interviews

Advantages

» Quantifiable data.

» Comparable data.

» Usually faster and less costly than other types of interviews.

» Less chance of interviewer bias and social desirability effects.

» More reliable.

Disadvantages

» Allow only limited responses.

» Impose researcher's concerns and priorities on participants.

Semi-structured interviews

Advantages

» Some of the same advantages as structured interviews.

» In addition, allows interviewer to clarify and probe and the participant to develop their responses.

» Compared to structured interviews, can add depth and detail.

Disadvantages

» Non-standard interviews.

» As a result the data are not directly comparable.

Unstructured interviews

Advantages

» Greater involvement of participants.

» Allows them more freedom to express themselves and to direct the interview into areas they see as important.

» More likely to reveal meanings and to produce valid data.

» Can be more suitable for sensitive individuals and sensitive topics.

Disadvantages

> Interviewer bias and social desirability effects more likely.

> Comparable data less likely.

Focus group interviews

Advantages

> Shows how people make sense of things and develop a shared viewpoint in a group context.

> When focus group members have experiences in common this can encourage discussion.

> In particular, sensitive experiences in common can sometimes lead to rich and valid data.

Disadvantages

> Social desirability effects may be strong in a group context.

> Not clear whether agreement between the participants reflects shared beliefs or group pressure.

Email interviews

Advantages

> Relaxed setting at home.

> Time to provide considered answers.

> Suitable for people with speech difficulties.

> Can be suitable for sensitive issues.

> Inexpensive and efficient.

Disadvantages

> Lack of immediacy.

> Representative samples unlikely.

> No body language or verbal emotional expression.

Key terms

Structured interview A questionnaire which is read out and filled in by the interviewer.

Semi-structured interview Similar to a structured interview, but the interviewer is allowed to probe with additional questions.

Unstructured interview Few, if any, pre-set questions, though researchers usually have certain topics they wish to cover.

Focus groups A group discussion guided by a moderator.

Moderator An interviewer who guides focus group discussions.

Interviewer bias The effect that the interviewer has on the participant's answers.

Social desirability effect The desire of the interview participant to reflect in their responses what is generally considered to be the right way to behave.

Non-directive interviewing An interviewing technique which seeks to avoid leading participants to answer in particular ways.

Rapport A friendly, trusting and understanding relationship.

Summary

1. There are various types of interviews, each with their advantages and disadvantages.

2. To a greater or lesser extent, all interviews are influenced by interviewer bias and social desirability effects.

3. Positivists prefer the quantitative data produced by structured interviews

4. Interpretivists prefer the qualitative data produced by unstructured interviews

5. The standard advice to interviewers is to avoid direction and develop rapport. However, on occasion, more active approaches may produce better results. Interviewers are advised that listening is a 'crucial skill'.

6. As with other research methods, ethical guidelines for interview participants include informed consent, confidentiality, privacy and protection from harm.

PART 4 SOCIAL SURVEYS AND QUESTIONNAIRES

Contents

Presidential elections, general elections and referendums in democratic societies are preceded by survey after survey asking people how they intend to vote. Sometimes these surveys get it right, sometimes they are dramatically wrong. Donald Trump defeated Hillary Clinton in the US presidential election despite survey predictions. And in the EU referendum in the UK, the majority voted to leave, contradicting the results of national voting intention surveys.

Surveys are a major part of market research. Companies survey existing and potential customers about their products and services. Many companies use online surveys asking customers to comment on the product they have bought and its packaging and delivery.

Sociological surveys cover a wide range of subjects from political views and religious beliefs to newspaper readership and television viewing. This part looks at social surveys conducted by sociologists. It examines the strengths and limitations of survey research and asks: Can sociologists do any better than voting intention surveys?

Social surveys are based on samples of the group of people to be investigated. A sample may be fairly general – for example, drawn from the UK population over 18. Or it may be more specific – for example, women from the UK over the age of 65. This part examines various methods of sampling. It asks whether they provide samples which are representative of the group in the wider society.

Questionnaires are the main method used to collect data in survey research. This part looks at the way questionnaires are constructed, the type of data they provide, and the quality of that data.

3.4.1 Social surveys

A **social survey** involves the systematic collection of the same type of data from a fairly large number of people. Most surveys use questionnaires to collect the data. A questionnaire is a list of written questions.

Questionnaires can be given by an interviewer – read out to the participant with the answers recorded by the interviewer. This is a **structured interview**. Or they can be given to participants to complete themselves. This is a **self-completion questionnaire**. Here is an example of a social survey.

The British Social Attitudes survey

Each year since 1983, the British Social Attitudes survey asks around 3000 people what it's like to live in Britain and what they think about how the country is run. Data come from two sources – a structured interview and a self-completion questionnaire.

The interviewer visits participants in their homes and reads out questions from the questionnaire and records the answers. This usually takes just over an hour. In addition, the interviewer leaves them with a self-completion questionnaire and asks them to record their answers by ticking boxes. This makes their responses easy to quantify and count as the following data from the 2015 survey indicate:

- 60 per cent of participants see themselves as working class.

- 31 per cent disagree with the statement that 'the government should spend more money on welfare benefits for the poor'.

- 37 per cent of workers experience stress 'always' or 'often'.

- 45 per cent say they are in favour of changing the electoral system to be fairer to smaller parties. (*British Social Attitudes 33,* 2016).

Participants in the survey are a random sample of adults over 18. The survey is designed to provide a **representative sample** – a sample which represents the population as a whole (*British Social Attitudes 33, Technical details*, 2016).

Key terms

Social survey The systematic collection of the same type of data from a relatively large number of people.

Structured interview A questionnaire read out by the interviewer who also records the answers.

Self-completion questionnaire A questionnaire completed by the research participant.

Summary

A social survey is usually based on presenting participants with the same questions in the form of a structured interview or a self-completion questionnaire.

3.4.2 Sampling

Nearly all social surveys are based on a **sample** of the population to be investigated. 'Population' is the term given to everybody in the group to be studied. The population might be adult males, female pensioners,

manual workers, 16–19-year-old students, parents with dependent children and so on. A sample is a selection of part of the population. Samples are necessary because researchers rarely have the time and money to study everybody in the particular population to be investigated.

Most researchers aim to select a sample which is representative of the population to be studied. This means that the sample should have the same characteristics as the population as a whole. Thus, if a researcher is studying the attitudes of British women, the sample should *not* consist of 1000 nuns, or 1000 women over 80 or 1000 divorced women, since such groups are hardly representative of British women.

With a representative sample, **generalisations** are more likely to be true – findings from the sample are more likely to be applicable to the research population as a whole.

Sample design and composition

Sampling unit Who should be included in a sample? In many cases it is fairly easy to define a

Activity

The researcher wants a representative sample of families with dependent children.

1. Why would the researcher want a representative sample?

2. How would the information in the picture help him to obtain one?

160

sampling unit – that is a member of the population to be studied. Dentists, males between 30 and 40 years of age, females who own their own businesses, people with one or more A-levels, can be defined without too many problems. However, other groups are not so easy – how would you define a semi-skilled manual worker or a person living in poverty?

Sampling frame Once the research population has been defined, the sample is selected from a **sampling frame** – a list of members of the population to be studied. In some cases, an appropriate sampling frame is readily available – for example, the Electoral Register (a list of people registered to vote) for a study of voting behaviour. In other cases, researchers may have to rely on listings, such as the Postcode Address Finder (a list of addresses complied by the Post Office – used by the British Social Attitudes survey) or telephone directories, which may or may not be suitable for their purposes. And all listings have drawbacks – not everyone is included, they are often out of date, certain groups are likely to be under-represented – for example, the poor are less likely to appear in telephone directories, and younger people on Electoral Registers as they are less likely to have registered to vote.

The design and composition of the sample will partly depend on the type of sample used. Some of the more common types are outlined below.

Types of sample

Random samples A **random sample** gives every member of the sampling frame an equal chance of being selected. Every name is given a number and then a list of random numbers is used to select a sample. This avoids bias in selection. It prevents the researcher from selecting a sample which provides a result which fits their theory, supports their hypothesis, that gives them what they expect and what they hope to find.

Random samples are not necessarily representative. For example, if the sample is intended to represent college students, it might include mostly female students. This can happen when the sample is randomly drawn even though females might make up only half the student population.

Stratified random sampling offers a possible solution to the problem of representativeness. The sample frame is divided into groups or **strata** which reflect the general population – for example age, gender, ethnicity and class groups. For instance, if the sample frame is based on women in the UK, the researcher might divide the women into ethnic and class groups and then draw a random sample from each of these groups.

This will be more likely to provide a representative sample of women. In practice, researchers will add strata they think are important to their research.

The annual Crime Survey for England and Wales provides an example of a stratified random sample. It is a nationally representative sample of around 35 000 adults and 3 000 children aged 10 to 15. The strata are age, gender, and region 'to ensure the sample reflects the profile of the general population' (*Crime in England and Wales*, ONS, 2017).

Quota samples A market researcher stands on a street corner looking for people to fill her quota. She has to find 20 women between the ages of 30 and 45 to answer a questionnaire on magazine readership. She fills her quota with the first 20 women passing by who 1) fit the required age group and 2) agree to answer her questions. The sample selection is not random – it is not randomly selected from a sampling frame. The researcher simply fills their quota from the first available bodies. This method is known as **quota sampling**. It is a type of stratified sampling in which the selection of people within each stratum is not random.

Quota sampling is often used for opinion polls and market research. It has its advantages – it is simpler, quicker and cheaper than stratified random sampling. However, it is less likely to produce a sample which

Activity

Selecting people for a quota sample.

With some reference to the picture, suggest why quota sampling is unlikely to produce a sample which is representative of the research population.

is representative of the research population. For example, where and when a quota is filled can make significant differences to the sample. Stopping people on the street during weekday working hours would exclude many people in paid employment. And the fact that researchers can choose who they interview can bias the sample still further. Faced with two young men one 'smart' and 'pleasant' looking, the other just the opposite, researchers would probably choose the former. In quota sampling, people in the same stratum do not have an equal chance of being selected.

Snowball samples Sometimes researchers have great difficulty obtaining people for their samples. First, lists for a sampling frame might not be available. Second, the research population might be so small that normal sampling methods would not supply the numbers needed. Third, members of the research population might not wish to be identified. Think of the problems in locating the following and getting them to form part of a sample: burglars, sex workers, and members of Masonic lodges. One possibility is to use a network of like-minded or like situated individuals. This is the basis of **snowball sampling**, so-called because if its similarity to rolling a snowball.

Snowballing works like this. The researcher finds someone who fits the bill. They are asked to find another person who fits and so on. In this way a network of members of the research population is built up and this forms the basis for the sample. In addition, if the researcher has established a good relationship with the first member of the sample, then they can vouch for the researcher with their friends and acquaintances.

Snowballing has the obvious advantage of creating a sampling frame when other methods have failed. However, it is unlikely to provide a representative sample since it is not random and relies on personal contacts and recommendations.

Volunteer samples As the name suggests, **volunteer samples** are made up of people who volunteer to take part in the research.

Advertisements, leaflets, posters, radio or TV broadcasts, newspapers or magazine articles, social media and emails announce the research and request volunteers for the sample. Annette Lawson (1988) wrote a newspaper article about her study of adultery. She used the article to obtain a volunteer sample by asking readers who had experienced

Activity

Deciding whether or not to take part in the survey.

With reference to the picture, why might volunteer samples be unrepresentative?

adultery to complete a questionnaire. 579 readers responded to her request.

Volunteer samples have the advantage that those who take part are likely to be interested in the topic and keen to participate. However, volunteer samples are unlikely to be representative because the sample members select themselves. Those who volunteer may have a particular reason for doing so – they may have a grievance or a strongly held point of view to express (Seale, 2012).

Online surveys and volunteer samples

Online surveys are questionnaires self-completed online. They are usually considerably cheaper and quicker than offline surveys. Samples are often larger and cover a wider geographical area.

There are two main types of online surveys. **Web surveys** direct the respondent to a website and **email surveys** send an email to the respondent. Web surveys are used to study larger groups. Here is an example of a web survey.

The Global Drug Survey

The Global Drug Survey is an annual web survey of drug users. The 2016 survey had over 100 000 respondents from over 50 countries. In the UK the survey was promoted online by *The Guardian* newspaper and *Mixmag*, which describes itself as 'The World's Biggest Dance Music and Clubbing Magazine'.

Who took part? The following is a summary of some of the characteristics of those who took part in the 2016 survey:

- Most came from Europe. Germany had the highest number, 31 per cent. The UK had 6 per cent.

- Two-thirds were male with an average age of 28.7 years.

- Just over one-third had a degree, 40 per cent were in full or part-time education and two-thirds in paid employment.

- 89 per cent were White.

- One-third lived with their partners, a quarter with their parents.

- 75 per cent were from urban areas.

- 62 per cent went clubbing at least every three months.

(*Global Drug Survey: Findings*, 2016)

The sample The sample is a volunteer sample. More particularly, it is a 'non-random opportunistic sample' which means it is a self-selected sample of people who are readily available at the time and choose to participate. The survey is available for only six weeks.

The survey is not based on a representative sample. It is not possible to find out how similar respondents are to other people who came across the survey and chose not to participate, or to those who didn't even come across the survey in the first place. But, since most participants were aged 18–30, this matches the age profile of the largest group of drug users in the UK.

However, the survey excludes or under-represents some groups with a high level of drug use – for example, the homeless, those in prison and those without online access. And it under-represents low-income groups and less well-educated groups (*Global Drug Survey: Methodology*, 2014).

Web surveys

Advantages

- Respondents can clearly see that they will remain anonymous. This is important for many people, especially when the topic is sensitive and/or the activity they are reporting taking part in is illegal.

- Web surveys are quicker and cheaper to administer than offline questionnaire-based surveys. When completed they can be downloaded immediately rather than waiting for postal questionnaires to arrive, or researchers to pick up self-completed questionnaires, or spending time reading out questionnaires in the form of structured interviews. When the findings of the Global Drug Study are released they are about two months old. The results of most offline national household surveys are at least 12 months out of date when they are released (*Global Drug Survey: Methodology*, 2014).

Disadvantages

- It is not possible to tell whether those who respond are representative of the population being studied. As a result, it is not possible to generalise from a web survey.

- Those who respond may have particular reasons for participating in the survey, reasons which are not known to the researcher.

- As a result, there may be important differences between those who choose to respond and those who choose not to respond.

Activity

Accepting and rejecting a request to take part in a survey on illegal drug use. Those in the left-hand picture who decided to take part have just read the invitation in Mixmag *and* The Guardian *to participate in the* Global Drug Survey.

Why might people be more likely to take part in a web survey than a telephone survey or a structured interview survey when the subject is illegal and/or sensitive?

Key terms

Sample A selection from the research population.

Sampling unit A member of the research population.

Sampling frame A list of members of the research population.

Random sample A sample which gives every member of the sampling frame an equal chance of being selected.

Stratified random sample A sample which attempts to reflect particular characteristics of the research population. The population is divided into strata in terms of age, gender etc., and the sample is randomly drawn from each stratum.

Quota sample A stratified sample in which selection from the strata is not random.

Snowball sample Members of the sample select each other.

Volunteer sample Members of the sample are self-selected.

Web survey Questionnaire answered on the researcher's website.

Email survey Questionnaire sent by email to the respondent.

Summary

1. Social surveys are based on samples of the population to be investigated.

2. Ideally samples should be representative – they should represent the larger group in the wider society.

3. With a representative sample, generalisations are more likely to be correct.

4. Whatever type of sample is used, there is no guarantee that it will be representative.

5. There is no way to tell whether those who respond to a web survey provide a representative sample of the population being studied.

3.4.3 Questionnaires

Questionnaires are the main method for gathering data in social surveys. They are usually designed to produce data that can be easily quantified.

Types of questions

There are two main types of questions – closed questions and open-ended questions or open questions.

Closed questions In closed questions, the range of responses is fixed by the researcher. The respondent has to select their answer from two or more given alternatives. Here is a very simple closed question which offers two possible answers. This type of question is easily quantified.

Do you believe in God? ☐ Yes
 ☐ No

Here is a more complex closed question in which the respondent has to select the answer which best fits their beliefs from six alternatives. It is taken from the *British Social Attitudes Survey*.

Again, the answers to this question are easy to quantify. The first column of figures shows the percentage of respondents who chose each alternative. The second column shows the actual number of respondents who chose each alternative.

Closed questions are the simplest way to produce numerical data. These data are suitable for statistical analysis. They make it possible to discover whether or not there is a **correlation** – a statistical link – between two or more variables or factors, for example, between educational attainment and social class.

Table 3.4.1 Belief in God

Year of research	2008	
I don't believe in God.	18%	356
I don't know if God exists and there is no way to find out.	19%	368
I don't believe in a personal God but I do believe in some kind of higher power.	14%	282
I believe in God some of the time but not at others.	13%	255
I have doubts but I feel that I do believe in God.	18%	357
I know God really exists and I have no doubts about it.	17%	332
Not answered	1%	24
Total		1974

Source: NatCen's *British Social Attitudes* survey, 2016.

Open questions ask respondents to answer questions in their own words. Several lines are left blank on the questionnaire for the respondent to write in their answer. Open questions give the respondent more freedom to answer questions in their own way.

Most researchers see closed questions as suitable for simple, factual information such as age, gender and income level. Open questions are usually seen as more suitable for data on meanings and beliefs where

Activity

What do you think about abortion?
☐ Good
☐ Bad
☐ No opinion

FAR TOO COMPLICATED TO ANSWER BY TICKING A BOX.

Any reasonable person is against keeping animals locked up in zoos.

Do you agree?

THEY'RE LEADING ME TO SAY YES.

Do you drink coffee often?

IS 16 CUPS A DAY OFTEN?

Questions to avoid when constructing a questionnaire.

What's wrong with each of these questions?

respondents are required to express how they feel. An open question allows them to do this in their own way.

Constructing a questionnaire

Most questionnaires are based on the idea that everybody is answering exactly the same questions. They are therefore all responding to the same things. Any differences in their answers should therefore indicate real differences between the respondents.

The questions must mean the same thing to all the respondents so that their answers can be directly compared. The researcher must make sure that the questions are clear and unambiguous. Words and phrases should be simple and straightforward.

Operationalisation and coding

Operationalisation Questionnaires are designed to measure things. And to do this, those 'things' must be **operationalised** – put into a form which can be measured. For example, how can the strength of religious belief be measured?

One way of operationalising religious belief is shown by the *British Social Attitudes* survey, which asks people to select one of six alternatives which go from 'I don't believe in God' to 'I know God really exists and I have no doubts about it'. Another way is to ask people about religious behaviour. For example, do they attend a place of worship and, if so, how often.

However, it is often difficult to assess whether operational definitions provide valid measurements. For example, does regular attendance at a place of worship indicate strong religious beliefs? It may do but there are non-religious reasons from attending a place of worship – to indicate respectability, to sing in a choir, because your friends do. And people who have strong religious beliefs do not necessarily attend a place of worship.

Coding answers Answers to questions are **coded**. This means they are classified into various categories. Answers to closed questions are pre-coded. For example, possible answers to the Belief in God questionnaire in Table 3.4.1 are pre-coded into six categories. The researcher simply has to count the number of people who choose each category. Quantifying the data is easy.

Open questions are coded after the answer has been given. It is sometimes difficult to code and quantify a written answer. Consider the following.

Question	Do you believe in God? Give reasons for your answer.
Answer	It depends what you mean by God. Do you mean a God that just exists apart from this world? Or, do you mean a God that controls what happens in this world? Sometimes, I think I believe in the first type of God.

This answer is difficult to code. Researchers usually have a list of categories in terms of which written answers are coded. Sometimes, however, written answers don't fit neatly into any of the categories provided.

Response rates

The **response rate** is the percentage of the sample that participates in the research. For example, if half the sample completes a questionnaire, then the response rate is 50 per cent. For instance, the response rate for the 2016 *Crime Survey for England and Wales* was 72 per cent for adults and 66 per cent for children aged 10 to 15 years (*Crime in England and Wales*, 2017). Here is the response rate for the 2015 *British Social Attitudes* survey.

Table 3.4.2 Response rate British Social Attitudes, 2015

	Number	Response rate
Sample size	8428	
Interview completed	4328	51%
Questionnaire completed	3670	43%

Source: Adapted from *British Social Attitudes 33, Technical details*, 2016.

The table shows that interviewers had a response rate of 51 per cent and the self-completion questionnaire a response rate of 43 per cent. A total of 658 respondents (15 per cent of those interviewed) did not return their self-completion questionnaire. Response rates vary widely. For example, Shere Hite's *The Hite Report on the Family* (1994) based on questionnaires in magazines had a mere 3 per cent response rate.

A low response rate may result in an unrepresentative sample. Those who do not respond may differ in important respects from those who do – for example, in terms of age, gender, ethnicity and social class.

Reasons for non-response

There are many reasons for non-response. In the case of surveys based on structured interviews, reasons for non-response include the following:

1. Failure to make contact because people have moved, are on holiday, in prison, working away from home or simply out when the researcher tries to get in touch.

2. Contact is made, but the interview cannot be conducted because the person is ill, deaf, experiencing some personal tragedy or can't speak English.

3. The person refuses to participate. Reasons may include no time, no interest, finds the subject too upsetting, sees no point in the research, is suspicious of, dislikes, or is embarrassed by the researcher.

Reasons for not responding to self-completion questionnaires are mainly no time, no interest, and it's easy to bin the questionnaire with little or no comeback.

In general, surveys based on structured interviews have a higher response rate than surveys based on self-completion questionnaires. And paper self-completion questionnaires usually have a higher completion rate than online questionnaires (Bryman, 2012).

Positivism and interpretivism

Positivism Social surveys and questionnaires fit straight into the positivist framework for sociological research. Surveys based on representative samples are seen to provide data for generalisations about behaviour in the wider society. Operationalising concepts puts them into a form which can be measured. Pre-coded questions and coding open-ended questions produce quantitative data. This makes it possible to use statistical tests to discover any correlations – possible links – between the data. And correlations might indicate cause and effect relationships.

Surveys based on questionnaires are seen as reliable because the same questionnaire can be given to all the participants so their answers can be directly compared. And the survey can be replicated – repeated under the same conditions – using the same questionnaire and a similar sample.

Interpretivism Interpretivists question the validity of responses to questionnaires. They argue that operationalising concepts has little chance of discovering the meanings which direct action. It simply imposes the researchers' interpretations on the meanings they intend to discover. Translating operationalised concepts into questions makes matters worse. The questions reflect the researchers' concerns and priorities rather than those of the participants. Coding further distorts social reality. Pre-coded questions give participants little opportunity to express themselves and to say exactly what they mean. And coding answers to open-ended questions further imposes the researchers' interpretations on the participants' answers. From an interpretivist view, this whole process takes the researcher further and further away from the meanings participants use to direct their actions.

Ethics, questionnaires and social surveys

In order to decide whether or not to complete a questionnaire, people should be given the information necessary for informed consent. This should include who the researcher is, the purpose of the research and how and why they have been selected to participate. It must be made clear that they are giving their consent voluntarily, that they can withdraw at any time and that they can decide not to answer particular questions. They must be told that their privacy and confidentiality will be respected – that they cannot be identified from the presentation or publication of the data they provide.

Questionnaires ask questions. It is important to try to make sure that the questions won't upset or offend. And it is important that the questions are clear and unambiguous, that participants are able to understand the words and phrases used and that the instructions for completing the questionnaire are straightforward. This not only provides good data, it is also an ethical issue. If participants can't understand the questions, they might feel stupid, defensive or offended and this might affect their answers.

For this reason, a pilot study is recommended to sort out any problems with the questionnaire before the main survey (*The Research Ethics Guidebook*, 2017).

Advantages and disadvantages of social surveys and questionnaires

Advantages

- Social surveys using questionnaires can be a cost-effective way to collect large quantities of data from large numbers of people over a relatively short period of time.

167

> The results of a questionnaire survey can be fairly easy to quantify especially if closed questions are used.

> The data can be analysed quickly and efficiently especially with the use of computers.

> Surveys tend to be seen as a reliable method because they are fairly easy to replicate – repeat using the same questions and a similar sample.

Disadvantages

Some researchers argue that the data produced by questionnaire surveys lack validity for the following reasons:

> Respondents may interpret the questions in different ways.

> The questions might not be relevant to their lives.

> When designing questionnaires, researchers impose their concerns and priorities rather than reflecting those of the respondents.

> When concepts and beliefs are operationalised they don't always measure what they are supposed to measure.

> What people say in response to questionnaires may not reflect their behaviour in everyday life.

Key terms

Operationalise Translating concepts into a form which can be measured.

Coding Classifying answers into various categories.

Closed questions Questions in which the range of responses is fixed by the researcher.

Open-ended/open questions Questions which allow the respondent to answer in their own words.

Correlation A statistical link between two or more variables or factors.

Response rate The percentage of the sample that participates in the research.

Summary

1. Questionnaires are the main method for collecting data in social surveys.

2. In theory, questionnaires provide directly comparable data.

3. Closed questions are pre-coded. They produce data which are easy to quantify.

4. Answers to open questions can be difficult to code and quantify.

5. It is difficult to assess whether operational definitions provide valid measurements.

6. Positivists favour social surveys based on questionnaires producing quantitative data.

7. Interpretivists argue that the kind of data produced by questionnaires often lack validity.

PART 5 FURTHER RESEARCH METHODS

Contents

This part looks at three additional research methods – longitudinal studies, case studies and experiments. Longitudinal studies examine the same group of people over fairly long periods of time. Case studies focus on a particular instance of something, for example one individual's life. Experiments are set up to test whether something is true, for example whether there is a relationship between two or more things. This part describes and evaluates these three research methods.

3.5.1 Longitudinal studies

Many sociological studies are like a snapshot. They show what's happening at a particular time. But things change, situations change, people change. Longitudinal studies are concerned with change.

A **longitudinal study** looks at the same group of people over a fairly long period of time. It reveals trends and identifies both change and continuity – what stays the same.

This unit looks at a major longitudinal study, the National Child Development Study. It then considers the advantages and disadvantages of longitudinal studies. Given the importance of this kind of research, it asks: Why aren't there more longitudinal studies?

The National Child Development Study

This is one of the most famous longitudinal studies. It has followed the lives of over 17 000 people born in Britain during one week in 1958. Since the original survey in 1958 there have been eight other major surveys of the same group, the most recent at the time of writing was in 2013 when

members were aged 55. The next survey is planned for 2018 when they will be 60. However, as time goes on, some members of the original group cannot take part or decide not to take part in the survey.

The data are collected by questionnaires and interviews. Parents and teachers provided information on children and, from age 16, most of the data were provided by members of the sample themselves.

The National Child Development Study examines the physical, educational and social development of members of the survey. It reveals very important

Activity – Social class and life chances

1958 FATHER–LAWYER

1979 SON– UNIVERSITY DEGREE

1990 WELL–PAID JOB

2000 OWN HOUSE

2004 TRANSPORT

1958 FATHER– LABOURER

1979 SON–NO QUALIFICATIONS

1990 UNEMPLOYED

2000 RENTED FLAT

2004 TRANSPORT

Each row shows a person at different stages of their life. The top row shows a man born into and remaining in the upper-middle class. The bottom row shows a man born into and remaining in the lower-working class. The pictures illustrate the life chances of the two men – their chances of obtaining desirable outcomes and experiences and of avoiding undesirable outcomes and experiences.

Question

The National Child Development Study shows that the class people are born into increasingly shapes their life chances. How do the pictures illustrate this?

changes from 1958 to 2013. For example, it shows an enormous increase in living standards but a substantial rise in inequality. A comparison of those born in 1958 with a study of those born in 1970 shows that the income gap between top and bottom has steadily widened and people's life chances – their chances of good health, good educational qualifications and a good job have become increasingly shaped by their class of origin – the class into which they were born. Those born into poverty had poor outcomes in terms of health, education and the labour market. And the numbers living in poverty doubled between the late 1970s and early 1990s.

The survey also looks at changes in family life. It shows a decline in marriage, a rise in cohabitation, and an increase in divorce and separation. It traces the effects of divorce and separation on children throughout their lives – they do less well at school, in the labour market and are more likely to go through breakups in their own partnerships (Elliot and Vaitilingam, 2008; National Child Development Study, 2016).

Ethics and longitudinal studies

Apart from the standard ethical guidelines, such as informed consent and confidentiality, longitudinal studies raise particular concerns. Investigators will probably change at several points, which involves new relationships with participants. Circumstances may change and new issues arise. Participants may have separated from their partners, their partners may have died, they may be experiencing longstanding illness and, as they grow older, they may be unable to give informed consent. These are sensitive issues. Researchers need to be aware of such possibilities and be prepared to deal with the grief, stress and/or embarrassment that talking about them may cause.

Advantages and disadvantages of longitudinal studies

Advantages Longitudinal studies provide a picture of developments over time. By studying the same individuals, researchers can be sure that any changes in behaviour and attitudes are not simply due to changes in the makeup of the sample. And this is the

problem. The original sample always decreases in size as the survey moves from year to year.

Despite this, longitudinal studies can reveal important social changes. For example, the National Child Development Study revealed a significant widening of social inequality. These findings provide important data to inform government policy on inequality. Longitudinal studies avoid asking people to recall events from much earlier in their lives when memory might fail them. In this respect, the data are more likely to be valid.

Disadvantages The main problem faced by researchers is **sample attrition**, the reduction of the original sample. The National Child Development Study began in 1958 with 17 000. By 1991 the number of participants was down to 15 600, by 2004 to 11 700 and by 2013 to 9000. Reasons for this reduction include death, emigration, refusal to participate and failure to trace. The survey makes considerable efforts to maintain contact. They send birthday cards to those whose address is known and search telephone directories and electoral registers hoping to find missing participants (Elliot and Vaitilingam, 2008; National Child Development Study, 2016). Despite their efforts, samples inevitably grow smaller and probably less representative. A further disadvantage of longitudinal studies is cost. Few organisations can afford an investigation which may last for 20 years or more. Even a survey over a shorter period of time can be very expensive.

Key terms

Longitudinal study A study of the same group of people over time.

Sample attrition The reduction of the original sample when it is used again.

Summary

1. Longitudinal studies provide a picture of developments over a fairly long period of time.

2. They provide data for studying social change.

3. The data are more likely to be valid compared to relying on people's long-term memory.

4. Longitudinal studies are costly and have the problem of sample attrition.

3.5.2 Case studies and life histories

A **case study** is a detailed study of a particular instance of something – for example, a study of a particular individual or community. A **life history** is a case study of an individual, usually based on a series of in-depth interviews. This unit gives two examples of life histories – the life of an English burglar and the life of a Cheyenne Native American. Sociology has been defined as the study of people in groups. This unit asks why study an individual's life? It also looks at a case study of a community and asks why study a single community?

Life histories

Mike Maguire (2000) conducted a series of interviews to build a life history of a 'specialist country house burglar'. The burglar was serving a long prison sentence. Maguire got to know him and gained his trust and friendship. He prepared for Maguire's visits to prison by writing notes. Each interview covered a different period of his life. According to Maguire, the life history method allowed him to 'probe more deeply than one-off interviews'.

The American anthropologist Margot Liberty produced a life history of John Stands In Timber, one of the last Cheyenne Native Americans who had lived their traditional way of life. According to Liberty, 'John's narrative provides White readers with a rare insight into the history and culture of his people. [He] has given us the history of the Cheyennes as they themselves recall and interpret it. ... His kind of inside view will never be achieved again' (Stands In Timber and Liberty, 1967).

A community

Paul Heelas and Linda Woodhead (2005) used Kendal, a town of around 28 000 in the Lake District in northern England, for a detailed study of spirituality and religion. Kendal was small enough to investigate systematically, but large enough to have a range of spiritual and Christian activities.

Heelas and Woodhead found a decline in traditional Christianity with its emphasis on a God-on-high who directs people how to live their lives. This was matched by a rise in spirituality with a focus on inner feelings and a self-directed life which combined mind, body and spirit. There was an emphasis on spirituality in activities such as yoga and tai chi with meditation, spiritual awakening and spiritual cleansing.

Advantages and disadvantages of case studies

Advantages

Case studies have a number of advantages:

- ▶ By focusing on a particular case, they can provide a richer and more detailed picture than research based on large samples.

- ▶ This may result in new insights and fresh ideas.

- ▶ Case studies can provide useful information for a larger research project.

- ▶ There is a better chance of a questionnaire or interview being relevant and meaningful if it is based, at least in part, on a case study.

- ▶ They are a valuable warning to sweeping generalisations. A single case study can call into question the findings of a much larger study. It can provide data which might lead to the modification or rejection of a theory.

Disadvantages

Case studies have sometimes been criticised as limited and unrepresentative. Since they are one-off instances, they cannot be used as a basis for generalisation. However, as noted above, this can sometimes be a strength – it can question the results of a larger study.

Key terms

Case study A study of a particular instance of something.

Life history A case study of an individual's life.

Summary

1. Case studies can produce new insights.

2. They can produce data which question existing generalisations and theories.

3.5.3 Experiments

There are two types of experiments in which people are asked to participate – **laboratory experiments** and **field experiments**. A laboratory experiment usually takes place in a closed room, cut off from outside factors such as noise or passers-by. A field experiment usually takes place in normal, everyday surroundings such as the street or a workplace.

171

Sociologists don't often use experiments, especially not laboratory experiments. The main reason for this is that a laboratory is an abnormal situation and people may well be responding to this abnormality rather than the experiment itself. Also, experiments are contrived, they are created by the researcher. Sociologists are concerned with normal behaviour in real world situations.

Laboratory experiments

A laboratory experiment is a setting and a situation which is designed to test an **hypothesis** – an assumption or proposition about the relationship between two or more **variables**. Variables are things that can vary such as temperature, sound or light. In a laboratory experiment they can be held constant – kept the same – or manipulated – changed. Experiments are usually designed to see if one variable – the **independent variable** – has a causal effect on another variable – the **dependent variable**. The variables and results of laboratory experiments are usually quantified.

The main aspects of the experimental method can be illustrated by the following example. This experiment is designed to test the hypothesis that noise has an effect on memory. The hypothesis is stated in a way in which it can be tested – the louder the noise the more it will reduce the ability to remember. Every variable in the laboratory except the level of noise – the independent variable – is held constant throughout the experiment, for example the temperature and lighting remain the same. The participant is given a list of 20 random numbers, asked to memorise them within one minute and then to recall them. The experiment is repeated five times with the noise starting from nothing – silence – then steadily rising in measured units. If the participant recalls fewer and fewer numbers, then this may provide support for the hypothesis – that the louder the noise the more it will reduce the ability to remember.

If the results of the experiment show a **correlation** (a comparable change) between the independent variable – the level of noise – and the dependent variable – the amount of recall – then this may show that one causes the other. But correlation does not necessarily mean causation. However, the ability to control variables in the closed system of a laboratory does help the researcher to judge whether the correlation is causative or coincidental, as does the use of quantitative measurements. This allows the replication of the experiment so results can be directly compared.

Activity

If two things are correlated they may increase or decrease together, or when one increases then the other decreases. This may be due to one causing the other, to a third factor which causes both, or due to chance.

Select one of the above possibilities for each of the following correlations and give reasons for your choice.

1. In Copenhagen for the 12 years following World War Two the number of storks nesting in the city and the number of human babies born went up and down together.

2. There appears to be a link between yellow grass and the sale of cold drinks. The yellower the grass, the more cold drinks are sold.

Social class and 'unethical behaviour'

The unit on non-participant observation looked at a study of social class and driving behaviour by Paul Piff and his colleagues, (Piff *et al.*, 2012). The results suggested that upper-class drivers were more selfish and uncaring than those lower down the social scale. See pp. 149–151.

Paul Piff conducted a number of laboratory experiments to see if they produced similar results. In one experiment participants watched a die being rolled randomly five times on a computer screen. They were asked to add up the five rolls. They were told that the higher their scores, the greater their chance of winning a $50 prize. In fact, the rolls were not random – they always added up to 12. Those who reported a score higher than 12 were usually the upper-class participants. They lied and cheated, they were greedy. Their behaviour was 'unethical'.

In a second experiment, participants were presented with a jar of individually wrapped candies (sweets). They were told they could take some if they wanted and the rest would be given to children in a nearby laboratory. The upper-class participants took most candy – candy which would otherwise go to the children. Again they were more greedy and selfish and their behaviour was again described as 'unethical' (Piff *et al.*, 2012).

Evaluation

Laboratory experiments have been very successful in the natural sciences such as physics and chemistry. However, most sociologists have serious doubts about their use with human beings. This is partly because people act in terms of their definitions of situations. They are likely to define laboratories as artificial situations and act accordingly. As a result, their actions may be very different from their behaviour in the 'real' world. An attempt to get round this is the **field experiment**, an experiment which takes place in people's everyday situations.

Field experiments

Field experiments are conducted in normal social situations such as the classroom, the factory and the street corner. The following example was devised to test the effect of social class on interaction between strangers (Sissons, 1970). An actor stood outside Paddington Station in London and asked people for directions. The actor, place and request were kept the same but the actor's dress varied from that of a businessman to a labourer. The experiment indicated that people were more helpful to the 'businessman'. It could therefore be argued that people were responding to what they perceived as the actor's social class. However, there are other possibilities. For example, the actor may behave more confidently in his role as businessman and people might respond to his level of confidence rather than level of class.

Field experiments are always going to be inexact and 'messy'. It is impossible to identify and control all the variables which might affect the results. For example, it is difficult, if not impossible, to control the social class of the people who were asked for directions in the above experiment. Most of them may have been middle class. If so, they may have been more helpful to the 'businessman' because he seemed 'more like them'.

Experimental effect – the Hawthorne effect

Whether in the laboratory or in more normal social contexts, people are often aware they are participating in an experiment. And this in itself is likely to affect their behaviour. This particular **experimental effect** is often known as the **Hawthorne effect** since it was first observed during a study at the Hawthorne Works of the Western Electricity Company in Chicago in the late 1920s. The researchers conducted an experiment to discover whether there was a relationship between the workers' productivity and variables such as levels of lighting and heating and the frequency of rest periods. The researchers were puzzled as the results appeared to make little or no sense. For example, productivity increased whether the temperature in the workplace was turned up or down. The only factor which appeared to explain the increase in productivity was the workers' awareness that they were part of an experiment – hence the term **Hawthorne effect**.

Experimenter bias

People act in terms of how they perceive others. They will tend to respond differently if the experimenter is young or old, male or female, Black or White and so on. People also tend to act in terms of how they think others expect them to act. This might explain the results in the experiment involving the actor dressed as a businessman and a labourer. He might be conveying two different expectations and this may affect the responses to his request for directions. For example, he may expect more help in his role as businessman and unintentionally convey this to the participants. The unintended effect of the experimenter on those being studied is known as **experimenter bias**.

Ethics and experiments

Experiments sometimes involve deception. Participants are not informed of the true purpose of the experiment. They are not given the information necessary for informed consent. If they were, the experiment might not work. Participants might change their behaviour if they knew what the experiment was about. For example, if the participants in Paul Piff's experiments described above knew that their honesty, decency and generosity were being measured, then they would probably have changed their behaviour.

Experiments are often used in psychology. The American Psychological Association justifies the use of deception in the following way. It can only be used if no other procedures are available. However, it cannot be used if it may cause 'physical pain or severe emotional stress'. Informed consent must follow after the data collection. Participants can then withdraw the use of their data (Behnke, 2009).

Advantages and disadvantages of experiments

Advantages

> Laboratory experiments allow researchers to control variables.

> They can provide quantitative data.

> They are reliable. They are fairly easy to replicate.

> Field experiments provide a more realistic setting.

Activity

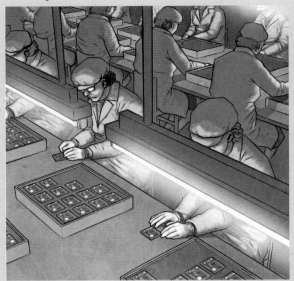

The Hawthorne Works – productivity increased whether the lighting was turned up or down.

Suggest reasons for the Hawthorne effect.

Disadvantages

> Laboratories are artificial environments.

> Participants' behaviour in laboratories may not reflect their behaviour in the outside world.

> The tasks they are asked to perform may appear meaningless.

> Although field experiments may provide more realistic contexts, it is not possible to control all the important variables.

> In addition, the problems of experimental effect and experimenter bias may arise.

Key terms

Hypothesis A statement that can be tested about the relationship between two or more variables.

Variables Factors which affect behaviour. Variables can vary, for example temperature can increase or decrease.

Replication Repeating an experiment or research study under the same conditions.

Correlation A statistical link between two or more variables.

Laboratory experiment An experiment conducted in a specially designed setting.

Field experiment An experiment conducted in everyday social settings.

Experimental effect Any unintended effect of the experiment on the participants.

Hawthorne effect Changes in the behaviour of participants resulting from an awareness that they are taking part in an experiment.

Experimenter bias The unintended effect of the experimenter on the participant.

Summary

1. There are two main types of experiments – laboratory experiments and field experiments.

2. Experiments are designed to test hypotheses.

3. Experiments are usually intended to measure the strength of relationships between two or more variables.

4. Ideally, laboratory experiments allow the researcher to control all the important variables.

5. Laboratories are artificial situations. Critics argue that as a result, findings from laboratory experiments may not apply to everyday social situations.

6. Field experiments help to avoid artificiality, but they do not provide the same control of variables.

7. Both laboratory and field experiments have been criticised for experimental effect and experimenter bias. As a result, their findings may be low in validity.

PART 6 SECONDARY SOURCES

Contents

So far this chapter has looked at methods which produce primary data – data which are created as a result of the research and were not there before the research began. This part looks at secondary data – data which existed before the research began. Two types of secondary data are examined. The first, documents, are an example of qualitative data. The second, official statistics, are an example of quantitative data.

3.6.1 Documents

This unit looks at **documents**, a type of secondary qualitative data, and asks how they might be analysed and what use they might be to sociologists. The significance of documents is that, for the most part, they have *not* been produced by sociologists using sociological research methods. Instead, they are produced by people as part of their normal lives – as members of families, as part of their paid employment, as part of their leisure activities. This is exactly the kind of data that sociologists look for. It is a ready-made form of evidence.

The term **documents** covers a wide range of material. It includes:

> written material – letters, diaries, autobiographies, novels, newspapers, magazines and government reports

> images – pictures, posters, photographs, paintings, flags, comics and cartoons

> radio and television broadcasts, music, films and social media.

Types of documents

Documents can be divided into various types – for example, personal documents such as letters, historical documents such as images from the past, and official documents such as government reports. Examples of these three types will now be examined.

Personal documents

Also known as life documents, personal documents include letters, diaries, family photographs and communications on social media. Personal documents can be an expression of people's hopes, feelings, worries and concerns – just the kind of data many sociologists are looking for.

This can be seen from Valerie Hey's (1997) study *The Company She Keeps: An Ethnography of Girls' Friendship*. Based on research in two London comprehensive schools, part of her data consisted of notes the girls wrote and secretly passed to each other during lessons. These notes revealed the girls' feelings and worries about their friendships. For example, 90 per cent of what they wrote concerned their relationships with each other.

The importance of personal documents can be seen from a classic sociological work entitled *The Polish Peasant in Europe and America* by William I. Thomas and Florian Znaniecki (1958, originally published in five volumes from 1918 to 1920). It is partly based on 764 letters exchanged between immigrants to the USA and their families in Poland. The letters give a valuable insight into village life in Poland and the experience of migration to the USA. The letters also represent the writers' world view, their picture of their lives, and their reflections on their relationships with families and friends (Stanley, L., 2010). Personal documents such as these provide kinds of data which are not available from the primary data provided by the standard sociological research methods.

Evaluation Personal documents provide a unique and valuable source for people's hopes and fears, wishes and desires, their world views and reflections on their situation. Like many documents, personal documents are often written for a particular audience. They may say more about the writer rather than the events they are describing. And the writer may not be representative of the group they belong to. Personal documents tend to be one-sided, prejudiced, and based on particular viewpoints and value judgements. But in many respects that's life, and life is what sociologists study.

Historical documents

For studying the past, historical documents are often the major and sometimes the only source of information. Max Weber's classic study *The Protestant Ethic and the Spirit of Capitalism*, first published in 1905, could not have been written without a range of historical documents.

According to Weber, the Protestant ethic – an approach to life and work – came from ascetic Protestantism (ascetic means abstaining from pleasure, severe self-discipline). This version of Protestantism saw work as a religious calling, success in business as indicating that a person had not lost favour in God's eyes, and profits as a source for further investment in business rather than a means of funding luxuries and 'frivolous' entertainment.

Weber builds a strong case for the Protestant ethic underlying and preceding capitalism by quoting from the speeches and writings of religious ministers such as John Calvin (1509–1564). He illustrates the spirit of capitalism with quotes from two books by Benjamin Franklin, *Necessary Hints to Those that would be Rich* (1736) and *Advice to a Young Tradesman* (1748).

Geoffrey Pearson's *Hooligan: A History of Respectable Fears* (1983) provides a more recent example of the use of historical documents. Pearson looks back to Victorian England and forward to the 20th century to show that 'for generations Britain has been plagued by the same fears and problems'. He looks at 'hooliganism' – street crime and violence – the fears and moral panics it generates and its 'discovery' time and time again as something new, in contrast to the 'good old days'. Pearson builds up a substantial case for this argument with a range of historical documents which include newspapers, magazines such as *Punch* and *Teacher's World*, contemporary novels and government reports.

Historical documents are a valuable source of data for studying social change. For example, Peter Laslett's (1965, 1977) research on the family in pre-industrial England was based on parish records from 1564 to 1821. And Michael Anderson's (1971) research on working-class families during the early stages of industrialisation was based on a sample of households from Preston in Lancashire using data from the 1851 census.

Evaluation As with personal documents, historical documents are often biased, prejudiced, one-sided, written for a particular audience and concerned with putting over a particular point of view. However, as long as researchers take them for what they are, historical documents provide a rich and valuable source of data. Thus Lord Ashley's announcement in the House of Commons in 1843 that, 'the morals of the children are tenfold worse than formerly' (quoted in Pearson, 1983) cannot be seen as a balanced assessment of juvenile morality. However, for Pearson's study of 'respectable fears', it is a very useful piece of data since it exemplifies a fear that has recurred throughout the past two centuries.

Official documents

Official documents include publications from government departments such as the Department for Education, from Parliamentary Select Committees such as the Defence Committee, and from government organisations such as H M Revenue and Customs. Official publications for 2017 include the *2017 Spring Budget Documents* produced by the Treasury, the *UK Trade Options Beyond 2019* published by the International Trade Committee, and an updated version of *Published Details of Deliberate Tax Defaulters,* a report from H M Revenue and Customs.

Evaluation Official documents can be very useful to sociologists as Chapter 2 Education illustrates. The section on educational policy in the UK relies partly on government policy documents. The sections on class,

Activity

This cartoon from 1653 shows a Puritan driving Father Christmas out of town. Christmas fun and games and even mince pies were banned in mid-17th century England.

How might this cartoon illustrate Weber's view of the Protestant ethic?

gender and ethnicity make use of research funded and published by the Department for Education. For some of the larger scale studies, sociologists do not usually have the resources – time, money and people – to conduct the research.

Government publications are not objective. This is clear from policy statements which outline and justify political party policies – for example, the reintroduction of grammar schools proposed by Theresa May's Conservative government. In such cases bias would be expected. However, bias can also be seen in government reports on their reforms. Governments pay for evaluations of the outcome of their policies – for example, have the reforms based on these policies been successful? A study based on policy evaluations from 2007 to 2013 commissioned by the British government found 'widespread evidence of outcome reporting bias' or 'spin' in favour of the government (Vaganay, 2016). The evidence for this included selective reporting – filtering out negative results and overemphasising positive results – particularly in the outcome reports' conclusions.

Visual documents

Visual documents include pictures, photographs, paintings, posters, flags, cartoons, films, TV programmes, video games and images on social media. This section looks at ways of analysing visual documents.

Formal content analysis This is a method used to analyse words and images. At its simplest it just counts how often particular words and images occur. Table 3.6.1 shows the results of a large-scale content analysis of the main characters in video games in the USA. It found that males, White people and adults were over-represented in comparison to the US population as a whole, while females, Black people, Hispanics and Native Americans were under-represented (Williams *et al.*, 2009).

Table 3.6.1 Main characters in video games, USA, percentages

	Males	White people	Adults
In video games	90%	80%	87%
In US population	51%	75%	59%

Semiotic analysis Semiology is the study of signs and symbols and how they work together to create meanings. Semiotic analysis is often used to analyse the images in advertising. Cigarette advertisements from the 1960s provide an example. The settings are

An advert for Lucky Strike cigarettes from the 1950s.

What meanings does this advert convey?

idyllic – waves lapping on golden beaches, sunshine and blue skies, meadows adorned with wild flowers, snow covered hills, lakes, rivers, babbling brooks and fronting the scene a packet of 20 cigarettes. The people in the ads are happy, smiling and laughing, they are young, vital, healthy and athletic. Their main pastimes are sporting – swimming, sailing, ice skating, cycling, golfing, skiing, mountain climbing. And more often than not they are smoking to their heart's content. The meanings are clear – happiness, health, vitality and cigarette smoking go together.

Discourse analysis A discourse is a way of knowing, thinking about and acting towards something. Discourse analysis is a way of identifying and analysing discourses. For example, in Victorian times the discourse on prostitutes portrayed them as 'fallen women' who enjoyed sex, alcohol and the 'low life', who dressed provocatively and tended to meet an early death as a result of suicide or murder (Nead, 1988; Rose, 2012).

As the following pictures show, images can be analysed using discourse analysis. They can be seen as illustrations of discourses.

177

Activity

Customers in a brothel.

A murdered prostitute.

How do the pictures illustrate the Victorian discourse on prostitutes?

Sociological analysis Societies are made up of different social groups – for example, regional, ethnic and class groups. To some extent, each group will give their own meanings to images, meanings which will be influenced by their position in society. From a sociological perspective, images can be analysed in terms of the meanings given to them by social groups, meanings which are shaped by the history and social situations of those groups.

Activity – Images and social groups

In 2015, a young White supremacist shot and killed nine African Americans in a church in Charleston, South Carolina. He was photographed with a Confederate flag, a flag which since the Civil War has been a symbol of the Confederacy which fought, in part, to preserve slavery. After the shooting, the state legislature voted to remove the flag from outside the statehouse. The picture illustrates the different meanings given to the Confederate flag by African Americans and White Americans in South Carolina.

Questions

1. What are the meanings given to the Confederate flag by Black Americans and White Americans?

2. Suggest reasons for the differences in their views of the flag.

Outside the statehouse in Charleston, South Carolina.

Types of content analysis

This section looks at various types of content analysis. Ray Pawson (1995) identifies four main types, 1) formal content analysis, 2) thematic analysis, 3) textual analysis, 4) audience analysis.

Formal content analysis This method attempts to classify and quantify the contents of a document in an objective way. At its simplest it counts words, phrases and images. As noted earlier, it was used to analyse the gender, ethnicity and age of the main characters in video games. A further example is provided by the Global Media Monitoring Project. Every five years the project presents a content analysis of women in the news media. In 2015 it had contributors from 114 countries. The 2015 report showed 'persistent and emerging' under-representation and portrayal of women in global news media (Global Media Monitoring Project, 2016).

Formal content analysis is a reliable method. It is fairly easy to replicate. However, it says little about the meaning of a document to an audience.

Thematic analysis This approach looks for the motives, intentions and ideologies of the authors which are seen to underlie documents. For example, a news broadcast may reflect the interests of particular groups. Aseel Baidoun (2014) conducted a thematic analysis of 31 press articles on the Gaza/Israeli conflict of 2013 from two Palestinian and two Israeli news agencies. He found that war correspondents were not neutral – they took sides. The Palestinian journalists repeatedly referred to the 'Israeli occupation army' indicating what they saw as Israel's illegal occupation of Palestinian land. The Israeli journalists referred the Palestinians as 'violent people' and 'terrorists'. Each side attempted to demoralise and dehumanise the other.

While thematic analysis may uncover meanings and motives, it has its problems. Who is to say that the sociologist's interpretation of underlying themes is correct? And who is to say that the audience interprets the articles in the same way as the researcher?

Textual analysis This approach involves a close examination of the 'text' to see how the words and phrases used encourage a particular reading of the document. The Glasgow University Media Group's (1976) study of TV reporting of strikes provides an example. Strikers tended to be reported using verbs such as 'claim' or 'demand' while management were reported using verbs such as 'offer' and 'propose'. As a result, managers appeared reasonable and ready to negotiate whereas the strikers appeared to be demanding and uncompromising.

As with thematic analysis, textual analysis relies on the researcher's interpretation which may not correspond to the audience's view.

Audience analysis Some researchers argue that the focus of document research should be the audience. They see audiences actively negotiating the meaning of messages with the outcome of negotiation ranging from acceptance, to indifference, to opposition (Pawson, 1995). Here is an example of audience analysis. Greg Philo and David Miller (2002) examined BBC and ITN TV news broadcasts of the Israeli/Palestinian conflict. The broadcasts focused on images of violence and the bleak prospects for peace. The researchers' audience sample included 300 young people aged 17–22. The responses of this sample show how TV news affected their knowledge and understanding of the conflict.

News broadcasts made little reference to the history and background of the Israeli/Palestinian conflict. Broadcasts referred to 'occupied territories' but provided no explanation of what they were. Only 9 per cent of the young people sampled knew it was Israelis occupying Palestinian land, 71 per cent had no idea what the term meant, and 11 per cent actually thought it was the Palestinians occupying Israeli land. Broadcasts showed Palestinians burning the American flag and mentioned their distrust of American peace proposals. There was little or no mention of why. For example, there was hardly a reference to the fact that the USA supplied some three billion dollars of aid to Israel each year, much of it in the form of military hardware. When asked to explain Palestinian distrust of the Americans, 66 per cent of the sample had no idea, 24 per cent thought America 'supported' Israel and only 10 per cent mentioned money and arms (Philo and Miller, 2002).

This study shows the importance of audience research. Sociology is the study of people in society. When researchers examine 'documents' such as TV news, a major concern is how they affect members of society. And this requires researchers to discover the meanings people give to those documents and the understandings they draw from them. To do this, sociologists must 'ask the audience'.

Assessing documents

John Scott (1990) offers four 'quality control criteria' for assessing documents:

- Authenticity – are they genuine?
- Credibility – are they true?
- Representativeness – are they typical?
- Meaning – are they comprehensible?

Authenticity Is the document original or is it a copy? If it is a copy, is it an exact copy? Has it been tampered with in any way like the famous photograph of Lenin, one of the founders of the Soviet Union.

One of the first questions to ask about some documents is whether or not they are forgeries. Are they intended to pass as something they are not such as a painting falsely claimed to be produced by a famous artist such as Picasso, Vermeer or Renoir? One of the most famous forgeries was Adolf Hitler's supposed diaries. In 1983, the German magazine *Stern* paid $4 million for 62 handwritten volumes which the seller claimed were written by Hitler. Research later showed they were forgeries.

Credibility Is the author of the document 'sincere' and honest or do they distort the evidence in order to mislead the audience? There are plenty of examples of distortion, deceit and outright lies in documents. This can be seen from the activity on fake news.

Representativeness To what extent is the document representative? For example, is a newspaper article typical of the articles which appear in that particular newspaper? The question of representativeness is particularly important in the case of historical documents as many have been lost or destroyed. Those that remain may be untypical. For example, a study of witchcraft in 17th-century New England was based on court records relating to 114 individuals. The researcher believes that these surviving records are only the 'tip of the iceberg', a tip which may well be unrepresentative (discussed in O'Connell Davidson and Layder, 1994).

Meaning What does a document mean? Researchers must be able to understand words and phrases when analysing written, spoken and sung material. Ideally, they should know the meanings intended by the writer/speaker/singer and what was understood by various members of the audience. In the example on the next page, Jay-Z translates words from three of his recordings (titles in brackets) for those who don't understand. They are taken from his book *Decoded* (2010).

Activity

Lenin addressing troops in Moscow. On the right of the podium are Trotsky and Kamenev.

When Stalin came to power he 'removed' Trotsky (who was murdered) and Kamenev (who was executed). They were then 'removed' from the photograph.

Why is it important to know that an original document has been altered?

Contemporary issues: Fake news

US presidential candidates Hillary Clinton and Donald Trump debating before the election in 2016.

The Macedonian town of Vales in eastern Europe has launched over 140 United States political news websites. Almost all support Donald Trump, mostly with fake news stories. Here are a couple of false news stories for Trump supporters about his opponent for the presidency Hillary Clinton.

A 'quote' from Hillary Clinton

Hillary Clinton is falsely quoted on one website as saying in 2013, 'I would like to see people like Donald Trump running for office. They're honest and can't be bought and sold'. In its first week on Facebook this post had 480000 shares, reactions and comments.

Source: Buzzfeed News online.

Your prayers have been answered

Under this headline the article claimed that Hillary Clinton would be indicted and tried in 2017 for crimes related to her supposed misuse of her personal email. This fake news produced 140000 shares, reactions and comments on Facebook.

Questions

1. Why is it important to study fake news?

2. Should fake news be censored? Think about freedom of expression in your answer.

3. How might fake news have influenced the US presidential election in 2016?

Activity

Jay-Z.

> 'Cheddar' means money.
> (from 'Public Service Announcement')
> 'Slingin' means selling drugs.
> (from 'Coming of Age')
> 'Blow' means showing off.
> (from 'Fallin')

1. How do these data indicate the importance of the researcher understanding words?

2. Did you need a translation?

Positivism and interpretivism

Positivism Positivists tend not to use documentary material as the main source of data for research projects. It is often difficult to quantify documents. It is also difficult to obtain representative samples of documentary material and to make generalisations from documentary data. This is particularly true of historical documents as the authors are not representative of the population as a whole. In many eras literate people were in a minority, they were usually the better-off, and documents were usually written by men.

The methods often used to analyse documents tend not meet positivist requirements. Methods such as thematic and textual analysis and semiology rely heavily on the interpretations of the researcher. In this respect they are not reliable and open to replication.

However, positivists would be likely to favour formal content analysis when suitable documentary data are available for quantification by counting words and images, for obtaining representative samples and for making generalisations.

Interpretivism In some respects, documents are just the kind of data that interpretivists are looking for. All documents are valid, from a heartfelt letter to the forged diaries purported to be written by Hitler. They are all instances of human behaviour. Most have not been produced or influenced by sociologists. Documents might present a false picture, either intentionally or unintentionally, they may distort, they may be based on ignorance and misunderstanding. But they are still valid in the sense that they are actual products of human behaviour.

Documents often provide the kind of data interpretivists value. For example, personal documents reveal hopes and fears, wishes and desires, expectations and meanings, outlooks and world views. They can provide qualitative data with a richness and depth sometimes not found in the data produced by sociological research.

Ethics and documentary research

Documents provide secondary data. Should the ethical guidelines used for gathering primary data also be applied to the use of secondary data? This is a matter for judgement and the law. The 1998 Data Protection Act prevents certain documents from being used without permission from the individuals concerned and from possible copyright holders.

The use of some documents raises issues of 'confidentiality, anonymity and consent' (Ali, 2012). For example, with reference to personal documents, particularly photographs, can individuals be recognised and identified? If so, should the people concerned, or if they have died their relatives, be informed and their permission requested? These are some of the questions which need to be considered when conducting documentary research.

Advantages and disadvantages of documents

Advantages

- They provide an enormous amount and variety of data.
- Valid data.
- Data which is not usually produced or influenced by sociologists.
- Evidence which may not be available from sociological research.
- In-depth and rich qualitative data.

Disadvantages

- Unlikely to provide an objective view.
- Often biased and one-sided. (This is not necessarily a disadvantage as it provides people's viewpoints.)
- Analysis of documents is often based on the researcher's interpretation. This may result in the imposition of the researcher's meanings and priorities.
- Often not possible to obtain quantified data and a representative sample which prevents generalisation.
- Research based on documents tends to be unreliable and difficult to replicate.

Key terms

Documents Secondary, mainly qualitative, data in written, visual and broadcast form.

Personal documents Letters, diaries, photographs and social media communications.

Historical documents Documents from the past.

Official documents Documents produced by government organisations and departments.

Formal content analysis Counting how often particular words, phrases and images occur.

Semiotic analysis The study of signs and symbols and how they combine to create meaning.

Discourse analysis Examining how words and images illustrate ways of knowing and thinking.

Sociological analysis In terms of documentary research, examining the meanings social groups give to documentary material.

Thematic analysis Interpreting the meanings, motives and ideologies which underlie documents.

Textual analysis Examining how words and phrases encourage a particular reading of a document.

Audience analysis Examining how audiences respond to and interpret documentary material.

Summary

1. Documents provide data on personal feelings and concerns, hundreds of years of history, official government statements and a wide range of images from photographs to flags to video games.

2. Images can be analysed and interpreted in a variety of ways including formal content analysis, semiotic analysis, discourse analysis and sociological analysis.

3. Various types of content analysis can be used to analyse documents. They include formal content analysis, thematic analysis, textual analysis and audience analysis.

4. Documents can be assessed in terms of:

   › authenticity – are they genuine?

   › credibility – are they true?

   › representativeness – are they typical?

   › meaning – are they comprehensible?

3.6.2 Official statistics

Official statistics are numerical data produced by national and local government. They cover a wide range of behaviour including births, deaths, marriages and divorces, the distribution of income and wealth, crime and sentencing, and work and leisure. The following are among the main sources of official statistics.

1. **Government departments** Departments such as the Home Office, the Department of Health and the Department for Work and Pensions regularly request information from organisations such as local tax offices, social services departments, hospitals, job centres and police stations. This information is then processed and much of it published.

2. **Surveys** The Office for National Statistics is the government agency responsible for compiling and analysing many of the UK's economic, social and population statistics. Surveys are a major source

of statistical data. Every 10 years the Office for National Statistics carries out the Census of the Population which covers every household in the UK. Each head of household must, by law, complete a questionnaire that deals with family composition, housing, occupation, transport and leisure. Other large scale surveys include the Integrated Household Survey, an annual survey of around 325 000 people covering topics such as education, housing, employment and health, and the Annual Survey of Hours and Earnings based on a 1 per cent sample of employees drawn from HM Revenue and Customs Pay As You Earn records (Office for National Statistics, 2016).

This unit critically examines two forms of official statistics – crime statistics and unemployment statistics. Do they really measure what they are intended to measure? In other words, do they provide valid data?

Crime statistics

The annual crime statistics are a widely used form of official statistics. They are reported by the media and commented on by the government of the day. There are two sets of statistics measuring crime – the Crime Survey for England and Wales and Police Recorded Crime.

The Crime Survey for England and Wales (CSEW) is an annual survey which asks a representative sample of around 35 000 adults and, since 2009, 3000 children aged 10 to 15, if they have been a victim of certain crimes. It takes the form of a structured interview. An interviewer reads out a list of crimes and asks the participants if they have been a victim of these crimes in the past 12 months.

The CSEW is an effective measure of trends in the crimes it covers as the methods used and the list of crimes have, until recently, remained basically the same since the survey began in 1981. The survey shows that crime increased steadily from 1981 to 1995 and then steadily declined to the year ending June 2016 – the most recent statistics available at the time of writing. These figures do not include homicide, sexual offences and crimes against children under 10 years old.

However, the downward trend is questionable since the figures do not include crimes against organisations and cybercrime (online crime). As the 2016 CSEW report states, 'The way in which criminals are operating is changing and they can now take advantage of new technologies such as the internet'. To take account of this, new questions on fraud and cybercrime were given to half the survey in 2016 but not included in the total estimate of crimes. The results gave an estimate of 5.6 million offences. Add this to the 6.4 million estimate of crimes in the 2016 survey and the result is a massive rise. In addition, there is evidence of widespread under-reporting of fraud. Some people do not realise they have been defrauded, others might be too ashamed to admit they have been victims – they feel a fool, they feel it was their fault (Deevy and Beals, 2013). Figures on fraud and cybercrime will be included in future CSEW surveys (Office for National Statistics, 20.10.2016).

Police Recorded Crime (PRC) As its name suggests, Police Recorded Crime consists of crimes actually recorded by the police. Most PRC is based on reports by the public of what they consider crimes.

PRC shows an overall reduction from 2003, when new counting rules were introduced, then a rise in 2015 and a further rise in 2016. 4.6 million crimes were recorded for the year ending June 2016, an annual rise of 7 per cent. Most of this rise was due to improvements in recording practices as a result of the following investigation (Office for National Statistics, 20.10.2016).

In 2014, Her Majesty's Inspectorate of Constabulary (HMIC), an independent body which assesses the police, published an investigation into police crime recording. It concluded that:

Over 800 000 crimes reported to the police have gone unrecorded each year. This represents an under-recording of 19 per cent. The problem is greatest for victims of violence against the person and sexual offences, where the under-recording rates are 33 per cent and 26 per cent respectively. This failure to record such a significant proportion of reported crime is wholly unacceptable. **HMIC, 2014**

The HMIC conducted an online survey of police officers and staff to see if there was any massaging of the statistics. 8600 said they were responsible for decisions about what crimes to record and around one fifth 'reported pressures not to record a crime in the last six months' and 'undue pressure' from higher ranking officers to make it appear that the police were meeting performance targets (HMIC, 2014). Since the publication of this report there has been a significant rise in police recorded crime. However, in 2014 the

Activity – Police Recorded Crime

In 2014 the House of Commons Public Administration Select Committee published a report entitled 'Caught red-handed: Why we can't count on Police Recorded Crime statistics'. They note that the misreporting of crime can deny 'crucial information' for police activity and government policy (House of Commons, 2014).

Question

In what ways might the misrecording of crime affect police activity and government policy?

UK Statistics Authority stated that statistics based on Police Recorded Crime did not reach the required standard to be designated as 'National Statistics'.

A further problem with police statistics is changes in the number and classification of crimes on the list of offences. For example, in 2016, PRC showed an annual rise of 24 per cent in violence against the person offences. About one third of this was due to the addition of two more offences under the heading of violence against the person. Add to this improvements in recording crime, and the increase was probably slight. Changes in the number and classification of offences means that trends over time cannot be identified (Office for National Statistics, 20.10.2016).

Another problem for identifying trends in crime is police priorities. For example, in recent years the police have prioritised weapons offences. Time, money and personnel have been directed at these offences and, at least partly due to this, recorded weapons offences have risen.

Unemployment statistics

The extent of unemployment is measured by the Labour Force Survey, a three-monthly survey based on interviews of around 100 000 individuals. Unemployed people are defined as 'those without a job who have been actively seeking work in the past 4 weeks and are available to start work in the next 2 weeks. It also included those who are out of work but have found a job and are waiting to start it in the next 2 weeks'. Using this measure, there were 1.6 million unemployed people in the UK from July to September, 2016 (Office for National Statistics, 16.11.2016).

The definition and extent of unemployment has long been a subject for debate. It has been argued that some official statistics are politically biased, that they are constructed to present governments in a favourable light. For example, according to the Labour Party, Conservative governments changed the method used to count unemployment over 30 times between 1982 and 1992. And, in practically every case, these changes resulted in a drop in the official level of unemployment (Denscombe, 1994).

More recently, in an article entitled 'The real level of unemployment 2012', Christine Beatty, Steve Fothergill and Tony Gore (2012) question the Coalition government's unemployment count. According to the Labour Force Survey, some 2.5 million people were unemployed. However, around 900 000 unemployed people were diverted on to incapacity benefits instead of unemployment benefits. Add them to the Labour Force Survey count of 2.5 million and the total unemployed comes to 3.4 million. Beatty *et al.* claim that their research 'assesses the real level of unemployment and provides alternative – and more robust – estimates of unemployment'.

Activity

One way of reducing unemployment.

Why is it important to know exactly how unemployment statistics are constructed?

Official statistics – validity and reliability

How valid and reliable are official statistics? If they are valid, they will provide a true and accurate picture of what they are intended to measure. If they are reliable, then the use of the same procedures for measurement will produce similar statistics.

Some official statistics are more likely than others to be valid and reliable. Take statistics on births and deaths and marriages and divorces. Definitions of all these events are clear and there is no disagreement about what is being measured. And there are standardised procedures for reporting and recording these events. As a result, the statistics are likely to be valid and reliable.

Other official statistics are less likely to be valid and reliable – for example, crime statistics. The Crime Survey for England and Wales is an annual survey based on a large representative sample. It asks participants whether they have been victims of various crimes over the past year. Until recently, the crimes listed have been largely the same since the survey began in 1981. Asking a representative sample similar questions year after year is likely to produce reliable data and, in terms of the crimes it covers, valid data.

But does the Crime Survey provide an accurate measure of the extent of crime in England and Wales? The answer is no. The survey does not cover crimes against children under 10 years old, sexual offences and homicide. Nor does it cover crimes against organisations such as business fraud and tax evasion. And, until 2017, it did not include cybercrime. As noted earlier, the inclusion of cybercrime will probably result in a massive rise in the estimated extent of crime.

Positivism and interpretivism

Positivism While recognising the problems of validity and reliability, positivists favour the quantitative data available from official statistics. They value statistics based on large representative samples which can provide reliable data from which to draw generalisations.

Interpretivism Interpretivists are more likely to focus on how statistics are constructed and to question their validity. Some go further and argue that statistics are simply meanings. For example, in *Discovering Suicide* (1978) J. Maxell Atkinson states that suicide is a social construction, a meaning, used by coroners to officially classify certain deaths as suicide. Based on observations in coroners' courts, Atkinson claims that coroners have a picture of a typical suicide death, such as hanging and drug overdose, and a picture of a typical suicide victim, such as a lonely, friendless and isolated individual. If a dead person fits these pictures then there is a greater likelihood of a verdict of suicide. Suicide is a meaning and there is no reality beyond that meaning. The job of the sociologist is simply to discover the meanings used to construct suicide statistics, and for that matter any other statistics.

Taking this view to its extreme, if meanings are social reality then it can be argued that it is not possible to get beyond meanings to some other reality which might provide a more valid picture. We are human beings and meanings are all we have.

Advantages and disadvantages of official statistics

Advantages

> Official statistics can be very useful for sociological research. Published statistics are readily available and cost little or nothing to use.

> Care is taken to select representative samples and sample sizes are often large. Surveys as large as the Crime Survey for England and Wales are usually outside sociologists' research budgets.

> Many government surveys are well planned and organised, with detailed questionnaires or interview schedules. As such, they meet the standards of sociological research.

> Surveys are often conducted regularly, for example on a three monthly, annual or 10-yearly basis. This can allow for comparisons over time and the identification of trends.

> Sometimes official statistics are the only major source of information on a particular topic.

Disadvantages

> Some official statistics are neither valid nor reliable.

> The definitions on which official statistics are based – for example, the definition of unemployment – can change. As a result, measuring trends over time may not be possible.

> Official statistics measure what governments decide is important. To some extent this is a political decision.

Key term

Official statistics Statistics produced by local and national government, government agencies and organisations funded by government.

Summary

1. Researchers need to know how official statistics are constructed in order to assess the validity of the data they provide.

2. The Crime Survey for England and Wales now includes questions on fraud and cybercrime.

3. Police Recorded Crime is now regarded as an inadequate measure of the extent of and trends in crime.

4. Some researchers argue that official statistics can be politically biased in order to present governments in a favourable light.

5. Despite their shortcomings, official statistics can provide valuable data for sociological research.

PART 7 MIXED METHODS AND TRIANGULATION

A mixed methods approach combines different research methods, for example participant observation and interviews. **Mixed methods** often produces different types of data – both quantitative and qualitative data. It sometimes uses both primary and secondary data. It can also combine aspects of positivist and interpretivist approaches. Mixed methods is sometimes known as methodological pluralism.

This part provides an example of a mixed methods approach. It also asks why mixed methods has become an increasingly popular research method.

Mixed methods – an example

Goth: Identity, Style and Subculture by Paul Hodkinson (2002) uses a variety of methods and several types of data. Hodkinson used participant observation at the Whitby Gothic Weekend. He described this festival as 'the ultimate experience in taking part in the Goth scene'. It gave him first-hand experience of 'pure Goth'. Questionnaires 'provided useful quantitative data' and open-ended questions 'some extremely valuable comments'. Unstructured interviews were 'open and flowing' and provided 'in-depth, quality information'.

Hodkinson also used secondary data and documentary research. He analysed Goth fanzines, websites, posters and music. He summarises his approach in the following quote.

My aim was to conduct in-depth and thorough qualitative research on the Goth scene in Britain, in order to examine and account for the cultural form taken by the group. In particular, the focus was on the norms, meanings, motivations and social patterns of those involved. In order to achieve maximum depth and quality of information and understanding, I adopted a multi-method ethnographic approach, which included participant observation, in-depth interviews, media analysis and even a questionnaire.

Hodkinson found that mixed methods provided a fuller and more rounded picture. For example, taking part in Goth online discussion groups 'widened the scope of my research'. Participant observation at gigs, clubs and festivals 'complemented and verified my interview data'. The closed questions on the self-completion questionnaires gave 'useful quantitative estimates' while the open-ended questions provided 'valuable comments'. Overall, mixed methods gave 'a thorough, detailed and cross-verified understanding of the Goth scene' (Hodkinson, 2002).

Mixed methods – uses

Mixed methods have a number of uses:

- Using one method can improve another method. For example, information from in-depth interviews can make a questionnaire more relevant to respondents.

- Data from one method might be developed by another. For example, participant observation can provide insights which might form the basis of a questionnaire survey which, in turn, might make generalisations possible.

- Different methods produce different types of data. This may provide a fuller, richer and more detailed picture.

- In practice, many sociologists do not think in terms of positivist versus interpretivist approaches. As a result, they see no problem combining

Activity

Participant observation at the Whitby Gothic Weekend.

1. With some reference to the picture, what might Hodkinson learn from participating in the Goth festival?

2. How might he combine what he learned with data from other research methods?

methods which others might see as more appropriate for one or other of these approaches.

> If there are contradictions between the data produced by different methods, then this raises issues. These will be examined in the next section.

Triangulation

Triangulation is a way of checking the validity of research findings. This can be done in a number of ways.

First, by using a mixed methods approach – for example, combining participant observation and interviews. If the two methods produce conflicting results, then this raises questions about validity. Has one or both methods produced incorrect data?

Second, triangulation can combine different types of data – for example, primary and secondary data and/ or qualitative and quantitative data. If one form of data contradicts the other, then this raises questions of validity and suggests that further research is needed to get a true picture.

Third, if the findings of one researcher are different from those of another, then one of them may have made an incorrect observation. Again this raises the question of validity and suggests the need for further research.

Triangulation can be a very useful for checking research results. It offers a means of improving validity. However, different findings do not necessarily mean that one is correct and another incorrect. They may simply be different perspectives with neither being right or wrong.

Here is an example of triangulation using different research methods, different types of data and different researchers. It was used by Sandra Walklate and her team in a study of the fear of crime in two high crime urban areas in northern England (Walklate, 2000).

The methods used were:

> Participant observation in pubs.

> In-depth unstructured interviews with professionals such as social workers.

> Documentary research – analysis of local newspapers.

> Structured interviews – in a house-to-house survey.

> Focus group discussions with survey participants.

> Postal questionnaires sent to local businesses and organisations.

> Telephone interviews with businesses and organisations who agreed to take apart.

Here are some comments from the research team on the use of mixed methods and triangulation. 'We were always moving between quantitative and qualitative data. The different research methods have uncovered different layers of social reality. We looked for confirmations and contradictions between those different layers.'

Key terms

Mixed methods Using more than one method for a research project.

Triangulation Using mixed methods to check the validity of research findings.

Summary

1. Many sociologists see advantages to using mixed methods.

2. They see it as producing a fuller and more rounded picture and as a way of checking the validity of research findings.

EXAM PRACTICE QUESTIONS

AS-LEVEL PAPER 2
RESEARCH METHODS

| 0 | 1 | Outline **two** problems of using questionnaires. | **[4 marks]** |

| 0 | 2 | Evaluate some of the problems of using unstructured interviews when conducting sociological research. | **[16 marks]** |

A-LEVEL PAPER 1
THEORY AND METHODS

| 0 | 1 | Outline and explain **two** arguments against the view that official statistics produce valid data. | **[10 marks]** |

For further A-level Paper 1 and Paper 3 questions on Theory and Methods please see Book 2.

4 METHODS IN CONTEXT

Chapter contents

In Chapter 2, you saw that sociologists study a wide range of topics within the field of education, such as the effects of teacher expectations on pupils' academic performance, the formation of counter-school cultures and the ways parents draw on their cultural, social and material resources to support their children's education. Chapter 3 examined the different research methods that sociologists use in order to gather data and evidence to address their research aims and questions. This chapter focuses on the methods that sociologists use to study education. What is distinctive about education as a field of sociological research? How do sociologists go about their research in sites such as schools, colleges, classrooms and students' homes? What practical and ethical issues are raised when undertaking research in educational settings?

The key **research characteristics** of the different groups of people within educational settings such as pupils, teachers and parents are examined. Are some methods more appropriate than others in research on primary school pupils or anti-school cultures? Are some groups of parents more likely than others to respond to self-completion questionnaires? Why might some teachers be reluctant to have an observer in their classroom?

The chapter then looks at the different research methods (such as observation, interviews and surveys) that sociologists use when researching education. Are some methods more suited to particular topics than others? In this chapter, answers to this and other important questions are suggested. A main focus of the chapter is the practical, ethical and theoretical implications of using a particular method to investigate a specific topic.

PART 1 CARRYING OUT RESEARCH IN THE CONTEXT OF EDUCATION

Contents

Part 1 of this chapter looks at some of the issues that sociologists have to consider when planning and carrying out educational research. It examines the different groups that sociologists study within educational organisations and explores the practical, ethical and theoretical issues that can arise when researching people in these settings. It also examines factors such as the power relationships and legal framework within which sociologists carry out educational research, and how these might impact on their work.

4.1.1 Researching schools and colleges

Educational research takes place in a range of educational establishments including:

 » primary and secondary schools (for example, private and state schools, day and boarding schools, comprehensive and grammar schools, special schools, free schools, academies and faith schools)

 » sixth form and further education colleges

 » universities.

Schools and colleges are located in different catchment areas and vary in terms of the social mix of their intake as well as their **culture** and **ethos**. Some studies are based on a single site while others are based on several sites and allow sociologists to compare and contrast schools when analysing their data.

This unit examines the practical, ethical and theoretical issues that sociologists have to consider when researching educational settings. It also looks at power relationships, and the legal and political context of educational research.

Research settings and participants

Sociological research into education can take place in different non-public locations or settings such as:

 » classrooms

 » staffrooms

 » specific departments

 » playgrounds and other social spaces

 » students' homes if the research involves parents.

Different groups of people participate in research on education and provide information to enable sociologists to address their research questions. These groups include:

 » classroom assistants, teachers, heads of department and head teachers

 » pupils and students

 » parents, guardians and carers

 » school governors

 » careers staff and counsellors.

Practical issues in educational research

Educational research (like all social research) requires time and money. The costs of travel, accommodation, phone calls, photocopying, stationery and transcribing, for example, must be budgeted for during the planning stage.

Sociologists have to bear in mind any possible time and resource constraints when designing their research and selecting their methods. For example, if a sociologist is studying students' involvement in **extra-curricular activities**, their research budget might not cover the relatively high costs of lengthy unstructured interviews but it might be enough for a short questionnaire survey. A sociologist who has a regular teaching timetable and administrative duties may not have enough time to carry out an ethnographic study of a school or sufficient funding to employ a researcher to do the fieldwork. In this case, they may use unstructured interviews instead. Another consideration is that schools and colleges operate on an academic year calendar and sociologists have to timetable their fieldwork around this.

It can be hard to find a quiet, private place in a school to carry out confidential interviews. Teachers and students may walk into a room where an interview is taking place and stay around for a while. As a guest at the school, a researcher might find it difficult to ask a teacher to leave the room.

Ethical issues in educational research

Ethical principles (see pp. 140–142) cover issues such as harm to participants, informed consent, invasion of privacy and deception. Researchers in education use agreed ethics standards, codes or guidelines, for example those produced by professional associations such as the British Sociological Association (BSA) or the British Education Research Association (BERA). The funders of a project such as the Economic and Social Research Council (ESRC) may also set their own standards of ethics.

Ethical guidelines on educational research protect not only research participants including students, teachers and parents but also researchers and their employers. Sociologists must apply the general ethical standards (for example, on informed consent) to their own study of education. How they do this will depend on the particular context (for instance, whether the participants are primary school pupils, university students or head teachers), the sensitivity of the topic and the methods they are using.

Informed consent

All research participants must be able to make an informed decision about whether they want to take part in a study (see p. 141). One way of informing prospective participants is by providing detailed information sheets about the study and how they will be involved. This information could include assurances about confidentiality, anonymity, privacy and participants' right to withdraw at any stage. Within the context of education, the language and vocabulary used in the information would need to be tailored to the particular group of participants, taking into account factors such as their age, competence and ability to understand abstract ideas.

Activity

Staff and students should be made aware that they are participating in research and informed consent should be sought from them.

Explain how far you agree that a researcher who is undertaking a study of a primary school based on participant observation should get informed consent from:

a) a coach driver on a school trip

b) all members of staff who use the staff room

c) all parents attending parents' evening

d) a pupil with whom the researcher has a casual conversation on the corridor.

The role of research ethics committees

Sociologists may have to submit their research proposals to a **research ethics committee** (REC) at their university (see pp. 140–141). RECs help to safeguard research participants (such as primary school children or students with special needs), advise on the ethical implications of a study and grant approval (or otherwise) to the research.

Theoretical issues in educational research

Theoretical issues concern questions about, for example, the validity, reliability and generalisability of data gathered during research. For instance, studies of counter-school cultures are usually based on participant observation in one secondary school (see, for example, Willis, pp. 29–32, 92–93, 105 and 120–121). This allows the researcher to build strong rapport with participants and gather rich and detailed data about the formation of student subcultures in that school. However, if teachers or pupils associate participant observers with inspectors, for example, this may reduce the validity of the data.

Power relationships within schools and colleges

Power relationships are built into the management structure of schools. Newly qualified teachers, for example, have less power than head teachers and senior managers. Power relationships also exist between teachers and pupils. In general, young people are used to complying with adults' wishes. These power relationships have implications for research ethics, for instance, in terms of informed consent and how far this is given voluntarily. They might also affect how honest participants are when responding to questions in unstructured interviews or questionnaires.

The legal framework

Researchers must comply with the requirements of legislation on working with children and child protection. As part of a school's safeguarding procedures, researchers who have contact with pupils may have to undergo a Disclosure and Barring Service (DBS) check.

Researchers must also comply with the requirements of the Data Protection Act 1988. For example, all personal data must not be kept longer than is necessary to complete a study. It must then be destroyed or securely archived.

Activity

Some issues raise both legal and ethical questions for sociologists. To what extent do you agree that a researcher must intervene if they become aware of instances of illegal drug use?

The political framework

Educational research takes place within a political context and many topics in educational policy and practice (such as funding and academies) are hotly debated by politicians, teachers, teaching unions and parents. Some issues are more politically sensitive than others at particular points in time, such as grammar schools in the run-up to the 2017 general election. This may affect the availability of funding and the willingness of prospective participants to get involved in a research project.

Key terms

Research characteristics The key features of a field of sociological investigation (such as education) including the research settings (such as primary school classrooms) and research participants (such as primary school pupils).

Culture (of a school) The norms and values of a particular school as reflected in, for example, its teaching and learning styles and behaviour management.

Ethos (of a school) The distinctive values and character of a particular school.

Extra-curricular activities Activities undertaken outside lessons at school such as clubs and debating societies or hobbies undertaken outside school such as swimming or rumba.

Research ethics committee A body in a university that scrutinises research proposals.

Summary

1. Sociologists carry out educational research in different types of school as well as sixth form colleges, further education colleges and universities.

2. Different groups – including staff, students and parents – participate in research on education. Research can take place in settings such as classrooms, staffrooms and students' homes.

3. Sociologists have to consider several practical issues when planning and carrying out research including the availability of time and money.

4. Researching education raises ethical issues such as harm, informed consent, privacy and deception.

5. Theoretical issues include the validity, reliability and generalisability of data gathered during research.

6. Other issues to consider when planning and carrying out educational research include power relationships in schools and colleges, and the legal and political frameworks within which the research takes place.

4.1.2 Researching staff in an educational context

When planning and carrying out research with staff in educational contexts, sociologists focus on several key issues including practical, ethical and theoretical considerations. This unit looks at these issues in more detail.

Practical issues in researching staff

Practical issues include selecting and accessing a research site, and negotiating access to participants.

Selecting and negotiating access to a research site

Initially, a researcher has to choose an appropriate educational establishment and negotiate access to this site to carry out the research. In practice, sociologists often draw on their personal contacts (such as friends or former colleagues) when trying to access a school or college. They might approach a local school to cut down on travel costs and time. However, a convenient local site may not necessarily be the most appropriate site (Walford, 2001). For example, the researcher may find that the sixth form is too small for a study of social class differences in students' higher education choices based on quantitative methods.

The head teacher, principal or chair of governors is usually the main **gatekeeper** with the power to grant or refuse access to the school or college. They are more likely to allow access if they recognise the purpose of the research or its relevance to schools. Researchers often give the gatekeeper an information sheet containing details about the research aims and methods, and provide assurances about confidentiality, anonymity, privacy and so on. The gatekeepers must be willing to support the project if it is to succeed. They must also feel confident that any account of the school, its staff, students and practices will be fair and balanced.

When negotiating access, some researchers offer to work as a supply teacher at the school or to teach a number of classes per week. This gives the researcher more of an **insider** perspective. One potential disadvantage of doing this is that the students might be less open in interviews because they see the researcher as an authority figure. This could reduce the validity of the data.

Powerful gatekeepers might have their own agenda in granting access. For example, the head teacher may give the researcher access only to trusted teachers or pupils to protect the school's image and this raises questions about the data's validity. Alternatively, the head might give the researcher access to a teacher who they want information about and this could create ethical problems for the researcher.

Gatekeepers differ in how far they control researchers' movement around a school and their access to teachers and students. David Gillborn and Deborah Youdell (2000) carried out research in two secondary schools in London over a two-year period to investigate some of the effects of league tables and marketisation on teaching (see pp. 52–53, 93 and 112). In one school, a deputy head teacher controlled their access to the school, the staff and students. In the other school, however, the researchers were able to observe assemblies, parents' evenings and staff meetings, and to talk to students and teachers informally during tutor group periods. As a result, Gillborn and Youdell developed closer rapport with students at this school.

Refusal of access

Negotiating access to an educational establishment can be a lengthy process and there are no guarantees of success. The gatekeepers' priority is the students under their care rather than a research project. They may block access because the research could impact on students' achievements (for example, during the run-up to public examinations), increase teachers' workload or cause stress (for instance, around the time of an Ofsted inspection).

Some research topics or issues are potentially more sensitive than others for the schools involved because they are viewed as undesirable or threatening in some way. Topics such as streaming, unauthorised absence, school-based factors linked to underachievement, racism, gender inequality in the classroom or bullying are all potentially sensitive. In these cases, staff may be reluctant to participate in a research project.

In the current climate of marketisation and competition (see pp. 39–43, 45–49 and 51–56), schools and colleges are concerned about their image and would be cautious about participating in research if the results could reflect badly on their reputation, market or league table position. Research findings may be misrepresented in the media to create a 'good' story (Hill, 2005). The possibility of getting negative publicity could discourage schools from participating in future studies. Other possible reasons for refusal include the fear of surveillance, scrutiny and exposure, and research fatigue.

Negotiating access to the teaching staff

Activity

Trying to negotiate access to classrooms takes time and there is no guarantee of success.

Why do you think some teachers might not want to participate in sociological research on education?

Getting access to the school is only the first step as there are several other layers of access, including teachers, students and parents. The researcher must negotiate access with relevant teaching staff such as individual teachers, heads of year or heads of departments and this can take time.

However, some teachers might view a sociologist with suspicion and think that they are carrying out an evaluation or that they are on the management's side.

Individual teachers may not want to participate in interviews because this is an additional demand on their time. They might not allow their students to take time out of GCSE or A-level lessons to participate in interviews or complete questionnaires because this would disrupt examination preparation. Teachers may refuse to let a researcher into their classroom because they dislike the idea of being observed in their workplace or feel defensive about possible criticisms.

Ethical issues in researching staff

Issues such as informed consent, anonymity and confidentiality are particular concerns in educational research. When seeking informed consent from staff, the researcher has to make sure that the teachers volunteered to participate in the research rather than being pressurised into it by a head teacher or head of department.

After collecting their data, many researchers provide feedback reports to the school, giving participants the opportunity to comment on the contents and findings. This can increase the validity of the data. However, it raises questions about what to feed back and to whom. For example, sociologists would not want to hide evidence of bullying or labelling but, in practice, it might be difficult to report back on these without identifying individuals.

As a condition of granting access, the head teacher may insist that the identity of the school is not revealed. However, although the school is not named in any publications, the people directly involved in the research will still know that it is their school. The head teacher and others may be able to identify individual teachers even though pseudonyms are used. By referring to a particular position in a school (such as the Head of Sociology or Chemistry), the researcher risks identifying the post holder. Teachers may feel angry about being identified in this way. It may damage their career prospects and make them (and their colleagues) reluctant to participate in other research.

Theoretical issues in researching staff

One issue is that, if teachers are aware of the research and its aims, they may not behave normally. In studies based on observation, this is referred to as the observer effect. If teachers change their behaviour in the classroom, the validity of the data is likely to be affected. Similarly, interviews with staff may be influenced by interview bias if, for example, teachers do not give honest answers because they think their comments might get back to the senior management team. Interviews are also subject to interviewer bias (see pp. 152–154) and the accent, dress, gender, ethnicity or skills of the interviewer may affect the development of rapport and interviewees' responses. In these cases, the validity of interview data may be reduced. Another issue is that, if senior managers give the researcher access only to trusted teachers, then the sample is unlikely to be typical of all teachers at that institution. Any data from interviews or observation are unlikely to be representative and it becomes difficult to generalise from the findings.

195

Summary

1. Practical issues when researching staff include selecting a suitable research site and negotiating access to it. Gatekeepers are more likely to allow access if they see the research as relevant to schools or colleges. They might refuse access because they believe the research could damage the institution's image or impact negatively on students' achievements.

2. Sociologists must also negotiate access to staff. Some teachers may not want to participate because they lack time, do not want to be observed in the classroom or fear possible criticism.

3. Good ethical practice means ensuring that teachers provide consent voluntarily. Sociologists must also ensure that individual teachers are not identifiable in publications. Providing feedback reports to research sites for comment can increase the possibility of revealing identities.

4. Theoretical concerns include questions of validity arising from the observer effect in classroom-based research, interview bias and interviewer bias. Other concerns include the extent to which the sample of teachers is representative and the implications of this for generalising.

4.1.3 Researching pupils and students

Most educational research involves pupils and students as research participants. They differ from each other in terms of their social characteristics such as their class, ethnicity, gender and age. They also differ in terms of individual characteristics such as their self-esteem, attitudes to school and authority figures, levels of articulacy and literacy skills. These features have implications for researchers who carry out research in educational settings. For example, researchers should take into account pupils' age and literacy skills when designing self-completion questionnaires. This unit looks at the issues involved in researching pupils and students.

Pupils and students as research participants

Depending on the topic, a particular research project might focus on individual boys or girls; peer groups; pupils with special educational needs; students of Asian heritage; middle-class students; white working-class boys; pupils in different bands; A-level students; or a specific year group.

Activity

Sociologists have to be alert to particular practical and ethical issues when researching primary school children.

Why do you think primary school children are seen as a potentially vulnerable group in sociological research on education?

Researching students and pupils raises particular issues. Most primary school children, for example, are less able than older people to understand and express abstract ideas (Hill, 2005). They might misunderstand a question or struggle to answer it. As a result, sociologists have to choose research methods that allow children to express their views and describe their experiences. Children also have less power than adults based on their age, social and legal status, and their position within the school hierarchy. This has implications for research in that children may be reluctant to disagree with adult interviewers. Children are also seen as a particularly vulnerable group because they may be open to adult influence and persuasion (Hill, 2005). Keith Punch (2009) argues that the research methods used with children need to be appropriate to the child's stage of development. The methods should also be sensitive to the issues arising from children's abilities, powerlessness and vulnerability.

Practical issues in researching pupils and students

A sociologist may have to ensure that funds and time are available to include children whose first language is not English and children with special needs, learning or speech difficulties (for example, the costs of having information sheets in Braille).

Negotiating access can be problematic in that some students might assume that the researcher will report back to teachers and, as a result, they will be treated differently at school. In many cases, members of counter-school cultures may be reluctant to cooperate with researchers.

Ethical issues in researching pupils and students

Ethical guidelines require researchers to safeguard children against potential risks to their emotional, physical or general wellbeing. Research with pupils and students raises particular ethical questions that may not apply when researching adults.

Informed consent

When researching children and young people, getting informed consent can involve two stages: first, permission from parents or guardians and second permission from the pupils or students themselves. In some cases, the head teacher may think that this two-stage process would take up too much time. A researcher depends on the goodwill of the host school and may find it difficult to insist on asking parents and students to sign consent forms if the head teacher views this as unnecessary. Older students, particularly sixth formers, may feel patronised if parental consent is required on their behalf and this may damage the rapport between researchers and students.

Children may not understand enough about the research to give informed consent. Pupils in the early years of primary school can be the most difficult group to inform because of their age. However, they still have the right to information about the project and to consent (or otherwise) to participating. It is important that any information provided (both written and spoken) is appropriate and clear, taking into account the participants' age, their level of understanding, reading abilities and whether they have learning difficulties.

In practice, student participation in research may not be entirely voluntary if, for example, a form tutor distributes copies of a questionnaire during a tutorial and expects all tutees to complete one. Students (who have less power than teachers) may have little choice but to cooperate with the research in a minimal way. Students and pupils may also experience peer pressure either to participate in a project or not to participate.

Confidentiality

In research with children, researchers should make the limits to confidentiality clear when negotiating consent. A researcher may gain '**guilty knowledge**' (De Laine, 2000) about, for example, the activities of a counter-school culture and will have to decide how to handle this information. The right to confidentiality may be broken if the researcher thinks that someone is in serious danger or at serious risk of harming others. If a pupil reveals something in an interview that leads a researcher to believe they are in significant and immediate danger, the researcher has a responsibility to take action.

Protection from harm

Ethical guidelines advise against the risk of causing harm, distress, humiliation or embarrassment to participants. A researcher may ask a question (for example, about examination results or friendship groups) that causes embarrassment to a student. A pupil might find it distressing to describe the experience of being bullied. The researcher must guard against anything that could stigmatise or label individuals or groups of students (such as those on free school meals or those with learning difficulties). They also have to ensure that students' involvement in a research project does not distract them from their education or affect their achievements.

Theoretical issues in researching pupils and students

In classroom-based observation, pupils may act differently if they know they are being observed, particularly during the early days of a study. In interviews with children, the interviewer's appearance, gender, age and ethnicity can affect the

197

results (see pp. 151–154). Some female students may feel intimidated by a male researcher and prefer to be interviewed by a female. This could affect the quality and quantity of the interview data. Some younger pupils may be unable to express their ideas fully in words. Pupils and students may censor themselves during interviews and say what they think the interviewer wants to hear. This is sometimes referred to as the social desirability effect. In these cases, the validity of the data is likely to be reduced.

If parents from particular social groups withhold consent to their children being involved in a study, this may impact on the representativeness of the sample. For example, some working-class parents who did not go to university may be more suspicious of researchers than middle-class university educated parents. If the sample of pupils who complete a questionnaire is not representative of the wider population, the sociologist will not be able to generalise.

Activity

Identify two possible differences between the research characteristics of secondary school students and those of:

a) university students

b) primary school pupils.

Key term

Guilty knowledge Information that a researcher acquires about, for example, a research participant's involvement in criminal or deviant acts.

Summary

1. Researching pupils and students raises particular issues that are less likely to arise when researching adults. For example, the methods should be sensitive to children's abilities, lack of power and vulnerability.

2. Practical issues include any additional costs of funding research to ensure that children with special needs are not excluded.

3. Negotiating access to members of counter-school cultures can be difficult. Some students may assume that the researcher will report back to the school.

4. Researching pupils and students raises ethical questions about their ability to understand the research aims and any abstract concepts, their powerlessness in schools and their potential vulnerability to persuasion.

5. Getting informed consent may involve parents and their children. Pupils may not understand enough about the research project to give informed consent. All information should be clear taking into account the participants' age and abilities.

6. Consent must be voluntary but pupils and students may feel under pressure from staff to participate in the research or from peers not to participate.

7. Confidentiality may be legitimately breached under certain circumstances.

8. Good ethical practice includes protecting vulnerable and powerless participants from harm or distress, for example during interviews on bullying or truancy.

9. Theoretical issues include questions about how far the sample of participants is representative, how far methods such as interviews and classroom-based observation generate valid data. And how far generalisations are possible.

4.1.4 Researching parents in an educational context

Sociologists are interested in exploring issues such as the impact of home background, parental expectations, and economic, social and cultural capital on educational achievement. They can gather valuable data on these issues by undertaking research with parents, guardians and carers. This unit looks at some of the practical, ethical and theoretical issues related to researching parents.

Practical issues in researching parents

One of the main practical considerations when researching parents is negotiating access.

Negotiating access

Teachers and students are relatively easy to locate because large numbers of them can be found in schools during term time. By contrast, parents are not located in one site and the researcher has to track them down. Martin Hughes (1994) argues that the process of negotiating agreement for an interview is often more time-consuming and complicated for parents than for teachers or students.

Activity

In practice, more mothers than fathers participate in educational research.

How might this affect the representativeness of the sample of parents?

When a sociologist is undertaking research in a school site, one way of accessing parents is to write to them, explaining what the research is about and inviting them to participate in interviews or complete questionnaires. However, schools are unlikely to provide students' home addresses and, if children are asked to deliver the letters to their parents, there is no guarantee that they will arrive. Another option is to ask teachers to select parents but one disadvantage of this approach is that they may select parents who they see as cooperative so the sample is unlikely to be representative.

Some studies of parents are not linked to a research project in a school site. In this case, snowballing may be used to generate a sample but it is likely to be unrepresentative and this makes it difficult to generalise (see p. 162).

Interviews with parents may be carried out in the students' homes. This is particularly advantageous when the research focuses on issues such as links between home background, material resources or cultural capital and educational achievement. By visiting the home, a researcher can gather additional information about the family and household context, and resources. However, home-based interviews with parents are relatively time consuming and expensive. It might also be difficult to find a quiet space to carry out a confidential interview.

Refusal of access

Parents may refuse to take part in research for several reasons. They may be too busy to fit an interview into their schedule, see the research as irrelevant or not want to discuss topics such as bullying or truancy with a stranger. They may fear that any negative comments will get back to the school. Some parents may feel intimidated by the idea of an interview with a sociologist or uncomfortable about inviting a researcher into their home. In some cases, students may persuade their parents not to get involved

because, for example, they associate the researcher with school.

Activity

Some sociologists compensate participants for giving up their time to complete questionnaires or interviews by entering them in a prize draw or offering them gift vouchers.

Identify two advantages and two disadvantages of compensating research participants in this way.

Ethical issues in researching parents

Obtaining informed consent is likely to be more straightforward with parents than young children as they are able to understand what the project is about, ask questions about it and raise any concerns.

Research intrudes on people's lives and some topics within the sociology of education are potentially sensitive. For example, parents may have to discuss personal and possibly distressing accounts of their children's experiences of bullying or racism in school or their own difficult encounters with their children's school.

If the researcher has contacted the parents via their children's school, issues of confidentiality and anonymity are particularly important. Before consenting, the parents must feel confident that nothing will be reported back to the school. Sociologists may protect parents' anonymity in published accounts of the research by using pseudonyms and excluding some details such as the age and gender of any children who are not participants in the research.

Theoretical issues in researching parents

Few researchers carry out ethnographic studies inside people's homes because, for example, it is difficult to get long-term access. Instead, they have to rely on what parents tell them in interviews or write on questionnaires. When discussing potentially sensitive topics during interviews, parents may not be entirely honest. For example, some middle-class parents may not disclose the extent to which they help with their children's assignments or the lengths they go in order to secure their preferred school choices. Other parents may feel defensive and exaggerate how much help they give with homework or the extent of their contact with the school. In these cases, the validity of the data will be reduced.

199

Parents who feel most strongly about the topic being studied (such as racism or sexism within education) may agree to participate and, for example, will return questionnaires fairly quickly. Other parents may have literacy problems which limit their ability to complete a questionnaire. Those parents who respond may not be typical of the sample and this will affect how far sociologists can generalise.

Activity

Self-completion questionnaires may not be suitable for all parents.

Explain why a low response rate among some groups of parents would be problematic in sociological research on education.

Summary

1. Research with parents allows sociologists to explore topics such as the impact of home background, parental expectations and different forms of capital on students' achievements.

2. Negotiating access to parents can be relatively time consuming and complex. The different ways of accessing parents (such as via schools and snowballing) have advantages and disadvantages.

3. Parents may refuse to participate in research because they are too busy, see the research as irrelevant or an invasion of privacy or fear that any negative comments will get back to the school. Some parents may feel intimidated by the idea of an interview with a sociologist.

4. Good ethical practice recognises that some topics (such as sexism, racism or bullying experienced by participants' children at school) are potentially sensitive and it may distress parents to discuss them.

5. Sociologists can protect parents' anonymity in publications by using pseudonyms and excluding some details.

6. One theoretical concern is that the validity of data may be reduced if, for example, parents underplay or exaggerate the help they provide with homework.

7. Parents who choose to participate in research may not be typical of the population. This raises questions about the generalisability of data.

PART 2 OBSERVATION IN SOCIOLOGICAL RESEARCH ON EDUCATION

Contents

Observation in settings such as schools, colleges, classrooms, staffrooms and playgrounds is a popular method in sociological research on education. It has been used to study topics such as teacher and student behaviour during lessons, gendered classroom interaction and counter-school cultures. It may involve either participant observation (which is unstructured) or non-participant observation (which can be either structured or unstructured). This part looks at these different types of observation (see pp.142–151). What sorts of data do they generate? What practical, ethical and theoretical issues do they raise for researchers in educational settings?

4.2.1 Participant observation

Participant observation allows a researcher to study teachers and students in schools, classrooms and other normal, everyday settings such as playgrounds and college libraries to see what they do rather than relying on what they say they do (see pp. 143–149). It may be carried out overtly but it may also be covert if the researcher takes on a role within the setting (such as a teacher, classroom assistant, cleaner or university student) in order to carry out research without informing participants.

Research based on participant observation has produced some vivid accounts of classroom interaction and counter-school cultures. This unit begins by looking at several examples of studies based on participant observation. It then examines some of the practical, ethical and theoretical issues related to using participant observation in sociological research on education.

Research example: researching a counter-school culture

Learning to Labour: How Working-Class Kids get Working-Class Jobs by Paul Willis (1977) is a classic ethnographic case study of 12 non-academic, working-class boys who belonged to a counter-school culture (see pp. 29–32, 92–93, 105, 120–121). Willis began studying the 'lads' at the start of their second term in the fourth year (Year 10) at Hammertown Boys, a secondary modern school on a council estate in the Midlands. He followed them during their last 18 months at school and into the first six months at work.

Willis studied the 'lads' by using observation and participant observation in classrooms, assemblies, in corridors and around the school. He attended lessons with the lads as a member of the class rather than as a teacher. During breaks at school and during their leisure activities, he spent time with the boys. He also attended careers classes and went on school trips. Other methods included informal interviews with individual boys, recorded group discussions (for example, on topics such as teachers, the school curriculum and vandalism) and diaries. He also recorded 'long conversations' with the lads' parents and with senior teachers, the boys' subject teachers and careers officers.

After the boys left school, Willis followed them into the workplace as they began working in jobs such as carpet laying, tyre fitting, plumber's mate and factory work. He undertook participant observation here,

working alongside each boy as he carried out his job. He also interviewed the boys individually at work and carried out interviews with foremen, managers and shop stewards.

Activity

Paul Willis met up with some of the lads for a group discussion at the university after he had finished the fieldwork and analysis, and the book was in draft form. The following extract is from the group discussion.

'**Perc**: "Truthfully I was a bit fed up of yer ... I enjoy talking to people, but sometimes I used to think, y'know, he's asking some bloody, y'know, right things. I used to think you was asking a bit much, personal things y'know."

Spanksy: "It was nice to be out of lessons."

Bill: "You were staff (at first), you were somebody in between, later on I took you as one of us ... The main difference is, you listen to us, you want to know what we've got to say, they (teachers) don't, none of them."

Joey: "When you first started asking questions something illegal must have come out and we'd told you things we'd done wrong and we never got any backlash off other members of staff which obviously meant you hadn't told anybody.'"

Source: Willis, P.E. (1977) *Learning to Labour: How Working-Class Kids get Working-Class Jobs*, Saxon House, Farnborough, pp. 195–197.

1. Drawing on this information:

    a) briefly describe how Paul Willis's relationship with the boys changed over time.

    b) identify two ethical issues raised by Paul Willis's study.

2. Drawing on this information and your own knowledge of research methods, explain

    a) what is meant by the term 'mixed methods'.

    b) two strengths of using participant observation to study a counter-school culture in a boys' secondary school.

    c) two limitations of using participant observation to study a counter-school culture in a boys' secondary school.

Research example: researching working-class masculinities

In *From Labouring to Learning: Working-Class Masculinities, Education and De-industrialisation*, Michael R.M. Ward (2015) spent two and a half years following the educational and social lives of 32 young men in a South Wales community (see pp. 31, 105–106, 121–122 and 129). He took an ethnographic approach studying their lives not only in school and college but also in their leisure activities, friendship groups and families. Ward actually 'participated in many of the same activities' of those he studied. He states, 'My interpretations and understandings were formed through personal knowledge and deep relationships with the young men'.

Ethnography is the study of the way of life of a group, their experiences and their view of the world. In Ward's words, 'Ethnography captures reality as it happens whereas interview-based studies are only participants' accounts of events rather than actually observed situations'. As this suggests, Ward's main method of data collection was participant observation. It gave him the 'richness of data' he wanted.

Ward observed the young men in school and college, actively participating in some lessons: 'on one occasion I helped to change a tyre on a car and on another groom a horse'. He hung round the common room, went on school trips and attended parents' evenings. He went beyond school and college 'in order to extend the gaze of research and gain a more meaningful and intricate understanding of how the young men understood and experienced their world'.

Ward's activities included, 'sitting in cars in car parks and driving round the town; attending sports events and nights out in pubs and night clubs; going to live music events and the cinema; shopping; birthday parties; frequenting takeaways and cafes; playing computer games; going to university open days … I also used Facebook as a means of keeping in touch'. Ward describes ethnographic research as a 'balancing act where researchers try to become immersed in their fieldwork to better understand a culture without becoming too immersed or "going native" and losing one's focus!'

Michael Ward came from a similar community to the young men he studied but was 10 years older than them. In the pub he put songs on the jukebox which he knew they liked – songs by The Killers, Muse and Bullet for my Valentine. After a few beers he couldn't resist choosing a song he liked, *Born To Run* by Bruce Springsteen. He had to buy a round of drinks for his 'uncool' behaviour.

Source: Ward, M.R.M. (2015). *From Labouring to Learning: Working-Class Masculinities, Education and De-industrialisation*, Palgrave MacMillan, Basingstoke.

Activity

1. How important do you think Michael Ward's gender and age were in helping him to build rapport with the research participants?

2. Drawing on this information and your own knowledge of research methods, explain

   a) two strengths of this study from an interpretivist perspective

   b) two limitations of this study from a positivist perspective.

Research example: researching education and social class

Gillian Evans (2006), a social anthropologist, undertook an ethnographic study of a primary school in Bermondsey, southeast London and, in her book, presents 'case studies of working-class children and their families'. The research focused on the relationship between social class and education (see p. 75).

Gillian Evans carried out fieldwork in Tenter Ground Primary School to understand how social relations are formed in the classroom and the school. She observed lessons, had discussions and conversations with teachers, observed interaction in the playground and classroom, attended school assemblies, spent time in the staffroom and accompanied one class on a school trip. In this way, she developed an understanding of the daily realities of school life.

Sometimes, she sat at the tables with the pupils, observed their interaction and made notes without intervening. Over time, she became more like a friend than a teacher or classroom assistant. For instance, she did not report children who engaged in disruptive behaviour unless there was a direct risk of harm.

When she began her research, Gillian Evans, a middle-class woman, lived in a two-bedroom flat on a council estate in Bermondsey. As a long-term resident, she was not a complete outsider and her daughters went to primary school close to Bermondsey. Some of the other residents saw her as a 'posh cow' and she learned not to advertise her education and experience in everyday interactions. Over time, her accent changed and she began to talk more like the local people. In this respect, doing the fieldwork changed her.

Gillian Evans spent time sitting in parents' homes, drinking tea, chatting and interviewing them. She was able to observe family members interacting at home and talked to parents in the school playground.

Activity

1. Identify and explain one way in which Gillian Evans can be seen as:

   a) an outsider in this community

   b) an insider.

2. Identify two ethical issues that a researcher would need to consider when undertaking fieldwork in parents' homes.

Practical issues when using participant observation

Resources

Compared to methods such as self-completion questionnaires and structured interviews, the fieldwork in a school-based participant observation study is time consuming. It can generate a huge amount of qualitative data (for example, from field notes, guided conversations and unstructured interviews) which need to be transcribed (put into written form) and analysed. The more time consuming a study, the more expensive it is likely to be.

Gaining access, entry and acceptance

Gatekeepers might be unwilling to host a study that involves a researcher being present in the educational setting for several years. Even if a school grants access, the senior management may not give the researcher much freedom to observe lessons, talk to students informally and hang around in order to gather data. The researcher may be reluctant to make fieldnotes in settings such as staffrooms or school canteens as this could disrupt naturally occurring behaviour. They may prefer to rely on memory and write their notes at the end of each day.

Activity

Fitting into a school setting can be difficult in an overt participant observation study.

Why might it be easier to blend in when carrying out a covert rather than an overt participant observation study in a school?

It can be difficult for an adult to blend into a classroom when carrying out overt participant observation. David Hargreaves (1967) had previously worked as a teacher before starting his participant observation at a boys' secondary school and spent some time teaching at the research site during his fieldwork. Although this may have helped him to gain acceptance among the staff, the boys may have seen him as an authority figure. When studying topics such as truancy, the researcher might adopt a covert role as an education welfare officer in order to blend in.

Compared to structured methods, participant observation relies more on the researcher's personal qualities. In order to build positive relationships, a researcher must be able to engage in different situations (such as classrooms and staffrooms) and interact with a range of different participants (for example, head teachers, teachers, support staff, pro- and anti-school pupils and older students). The researcher's social characteristics (including their age, class, gender, ethnicity and accent) may help or hinder them in building rapport with diverse research participants in educational settings. Developing rapport, gaining trust and establishing good field relationships take time but they influence the quality and quantity of the data gathered.

Ethical issues when using participant observation

The issue of informed consent in ethnographic research within educational settings generates debate among sociologists. One view is that during studies based on overt participant observation, it is not possible for teachers and students to give informed consent because even the researchers do not know at the outset how the research might unfold. Covert participant observation with potentially vulnerable pupils is seen as unethical because it is not based on informed consent.

Another ethical issue arising from the use of participant observation is that teachers may make comments during casual conversations in the staffroom without realising that they are providing the researcher with data.

A school-based participant observer may face an ethical dilemma if they observe rule breaking among students. If they report this to staff, they risk losing students' trust. If they do not report it, they risk being seen by teachers as condoning rule breaking. A participant observer may also have to decide whether to intervene if they observe a fight or verbal abuse in the playground. They must also write up any incidents involving rule breaking without revealing identities.

Theoretical issues when using participant observation

Supporters of participant observation see it as one of the best ways of generating valid data about school processes such as labelling or the formation of anti-school cultures. It allows a researcher to build rapport with groups of staff and students over time and to understand how they make sense of their lived experiences. Interpretivists see participant observation as the most appropriate method for providing a true picture of the meanings that guide

Activity

A discussion of the observer effect during David Hargreaves's study of life in a boys' secondary modern school based on participant observation.

1. Identify two possible reasons why some teachers might not behave naturally when a researcher is in the classroom.

2. Explain one reason why the observer effect is problematic in classroom-based research.

teachers' and students' behaviour. It provides information about school structures, processes, cultures and group interaction that standardised methods such as questionnaires are unable to gather. For example, it could illuminate students' motives for truanting and allow a researcher to observe peer pressure to truant as it unfolds.

Critics highlight several limitations of participant observation as a means of gathering data in sociological research on education. They argue that the observer effect can impact on teachers' and students' behaviour in classrooms particularly during the early stages of the fieldwork. In this case, the validity of the data will be reduced. However, the more accustomed teachers and students are to having an observer in the classroom, the less impact the researcher is likely to have on their behaviour.

Critics also argue that a participant observer may come to identify so closely with the members of a counter-school culture that behaviour related to sexism, racism or homophobia, for example, is glossed over. Any loss of objectivity may reduce the validity of the observations.

Positivists emphasise measurement and statistical relationships. From a positivist perspective, participant observation in schools is unsystematic, and the data are rarely quantified. Instead, it relies on the observers' subjective interpretations. Any interactions that they note and discuss in their analyses will be selective and might reflect their own preoccupations (for example, that schools are patriarchal or that banding leads to inequality of opportunity). It is also difficult to replicate a study to check the reliability of the data. Participant observation studies in school settings usually focus on small, unrepresentative samples so it is not possible to generalise from the findings.

Summary

1. Participant observation produces rich and detailed accounts of school life, student cultures and classroom interaction. It is used in ethnographic and mixed methods research.

2. Participant observation in educational settings is relatively time consuming and expensive.

3. Gaining access and acceptance can be problematic and a participant observer must be skilled in building rapport with teachers and students.

4. With overt participant observation, it may not be possible to get informed consent at the outset because it is not clear how the study will unfold.

5. Covert participant observation of potentially vulnerable students is seen as unethical because it is not based on informed consent.

6. Researchers may experience ethical dilemmas during fieldwork if, for example, they observe rule breaking among pupils.

7. Interpretivists see participant observation as providing a true picture of the meanings that guide pupils' and teachers' behaviour. However, the observer effect may distort the situation and reduce validity.

8. Positivists argue that participant observation studies in educational settings are unsystematic and based on the observer's subjective interpretations. They focus on small, unrepresentative samples and cannot be replicated to check reliability so generalisations are inappropriate.

Activity

1. Explain two strengths of using participant observation to investigate the effects of banding on students in a secondary school.

2. Explain two limitations of using participant observation to investigate gendered classroom interaction in a primary school.

4.2.2 Non-participant observation

With non-participant observation, the researcher usually sits in a classroom and observes without participating in activities or school life (see p. 149). It may be structured or unstructured, depending on whether the researcher uses a systematic observation schedule. What sorts of data do these different approaches generate? How useful are they in sociological research on education? This unit begins by looking at examples of research based on non-participant observation. It then examines

205

some of the practical, ethical and theoretical issues related to using non-participant observation in classrooms and schools.

Unstructured non–participant observation

Unstructured observation in classrooms has been used to study topics such as students' interactions with their peers and teacher, the effects of marketisation and league tables on teaching, and the way students construct gender in the classroom. A researcher may also observe primary school pupils' gendered behaviour in a school playground from an upstairs room in the school.

Research example: researching the construction of gender in the classroom

In *Boys, Girls and Achievement*, Becky Francis (2000) explores the ways in which students aged 14 to 16 years construct gender in the classroom. She used a combination of research methods including observation of GCSE English and maths classes to record classroom interaction and pupil behaviour in three secondary schools in London. In total, Becky Francis observed 12 different classes and, for each class, she observed a lesson three times. Although she informed the teachers about the project's aims, she did not inform the students that she was focusing on gender. She acknowledges that this raises questions about informed consent and power in the research process. However, if

Then and now: Becky Francis, *Boys, Girls and Achievement* (2000)

"It is interesting to reflect back on my study today. Since that time I have continued with mixed-methods research, because gathering data in different ways and from different perspectives sheds so much more light on an issue than just a single methodological approach. Most recently, I have been involved with very large-scale longitudinal studies, including both qualitative and quantitative research. But each time I embark on an educational research project that doesn't involve classroom observation, I find that it misses the richness and directness that direct observation provides.

There are of course issues of power and ethics involved with observation that it is important to consider – and to try to address. In this, I think sociological researchers are more sensitive than other scientists (including social scientists). For example, in different branches of psychology it is quite common not to reveal all the circumstances of the experiment in which subjects are asked to participate. This is often seen as legitimate in the interests of the pursuit of science. I think it is right that we balance such interests with attempts to ensure that the subjects of our research are not disempowered. Working with young people in schools adds an additional ethical dimension – school relies on young people obeying adults, and of course they have no choice about attending school either! I have found that piloting research approaches and interview questions with young people can help to ensure sensitivity, enabling a

change of question or even method if this seems more appropriate. (For example, at times I have changed from focus group to individual interviews if topics seem too personal; or from individual interviews to focus groups on topics where young people appear to appreciate 'strength in numbers').

But it's the revelations within qualitative work with children that still trouble me. We researchers tell young people that their interviews are confidential. Yet sometimes children reveal awful things that need addressing: being smacked by a teacher, for example; or that they are being bullied. Each time something like this happens, it requires a judgement from the researcher. And how would you feel as an interviewer if your respondent says something racist or homophobic – do you just continue to listen, because your role is to accurately capture the respondent's views, rather than exercise a judgement or hierarchical power relationship? Or does not intervening to challenge those views legitimate and perhaps even perpetuate them? These are dilemmas for all researchers, but especially for feminist researchers concerned to avoid disempowering respondents, while also contesting inequality."

Activity

1. Why does Becky Francis continue to use a mixed methods approach?

2. What ethical dilemmas does she refer to?

3. How does Becky Francis try to ensure sensitivity when researching young people in schools?

she had provided students with more details, this could have impacted on their gendered behaviour.

'This was the first time I had been an observer in a secondary school classroom, and I initially found that taking my place at the back or front of the classroom was an embarrassing and threatening experience ... I felt very vulnerable and consequently quite nervous. I expected to hear personal comments about me being loudly whispered, rubbers to hit me on the head and tampons to fly into my lap. In fact, I was amazed how little attention pupils gave me in the classroom. Some asked me if I was an inspector, and this may provide a clue to the pupils' apparent acceptance at being observed: observation by inspectors and the like is more common now than when I was at school during the 1980s...

Teachers also responded to my presence in class in different ways. One male teacher used me as a disciplinary tool, saying to a girl who was messing about with a boy at the back of the class (with a sideways look at me), "do you know you're being observed?" Some were clearly concerned that I was observing their teaching practice as well as the pupils' behaviour ...'

Source: Francis, B. (2000) *Boys, Girls and Achievement*, Routledge Falmer, London, pp. 27–29.

Becky Francis points out that having an observer in the classroom can feel intimidating or threatening to teachers. It can add more pressure in a job that is already very pressurised.

Activity — Using unstructured non-participant observation in classrooms

Drawing on this information, explain one way in which limiting the information given to the pupils raises issues about

a) research ethics

b) power in the research process.

Structured non-participant observation

Structured or systematic observation has been used to study topics such as the process of teaching and learning, teacher and pupil behaviour in classrooms, and playground behaviour.

During structured observation, the researcher uses an observation schedule or a coding scheme which tells them what to look for and how to record their observations. It is seen as an objective, systematic technique for analysing classroom interaction and measuring differences in teaching styles.

Ned Flanders (1970) developed a ten-category system to code interaction in classrooms (the Flanders Interaction Analysis Categories or FIAC) by keeping track of pre-selected events (e.g. teacher and student talk). Seven of these categories refer to teacher talk (e.g. the teacher praises or encourages pupils; asks questions; criticises; or gives directions). Two categories refer to pupil talk

Activity

The FIAC codes teacher and student talk in the classroom.

1. Identify two strengths of the FIAC from a positivist perspective.

2. Identify two limitations of the FIAC from an interpretivist perspective.

(e.g. pupils respond to the teacher; or initiate talk by, for instance, expressing their own ideas). One category is used to indicate periods of silence or confusion.

The FIAC can be used by a trained non-participant observer who sits in the classroom (or views a video) and records events on an observation form. At regular intervals (for example, every three seconds), the observer systematically codes the type of activity taking place. The FIAC allows a researcher to measure and compare the proportion of time that the teacher and pupils spend talking during a lesson.

Practical issues when using non-participant observation

Structured non-participant observation is cheaper and quicker than unstructured observation because the researcher does not need to spend time building rapport with students and teachers.

The use of an observation form with pre-set categories makes it easier to record data in classrooms compared to unstructured observation. If the focus is on verbal communication, however, the noise level in some classes may make it difficult to record all interactions. Some researchers video record lessons so they can review the material rather than relying on fieldnotes.

Ethical issues when using non-participant observation

Informed consent can be problematic when using non-participant observation. One issue is that it can be difficult to get consent to video record young children in schools for research purposes. Another is that researchers may not provide students with full information about their research topic when, for example, studying areas related to gender. Critics argue that this involves deception and goes against the principle of informed consent.

Theoretical issues when using non-participant observation

Sociologists who adopt a positivist approach favour structured non-participant observation to investigate classroom behaviour because the procedure is seen as more systematic and objective than unstructured observations. The researcher does not interact with pupils in the classroom and is less likely to become over-involved or go 'native'. They can count and quantify the frequency and proportion of teacher talk, student talk, silence or confusion during a particular lesson. They can also compare different teaching styles across classrooms, departments and schools. With pre-set categories, a study can be replicated to check the reliability of the findings before making generalisations.

Critics, however, argue that the observer effect may come into play with structured observation in classrooms, reducing the validity of the findings. Pupils in an anti-school culture, for example, may exaggerate their behaviour to impress their peers and, in this case, the data will not provide a true picture. Critics also point out that an observer must first interpret classroom behaviour in order to code it and two observers may interpret the same behaviour differently. For example, when categorising behaviour, the observer might find it difficult to decide whether a pupil is genuinely asking a question or trying to sidetrack a teacher.

Sociologists who adopt an interpretivist approach argue that data based on systematic observations of teachers, pupils and lessons lack the rich detail of unstructured lesson observations. By using an observation schedule, researchers impose their own meanings on classroom interaction. They also ignore the meanings behind teachers' and pupils' behaviour and how they experience classroom interaction. More qualitative methods are needed to capture this.

Activity

1. Explain one strength of using systematic classroom observations to investigate the relationship between class size and pupil behaviour.

2. Explain one limitation of using systematic classroom observations to investigate the relationship between class size and pupil behaviour.

Summary

1. Non-participant observation in classrooms may be structured or unstructured. Structured non-participant observation is quicker and cheaper because the observer spends little time building rapport with teachers and students.

2. Non-participant observation may involve deception which raises questions about informed consent and the power imbalance between the observer and observed.

3. Positivists favour structured non-participant observation which provides a systematic way of analysing classroom interaction and measuring differences in teaching styles. It is based on a classroom observation schedule and can be replicated to check the reliability of the data before generalising.

4. Critics argue that structured non-participant observation in classrooms is subject to the observer effect which reduces validity. It also involves the observer imposing their own meanings on classroom interaction.

5. Interpretivists prefer unstructured non-participant observation which generates rich and detailed qualitative data that capture the meanings behind classroom interaction.

PART 3 INTERVIEWS IN SOCIOLOGICAL RESEARCH ON EDUCATION

Contents

Interviews with parents, teachers and students are one of the most popular methods in sociological research on education. They can take place in a range of settings including empty classrooms, staff offices, students' homes, parents' workplaces, university premises or public locations such as parks or cafes depending on factors such as the participants' age and preferences. Interviews have been used to study a wide variety of topics including the strategies that parents use to support their children's education, teachers' perspectives on 'laddish' behaviour among girls and boys in schools, and the significance of social class to students' friendship networks. What are the practical, ethical and theoretical implications of using interviews in educational research? What questions do interviews raise about power relationships between researchers and participants? Why do interviews with primary school pupils raise particular issues for sociologists? This part examines the different types of individual interview as well as focus group interviews. It looks at some of the issues that researchers have to consider when using interviews in educational research.

4.3.1 Individual interviews

Individual interviews may be structured, semi-structured or unstructured, depending on how far the questions are standardised in advance (see pp. 151–158). This unit examines an example of the use of individual interviews in sociological research on education. It then looks at some practical, ethical and theoretical issues related to the different types of one-to-one interview.

Research example: researching Black Caribbean middle-class families

In *The Colour of Class*, Nicola Rollock *et al*. (2015) examine the way in which Black Caribbean middle-class families use their social and cultural resources to support their children's education, for example when choosing schools or when faced with low teachers' expectations of their children's academic capabilities. The main aim of the study was to explore and analyse the educational perspectives, strategies and experiences of Black Caribbean middle-class families. The research team focused mainly on the parents' role and the home setting rather than on schools and investigated how race intersects with social class status to shape experiences.

The study was based on qualitative semi-structured interviews with a sample of 62 parents who defined themselves as Black Caribbean. Participants were recruited through several sources including announcements on family and education websites, Black social groups and professional websites. The researchers also drew on their existing contacts through snowballing (see p. 162).

The selection criteria for parents included having one or more child aged between eight and 18 years. This age group was chosen because it includes key points of transition in children's education. The researchers drew on the NS–SEC classification (see pp. 8 and 67) to measure class. They interviewed parents in professional or managerial occupations including teachers, psychologists, social workers, managers and solicitors. The researchers used pseudonyms for the parents and did not include details of any children who were not within the selection criteria (eight to 18 years) to protect parents' anonymity.

Although the researchers made an effort to include men in the sample, they ended up interviewing only 13 fathers. Most of the interviews took place in London between 2009 and 2011. The researchers carried out follow-up interviews with 15 parents one year later in order, for example, to revisit some of the original themes in greater depth.

In their book, the authors discuss the ethical issues related to having a research team made up of three White professors (one woman and two men) and a Black female researcher. The latter team member, Nicola Rollock, shared the same Caribbean cultural heritage and social class position as the parents in the study and could connect to issues raised during the interviews. The three White team members were outsiders and questioned their ethnic privileges, the power linked to their Whiteness, and how far they grasped the experiences of racism. The research team offered interviewees a choice in terms of the ethnicity of the interviewer. One advantage of having outsiders on the team was that interviewees often explained their experiences fully, knowing that these would be outside White people's experiences.

Activity

Drawing on this information and your own knowledge of research methods, explain:

a) one ethical issue that White researchers may face when investigating the educational perspectives of Black Caribbean heritage parents

b) two strengths of this study from an interpretivist perspective

c) two limitations of this study from a positivist perspective.

Practical issues when using one-to-one interviews

Using qualitative semi-structured and unstructured interviews in educational research is time consuming and labour intensive compared to structured interviews. This may deter a sociologist from using them if their time is limited. Lack of time could also deter busy parents and teachers from participating in **qualitative interviews**.

Funding affects the number of interviews that can be carried out. For instance, if a sociologist is studying marketisation in education, the budget might not cover the costs of piloting, carrying out and transcribing numerous unstructured interviews with teachers but it might be enough for computer-assisted structured interviews.

Students may be absent on the day of their scheduled interview. Some groups of students (such as those who truant or refuse to attend school) are more likely to be absent than others.

Schools are unlikely to release parents' contact details but assuming that the sociologist has been able to obtain them, it can be difficult to arrange a convenient time for home-based interviews with parents. Teachers have to fit interviews around their teaching timetables and schools may be reluctant to allow pupils to be withdrawn from lessons in order to participate in interviews. It is not always easy to find a quiet space in a school or college and background noise can affect the sound quality when recording interviews.

Interviewing primary school pupils raises particular issues for sociologists. They differ from young people, parents and teachers in terms of their language development, ability to understand complex ideas and their attention span. Interviews with younger pupils should be relatively short in order to avoid tiring them. The questions should be appropriate to the participants' age and development, for example, in terms of the complexity of language and use of abstract concepts. One advantage of interviews over self-completion questionnaires is that the researcher can rephrase a question if a pupil does not understand it. Some researchers encourage pupils to create drawings during interviews as a way of helping them to express their ideas.

Ethical issues when using one-to-one interviews

Qualitative interviews have advantages when studying **oppositional groups** in educational settings. For example, semi-structured interviews allow the researcher to build rapport and trust. Members of a counter-school culture may be more likely to provide information to a skilled and sensitive interviewer rather than complete a questionnaire. Qualitative interviews also have advantages when studying sensitive topics in educational contexts. Participants are more likely to discuss sensitive or painful experiences (for example, their own or their children's experiences of racism or bullying at school) with a sympathetic and understanding interviewer.

Before interviewing pupils in schools, sociologists may have to undergo a DBS check and obtain parental consent. Getting informed consent can be more problematic with semi-structured and unstructured interviews than with structured interviews. Qualitative interviews are not based on a standardised set of questions so it is not always clear at the outset what the participant is consenting to. An interview with students about parental involvement in homework, for example, may veer into unanticipated areas or touch upon sensitive issues such as divorce or bereavement that cause emotional distress. As a result, it is important that participants are made aware that they can stop the interview at any time.

Power, status and age differences come into play when researchers interview school pupils. Children and young people may see researchers in educational settings as authority figures. In this case, they may be reluctant to contradict or disagree with an adult or they may provide answers they think the researcher is looking for. (This social desirability effect can reduce the validity of interview data.) Some researchers avoid undertaking interviews in school settings, where possible, or ask older students to choose the venue as a way of giving them some control. On the other hand, participants have more opportunity to control the direction of the discussion in qualitative interviews compared to structured interviews so power relationships are less pronounced.

During an interview, students or parents may ask an interviewer for advice (for example, about local schools or GCSE options) and there are ethical questions attached to either providing advice (Pugsley, 2002)

or withholding it. Parents and teachers may ask the researcher what their children or students have said. Researchers may also face an ethical dilemma about confidentiality if a student reveals that they are being bullied or sexually harassed at school.

Theoretical issues when using one-to-one interviews

Nicola Rollock *et al.* (2015) argue that one of the main strengths of qualitative research based on interviews is that it provides rich data, insights and nuances about people's lives that could not be gained by using statistical research alone. It also provides detailed insights into the everyday processes (such as labelling) behind the patterns of educational underachievement and achievement. These strengths lead interpretivist sociologists to favour qualitative rather than standardised interviews in educational research.

Semi-structured and unstructured interviews are more suited to research that aims to discover meanings and lived experiences, for example what it means to pupils to belong to a counter-school culture or how sixth formers experience the process of withdrawing from school before completing their A-levels. The atmosphere is less formal so participants are more likely to open up and provide rich, valid data. On the other hand, membership of an anti-school culture will influence how participants view the researcher (for example, as an authority figure) and respond to questions.

Activity

Sociologists are interested in how families use their social, cultural and financial resources to support their children's education.

Explain one reason why interviews might not provide a valid picture of how far parents support their children's education.

Some teachers and parents may agree to be interviewed because they feel particularly strongly about the issue being investigated (such as bullying, cuts to public spending on education or marketisation policies). They may use the interview as an opportunity to air their grievances. In this case, the data may not be representative of other teachers' or parents' views.

Teachers and parents may not open up on some topics during an interview (for example, their perspectives on new policies introduced by senior managers such as banding or mixed-ability teaching) particularly if they have concerns about confidentiality. If they are reluctant to express their criticisms, this may reduce the validity of the data.

Interview bias is a potential problem and participants may provide socially desirable responses rather than reveal their true thoughts on controversial topics. Teachers, for example, may be guarded in what they reveal about their perceptions of social class, gender or ethnicity and any discrimination based on these factors. The social desirability effect can reduce the validity of data, particularly in unstructured interviews where participants and interviewers have a relatively close relationship. On the other hand, less structured interviews provide more opportunities for researchers to build rapport with teachers, students and parents. They can provide a more supportive setting for participants to discuss sensitive feelings and experiences, which may increase the validity of the data.

Interviewer bias arising from the interviewer's social characteristics such as their age, gender, ethnicity or class is another potential problem. The level of formality of an interview and the interviewer's manner, appearance, dress and accent can influence pupils. Students may be more open with young, casually dressed researchers while some head teachers may identify more with older, smartly dressed researchers.

Structured interviews are a type of social survey. Closed questions generate data that can be quantified, for example 34 per cent of Year 12 students stated that they planned to apply to their local university. All participants answer the same standardised questions so their responses are comparable, for example 54 per cent of working-class and 28 per cent of middle-class students in Year 12 stated that they planned to apply to their local university. In this way, the researcher can identify patterns and correlations (or statistical links) in the data. Structured interviews can be replicated to check for reliability and allow generalisations about issues such as social class and university applications. Positivists argue that qualitative interviews generate responses that are difficult to code, compare and

generalise from. As a result, positivists favour the use of structured interviews.

Structured interviews have limitations in educational research. First, participants have less opportunity to develop their answers, for example to discuss the circumstances around their university application. Second, sociologists devise the questions in advance according to what issues they see as important and interviewees answer these questions. Fresh issues about students' university applications, for example, are less likely to emerge than during qualitative interviews or participant observation. Some interpretivists prefer participant observation rather than structured interviews because it takes place in real social settings such as classrooms and playgrounds and allows direct observation of interaction.

Activity

1. Explain two strengths of using structured interviews to investigate the relationship between social class, parental support and educational achievement.

2. Explain two limitations of using unstructured interviews to investigate the factors influencing Year 11 students' A-level subject choices.

Key terms

Qualitative interviews Semi-structured and unstructured interviews that generate data in the form of verbatim (or word-for-word) quotations.

Oppositional groups Groups that oppose the status quo or resist authority such as counter-school cultures.

Summary

1. Semi-structured and unstructured interviews are more time consuming, labour intensive and costly than structured interviews in educational research.

2. When interviewing pupils, sociologists must take into account their language development, conceptual understanding and attention span.

3. During qualitative interviews, researchers can build rapport with interviewees when, for example, discussing sensitive topics such as bullying. This may increase validity.

4. Negotiating informed consent may be problematic in qualitative interviews as the discussions could move into unanticipated directions. However, participants have more

opportunities to control the direction of discussions than in structured interviews.

5. There are ethical problems in giving (or withholding) advice during interviews with parents and students.

6. Qualitative interviews are favoured by interpretivists because they provide detailed insights into everyday school processes and the lived experiences of teachers, pupils and parents. However, they are subject to interview and interviewer bias.

7. Structured interviews generate quantitative data and allow researchers to identify patterns between, for example, social class, gender and students' higher education destinations. Positivists see them as replicable, reliable and generalisable. However, participants cannot develop their answers or introduce fresh issues.

4.3.2 Focus group interviews

Sociologists often use focus groups (or group interviews) with students, teachers or parents together with individual interviews or participant observation, for instance, in mixed methods research on education (see pp. 140 and 186). In some cases, they use focus groups to inform the development of interview schedules or hypotheses. This unit looks at an example of a group interview and then examines some of the practical, ethical and theoretical issues related to their use.

Research example: researching social class and friendship networks in school

In "When you see a normal person …": social class and friendship networks among teenage students', Maria Papapolydorou (2014) investigated the significance of social class to students' friendship networks in school. She carried out research with Year 12 students aged 16 to 17 years from four secondary schools in London and used focus groups as well as semi-structured, individual interviews. Each focus group lasted between one and two hours and the students had some control over the direction of the discussions. In the following extract from one of the focus groups, the participants can be observed interacting at first hand within a friendship group.

James: *Yeah, I actually find it funny because say we go to a party with a lot of posh people and you go and sit on the sofa next to them … All these posh people would get up and move away. And I'm like why are you moving for? And they are like 'Oh because you are gonna rob us'.*

Researcher: *Are you serious?*

James: *Yeah, they do. They do.*

Researcher: *But how can they tell …?*

James: *They can because … I sit there and my body posture … I'm open.*

Researcher: *So by your body posture?*

James: *Yeah, I'd just sit there open. I'd just sit casually. Like that [he demonstrates]. I'd just sit like that.*

Andy: *Just like that, yeah.*

James: *Yeah and they'd move away. All right then. And when, when they say that I'm like…*

George: *That's the silliest thing. The silliest thing.*

James: *I just think to myself because they think that I'm gonna rob them … then I just think to myself I'm gonna rob them for the sake of it. And I've done it.*

(James, White British, working-class boy; Andy, Black African, working-class boy; George, mixed heritage: Black African and White British, working-class boy).

Source: Maria Papapolydorou (2014), *British Journal of Sociology of Education,* pp. 567–568.

Activity

1. Identify one possible ethical dilemma the researcher may have experienced during this focus group discussion.

2. Identify one example to show that the students have some control over the direction of this discussion.

3. Explain two limitations of using focus groups to investigate the significance of social class to students' friendship networks in school.

Practical issues when using group interviews

A group interview can be particularly useful with primary school pupils who are used to working in small group settings. It encourages them to interact within a peer group rather than just responding to an interviewer's questions. However, group interviews may be less appropriate than individual interviews for pupils who lack confidence. The interviewer must manage the group carefully so that individuals do not dominate the discussion.

Activity

In group interviews, the researcher's role is to encourage discussion rather than control it so there is less of a power imbalance than with individual interviews. However, the researcher must be able to manage a group interview.

In each case above, explain how the interviewer might respond to the participant (e.g. verbally or using non-verbal communication such as eye contact).

Group interviews with students, teachers or parents can save time and money compared to individual interviews. However, it can be time-consuming to transcribe the contents particularly with single gender groups or when participants talk over each other.

It can be difficult to get all the pupils together at the same time. If a researcher wanted to investigate students' experience of truancy, for example, those who truant regularly may be absent when the interview is scheduled and a school setting might not encourage an open discussion.

Ethical issues when using group interviews

Some pupils may be more likely to disclose sensitive feelings in a small group of people like themselves (for example, within a supportive group who have all experienced bullying or exclusion from school) rather than in a one-to-one interview. Group interviews may provide support to, and empower, vulnerable research participants with shared experiences of, for instance, racism, sexism or homophobia in schools. However, group interviews may be unsuitable for some sensitive or personal topics and participants may find the discussion too embarrassing or hurtful. Teachers may feel exposed when participating in a group interview with their head teacher or senior managers.

In school-based research with groups of classmates, the researcher cannot guarantee confidentiality or safeguard participants' identity. Some participants may be offended by comments or reluctant to discuss topics such as material deprivation or their home setting in front of their peers. In group interviews, it is more difficult for the researcher to minimise harm experienced by participants. Getting informed consent can be problematic as the discussion may veer into unexpected directions.

Theoretical issues when using group interviews

One strength of group interviews is that they are usually semi-structured or unstructured so the researcher can build up relationships with participants and observe the group (such as peers or colleagues) interacting at first hand. Participants have more control over the direction of the discussion and this can increase the validity of the data.

In a group setting, some participants may experience peer pressure to conform to the majority view. For example, they might not want to admit to working hard at school. Peer pressure can reduce the validity of the data if it discourages participants from giving a true account of their perspectives. During a group interview with boys who belong to a counter-school culture, for instance, participants may be influenced by the norms of their peers. The boys may, for example, try to shock the researcher, impress each other and express more macho views about girls than they would in other contexts such as in front of their teachers, parents or female friends. The researcher's gender, ethnicity, age and social class might influence the results. (See also the evaluation of Louise Archer's data from her study of Muslim boys and education on pp. 116–117.)

From an interpretivist perspective, focus groups can provide rich qualitative data about, for example, friendship groups or laddish behaviour. They can also illuminate how groups of friends, peers or colleagues interact in real social settings. From a positivist perspective, focus groups are not useful for testing hypotheses or for research questions that require quantitative findings or measurement. They are based on small samples and participants may not be representative of other students, parents or teachers. The lack of standardisation makes it difficult to replicate them to check reliability in order to generalise from them.

Activity

1. Explain two strengths of using group interviews to investigate pupils' perspectives on the significance of working hard academically.

2. Explain two limitations of using group interviews to investigate the factors influencing parents' choice of primary schools.

Summary

1. Interviews with groups of students, teachers or parents can save time and money compared to individual interviews.

2. They can work well with primary school pupils who are used to working in groups. However, the researcher must ensure that nobody dominates the discussion.

3. In school-based group interviews, the researcher cannot safeguard identities or guarantee confidentiality.

4. Participants have some control over the direction of the discussion, which increases the validity of data. However, peer pressure may reduce validity.

5. Interpretivists favour group interviews in educational research as they generate detailed qualitative data.

6. Positivists argue that group interviews are based on small samples of students, teachers or parents. Lack of standardisation makes them difficult to replicate in order to check reliability so generalisations are inappropriate.

PART 4 SOCIAL SURVEYS AND QUESTIONNAIRES IN SOCIOLOGICAL RESEARCH ON EDUCATION

Contents

In social survey research, data are collected by using self-completion questionnaires or structured interviews (see pp. 151–152 and 156–157 and Chapter 4, Unit 4.3.1 for a discussion of structured interviews). Questionnaires have been used to study a variety of topics within the sociology of education including laddish attitudes and behaviour among girls and boys in schools, the sources of information that students use when making decisions about higher education, and primary school pupils' enjoyment

and beliefs about reading and other school-related pursuits. Questionnaires are sometimes used in mixed methods research within the field of education alongside qualitative methods such as semi-structured interviews or focus groups. Do researchers experience fewer ethical dilemmas when using self-completion questionnaires compared to more qualitative methods such as unstructured interviews? How valid are the data generated by questionnaires? What are the practical, ethical and theoretical strengths and limitations of using questionnaires in sociological research on education? This part looks at some of the issues that sociologists have to consider when using questionnaires in educational research.

4.4.1 Social survey research and questionnaires

In some ways, questionnaire surveys are a particularly suitable method to use in school and college settings. For example, teachers and students – the potential respondents – are concentrated in one site and researchers can collect large amounts of information from them quickly and cheaply. In theory, a researcher could select random samples of teachers, students and parents from sampling frames such as school registers or lists of parents and teachers. In practice, however, schools may be unwilling to release this information for data protection reasons. This unit looks at an example of questionnaire-based sociological research in an educational setting. It then focuses on the practical, ethical and theoretical implications of using questionnaire surveys.

Research example: researching higher education decision-making

In an article entitled '"Hot", "cold" and "warm" information and higher education decision-making', Kim Slack *et al.* (2014) explore the different sources of information (such as family, friends, university visits, prospectuses and the National Student Survey) that students from advantaged and less advantaged backgrounds in England use in relation to their higher education (HE) choices. The researchers adopted a mixed methods approach, gathering quantitative data from a questionnaire and qualitative data from focus groups.

'The data collection was in February and March 2010, after the prospective students would be expected to have submitted applications for university courses. The survey included a range of educational institutions to achieve social and geographic spread: prospective students from comprehensive, selective 11–18 state and independent schools (n = 20); sixth-form and further education (FE) colleges (n = 5); and university colleges and universities (n = 5).

The questionnaires were distributed through named contacts at each institution and 1544 were completed ... The questionnaire asked students about the usefulness of knowing a list of information items when undertaking their search for information about HE (on a scale of one to four), whether they tried to obtain this information, and, if so, whether they succeeded.

Additional questions asked what types of sources of information they used when undertaking searches

and whether these were useful (on a scale of one to four). Information was collected on two socio-economic indicators: whether the student was first or second generation and the student's opinion of which of three categories their family income belonged to.'

Source: A.K. Slack, J. Mangan, A. Hughes and P. Davies (2014) '"Hot", "cold" and "warm" information and higher education decision-making', *British Journal of Sociology of Education*, vol. 35, no. 2, pp. 204–223.

Activity
Drawing on this information and your own knowledge of research methods, explain:

a) two strengths of using a questionnaire to investigate the sources of information that students from different backgrounds use when making HE choices

b) two weaknesses of using a questionnaire to investigate the sources of information that they use when making HE choices

c) one advantage of using a mixed methods approach in this study.

Practical issues when using questionnaires

Postal questionnaires or questionnaires completed during tutorials are cheaper and less time consuming than structured interviews. For example, self-completion questionnaires, an accompanying letter and reply-paid envelope could be sent to a large sample of primary school head teachers in England and Wales to investigate their views on marketisation, selective education or academies. Factors such as time and cost will influence researchers' decisions about the sample size.

If the gatekeeper at a school believes that filling out a questionnaire would take up too much lesson time or hamper students' academic progress (for example, during the run-up to public examinations when it disrupts revision), access may be denied. However, gatekeepers may agree to host a study based on questionnaires rather than a two-year ethnography.

Copies of a questionnaire can be distributed easily to large samples of students, teachers and parents. One way of delivering a questionnaire to students is for the researcher to hand out copies to all members of a class (for example, during a tutorial), remain in the room during completion and collect the completed questionnaires. If the researcher is there to supervise completion, they can answer any questions and ensure that students do not discuss their answers. The response rate is also likely to be high. However, some students may not answer honestly if they think their handwriting might identify them.

Another option is for a designated person (for example, a head of year) to distribute the questionnaire to students and ask them to post completed copies in a post box in school. This would safeguard anonymity but students may not bother to respond to a long questionnaire or treat it as a joke. If the delivery is staggered over time, students or teachers may discuss the questions and their answers.

A self-completion questionnaire is not necessarily appropriate for all topics (such as literacy skills) or groups of students. Younger pupils in primary schools, students for whom English is a second language or those with literacy problems may struggle to read and answer the questions. Some students may be unable to follow the instructions or to answer questions about, for example, household income or parents' qualifications. They may misunderstand questions, miss them out or write illegible answers. Others may get tired or bored, write very little or give up. Students who truant or those from traveller communities may not be present in school to receive a copy of the questionnaire.

It can be difficult to access the parents of students from a particular school or college. A school may not be willing to provide lists of home addresses but it may post copies of the questionnaire to parents, for example, with other correspondence. Alternatively, pupils could be asked to deliver the questionnaire, a letter and a pre-paid envelope to their parents but there is no guarantee that parents will receive them.

The non-response rate from parents may be relatively high because, for example, they do not want to answer personal or sensitive questions (for instance, about their income or employment status), they see it as of little benefit to their children, they have literacy problems, their first language is not English or they feel they might be identified by their answers. Parents and teachers might not return the questionnaire if it takes too long to complete.

Ethical issues when using questionnaires

Compared to ethnographic approaches, self-completion questionnaires may seem to raise few ethical concerns. There are issues about informed consent, however, when using them in educational settings. Although younger pupils may be able to complete a questionnaire, it can be difficult to get informed consent from them if they do not fully understand the details of the research. If a researcher or teacher distributes a questionnaire during a lesson, students may feel pressurised to complete it even though they would prefer not to do so. This would go against the principle of informed consent. On the other hand, it may be easier for students to withdraw from research based on self-completion questionnaires compared to interviews because they can simply draw or scribble on the questionnaire, or throw it away without any repercussions.

Self-completion questionnaires can be filled in anonymously. The findings of questionnaire surveys are usually presented and published in statistical form. As a result, there is less chance of individual teachers, students or parents being identified compared to qualitative research that uses verbatim quotations from individual participants.

Activity

PLEASE ANSWER EACH QUESTION BY TICKING ONE OF THE BOXES.

Self-completion questionnaires may not be appropriate for all students or topics.

1. Identify three practical factors that a sociologist should take into account when designing a self-completion questionnaire for primary school pupils.

2. Identify two ethical issues that a researcher should consider when using questionnaires with primary school pupils.

217

Theoretical issues when using questionnaires

Closed questions can provide quantitative data on students' social class background by asking about, for example, their eligibility to free school meals, parents' income, occupation and educational qualifications. It is possible to link this to other statistical data, for instance, primary school pupils' achievements in SATs or sixth formers' A-level results in order to test hypotheses about the relationship between social class and educational achievement. The researcher can identify any correlations between two or more variables, for example between ethnicity and educational attainment or gender and attitudes towards laddish culture in higher education.

As all questions are standardised, a researcher can compare students or teachers within a school. It is also possible to compare large samples of parents, students or teachers across different types of school (for example, comprehensive and grammar schools or state and private schools) and schools with contrasting intakes (for example, schools in which the majority of students are working or middle class).

With postal questionnaires, the researcher is not present so there is no social desirability effect, interview effects or interviewer bias. They are anonymous so respondents may be more likely to answer honestly.

Positivists favour the use of questionnaires to test hypotheses. Questionnaires allow measurement and the establishment of patterns and trends. The questions are standardised so any differences in respondents' answers should reflect real differences between them. Questionnaires can also be replicated to check reliability before making generalisations. However, when designing questionnaires, it is difficult to define and operationalise abstract concepts such as social class, cultural capital and educational underachievement in order to measure them.

Interpretivists argue that questionnaires are based on the assumption that sociologists know in advance what is important. They do not allow sociologists to discover the meanings that direct behaviour. If a researcher wanted to explore head teachers' perspectives on the gendered nature of their role, pre-structured self-completion questionnaires would provide limited data. Instead, the researcher could use qualitative methods such as semi-structured interviews that allow them to probe and give participants some control of the discussion.

Some sociologists question the validity of data from questionnaires in educational research. One issue is that participants' answers (for example, to questions on teaching behaviour or sexism in the classroom) may not reflect their actual classroom behaviour. Another issue is that peers may influence participants' responses. If pupils discuss their answers while completing a self-administered questionnaire, this may reduce the validity of the findings.

Activity

Questionnaires may not be appropriate for students who truant.

Explain one reason why a low response rate among some groups of students is problematic in survey research.

Members of some groups of students (for example, students who truant or are frequently excluded) are more likely to be absent regularly. Ian Law and Sarah Swann (2011) used several methods including a quantitative survey but found that 'very few of the gypsy and traveller Year 10 pupils on school rolls were in school' so few were included in the survey. Students who belong to an anti-school culture may see the questions as irrelevant to their lives, treat the questionnaire as a joke or not bother to respond. If the respondents are largely made up of pro-school students, senior teachers or university-educated parents, for example, this bias may result in an unrepresentative sample and make generalisation difficult.

Summary

1. Social surveys collect data via self-completion questionnaires and structured interviews. They are sometimes used in mixed methods research on education.

2. Self-completion questionnaires are cheaper and less time consuming than structured interviews and can be distributed to large samples of pupils, teachers and parents. However, they are not necessarily appropriate for all topics or groups within the educational context.

3. Accessing parents can be difficult and the non-response rate may be high.

4. Negotiating informed consent with younger pupils can be problematic and students may feel pressurised to complete questionnaires that are distributed during lessons.

5. Self-completion questionnaires are anonymous and individuals are less likely to be identified in any publications compared to qualitative methods.

6. Closed questions generate quantitative data that allow comparisons between groups of students, teachers or parents. With standardised questions, a questionnaire can be replicated to check reliability before making generalisations. Consequently, surveys are favoured by positivists. However, it is difficult to operationalise complex concepts when designing questionnaires.

7. Interpretivists argue that surveys do not allow researchers to discover the meanings behind behaviour among, for example, counter-school cultures.

8. Data from surveys may be invalid if participants' answers do not reflect their behaviour.

9. If members of some groups (such as travellers) do not respond to a questionnaire, the sample may be unrepresentative, making it difficult to generalise.

PART 5 FURTHER METHODS USED IN SOCIOLOGICAL RESEARCH ON EDUCATION

Contents

This part examines the use of longitudinal studies and experiments to study education. Longitudinal studies may be based on methods such as observation, semi-structured interviews or surveys. Experiments are devised to test hypotheses. What are the strengths and limitations of these methods in sociological research on education? This part also explores some of the practical, ethical and theoretical implications of using longitudinal studies and experiments.

4.5.1 Longitudinal studies

Traditionally, longitudinal studies in education were associated with survey research. More recently, however, sociologists have been carrying out qualitative longitudinal research to explore, for example, the construction of pupils' identities during schooling, young people's transitions from school to post-compulsory education and the changes experienced by schools due to new education policies. This unit examines some of the practical, ethical and theoretical issues linked to the use of longitudinal research.

Qualitative longitudinal research

Qualitative longitudinal research in education might involve visiting a school annually for several years to carry out semi-structured interviews with the same sample of students, teachers and senior managers. In *Choice, Pathways and Transitions Post-16: New Youth, New Economies in the Global City*, Stephen Ball *et al.* (2000) explored young people's transitions from compulsory schooling to post-compulsory education and training. They undertook a longitudinal study of a sample of students from a mixed comprehensive school and a Pupil Referral Unit in South London. The same students were interviewed over several years. Consequently, the researchers were able to analyse the young people's transitions over time and follow up issues from the previous round of interviews.

Activity

Qualitative longitudinal research has been used to explore young people's transitions from compulsory schooling to post-compulsory education and training.

Explain how longitudinal studies allow sociologists of education to analyse continuity and change over time.

Quantitative longitudinal research

Quantitative longitudinal research usually involves collecting statistical data from the same group of survey respondents over time. The National Child Development Study (NCDS) has been running for decades and examines the educational, social and physical development of a cohort born in one week in Britain in 1958 via a survey (see pp. 169–170).

Sociologists use secondary data from this longitudinal study to investigate topics related to education, life chances and social mobility. Vikki Boliver and Adam Smith (2012) drew on survey data from the NCDS to investigate whether working-class children who attended grammar schools were more likely to experience upward social mobility than those who attended comprehensives.

Practical issues when using longitudinal research

Longitudinal studies in educational settings (particularly those based on qualitative methods) may not be feasible because they require a lot of resources (money, time and researchers). Gatekeepers in a school may not agree to host a longitudinal study because it would require a long-term commitment.

Some participants will inevitably withdraw from a school-based longitudinal study. Teachers may move to take up jobs in other schools or switch careers. Students and parents may withdraw from the research because they lose interest in it.

Ethical issues when using longitudinal studies

General ethical guidelines apply to the use of longitudinal studies in educational research. One particular issue is that at each wave of a longitudinal study, informed consent is needed from the participants.

Theoretical issues when using longitudinal research

With qualitative longitudinal research in particular, a researcher can build rapport with the staff and students in a school or college over time. This would help them to gather rich data during interviews or observation. They may, however, find it difficult to remain independent if they have established positive relationships. If they become too involved, their interpretation of the data may be affected.

If a researcher returned to a school once or twice a year, participants may not have to rely so much on memory when responding to questions. For example, in a longitudinal study of students' career decision-making, there is less chance that participants would have to recall experiences, choices and decisions from five or 10 years ago. This is likely to increase the validity of the data.

If participants withdraw from a quantitative longitudinal study, the original sample will decrease in size over time and may become less representative. In this case, it would be difficult to generalise.

Longitudinal studies allow researchers to analyse continuity and change over time. A researcher could use a longitudinal study in a school setting to examine the impact of new policies such as the introduction of the EBacc or the switch to academy status on students' attainments.

Interpretivists argue that qualitative longitudinal research allows researchers to explore processes over time. They can link micro processes such as teachers' perspectives on the change to mixed-ability teaching and how they experience this to macro processes such as the wider policy or institutional contexts. Positivists, however, favour quantitative longitudinal research based on surveys that allow measurement and correlations between, for example, students' social class and their attainments before and after mixed-ability teaching was introduced.

Summary

1. Longitudinal research is relatively time consuming and expensive. School gatekeepers may not commit to a long-term study.

2. Inevitably, some participants will withdraw from a longitudinal study. If the sample becomes less representative, it may be difficult to generalise.

3. Informed consent is needed at each wave of a longitudinal study.

4. Qualitative longitudinal research allows researchers to build rapport with school-based participants over time and to gather detailed data.

5. Participants are not so reliant on memory so the data may be more valid.

6. Longitudinal studies enable researchers to analyse continuity and change over time.

7. Interpretivists argue that qualitative longitudinal research allows researchers to link micro processes (such as how teachers experience change) and macro processes (such as the school context).

8. Positivists prefer survey-based quantitative longitudinal research that allows measurement, correlations and generalisations.

4.5.2 Experiments

Experimental research in the field of education has focused on areas such as teacher expectations and the self-fulfilling prophecy. This unit looks at examples of laboratory and field experiments. It then examines some of the practical, ethical and theoretical implications of using experiments in research on education.

Laboratory experiments

Laboratory experiments (see pp. 171–173) are not widely used in sociological research on education. Sociologists argue that laboratories are artificial settings and experiments are not naturally occurring events. This will affect teachers' and students' definitions of the situation and their actions. In this case, experiments can tell us little about how participants behave in classrooms in the real world.

Research example: researching teacher expectation and social class

Dale Harvey and Gerald Slatin (1975) carried out research to assess how far teachers' expectations of pupils' performance were related to their perceptions of the children's social class. The experiment involved a sample of 96 teachers from four elementary schools (which are similar to primary schools) serving 'lower class' and 'middle-upper-class' neighbourhoods in a US city. They asked this sample to judge the potential (for example to succeed or fail academically) and the socio-economic background of a set of 18 anonymous photographs of Black and White school children aged 8–12 years.

Harvey and Slatin found that perceived socio-economic class was more strongly associated with success among the White children and with failure among the Black children. However, the experiment did not show that the middle-class bias in teachers' perceptions affected students' academic performance in real world classrooms or that this bias would be communicated to children. It is also difficult to generalise from a small sample of teachers.

Activity

1. Why do you think the researchers used photographs rather than real children in their experiment?

2. How far are teachers' responses to photographs a valid measure of the judgements they make in the classroom?

Field experiments

Field experiments are carried out in everyday settings such as classrooms and provide more realistic environments than laboratories.

Research example: researching teacher expectations in the classroom

Robert Rosenthal and Lenore Jacobson (1968) carried out an experiment at Oak School, a public elementary school in the USA (see p. 90). They aimed to test whether teachers' positive expectations of pupils' potential affect their achievements. The study had a longitudinal aspect in that the researchers tested pupils' scores several times (in a pre-test of intelligence that would apparently identify children who were most likely to show greater intellectual growth within the next year, re-tests during the following school year and two years after the pre-test). So the researchers were able to monitor changes in the scores over time.

Activity

Rosenthal and Jacobson tested whether teachers' positive expectations of pupils' potential affect their achievements. They gave teachers false information. The names on the list were a random sample of pupils, not those likely to show most academic progress.

1. What was Rosenthal and Jacobson's hypothesis?

2. Why did their study include a longitudinal element?

This study has come under strong criticism on ethical grounds (see below). It has also been criticised on methodological grounds. For example, Rosenthal and Jacobson were interested in whether the gains in IQ test scores among the experimental group (those identified as most likely to show greater academic progress) were reflected in their classroom behaviour. Instead of observing the pupils' classroom behaviour themselves, however, they relied on teachers' accounts of this.

Practical issues when using experiments

Field experiments in educational research are likely to be more expensive than laboratory experiments and other methods. For example, in order to set up a field experiment to test the relationship between class size and primary school pupils' performance in English and maths, it would prove expensive to employ the additional teachers and build the extra classrooms needed in order to test hypotheses. Gatekeepers and parents may also be unwilling to allow pupils to be subjected to field and laboratory experiments.

Ethical issues when using experiments

One potential problem with experiments is deception. For example, Rosenthal and Jacobson misinformed the teachers about the true nature of the research and its purpose so they were not in a position to give informed consent. Also, informed consent was not sought from the children or their parents. A further problem is that the 20 percent of pupils who were randomly allocated to the experimental group may have been advantaged compared to the majority of pupils. For example, they may have received more teacher attention than the pupils allocated to the control group. In this case, the control group may have been harmed if their progress was negatively affected by the research.

Theoretical issues when using experiments

Laboratory experiments can be used to test hypotheses about, for example, the relationship between teachers' expectations and their non-verbal behaviour. They can be replicated to test the reliability of the findings and, if the findings are reliable, generalisations can be drawn. They are, therefore, favoured by positivists. However, experimental research on labelling has not produced consistent findings.

In field experiments, the researcher cannot control all variables. Rosenthal and Jacobson, for example, had no control over parental expectations or whether parents were tutoring their children at home. Other critics point out that it is difficult to generalise beyond the types of school involved in an experiment, for example to generalise to smaller or larger schools.

One of the main problems with experiments in educational research is that the findings lack validity. There are several reasons for this. First, a laboratory is an artificial setting and an experiment cannot capture the real world of education or classroom interaction. Second, experiments are subject to the Hawthorne or experimental effect (see pp. 173–174) so, if teachers and students know that they are involved in an experiment, this may affect their behaviour. Third, experiments are subject to experimenter bias and in field experiments, for example, the researcher may affect the participants' behaviour. Interpretivists favour more qualitative methods that capture the lived experience of classroom interaction from teachers' and pupils' perspectives.

Summary

1. Laboratory experiments do not reveal how teachers and students behave in classrooms.

2. Field experiments take place in everyday settings such as classrooms. However, the researcher cannot control all variables.

3. Experiments that involve deception go against the principle of informed consent.

4. Experiments are used to test hypotheses about, for example, teachers' expectations and social class. They are favoured by positivists because they can be replicated to test the reliability of the findings before making generalisations.

5. Findings from experiments in educational research lack validity due to the artificiality of laboratory settings, the experimental effect and experimenter bias. Interpretivists prefer qualitative methods that capture teachers' and students' lived experiences in classrooms.

Activity

1. Explain one strength of using a field experiment to investigate the relationship between teachers' expectations and pupils' achievements.

2. Explain one limitation of using laboratory experiments in educational research on labelling.

PART 6 SECONDARY SOURCES IN SOCIOLOGICAL RESEARCH ON EDUCATION

Contents

Secondary sources are a valuable source of information for researchers within the sociology of education and most studies draw on them in one form or another. Qualitative secondary sources include policy documents such as a school's written policy on teaching and learning or school trips. Quantitative secondary sources include official statistics on authorised and unauthorised absence published by the Department for Education (DfE). In practice, however, many documents include both types of data. How useful are the different qualitative and quantitative sources? What are their strengths and limitations? This part focuses on some of the practical, ethical and theoretical implications of using secondary sources in sociological research on education.

4.6.1 Documents

In addition to generating data through research methods such as school-based interviews with teachers and pupils, sociologists often draw on qualitative secondary sources of information in the form of written documents (see pp. 175–183). Public documents are readily available and include schools' policy documents and publicity material. By contrast, personal documents such as school reports on pupils, students' written work or notes passed between them during lessons are more difficult to access. This unit looks at the different types of document available to sociologists and their uses in research on education.

Public documents

Some public documents have been put together by a school, college or university and may be downloaded from their websites at no cost. Publicity documents, for example, include school prospectuses and newsletters. Public documentation also includes school policy documents on equality and diversity, safeguarding and behaviour management (covering, for example, school uniform and exclusions). Other examples of public documents include Ofsted inspection reports published by the DfE, government policy statements and legislation.

Public documents have several uses in sociological research on education. When shortlisting prospective research sites in which to carry out case studies, a researcher may draw on information from school prospectuses to build a picture of the context of particular schools. For example, they may want to identify 'average' schools so access to Ofsted inspection reports would provide useful contextual data. If a researcher was exploring the impact of school culture and ethos on academic attainment, they could glean information about this from its publications.

In *How Schools Do Policy: Policy Enactments in Secondary Schools*, Stephen Ball *et al.* (2012) explored the education policy process in schools in England. They focused on how policies (for example, on behaviour management) were interpreted, enacted and dealt with (or ignored) in four case studies of state secondary schools over two years. As part of the fieldwork, they undertook semi-structured interviews with head teachers and teachers. They also carried out an audit of policies in each school and collected information from sources such as Ofsted inspection reports and school brochures. They collected a range of school documentation and examined 'handbooks, websites, parent newsletters, student diaries and teacher planners'. In each school, the researchers had access to the intranet where many documents could be found.

Official documents

Official documents include publications from government departments such as the Department for Education (DfE) and Ofsted. The DfE funds research

projects and publishes research reports (for instance, the *Teacher Workload Survey 2016* and *Parents' Views and Demand for 30 Hours of Free Childcare*). Sociologists can draw on government-funded research findings in their own studies. For example, a sociologist researching students who withdraw from A-level study before completion may discuss relevant research published by the DfE in their literature review. Sociologists can also draw on government policy documents when researching educational policy such as marketisation and its impact on schools, classrooms and parents.

Personal or life documents

In *The Company She Keeps: An Ethnography of Girls' Friendship*, Valerie Hey (1997) studied girls' friendship patterns in two London comprehensive schools (see p. 175). She used a mixed methods approach combining documentary research (analysing the notes that the girls exchanged during lessons) with participant observation, case studies of several girls' networks, informal interviews, discussions and diaries in which some of the girls recorded their social activities for a week.

After lessons, Hey gathered up crumpled notes thrown on the floor or left on desks. One teacher retrieved notes from her waste paper basket and gave them to Hey. The teacher referred to the notes as 'little pieces of garbage'.

Notes were regularly exchanged. In one history lesson, 15 notes were exchanged between three girls. The correspondence could continue from lesson to lesson – in one instance, there were 50 separate note exchanges that lasted over a week.

Around 90 per cent of what the girls wrote was concerned with their relationships with each other. In Hey's words, the notes provided 'visible evidence of the extensive emotional labour invested by the girls in their friendships'. They reflected the themes that emerged from her research – the girls' 'intimacy, secrecy and struggle'. They illustrated how the girls were 'intensely preoccupied by the micro-politics of their relationships', they revealed the 'passionate fallouts' and their 'sense of unease about friendships'.

For Valerie Hey, the notes were 'sociologically fascinating'. They were not 'second hand' data from questionnaires or interviews. They were not the researcher's perceptions derived from participant observation. They were 'first hand' and direct expressions and concerns about relationships untouched by the researcher.

Activity

Part of Valerie Hey's data came from notes that the girls exchanged during lessons.

1. Explain two strengths of using discarded notes to study girls' friendship patterns in schools.

2. Explain two limitations of using these notes to study girls' friendship patterns in schools.

Then and now: Valerie Hey, *The Company She Keeps* (1997)

"My original study arose because of my familiarity with the classroom setting. As an ex-school teacher I was fascinated by the cultural work going on in front of me as children made creative use of any informal time to chat, draw and make jokes in their social groups. My approach to research was influenced by both feminist sociology and cultural studies approaches to exploring and explaining how people 'made themselves up' through the kinds of identity work done in their everyday lives.

Girls were often ignored in landmark sociological and educational studies and yet my own experience and research revealed a richly textured series of activities that mattered a great deal to young girls in their schools. What kind of labour was entailed in making friends and what sort of emotional efforts were invested in 'becoming' a female 'somebody'? These concerns focused how I interpreted the fragments and sequences of their 'notes'. What I found there was that such marginalia – by this I mean material central to their lives but not formally 'taught' at school – entailed ethical worries about intensely important friendships. The girls were exploring questions of loyalty, belonging, modes of sexuality and conformity entangled in worries about social popularity and inclusion. I found vernacular communications steeped in everyday vocabularies of fun, rudeness, as well as less benign aspects such as classism, racism, and heterosexism. At stake were fears about their 'acceptance' as members of specific white working-class or middle-class friendship networks – social worries in effect reproducing, as well as at times expressing playful resistance to, dominant social forces and their expectations.

All of these preoccupations with 'fitting in' have intensified I think in a brutally competitive individualistic economic, cultural and social order. Worries about being educationally and socially 'successful' multiply all the time driven by the digital, hyper-responsive world of social media. My 'little bits of garbage' were pieces of ephemera – sometimes with sentiments that were vicious – but they did not usually become an archive of abuse. Now in the contemporary moment – in the context of 'sexting', on-line harassment and vicious assumptions about body norms – the ubiquity of pornography in particular presents young girls and young women and their teachers with new responsibilities to challenge the masculinist modes of evaluating and constructing the world of young emergent sexualities. The paucity of serious attention to this fact in schools and colleges is shocking.

Moreover, in a context where certain minority faiths have become demonised, I am not sure I would have been able to handle contemporary digital data and its sheer volume of messages. I do know that the workings of contemporary society drive social antagonism into fiercer forms of 'othering' and classrooms are one major site for both their performance and challenge."

225

Hey was concerned about the ethics of collecting and using private and personal documents without permission. She sometimes felt 'like a thief' and 'a spy'. However, not all the notes were gathered without permission. Hey asked some of her 'key informants' if they had any more examples. To her surprise, some of the girls had stored notes for years and gladly gave her access to them.

Practical issues in using documents

Public documents such as school or university prospectuses are usually freely available via the internet. Government research reports are similarly easy to access and sociologists may refer to them if they lack sufficient resources to undertake the research themselves. Government documents (for example Ofsted inspection reports) may be the only source of readily available data on a topic. By contrast, personal documents such as written notes or students' reports are usually more difficult to access.

Ethical issues in using documents

Sociologists do not usually encounter ethical problems when accessing and using public documents other than those relating to anonymity in their research publications. Accessing and using personal documents such as discarded notes without permission, however, is seen as unethical because the person who produced the document has not given informed consent. However, if students are aware that a sociologist is planning to collect and analyse the contents of these notes for research purposes, they may be more guarded in what they write or stop discarding them.

Theoretical issues in using documents

Official government publications are not necessarily objective because they reflect the biases of the political party in power when they were produced. For example, policy statements from Theresa May's Conservative government that outlined and justified the reintroduction of grammar schools can be seen as one-sided in their arguments. Government reports on their own reforms can also be biased in their evaluations of the success of the policies. Ofsted inspection reports do not necessarily provide valid or reliable ratings of schools and classroom observations.

School, college and university prospectuses and brochures are often put together with a particular purpose and audience in mind (for example, to market the institution to prospective students and their parents). They may present a distorted or biased picture of the institution. In this case, the contents cannot be taken at face value.

From an interpretivist perspective, the notes that Valerie Hey analysed in her research on girls' friendships are valid in that they are naturally occurring data, the products of human behaviour. They were not produced for a sociologist (as would be the case if a researcher asked participants to keep diaries for a week) or influenced by interviewer or interview bias (as might be the case during an interview on friendships). The notes reveal real issues of concern to the girls and provide rich qualitative data. Critics, however, argue that the researcher's analysis of the notes' contents is based on their interpretation. As a result, the researcher may impose their own meaning onto the notes and the true meaning from the girls' perspective is lost. Additionally, the notes that the researcher managed to collect may not be representative and, in this case, it would be difficult to generalise from them.

Summary

1. Public documents (such as school prospectuses) and official documents (such as DfE publications) are usually more readily available than personal documents (such as discarded notes).

2. Using personal documents without permission raises ethical questions about informed consent.

3. Official government publications may lack objectivity and reflect party political biases.

4. School prospectuses, for example, are designed for marketing purposes and may provide a distorted picture of institutions.

5. Interpretivists argue that personal documents such as notes that were not produced for research purposes provide rich and valid qualitative data.

6. Critics argue that a researcher's analysis of the contents of personal documents is based on their own interpretations.

4.6.2 Official statistics

A vast quantity of official statistics on education is published by government departments each year (see, for instance, p. 68). Statistical data are available, for example, on the social characteristics of young people aged 16 to 18 years in England who are not in education, employment or training (NEETs), authorised and unauthorised absence and students' attainments in public examinations. This unit examines some of the uses and limitations of official statistics in sociological research on education.

Uses of official statistics

Official statistics from the DfE on authorised and unauthorised absence in state-funded primary, secondary and special schools are a valuable source of quantitative secondary data. Researchers have used them to examine the social factors associated with absenteeism such as family structures, poverty and socio-economic status operationalised (or measured) in terms of receipt of free school meals (FSM). Official statistics can also be used to investigate how absence impacts on students' academic achievements.

Official statistics published by the DfE on school exclusions and on pupil attainment in England present the information according to pupils' social characteristics such as their age, gender, ethnicity, FSM eligibility, year group and level of deprivation. Sociologists can make comparisons between groups, for example in the GCSE achievements of pupils living in the most and least deprived areas. They can also measure changes in the attainment of

Activity

Official statistics on student attainment in public examinations are a key source of quantitative secondary data.

Explain one advantage of using official statistics to study changes in the gender education gap.

different groups and identify trends in attainment over time. This would help them to assess the impact of changing government policies on attainment.

Official statistics on pupils' achievements in public examinations such as GCSEs are a key source of quantitative secondary data for sociologists researching gender and education. They allow researchers to identify trends in attainment by gender over time and to examine the impact of government policies (such as the introduction of the national curriculum and the EBacc or changes to assessment schemes) on the **gender education gap**. However, although these statistics provide measurement, more qualitative methods are required in order to explain the differences in attainment by gender and the meanings behind them.

The DfE also publishes annual school performance tables (or league tables as they are known) in England. Secondary school league tables in England, for example, provide statistical information on a range of issues such as students' achievements at Key Stage 4 in particular schools and how they compare with other schools in the local authority and in England. The performance tables also provide Ofsted ratings of individual schools.

Practical issues when using official statistics

Official statistics on education published by the DfE are readily available and can be accessed quickly via the internet without charge. Sociologists do not have the resources to compile these statistics themselves.

227

Ethical issues when using official statistics

The DfE complies with the Code of Practice for Official Statistics which requires it to take reasonable steps to protect the confidentiality of individuals. Individual pupils who have been excluded from school, for example, are not identified.

Theoretical issues when using official statistics

Official statistics published by the DfE on NEETs and pupil absence are designated as National Statistics which means that they are produced according to sound methods and are considered reliable. From a positivist perspective, they provide important facts and figures about social issues such as truancy.

Official statistics on pupil absence

A sociologist could draw on official statistics to examine national patterns and trends in authorised and unauthorised absence over time. For example, they could compare the absence rates for pupils according to characteristics such as their ethnicity, deprivation levels, FSM eligibility and year group. Such comparisons show, for instance, that the rates of unauthorised absence are much higher for pupils living in the most deprived areas than in the least deprived areas. They could also compare pupils' absence by region or Local Authority.

Sociologists could use these data to examine the impact of policy changes on attendance and absence. One problem, however, is that definitions of 'persistent absentees' change over time so it is difficult to identify long-term trends. Another issue is that data on pupils' social class as measured by their parents' occupations is not available, and eligibility to FSM is often used as a proxy for social class. This is problematic because some middle-class children may receive FSM if their parents are unemployed and some working-class children who are entitled to FSM may not claim them.

The official statistics on pupil absence are based on universal samples and collect pupil level absence data via the **school census**. They include all state schools and are seen as representative. From a positivist perspective, they are a reliable source of quantitative secondary data from which generalisations can be drawn.

Some sociologists question the validity of the official statistics on unauthorised absence. For example,

family holidays can be authorised by the school in exceptional circumstances and a head teacher has the discretion to grant permission. In practice, however, different head teachers may not interpret 'exceptional circumstances' consistently. Some schools may feel pressurised to under record unauthorised absence to avoid damaging their public image and market position. Critics question the reliability of the statistics and whether they provide a true measure of unauthorised absence.

Statistics on unauthorised absence may be used in studies of truancy. However, the official definition of unauthorised absence may not correspond to a sociologist's definition of truancy. For example, if a parent takes a child out of school without the head teacher's permission in order to go on holiday, this would count as an instance of unauthorised absence within the official statistics but it would not necessarily count as an instance of truancy according to the sociologist's definition because it is condoned by the parent. Sociologists might also be interested in identifying students who attend the morning and afternoon registration sessions on a particular day but fail to attend one or more lessons. Official statistics would not record this as unauthorised absence (although individual lessons registers would record their absence).

Interpretivists are interested in understanding students' lived experiences of truancy. The statistics cannot tell us anything about the lived experiences of students who truant, what it means to them or their parents. This would require more qualitative or ethnographic methods. Interpretivists argue that official statistics on unauthorised absence are socially constructed. They are published as statements of fact but, in reality, they are the outcomes of decisions and choices made by the students, parents and teachers involved.

School league tables

One problem with school league tables is that the performance measures change so it is difficult to compare results over time. Since 2016, school league tables have measured school performance in terms of 'Progress 8'. This measure takes into account pupils' performance in eight GCSE subjects compared to that of other pupils with the same prior attainment at Key Stage 2. However, it does not take account of pupils' socio-economic backgrounds. Critics argue that this value added measure rewards schools with advantaged intakes but penalises schools serving disadvantaged communities. Other problems include the practice of removing lower attaining pupils from schools before their Year 11 examinations or using qualifications such as the European Computer Driving Licence to boost a school's Progress 8 score. Consequently, school league tables should be treated with caution.

Activity

1. Explain one strength of using official statistics to investigate truancy.

2. Explain one limitation of using official statistics to investigate the relationship between gender and educational achievement.

Key terms

Gender education gap The difference in the educational attainments and examination results of female and male students.

School census A survey that collects data from state schools in England about individual pupils (such as eligibility to FSM and attendance) and the schools themselves (for example, their educational provision).

Summary

1. Official statistics from the DfE are a valuable, accessible and cheap source of quantitative secondary data.

2. They allow sociologists to compare groups and measure trends (for example, attainment by gender) over time. However, more qualitative methods are needed to explain the meaning behind the statistics.

3. Individuals' confidentiality is protected within the statistics.

4. National Statistics are produced according to sound methods and are seen as reliable. From a positivist perspective, they provide factual data about education. They enable comparisons between groups, examination of trends and generalisations.

5. Some sociologists question the validity and reliability of official statistics on unauthorised absence and data on school performance.

6. Official statistics may use definitions (for instance, of unauthorised absence) that are unsuitable for sociologists' purposes.

EXAM PRACTICE QUESTIONS

AS-LEVEL PAPER 1 METHODS IN CONTEXT

0 1   Read **Item A** and answer the question that follows.

Item A

Investigating pupils' cultural background and educational achievement

Some sociologists believe that the cultural background of pupils has a significant impact upon the achievement of pupils in school. Differences in both class and ethnic background can affect whether children start their school careers with the skills and knowledge that will make it easy for them to succeed.

Sociologists may study the cultural background of pupils by using questionnaires to collect information from parents. Questionnaires can be seen as having practical, ethical and theoretical advantages for studying this topic. For example, it is easier and more convenient to access a sample of parents using questionnaires than using most other methods; it is clear that parents are giving consent if they are willing to fill in the questionnaires and this method may provide the best chance of getting a representative sample of parents. However, gaining access to a suitable sampling frame can be difficult, and getting parents to cooperate and ensuring that their answers give a true representation of cultural differences are further problems. Therefore, some sociologists prefer using qualitative methods to study the cultural background of pupils.

Applying material from **Item A** and your own knowledge of research methods, evaluate the strengths and limitations of using questionnaires to study how the cultural background of pupils might influence educational achievement.

        [20 marks]

A–LEVEL PAPER 1
METHODS IN CONTEXT

0 2 Read **Item A** and answer the question that follows.

Item A

Investigating school subcultures

Pupils in schools often associate with other groups of pupils who they see as being similar to themselves. These groups can develop into distinct subcultures with their own norms and values which may complement or conflict with the values of the school and of its teachers. Class, gender and ethnicity can be important in subculture formation, but a wide range of other factors can be important too.

Since subcultures are social groups, one way to gain information about them is to use group interviews or focus groups. These can allow researchers to explore the interaction between members of the same subculture. This interaction may also enable the researchers to obtain a more in-depth understanding of subcultures than they would be able to do in one-to-one interviews. However, the responses of pupils in a group interview might be influenced by the presence of their peers.

Applying material from **Item A** and your own knowledge of research methods, evaluate the strengths and limitations of group interviews for studying pupil subcultures.

[20 marks]

5 FAMILIES AND HOUSEHOLDS

Chapter contents

Families (groups of people related by blood, marriage or adoption) and households (people who live together) are two of the most basic groupings in society. As such they have been a key concern for sociologists. The family has long been seen as a vital institution and early sociologists tended to emphasise its positive contribution to society. More recent theories, however, have challenged the assumption that the family always played a positive role and have considered whether social changes have undermined family life. In the UK in the 1950s, divorce was rare and births outside marriage were still regarded as slightly scandalous. Today, divorce is commonplace, less than half of births take place within marriage and same-sex marriage is legal and accepted as normal by many people.

Some traditionalists regard such changes as a disastrous collapse in moral standards. Others welcome them as evidence of increasing choice allowing people to live their personal life according to their own preferences rather than being tied down by convention.

As well as looking at these changes in families and households, this chapter also discusses changing relationships within the family, particularly between partners and between parents and children. It asks how far these relationships have changed and whether they have become more equal. In addition, the chapter looks at government policy concerned with families and at demographic change in the UK, both of which have a significant impact on families and households.

PART 1 CLASSIC PERSPECTIVES ON THE ROLE OF THE FAMILY AND SOCIAL CHANGE: FUNCTIONALISM, MARXISM AND FEMINISM

Contents

The family has often been regarded as the cornerstone of society, as the basic unit of social organisation. Early sociologists, such as functionalists, saw the family playing a vital role in society, carrying out tasks like socialising children. However, from the 1960s onwards, a number of sociologists argued that the family was not the beneficial institution that functionalists assumed. For example, Marxists argued that it served the interests of the rich and powerful rather than society as a whole. And feminists questioned whether women benefitted from family life to the same extent as men. This part of the chapter asks who gains and who loses from family life. It questions whether the family is the cornerstone of society in view of the instability and conflict that is evident in many aspects of family life today.

5.1.1 Functionalist perspectives on the family

The sociological theory of functionalism was introduced in Chapter 1. Briefly, functionalists see society as a system made up of interrelated parts. The parts work together to maintain society as a whole. The job of the sociologist is to examine the function of each part – that is, how it contributes to the maintenance of the social system.

As with functionalist analysis in general, the functionalist view of the family tends to focus on the positive contributions families make to the maintenance of the social system. This unit looks at two of the main functionalist theories of the family and asks whether they are still credible in the light of all the changes that have occurred in families and of criticisms put forward by other sociologists.

George Peter Murdock: the family – a universal social institution

In a study entitled *Social Structure* (1949), George Peter Murdock examined the institution of the family in a wide range of societies. Murdock took a sample of 250 societies, ranging from small hunting and gathering bands to large-scale industrial societies. He claimed that some form of family existed in every society, and, on the evidence of his sample, concluded that the family is universal.

Murdock defined the family as follows:

The family is a social group characterised by common residence, economic cooperation and reproduction. It includes adults of both sexes, at least two of whom maintain a socially approved sexual relationship, and one or more children, own or adopted, of the sexually cohabiting adults.   Murdock, 1949

Thus, the family lives together, pools its resources and works together, and produces offspring. At least two of the adult members conduct a sexual relationship according to the norms of their particular society.

The family unit described by Murdock is known as the **nuclear family** and consists of a husband and wife and their children. Units larger than the nuclear family are usually known as **extended families**. Such families can be seen as extensions of the basic nuclear unit, for example through the addition of members of a third generation (the parents of the husband or wife) or members of the same generation (either spouse's siblings).

Murdock found that the nuclear family was present in every society in his sample, either on its own or as the basic unit within an extended family. This led him to conclude that 'the nuclear family is a universal human social grouping' (Murdock, 1949).

From his analysis, Murdock (1949) argued that the family performs four basic functions in all societies, which he termed **sexual**, **reproductive**, **economic** and **educational**. These functions are essential for social life since without the sexual function sexual urges would be unregulated, without the reproductive function there would be no members of society, without the economic function (for example, the provision and preparation of food) life would cease, and without education (a term Murdock uses for socialisation) there would be no culture. Human society without culture could not function.

Clearly, the family does not perform these functions by itself. However, it makes important contributions to them all and Murdock believed that no other institution can perform these functions as successfully.

The family's functions for society are inseparable from its functions for its individual members. The sexual function provides a good example of this. Husband and wife are (at least in theory) exclusive sexual partners. This provides sexual gratification for the couple and strengthens the bond between them. The sexual function also helps to stabilise society by limiting sexual activities to married couples.

Similarly, Murdock claims that the economic function is best achieved by family members living together. He refers in glowing terms to the division of labour within the family, whereby the husband specialises in certain activities, the wife in others. For example, in hunter-gatherer groups men hunt while their wives gather nuts, roots and berries.

Evaluation of Murdock

Murdock's picture of the family is rather like the multifaceted, indispensable Swiss army knife. The family is seen as a multifunctional institution that is indispensable to society. Its 'many-sided utility' accounts for its universality and its inevitability.

In his enthusiasm for the family, however, Murdock did not seriously consider whether other social institutions

could perform its functions and he did not examine alternatives to the family.

In addition, Murdock's description of the family is almost too good to be true. It does not acknowledge the possibility of conflict or exploitation in the family.

Murdock has also been attacked for arguing that the family (as defined by him) is a universal institution.

Yanina Sheeran (1993) argues that the **female-carer core** (a mother caring for one or more children) is the most basic family unit.

The female-carer unit is the foundation of the single-mother family, the two-parent family, and the extended family in its many forms. Thus, it is certainly the basis of family household life in Britain today, and is a ubiquitous phenomenon, since even in South Pacific longhouses, preindustrial farmsteads, communes and Kibbutzim, we know that female carers predominate. **Sheeran, 1993**

In Britain, for example, Sheeran maintains that children usually have one woman who is primarily responsible for their care. This primary carer is often, but not always, the biological mother but could be another relative or adoptive mother.

Sheeran seems to be on strong ground in arguing that a female-carer core is a more basic family unit than that identified by Murdock, since in some societies families without an adult male are quite common. (Her theory does not, however, account for lone-parent families headed by a man.)

Another type of household that may contradict Murdock's claims about the universality of the nuclear family, as defined by him, is the gay or lesbian household. By definition, such households will not contain 'adults of both sexes' who are partners (Murdock, 1949). Furthermore, Judith Stacey (2011) notes that in the USA transgender people can marry people of the same or opposite sex and this is also true in the UK. Stacey also argues that the example of the Mosuo people of southwest China undermines the view that the family, as understood by Murdock, is universal.

Talcott Parsons — the 'basic and irreducible' functions of the family

Talcott Parsons (1959, 1965b) studied the family in modern American society. However, his ideas

Activity

1. Based on the Contemporary issues box below, in what ways does Stacey's research contradict the ideas of Murdock?

2. What aspects of these practices would be considered strange or unacceptable in Britain today?

Contemporary issues: Judith Stacey on the Mosuo people

In 2007 the US sociologist Judith Stacey (2011) visited a remote region of south-west China to study the family life of the Mosuo people who she had heard were the only people in the world who did not practice marriage. At age 13, girls in this culture take part in a 'skirt' initiation ceremony after which they are given a sleeping room of their own known as their 'flower chamber'. From this point onwards, the women are free to take as many male lovers as they choose. Both men and women continue to live with their mother's family but at night men can visit women's flower chambers so long as they return to their own home during the day.

Children are raised by all the women living in the maternal home and adult children live their whole lives in extended households with several generations living together. Fathers owe no particular obligations to their children and indeed the paternity of children is not considered important. Similarly, **heterosexual sexual** partners have no major obligations to one

another although they can, if they wish, undergo a short ceremony and exchange gifts if they want to publicly declare their love. Children generally grow up to be well-adjusted and have little interest in finding out who their natural fathers are.

Guozguang ball of the Mosuo people where women choose their sexual partners whom they neither marry nor live with.

can be applied more broadly, since he argued that the American family retains two 'basic and irreducible functions' that are common to the family in all societies. These are the 'primary socialisation of children' and the 'stabilisation of the adult personalities'.

Primary socialisation refers to the process by which children learn the culture of their society during the early years of childhood. This takes place mainly within the family. **Secondary socialisation** occurs during the later years when other agencies (such as the peer group and the school) exert increasing influence.

There are two basic processes involved in primary socialisation: the **internalisation of society's culture** and the **structuring of the personality**. If culture were not internalised – that is, absorbed and accepted – society would cease to exist, since without shared norms and values social life would not be possible. However, culture is not simply learned, it is

'internalised as part of the personality structure'. The child's personality is moulded by the central values of the culture to the point where they become a part of him or her. In the case of American society, personality is shaped in terms of the values of independence and the desire to be successful.

Parsons argued that families 'are "factories" which produce human personalities'. He believed that the family was the only institution which provides the warmth, security and mutual support necessary to fulfil this function.

Once produced, the personality must be kept stable. This is the second basic function of the family: the **stabilisation of adult personalities**. The emphasis here is on the marriage relationship and the emotional security the couple provide for each other. This function is particularly important in Western industrial society, since the nuclear family is largely isolated from the wider family. It does not have the security

235

Activity

Using this picture, suggest how playing with their children might stabilise adult personalities.

once provided by the close-knit extended family. Thus the married couple increasingly look to each other for emotional support.

Adult personalities are also stabilised by their role in socialising their children. This allows parents to act out 'childish' elements of their own personalities which they have retained from childhood but which cannot be indulged in adult society. For example, father is 'kept on the rails' by playing with his son's train set. According to Parsons, the family therefore provides a context in which husband and wife can express their childish whims, give and receive emotional support, recharge their batteries, and so stabilise their personalities.

Talcott Parsons – the 'isolated nuclear family'

Talcott Parsons argued that the move from pre-industrial to industrial society led to a shift from the extended family to the nuclear family. The **isolated nuclear family** is the typical family form in modern industrial society (Parsons, 1959). It is 'structurally isolated' because it does not form an integral part of a wider system of kinship relationships, with people related by blood, marriage or adoption. There are social relationships between members of nuclear families and their kin, but these relationships are more a matter of choice than binding obligations.

Parsons argued that there is a functional relationship between the isolated nuclear family and the economic system in industrial society. In particular, the isolated nuclear family is shaped to meet the requirements of the economic system which depends on geographical

mobility – the ability to move to a different area so that businesses can recruit the specialist workers they need.

The isolated nuclear family is suited to this need for geographical mobility. It is not tied down by binding obligations to a wide range of kin and, compared to the pre-industrial families, it is a small, streamlined unit.

Criticisms of Parsons

1. As with Murdock, Parsons has been accused of idealising the family with his picture of well-adjusted children and sympathetic husbands and wives caring for each other's every need. It is an over-optimistic theory which may have little relationship to reality.

2. His picture is based largely on the American middle-class family, which he treats as representative of American families in general, ignoring differences based on social divisions. For example, Parsons fails to explore possible differences between middle-class and working-class families, or different family structures in minority ethnic communities.

3. Parsons' view of the socialisation process can be criticised. He sees it as a one-way process, with the children being pumped full of culture and their personalities being moulded by powerful parents. He tends to ignore the two-way interaction between parents and children.

4. More recent theories of the family, such as those put forward by Giddens (1992), argue that the significance of families and the rigidity of family structures have declined with increasing choice for individuals (see Part 2.1). From this perspective, it is misguided to look for a single, dominant family structure since family life is increasingly diverse and fluid.

5. Parsons has also been heavily criticised from a feminist perspective. Lynn Jamieson (2005) accuses Parsons of ignoring the way that families 'were key mechanisms for sustaining gender inequalities and the subordination of women' (Jamieson, 2005).

6. Jamieson also argues that through his concentration on structures Parsons paid no attention to the meanings of family life for those involved. His theorising was not backed up by detailed research so he saw families as abstract entities without examining whether the reality of family life conformed to his assumptions. (See the discussion of personal life on pp. 258–262).

Key terms

Nuclear family A family of two generations (parents and children) related by blood or marriage who live together.

Extended family Any family containing relatives other than parents and children, for example, aunts, uncles and grandparents.

Female carer-core Mothers and children, sometimes seen as the most basic family unit.

Primary socialisation The first stage of the process by which children learn the culture of their society which takes place within the family.

Secondary socialisation The later stages of the process by which people learn the culture of their society which takes place within the education system and other contexts.

Stabilisation of adult personalities To Parsons, the role of the family in maintaining the psychological health of adults by providing warmth and security and allowing them to act out childish elements in their personality.

Summary

1. Functionalist perspectives emphasise the positive role that families play and see them as vital to maintaining stability in society.

2. Murdoch sees the nuclear family as a universal institution – it is found in all societies. He believes that it performs four key functions:

   ▹ Sexual
   ▹ Reproductive
   ▹ Economic
   ▹ Educational (socialisation).

3. Murdock has been criticised for claiming that the nuclear family is the basic family unit. For example, Sheeran sees the female-carer core as the basic family unit.

4. Parsons believes that all families have two 'basic and irreducible' functions:

   ▹ primary socialisation
   ▹ the stabilisation of adult personalities.

5. He claims that the family has moved from an extended form to an isolated nuclear form in modern industrial societies. This streamlined family helps to provide a geographically mobile workforce.

6. There have been many criticisms of Parsons – for idealising the nuclear family, ignoring the increasing variety of family forms, showing no awareness of gender inequality within the family and ignoring the meanings of family life to its members.

5.1.2 'March of progress' theories

Parsons' general view that family structures have changed from extended to nuclear during the transition from pre-industrial to industrial societies has been carefully researched by a number of sociologists and historians. Some researchers have raised questions about the historical accuracy of Parsons' claims but have supported his general view that family life progressively adapts to changes in society and the economy. Theories which support this view are known as **'march of progress' theories**. But has the family really developed in a particular direction and if so are the changes in line with Parsons' predictions?

Young and Willmott and the stages of family life

Michael Young and Peter Willmott conducted studies of family life in London from the 1950s to the 1970s. In their book *The Symmetrical Family* (1973), they attempt to trace the development of the family from pre-industrial England to the 1970s. They disagreed with Parsons over some of the details of how families have developed, for example by arguing that the extended family survived much longer than Parsons had claimed. However, they agreed that the family adapted to economic and social changes. They saw these changes in a positive light and it is for this reason that their ideas have sometimes been seen as 'march of progress theories'.

Using a combination of historical research and social surveys, they suggest that the family has gone through three main stages.

Stage 1 – the pre-industrial family

Stage 1 is represented by the pre-industrial family. The family is a unit of production: the husband, wife and unmarried children work as a team, typically in agriculture or textiles. This type of family was gradually replaced during the industrial revolution. However, it continued well into the 19th century and is still represented in a small minority of families today, the best examples being some farming families.

Activity

Spinning in a cottage in the early 1700s.

Around 1720, Daniel Defoe (author of Robinson Crusoe) journeyed to Halifax in West Yorkshire. This is what he saw.

'Among the manufacturers' houses are likewise scattered an infinite number of cottages or small dwellings, in which dwell the workmen which are employed, the women and children of whom, are always busy carding, spinning etc. so that no hands being unemployed, all can gain their bread, even from the youngest to the ancient […].'

In what ways do the picture and Daniel Defoe's account illustrate the Stage 1 pre-industrial family?

Source: *A Tour through the Whole Island of Great Britain*, Daniel Defoe, 1971

Stage 2 – the early industrial family

The Stage 2 family began with the industrial revolution, developed throughout the 19th century and reached its peak in the early years of the 20th century. The family ceased to be a unit of production, since individual members were employed as wage earners outside the family.

Throughout the 19th century, working-class poverty was widespread, wages were low and unemployment was high. Young and Willmott argue that the family responded to this situation by extending its network to include relatives beyond the nuclear family. This provided an insurance policy against the insecurity and hardship of poverty.

The extension of the nuclear family was largely conducted by women. The basic tie was between a mother and her married daughter and, in comparison, the conjugal bond (the husband–wife relationship) was weak. Women created an 'informal trade union' which largely excluded men

who mixed more with their male peers, for example in local pubs. Mothers and daughters often lived close to each other and would meet frequently. Mothers offered their daughters advice and practical help in looking after children and running the household.

The Stage 2 family began to decline in the early years of the 20th century, but it was still found in many low-income, long-established working-class areas in the 1950s. Its survival is documented in Young and Willmott's famous study entitled *Family and Kinship in East London*. The study was conducted in the mid-1950s in Bethnal Green, a low-income borough in London's East End. Bethnal Green was a long-settled, traditional working-class area. Children usually remained in the same locality after marriage. At the time of the research, two out of three married people had parents living within two to three miles. The study found that there was a close tie between female relatives. Over 50 per cent of the married women in the sample had seen their mother during the previous day, over 80 per cent within the previous week.

Stage 3 – the symmetrical family

In the early 1970s Young and Willmott conducted a large-scale social survey in which 1928 people were interviewed in Greater London and the outer metropolitan area. The results formed the basis of their book, *The Symmetrical Family*.

Young and Willmott argued that the Stage 2 family has largely disappeared. For all social classes, but particularly the working class, the Stage 3 family predominated. The Stage 3 family was a nuclear family which was relatively self-sufficient and home-centred with many leisure activities taking place within the home, for example watching TV. The conjugal bond was strong and relationships between husband and wife involved close cooperation based on companionship.

Young and Willmott used the term symmetrical family to describe the nuclear family of Stage 3. 'Symmetry' refers to an arrangement in which the opposite parts are similar in shape and size. Within the symmetrical family, conjugal roles are similar, in terms of the contribution made by each spouse to the running of the household, although not the same – wives still have the main responsibility for raising the children, even if husbands help. They share many of the chores, they share decisions, they work together, yet there is still men's work and women's work.

Activity

Changing conjugal roles.

1. In what ways does this image represent Young and Willmott's views on the symmetrical family?

2. Does the image reflect the 'typical' British family today?

Conjugal roles are not interchangeable but they are symmetrical in important respects.

Evaluation of Young and Willmott

A number of features of Young and Willmott's work are open to criticism. Many feminists have attacked the concept of **the symmetrical family**, arguing that there has been little progress towards equality between husbands and wives (see Unit 5.5.2, pp. 305–309). Later research by Peter Willmott himself has not used or supported the concept of the symmetrical nuclear family. In the 1980s Willmott (1988) found little evidence of the disappearance of extended family networks. His research showed that contacts with kin remained important in both the middle and working class; two-thirds of the couples saw relatives at least weekly, telephones and cars enabled frequent contact and visits to relatives remained very important as a source of care and support.

Even more significantly, 'march of progress' theories tend to assume that a single family type is dominant at a particular time. However, much research and theorising about families questions this idea and suggests family diversity has become the norm (see pp. 274–291).

Key terms

March of progress theory A theory of the family which assumes that it develops in a progressive way responding and adapting to wider social changes.

Symmetrical family A family in which both husband and wife are in employment and both do some housework and provide childcare.

New individualism A renewed emphasis upon the needs and interests of individuals rather than the collective well-being of the family or community.

Summary

1. March of progress theories argue that the family has adapted to changes in western industrial societies and that these changes represent progress.

2. Young and Willmott argued there have been three main stages in family life, stage 1 being the preindustrial family which was a unit of production, stage 2 being the extended family which survived in working-class areas such as

Then and now: Bethnal Green revisited

In a study published in 2006 Michael Young, along with Geoff Dench and Kate Gavron (Dench, Gavron and Young, 2006) carried out a follow-up to Young and Willmott's study of family life in Bethnal Green in the 1950s.

Dench *et al.* found that the earlier family patterns had largely disappeared. Life in Bethnal Green had

Bethnal Green today.

become much more fluid and varied than it was in the 1950s. For example, the survey they conducted found that 21 per cent of the sample were living in single-person households. A further 9 per cent lived in households which consisted of unrelated adults. Dench *et al.* argue that a **new individualism** had developed in which individuals relied less on other family members and more on the welfare state.

Compared with the 1950s, cohabitation, divorce, separation and single parenthood were all more common. However, there had also been a 'slide back towards conventionality'. People still valued conventional marriage, and there was a widespread feeling that family patterns had moved too far from traditional patterns. Many people believed that casual relationships were acceptable before children were born, but once you became a parent, more stable households were preferable.

Yet according to Dench *et al.*, this new individualism had affected White family life but had had little noticeable impact on Bangladeshi family life. Out of the sample of over 1000 Bangladeshis, only four lived in single-person households.

Bethnal Green into the 1950s, and stage 3 being the nuclear, symmetrical family dominant in the second half of the 20th century.

3. Critics have argued that march of progress theories exaggerate the fit between the family and a particular time period and they question whether a single family type is, or ever has been, dominant in western industrial societies.

4. When Young returned to Bethnal Green with other researchers in more recent research he found much more variety in family life than had existed in the 1950s. He saw this as evidence of a new individualism.

5.1.3 Marxist perspectives on the family

This unit covers Marxist perspectives on the family and criticisms of these approaches. Marxist perspectives on the family are based upon the theories of Karl Marx (see Chapter 1 Part 2 for an introduction to these). They see the family as part of the superstructure

of society which is shaped by the economic base. Marxists believe the form the family takes tends to reflect the economic system of society and in unequal societies, such as capitalist societies, the family takes a form which benefits the ruling class. However, according to an influential Marxist view, the family did not exist in the earliest, pre-capitalist societies.

Friedrich Engels – the origin of the family

The earliest view of the family from a Marxist perspective is developed in Friedrich Engels' *The Origin of the Family, Private Property and the State* (Engels, 1972, first published 1884).

Engels believed that during the early stages of human evolution, the forces of production were communally owned and the family as such did not exist. This era of **primitive communism** was characterised by promiscuity (people had as many sexual partners as they wished) and they lived in what he called the **promiscuous horde**. There were no rules limiting sexual relationships and no institution of marriage.

The evolution of the family

Engels argued that, throughout human history, more and more restrictions were placed on sexual relationships and the production of children. He speculated that marriage and the family evolved out of promiscuity through a series of stages ranging from **polygyny** (in which men have more than one wife), to its present stage, the **monogamous nuclear family** (in which one man is married to one woman). Each successive stage placed greater restrictions on the number of sexual partners available to the individual.

The monogamous nuclear family developed with the emergence of private property, in particular the private ownership of the **forces of production**, and the introduction of the state. The state instituted laws to protect the system of private property and to enforce the rules of monogamous marriage. This form of marriage and the family developed to solve the problem of how private property should be inherited or passed on. In order for men to be able to pass down their property to their offspring, they had to be sure of the paternity of their children. They therefore needed greater control over women so that there could be no doubt about who the father was. The monogamous family provided the most efficient device for this purpose. In Engels' words:

> *It is based on the supremacy of the man, the express purpose being to produce children of undisputed paternity; such paternity is demanded because these children are later to come into their father's property as his natural heirs.* Engels, 1972, first published 1884

Evaluation of Engels

Modern research has suggested that many of the details of Engels' scheme are incorrect. For example, monogamous marriage and the nuclear family are often found in hunting and gathering bands. Since humanity has lived in hunting and gathering bands for the vast majority of its existence, the various forms of group marriage suggested by Engels (such as the promiscuous horde) may well be figments of his imagination. However, Gough (1972) argues that Engels did identify the general direction in which family life changed. Although nuclear families and monogamous marriage exist in small-scale societies, they form a part of a larger kinship group. When individuals marry, they take on a series of duties and obligations to their spouse's kin. And the group character of wider kinship groups gradually weakens with the development of private property.

Deborah Chambers (2012) notes that feminist writers have criticised Engels for emphasising economic relations of production over reproduction (childbearing and childrearing). He was not particularly concerned with the restrictions placed on women by the demands of housework and childcare; instead he concentrated on issues related to property ownership. However, Chambers believes that Engel's work was very important as a pioneering study which linked *production* and *reproduction* and explored gender inequality in the family in terms of historical and political factors. As such it laid the groundwork for many later studies, including the next to be considered.

Eli Zaretsky – personal life and capitalism

Eli Zaretsky (1976) analysed more recent developments in the family from a Marxist perspective. He argued that the family in modern capitalist society creates the illusion that the 'private life' of the family is quite separate from the economy. Before the early 19th century, the family was the basic unit of production. For example, in the early capitalist textile industry, production of cloth took place in the home and involved all family members. Only with the development of factory-based production were work and family life separated.

Following the ideas of Marx, Zaretsky believed that people in capitalism did not feel fulfilled at work where they were being exploited by capitalists. In contrast, family life seemed like a welcome escape. The private life of the family was experienced as much more fulfilling than public life in the workplace.

Zaretsky welcomes the increased possibilities for a personal life for the proletariat as working hours in factories were gradually reduced from the 19th century onwards. However, he believes the family is unable to provide for the psychological and personal needs of individuals. He says, 'it simply cannot meet the pressures of being the only refuge in a brutal society'. It might cushion the effects of capitalism but it cannot compensate for the general misery caused by living in a capitalist society and it in fact helps to keep the system going.

Zaretsky sees the family as a major prop to the capitalist economy. The capitalist system is based upon the domestic labour of housewives (housework and childcare) who reproduce future generations of workers who are needed by capitalists. Furthermore, he also believes the family has become a vital unit

241

of consumption. The family consumes the products of capitalism and this allows the bourgeoisie (the ruling class in capitalism) to continue producing profit. To Zaretsky, only a more equal socialist society will end the artificial separation of family private life and public life, and allow the possibility of personal fulfilment.

Evaluation of Zaretsky

Jennifer Somerville (2000) argues that Zaretsky exaggerates the importance of the family as a refuge from life in capitalist society. She suggests that Zaretsky underestimates 'the extent of cruelty, violence, incest and neglect' within families. He also exaggerates the extent to which family life is separated from work. According to Somerville, during the early stages of capitalism, most working-class women had to take paid work in order for the family to survive financially, and relatively few stayed at home as full-time housewives. There is no doubt though that consumption by and in families is important in contemporary capitalist societies.

Arlie Hochschild — emotional life, commodification and alienation

Arlie Hochschild (2011) uses Marxist theory (along with other theories) in her studies of emotional life in capitalist societies.

Commodification

Hochschild follows Marx in arguing that in capitalism almost every aspect of social life is **commodified** — that is, it is turned into something that can be bought and sold. Capitalism seeks profit wherever it can and expands into new areas when profits cannot be raised in existing markets. In recent decades, emotional life has increasingly become a commodity. This means that things that used to be thought of as private and personal and distinct from economic life have become just another commodity to buy and sell. For example, you can buy the chance to find love by joining a dating agency. In this process, people can become alienated from their emotional attachment to others and even from their own feelings.

Alienation

Alienation involves a sense of detachment from something. It occurs when people lack or lose a sense of connection to something or someone, perhaps even feeling a stranger to themselves. Marx believed that capitalism created alienation because workers produced products for capitalists and did not own the products of their own labour. They had to compete with other workers rather than cooperate with them and they couldn't express themselves through work which was imposed on them by capitalists. To Hochschild, this process has extended further than ever, alienating people from their own feelings and from their connections to others, including family members.

Examples of alienation

Hochschild examined case studies involving over one hundred in-depth interviews with individuals about the emotional impact of personal service work where commodification had occurred. She sees the case studies as revealing 'the human story behind a world of everything for sale' (Hochschild, 2011). The personal service workers included birthday party planners (who freed parents of the emotional responsibility of entertaining their children and their friends), love coaches who advised people on falling in love, care workers who were 'paid to love' and a boat captain paid to scatter the ashes of relatives after their cremation. In all these cases, commodification had extended into areas previously associated with family life and alienation had developed in the process.

Hochschild also interviewed Indian surrogate mothers who were pregnant with the children of clients from the USA and Canada. One interviewee described how she tried to keep a sense of detachment from the baby, the clients and even her own womb. She had decided to rent out her womb to pay her husband's medical bills which she would not otherwise be able to afford. She was very aware that others thought surrogacy was shameful, so she moved to a different village away from neighbours and relatives. The clinic which employed women as surrogates treated them very much as commodities. Their aims were to produce more babies, improve quality by controlling the diet and sexual activity of the women, and to make the whole process more efficient and emotion-free. To Hochschild, the women were engaged in a form of **emotional labour**, alienating themselves from their own bodies and the babies they carried to protect themselves from 'a sense of loss and grief' they might experience upon surrendering the babies after birth.

Activity

Surrogate mothers in India.

Why might being a surrogate mother produce particularly intense feelings of alienation compared with other jobs?

Evaluation of Hochschild

Hochschild's work, like that of Zaretsky, shows how family life has become part of consumer capitalism with emotion work in the form of personal services being bought and consumed by families. It also demonstrates how alienation in capitalist societies extends into intimate personal life. Contrary to Zaretsky's views, this suggests that family life and intimate relationships are not a refuge from the harshness of capitalist relationships. While Hochschild believes that individuals do not just act as passive victims — they actively struggle with controlling their emotions so they can defend their own sense of self-worth — individuals cannot escape from work and avoid alienation in their personal, intimate and family life. Emotional labour pervades all aspects of social life in capitalist societies.

Key terms

Primitive communism Very early societies in which no surplus was produced and no classes existed. Because of this there was no need for families.

Polygyny When men are permitted to have more than one wife at the same time.

Forces of production Those things required to produce goods such as land, machinery, capital, technical knowledge and workers.

Monogamous nuclear family A family of parents and children where the adult partners only have sex with each other.

Promiscuous horde A situation in which there are no taboos on having multiple sexual partners from within the same society.

Commodification A process in which more and more things become available for sale and purchase.

Alienation A process in which people come to feel detached from themselves, from other people or from things.

Emotional labour The work involved in trying to influence the emotions of other people.

Summary

1. Marxists believe that the family is shaped by the economic system and in unequal societies it serves the interests of the ruling class rather than society as a whole.

2. Engels believes that in the earliest, primitive communist societies people lived in promiscuous hordes because there was no private property and therefore no need for families to establish the paternity of children. This changed when men began to accumulate property and they wanted to pass it down to their heirs. The family was developed in order to control women's sexuality.

3. Engels has been criticised for over-emphasising economic factors in shaping family life and for having a faulty understanding of the historical development of the family.

4. Zaretsky believes that the private life of the family and work became separated in capitalist societies. This provided an escape from the exploitation at work but it has meant that the family serves as a prop to capitalism by reproducing labour power (workers) at no cost to the capitalists and by making alienating work more bearable.

5. Zaretsky has been criticised for neglecting exploitation and conflict within the family.

6. Hochschild believes that capitalist values and relationships have penetrated more and more into the private life of the family. Emotional life and personal relationships have become increasingly commodified. This has increased alienation.

5.1.4 Feminist perspectives on the family

Like Marxists, feminists have been highly critical of the family. However, unlike other critics, they have tended to emphasise the harmful effects of family life upon women. Feminists see society as **patriarchal** – that is, dominated by and run in the interests of men. In studying patriarchy within the family, feminists have developed new perspectives and highlighted new issues.

Feminists have, for example, introduced into sociology the study of areas of family life such as housework and domestic violence. They have challenged some widely-held views about the inevitability of male dominance in families and have questioned the view that family life is becoming more egalitarian or equal. Feminists have also highlighted the economic contribution to society made by women's **domestic labour** (housework and childcare) within the family.

Above all, feminist theory has encouraged sociologists to see the family as an institution involving power relationships. It has challenged the image of family life as being based upon cooperation, shared interests and love. Although feminists don't agree about everything, and we will explore different feminist perspectives in this unit, they do agree that gender inequality is a fundamental characteristic of family life.

Marxist feminist perspectives on the family

Marxists such as Engels and Zaretsky acknowledge that women are exploited in marriage and family life but they emphasise the relationship between capitalism and the family. Marxist feminists widen the focus to consider the relationship between patriarchy and the family as well.

The production of labour power

Margaret Benston stated:

> *The amount of unpaid labour performed by women is very large and very profitable to those who own the means of production. To pay women for their work, even at minimum wage scales, would involve a massive redistribution of wealth. At present, the support of the family is a hidden tax on the wage earner – his wage buys the labour power of two people.* Benston, 1972

When a husband pays for the production and upkeep of future labour by supporting a wife who raises children to the point where they can become workers, this acts as a strong discipline on his behaviour at work. He cannot easily withdraw his labour to go on strike with a wife and children to support. These responsibilities weaken his bargaining power and commit him to wage labour.

Not only does the family produce and rear cheap labour, it also maintains it at no cost to the employer. In her role as housewife, the woman attends to her husband's needs, thus keeping him in good running order to perform his role as a wage labourer.

Fran Ansley (1972) translates Parsons' view that the family functions to stabilise adult personalities into a Marxist framework. She sees the emotional support provided by the wife as a safety valve for the frustration produced in the husband by working in a capitalist system. Rather than being turned against the system which produced it, this frustration is absorbed by the comforting wife. In this way, the system is not threatened. In Ansley's words:

> *When wives play their traditional role as takers of shit, they often absorb their husbands' legitimate anger and frustration at their own powerlessness and oppression. With every worker provided with a sponge to soak up his possibly revolutionary ire, the bosses rest more secure.* Quoted in Bernard, 1976

Ideological conditioning

The social reproduction of labour power does not simply involve producing children and maintaining them in good health. It also involves the reproduction of the attitudes essential for an efficient workforce under capitalism. Thus, David Cooper (1972) argues that the family is 'an **ideological conditioning** device in an exploitative society'. Within the family, children learn to conform and to submit to authority. The foundation is therefore laid for the obedient and submissive workforce required by capitalism.

Criticisms of previous views

Some of the criticisms of previous views of the family also apply to Marxist approaches. There is a tendency to talk about 'the family' in capitalist society without regard to possible variations in family life between social classes, ethnic groups, heterosexual and gay and lesbian families, lone-parent families, and over time. As Morgan (1975) notes in his criticism of both functionalist and Marxist approaches, both assume that families are based on nuclear families in which the husband is the main breadwinner and nearly all housework is done by wives. This pattern is becoming less common and the critique of this type of family may therefore be becoming less important.

Marxist feminists may therefore exaggerate the harm caused to women by families and they say little about how the experience of racism might influence families. They also tend to portray female family members as the passive victims of capitalist and patriarchal exploitation. They ignore the possibility that women may have fought back against such exploitation and succeeded in making family relationships less unequal. As we shall see, some liberal feminists are more prepared to accept that progress has been made towards greater gender equality in family life.

Activity

Part of the global Million Women Rise march, London, 2009.
What might these feminists see as the solution to the exploitation of women?

Radical feminist perspectives on the family

To radical feminists, society is seen as fundamentally **patriarchal**, rather than capitalist, and women are held to have different interests from those of men. While there are many varieties of radical feminism, Rosemary Tong (2016) argues that they all agree that 'women's oppression *as women* is more fundamental than other forms of human oppression'. Women are systematically dominated and oppressed in every area of society, from politics and the jobs market to the family.

Radical feminists do not agree on the source of male domination, but most do see the family as important in maintaining male power. A number of radical feminists emphasise domestic violence against women as a source of female oppression (see pp. 315–320).

However, many different aspects of family life are seen as oppressive by some radical feminists, as the discussion of Germaine Greer will demonstrate.

Germaine Greer – *The Whole Woman* and the family

Germaine Greer (2000) is a radical feminist who argues that family life continues to disadvantage and oppress women.

Women as wives

Greer argues there is a strong ideology suggesting that being a wife (or as she puts it, a 'female consort') is the most important female role. The wives of presidents and prime ministers get considerable publicity, but they have to be very much subservient to their husbands. Such a role demands that the woman

> *must not only be seen to be at her husband's side on all formal occasions, she must also be seen to adore him, and never to appear less than dazzled by everything he may say or do. Her eyes should be fixed on him but he should do his best never to be caught looking at her. The relationship must be clearly seen to be unequal.*   Greer, 2000

This inequality extends to all other, less celebrated relationships, but this does little to undermine the enthusiasm of women for getting married. Greer complains of the 'ghastly figure of the bride', and notes that the average wedding costs over many thousands of pounds. However, the honeymoon period will not last for ever, and inequalities will soon appear:

> *Having been so lucky as to acquire a wife, [the husband] begins to take the liberties that husbands have traditionally taken, comes and goes as he pleases, spends more time outside the connubial home, spends more money on himself, leaves off the share of the housework that he may have formerly done. She sees her job as making him happy; he feels that in marrying her he has done all that is necessary in making her happy.*   Greer, 2000

Yet Greer argues all this is a 'con' because it is men who need marriage more. Married men score much higher on all measures of psychological well-being than unmarried men, whereas single women tend to be more content than married women. Wives are seen as having a duty to keep their husbands interested in sex with them, even though they may no longer 'fancy' their husband. However, they have no realistic chance of maintaining

Activity

What would Germaine Greer make of this scene?

his sexual interest because 'Wives are not sexy. Male sexuality demands the added stimulus of novelty'.

Women as mothers

If women get little fulfilment from being wives, perhaps motherhood offers women better prospects? Greer does not deny that motherhood can be intrinsically satisfying, but she claims that it is not valued by society. She says: 'Mothers bear children in pain, feed them from their bodies, cherish and nourish and prepare to lose them'.

Children are expected to leave their mother's home when quite young and to owe their mother little or nothing. Many of the elderly who die of hypothermia are mothers, yet their children accept no responsibility for helping or supporting them. Society attaches no value to motherhood. Greer says:

> *'Mother' is not a career option; the woman who gave her all to mothering has to get in shape, find a job, and keep young and beautiful if she wants to be loved. 'Motherly' is a word for people who are frumpish and suffocating, people who wear cotton hose and shoes with a small heel.*
>
> **Greer, 2000**

This is reflected in 'the accepted ideal of feminine beauty', according to which women are 'boyishly slim and hipless' and the 'broad hips and full bosom of maternity' are seen as 'monstrous'. Women are expected to 'regain their figure' as quickly as they can after childbirth.

In childbirth, medical attention focuses on the well-being of the baby, while the mother's health takes a back seat. After birth, women find that 'mothers and babies are not welcome in adult society, in cinemas, theatres, restaurants, shops or buses'. Women are often expected to return to work 'to service the family debt', and end up exhausted.

Women as daughters

According to Greer, then, family life does little to benefit women in their adult roles as mothers and wives. However, it is also unrewarding for them as daughters. Greer suggests recent evidence shows that daughters are quite likely to experience sexual abuse from fathers, stepfathers and other adult male relatives. Greer sees this as a particularly horrendous extension of patriarchal relations within families.

Such abuse is 'very much commoner than we like to believe' and is not confined to 'a special group of inadequate individuals'. Instead, it is an extension of male heterosexuality. Greer says: 'It is understood that heterosexual men fancy young things, that youth itself is a turn-on, but no one is sure how young is too young. Why after all are sexy young women called "babes"?'

Evaluation of Greer

Given the dismal prospects for women within patriarchal families, Greer argues that the best bet for women is segregation by living in households free of adult males. The only alternative is for women to continue to accept their 'humiliation' by men in conventional families.

Germaine Greer's work is very provocative and makes some important points about the position of women in contemporary society. However, it does make sweeping generalisations, many of which are not backed up by research evidence.

Jennifer Somerville (2000) is very critical of Greer. Somerville argues that Greer underestimates the progress made by women over recent decades. She also argues that Greer offers little in the way of practical policy proposals that might make a real difference to women's lives and she fails to discuss the effectiveness of policies that have been introduced.

Greer is just one of many radical feminists with others offering a range of solutions to the problem of patriarchy, including females replacing males in the dominant positions in society and the creation of artificial wombs so women are not burdened by child bearing. Less radical solutions are put forward by liberal feminists.

Activity

A bride.

1. Why do you think that Germaine Greer refers to 'the bride' as a 'hideous figure'?

2. Do you agree with her? Give reasons for your answer.

Liberal feminism

The term 'liberal feminist' describes a wide range of moderate feminists who support equal rights for women and who believe that this can be achieved through gradual reform rather than revolutionary change. They tend to emphasise the importance of legislation to guarantee equal opportunities and cultural change to reduce or eliminate sexism and gender discrimination. As Rosemarie Tong argues, 'Liberal feminists wish to free women from oppressive gender roles – that is those roles used as excuses for giving women a lesser place, or no place at all' (Tong, 2016). To most liberal feminists, gender roles within the family play a key part in shaping differences and inequalities between men and women. Jennifer Somerville is a case in point.

Jennifer Somerville – a liberal feminist perspective on the family

Compared to Greer, Jennifer Somerville (2000) herself offers a less radical feminist critique of the family and identifies more specific policies which might improve the position of women. Her proposals involve relatively modest reform rather than revolutionary change. For these reasons Somerville can be seen as a liberal feminist, although she does not use this term herself.

The family and reform

Somerville argues that many young women do not feel entirely sympathetic to feminism, yet still feel some sense of grievance. To Somerville, many feminists have failed to acknowledge the progress that has been made for women. For example, women now have much greater freedom to take paid work even if they are married and have young children. They also have much more choice about when or whether they marry or cohabit, become single mothers, enter lesbian relationships, or live on their own.

The increased choice for women and the tendency for families to have both partners in employment have helped to create greater equality within marriage. Despite this, however, Somerville argues 'Women are angry, resentful, but above all disappointed in men'. Many men do not take on their full share of responsibilities and often these men can be 'shown the door'.

Somerville raises the possibility that women might do without male partners, especially as so many prove inadequate, and instead get their sense of fulfilment from their children. Unlike Germaine Greer, though, Somerville does not believe that living in households without adult males is the answer. She says, 'the high figures for remarriage suggest that children are not adequate substitutes for adult relationships of intimacy and companionship for most women'. Such a solution fails to 'mention desire – that physical and energizing interest in the Other – which defies being tailored to the logic of equality and common sense'.

Principled pragmatism

From Somerville's viewpoint, heterosexual attraction between men and women and the need for adult companionship mean that heterosexual families will not disappear. However, nor will conflict and inequality between women and men in relationships. These will lead to more women cohabiting, living in non-family households or on their own; but most will return to giving a permanent partnership a try at some point.

What is therefore needed is a 'principled pragmatism' in which feminists devise policies to encourage greater equality within relationships and to help women cope with the practicalities of family life. One area that Somerville thinks is particularly important is the introduction of new policies to help working parents so that they can balance work and family life and so that both parents can play a full role in childcare. At present, many jobs lack the flexibility needed to combine work with effective parenting.

Somerville therefore believes that family life is in crisis because feminist ideals have only been partly achieved and society's institutions still make it difficult to attain genuine equality between heterosexual partners. If that institutional framework can be changed, for example by increased flexibility

Sheryl Sandberg, Chief Operating Officer of Facebook, at the World Economic Forum in 2013. But are her experiences typical of 'ordinary' women?

in paid employment, then the liberal feminist dream of egalitarian relationships between men and women will move closer to being a reality.

Evaluation of liberal feminism

Somerville's work recognises that significant changes have taken place in family life, and it offers the realistic possibility of gradual progress towards greater equality within the family. However, to radical feminists such an approach will fail to deal with the persistence of patriarchal structures in society and a patriarchal culture in family life. Linda McKie and Samantha Callan (2012) argue that liberal feminism has failed to deliver fully on its promises. According to them, when women become mothers this can be a turning point which leads to women adopting traditional gender roles. Mothers (and in some contexts their daughters) still end up doing a disproportionate share of housework, caring work and **emotion work** (for example writing and sending birthday and Christmas cards).

Contemporary issues: Neoliberal feminism?

Angela McRobbie (2013) raises questions about the success of liberal feminism in a recent article. She argues that a new form of feminism has emerged which serves the interests of middle and upper-class women and capitalism, but not women from working-class backgrounds. This new form of feminism has undermined the traditional role of feminism in promoting greater equality and instead has become closely tied to **neoliberalism**. (Neoliberalism is the contemporary form of capitalism based on free markets and free trade, which can lead to extreme inequality.) Motherhood is the central issue to neoliberal feminists.

Neoliberals support a capitalist system in which the state has a minimal role in regulating the economy and the welfare state is cut back as far as possible. According to McRobbie, cutting welfare is linked to the celebration of independent, self-sufficient and well-functioning families in which mothers play a central role. Women are called on to be 'exemplary mothers' socialising their children effectively while at the same time being strong, successful and independent women. If women juggle motherhood and careers they can take advantage of the sort of opportunities that liberal feminists have striven for (for example opportunities for high-flying careers and high-quality childcare). If they take time away from work to raise children, then they can achieve

fulfilment by being 'professional mothers' using their education and professional experience to invest time and effort in the future success of their children. The daily grind of housework and childcare is no longer portrayed as drudgery (as in traditional feminist writing) but as an opportunity to exercise professional skills (albeit often with paid-help from cleaners, childminders or nannies to reduce the burden).

McRobbie refers to a book by Sheryl Sandberg, the Chief Operating Officer of *Facebook*, which advises women on using business techniques to run households, raise children and still have very successful careers. At the same time the professional mother, whether full or part-time, is expected to maintain her (hetero)sexual desirability, getting exercise, keeping slim, keeping up with fashion and spending time and money on make-up and personal grooming. She aspires to be 'a yummy mummy' impressing her peers with her femininity as well as her success. For example, women can use 'jogging buggies' to keep fit while bonding with their young children.

As well as in books like Sandberg's, these ideas are promoted in The *Daily Mail's Femail* section, on the website *Mumsnet*, in magazines such as *Elle* and *Red*, TV programmes such as *Loose Women* and so on. The messages are reinforced by social media particularly *Instagram* and *Facebook*. This new neoliberal version of feminism draws on aspects of the old liberal feminism – for example telling women to demand caring male partners who will help with childcare and housework – but it stops short of supporting equality for all women. The neoliberal image of the independent, successful career woman with an egalitarian relationship does not extend to working-class women. There is little or no concern with state welfare to support single mothers, mothers struggling on low income or in insecure work. Indeed, such women are seen as not 'trying hard enough' and failing to live up to the ideals of motherhood with its 'routines of play dates, coffee shops and jogging buggies'.

According to McRobbie, the neoliberal form of feminism does more for the interests of capitalists than women, especially working-class women. While it encourages opportunities for middle-class women (at least to some extent) working-class women are looked down on as unfashionable and as lacking the 'right' (middle-class) lifestyle. Furthermore, opportunities for middle-class mothers to spend quality time with their children, to keep slim and fashionable or to pursue their careers, rely on working-class childminders, nannies and cleaners. Therefore, neoliberal feminism is no substitute for

more radical forms of feminism which promote greater equality for all women, and which acknowledge class as well as gender inequality.

The Quest Jogging Stroller: With shock-absorbing tyre suspension and a built-in sound system, it is designed so you can bond with your baby while jogging to keep fit.

Questions

1. How does the Quest Jogging Stroller reflect the concerns of neoliberal feminists?

2. Are mothers who use them more 'worthy' than those who use cheap buggies?

Key terms

Patriarchal A patriarchy is a society or group that is dominated by and run in the interests of men.

Domestic labour Work done within the home such as housework and childcare. It may be unpaid but it creates value just as paid work does.

Ideological conditioning The process by which people are taught distorted beliefs which serve the interests of powerful groups in society, particularly capitalists.

Radical feminism The most extreme version of feminism which tends to see society as being completely dominated by men and which sees the interests of men and women as being very different.

Oppression Keeping people in a state in which they are disadvantaged, exploited, and denied opportunity and freedom.

Liberal feminism A version of feminism which is relatively moderate and believes that the position of women in society can be improved through reform rather than radical or revolutionary change.

Neoliberalism The latest stage of capitalism which supports free markets and a minimal role for the state.

Neoliberal feminism According to McRobbie, a version of feminism which is pro-capitalist.

Summary

1. There are many different versions of feminism, but they all emphasise the negative effects of family life on women.

2. Marxist feminists believe that the family benefits men and capitalists in a variety of ways.

   › Women's labour reproduces the workforce at no cost to capitalists.

   › It serves as an ideological conditioning device persuading workers to accept capitalism.

3. Radical feminism comes in a variety of forms but all agree that revolutionary change is needed to end the oppression of women.

4. Germaine Greer believes that whether as mothers, wives or daughters, women's roles

within the family lead to exploitation. She argues that women would be better off living separately from men. Greer has been criticised for failing to take account of the progress made by women in securing greater equality.

5. Liberal feminists accept that women have made progress through gradual change but argue that more progress is still needed if women are to become equal within the family.

　❯ Jennifer Somerville argues that men still fail to provide a fair contribution to family life.

　❯ Liberal feminism is criticised for failing to acknowledge the continuing strength of patriarchal structures and for not accepting that more radical changes are needed to address the underlying reasons for the exploitation and oppression of women in families.

6. Angela McRobbie argues that a new neoliberal form of feminism is dominant which benefits capitalism and middle-class career-oriented women and 'professional mothers' but is based on the exploitation of working-class women.

PART 2 CONTEMPORARY PERSPECTIVES ON THE ROLE OF THE FAMILY AND SOCIAL CHANGE: MODERNITY, POSTMODERNITY AND INTERPRETIVIST PERSPECTIVES

Contents

The perspectives examined in part one Part 1 of this chapter all tend to assume there is a single dominant family type in contemporary society and the family has a specific role in society. The theories examined in this part challenge these assumptions. They ask questions such as: Do most young people expect to marry a person of the opposite sex, have children and live in a nuclear family? Do they have any family plan for their lives? Are family relationships the most important relationships in people's lives?

This part begins by examining theories which argue that families have changed in response to wider economic and social changes. Some sociologists characterise these changes as involving a transition to a new type of modern society (described variously as late modern, the second modernity or the risk society). Others argue that a complete transformation is taking place with a shift from a modern society to a postmodern society (see pp. 16–19). But, however these sociologists analyse social change, they agree that there has been a trend towards the acceptance of a greater variety of family types in Western societies. In their different ways, they also argue that this results from increased choice over family and personal relationships. Individuals feel less obligation to slavishly follow a single model of family and personal life. As a result, families are seen as becoming less stable and predictable and more diverse.

The personal life approach examined at the end of this part of the chapter moves away from grand theorising and instead focuses on personal relationships involving friends as well as family members. This approach emphasises the meanings individuals attach to personal relationships and is less concerned with changes in society as a whole. It asks questions such as how is personal life lived? How is it experienced by individuals? What really matters to people in personal relationships?

5.2.1 Modernity, late modernity and the family

This unit reviews the perspectives examined in Part 1 of the chapter in terms of the way in which their ideas on the family are linked to the concept of modernity. It then considers perspectives which argue that society is changing and moving into later stages of modernity resulting in major changes in family relationships. It raises questions about whether the meaning of sexuality and the nature of love are changing.

Modernity and the family

The idea of modernity involves a belief in human progress. From this point of view, social change has a direction and this direction is towards better and more efficient and effective institutions. This can come about through evolutionary change or through planning. Talcott Parson's view of the family (see pp. 234–236) is an example of the evolutionary view. As discussed in the previous part, Parsons believes that a change from the **extended family** to the **isolated nuclear family** in modern, industrial societies meant that the family was well adapted to the demands of that type of society. Because the isolated nuclear family is not dependent on extended kin, it was easier for families to be geographically mobile and therefore to move wherever family members were needed by employers. Similarly, 'march of progress' theories (p. 237) believe that the move towards the **symmetrical family** in modern societies was a progressive change encouraging more equal relationships between husbands and wives.

Theorists such as Anthony Giddens believe that modernity has itself changed and has entered a new phase of **late modernity**. This doesn't involve a complete break with modernity, but there are still significant changes and these have important effects on family life. Giddens (and Beck and Beck-Gernsheim who are discussed below) do not assume that these changes are necessarily beneficial and progressive. While Giddens sees them in a broadly positive light, the other theorists are less optimistic.

Anthony Giddens: *The Transformation of Intimacy*

In an influential book, the British sociologist Anthony Giddens (1990) argues that major changes have taken place in intimate relationships between people (particularly relationships between sexual partners). He relates these changes to the development of what he calls **late modernity**.

Modern love

According to Giddens, in the modern era, marriage and family life were based on an idea of **romantic love** which began to develop first among the aristocracy. Romantic love involves idealising the object of one's love and, for women in particular, telling stories to oneself about how you could become fulfilled through the relationship.

In theory, romantic love should be egalitarian (based on equality) because the bond is based upon mutual attraction. In practice, however, it has tended to lead to the dominance of men. Sex is important in romantic love, but a successful sexual relationship is seen as stemming from the romantic attraction, and not the other way round. In the ideal of romantic love, a woman saves herself and preserves her virginity until the perfect man comes along.

On the basis of romantic love, partners are bound together until death. They marry, if possible have children and remain faithful. The idea of romantic love is therefore the foundation of family life. Of course, Giddens is aware that things didn't always work out that well, and inequalities between men and women and other issues could cause relationship problems. However, a stable marriage based on romantic love was still the ideal in modern society.

Plastic sexuality

Giddens believes that in the later decades of the 20th century the era of modernity began to give way to a new era of **late modernity**. Broadly speaking, this involved people losing the belief that there was a single, right and best way to live your life and instead exercising more choice over a wider range of options. This involves the development of what Giddens calls **reflexivity** – the ability to reflect upon your life and make choices about the best way forward instead of sticking to a preordained script. In other words, people began to question whether your sex life, child-rearing and marriage should necessarily be entangled with one another and whether you should stay with the same partner for life. The idea of **plastic sexuality** began to develop. This involves sex being freed from its association with childbirth altogether. People have much greater choice over when, how often and with whom they engage in sex. Sex becomes a type of leisure pursuit.

Activity

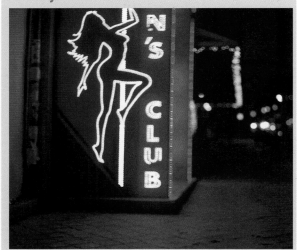

Has the sex industry contributed to changing the meaning of sex?

1. How far do you agree with Giddens that sex has become a leisure pursuit which is no longer tied to conceiving children?

2. Do his views apply equally well to men and to women?

Confluent love and the pure relationship

The emergence of plastic sexuality changes the nature of love. Romantic love is increasingly replaced by **confluent love**. Confluent love is love which lasts only so long as it benefits the lover.

In earlier eras, divorce was difficult or impossible and it was difficult to engage openly in premarital relationships. Now people have much more choice and they are not compelled to stay together if a relationship is not working.

The ideal on which people increasingly base relationships is the **pure relationship**, rather than a marriage based on romantic passion. Pure relationships are based on the active choice of the partners. They stay together 'until further notice' as long as both get sufficient benefit from the relationship to make it worthwhile.

In general, Giddens sees pure relationships as having the potential for creating more equal relationships between men and women. They have an openness and a mutual concern and respect which makes it difficult for one partner to be dominant. However, he recognises that a whole range of emotional, psychological and physical abuses can occur within

contemporary relationships. The pure relationship is more of an ideal than something most intimate couples have achieved, but there is still a trend in this direction.

Modernity and self-identity

Giddens sees **reflexivity** as a key, perhaps the key, characteristic of modernity. In pre-modern times institutions were largely governed by tradition. They carried on in certain ways because they had always operated that way in the past. Modernity involves the increasing application of reason. Reason is used to work out how institutions can work better. Reflexivity describes the way in which people can use reason to reflect upon the institutions that are part of the social world and try to change them for the better.

Increasingly, such reflexivity reaches into all areas of social life, including very personal areas such as sexuality. For example, an increasing number of self-help books, magazine columns and so on are written to help people reflect upon and try to improve their sex lives.

Reflexivity extends into the creation of self-identity. People can increasingly choose who they want to be. They are no longer stuck with the roles into which they were born or confined by the dictates of tradition.

Activity

Dating sites are becoming increasingly popular. There are a number of so-called affair sites designed for people looking for an affair.

Can affair sites be seen as evidence for or against:

a) plastic sexuality?

b) the pure relationship?

c) 'the reflexive project of self'?

Explain your answers.

Giddens argues there is a 'reflexive project of the self' in which individuals think about what sort of person they want to become and continually review their progress towards their ideals. People want to discover who they really are, and trying out different relationships can be an important part of this process. Seeking a pure relationship may, for example, allow an individual to try to decide whether they are truly homosexual, heterosexual or bisexual.

People have a far greater choice of lifestyles than in the past, and trying different ones may be part of creating a self-identity. When people ask themselves 'Who shall I be?' they also ask themselves 'How shall I live?' Family and personal relationships are a very important part of this.

Evaluation of Giddens

Giddens's theory appears to explain the increasing rates of divorce and other relationship breakdowns and the greater variety of family forms. If people are continually searching to find their true selves and the perfect 'pure' relationship, it is unsurprising that many relationships will fall short of the ideal and will break down as people try out new alternatives. But his ideas can also explain why marriage, whether heterosexual or not, remains popular in the quest for the pure relationship.

However, the feminist Lynn Jamieson (1999) argues that there is little evidence that 'pure relationships' have become widespread, claiming that gender inequalities still make it very difficult for women to gain equality in sexual relationships with men. To Jamieson (1997) Giddens ignores the wider structural factors, particularly patriarchy, which help to produce inequality.

Other sociologists, while agreeing with Giddens that there is now more choice, see this as resulting from somewhat different processes from those discussed by Giddens. Furthermore, some see the changes in a much more negative light than Giddens does.

Ulrich Beck and Elisabeth Beck–Gernsheim: *The Normal Chaos of Love*

The German sociologists Ulrich Beck and Elisabeth Beck-Gernsheim (1995, first published in German in 1990) put forward another influential interpretation of changes in relationships and family life. Beck and Beck-Gernsheim follow a similar line of argument to Giddens in claiming that changes in family life and

relationships are being shaped by the development of modernity bringing with it greater choice for individuals. However, they use the term the second modernity to describe this phase and see its central characteristic as being **individualisation** rather than reflexivity. They also see the changes as having rather different consequences from those suggested by Giddens.

Individualisation

Individualisation involves an extension of the areas of life in which individuals are expected to make their own decisions. Beck and Beck-Gernsheim link this to an increase in personal mobility, both social and geographical. As modern societies opened up, moving location and moving jobs became easier, and this presented individuals with more choices about how to run their lives. Improved labour market (job) opportunities for women have been particularly important leading to new uncertainties about gender roles which have affected intimate relationships.

Choice in families and relationships

As individuals gained more personal choice they were freed from the restrictions produced by an obligation to live in traditional families, but they also lost the support and security that came with traditional family life. Instead, individuals now have to try to *create* personal relationships that will provide for their needs.

Beck and Beck-Gernsheim say the nuclear family seems to offer 'a sort of refuge in the chilly environment of our affluent, impersonal, uncertain society, stripped of its traditions and scarred by all kinds of risk. Love will become more important than ever and equally impossible'. Love is important because people believe they can express and fulfil their individuality through a loving relationship. Love offers the promise of an 'emotional base' and a 'security system', which are absent in the world outside. However, contemporary societies make the formation of relationships based on love very problematic.

Love has come to depend on individuals finding a successful formula. It can no longer be based upon norms and traditions, since these no longer exist in a form that is generally or even widely accepted. In their search for love, people often try out a number of arrangements, such as cohabitation, marriage and divorce. Each time they have to devise their own arrangements, negotiate them and justify them. This often leads to conflict with partners and lovers.

The causes of conflict

The amount of choice in itself causes the potential for conflict, but there are other factors that make it even more likely. Earlier periods of industrial modern societies were based upon relatively clear-cut gender roles involving a male breadwinner and a female carer and homemaker. With increased opportunities for women in education and employment, this has changed. Now, both men and women seek fulfilling careers. Furthermore, work has become more demanding with longer hours and employers demanding more of their employees. This makes it difficult to devote sufficient time and energy to family life.

The family is the arena in which these contradictions and conflicts are played out. Men and women argue over who should do the housework, who should look after the kids and whose job should take priority. The results of the arguments rarely satisfy both parties. In the end one person's career or personal development has to take a back seat. In a world where individualisation has proceeded so far, this is bound to cause resentment.

Beck and Beck-Gernsheim believe these contradictions lead to what they call 'the normal chaos of love'. Love is increasingly craved to provide security in an insecure world, but it is increasingly difficult to find and sustain. The quest for individual fulfilment by both partners in a relationship makes it difficult for them to find common ground.

Evaluation of Beck and Beck-Gernsheim

Beck and Beck-Gernsheim may be right to suggest that greater choice over relationships can create problems in making them work. There are certainly plenty of relationship breakdowns in contemporary society. However, they have been criticised for being too pessimistic about relationships and family life (Chambers, 2012). Some couples do manage to work out their differences and produce mutually satisfactory relationships.

Some sociologists have been sceptical about the individualisation thesis. Vanessa May (2011) criticises it for exaggerating the decline of traditional norms and values. May argues, for example, that class differences still shape family life and marriage and family relationships are still strongly valued by most people. An example of this is the strength of feeling over the effects of divorce on children. Another is that people still overwhelmingly leave their property to family members when they die (Gilding 2010, cited in May, 2015).

Carol Smart (2007) questions the idea of individualisation, arguing that individuals are too wrapped up in networks of relationships with family and friends to simply act as individuals (see p. 258). She believes that the idea of the independent, autonomous individual is a myth because every aspect of a person's life and identity is entangled with the lives of others.

Activity

Celebrity couple Angelina Jolie and Brad Pitt (collectively known as 'Brangelina') pictured here in 2013 were married in 2014 but announced their divorce in 2016.

1. Many relationships and marriages between high profile and celebrity couples are short-lived, however idyllic they may seem at the start. Can Beck and Beck-Gernsheim's theory of 'the normal chaos of love' explain this?

2. Is this theory more convincing for rich celebrity couples or relatively poor 'ordinary' couples?

Key terms

Late modernity According to Giddens the latest phase of modernity characterised by greater individualisation and reflexivity.

Modernity A phase in the development of society in which rationality is particularly important.

Romantic love A form of love in which you idealise the one you love and believe they are necessary for a fulfilling life.

Reflexivity The ability to reflect upon your life and make choices about the best way forward.

Pure relationship A relationship in which people stay together because the relationship is mutually rewarding rather than out of a sense of duty.

Plastic sexuality A form of sexuality in which the purpose of sex is not primarily to conceive children but is more about self-fulfilment.

Confluent love Love which only lasts as long as it provides satisfaction.

The second modernity The most recent phase of modernity according to Beck and Beck-Gernsheim involving individualisation.

Individualisation An extension of the areas of social life in which individuals are expected to make their own decisions rather than relying on tradition and social norms.

Summary

1. Theorists of modernity such as Parsons believed that both societies and families were progressing with the nuclear family becoming the dominant form.

2. The idea of late modernity suggests we are moving into a new phase of modernity.

3. Giddens believes that family life is characterised by greater choice because of growing reflexivity (allowing people to choose their own paths in life more than ever before).

4. Giddens thinks that relationships are increasingly freely-chosen *pure relationships* rather than relationships based on a sense of obligation.

5. Beck and Beck-Gernsheim are pessimistic and see the changes in family life as driven by individualisation which offers too many choices leading to conflict in relationships.

6. Beck and Beck-Gernsheim have been criticised for underestimating the continuing appeal of traditional family structures and the importance of social networks as opposed to the pursuit of self-interest.

5.2.2 Postmodernity and the family

Unlike Giddens and Beck and Beck-Gernsheim, postmodernists believe contemporary societies such as the USA have developed the **postmodern family**. From this point of view, societies have moved beyond modernity with its emphasis on rationality, reflexivity, planning and progress and entered a new era of **postmodernity**. An important characteristic of postmodernity is that most people lose faith in claims that there is a single, best, way of living your life and they turn against the idea that their identity and lifestyle have to be planned and that they have to follow a predictable and progressive path. This has important implications for all aspects of social life, including families.

Judith Stacey — the postmodern family

Like the other writers examined in this unit, the American postmodernist Judith Stacey (1996, 2011) associates changes in the family with a movement away from a single dominant family type to greater variety in family relationships. She believes that today, families in Western societies are varied, constantly changing and tend to lack a fixed shape, form or structure. Elements of traditional family life might be preserved but they often exist alongside novel features. The old and the new are frequently blended together as families improvise new ways of living in a rapidly changing world. In more recent writing, (2011) she argues that in a globalised world a wide variety of family forms exists not just in the USA and Europe, but in most of the rest of the world as well.

The shift to the postmodern family

Stacey does not see the emergence of the postmodern family as another stage in the development of family life; instead, it has destroyed the whole idea that the family progresses through a series of logical stages. It no longer makes sense to discuss what type of family is dominant in contemporary societies because family forms have become so diverse. Furthermore, there can be no assumption that any particular form will become accepted as the main, best or normal type of family.

Stacey believes this situation is here to stay. It will be impossible for societies to go back to having a single standard (such as the heterosexual nuclear family) against which all families are compared and judged. Societies will have to come to terms with such changes and adapt to cope with the greater variety and uncertainty in family life.

Although some commentators deplore the decline of the conventional, heterosexual nuclear family, diversity is permanent and social attitudes and social policies will have to adjust to this diversity if people are to have fulfilling lives. If, on the other hand people are forced against their will to live in conventional families, it will just lead to more misery and 'unhappy families' (Stacey, 2011).

Postmodern families in Silicon Valley

Stacey's claim that the postmodern family is now typical in Western societies is based upon her own research into family life in Silicon Valley, conducted during the mid-1980s. Silicon Valley in California is the 'global headquarters of the electronics industry and the world's vanguard post-industrial region' (Stacey, 1996). Usually, trends in family life in the USA take on an exaggerated form in Silicon Valley. For example, divorce rates in this area have risen faster than in other areas of the country. Trends there are generally indicative of future trends elsewhere.

Stacey's research focused on two working-class extended-kin networks in Silicon Valley, and uncovered the way in which these families had become adaptable and innovative in response to social changes. The two individuals central to the two kinship networks studied by Stacey were Pam and Dotty: working-class women who had to adapt their family life to changing personal circumstances and the changing society that surrounded them.

Pam and Dotty

Both Pam and Dotty got married to manual workers around the end of the 1950s and the start of the 1960s. Both were unhappy with aspects of their marriage. Both husbands took little part in family life

Activity

Silicon Valley is home to many of the leading technology companies in the USA – Apple, Google, Facebook, Visa and PayPal all have their headquarters in the area.

Suggest reasons why the postmodern family should be pioneered in Silicon Valley.

and were unwilling to help with housework. Dotty's husband, Lou, physically abused her. For these reasons both women left their husbands.

Pam got divorced, studied for a degree, and pursued a career working for social services. Some time later, Pam became a born-again Christian and remarried. Her second marriage was a more egalitarian one and her family network was far from conventional. For example, she formed a close relationship with her first husband's live-in lover and they helped each other out in a range of practical ways.

Dotty eventually took her husband back, but only after he had had a serious heart attack that left him unable to abuse her physically. Furthermore, the reconciliation was largely on Dotty's terms and her husband had to carry out most of the housework. Dotty meanwhile got involved in political campaigns in the community, particularly those concerned with helping wives who had been the victims of domestic violence. Later, her husband and two of her adult children died. One of her deceased daughters left four children behind and Dotty successfully obtained custody of the children. Dotty then formed a household with one of her surviving daughters, who was a single mother.

These complex changes in the families of Pam and Dotty showed how two working-class women developed their family life to take account of changes in their circumstances in a rapidly changing environment. In the process, they moved away from living in traditional nuclear families.

Gay and lesbian families

Stacey argues that gay and lesbian families have also played a crucial role in changes in family life. In the early 1970s gay and lesbian organisations were often strongly anti-family, but by the late 1980s this attitude had been reversed. There was a major 'gayby boom' – that is, a boom in babies and children being looked after by gay and lesbian couples.

Gay and lesbian families are themselves extremely diverse, but because of the prejudice they sometimes face they have had to consider the best way to develop their intimate relationships. This forced reflection has made these families more creative and imaginative in developing family forms to suit their circumstances. It has made them more likely to include people from outside conventional nuclear family relationships in their family circle, including single people.

Within this creativity and flexibility, gay and lesbian couples have increasingly asserted a right to claim, if they wish, aspects of more conventional family relationships for themselves. This has involved, for example, claiming custody of children, lesbian women intentionally becoming pregnant so that they can raise a child with their partner, and trying to have same-sex marriages legally recognised. Slowly, they have made gains on all these fronts.

Stacey believes children raised in gay and lesbian families are less likely to be hostile to homosexual relationships and more likely to try them for themselves. However, she regards this as an advantage rather than a problem. This is because it discourages intolerance of families who are different, and in a world of increasing family diversity this is essential. It also allows people more freedom to explore and develop their sexuality, free from what Adrienne Rich has called '**compulsory heterosexuality**' (cited in Stacey, 1996).

Stacey does not believe that the development of the postmodern family has no disadvantages. She acknowledges that it creates a certain degree of unsettling instability. Nevertheless, she generally welcomes it as an opportunity to develop more egalitarian and more democratic family relationships.

Evaluation of Stacey

As we will see later in the chapter (Part 4), it is questionable how far the undoubted diversification of families has supplanted more conventional families. It is possible that Stacey exaggerates the extent of change. Neither gay and lesbian families, nor families in Silicon Valley, are likely to be typical American families or typical of families in Britain and elsewhere. Furthermore, the belief that 'traditional' families are the 'best' family form, especially for raising children arguably remains strong. New Right theories of the family (see Part 3) would certainly question whether diversity is a good thing.

Nevertheless, Stacey seems to be on strong ground in arguing that there is greater diversity and that it seems very unlikely that societies such as the USA and UK will ever return to a situation in which conventional marriage and the nuclear family are as dominant as they were in the past.

Activity

Elton John, David Furnish and their children.

1. In what ways does this photo suggest that families and personal relationships are becoming more the choice of individuals than the product of social norms?

2. Does the photo suggest the ideology of the nuclear family still has influence?

Key terms

Postmodernity According to some sociologists, a phase in the development of society in which there is no longer a belief in a single best way of organising social life and in which the idea of progress Is rejected.

Postmodern family The family under postmodernity which changes rapidly and has no fixed structure.

Compulsory heterosexuality A situation in which alternatives to heterosexuality are considered socially unacceptable.

Summary

1. Some sociologists believe that we have moved beyond modernity altogether into a postmodern era.

2. This involves a break with the idea of progress and to Stacey means a breakdown of the idea that the family moves through stages.

3. Stacey believes that families change rapidly and take a variety of forms as their members react to circumstances.

4. Her research in Silicon Valley suggests that working-class families are creating new, flexible family forms.

5. Gay and lesbian families are also at the forefront of change since they cannot easily fall back on the heterosexual model of family life.

6. Critics suggest that Stacey may exaggerate the pace and extent of change and underestimate the value that people still place on traditional nuclear family relationships and structures.

5.2.3 The sociology of personal life

A number of sociologists have recently begun to argue that the sociology of the family (along with other areas of sociology) needs to be reconceptualised in terms of the sociology of personal life. Vanessa May (2011) argues that personal relationships are not confined to families and should not be exclusively studied in terms of the sociology of the family. She does not question the view that family relationships are central to personal life, but she argues that personal life also involves relationships with other people outside traditional families as well.

May believes that an emphasis upon the continuing importance of relationships between people provides a more realistic view of contemporary social life than the theories of Giddens (1992) and Beck and Beck-Gernsheim (1995) which focus more on individuals than relationships. In Smart's work, understanding the meanings that people give to these relationships is a crucial aspect of the sociology of personal life and as such it can be seen as an interpretative approach. This approach asks important questions about what personal life means to individuals and how they see their relationships. After all, to most people, the structure of their family is not as important as how they get along with those they are closest to.

Carol Smart: *Personal Life*

In *Personal Life*, Smart (2007) argues that the early sociology of the family tended to concentrate upon the White, nuclear heterosexual family in Western culture. Gradually the terminology in the sociology of the family has shifted, introducing concepts such as households, discussing families of choice (which can encompass friends as well as kin) and thinking in terms of practices rather than structures and institutions.

However, despite this, the sociology of the family, kinship and households still puts most emphasis on those who are connected by marriage or birth and/or those who live together under one roof. Smart, though, believes that people no longer necessarily see their personal life as structured in this way. For example, with technological developments it is easier for people to have significant relationships with people who live far away. Relationships between people who are not related can also be very strong and family life is not necessarily the centre of everyone's relationships.

The main features of personal life

Smart argues that the 'personal' is different from the 'individual'. She defines the *personal* as a part of social life which 'impacts closely on people and means much to them'. It involves those aspects of life which evoke significant feelings. People may try to shape their personal life, but Smart does not assume that people can do whatever they want. People's **agency**, their ability to choose how to act, is always constrained by their relationships with other people. Smart draws on the work of the symbolic interactionist George Herbert Mead to emphasise the importance of interaction between people in understanding personal life. (See pp. 13–14 for a description of symbolic interactionism.)

The idea of personal life does not see kin as necessarily more important than friends and allows for the idea of **families of choice**. It also incorporates relatively neglected areas of social life such as emotions, bodies and sexuality into the study of the family and other personal relationships. Subjective aspects of social life such as emotions and memories are particularly important in the sociology of personal life.

Activity

Are friendship groups 'chosen families'?

What aspects of Smart's study of personal life are reflected in this image?

Core concepts in the study of personal life

Developing her arguments further, Carol Smart identifies five core concepts in the study of personal life. These are illustrated in Figure 5.2.1 All are concepts which tend to be neglected in more conventional studies of family life.

1. **Memory** is a selective process. The more meaningful an event, the more likely it is to be remembered, and meaningfulness often involves personal relationships. Emotions such as passion, love, feelings of rejection, fear, jealousy and a sense of security can be closely related to the history of your own family. Families often provide the context which influences what we remember, and shared memory is an important part of connections between family members.

2. **Biography**, or **life history**, the story of an individual's life, is also important in understanding personal life. Biography can provide in-depth descriptions for the researcher and help in understanding movement through the life course. It is particularly useful to study the biography of different family members to appreciate how they might experience the same events in different ways.

Figure 5.2.1 Overlapping core concepts

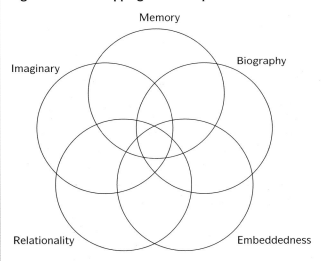

Source: C. Smart (2007) *Personal Life*, Polity Press, Cambridge, p. 37.

Activity

Suggest how two or more of these core concepts could be used to understand the meaning of:

a) family holidays

b) family outings

c) family arguments.

By embracing core concepts such as those outlined above, Smart believes that the study of personal life can become both deeper and more complex. It can seek meaning in the everyday.

259

3. **Embeddedness** is important to Smart partly because it helps to counterbalance the excessive emphasis on individuals in theories like those of Giddens and Beck and Beck-Gernsheim. It shows how the experiences of individuals are made meaningful through being embedded in webs of relationships with other people, whether family, kin or friends.

4. **Relationality** is concerned with how people relate to one another and it plays down the significance of formal structures within and outside families. The idea of relationality emphasises that the nature of the relationship is more important than the position of a person within a family structure and that emotionally significant relationships are not confined to kin.

5. **Imaginary** is concerned with how people's relationships and memories exist as much in the imagination as in reality.

Love, commitment and emotions

Using the general framework discussed above, Smart goes on to discuss several aspects of personal life. One of these is *love*. Some theorists are quite disdainful about love. For example, feminists tend to see it as no more than a patriarchal ideology which persuades women to accept the authority of men. Beck and Beck-Gernsheim (1995) are sceptical about the possibility of love in an individualised society.

Smart uses data from research she conducted in which 54 in-depth interviews were carried out with same-sex couples about their civil partnerships or commitment ceremonies, to discuss love, commitment and emotions. Twelve of the couples saw the ceremony to form a civil partnership as transforming the meaning of their love and bringing it to a higher level. Thirty-seven of the couples saw it as the culmination of a **growing commitment** that had developed over time. These couples were less likely to talk directly about love, and relied more on their shared history rather than their future relationship to give meaning to the ceremony. Three of the couples saw the ceremony primarily in terms of how it enlisted recognition and support from their wider networks of friends and family.

Smart's research demonstrated the importance of personal meanings and emotional attachments and the centrality of networks beyond the immediate family and people's households in their lives. In other parts of her work Smart discusses a wide variety of other aspects of personal life. These include the social significance of *family stories* and *family secrets*.

Then and now: Carol Smart, *Personal Life* (2007)

"*Personal Life* was published in 2007. It was the culmination of many years of research, both **empirical** and theoretical, and so it is important to recognise that its intricate roots go much further back than the date of publication. When I was a sociology student I could never relate to courses on 'The Family' (as they were then called) because the idealised image of families we were presented with bore no resemblance at all to my own family or the families of my friends. Yet, paradoxically, as a teacher I was always keen to put on courses for students on families and relationships. This was because by then I had become fascinated by how close relationships work and because I wanted to explore and expose the complexities and challenges of these important relationships. These interests set in train a number of empirical projects which gave me the opportunity, over several decades, to talk to hundreds of people about their relationships. So *Personal Life* is not a single study, but rather distilled insights from many of my projects.

Given this history to the book, I was somewhat taken aback to discover that some sociologists felt that I had abandoned my interest in family life and that I was trying to devalue the study of families – simply because I was trying to stretch the study of important relationships beyond the conventional limits of families by using the term personal life. It remains a mystery to me how anyone could come to the conclusion that *Personal Life* is not substantially about family life. It is true that it is more than just this, of course. Yet I prefer to think of it as being about 'family life *plus*', although we should always remember that families do not provide the primary source of relationships for all people or for all time.

It was because I felt it was more important to study what people do, and how they relate to one another, that I moved decisively away from the study of the structures of the family and the kind of sociology I had been taught as an undergraduate. Instead I moved towards studying what David Morgan (1996; 2011) has called family practices. This **epistemological** shift away from structures towards practices opened up a completely new way of understanding relationships as well as providing much more engaging methods of researching families, kinships and friendships. These included such things as basing discussions of relationships on photographs to evoke memories and stories; using vignettes or hypothetical situations as ways of eliciting sensitive ideas; and using written accounts of family histories. It even led me to the study of family secrets as a way of getting 'behind' the public front of family life.

Since the book was published, families and relationships have inevitably continued to change. Same-sex marriage is now well established in England, Wales and Scotland (although not in Northern Ireland). Assisted reproduction (in the form of egg, sperm and embryo donation) and surrogacy are changing the shape of many families as children born from such methods may not be genetically related to one or both of their parents. This in turn means they are not genetically related to their grandparents. We need to understand how these new relationships work and from my perspective, and from the perspective of *Personal Life*, this is a much more important question than simply bemoaning the fact that families in 2017 don't look like the families formed in 1917 or 1957.

In the second chapter of the book I stated that family 'relationships are very sticky' and I went on to say 'it is hard to shake free from them at an emotional level and their existence can continue to influence our practices and not just our thoughts' (2007: 45). I still stand by that statement but wish to underline that this does not mean that such relationships are ideal, unremittingly positive or even supportive. I wanted this 'warts and all' perspective on family/kin/friend relationships to be more clearly understood without throwing the baby out with the bathwater – to use an overworked cliché. I hope that this at least is what future students will take from the book. **"**

Carol Smart
November 2017

Evaluation of Smart

Despite the diversity of the topics studied by Smart, they all illustrate the importance of connections between people. Indeed, Smart describes the central theme of her work on personal life as the **connectedness thesis**. It therefore demonstrates the limitations of theories of individualisation such as those put forward by Giddens (1992) and Beck and Beck-Gernsheim (1995). Smart believes that by looking at personal life, a much more in-depth understanding of families can be gained than through the rather generalised theories of individualisation in late modernity or the second modernity. In the process, the connections between individual lives and wider social changes can be understood.

Many sociologists have welcomed Smart's approach. Deborah Chambers (2012) sees it as useful because it does not prioritise relationships based on family and marriage over other relationships which may be equally or more significant; it gets away from any idea that nuclear families are the norm or the ideal and it encourages small-scale qualitative research which acknowledges the importance of meanings. However, the relatively narrow focus of the research based on this approach can lose sight of wider patterns of social change. It could be seen as sometimes focusing on relatively marginal aspects of personal life or as being such a generalised approach that it lacks a clear focus.

Key terms

Personal life The most meaningful parts of people's lives which involve relationships with other people they are close to.

Agency The capacity of individuals to act and make a difference to the world around them.

Chosen families Families that consist of the people that people feel closest to regardless of whether they are family members.

Connectedness thesis The theory that it is important to understand individuals through the networks of personal relationships they are involved in rather than simply as isolated individuals.

Empirical based on experience or observation.

Epistemological relating to how knowledge of a given subject is obtained.

Summary

1. Significant personal relationships exist outside families and these may be at least as important to people as family relationships.

2. Connections between people are crucial to understanding members of society.

3. Carol Smart believes that an individual's agency, their capacity to act, is always limited by their relationships with others.

4. Families are no longer determined by kinship and marriage relations but are chosen.

5. Smart believes that the sociology of personal life should study subjective aspects of people's lives such as memory and the imagination, and should look at how personal life is embedded in connections to other people.

6. Sociologists should take emotions such as love seriously but studying love shows that it has different meanings for different people.

PART 3 FAMILIES AND SOCIAL POLICY

Contents

The family is usually thought of as a private sphere, something in which politicians should not interfere. However, in reality a wide range of laws and policies have a profound effect on family life. Some are directly concerned with families (for example, marriage and divorce laws, rules on adoption, child protection measures and the intervention of social services in families). Other policies may have a less direct effect but taxation, welfare, housing and education policies all influence the way in which people organise their family life. The policies adopted can encourage people to live in certain types of household and discourage them from living in other types. They can make certain types of family arrangements seem legitimate and respectable while making others seem deviant and disreputable.

This part of the chapter examines social policies in Britain. It considers a range of perspectives on family life of which the most significant is that of the New Right which has influenced a number of British governments, particularly Conservative ones. The details of British family policies under successive governments are then examined and we finish by asking whether the policies encourage or discourage people from living in traditional nuclear families. Are governments really biased in favour of nuclear families or have they now come to accept that anything goes in terms of family life?

5.3.1 The New Right and family policy

One of the most influential perspectives on family policy in Britain over recent decades has been that of the **New Right**. In the UK, the term the 'New Right' is applied to predominantly Conservative politicians, academics, and writers who believe in liberal, free-market economic policies which emphasise individual freedom and discourage excessive state intervention in most areas of social life. They support low taxes and argue for a limited role for the welfare state. They are opposed to the government running companies and therefore support privatisation (transferring businesses from government control to private ownership). They believe that individuals and families should be as self-reliant as possible. Family members should look after each other and should only get help from the state when there is no alternative. However, they argue strongly for intervention in dysfunctional families which they regard as being harmful to society.

The New Right are strongly in favour of traditional heterosexual nuclear families which they see as the foundation of society. They oppose family diversity, particularly lone parent families and gay and lesbian families.

The New Right are generally despondent about the apparent breakdown of the family suggested by high rates of single parenthood and divorce. They believe that these trends undermine the independence of families, make them more reliant on state benefits and harm children who may lack a stable family environment when growing up.

Margaret Thatcher and the New Right

Writing particularly about Conservative governments under Margaret Thatcher (the Prime Minister from 1979 to 1990) Abbott and Wallace (1992) argue that these administrations supported New Right thinking on the family. They mixed very conservative views on family morality with a belief in free markets – markets in which the government does not interfere. To them, the family operated properly when it remained stable and the wife was responsible for socialising children so that they conformed to society's norms and values. The husband, as principal breadwinner, would be disciplined by the need to provide for his family. He could not, for example, go on strike when his family relied on his salary.

Margaret Thatcher and her New Right supporters saw the family as being under threat from permissiveness (such as greater acceptance of extramarital sex), social change and the policies of previous governments. Other problems included mothers who went out to work instead of putting the well-being of their children first, rising divorce rates, homosexuality and lone parent families. These changes were believed to be threatening the stability of society and playing a major role in causing social problems such as crime, delinquency and drug abuse.

Activity

Margaret Thatcher, Prime Minister from 1979 to 1990. In a 1988 speech she said 'The family is the building block of society. It is a nursery, a school, a hospital, a leisure place, a place of refuge and a place of rest. It encompasses the whole of society. It fashions beliefs. It is the preparation for the rest of our life. And women run it.'

1. In what ways does this quotation reflect the New Right view of social policy and the family?

2. How far do you agree with the claims made in the quotation?

Charles Murray — the family and the underclass

An influential version of New Right thinking was developed by Charles Murray (1984) who argued that families had been badly affected by over-generous welfare payments particularly to lone parents. According to Murray, this created perverse incentives for young women to become pregnant and young men to neglect responsibility for their children. The benefits system made it possible for lone parent mothers to raise children by relying on benefits rather than working or being supported by the income of the children's fathers. Because of this, young men were freed from family responsibilities and did not feel a need to support their children who might also become dependent upon benefits (a situation known as **welfare dependency**). There was little incentive for either single parent women or young men to take paid employment because much of what they earned could result in a loss of the 'generous' benefits they received, for example housing benefit and income support.

According to Murray, lone parenthood is harmful to society because it encourages irresponsible behaviour amongst children who copy their parents. The daughters of single mothers are quite likely to become lone mothers themselves following in their mother's footsteps by having children outside of stable relationships. The sons of single mothers lack an adult role model of a hard-working and responsible father taking care of his family. As a result, they don't learn the importance of these characteristics and tend to become dependent upon benefits themselves. Murray also believes that freed from parental responsibility, young fathers are likely to become involved in crime to supplement their income from benefits.

Murray claims that these groups who are reliant upon benefits form a distinct group or an **underclass** outside and below the rest of the class structure. The underclass is characterised by a set of attitudes, values and lifestyles which does not value traditional family life or respect the law. The underclass is harmful to society because it produces criminal and antisocial behaviour and it is costly because the lifestyle of the underclass is largely sustained through the benefits system at the expense of the taxpayer.

Evaluation of Murray

Tony Fitzpatrick (2011) argues that Murray puts forward no serious evidence to support his arguments about the effects of lone parenthood, or even to support his claim that a distinctive underclass culture actually exists. Fitzpatrick also argues that Murray ignores the importance of poverty and social exclusion in explaining the position of the so-called underclass. To Fitzpatrick, Murray's ideas are simply a politically motivated justification for cuts to benefits.

Research into the effects of lone parenthood has not tended to support Murray's central claims about the effects of lone parenthood and has suggested that it is low income rather than lack of a cohabiting partner that is largely responsible for problems faced by some lone mothers (see pp. 279–284).

263

New Right solutions

In line with Fitzpatrick's analysis, the New Right do tend to argue that welfare benefits should be cut for lone parents to discourage lone parenthood and encourage the formation of nuclear families. They also favour tax incentives for marriage. They believe that is important that fathers contribute to the costs of raising children, even if they do not live with the mother of their child. In general, their ideas are based upon the view that families should be self-reliant. In their view, an over-generous welfare state discourages self-reliance. However, they do generally accept that the state sometimes needs to intervene to deal with 'problem' families, especially when children are being harmed or are getting involved in crime or anti-social behaviour. They also believe that the state may sometimes need to intervene to actively discourage family break-up and 'undesirable' types of family, which in the 1980s and 1990s some of the New Right saw as including gay and lesbian families.

The influence of the New Right

The New Right were most influential in the UK when Margaret Thatcher was Prime Minister and in the USA under President Reagan (1981–1989). Their ideas had a significant influence upon policies at that time although they were never totally dominant. Later Conservative governments (and to a lesser extent the Coalition government of 2010 to 2015) have also been influenced by New Right thinking and even Labour governments have adopted some ideas from this perspective. Nevertheless, the influence of the New Right has declined partly because there has been a shift amongst right-wing politicians towards neoliberalism.

Neoliberalism supports the economic views of the New Right (low taxes, low benefits and minimal state intervention in the economy) but with less emphasis on the desirability of nuclear families and traditional morality. Nevertheless, some politicians, commentators and sociologists (e.g. Patricia Morgan) continue to support New Right thinking.

The influence of New Right policy on government policy has been patchy. Writing in 1992, Abbot and Wallace argued that the New Right had limited success in getting the Thatcher governments to introduce their policies. Nevertheless, the 1988 budget changed taxation so that cohabiting couples could no longer claim more in tax allowances than a married couple. **Section 28** of The Local Government

Act 1988 prohibited councils from promoting homosexuality and council-controlled schools from promoting 'the teaching in any maintained school of the acceptability of homosexuality as a pretended family relationship' (cited in Stonewall, 2016). (This was repealed after a long campaign in 2003.)

However, in many other ways the New Right failed to achieve the changes it wanted. In terms of moral policies, divorce was actually made easier in 1984, and further legislation gave 'illegitimate' children the same rights (for example inheritance rights) as those born within marriage.

Activity

Scrap Section 28 banner at Gay Pride London, 1998

Jenny Lives with Eric and Martin is a book published in 1983 by the Danish author Susanne Bösche which was designed to help children get used to the idea that some children do not live in conventional family households. The Conservative government of the time objected to a copy being purchased by the Inner London Education Authority and ultimately this led on to the introduction of Clause 28, which banned the teaching of homosexuality as a 'pretended family relationship'.

1. Do you think anybody would raise objection to a book such as this in schools today?

2. Keeping in mind your answer to part 1, to what extent do you think different types of family are accepted as 'normal' in the education system?

Evaluation of the New Right

New Right views on the family have been criticised by feminists for supporting patriarchy by assuming that mothers rather that fathers should give up work to care for children (see pp. 244–249). Charles Murray's view that lone parenthood is bad for children has not been supported by research (see pp. 281–283). Many commentators have seen cuts in welfare for lone parents as undesirable because they increase child poverty. As the next part of the chapter will show, whatever the preferences of the New Right, families and households have become more diverse. Simply telling people they should follow traditional morality is unlikely to change their behaviour and following policies which support nuclear families risks disadvantaging people (including children) living in other types of household. Partly for these reasons, different policies were developed by the Labour governments after 1997. (For more evaluation of the New Right see pp. 270–273.)

Key terms

New Right Politicians, academics and commentators who see traditional heterosexual nuclear families with the man as main breadwinner as the ideal and who believe that state intervention in economic and social life should be minimised – except in 'dysfunctional' families. They support free market economics.

Welfare dependency To New Right thinkers, a situation in which individuals come to rely on 'hand outs' from the state preventing them from taking responsibility for themselves and their own family.

Underclass According to Charles Murray, a group at the bottom of society characterised by lone parenthood, unemployment and criminality which is dependent on welfare and which undermines traditional nuclear family life while encouraging irresponsible behaviour.

Neoliberalism The term now usually applied to right-wing thinkers who are in favour of free markets. The term 'neoliberalism' doesn't imply support for traditional nuclear families in the same way as the term 'New Right'.

Section 28 Part of *The Local Government Act 1988* which banned councils from promoting homosexual relationships as being similar or equivalent to heterosexual family relationships.

Summary

1. The New Right support traditional heterosexual families with the man as main breadwinner.

2. They were most influential when Margret Thatcher was Prime Minister but they continue to have some support and influence today.

3. Charles Murray suggests that welfare spending has made the growth of lone parenthood possible and has created an underclass based on welfare dependency.

4. Their influence helped to produce changes in taxation to help married couples and *Section 28* banning councils from promoting gay and lesbian family relationships as 'normal' family relationships.

5. In other respects, Abbot and Wallace suggest the influence of the New Right was limited under Thatcher although several governments have cut benefits for lone parents.

5.3.2 Family policy and UK governments 1997–2017

Between 1997 and 2010 Labour governments were in power. From 2010 to 2015 a Conservative-led coalition with the Liberal Democrats formed the government after which there were two Conservative governments. There were important shifts in policy with these successive governments but all involved some move away from New Right thinking and policies, particularly under Labour and the Coalition administrations.

The family and Labour governments 1997–2010

The Labour governments of 1997–2010 (in which Tony Blair was Prime Minister from 1997–2007 and Gordon Brown was Prime Minister from 2007 to 2010) shifted the emphasis in family policy. Tony Blair continued to praise traditional families (Silva and Smart, 1999) and a 1998 government Green Paper (consultation document) entitled *Supporting Families* suggested a number of measures to support marriage and reduce divorce rates. Nevertheless, the influence of New Right thinking declined so the government moved further away from its ideas towards a greater acceptance of diverse forms of family.

Family values and social liberalism

There were two main aspects of Labour policy: social liberalism and a belief in supporting and controlling families.

Clem Henricson (2012) defines **social liberalism** as involving a belief in gender equality and acceptance of a wide variety of different types of family. In many ways, this is the polar opposite of the New Right view. Social liberalism was reflected in a range of measures introduced by the Labour governments:

- Gender equality was promoted with the extension of maternity leave – which became some of the most generous in Europe – and through measures allowing the transfer of parental leave between father and mothers.

- Government financial support for childcare was considerably extended and the Childcare Act of 2006 required councils to make sure there were enough childcare places available for mothers in their area.

- In 1998 the Human Rights Act was introduced which made discrimination against different types of family illegal.

- The government also removed the requirement to be married to have NHS fertility treatment or the right to adopt children.

- Discrimination against homosexuality was prohibited in the provision of goods and services by *The Equality Act (Sexual Orientation)* regulations of 2007 and Civil Partnerships for same-sex couples became legal from 2005.

Henricson sees these changes as involving a major shift in policy away from family policies favouring the traditional family with a male breadwinner. However, a second aspect of Labour policies involved stronger attempts to intervene in family life involving greater 'support and control'.

Support and control

This strand of Labour policy was particularly concerned with parenting and it was linked to a wider policy designed to reduce and eventually eliminate child poverty (Henricson, 2012). Child poverty was reduced by more than 25 per cent under these Labour governments. One direct way in which financial support was given was through Child Tax Credits which boosted the income of parents with low or moderate levels of income. However, many of the new measures were also aimed at providing support and incentives for 'good' parenting. These measures were targeted mainly at those on low income or those who were defined as being 'socially excluded'.

These measures included:

- Sure Start Centres, which provided child services, parenting courses, opportunities for pre-school education and play for children

- Family Intervention Projects, which were established in some areas to work intensively with 'families at risk' of social exclusion.

There were also policies designed more to 'control' families rather than 'supporting' them when parents did not meet the government's expectations as parents. The most notable of these was the *Parenting Order* (introduced in 2003) which could require parents to have guidance and counselling if their children acted in anti-social ways, truanted from school or broke the law. Some benefits (particularly maternity benefits), were made conditional on accepting health and parenting advice.

Despite the extensive intervention in the role of parents, there was less intervention in family roles involving care of the elderly. State Pensions were increased but little was done to either fund state care for the elderly or to support families in looking after elderly relatives (arguably leaving children, particularly daughters, to shoulder much of the burden).

Evaluation of Labour family policies

Clem Henricson (2012) argues that the Labour government shifted policy towards a more interventionist approach to families as well as reducing child poverty, producing greater equality between men and women in family relationships, and making it easier for women with children to take paid employment. Labour governments also removed some policies which favoured traditional family forms. Henricson therefore describes these policies as socially liberal but also interventionist.

However, Alan Barlow, Simon Duncan and Grace James (2002) were more critical, arguing that the Labour governments claimed to support moral tolerance but still preferred children to live with their biological parents because this reduced reliance upon benefits. According to Barlow, Duncan and James, despite a toning down of the rhetoric criticising unconventional families and non-family groups, New Labour continued to idealise stable, long-lasting marriage and nuclear families as the best family structure for raising children.

Activity

Tony Blair with his family after election victory in 2001.

Extracts from a speech made by Tony Blair in 2002:

'There are over 1.6m lone parents with 2.8m children in Britain – and over half of those children are growing up at risk of poverty. Those children's best chance of a better future is for their parents to find routes into work.

But they face very real barriers – the shortage of childcare, the need for new skills, perhaps a lack of confidence from being out of the job market, and the need to find a job which fits in with their caring responsibilities.

So we're investing in the support they need.

- £146m for the New Deal for Lone Parents – 1300 Personal Advisers, who have given 315 000 parents help and advice; almost half have found work.

- From 2003 a guaranteed minimum income of £179 a week for a lone parent working 16 hours a week.

- Over £300m invested in childcare since 1997, creating places for more than 900 000 children.

That investment is our side of the bargain – helping lone parents to help themselves. In return, we expect them to come and discuss with personal advisers how they can get back to work.'

1. Based on the extracts from Tony Blair's speech, what was his government's approach to lone parenthood?

2. How far does this approach seem to fit a philosophy of social liberalism?

Coalition and Conservative family policies since 2010

The Labour Party lost power in 2010 but the Conservatives failed to win an overall majority in the House of Commons. Therefore, a Coalition government was formed with a Conservative Prime Minister (David Cameron) and a Liberal Democrat Deputy Prime Minister (Nick Clegg). In the 2015 election the Conservatives won an overall majoritywith David Cameron as Prime Minister. He resigned in 2016 in the aftermath of the Brexit vote for the UK to leave the EU and was replaced by Theresa May as Conservative Prime Minister.

Policies supporting traditional family structures

One of Cameron's particular concerns was the **couple penalty**, a situation in which a couple who are married or who cohabit pay more in taxes or get less in benefits that a couple who live apart. The Coalition agreement between the Conservatives and Liberal Democrats in 2015 watered down a Conservative manifesto pledge to abolish the couple penalty, but it did promise to reduce it (cited in Hayter, 2010). As in other areas of policy, Cameron was somewhat constrained by having to compromise with Liberal Democrat partners in the Coalition, though the Conservatives were the dominant party.

Adam and Brewer (2010) analysed the impact of the detailed policies proposed in the Conservative manifesto of 2010. They found that the proposals would have some impact upon the couple penalty, but only a very marginal one. The number of people

267

facing a couple's penalty would fall by just 1 per cent under the Conservative proposals and the amount the penalty would fall would be just 0.2 per cent. It can therefore be argued that the policy was more symbolic than anything else and would make little real difference to the actual income of couples in comparison to people living on their own or in lone parent families.

However, in 2015 the government did introduce a modest tax break for married couples and civil partners making it possible for them to transfer some of their tax-free income (up to £1060) from one partner to another. This favoured couples where one was the main breadwinner and the other was not working or was working part time, but the allowance had a maximum saving of just £212 per year. Initially it benefited some 4 million couples (Chapman *et al.*, 2015).

Policies which did not support traditional family structures

Unlike policies concerned with the couple penalty, childcare policies introduced by Coalition/Conservative governments between 2010 and 2017 gave additional support to two-parent families where both parents worked. Another policy which came into effect in 2015 was shared parental leave which allowed the entitlement to parental leave to be shared between mothers and fathers. After the Conservatives took power on their own in 2015, they introduced measures which meant that from September 2017 parents could have 30 hours' free childcare per week for three and four-year olds during term times. This made it easier for both parents to work rather than supporting traditional female childcare and male breadwinner roles.

David Cameron's most controversial measure which contradicted traditional views that families should be based on heterosexual marriage was the introduction of same-sex marriage in 2014.

Policies affecting choices over family formation and intervention in families

In some ways, Conservative/Coalition policies actively intervened in family life by restricting the ability of couples to live together and creating a financial penalty for large families. One policy, designed to reduce immigration, stipulated that spouses of British citizens who did not have UK citizenships could only come to Britain if their husband or wife had an income of £18600 per year or more. This discriminated against those on low incomes by preventing them from living in the UK with their partner. In another measure, in 2017 the government withdrew child benefit from new claimants for third or additional children. The policy was designed to discourage benefit-reliant families from having children they could not afford to support.

However, the Coalition government did reduce direct intervention in family life in some areas. For example, there were significant cuts in the funding of Sure Start centres and cuts in programmes of parental education introduced by the Labour government. Instead, in 2011, David Cameron announced a £450 billion programme targeted on 120000 'problem families' affected by issues such as truancy, anti-social behaviour and addiction (Wintour, 2011). While this was in part a continuation of Labour policies, the greater concentration on a smaller number of families reflected greater emphasis on *control* rather than *support*.

Contemporary issues: Sure Start and lone parent families

Sure Start centres were introduced under the New Labour governments of 1997–2010, but funding for them was cut and some were closed under Coalition and Conservative governments from 2010. In 2017 The Labour Party spokesperson responsible for Education was the Shadow Minister Angela Rayner. In a speech in September 2017, she promised that if Labour got into power they would invest £500 million in reversing cuts to the Sure Start programme (Elgot, 2017). Angela Rayner spoke passionately in the speech in support of Sure Start. She herself had used one

of the centres after she became pregnant at 16, left school and tried to support herself and her son as an unskilled care worker. In her speech, Rayner argued that Sure Start had enabled her son to get on in life by helping to provide him with opportunities which her own mother (who couldn't read or write) never had. In an interview with LBC radio she explained that Sure Start had helped her learn about the importance of reading to her children, cuddling them and telling them that you loved them.

A different view is taken by Lisa McKenzie, who like Rayner is from a working-class background and became a lone mother at a young age. McKenzie became an academic researcher and carried out research in St Ann's, a working-class area of Nottingham where she grew up. She found that many of the women there were less enthusiastic about Sure Start than Rayner (McKenzie, 2010). Although some of the women she interviewed valued the services, others believed that there was a stigma attached to using them, or that they were only suitable for those that 'couldn't cope'. Two women felt that the centres put too much pressure on them to breast feed. Responding to Angela Rayner's speech on Twitter, McKenzie commented that Sure Start centres were 'part of the New Labour programme of carrot and stick in not being working class' and 'Sure Start was always a nasty assessment centre to police w-class mothers'.

Questions

1. Explain the differences between the views of Angela Rayner and Lisa McKenzie.

2. Whose arguments do you find more convincing? Justify your answer.

3. What does the above evidence tell you about Labour Party policies towards family life?

A Sure Start Centre in St Ann's, Nottingham.

Evaluation of Conservative policies

A detailed analysis conducted by James Browne and William Elming (2015) of the Institute for Fiscal Studies looked at the effect of policies under the Coalition government of 2010–2015. It found little evidence that the tax and spending policies of the Conservative-led government would actually benefit more traditional families consisting of a married couple with children and the man as the main breadwinner. Two-earner couples without children were the only household type to benefit from the changes. One-earner couples with children fared worse than two-earner couples with children. However, lone parents generally did worse than two-parent families. Single people and pensioners lost less from the changes than most other groups. Overall, this research does suggest that Coalition policies were matching Conservative rhetoric only to a limited extent. Although lone parents were dealt with more harshly than two-parent families, pensioners and single people were most favoured by the changes.

This evidence, along with policies on the benefits cap and immigration, suggests that in most respects Conservative family policy was largely driven by a desire to save money from the benefits bill (and to a lesser extent to cut immigration) rather than a desire to encourage (or discourage) traditional family forms. The minimal incentives for traditional gender roles created by the married couples tax allowance were more than outweighed by the extra help with childcare making it more affordable for both parents in two-parent households to work. Therefore, tax and benefits policies seem to be based more upon a desire for political popularity than any underlying principles relating to family life.

There was less emphasis than under Labour governments on supporting *all* families, with substantial benefit cuts and the introduction of a benefit cap. Nevertheless, with the introduction of same-sex marriage in 2014, Conservative and Conservative-led governments have moved some way towards the acceptance of family diversity.

269

Key terms

Social liberalism Policies or views supportive of diverse family forms and greater equality within families.

Parenting order A 2003 policy which allowed the authorities to require the parents of children in trouble with the law to undergo education or counselling.

Couple penalty A situation in which couples are betteroff living apart than they are living together as a result of tax and benefits rules.

Summary

1. Labour governments of 1997–2010 followed socially liberal policies supporting family diversity and greater equality based on sexuality and gender.

2. There were more attempts to support families and cut child poverty but also to control families which were seen as failing children.

3. Critics argue that the Labour leadership still idealised the traditional nuclear family.

4. The Conservative Prime Minister of 2010–2016 wanted to end the couple penalty and support traditional families but a small tax break for married couples was only introduced in 2015.

5. Cameron introduced same-sex marriage and moved the Conservatives towards greater social liberalism in some respects than previous Conservative governments.

6. Many Coalition and Conservative policies were concerned with saving money and critics argue that these hit the finances of most families and households.

5.3.3 Policy bias and traditional nuclear families

Rather than looking at the policies of particular governments, some sociologists have tried to characterise and evaluate the overall direction of government policies over recent decades. Perhaps unsurprisingly, New Right theorists have seen policies as biased against nuclear families, particularly those with male breadwinners, while others have argued the opposite. But how strong are the claims of these competing groups and what does the evidence suggest about the overall direction of policy under both Conservative and Labour governments?

The New Right, social policy and bias against the nuclear family

Some New Right sociologists argue that government policies seriously undermine heterosexual nuclear families with traditional gender roles. Patricia Morgan (2007, 2014) argues that a range of measures have destabilised this type of family and have even provided incentives to live outside such families. She goes so far as claiming there has been a 'war' between the state and the family which has been very damaging to family life (2007).

This 'war' has involved a number of features:

1. **'Abolishing marriage'**. Morgan argues that tax and benefits rules have been changed to remove any advantages for married couples.

2. **Divorce and lone parents.** Since the 1960s, divorce has become progressively easier to obtain so that now divorce is possible without either party being held responsible for the breakdown of the marriage. Furthermore, Morgan believes that benefits systems have been geared towards supporting lone parents better than two-parent families on low income. Amongst married couples with two-earners, the combined income often means that they are not entitled to the same levels of state support as lone parents.

3. **The state as breadwinner**. As a result of the above, the *state* has come to be seen as the breadwinner rather than husbands and fathers. The benefits system has made it increasingly likely that lone parents are reliant upon benefits and, in this situation, there is little incentive for fathers to openly live with the mothers of their children. If the parents live together, whether they rely completely on benefits or are on low income, they end up with less income than if they live apart. This leads to 'casualisation of relationships'. Alternatively, they end up 'faking it' – living together but pretending to live apart by lying to

the authorities. Either way, it discourages marriage and two-parent families.

4. **The state as child carer**. According to Morgan, the New Labour Government went even further than the preceding Conservative governments in establishing lone mothers as the basic family type. This was because it provided increasing support for childcare so that mothers no longer needed the support of a breadwinner so they could stay at home with young children. State funded childcare in nurseries allowed mothers to work even if they had pre-school children.

Morgan therefore argues that social policies of successive governments have systematically encouraged lone parenthood particularly for those on low income, and they have therefore undermined traditional family relationships. Writing in 2014, she argued that these types of policy had the following effects:

» Around 50 per cent of those born could expect their parents to separate by the time they reached 15.

» Marriage rates had fallen dramatically.

» The number of family-breakdowns had doubled since the 1980s.

» Cohabitation had become more common but the relationships of cohabitees broke up at four times the rate of those who were married.

» Children of lone parents or those whose parents split up suffered badly in terms of their development and life chances. This was because boys lacked male role models and mothers and daughters didn't have a 'protector'.

» Morgan further argues that the fall in marriage rates has a negative impact on the health of adults, puts more demand on housing by creating smaller households and puts additional strain on health and other public services.

Evaluation of new right perspectives on policy bias

New Right perspectives on the family have been extensively criticised.

First, feminist perspectives argue that social policies encourage traditional gender roles within families and act to keep women subservient to their husbands (see p. 244 for a discussion of feminist views on the family).

Second, many sociologists have questioned the claim that lone-parent families are bad for children. They argue that children may well be better off living with one parent than living with two parents if the parents are unhappy together or if one of them is abusive. Furthermore, many of the apparently negative effects of lone parenthood may be due to low income or poverty rather than family structure (see pp. 281–283).

Third, the New Right may greatly exaggerate the impact of specific policies on family life. Most of the change described by Morgan could be attributed to wider social changes rather than government policy and some of those changes could be seen in a positive way. For example, Anthony Giddens (1992) believes that increased choice is characteristic of late-modern society and this is good thing because it allows people to form the most satisfying relationships and to avoid being stuck in unhappy ones (see pp. 251–253).

Fourth, some sociologists believe that there are many policies which, far from being biased against traditional family structures, are biased in favour of them. These arguments will now be examined.

Policy as biased in favour of conventional families

Feminists and other radical critics of government policies have also sometimes seen government policies towards families as biased. However, unlike the New Right, they have argued that policies tend to favour the traditional nuclear family in which there are two parents: a male breadwinner and a wife who stays at home when there are young children.

Allan (1985) argues that: 'Much state provision … is based upon an implicit ideology of the "normal" family in which there are two heterosexual parents, wives are economically dependent on husbands and it is wives who are mainly responsible for childcare and looking after elderly relatives'.

There are several examples which seem to support Allan:

1. School hours and the long summer school holidays make it difficult for children to be cared for by a parent or parents who are working in full-time jobs. Responsibility for caring for children is more

271

likely to fall on women meaning that husbands (or male partners) are still regarded as the main breadwinner. To some extent, increasing state support for childcare has counteracted this problem but most support is given in term-time and it can still be difficult to find affordable and flexible childcare.

2. Care of relatives is still predominantly seen as a female responsibility and government policies in recent decades may well have forced women into taking on more such responsibilities. For example, after the 2015 election the Conservative governments under David Cameron and later Theresa May cut government spending sharply leading to major reductions in the budgets for social care of the elderly in their own homes. The Institute for Fiscal Studies (2017) reported that between 2009–2010 and 2015–2016 spending per adult on social care fell by 11 per cent in real terms.

3. According to Lorraine Fox Harding (1996) public housing policy generally makes children's needs the priority. However, she believes that in practice married couples with children tend to be favoured over lone parents with children. Lone parents are usually provided with the least desirable housing. Furthermore, most dwellings are constructed for the nuclear family with very little social housing built to accommodate groups larger than conventional nuclear families.

4. Fox Harding (1996) also argues that families are increasingly expected to care for their adult children, because of cuts to benefits which make it difficult or impossible for young adults to live independently. Since Fox Harding was writing, there have been further benefit cuts, as well as the requirement for students to pay university fees and the replacement of student grants with loans. Certainly, there has been a shift towards adults who are not leaving home in their 20s or even 30s and continuing to be reliant upon parents (Williams, 2016).

5. David Cameron, the Conservative Prime Minister introduced a transferable tax allowance in 2015 which was only available to married couples (although the maximum benefit was only £4 per week for a married couple).

Activity

Cuts to council budgets under the Conservative government from 2015 led to a shortage of social care for the elderly people being supported to live in their own homes.

What effects are cuts to social care likely to have on families and gender roles within families?

Evaluation – are policies biased for or against traditional nuclear families?

Clearly there are arguments both for and against the view that social policies in the UK favour traditional family structures and family roles (particularly heterosexual, nuclear families with men as the main breadwinner). The reality may be more complex than either side of the argument suggests for the following reasons:

1. Many policies are not aimed solely at influencing family life. For example, policies under Coalition and Conservative governments from 2010 have been primarily concerned with saving money rather than encouraging or discouraging particular types of family.

2. Overall, there has undoubtedly been a move away from New Right approaches to welfare. An example is the gradual liberalisation of divorce laws, but there have also been some moves back towards supporting traditional families (such as the transferable tax allowance for couples, introduced by David Cameron).

3. Many policies are open to interpretation in terms of whether they are supporting the idea of nuclear families or not. A case in point is the introduction of same-sex marriage, which is discussed below.

For these reasons, it is dangerous to generalise about the direction of social policies affecting families.

Contemporary issues: Same-sex marriage and civil partnerships

Protestors opposing and supporting same-sex marriage.

In 2004, the Labour government introduced **civil partnerships** for same-sex couples. In 2014 **same-sex marriage** was introduced for gay and lesbian couples. From a New Right perspective, Patricia Morgan (cited in the *Daily Telegraph,* 2013) argued that these arrangements (and particularly same-sex marriage) undermine traditional nuclear families. She claims that it promotes the view that marriage is not linked to becoming a parent. According to Morgan, same-sex marriage is only concerned with couple relationships and not with having children and this view has resulted in a significant decline in marriage rates in countries where it has been legalised such as Spain, Sweden, Norway and the Netherlands. Morgan claimed that same-sex marriages were more likely to be open (allowing additional sexual partners) rather than exclusive like other marriages, and, once they were allowed, heterosexual marriages would end up being open as well. Open marriage in which partners are not faithful are more likely to break down and thus same-sex marriage would destabilise marriage in general.

On the other hand, the coalition government (2010–2015) argued that same-sex marriage would have the opposite effect. The then Home Secretary and later Prime Minister Theresa May told the *Daily Telegraph* (2013) that same-sex couples could act like 'missionaries' for the virtues of marriage and bolster heterosexual marriage as well.

While is too early to evaluate the long-term impact of civil partnerships and same-sex marriage on heterosexual marriage, marriage rates in England and Wales rose in 2014 (ONS, 2017) contrary to Morgan's controversial predictions. Morgan's argument that same-sex marriage breaks the link between marriage and child rearing is not necessarily true since many same sex couples do have children through new reproductive technologies, adoption or from previous relationships. Although some civil partnerships have been dissolved since they were introduced in 2004, by the end of 2015 over 93 per cent of male civil partnerships and over 87 per cent of female civil partnerships in England and Wales had not ended in dissolution. (ONS, 2016).

Qualitative research by Em Temple-Malt (2017), which involved interviewing 42 civil partners, found that most of the younger civil partners saw their decision to form a formal partnership as an expression of their love and commitment with some saying it showed that they wanted to stay together for the rest of their lives. Temple-Malt comments that they were 'using the same kinds of terminology' as heterosexuals when entering into marriage. Some of the older civil partners emphasised more practical reasons for forming civil partnerships, but none of them saw themselves as forming open relationships or expected their civil partnership to be short-lived.

Question

Evaluate the arguments put forward by Morgan about the likely effects of same-sex marriage on heterosexual marriage and family life.

Key terms

Civil partnerships Legally recognised relationships for same-sex couples which became possible in the UK in 2004.

Same-sex marriage Legally recognised marriage for same-sex couples which became possible in the UK in 2014.

Summary

1. The New Right see many policies as biased against traditional nuclear families.

2. From a New Right perspective, Patricia Morgan argues that tax and benefits in the UK discourage marriage, encourage lone parenthood, and lead to the state taking over responsibility from families for providing for family members and caring for children.

3. Critics of New Right views argue that many policies actively encourage traditional gender roles and nuclear families and that they discourage lone parenthood. They also deny that lone parenthood is harmful.

4. Others argue that policies over housing, school hours, and benefits encourage traditional nuclear families and family relationships. David Cameron explicitly changed tax law to encourage heterosexual marriage.

5. Many policies are not primarily aimed at influencing families but are more concerned with saving money.

6. The impact of policies on families is often open to interpretation but there has certainly been some shift in policy towards accepting diverse types of family and household.

7. Patricia Morgan argues that same-sex marriage undermines heterosexual marriage, but there is a lack of convincing evidence to support this and others argue that same-sex marriage strengthens heterosexual marriage.

PART 4 CHANGING FAMILY PATTERNS

Contents

Over the past half a century or so there have been major changes in family and household patterns in the UK. (Families consist of groups related by blood, marriage or adoption whereas households are groups who live together.) Going back to the 1960s and 1970s, the traditional nuclear family consisting of a married heterosexual couple and their children was dominant. Most people got married at a relatively young age and divorce was uncommon. Births outside marriage were frowned upon and same-sex partnerships were illegal in Britain until 1967 and were therefore often hidden. Civil partnerships and marriage were not available for same-sex couples. Because of these family patterns, most people lived in households headed by two parents and lone parenthood and single person households were much less common than today. There were also fewer step families and couples who did not have children than in contemporary society.

Since then, family life and relationships have become much more diverse and the way that individuals pass through different stages of life (the **life course**) more unpredictable. But why have these very significant changes taken place? What can sociology tell us about these changes and the reasons behind them? Is it just a question of changing attitudes and values or are there deeper reasons? Do these changes represent a serious threat to the future of marriage? All these issues are complex and inter-connected but research does help to produce some tentative answers.

5.4.1 The growth of family diversity

The assumption has often been made that a single type of family is the 'normal' or dominant one at a particular point in time. In the 1980s though, social scientists began to question this and to recognise increased diversity or variety in living arrangements and family types. But what is the evidence for this and if it has occurred why has it happened and what is its significance?

The 'typical' family

Although there has always been a diversity of family types (Anderson, 1980) 'march of progress theories' (see p. 237) assumed that a single family type (for example the extended or the nuclear family) has been dominant in any particular era. These theories suggest that the British family has gone through a series of stages as family life has adapted to changing economic circumstances.

In the 1980s Ann Oakley (1982) described what was then the image of the typical or **conventional family**. She says, 'conventional families are nuclear families composed of legally married couples, voluntarily choosing the parenthood of one or more (but not too many) children'. Traditionally, the husband is the main breadwinner in this type of family with the wife being mainly responsible for domestic tasks (while often being employed part-time as well). Oakley suggested that there were strong norms at that time which suggested that this was the type of family that people *should* live in, although as a feminist she was highly critical of this model of family life, seeing it as oppressive to women.

The 'conventional family' described by Oakley is very much in line with the functionalist view of the 'isolated nuclear family' which Talcott Parsons as being typical of and well adapted to modern industrial societies. However, as we have already seen (p. 236) it is questionable whether this was ever the norm in the way that Parsons claimed and changes over recent decades suggest that the 'conventional family' has become less common. For example, the growing employment of married women since the 1950s has undermined the idea of the male breadwinner and the female housewife. Furthermore, many sociologists have pointed to the increasing diversity of family forms.

Activity

A typical 'conventional family'?

1. In what ways does this image represent a 'conventional family'?

2. Suggest as many ways as you can in which families today may diverge from this image.

Family and household diversity in Britain

Robert and Rhona Rapoport (1982, 1989) were among the first to argue that family diversity was a growing trend in Britain, Europe and globally.

They identified five distinct elements of family diversity in Britain:

1. **Organisational diversity**. By this they mean there are variations in family structure, household type, and patterns of kinship network, and differences in the division of labour within the home.

   For example, there are the differences between conventional families, lone-parent families, and **dual-worker families**, in which husband and wife both work. There are also increasing numbers of **reconstituted families**. These families are formed after divorce and remarriage or cohabitation with a new partner and may include one or more children of either or both partners. Where the partners marry they become stepfamilies.

2. The second type of diversity is **cultural diversity**. There are differences in the lifestyles of families of different ethnic origins and different religious beliefs. (We discuss ethnic family diversity in more detail in pp. 285–289.) Differences in lifestyle between Catholic, Protestant and Muslim families and those from other religions may also be an important element of diversity.

3. There are differences between upper-class, middle-class and working-class families, for example in terms of relationships between adults and the way in which children are socialised.

4. There are differences that result from the stage in the **life cycle** of the family. Newly married couples without children may have a different family life from those with dependent children or those whose children have achieved adult status. (See later in this unit for discussion of the **life course**.)

5. The fifth factor identified by the Rapoports as producing family diversity is **cohort**. This refers to the period when family members were born. Cohort affects the life experiences of the family. Those families whose children were due to enter the labour market in the 1980s may be different from those entering the labour market in the 2010s. For example, rising house prices may make it more difficult to buy a house and start a family today than in the past.

In addition to those aspects of diversity mentioned by the Rapoports, several additional types of organisational diversity have been highlighted by sociologists. Gay and lesbian households have added to the diversity of household and family types. Another trend is groups of friends living together. They are sometimes seen as part of a **chosen family**, a family based on choice rather than blood relations or marriage. Furthermore, there has been an apparent growth of couples who live apart. These are referred to as partners who are **living apart together** or **LATs**.

Contemporary issues: De-standardisation of the life course

The Rapoports used the concept of the **life cycle** implying a fixed series of stages through which individuals pass in terms of their family life. Typically, these might be being a dependent child, becoming independent (for example attending university) cohabiting with a partner, marrying, having and raising children, children growing up and leaving home, being widowed and finally dying. These are often seen as biologically-based and linked to ageing. However, increasingly sociologists use the term life course to indicate that these stages have become more flexible and less predictable.

Lorraine Green (2015) points out that many sociologists now argue that there has been a **de-standardisation of the life course** so that many people do not pass through the stages of family life at the same ages or even in the same order. For example, marriage and childrearing have been decoupled so people may get married after having children and new reproductive technologies mean that women potentially have more flexibility about what age they have children. Children may stay dependent on parents longer than in the past, with this often extending into adulthood, and healthy older people may enjoy lifestyles similar to those more associated with young single people.

A couple marrying later in life.

Questions

1. Suggest three ways in which the life course might be 'de-standardised' in relation to family life.

2. Suggest reasons why most people might still tend to follow a fairly standard life course in terms of their family life.

Statistical patterns

Official statistics suggest both a medium-term and a long-term trend towards family and household diversity. Table 5.4.1 opposite shows the percentages of different types of families between 1996 and 2016.

Table 5.4.1 shows that the proportion of families which are nuclear families (married heterosexual couples with dependent children) has been declining from just under a third of families to just over a quarter from 1996–2016 (from 33.1 per cent to 25.8 per cent). Table 5.4.1 also shows the rise in cohabitation, lone parent families and same-sex cohabiting couple families along with the emergence of families headed by same-sex civil partners. These data do not include figures for the growing proportion of households which

Table 5.4.1 Percentage of families of different types by presence of children: England 1996–2016

	1996	2006	2016
All families	**100.0%**	**100.0%**	**100.0%**
No children	40.7%	43.6%	42.6%
Dependent children	44.6%	42.9%	42.4%
Non-dependent children only	14.8%	13.5%	15.0%
Married couple family	**76.1%**	**69.9%**	**67.0%**
No children	35.0%	34.7%	32.6%
Dependent children	31.3%	26.8&	25.8%
Non-dependent children only	9.8%	8.5%	8.6%
Opposite sex cohabiting couple family	**9.3%**	**14.5%**	**17.1%**
No children	5.6%	8.5%	9.4%
Dependent children	3.5%	5.5%	6.7%
Non-dependent children only	0.3%	0.5%	0.9%
Lone parent family	**14.5%**	**15.1%**	**15.2%**
Dependent children	9.8%	10.5%	9.9%
Non-dependent children only	4.7%	4.6%	5.4%
Civil partner couple family (with and without children)	**0.0%**	**0.1%**	**0.2%**
Same sex cohabiting couple family (with and without children)	**0.3%**	**0.5%**	**0.9%**

Source: Derived from the Labour Force Survey (ONS, 2017).

Activity

1. Describe the main trends shown in Table 5.4.1.

2. To what extent do these trends support the idea that family and household diversity are increasing?

are single-person households (28 per cent in 2014) (ONS 2016).

In terms of long-term trends, the changes are even more marked. For example, only 6 per cent of households were lone-parent households in the UK in 1961 and 12 per cent were one-person households; both household types are much more common today.

However, these statistics need careful interpretation and as we shall see, some sociologists argue that the extent of diversification can be exaggerated.

Elizabeth Beck-Gernsheim – individualisation, diversity and lifestyle choice

Many different explanations have been put forward for increased diversity in families and households.

For example, New Right theorists have argued that an over-generous welfare state has created family instability (see p. 271), liberal feminists have welcome diversity as something which reflects greater choice for women (see p. 274) and theorists of postmodernity and late modernity have linked it to broad changes in society as a whole (see pp. 251–257). One theorist (see pp. 253–254) who has specifically addressed increased diversity is Elizabeth Beck-Gernsheim whose ideas will now be discussed.

In her book *Reinventing the Family: In Search of New Lifestyles* (Beck-Gernsheim, 2002), Elizabeth Beck-Gernsheim notes that surveys suggest that some groups do 'retain a traditional image of the family' (Beck-Gernsheim, 2002, p. 22). However, traditional family roles and relationships are becoming unclear. For example, even the concept of marriage, traditionally the foundation of the family, is losing its sense of exclusivity. People in a relationship are often now referred to as 'couples', 'partnerships', 'relationships' or 'life companions' rather than as married couples. In the process, the assumption that people will live in families is breaking down.

There is growing acceptance of bringing up children in a variety of domestic settings other than the father-mother-child unit and this introduces a wide range of possible new household and family types. Widowed and divorced mothers and fathers may be bringing up children alone, unmarried heterosexual couples may be living with their own children as may gay or lesbian partners.

Advances in medicine have challenged even the idea of parenthood. For example, the sperm donor or the surrogate mother may be biological parents but have no responsibility for the children.

Furthermore, increases in divorce create a wide variety of possibilities for who is seen as belonging to one family or another. With remarriage being increasingly common, 'each member has their own definition of who belongs to the family; everyone lives out their own version of the patchwork family' (Beck-Gernsheim, 2002, p. 34). In the **patchwork family** adults have a succession of different partners and this contributes greatly to complexity and diversity. For example, children may or may not regard siblings, stepsiblings, and half brothers and sisters as forming part of their family. The patchwork family, then, involves a situation in which there are a variety of diverse but sometimes overlapping families based upon the perceptions of individuals who share a household. Indeed, an individual may see themselves as belonging to several different families simultaneously as illustrated in the image.

Beck-Gernsheim sees these changes in family life as being both a cause and a consequence of greater **individualisation** in society as a whole. Society is increasingly characterised by individual choices. This creates 'greater fluidity and uncertainty in kinship relations' (p. 39). They become a part of lifestyle choice rather than being based upon a model or ideal to follow.

Beck-Gernsheim does not deny that some traditional families will remain although they will become less common and for many will be only temporary as people increasingly creating their own unique sets of relationships which often will not conform to a specific category or family type. (For more details of Beck-Gernsheim's work see p. 253).

Evaluation of Beck-Gernsheim

Beck-Gernsheim's work seems accurately to describe many changes which are taking place in contemporary family life. However, her work, along with the whole idea of family diversity, should be regarded with some caution. The evidence and arguments about a trend towards diversity will be evaluated below (see pp. 290–291). First, particular types of diversity will be critically examined.

Activity

Patchwork families.

Source: Elizabeth Beck-Gernsheim, (2002) *Reinventing the Family: In Search of New Lifestyles,* Polity Press, Cambridge.

1. Produce two images portraying two different 'patchwork families'.

2. Beck-Gernsheim sees patchwork families as being a product of individualisation. Suggest three alternative explanations for an increase in the number of patchwork families.

Key terms

Conventional family A nuclear, heterosexual family consisting of a married couple and one or two (but not too many) children.

Cultural diversity Variations in the lifestyle of families, for example variations in the lifestyle of families of different ethnic origins.

De-standardisation of the life course A process in which the timing and order of the different stages in life becomes less predictable.

Dual worker family A family in which both adults have paid employment.

Individualisation An increased emphasis on individual choice.

LATs People who are 'living apart together', that is partners who maintain separate households.

Life course The process of moving through the different stages of life such as birth, adulthood, marriage, retirement and so on.

Life cycle The different stages of life. The concept of life cycle treats these stages as more predictable than the idea of life course.

Organisational diversity The range of different structures that families can have.

Patchwork family A family made up of a variety of current and former partners and your own or their relatives. There is choice about who an individual sees as belonging to the patchwork family.

Reconstituted family A family formed after divorce and remarriage or cohabitation with a new partner which may include one or more children of either or both partners.

Summary

1. The nuclear family is not as dominant as it was in the 1960s and 1970s in Britain. A wide variety of different types of family and household have become more common in the decades since then.

2. Talcott Parsons believes that the nuclear family was typical of modern industrial society but from the 1980s, writers such as Rhona and Robert Rapoport thought that diversity was becoming more characteristic of British families.

3. The Rapoports identified five types of diversity: organisational diversity, cultural diversity, class diversity, diversity related to the life cycle and diversity based on cohort.

4. Diversification has also involved increases in cohabitation, lone parent families, gay and lesbian families, and reconstituted families.

5. Living apart together and chosen families are new alternative family forms.

6. The idea of the life course suggests that stages in life, including family life, are less predictable than they used to be.

7. Statistics suggest both medium and long-term trends towards family and household diversity.

8. The increased diversity has been caused by a range of factors but Elizabeth Beck-Gernsheim attributes it primarily to individualisation – an increased emphasis on individual choice.

5.4.2 Sexuality, new reproductive technology, lone parenthood and living alone

It has never been the case that everyone lives in families headed by a heterosexual married couple. There have always been exceptions, but those exceptions seem to be becoming increasingly common and accepted. These include households based on non-heterosexual sexualities, based on a single parent rather than two parents, and households where only a single person lives. But why have these types of household been growing and what does this tell us about changes in the family? And what are the consequences of their growth? Is it something to be welcomed, or does it represent a danger to social stability?

Sexuality, chosen families and diversity

Differences in sexuality and gender identity have contributed to increasing diversity according to many sociologists. **LGBTI** (lesbian, gay, bisexual, transgender and intersex) groups add significantly to family diversity although most research thus far has been on gay and lesbian households.

The growth of LGBTI families

Gay and lesbian families and households have become more commonplace – certainly there are more openly gay and lesbian households than there were several decades ago. Furthermore, legal changes have created the new family form of **civil partnerships** (which were introduced in the UK in 2005 and are only available to same-sex couples) and same-sex marriage (which became possible in March 2014). Between 2005 and 2015 there were approximately 61 500 civil partnerships in the UK (ONS 2016). Between March 2014 and October 2015 there were just over 15 000 same sex marriages in England and Wales.

Changing attitudes and the heteronorm

Sociologists generally argue that households which incorporate long-term gay or lesbian relationships should be seen as constituting families. According to Weeks *et al.* (1999), gay men and lesbians often look upon their households, and even their friendship networks, as being **chosen families**. Furthermore, some see their relationships as involving a greater degree of choice than those in more conventional heterosexual

279

families. They choose whom to include in their family and negotiate what are often fairly egalitarian relationships. Some see their families as an alternative type of family which they are consciously developing. Weeks *et al.* argue that this may be part of wider social changes in which 'we culturally prioritise individual choice and the acceptance of diversity. Commitment becomes increasingly a matter of negotiation rather than ascription'. (Their views are similar to those of Anthony Giddens – see p. 251 for details.)

Sasha Roseneil (2005) develops the idea of chosen families further. She uses the term **heteronorm** to refer to the belief that the 'normal' form of intimate relationships is between heterosexuals. Roseneil believes that the heteronorm is increasingly breaking down. She argues that this is particularly true of lesbian and gay intimacies where 'Friends become

lovers, lovers become friends and many have multiple sexual partners of varying degrees of commitment (and none)'. Indeed, an individual's 'significant other' may not be someone with whom she or he has a sexual relationship' (Roseneil, 2005, p. 244).

Rosneil points to television series such as *Friends*, *Seinfeld*, *Ellen* and *Will and Grace* as examples where it is the 'sociability of a group of friends rather than a conventional family, which provides the love, care and support essential to everyday life in the city' (Roseneil, 2005, p. 242). Therefore, the heterosexual couple who live together is no longer the basic unit of society.

According to Roesneil, this shift has resulted from social changes such as the rise in divorce, the increase in births outside marriage and heterosexual relationships, the increase in single-person households and the growth of lone parenthood.

Contemporary issues: Civil partnerships and the 'pure relationship'

Em Temple-Malt (2017) conducted interviews with 42 same-sex civil partners and explored the reasons why they had decided to form a civil partnership. She considered how far the research seemed to support the idea of the 'pure relationship' put forward by Giddens, which argued that relationships were increasingly based on individuals pursuing their own self-interest (see p. 252). Giddens saw same-sex couples as 'pioneers' of pure relationships. He argued that this type of relationship could not be based on traditional gender roles (since both partners were the same sex) and they would be based more on negotiation and would be more equal than heterosexual. Giddens predicted that eventually heterosexual relationships and same-sex relationships would converge with more open, negotiated and egalitarian relationships developing in both groups.

Temple-Malt found some evidence for Giddens's ideas. Among the younger same-sex partners (in their mid-30s to mid-40s) most gave similar reasons for forming a partnership as married heterosexuals. They saw it as a public expression of their love and as a relatively 'normal' thing to do. However, older civil partners were more likely to give 'protective' reasons for their decision. Many said that their families had not been supportive so they felt they could not trust them. They wanted formal legal protections (for example over property

A civil partnership ceremony using traditional ways of dressing for heterosexual marriage.

Civil partners wearing less traditional wedding outfits.

rights). Although these couples prioritised the couple relationship over their relationship with wider kin, this was not so much out of free choice as something that was forced on them because of hostility from their families of origin.

Em Temple-Malt's research illustrates the dangers of making general predictions about family change and ignoring the specific factors affecting certain types of relationship. In intimate relationships, 'choosing' who to see as your family can be shaped by discrimination and rejection as much as by more general changes in attitudes towards acceptance of different types of relationships and sexualities.

Questions

1. Suggest reasons why some couples forming a civil partnership might wear clothes similar to those worn by couples in traditional heterosexual wedding ceremonies.

2. Suggest reasons why some couples forming a civil partnership might wear clothes dissimilar to those worn by couples in traditional heterosexual wedding ceremonies.

New reproductive technologies

New reproductive technologies add an entirely new dimension to family diversity. This may take the form of third-party assisted reproduction involving the donation of eggs, sperm or embryos or surrogacy (Chambers, 2012). In 1978 the first 'test-tube baby', Louise Brown, was born. The process is called *in vitro fertilisation* and involves fertilising an egg with a sperm in a test-tube, before then implanting it in a woman's womb. The woman may or may not be the woman who produced the egg. Sperm and egg donation raises important questions about parenthood and whether the biological role of conception and carrying the foetus is more or less significant than the social role of raising a child. Surrogacy involves a woman carrying a foetus for another couple. This raises questions about who the parents of a child are, and about what constitutes a family.

Carol Smart (2007) discusses research suggesting the nature of the family and kinship are being changed by New Reproductive Technology, with egg donors, surrogate mothers and sperm donors all having claims to family membership.

John Macionis and Ken Plummer (1997) note how new reproductive technologies have also been used by lesbians, gay men, and single and older women. By making gay and lesbian parenting possible without a prior heterosexual relationship, a wider variety of unconventional family types are created. The biological restrictions on forming or enlarging families by having children have been greatly reduced.

The existence of these new technologies therefore adds considerably to the range of potential family types and thus contributes to growing diversity.

Lone parenthood

Lone parenthood is one of the most significant alternatives to nuclear families and the consequences of lone parent families for individuals and for society have been the subject of considerable debate.

The increase in lone parenthood

Lone parent families have become increasingly common in Britain. Between 1972 and 2016 the percentage of children living in lone-parent families increased from 7 per cent to 22 per cent (*Social Trends* 1998; ONS, 2016).

Although useful, these figures need to be interpreted with caution. They provide only a snapshot picture of the situation at one point in time and do not record changes in family situations. Many more children than the above figures seem to suggest spend *part* of their childhood in a lone parent family, but many fewer spend *all* of their childhood in one. Children may start their life living in a lone parent family. However, the lone parent may well find a new partner and marry or cohabit with them.

It should also be noted that many children who live in a lone parent household do spend time with their other parent. Furthermore, even in two-parent families, one parent (usually the mother) might be responsible for the vast majority of the childcare. In terms of children's experience, then, the distinction between lone parent and two-parent households is not clear-cut.

The causes of lone parenthood

Lone parenthood can come about through a number of different routes. People who are married can become lone parents through divorce, separation or being widowed, or individuals may become a parent outside of a cohabiting relationship.

In this context, the growth of lone parenthood is closely linked to other trends, particularly the increasing divorce rates. However, it may also be strongly linked to rising rates of cohabitation. Ann Berrington (2014) used data from the General Household Survey and General Lifestyle Survey to show that an increasing proportion of never-married lone mothers have previously cohabited. In 2005–2009 among lone mothers in their 30s for example, only one in six had never been married or cohabited.

Allan and Crow (2001) note that the increase in lone parenthood is clearly due to two factors: an increase in marital breakdown (particularly divorce), and a rise in births to unmarried mothers. They claim that both these trends more broadly 'reflect an acceptance of diversity and individual choice which was far less pronounced in previous eras'.

David Morgan (1994) suggests the rise in lone parenthood could partly be due to changing relationships between men and women. He says important factors causing the rise could include 'the expectations that women and men have of marriage and the growing opportunities for women to develop a life for themselves outside marriage or long-term cohabitations'.

There is widespread agreement that the stigma attached to lone parenthood has been decreasing.

According to David Morgan (1994), the reduction in stigma is reflected in the decreasing use of terms such as 'illegitimate children' and 'unmarried mothers', which seem to imply some deviation from the norms of family life, and their replacement by concepts such as 'lone-parent families', which do not carry such negative connotations. The reduction in the stigma of lone parenthood could relate to 'the weakening of religious or community controls over women'. However, there is little evidence that a large number of lone parents see their situation as ideal and actively choose it as an alternative to dual parenthood.

Allan and Crow (2001) argue that most lone parents don't reject a two-parent model at all: on average they only stay lone parents for about five years. Most do not wish to be lone parents, and would prefer to live with a partner.

The consequences of lone parenthood

Lone parenthood has increasingly become a contentious issue, with some arguing it has become a serious problem for society. Deborah Chambers (2001) discusses what she sees as a **moral panic** (an exaggerated and illogical concern about supposed social problems) in relation to lone parents. She argues that in the 1990s, in the Conservative Party and the tabloid press there was a widespread discourse suggesting that lone parenthood posed a major threat to the well-being of society. According to Esther Dermott and Marco Pomati (2016) the level of overt hostility to lone parents may have reduced in recent years; however, there is still some stigma attached to being a lone parent.

Part of the stigma has arisen from lone parents being seen in some quarters as 'bad parents'. However, research by Dermott and Pomati has found that:

> lone parents are more likely to sit down and eat a meal with their children every day than couple parents

> lone parents are more likely to cut down on personal spending, for example by skimping on food to help their children, than couple parents

> lone parents are more likely to help children with homework than couple parents.

On the other hand, lone parents are slightly less likely to read to their children and are less likely to take part in games and sports with them than couple parents (but financial constraints and the absence of fathers in most homes probably account for the lower participation in leisure activities). Overall, Dermott and Pomati conclude that there is no significant difference in the extent to which lone and couple parents engage in 'good' parenting.

However, there is no doubt that lone parenthood leads to financial difficulties for many families. According to official figures discussed by the organisation Gingerbread (2017), lone parent families have nearly twice the rate of poverty of couple families with 47 per cent living on 60 per cent or less of median income (the middle level of income for all households) compared with 24 per cent of couple families. Of course, not all lone-parent families are poor. A few are very affluent, but the majority do have low income and Gingerbread points out that they are more likely to rely on benefits and more likely to live in social housing than other types of family.

More controversial than the low average living standards of lone parents is the question of the psychological and social effects on children raised in such families. A range of studies have suggested that the children of lone parents suffer more psychological problems and experience less social success than other children (McLanahan and Booth, 1991).

Activity

Figure 5.4.1 The number of people living alone by age

The number of **people living alone** differs by age

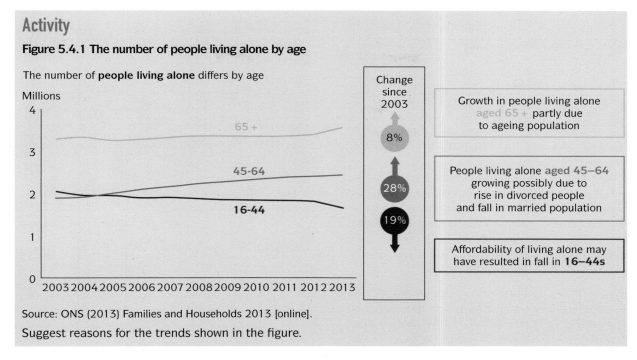

Source: ONS (2013) Families and Households 2013 [online].

Suggest reasons for the trends shown in the figure.

However, it may be that many of these effects are the result of low income rather than lone-parenthood as such.

Statistical research by Nick Spencer (2005) used data from over 15 000 children in the British government's *Children and Families Study* to examine the independent effects of living in a lone parent family. He examined whether living in lone parent families accounted for poorer health, less good educational achievement and increased risk of involvement in antisocial behaviour. Overall, he found that it was not family structure but material deprivation which accounted for these outcomes.

Single-person households

An alternative to living in a family is to live on one's own. Many single-person households may be formed as a result of divorce, separation, the break-up of a partnership involving cohabitation, or the death of a partner. However, others may result from a deliberate choice to live alone. There is statistical evidence that single-person households are becoming more common. Between 1972 and 2016 the proportion of one-person households rose from 18 per cent to 28.4 per cent (ONS, 2016).

In part, the long-term increase is due to the ageing of the population, but it is also a result of an increase in the proportion of those of working age living alone. However, recent trends (shown in Figure 5.4.1) reveal that there has been a decline in the number of younger adults (16–44) living alone which the Office for National Statistics attributes to the cost of housing. This encourages more people to house share or to continue living with parents in early adulthood.

Contemporary issues: Solo–living and individualisation

Lynn Jamieson, Fran Wasoff and Roona Simpson (2009) used data from European Social Surveys and from research by other writers to discuss the significance of living alone (or as they prefer to call it **solo-living**). They argue that the work of writers such as Beck and Beck-Gernsheim (1995) (see pp. 283–284 for details) suggests that solo-living is part of a trend towards **individualisation**. When individuals enter partnerships seeking their own satisfaction, the likelihood of conflict is increased and this makes relationships more unstable. This rather pessimistic view suggests that solo-living results from the difficulties of producing successful relationships.

Jamieson *et al.* conducted qualitative research which found that both young men and young women in their 20s identified some advantages to solo-living, but women were generally keener than men on finding a partner. She says, 'Young men were much more likely to associate and celebrate a life-style of sexual freedom and freedom to roam with solo-living than were young women' (Jamieson *et al.*, 2002). However, the research also suggested that for those who had lived on their own for a long time, women were more likely than men to see solo-living positively and to have established rich social networks. They say 'living alone can be a pleasurable and transformative experience for some women encouraging commitment to living alone but not withdrawal from a wider social life' (Jamieson *et al.*, 2009).

Nevertheless, they do not conclude that solo-living is a long-term choice for most people. Social surveys show that most people come to live on their own when a relationship ends and only a small minority continue to live alone for a long time. They therefore conclude that those who live alone should not be seen as a homogeneous group with the same motivations but are diverse. Only for a minority is solo-living seen as a desirable alternative to other lifestyles.

One depiction of solo-living.

Questions

1. The image above seems to portray solo-living in a negative light. In what ways might ideologies or social theories supporting the nuclear family regard solo-living as bad for society and bad for the individual?

2. Suggest some ways in which social theories (for example feminist theories and theories of modernity) might see solo-living in a positive way.

Key terms

Chosen families The group of people an individual regards as family members. It can include friends as well as relatives and kin.

Civil partnership A legal relationship between two partners with similar rights as marriage.

Heteronorm The belief that intimate relationships between heterosexual couples are the normal form that intimate relationships take.

Individualisation A process in which people become more concerned with individual self-interest and personal development than with the collective good or with conforming to social norms.

***In vitro* fertilisation** Fertilising an egg with a sperm in a test-tube.

LGBTI Lesbian, gay, transgender, bisexual and intersex groups and individuals.

Moral panic An exaggerated and illogical concern about supposed social problems which is often the result of media sensationalism.

New reproductive technologies Technological methods of allowing individuals and couples to have children when they would not otherwise be able to do so.

Summary

1. Lesbian, gay, transgender, bisexual and intersex groups add to a diversity of family types.

2. Same-sex civil partnerships were introduced in 2005 and same-sex marriage in 2014 and this reflected the growing number of openly gay and lesbian relationships and households.

3. Gay and lesbian households sometimes use the idea of the chosen family in which you can regard friends as well as relatives as part of your family.

4. The developments of gay and lesbian households have challenged the idea of heterosexuality as the norm.

5. Research into same-sex civil partnerships suggests there are a range of reasons for people entering these relationships.

6. New reproductive technologies open up a number of new possible family relationships.

7. Lone-parenthood has increased significantly in Britain.

8. Increased divorce and changing attitudes which reduce the stigma associated with lone- parenthood are important factors causing the increase.

9. Research suggests that the economic effects of lone-parenthood are more important than the lack of two parents in causing any negative effects for children.

10. The number of single-person households (or people who are solo-living) has increased significantly.

11. Some sociologists have attributed this increase to individualisation.

5.4.3 Ethnicity and family diversity

Ethnicity can be seen as one of the most important sources of family diversity in Britain. Ethnic groups with different cultural backgrounds may introduce family forms that differ significantly from those of the ethnic majority. But have the family relationships of minority ethnic groups remained distinctive or have they been modified in a British context?

Statistical evidence

Statistical evidence does suggest there are some differences in the prevalence of different household types in different ethnic groups.

Figures from The Labour Force Survey (Platt, 2009) averaged over the period 2004–2008 found significant differences in the proportions of different household types in different ethnic groups. Table 5.4.1 shows that just 11 per cent of Pakistani, 14 per cent of Bangladeshi households and 7 per cent of Indian households consisted of lone parents with dependent children, compared with 28 per cent of Black Caribbean and 22 per cent of Black African families. Perhaps surprisingly, there was a lower proportion of lone parents among White British households (9 per cent) than among Pakistani and Bangladeshi households.

Among all Asian groups, a high proportion of households consisted of couples with dependent children.

Activity

1. Briefly describe the main patterns shown in the table below.

2. How far do they support the view that ethnicity contributes to family diversity?

Table 5.4.1 Family type and average family size

Ethnic group	Family type, row percentages				Family size	
	Single person	Couple, no dependent children	Couple, dependent children	Lone parent	Average family size	% families 4 + people
White British	36	35	20	9	2.2	16
Other White	45	30	18	7	2.0	13
Mixed White and Caribbean	42	8	21	29	2.2	17
Mixed White and African	44	12	23	21	2.2	21
Mixed White and Asian	43	21	22	14	2.2	19
Other mixed	48	18	19	15	2.0	12
Indian	30	30	33	7	2.6	28

Ethnic group	Family type, row percentages				Family size	
	Single person	Couple, no dependent children	Couple, dependent children	Lone parent	Average family size	% families 4 + people
Pakistani	24	19	45	11	3.2	43
Bangladeshi	20	14	52	14	3.6	49
Other Asian	40	21	32	7	2.3	23
Black Caribbean	41	14	16	28	2.1	16
Black African	44	9	25	22	2.4	24
Other Black	43	13	23	21	2.3	21
Chinese	56	21	17	6	1.9	13
Other	43	18	28	11	2.3	22
All groups	37	33	20	10	2.2	17

Source: Platt, L. (2009) *Ethnicity and Family: Relationships Within and Between Ethnic Groups. An Analysis Using the Labour Force Survey, Equality and Human Rights Commission*, London [online].

Activity

A 'fusion' wedding mixing Indian and British influences.

Questions

1. Taking account of the statistics on 'mixed' families in the table and the photograph above, suggest ways in which 'mixed' weddings contribute to family diversity in the UK.

2. Suggest reasons why some ethnic groups are more likely to live in 'mixed' households than others.

Family diversity, ethnicity and 'modern individualism'

Richard Berthoud (2000) provides a useful starting point for analysing family diversity and ethnicity in Britain and for discussing ways in which family life is changing in different ethnic groups. Berthoud distinguishes between three broad ethnic groups: White British, British South Asians (including Pakistanis, Bangladeshis and Indians) and the British Black Caribbean community. He argues that each group has the following characteristics:

1. The South Asian population in Britain have a relatively 'traditional' family life. They have high rates of marriage and high fertility rates resulting in families with four or more children being quite common. Very few British South Asians cohabited outside marriage and rates of divorce were very low. Pakistani and Bangladeshi wives were more likely to act as full-time homemakers than other ethnic groups. One distinctive feature of this ethnic group was the prevalence of arranged marriages with more than a third of Sikhs and Muslims saying that their partner was chosen through this process. In this group, there are also relatively high rates of cohabitation with parents after marriage so three-generational households were not uncommon.

2. White British families have lower marriage rates and lower fertility with a smaller family size than

South Asians. Marriage outside the White British ethnic group is relatively common, arranged marriages are virtually non-existent and White British adults are unlikely to live with their parents once they have married themselves. White British groups also tend to have quite high rates of divorce.

3. According to Berthoud, British families of Caribbean origin have much lower rates of marriage than other ethnic groups and approximately similar fertility rates to White British people. However, this ethnic group has relatively high rates of lone parenthood with about half of mothers being never-married lone parents. The British Caribbean community also has high rates of mixed marriage with many having White British partners.

Berthoud accepted that there was considerable family diversity within each ethnic group but nevertheless argued that these distinctions between ethnic groups were adding to family diversity in the UK. However, he claimed that families from all ethnic groups were heading in the same direction towards what he called '**modern individualism**' and away from '**old-fashioned values**'. That is, in all groups there was a move away from stable, life-long marriage in which the family was prioritised over the needs of the individual. The direction of travel was the same for all groups, but according to Berthoud British South Asian families tended to be behind the trend with Black Caribbean families ahead of it.

To what extent, then, does other research support the ideas of Berthoud? More detailed studies of particular ethnic groups incorporating qualitative ethnographic data can be used to evaluate Berthoud's claims.

British Asians and diversity

Research into British Asian families has provided very informative evidence about the extent to which they remain a distinctive family type in Britain. It should be remembered though that South Asians encompass those of different religious and national origins and there is therefore considerable diversity within the British Asian population.

Ghazala Bhatti – British Asian families and social change

Ghazala Bhatti (1999) carried out research into 50 British Asian families living in a town in southern England. The research was largely based upon in-depth interviews: 44 of the families were Muslim with Pakistani or Bangladeshi backgrounds, and six were of Indian origin, four were Hindu and two Sikh.

Bhatti found there was a continuing emphasis on loyalty to the family and on trying to maintain traditional practices related to marriage. For example, *izzat* or family honour was also taken very seriously, with particular emphasis being placed on the behaviour of daughters. Bhatti found that mothers saw their family roles as being of paramount importance. She says: 'Motherhood bestowed status upon these women and they saw child rearing as their most important role and duty in life'. Paid work was seen as much less important than caring for children and others. Fathers, on the other hand, saw their family responsibilities more in terms of a traditional breadwinner role.

However, Bhatti did find some evidence for changing attitudes in younger generations and of conflict between different generations. In four of the families studied, 'open clashes had developed between parents and children'. In all these cases, the elder brother had 'decided to marry an English girl instead of somebody of his own kin'. The parents of these children all felt that they had failed as parents and worried about whether their younger children would follow a similar path.

However, Bhatti stresses that these families are 'not the norm'. There were some tensions between the generations in many of the other families, but for the most part these were minor and generally the children seemed happy to adhere to traditional patterns of family life. Bhatti therefore found that the distinctiveness of Asian families was largely continuing and therefore contributing to the family diversity of Britain.

Kaveri Qureshi, Katharine Charsley and Alison Shaw, British Asians and family diversity

Kaveri Qureshi, Katharine Charsley and Alison Shaw (2015) argue that British Asian families have often been considered to be the ethnic group in the UK with the lowest rates of divorce, lone parenthood and separation. This was reflected in research in the 1990s. However, Qureshi *et al.* argue that significant changes have taken place since the 1990s. For example, census figures found that the proportion of British Pakistani families with dependent children which were headed by lone parent had risen from 10 per cent in 1991 to 17 per cent in 2011. The proportion of lone parent British Bangladeshi families rose from 10 per cent to 16 per cent over the same period while there was a rise from 5 per cent to 11 per cent amongst British Indian families. Statistics from elsewhere suggest a long-term trend towards higher divorce and separation rates amongst British Asians. Kaveri Qureshi also carried out qualitative research in Peterborough and London between 2004

287

and 2011 into British Asian families and found further evidence of change in family life. The research involved ethnographic research using life-history interviews and observation with a total of 28 families.

They found that the pioneering first-generation migrants from Pakistan were quite strongly opposed to divorce and separation but this was not the case for younger generations. The older migrants tried to hide marital problems from other family members. For example, some wives believed that their husbands had been unfaithful if they had arrived in the UK without initially bringing their spouse (husband or wife) and other difficulties often arose from low-income in the early years after migration. For the older generation, divorce was not unthinkable and it did occasionally occur, but there was strong resistance to it unless there were compelling reasons such as domestic violence or infertility.

For British Pakistanis in their 20s and 30s there were rather different causes of marital conflict. Roughly half of British Pakistanis married a partner from Pakistan and the cultural differences between the couple could cause marital conflict. Sometimes there could be a lengthy wait before the marriage partner in Pakistan could obtain a visa and the period of separation between the newly married couple was often problematic. It could be five years before a permanent visa was granted so conflict could result from the unfulfilled need 'for love, intimacy and fulfilment' (p. 20). Traditionally, it was thought amongst British Pakistanis that only men could initiate divorce, but some women in the study had researched the Qur'an and concluded that it was possible for women to do this as well.

Most of the parents in the sample did support arranged marriage but an increasing number accepted the possibility that their children could divorce and remarry if they were not happy.

Qureshi *et al.* conclude that British Pakistani families are changing and in the process they are becoming less distinctive and more accepting of divorce. Nevertheless, attitudes to family life are not as individualistic as amongst the population as a whole and arranged marriages and a desire for family stability remain strong features of British Pakistani family culture.

Black Caribbean families

Research into the family life of Black Caribbean families both in the UK and in the Caribbean has found considerable diversity in their cultural patterns. Jocelyn Barrow (1982) argues that there are three main family types in the Caribbean:

1 The **conventional nuclear family**, or 'Christian marriage', which is often little different from nuclear families in Britain. Families of this type tend to be typical of the more religious or economically successful groups in the population.

2 The **common-law family**, which is more frequently found among the less economically successful. An unmarried couple live together and look after children who may or may not be their biological offspring.

3 The **mother household**, in which the mother or grandmother of the children is head of the household and, for most of the time at least, the household contains no adult males. This type of household often relies a good deal on the help and support of female kin living nearby to enable the head of the household to fulfil her family responsibilities.

Caribbean families in Britain

To a large extent, research has shown that a similar mixture of family types exists among Caribbean groups in Britain with nuclear families, common-law (or cohabiting) families and mother households (or lone mother households) all being common. However, Tracey Reynolds (2002) argues that the concentration on female-headed households among Black Caribbean families in Britain is rather misleading. She emphasises the diversity and fluidity of Black Caribbean families. In part, this reflects cultural diversity within the Black Caribbean community. Family patterns vary between Caribbean islands and these variations are reflected in Britain. For example, in Jamaica, female-headed households are dominant, but in Barbados and Antigua nuclear households are more common.

In Britain (and in the Caribbean) Black Caribbean family diversity is increased by the existence of **visiting relationships**. Even where there is no adult male in the household, the female head of household may still have a male partner, who does not live with her but visits frequently. The visiting man may play a full and active role as a parent.

Sometimes visiting relationships are maintained because they have advantages in terms of claiming social security benefits. However, Reynolds's own research suggests they are often seen as a stepping-stone towards a stable, cohabiting relationship, which might ultimately lead to marriage. Other women, though, valued the independence that a visiting relationship brought and had no desire to cohabit with and marry their partner.

Reynolds concludes that the: *tendency in policy research to present Black, female-headed households as the unitary Black family model disguises the fluid and adaptive nature of Black family relationships and living arrangements and also the fact that, similar to families in other racial and ethnic groups, the Black family has diverse family and household patterns.*

Reynolds, 2002, p. 69

Activity

A multi-generational Black family.

1. How well does the image above correspond to Barrow's analysis of different types of Black Caribbean family?

2. Would you agree with Reynolds's conclusions about the structure of Black Caribbean families?

Ethnicity and family diversity – conclusion

The general picture provided by these studies suggests that immigrants and their descendants have adapted their family life to fit British circumstances, but they are still influenced by family patterns in their country of origin. This would suggest that the presence of a variety of ethnic groups has indeed contributed to the diversity of family types to be found in Britain. These minority ethnic groups have succeeded in retaining many of the culturally distinctive features of their family life.

Nevertheless, there is also evidence of changes taking place in the families of minority ethnic groups, and British culture may have more effect on future generations. Each ethnic group also contains a variety of different family types, which are influenced by factors such as class and stage in the life cycle as well as ethnicity.

For this reason, Berthoud's argument that Black Caribbean families are in front of the trend to modern individualism and British Asian families are behind it

is an over-simplification. Alison Shaw (2014) therefore argues that there is no 'straightforward cultural convergence' but a 'complex process' in which the ongoing cultural transitions of different ethnic groups interact with the changing culture of Britain as a whole.

Key terms

Common-law family In the context of Black Caribbean families an unmarried couple who live together and look after children who may or may not be their biological offspring.

Ethnicity Cultural differences based on membership of groups which define themselves in terms of a relationship with a homeland.

Modern individualism To Berthoud the prioritising of individual self-interest over the interests of families.

Mother household In the context of Black Caribbean families a household in which the mother or grandmother of the children is head of the household and, for most of the time at least, the household contains no adult males.

'Old-fashioned values' To Berthoud a belief in the importance of traditional, stable, family life based on heterosexual (opposite sex) marriage.

Visiting relationships In the context of Black Caribbean households a situation where the female head of household may still have a male partner, who does not live with her but visits frequently. The visiting man may play a full and active role as a parent.

Summary

1. Ethnicity is an important source of family diversity in Britain.

2. Statistical evidence suggests that there are differences in the family life of ethnic groups with British Asians more likely to live in families headed by married couples and Black Caribbeans more likely to live in lone-parent families.

3. Richard Berthoud argues that compared to White British people, South Asians have a relatively traditional family life whereas Black Caribbean people have moved further towards modern individualism.

4. Qureshi *et al.* found that British Pakistani families were changing, for example by becoming more accepting of divorce than they had been previously, but also that they retained a strong desire for family stability.

5. Research into Black Caribbean families suggests that mother households are more common both in the Caribbean and in Britain than for other ethnic groups.

6. However, research also suggests that Black Caribbean families and households are highly diverse.

7. Minority ethnic groups have contributed to family diversity but they are themselves highly diverse and have changing patterns of family life.

5.4.4 Family and household diversity

So far, all the evidence in this section suggests that there has been a decisive shift towards family and household diversity in Britain. However, this has been challenged by some sociologists, including those who question the extent of diversity and those who argue that there is still a dominant type of family in the UK. But are they on strong ground? Has the shift towards diversity really been exaggerated?

Robert Chester — questioning diversity

In an early contribution to the debate, Robert Chester (1985) pointed out that statistics on family and household type can be misleading. They are usually based on the percentage of *households* of different types. But this does not take account of the number of *people* living in the household and you get different figures if you calculate the percentage of people who live in different types of household. For example, single-person households by definition have only one person living in them whereas married couple households with one or more dependent children have at least three members.

The statistics based on the percentage of *people* living in different types of household give a different impression from those based on the percentage of *households* of different types. For example, in the UK in 2010 (*Social Trends,* 2011) 20 per cent of *households* consisted of a couple with dependent children, but 36 per cent of *people* lived in this type of household. On the other hand, 29 per cent of *households* consisted of a person living alone, but only 12 per cent of *people* lived alone. Therefore figures based of

percentage of household exaggerate the significance of single person households and do not fully reflect the significance of family households.

The second point made by Chester was that life cycles make it inevitable that at any one time some people will not be a member of a nuclear family household. Many of those who lived in other types of household would either have experienced living in a nuclear family in the past, or would do so in the future. Most young single people living alone and many lone parents eventually move in with a partner, and many elderly people living alone have been widowed.

Evaluation of Chester

Chester makes some valid points about the ways in which the shift to diversity can be exaggerated but, since he was writing, there has been a slow but steady drift away from living in nuclear families in Britain. Deborah Chambers (2012) acknowledges that there are many types of family diversity but emphasises that 'the nuclear family remains a powerful icon of tradition and stability' (Chambers, 2012, p. 2). There is something of a 'moral panic' over the idea that the family is in decline and greater diversity has created 'anxiety about a collapse of moral standards caused by the deterioration of "proper family values"'. To Chambers, changes have occurred and there is an increasing variety in households, but this certainly does not mean that conventional family structures are disappearing or are in danger of collapse.

The beanpole family as the new norm?

Some sociologists go further than arguing that the idea of family diversity can be exaggerated and claim that there is still a dominant family type in Britain today. From this point of view, some family links remain particularly important. One such view is put forward by Julia Brannen (2000) who claims that the **beanpole family** is the dominant family type in Britain.

Drawing on her own research (Brannen *et al.*, 2000), Brannen argues that there are strong **intergenerational links** (links between generations) in contemporary British families. This is partly because people are living longer and therefore there are more families with three or even four generations alive than there were in the past.

Brannen *et al.* (2000) found that grandparents are increasingly providing informal childcare for their grandchildren. In addition, grandparents often give financial help to their children and grandchildren.

According to Brannen *et al.*'s research, adults still provide practical or emotional support for elderly parents in many families, and sometimes help them out financially as well. Although these family links are generally regarded as optional, they are commonplace and play a crucial role in maintaining family cohesion. Brannen (2003) claims that these intergenerational links tend to survive changes in families such as those resulting from divorce. For example, lone parents may rely more on help with childcare from grandparents than parents living with a partner do.

In contrast to the intergenerational links, Brannen *et al.* found that **intragenerational links** (links between those from the same generation, for example siblings and cousins) were somewhat weaker. Brannen therefore characterises contemporary family structures as being long and thin – she compares them to a beanpole. She concludes:

> *Many multigenerational families are now long and thin – typically described as beanpole families; they have fewer intragenerational ties because of high divorce rates, falling fertility and smaller family size, but more vertical intergenerational ties because of increased longevity.*
> Brannen, 2003

Evaluation of Brannen

Brannen's work emphasises the continuing importance of family relationships in contemporary Britain. Furthermore, the idea of the beanpole family is supported by other research which suggests that grandparents play an important role in family life. However, Brannen does generalise about families and takes little account of the increasing diversity of family and household types.

Key terms

Beanpole family A family in which there are strong intergenerational links between children, parents and grandparents, but weaker intragenerational links.

Intragenerational links Links between family members of the same generation, for example brothers and sisters.

Intergenerational links Links between family members of different generations, for example grandparents and grandchildren.

Summary

1. Robert Chester believes that the move towards family diversity can be exaggerated by looking at statistics on the proportion of different households in the country rather than the proportion of people living in different types of household.

2. Chester points out that the stages of the life cycle mean that many people who are not living in nuclear families at any one point in time will nevertheless spend much of their life living in a nuclear family.

3. Deborah Chambers believes that the decline of the nuclear family can be exaggerated but accepts that there is greater variety in family life than in the past.

4. Julia Brannen believes that the beanpole family with strong intergenerational links but weak intragenerational links is the most common type of family in Britain today.

5. Brannen can be criticised for taking little account of increasing diversity.

5.4.5 Partnerships

Partnerships can take several forms. Traditionally, heterosexual marriage was the most common type of partnership but, from the 1960s onwards, cohabitation outside marriage by heterosexual couples became more common. Today, an emerging type of partnership involves 'living apart together' where a couple (married or otherwise) maintain their relationship despite living in different places. Same-sex partnerships existed in the 1960s but they were not always open and there was more widespread disapproval of these relationships than there is now. More recently, same-sex couples have been able to enter civil partnerships and since 2013 to get married as well. But why are these changes taking place and do they suggest growing instability in partnerships and family life? This unit explores these issues.

Marriage

Many social and political commentators in Western societies have expressed concern about what they see as the decline of marriage. For example, Brenda Almond (2006) believes there is an increased emphasis on the needs of individuals and less emphasis on society's need for the rearing of children in stable relationships, particularly marriages. As a result, fewer people are getting married. Similarly, the New Right sociologist Patricia Morgan claims that decline in marriage is a serious threat to the family (see Part 3 in this chapter). The statistics do show a long-term decline in marriage but why this is and its significance are disputed.

Marriage rates

Figure 5.4.2 shows trends in marriage rates in England and Wales from 1934 to 2014 and shows that there has been a long-term decline in rates since the early 1970s. In 2014 the marriage rates (marriages per 1000 unmarried men/women) were 23 for men and 20.9 for women (ONS, 2017). There had been small rises from 2009–2012 but the 2014 figures were the second lowest on record (the lowest were in 2013) and they were a fraction of the 1972 figures when the rates were 78.4 for men and 60.5 for women.

Although most sociologists assume that the figures discussed above demonstrate a decline in the popularity of marriage, some have questioned this arguing that it merely indicates the postponement of marriage. They point out that most people do get married eventually. According to Jon Bernardes, writing in 1997, approximately 90 per cent of women got married in the UK at that time compared with 70 per cent or so in Victorian times.

Nevertheless, the evidence does suggest that people are tending to get married later and this is one factor which helps to explain the decline in marriage rates. Both men and women are tending to delay marriage until later in life. In 2013, average age at first marriage was 32.5 for men and 30.6 years for women; an increase of almost eight years for both sexes when compared with 1973. However, since first marriage rates are declining in all age groups it is not just a question of delaying marriage; each successive generation is less likely to get married.

Reasons for changing patterns of heterosexual marriage

A number of sociologists see the decline in marriage rates as being the result of changing attitudes. Some see these changes in a negative light; others see them more positively.

Activity

1. Describe the trends shown in Figure 5.4.2.

2. Suggests reasons for the trends in marriage rates.

Figure 5.4.2 Marriage rates for men and women (1934–2014), England and Wales

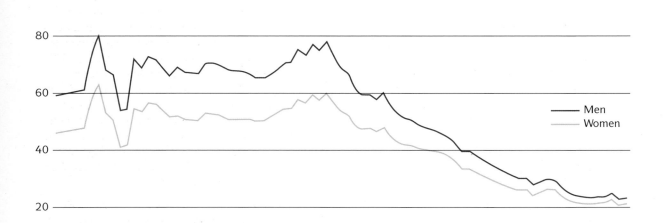

Rate: marriages per 1000 unmarried men/women aged 15 and over

Source: Office for National Statistics

Social change and changing attitudes

Brenda Almond (2006) believes that the family is fragmenting. She argues that there has been a shift away from concern with the family as a biological institution based upon the rearing of children, towards the family as an institution which emphasises 'two people's emotional need or desire for one another' (Almond, 2006, p. 107).

There is an increased emphasis on the needs of individuals and less emphasis on society's need for the rearing of children in stable relationships. In these circumstances, people are less likely to take on the commitment of marriage and more likely to stay single or cohabit instead. Almond believes that the decline of the family is damaging to society, and steps should be taken to reverse the trend.

From a different perspective, Anthony Giddens (1990) argues that in the latest phase of societal development (which he calls **late modernity**) the **pure relationship** becomes the norm. This involves partners only staying together for as long as the relationship meets their needs rather than seeing it as a lifelong commitment. Although marriages can be ended through divorce, it is easier if the partners are not married, so cohabitation or living apart together have become popular alternatives to marriage. Giddens does not see these changes as harmful, indeed he welcomes them as offering greater freedom and because they allow people to escape unsatisfactory or even abusive relationships. (There are more details of Giddens's work on pp. 251–253.)

Whatever the merits of the contrasting views of Almond and Giddens, there is strong statistical evidence that fewer people see marriage as an obligation for those who wish to form a partnership. The British Social Attitudes Survey (2013) found that between 1989 and 2012 the percentage agreeing or strongly agreeing that people who want children should get married fell from 74 per cent to 42 per cent. Similarly, by 2012 only 11 per cent thought premarital sex was 'Mostly' or 'Always' wrong compared with 27 per cent in 1983.

Secularisation

One factor closely linked to these changes in attitudes is the decline of religious beliefs (a process known as secularisation). Generally, religions are important for sanctifying marriage but religious beliefs are seen by many sociologists (for example Steve Bruce, 2011) as being in decline in the UK. Statistical evidence suggests a strong link between religion and attitudes to marriage. For example, the 2013 British Social Attitudes Survey (2013) found that only 2 per cent of those with no religion thought that pre-marital sex was wrong compared with 10 per cent of Anglicans, 11 per cent of Roman Catholics, 21 per cent of other Christians and 54 per cent of those who believed in a non-Christian religion. The same survey also noted a decline in religious belief among those from younger generations.

Gender roles and feminist perspectives on marriage rates

Elisabetta Ruspini (2015) is one of many sociologists who argues that transformations in family life, including declining rates of marriage, are closely linked to changing gender roles, particularly the changing position of women. Ruspini argues that there was a dramatic change in the position of women between the end of the Second World War and the 1960s and 70s. The wider availability of reliable contraception with the development of the pill allowed women greater control over reproduction. This reduced the likelihood of getting pregnant and therefore any need to get married to legitimise a pregnancy.

Just as importantly, political movements including the women's liberation movement of the 1960s and 70s encouraged cultural shifts which gave women a greater sense of independence. Consequently, women made greater investments in education and had 'growing aspirations for self-achievement in work … a greater involvement in working life; the possibility to decide regarding reproduction choices; and the free expression of their sexuality' (Ruspini, 2015, p. 13). Women also demanded greater equality with men. All these changes meant that many women no longer felt obliged to get married before starting a sexual relationship, or to marry before gaining educational qualifications or establishing a career. Marriage was therefore likely to be delayed until later in life with the possibility of choosing not to get married at all also becoming an option for women.

These changes are generally seen in a positive light by feminists because they offer women more choices, but from a New Right perspective they are seen negatively for undermining marriage. For example, Patricia Morgan (see p. 272) partly blames the welfare system

293

for the fall in marriage rates arguing that it makes it financially possible for women to become lone parents. She also believes welfare creates financial disincentives for mothers living on benefits to live with the father of their children.

Cohabitation

Cohabitation involves couples who are not legally married living together in a sexual relationship. Detailed statistics are not collected every year on cohabitation, but the available statistics do show a significant rise. The 2011 census showed that the number of households with one cohabiting couple rose almost 30 per cent between 2001 and 2011 from 1.8 to 2.3 million.

Two views of cohabitation

Whilst there is no doubt that cohabitation has become increasingly common, there is no agreement about the significance of this trend. Patricia Morgan (2003) sees it as part of a worrying trend in which marriage is going out of fashion and the family is in serious decline. Morgan believes that cohabitation used to be seen primarily as a prelude to marriage but increasingly it is part of a pattern which simply reflects an 'increase in sexual partners and partner change' (2003). She quotes statistics from the British Household Panel Survey showing that fewer than 4 per cent of cohabiting couples stay together for more than 10 years as cohabitants (although her own figures show that around 60 per cent get married).

A different view is taken by Joan Chandler (1993). She believes that more people are choosing to cohabit as a long-term alternative to marriage. Chandler sees this as being reflected in the increasing proportion of children born out of marriage – partners no longer feel as much pressure to marry to legitimise a pregnancy. Although more children are born to unmarried mothers, an increasing proportion of these births are jointly registered to a man and woman and most of them share the same address (suggesting they are cohabiting).

Although Chandler sees cohabitation as increasingly popular, she does point out that it is nothing new. Unofficial self-marriage (where people simply declare themselves to be married – sometimes called 'living over the brush') was very common in past centuries. She quotes research which estimates that as many

as a quarter to a third of couples lived in this sort of relationship in 18th-century Britain.

Evidence on cohabitation

Some evidence about the nature of cohabitation is provided by Eva Beaujouan and Máire Ní Bhrolcháin (2011). Using data from the General Household Survey they found the following:

❯ There is an increasing trend for people to live together before they married. In 1980–1984 only about 30 per cent did so but by 2004–2007 this had increased around 80 per cent.

❯ Cohabiting couples have tended to live together for longer. By 2004–2007 cohabiting couples who married lived together for about four years whereas in the 1980s most premarital cohabitation lasted less than two years.

❯ Many relationships based on cohabitation lead to marriage. Half of all those who started cohabiting in 1995–1999 were married 10 years later, with just under 12 per cent continuing to cohabit without being married.

This research suggests that for most, cohabitation is a long-term commitment. It is as likely to end in marriage as not, but just as within marriage, a significant proportion of relationships do not last. Beaujouan and Bhrolcháin make the point that the increase in cohabitation has been very similar to the decline in marriage. Consequently, there has been no significant reduction in the proportion of people entering partnerships of one kind (marriage) or another (cohabitation). They found that around 89–91 per cent of men and 94–96 per cent of women reaching 40 in the previous two decades had been in at least one partnership, figures as high as at any time in the 20th century (Beaujouan and Bhrolcháin 2011, p. 7).

Living Apart Together

An increasingly discussed alternative to conventional marriage is **Living Apart Together** (LAT). This involves couples who do not live together but maintain a sexual relationship and, other than the lack of co-residence, act as partners. Simon Duncan and Miranda Phillips (2009, cited in Smart, 2011) point out it is difficult to define this lifestyle and it is very similar to a couple 'going steady' while expecting to live together at some stage. Duncan and Phillips therefore distinguish between **dating LATs** who are developing their relationship prior to possible cohabitation or marriage, and **partner LATs** who see their relationship as longterm but do not anticipate living together. Smart (2011) points out that opinions are divided over whether LAT 'is a modern solution to the problem of keeping some independence in separate resources, while still having a deep and meaningful permanent relationship'—and is therefore a matter of choice—or whether it is 'a necessity arising out of contemporary conditions of working and caring' (for example, the need for couples to work in separate cities so they can keep their jobs or get promotion). To the extent that LAT is a choice rather than a necessity, it could be seen as a genuine threat to traditional families and to marriage. It could suggest that more people than in the past prioritise individual autonomy over cohabitation whether with a spouse or an unmarried partner. If it is simply a matter of necessity, it does not appear to pose a significant threat to the popularity of marriage or the stability of families.

Contemporary issues: Why people 'live apart together'

Detailed research on LATS has been carried out by Simon Duncan, Miranda Phillips and Sara Roseneil (discussed in Roseneil, 2016). In 2011– 2012 they conducted the first large-scale British study of LATs involving a representative survey of 572 LATs of whom 50 took part in semi-structured interviews. Even more detailed interviews were conducted with 16 respondents involving the development of a life history in order to examine the psycho-social reasons for their LAT relationship.

This research found that LATs were found in all social classes and were ethnically diverse but most were relatively young – 43 per cent were aged 16–24 and just 11 per cent over 55.

When giving reasons for choosing this lifestyle:

- 31 per cent said it was too early to cohabit
- 31 per cent said it was due to constraints or their situation such as lack of money or having jobs in different places
- 3 per cent were waiting to get married/civil partnered
- 1 per cent were living apart in order to maximise welfare benefits.

Overall, this research therefore found that around 3 per cent of the population of Britain actively chose to be LATs because they saw it as a desirable lifestyle. The most in-depth interviews suggested that the main reasons for this choice were:

- to avoid emotional pain or abuse
- to protect children from the potential problems of living with a new partner

- to avoid too much emotional intensity which might threaten their relationship
- to give themselves and their partner the autonomy to realise their own life goals.

The research therefore provides some support that people are becoming more individualistic, but also suggests that more traditional attitudes to family life (such as protecting children) also remain important.

Living apart together.

Questions

1. How might information technology affect LAT relationships?

2. Suggest reasons why LAT relationships

   a) are likely to become more common

   b) may not become more common.

Marital breakdown

Another possible threat to contemporary marriage and family life is the apparent rise in marital breakdowns. The usual way of estimating the number of such breakdowns is by using divorce statistics, but these statistics do not, on their own, provide a valid measure of marital breakdown.

Marital breakdown can be divided into three main categories:

1. **Divorce**, which refers to the legal termination of a marriage.

2. **Separation**, which refers to the physical separation of the spouses: they no longer share the same dwelling.

3. So-called **empty-shell marriages**, where the spouses live together, remain legally married, but their relationship has broken down and their marriage exists in name only. These three categories must be considered in any assessment of the rate of marital breakdown.

Divorce statistics

Figure 5.4.3 Divorce rates for men and women (1950–2014), England and Wales

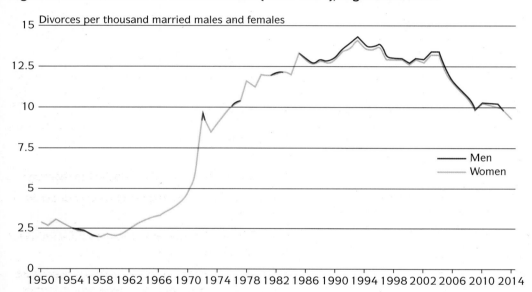

Source: Office for National Statistics

Despite minor fluctuations, there was a steady rise in divorce rates in modern industrial societies for most of the 20th century. In 1911, there just 859 petitions for divorce in England and Wales. In 1950 the **divorce rate** (the number of divorces per thousand married men and women) stood at 2.8. It peaked at 14.3 for men and 14.1 for women in 1993. It has declined somewhat since then and stood at 9.3 for both men and women in 2014 (ONS, 2016). The chances of getting divorced have increased over the last half century or so. According to the ONS, 22 per cent of those who got married in the early 1970s were divorced within 15 years of marriage, but for those married in 1995 the figure stood at 33 per cent. There is evidence of some decline in this figure in recent years (ONS, 2016).

However the figures are presented, there was a dramatic increase in divorce in the 20th century,

although there has been a consistent downward trend since 2003. Nevertheless, overall divorce rates remain at historically high levels.

The overall rise is not confined to Britain. The USA has an even higher rate than Britain, and nearly all industrial societies have experienced an increase in the divorce rate over the longterm.

Separation statistics

Reliable figures for separation of still married couples are unobtainable. In Britain, some indication is provided by data from the census, which in 2001 suggested that around 2.4 per cent of people are separated and living alone. By 2011 this had risen slightly to 2.6 per cent.

Activity

Figure 5.4.4 Number of marriages and divorces (1934–2014), England and Wales

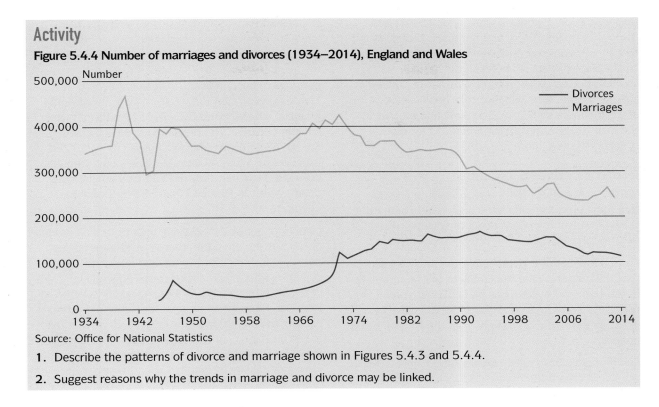

Source: Office for National Statistics

1. Describe the patterns of divorce and marriage shown in Figures 5.4.3 and 5.4.4.

2. Suggest reasons why the trends in marriage and divorce may be linked.

Empty-shell marriages

Estimates of the extent of empty-shell marriages can only be based on guesswork. Even where data exist, the concept is difficult to operationalise (that is, put into a measurable form). For example, if a couple express a high level of dissatisfaction with their relationship, should this be termed an empty-shell marriage? Historical evidence suggests that the stigma attached to divorce and separation meant that couples were more likely to stay together when their marriage had broken down than they are now.

In view of the problems involved in measuring marital breakdown, it is impossible to be completely confident about overall rates of breakdown. However, levels of divorce are now so high that it is probably true that more marriages break down today than they did several decades ago.

Explanations for marital breakdowns

In *When Marriage Ends* (1976), Nicky Hart argued that any explanation of marital breakdown must consider the following factors:

1. Those which affect the value attached to marriage.

2. Those which affect the degree of conflict between the spouses.

3. Those which affect the opportunities for individuals to escape from marriage.

We will first consider these factors from a functionalist perspective. From this viewpoint, behaviour is largely a response to shared norms and values. It therefore follows that a change in the rate of marital breakdown is to some degree a reflection of changing norms and values in general, particularly those associated with marriage and divorce.

The value of marriage

Functionalists such as Talcott Parsons and Ronald Fletcher (1966) argue that the rise in marital breakdown stems largely from the fact that marriage is increasingly valued. People expect and demand more from marriage and, consequently, are more likely to end a relationship which is not acceptable than they were in the past.

Research suggests that people do still attach a high value to marriage. From their analysis of the British

Social Attitudes Survey, Barlow *et al.* (2001) and Barlow, Burgoyne, Clery and Smithson (2008) found that most people do regard marriage as more than 'just a piece of paper'. However, they also regard cohabitation as an acceptable alternative. These surveys did not find evidence that people were attaching more significance to marriage than in the past, therefore other explanations for marital breakdown seem more plausible.

Conflict between spouses

Hart (1976) argues that the second set of factors that must be considered in an explanation of marital breakdown is those which affect the degree of conflict between the spouses.

From a functionalist perspective, it can be argued that the adaptation of the family to the requirements of the economic system has placed a strain on the marital relationship. It has led to the relative isolation of the nuclear family from the wider kinship network.

Similar points have been made by sociologists who would not regard themselves as functionalists. Graham Allan and Graham Crow (2001) believe 'marriage is less embedded within the economic system' than it used to be. Husbands and wives now usually have independent sources of income from paid employment. Since fewer people now rely as much as they used to on membership of the family to maintain their income, they are less willing to accept conflict with their spouse and more willing to contemplate divorce (Allan and Crow, 2001).

Gender, feminism and divorce

These changes particularly affect the willingness of married women to contemplate divorce. Feminism may have had some impact both by making divorce more possible because women are more financially independent and they are therefore more likely to contemplate divorce when they are unhappy with inequality within marriage. Women are more likely to instigate divorce proceedings than men, which may indicate that they are more likely to be dissatisfied with marriage than their husbands. In 2012, 65 per cent of divorces were granted to wives (Daubney, 2015). This was a dramatic change in comparison with 1946, when wives accounted for 37 per cent of petitions for divorce and husbands for 63 per cent.

However, research by Lynn Prince Cooke and Vanessa Gash (2010) using data from the British Household Panel Survey found no evidence that when women had paid employment they were more likely to get divorced. Furthermore, there was no significant relationship between the relative earnings of husbands and wives and divorce rates. This suggested that the degree to which wives had financial independence was not a significant factor affecting divorce. The researchers argued that it is now so common for married women to work, so it is no longer a major factor in determining who gets divorced. However, they did find very much higher divorce rates in families where the husband was unemployed.

Leah Ruppanner (2012) using data from the *European Social Survey* found that there was greater conflict between husbands and wives over housework in countries with a high divorce rate and with high rates of female employment. One such country was the UK. However, Ruppanner argued that rather than conflict causing the higher divorce rate, it could be that the easier availability of divorce and paid employment for women was itself the cause of the conflict. Women were more likely to complain about their partner doing too little housework if they were financially independent and divorce was more easily available.

Modernity, freedom and choice

Colin Gibson (1994) combines several arguments in claiming that the development of modernity has increased the likelihood of conflict between spouses because it encourages individualism and choice. The way modernity has developed puts increasing emphasis upon the desirability of individual achievement.

Gibson argues that people now live in an 'enterprise and free-market culture of individualism in which the licence of choice dominates'. He adds: 'A higher divorce rate may be indicative of modern couples generally anticipating a superior standard of personal marital satisfaction than was expected by their grandparents.'

People increasingly expect to get most of their personal satisfaction from their home life, and 'television programmes reinforce the feeling that togetherness is the consummate life style'. However, the emphasis on togetherness is somewhat undermined by the idea that you should pursue your own self-interest so 'conflict between spouses becomes more likely if self-fulfilment is not delivered by the marriage'.

Individualistic modernity emphasises consumer choice, and, if fulfilment is not forthcoming through your first choice of marriage partner, then you are more likely to leave and try an alternative in the hope of greater satisfaction. You will simply shop around for a better option. Women have greater independence than in the past so they feel able to leave a marriage which does not live up to their expectations. (For a general discussion of the relationship between modernity and changes in the family, see pp. 251–257)

While plausible, this approach is not backed up by specific empirical research and as such it is hard to evaluate. However, it does broadly fit with research which suggests that divorce might be connected to factors such as women's dissatisfaction with their husbands' contribution to family life.

The ease of divorce

So far, we have considered the factors which affect the value attached to marriage and those which affect the degree of conflict between spouses. The third set of factors that Hart considers essential to an explanation of marital breakdown are those which affect the opportunities for individuals to escape from marriage. This could be related to the stigma attached to divorce, financial considerations and legal factors.

The stigma of divorce

There is substantial evidence that any stigma attached to divorce is declining.

A 2013 survey by YouGov (National Family Mediation, 2013) found that almost two-thirds of people thought there was no longer stigma attached to divorce with just one in 25 strongly agreeing that divorce was socially taboo. 18–24 year olds were less likely to say that divorce was taboo than 25–54 year olds, indicating a liberalisation of attitudes in younger cohorts.

Colin Gibson (1994) believes secularisation (the decline of religion) has weakened the degree to which religious beliefs can bind a couple together and thereby strengthen marriage. He also argues that there has been a decline in any set of shared values that might operate to stabilise marriage. Society is too pluralistic in terms of gender, class, ethnicity, age and religion to sustain a common culture which guides people's morals. In the absence of any central, shared beliefs in society, there is little or no stigma attached to divorce.

Divorce legislation

The changing attitudes towards divorce have been institutionalised by various changes in the law which have made it much easier to obtain a divorce.

In Britain before 1857 a private Act of Parliament was required to obtain a divorce. This was an expensive procedure beyond the means of all but the most wealthy. Since 1857 the costs of obtaining a divorce have been reduced and the grounds for divorce have been widened.

Divorce legislation was influenced by the idea of **matrimonial offence**, the notion that one or both spouses had wronged the other. However, The Divorce Reform Act, which came into force in 1971, no longer emphasised the idea of matrimonial offence and so avoided the need for 'guilty parties'. It defined the grounds for divorce as 'the irretrievable breakdown of the marriage'. This made divorce considerably easier and accounts in part for the dramatic rise in the number of divorces in 1971 (see Figure 5.4.4).

New legislation relating to divorce was introduced at the end of 1984. This reduced the period a couple needed to be married before they could petition for divorce from three years to one year.

The Family Law Act of 1996 introduced several new measures. It no longer had to be demonstrated that the marriage had broken down. Instead, the partners simply had to assert the marriage had broken down and then had to undergo a 'period of reflection' to consider whether a reconciliation was possible.

Despite a reduction in costs, divorce was still an expensive process during the first half of the 20th century. It was beyond the means of many of the less wealthy. This was partly changed by the legal aid and Advice Act of 1949, which provided free legal advice and paid solicitors' fees for those who could not afford them. However, legislation which passed through parliament in 2012 led to an end to legal aid in divorce cases except for those claiming to be victims of domestic violence.

The economics of divorce were further eased by the extension of welfare provisions, particularly for lone parents with dependent children. The Child Support, Pensions and Social Security Act of 2000 (which was implemented in 2002) provided for absent parents to contribute a fixed proportion of their take-home pay towards maintenance costs. This varied from 15 per cent for one child to 25 per cent for three children. Although many consider these provisions far from generous, they do help to provide lone-parent families with the means to exist.

The long-established principle of 'spousal maintenance' sometimes also makes divorce more affordable. Courts can instruct the divorcing spouse in the stronger financial position to support their ex-partner for life or for a fixed period of time (although it ends on remarriage). This can be particularly beneficial to divorcing wives or husbands who gave up career opportunities to allow them to raise children.

The normalisation of divorce?

Carol Smart (2011) makes several useful points in reaching conclusions about divorce and marital breakdown. Smart attributes the rises in divorce to a combination of changes in divorce legislation, greater economic independence for women, and divorce becoming less stigmatised. However, she points out that the divorce rate has stopped rising. She therefore argues that 'The fear that rising rates of divorce might bring about the end of family life now seem unfounded, and as both divorce and separation have become much more commonplace there is growing evidence that family life can adapt to these changes without disintegrating. This means that whereas divorce was once interpreted as a worrying social problem, sociologists are now more inclined to understand it is one transition amongst others that occur during the life-course. In this sense, divorce and separation have become "normalised"' (Smart, 2011, p. 44).

That is not to say that divorce does not create problems for those involved, whether as parents or children. She suggests that there is a particularly strong financial impact on women and statistically men are more likely to remarry. Divorce can create difficulties for children who may no longer have day-to-day contact with both parents. However, she finds reasons for optimism because of 'evidence that

couples are beginning to construct post-divorce family life according to more collaborative principles which are giving rise to new patterns of parenting across households' (Smart, 2011, p. 45). It has become more common, for example, for both parents to continue to share responsibility for children after divorce and for grandparents to retain their close involvement as well. From Smart's point of view, the growth of marital breakdown has increased instability and fluidity in families but it has not destroyed them or prevented bonds between different generations remaining strong.

How much has marriage declined?

While there is clear evidence that marriage rates have declined and that it tends to take place at a later age than in the past, its decline should not be exaggerated. There are several reasons for this:

1. Remarriage rates are relatively high.

2. There is considerable ethnic diversity in the UK and patterns of marriage vary between ethnic groups.

3. Some sociologists argue that marriage is still highly valued and most people do aspire to get married at some point in their lives.

Recent figures, though, show further increases in the proportion who have never married. Data produced by Eva Beaujouan and Máire Ní Bhrolcháin (2011) showed that in 2004–2007 only 75.9 per cent of men and 84.2 per cent of women had married by the age of 40. This was significantly less than in 1990–1994 when 87.3 per cent of men and 93.7 per cent of women had married. Nevertheless, with the rise of cohabitation, civil partnerships, same-sex and living apart together, forming partnerships still remains popular in Britain. Heterosexual marriage is not quite as popular as it once was, but the desire to have a partner still has a strong appeal.

Activity

Divorce and children.

Would you agree with Smart that divorce has become 'normalised'? Give reasons for your answer.

Key terms

Dating LATs A couple who are living apart together and who are developing their relationship prior to possible cohabitation.

Divorce The legal ending of marriage.

Divorce rate The number of divorces per thousand married couples.

Empty-shell marriage A marriage in which the relationship between the spouses has broken down.

Late modernity According to Giddens, the most recent phase of modernity.

Marriage and partner LATs A couple who are living apart together, and who see their relationship as long-term but do not anticipate cohabiting.

Marital breakdown The ending of a meaningful relationship between a married couple.

Matrimonial offence In divorce, the idea that a spouse has acted in such a way that their partner is entitled to seek a divorce.

Pure relationship According to Giddens, a relationship in which people stay together only as long as they gain personal satisfaction from the relationship.

Separation Married couples living apart because their relationship has broken down.

Summary

1. Partnerships can take many different forms including heterosexual marriage, living apart together and same-sex partnerships.

2. Marriage rates have been declining over recent decades and the average age at marriage has been going up.

3. Some commentators see the decline of marriage as a crisis for the family as an institution, although Giddens sees it as a welcome indication of the development of greater freedom in pure relationships.

4. Secularisation and changing gender roles have also been seen as important in explaining the decreasing frequency of marriage.

5. Cohabitation has grown in recent decades but sociologists do not agree over the extent to which couples who cohabit are committed to their relationship.

6. Living apart together (LAT) is an alternative to cohabitation or marriage.

7. Many couples live apart together for practical reasons but some prefer the arrangement to living together as a way of retaining greater independence.

8. Marriages can break down through divorce, separation or empty-shell marriages.

9. Divorce statistics show a long-term rise but the trend has been downwards in most recent decades.

10. There is little evidence that divorce has increased because couples attach more importance to marriage. Increased conflict between spouses, the greater independence of wives and the influence of feminism may all play a part in a high divorce rate.

11. Gibson attributes high divorce to increased freedom and choice in modern societies.

12. A major explanation for divorce increases is the relaxation of divorce legislation and measures which make divorce more affordable. Carol Smart believes that divorce has increased instability in families but it does not threaten the future of marriage and family life and strong relationships between family members can survive divorce.

13. The decline of marriage should not be exaggerated because most people still value marriage, remarriage rates are high and some minority ethnic groups have strong commitment to marriage.

14. Nevertheless, there is clear evidence that with successive generations, fewer people in Britain are getting married.

PART 5 GENDER ROLES, DOMESTIC LABOUR AND POWER RELATIONSHIPS WITHIN THE FAMILY

Contents

This part of the chapter is concerned with relationships between adult partners and particularly with inequality between men and women. Some of the earliest functionalist writers on this issue assumed that differences between men and women were natural and even beneficial for society. This was increasingly questioned by feminists who rejected this functionalist view entirely and instead saw differences and inequalities between men and women in relationships as the product of **patriarchy**. Feminists started producing detailed research which questioned traditional views of gender roles in families and households in the 1970s. Gradually the questions they addressed were broadened to encompass many different aspects of inequality within relationships ranging from who did particular household tasks, to issues relating to power, money management and the use of violence. This part therefore asks questions such as: How have gender roles changed? Are men and women really equal now? Are fathers now as emotionally involved with their children as mothers? What factors affect inequality within heterosexual relationships? What causes domestic violence?

5.5.1 Classic perspectives on conjugal roles

The first unit defines conjugal roles and examines some of the research which initially framed sociological debates about relationships between men and women in families.

The term 'conjugal roles' refers to relationships between male and female partners in intimate relationships.

Conjugal roles can roughly be divided into two types:

> **Joint conjugal roles** are conjugal roles where the partners share responsibility for domestic tasks and both do paid employment. Joint conjugal roles are generally characterised by relative equality and it may lead to a strong bond between the partners. If a couple are married this is termed the **conjugal bond**. Joint conjugal roles may also be connected to the sharing of leisure time.

> **Segregated conjugal roles** occur when husbands and wives tend to have different roles within their marriage, for example with one doing most of the housework and childcare and the other concentrating on paid employment.

The assumption has often been made that there has been a long-term shift from segregated to joint conjugal roles and there is some evidence to support this. Furthermore, the Shared Parental Leave regulations introduced in 2014 made joint conjugal roles easier to achieve by allowing parental leave after the birth of a child to be shared between the mother and the father. However, the evidence also suggests that the picture is much more complicated than this, partly because there are many different aspects of conjugal roles.

Talcott Parsons — biology and the 'expressive' female

Talcott Parsons (1955) saw the isolated nuclear family as the family type which was typical of modern industrial societies. This family type specialised in two basic functions:

1. The **socialisation** of the young

2. The **stabilisation of adult personalities** (see p. 234)

According to Parsons, for socialisation to be effective, a close, warm and supportive group was essential. The family met this requirement and, within the family, the woman was primarily responsible for socialising the young. Parsons believed that women should take on this role because women's biology meant that they gave birth to and breastfed children and they were therefore naturally better at caring for children. Parsons characterised the woman's role in the family as **expressive**, which meant she provided warmth, security and emotional support. This was essential for the effective socialisation of the young.

It was only a short step from applying these expressive qualities to her children to applying them also to her husband. This was her major contribution to the second function of the isolated nuclear family: the stabilisation of adult personalities. The male breadwinner spent his working day competing in an achievement-oriented society. This **instrumental** role led to stress and anxiety. The expressive female relieved this tension by providing the weary breadwinner with love, consideration and understanding.

Parsons argued that there had to be a clear-cut division of labour by gender for the family to operate efficiently as a social system, and that the instrumental and expressive roles complemented each other and promoted family solidarity.

Conjugal roles as a social construct

Parsons' views have, unsurprisingly, been heavily criticised by feminists (and others) who see gender roles as a **social construction**. A social construction is a feature of society that most people take to be natural but which has actually been produced through social processes. For example, Jacqui Gabb (2008) argues that you learn to be a mother. The role of a mother is not biological – it does not come naturally – it is the product of the culture of a particular society. As Gabb puts it, motherhood is something a person 'does' rather than something a person 'is'. Women are taught how to be a 'good mother' by their own

mothers, other women, the media and elsewhere. For example, TV programmes such as *Supernanny* (in which a nanny was brought in to help parents control children who misbehaved) encourage feelings of guilt for women who are not 'good mothers'. Women learn what is expected of them and there are strong social pressures to conform to these expectations.

Based on interview research she conducted with young mothers and their male partners, Gabb noted how many women experienced the emotional aspects of motherhood and their commitment to their children as 'natural'. However, not all women experienced it in this way and many men also experienced a sense of loss at their lack of closeness to their children in their early years. But it is generally mothers who carry out or enact most of the care for young children and, in the process, they become mothers. Repetition of the tasks and the emotional responses expected changes them so that they take on, or are 'made up' as mothers. Following the work of Arlie Hoschild (2003 cited in Gabb, 2008) Gabb believes that there are certain **feeling rules** that mothers learn to follow. That is, there are informal rules in society about what you *should* feel in different circumstances and most people learn to conform to these rules. Their experience of the feelings is real, but they only have those feelings because it is expected of them. One feeling rule is that you should love your children. This is expected of both mothers and fathers but they are expected to express this love in different ways.

For example, interviewees in Gabb's study saw it as normal for there to be close physical contact between mothers and their young children, whereas this was regarded as potentially problematic for fathers. There were different attitudes among some participants about whether it was appropriate for men to have a bath with their children with some expressing concerns about possible sexual abuse. As men learn to keep their distance from children to avoid any possibility of being suspected of abuse, and women learn that close physical contact is expected as an expression of love, men and women are made up differently and start to adopt different parental roles.

Contemporary issues: Learning to be mothers

Supernanny is not just a TV show which ran for six seasons but also a website and an app for mobile phones so parents can have 'expert' advice wherever they go. *Supernanny* is a source of a very wide range of advice. For example, the TV programmes covered issues such as how to stop children hitting,

swearing and spitting, being overprotective of children as parents so you find it difficult to leave the house, dealing with tantrums at mealtimes and bedtimes and getting children to have a healthy relationship with food. The *Supernanny* website (https://www.supernanny.co.uk/) offers many recipes for 'healthy' meals and advice on discipling children without using smacking. The app includes a 'naughty step timer', illustrative YouTube clips and hundreds of articles on good parenting.

Supernanny.

Questions

Using the information in this Contemporary issues box and the *Supernanny* website, answer the following questions.

1. How do various types of media associated with *Supernanny* act to socialise parents into particular styles of parenting?

2. What kind of parenting is *Supernanny* encouraging?

3. What kind of 'feeling rules' might *Supernanny* be encouraging?

4. Explain how the example of *Supernanny* can be used to support the view that the feelings associated with motherhood are socially constructed rather than natural.

Young and Willmott – the symmetrical family and conjugal roles

Husbands and wives in the symmetrical family

If Gabb is correct, conjugal roles in terms of childcare are not natural but are shaped by societal expectations and will change over time. The same argument can be applied to other aspects of conjugal roles including housework. Based upon survey research in London, in the early 1970s Young and Willmott (1973) claimed that the **symmetrical family** was developing in Britain (see p. 239 for more details). The symmetrical family was defined as a nuclear family in which the roles of husband and wife (conjugal roles) were becoming increasingly similar and more equal. Young and Willmott believed that spouses – wives and husbands – were increasingly sharing domestic tasks and leisure activities and both were contributing to household income.

Although the wife still had primary responsibility for housework and child rearing, husbands became more involved, often washing clothes, ironing and sharing other domestic duties. In 72 per cent of family households studied by Young and Willmott in London in the 1970s, men contributed to the housework. Furthermore, husband and wife increasingly shared responsibility for decisions that affected the family. They discussed matters such as household finances and their children's education to a greater degree than in the past.

Reasons for the rise of the symmetrical family

Young and Willmott argued that the symmetrical family developed for several reasons:

1. Increased employment opportunities for women made it more likely that women would become breadwinners alongside their husbands.

2. Increasing geographical mobility has tended to sever kinship ties with other family members and strengthen the bond between husbands and wives.

3. The reduction in the number of children provided greater opportunities for wives to work.

4. With two earners, in **dual earner families** living standards rose and the husband was drawn more closely into the family circle, since the home was a more attractive place with better amenities and a greater range of home entertainments.

Evaluation of Young and Willmott

Young and Willmott's views on the symmetrical family have been heavily criticised. Ann Oakley (1974) argues that their claim of increasing symmetry within marriage is based on inadequate research.

Although their figure of 72 per cent (for men doing housework) sounds impressive, she points out that it is based on only one question in Young and Willmott's interview schedule:

Do you/does your husband help at least once a week with any household jobs like washing up, making beds (helping with the children), ironing, cooking or cleaning?

Oakley notes that men who make only a very small contribution to housework would be included in the 72 per cent She says:

A man who helps with the children once a week would be included in this percentage, so would (presumably) a man who ironed his own trousers on a Saturday afternoon.

Housework and childcare — a feminist view

A rather different picture of conjugal roles emerged in Oakley's own research (1974). She collected information on 40 married women who had one child or more under the age of five, who were British or Irish born, and aged between 20 and 30. Half of her sample were working class, half were middle class, and all lived in the London area.

She found greater equality in terms of the allocation of domestic tasks between spouses in the middle class than in the working class. However, in both classes few men had high levels of participation in housework and childcare: few marriages could be defined as egalitarian. In only 15 per cent of marriages did men have high levels of participation in housework; for childcare, the figure was 30 per cent.

Since these pioneering pieces of research, more sophisticated methods have been developed for examining the domestic division of labour and other aspects of inequality. These will be discussed in the next unit.

Key terms

Conjugal bond The relationship between husband and wife or other intimate partners.

Joint conjugal roles Conjugal roles where the partners share responsibility for domestic tasks and both do paid employment.

Segregated conjugal roles Conjugal roles when partners tend to have different roles within their marriage, for example with one doing most of the housework and childcare and the other concentrating on paid employment.

Socialisation The process through which a person learns the culture of their society.

Stabilisation of adult personalities To Parsons, the role of the family in maintaining the psychological health of adults by providing warmth and security and allowing them to act out childish elements in their personality.

Expressive role A family role in which caring and emotion are important.

Instrumental role A family role in which achieving particular objectives is important.

Expressive role A family role in which caring and emotion are important.

Social construction A feature of society that most people take to be natural but which has actually been produced through social processes.

Feeling rules Informal rules (norms) in society about what you should feel in different circumstances.

Symmetrical family A family in which both husband and wife do paid employment and both do some housework and provide childcare.

Dual earner family A family in which both partners do paid employment.

Summary

1. Conjugal roles are the roles of partners in intimate relationships.

2. Joint conjugal roles are more equal than segregated roles.

3. Parsons believes that segregated roles are natural and are functional for society in the nuclear family of modern industrial society.

4. Social constructionists argue that conjugal roles are learned rather than natural.

5. Young and Willmott found that by the 1970s in Britain there had been a move towards more joint conjugal roles in the symmetrical family.

6. Ann Oakley found little evidence for more joint roles in her 1980s feminist research into housework.

5.5.2 The domestic division of labour

As discussed above, the earliest research on inequality in the home between partners focused on the tasks carried out by men and women and the way these are divided up. The organisation of tasks such as housework and childcare is known as the **domestic division of labour**. Young and Willmott and Ann Oakley used very simple and quite crude methods to measure the domestic division of labour and they also used unrepresentative and in Oakley's case quite small samples. As time has gone on, more representative samples have been used in most studies and ways of measuring the domestic division of labour have become more varied and more sophisticated. Running a home and raising a family require people to do a very large range of complex tasks but they also require a great deal of thought and emotional investment.

It has been widely assumed that the household division of labour has become somewhat fairer and less unequal since the very early research by Young and Willmott and Ann Oakley. This unit examines whether this assumption is true once the complexities of the domestic division of labour are taken fully into account.

Survey research on household tasks

Survey data have produce useful findings which make it possible to make simple comparisons about conjugal roles over time. The British Social Attitudes Survey (2013) used a nationally representative sample to look at trends in the domestic division of labour. These are shown in Table 5.5.1. The table demonstrates that there has been a gradual but significant move towards men doing a greater share of household tasks although considerable inequalities remain.

Table 5.5.1 Household tasks undertaken by men and women, 1994–2012[2]

Individual reported as always/usually undertaking task	1994	2002	2006	2012
Does the laundry	%	%	%	%
Always/usually man	1	6	5	6
Both equally	18	15	17	20
Always/usually woman	79	78	74	70
Makes small repairs around the house	%	%	%	%
Always/usually man	75	71	73	75
Both equally	18	17	14	10
Always/usually woman	5	7	8	7
Cares for sick family members	%	%	%	%
Always/usually man	1	3	3	5
Both equally	45	36	44	38
Always/usually woman	48	48	43	36
Shops for groceries	%	%	%	%
Always/usually man	6	8	8	10
Both equally	52	45	47	43
Always/usually woman	41	45	41	44
Does the household cleaning	%	%	%	%
Always/usually man	n/a	5	6	8
Both equally	n/a	29	30	29
Always/usually woman	n/a	59	58	56
Prepares the meals	%	%	%	%
Always/usually man	n/a	11	11	16
Both equally	n/a	29	27	27
Always/usually woman	n/a	58	58	55

The percentages in the table do not add up to 100 per cent because it does not show the very few responses that say they can't choose or the task is done by someone else.
n/a = not asked

Source: British Social Attitudes (2013) 'Attitudes have changed but have behaviours'? [online]

In 2012 in a majority of households within the sample, *laundry*, *preparing meals* and doing the *household cleaning* was usually or always done by women. In three quarters of households, *small repairs around the home* was usually or always done by men. Only in a small minority of households were men mainly or always responsible for *caring for sick family members* or *preparing the main meal of the day*. Nevertheless, in all areas of domestic work apart from making small repairs, there was a shift towards men taking on more tasks.

If you take a longer time frame, the changes have been more significant. Crompton and Lyonette (2008) used data from the British Attitudes Survey and other sources and found that found that there was a significant shift towards men doing a greater share of housework between the 1960s and 1990s. Since the 1990s though, men's contribution has not increased to any great extent.

The changes should not therefore be exaggerated but this evidence makes it clear that simply in terms of the division of labour, British households come nowhere near to gender equality. However, simply measuring who does what is not the only way to determine how unfair and unequal domestic life is. As we shall see shortly, time-use is also important.

Time and gender roles

Another way to study gender roles is to examine time spent on different tasks.

Research conducted for Oxfam by OnePoll (Oxfam, 2016) based on a sample of 2000 people living with partners found that on average women in a partnership spent 31 per cent more time caring for children and 28 per cent more time doing housework than men. Women spent more time on every type of task than men apart from putting out the bins and DIY. Women spent no less than 54 per cent more time doing laundry than men. As a result, women have less time to do other things. On average, women spend the equivalent of about two working days per month more

than men on housework, meaning they can devote less time to personal leisure and/or earning money and pursuing a career.

The Office for National Statistics (2016) also produces data on unpaid household work. Their time-use survey found even bigger disparities in male and female contributions than OnePoll. According to the ONS, in 2015 men did an average of 16 hours per week of unpaid work whereas women did an average of 26 hours. In other words, women did an extra working day of unpaid work every week. The difference between the surveys is partly explained by the broader scope of the ONS survey which included travel to work, care of adult family members and providing transport for family members (i.e. giving lifts). It also includes all adult men and women, not just those in partnerships. Men did spend more time giving lifts than women but this was the only type of unpaid work they devoted more time to. Although some of the respondents were not in a relationship, most were and the figures provide a useful indication of gender roles in society as a whole.

Taking typical pay levels for different types of work, the ONS calculated that if people were given a wage for their unpaid work then men would earn an extra £259 per week and women £166. This perhaps helps to explain why women have lower earnings than men despite sex discrimination and equal pay legislation being introduced more than 40 years ago in the 1970s.

Table 5.5.2 Average hours of unpaid work done per week in each category for men and women, UK, 2015

	Female	Male
Cooking	7.28	3.65
Transport	5.85	7.21
Childcare	4.67	1.89
Housework	4.66	2.42
Laundry	2.4	0.39
Volunteering	0.36	0.2
Adult care	0.32	0.23

Source: ONS (2016) 'Women shoulder the responsibility of unpaid work' [online].

Factors influencing the domestic division of labour

Rosemary Crompton and Clare Lyonette (Crompton and Lyonette, 2008) have examined a variety of research on the domestic division of labour and have considered explanations for the continuing inequality which means that women continue to do most domestic tasks. They identify two main theories:

1. **Economistic or material theories** take the view that it may be rational for women to do a greater share of the housework if men earn more and total family income is increased if they devote more time to paid employment than women.

2. An alternative theory, which they call the **normative** or **gender construction theory**, which suggests that the division of household labour is not rational at all but is shaped by dominant ideas about gender roles. From this point of view, women will tend to do more housework because that is what society expects of women regardless of who has the higher rate of pay.

Economistic/materialistic theories seem to be supported by the continuing inequalities in the wages earned by men and women.

According to the ONS Annual Survey of Hours and Earnings (2016) there is a significant difference between the earnings of men and women. The **gender pay gap** is the difference in average hourly earnings of men and women as a percentage of the average earnings of male workers. In 2016 the gender pay gap was 9.4 per cent, the lowest since the data started being produced in 1997. However, for part-time work, women earned more than men, with a gender pay gap in favour of women of some 6 per cent. In terms of material self-interest, it therefore makes sense for the man to work full-time and the woman in a relationship to work part-time if, for example, one of the partners wanted to devote time to childcare.

Further evidence to support this view can be found in research by Man-Yee Kan and Heather Laurie (2016) using data from the UK Household Longitudinal Study, a government survey. Kan and Laurie found that inequality in gender roles was reduced when women were employed and when women had a degree (which was likely to increase their earnings relative to their male partner). Furthermore, Crompton and Lyonette (2008) also found evidence that material factors were important. They found that women who had full-time paid employment and who had high wage rates did

tend to do a lower proportion of domestic tasks than other women, as would be predicted by economistic or material theories.

Gender construction theory is supported by a range of evidence and arguments. The data analysed by Kan and Laurie (2016) found that there was a statistical link between attitudes to gender and gender inequality in domestic labour. The more traditional the attitude of men was towards gender roles, the lower the proportion of housework they tended to do. Furthermore, the research found that women who had traditional attitudes towards gender roles tended to do a higher proportion of the housework than was typical. The research also suggested that gender inequality was influenced by cultural differences between ethnic groups. Across all ethnic groups in their data, women did about 70 per cent of housework, but it was higher than this in Pakistani couples (women did about 83 per cent of the housework) and lower among couple of mixed ethnicity (where women did approximately 65 per cent of the housework).

Activity

Conjugal role reversal?

1. What is your reaction to the photograph above?

2. What does your reaction suggest about the importance of normative factors in shaping conjugal roles?

This research therefore suggests that both types of factor play a role in explaining continuing inequality in the domestic division of labour. Crompton and Lyonette (2008) also found evidence to support gender construction theory. More egalitarian gender roles within the home were found amongst lower age groups, the better educated, those from higher social classes and those who had expressed less traditional views about who should do the housework. Furthermore, even when taking into account factors such as the amount of paid work done by each partner and the rates of pay, there was still a significant normative effect whereby women continued to do a higher proportion of domestic tasks than was rational (or, for that matter, fair). They conclude that, 'in aggregate, women remain normatively associated with domestic work and caring' (p. 74) and this was continuing to restrict the choices that women were making about how much they should work.

Key terms

Domestic division of labour The way that tasks are divided up between members of a household.

Economistic/material theories Theories which explain the domestic division of labour in terms of the financial interests of the household.

Normative/gender construction theory Theories which explain the domestic division of labour in terms of socially constructed gender roles.

Gender pay gap The difference in average hourly earnings of men and women as a percentage of the average earnings of male workers.

Summary

1. Survey research into household tasks shows that men have increased the range and frequency of household tasks they do but women still do the bulk of these tasks.

2. Gender differences remain in terms of which household tasks men and women tend to do.

3. Women continue to spend more time on household tasks than men and have less personal leisure time.

4. Evidence suggests that both economic factors and norms about gender roles play a part in causing the gender differences in the domestic division of labour.

5.5.3 Childcare and emotion work

There is much more to domestic life than simply carrying out household tasks such as ironing and putting the bins out. Caring for others (both physically and emotionally) is also very important. This isn't normally thought of as work in a family context but what if you do think of it that way? Who does this work and how demanding is it?

Childcare

Looking after children can be physically and emotionally demanding. In the past, women generally took more responsibility for childcare, but is this still the case today?

Mary Boulton – responsibility for children

Mary Boulton (1983) argues that studies which focus upon the allocation of tasks in the home exaggerate the extent of men's involvement in childcare, and she denies that questions about who does what give a true picture of conjugal roles. To her, childcare:

> *is essentially about exercising responsibility for another person who is not fully responsible for herself and it entails seeing to all aspects of the child's security and well-being, her growth and development at any and all times.* Boulton, 1983

Boulton claims that, although men might help with particular tasks, it is their wives who retain primary responsibility for children. It is the wives who relegate non-domestic aspects of their lives to a low priority.

The Millennium Cohort Study

Some empirical support for Boulton is provided by The Millennium Cohort Study (Dex and Ward, 2007) a longitudinal study based upon detailed quantitative research on a sample of babies born in 2000 and 2001. Over 28 000 parents were questioned when the baby was 9–10 months old and over 23 000 when the child was three. It found that when a three-year-old child was ill, 69.6 per cent of mothers said that they did most of the childcare whereas in only 1.1 per cent of cases did their partner take main responsibility. In 28.6 per cent of cases the responsibility was shared.

Activity

A mother caring for a sick child.

1. In your experience, are mothers still more likely to look after sick children than fathers?

2. List all the factors that might influence which parent takes responsibility for a child when they are ill.

3. Which, if any, of the factors you have identified can be linked to the feminist concept of 'patriarchy'? How are they linked?

Furthermore, the 2005 *Time Use Survey* (Lader *et al.*, 2006) found that on average women spent more than twice as much time on childcare as men.

Fathers and childcare

Annette Braun, Carol Vincent and Stephen J. Ball (2011) point out that many surveys suggest men think they should be more involved in childcare and quantitative research in a variety of surveys does suggest that fathers are doing more than in previous generations. However, their own research suggests that men's involvement is still limited and the research also suggests reasons for this.

Braun, Vincent and Ball did an in-depth study on working-class fathers from London with pre-school children using interviews with 70 families including 16 interviews with individual men. They also discuss evidence from an earlier study of middle-class fathers in the same areas of London (Vincent and Ball, 2006, cited in Braun, Vincent and Ball, 2011).

Half of these 16 working-class fathers were classified as 'active fathers' who were *highly involved fathers* although four of these still displayed a tendency to refer to the mothers for 'instruction and reassurance' (Braun, Vincent and Ball, 2011, p. 24). The others were classified as *background fathers* who did not

spend much time with the children and saw the mother as primarily responsible for them. In the case of four of the active fathers, their partner was the main breadwinner and these fathers tended to feel that ideally *they* as the man of the house should be the main earner. Indeed, throughout the sample there was a strong **provider ideology** linking the breadwinner role with masculine identities.

There was only one father in the sample who had made any change in their work to spend more time looking after children. For most of the other fathers in the two research projects, childcare was largely seen in terms of their relationship with their partner. Contributing to childcare was a way of helping their partner rather than something that was primarily their responsibility to their children. Most saw financial provision as an important part of their role as fathers while spending time with children was not given the same importance as it was by mothers.

Many of the men also discussed how uncomfortable they felt looking after their child or children in public places when their partner was not present. Active fathers were 'very aware and self-conscious of "moral-panics" linking lone men and children to paedophilia' (Braun, Vincent and Ball, 2011, p. 29). Many of them avoided taking their children to organised activities (such as play groups) where they felt out of place and isolated.

Conjugal roles and emotion work

Drawing on the work of various sociologists, Jean Duncombe and Dennis Marsden (1995) argue that some forms of domestic work cannot be measured in conventional surveys. In particular, alongside such tasks as housework and childcare, members of households also carry out **emotion work** (a term first used by Arlie Hochschild (1983) to describe the sort of work done by female airline cabin crew when trying to keep passengers happy).

Duncombe and Marsden examine the implication of this idea for relationships between heterosexual partners.

Their research was based on interviews with 40 White couples who had been married for 15 years. They asked the couples, separately and together, how their marriage had survived for so long in an age of high divorce rates. They found that many women expressed dissatisfaction with their partner's emotional input into the relationship and the family.

Many of the women felt emotionally lonely. Several of the men concentrated on their paid employment, were unwilling to express feelings of love for their partner, and were reluctant to discuss their feelings more generally. Most of the men did not believe there was a problem. They did not acknowledge that emotion work needed to be done to make the relationship work. Duncombe and Marsden found that many of the women in the study were holding the relationship together by doing the crucial emotion work.

As the relationship goes on they may start pretending to their partners and others that the relationship is satisfactory and they are happy with it. They 'live the family myth' or 'play the couple game' to maintain the illusion of a happy family. This places a considerable emotional strain on the woman, but it is the price to pay for keeping the family together.

Women's greater participation in emotion work can be 'a major dimension of gender inequality in couple relationships'. With married women increasingly having paid employment, they can end up performing a **triple shift**. Having completed their paid employment, they not only have to come home and do most of the housework, they also have to do most of the emotion work as well.

Activity

The triple shift and emotion work.

1. Suggest how the mother in this photograph might be engaging in one part of the 'triple shift'.

2. What different kinds of emotion work might a mother and wife such as the one in this photograph carry out in preparing, serving and eating a family dinner?

Contemporary issues: New fatherhood and falling back into gender

Many sociologists and other commentators have argued that there is a trend towards *new fatherhood*. According to Tina Miller (2011) the new father is viewed as someone who does not conform to traditional masculine roles in parenting. Rather than **doing gender** in a conventional way, new fathers act in ways which involve **undoing gender** by engaging in parenting practices which challenge and change traditional ideas about masculinity, femininity and parenting.

Miller set out to test whether new fathers were a reality by conducting unstructured interviews with 17 men who were becoming fathers for the first time. All the participants had full-time jobs, most were in middle-class employment and all the mothers worked as well.

Miller found that the men wanted to be 'hands-on' and to be emotionally close to their children. They expressed a desire to share all aspects of caring for their children (with the exception of breastfeeding). They wanted to be 'good fathers' and many said that they wanted to be much more

involved with their child than their own fathers had been with them.

However, Miller noted that they always expressed their desire for involvement in terms of supporting their partners and they assumed that they would have a 'supportive' role rather than the primary caring role. In their early fathering experiences, particularly during the paternity leave of two weeks or more which all the men took, there was a 'real sense of learning and sharing'. However, this was short-lived and once the man returned to paid work many felt that they 'became out of touch' with the needs of the child, and they felt unable to continue such an intense sharing of responsibility with their partner. Over time, both the fathers and the mothers ended up **falling back into gender**, that is, resuming relatively traditional gender roles.

Miller believes that dominant forms of masculinity (hegemonic masculinity) continue to make it very difficult for men to become equal partners as parents with mothers and to undo gender roles. This

311

is because cultural norms about gender encourage men to value their role as breadwinners. However, other factors such as the limited paternity leave and higher wages for men also push men back towards traditional masculine roles. Therefore, despite some changes in parenting, 'for the most part it remains the mother who is left holding the baby'.

Questions

1. Suggest reasons why mothers are more likely to go to playgroups than fathers.

2. Drawing on your own knowledge, suggest why it can be easy to 'fall back into gender' once a couple become parents.

New fatherhood.

Key terms

Provider ideology The belief that it is right that men should be the main income earner for families.

Emotion work The work involved in trying to influence the emotions of other people.

Triple shift The three types of work that women are required to do – paid employment, housework and emotion work.

Doing gender Acting in ways which follow traditional socially constructed expectations of the behaviour of men and women and thereby reinforce those expectations.

Undoing gender Acting in ways which do not follow traditional socially constructed expectations of the behaviour of men and women and thereby undermine those expectations.

Falling back into gender Reverting back to following traditional socially constructed expectations of the behaviour of men and women after becoming a parent.

Summary

1. Mary Boulton argues that gender inequality in relation to childcare is more about who has responsibility for children than who does most tasks.

2. Survey research suggests mothers are more likely than fathers to look after children who are ill.

3. Research by Braun *et al.* suggests that in most families fathers are seen as helping mothers with childcare and a strong provider ideology for men remains.

4. Duncombe and Marsden believe many women do a triple-shift involving emotion work as well as housework and paid work.

5. Tina Miller's research suggests that despite the best intentions of couples to share parenting and other domestic responsibilities, they tend to 'fall back into gender' after their first child is born.

5.5.4 Power and money

Another approach to studying conjugal roles is to examine power within heterosexual relationships. This has usually been attempted through an examination of who makes the decisions. Power is often closely linked to control over financial resources which in turn is linked to different systems for managing household resources. In studying power and money, sociologists have asked who really gets their own way in relationships and who gets most opportunity to spend money on what they want.

Power

A study by Irene Hardill, Anne Green, Anna Dudleston and David Owen (1997) examined power in dual-earner households in Nottingham using semi-structured interviews. The households were classified into those where the husband's career took precedence in making major household decisions (such as what part of the country to live in), those where the wife's career took precedence, and those where neither career clearly took precedence over the other.

In 19 households, the man's career came first, in five the woman's career took precedence, and in six neither career was clearly prioritised. It was most likely to be the man who decided where the couple were to live, and men tended to make decisions about cars. However, husband and wife usually made a joint decision about buying or renting a house. Although men dominated decision-making in most households, this was not the case in a significant minority of households where there appeared to be more egalitarian relationships.

Activity

Power and decision-making.

1. Is studying control over the TV remote control a good way of measuring power in couple relationships?

2. Suggest other ways in which power could be measured in relationships.

Judith Treas and Tsui-o Tai (2011) examined cross-national data from 31 countries including the UK and found that there has been a widespread move towards greater apparent equality. They found that some 75 per cent of couples made joint decisions on how to bring up children, what to do at weekends and expensive purchases. Interestingly they found that the higher the income of wives in comparison with their husbands, the more power women tended to exercise. This suggests that money can be crucial in understanding power in couple relationships.

Money

The way that married couples and cohabiting partners manage their money can reveal a great deal about inequality. Research shows that couples use a wide variety of ways to manage money and these different approaches to money management have important implications.

Jan Pahl – systems of money management

Jan Pahl (1989, 1993) was the first British sociologist to conduct detailed studies of how couples manage their money. Her study was based upon interviews with 102 couples with at least one child under 16. The study found four main patterns of money management:

1. **Husband-controlled pooling** was the most common pattern (39 couples). In this system, money was shared but the husband had the dominant role in deciding how it was spent.

2. **Wife-controlled pooling** was the second most common category, involving 27 couples. In this system, money was shared but the wife had the dominant role in deciding how it was spent.

3. **Husband control** was found in 22 couples. Among these couples the husband was usually the one with the main or only wage, and often he gave his wife housekeeping money.

4. **Wife control** was the least frequent pattern, found in just 14 couples. This was most common in working-class and low-income households. It was most common in poorer households where the responsibility for managing the money was more of a burden than a privilege.

Inequality and money management

According to Pahl, the most egalitarian type of control is wife-controlled pooling where there tends to be a great deal of joint decision-making. Wife-controlled

313

systems appear to give women an advantage over men. However, they tend to be found in households where money is tight and there is little, if anything, left over after paying for necessities. Often women will go short themselves (for example, by eating less, delaying buying new clothes and spending little on their leisure) rather than see their husband or children go short. Husband-controlled systems tend to give husbands more power than their wives. In these households, men usually spend more on personal consumption than wives. Where husband-controlled pooling occurs, men tend to have more power than women, but the inequality is not as great as in systems of husband control.

Overall, then, Pahl found that just over a quarter of the couples had a system (wife-controlled pooling) associated with a fair degree of equality between the partners. This would suggest that in domestic relationships, as in some other areas, women have not yet come close to reaching a position of equality.

Survey research

Research by Vogler, Brockmann and Wiggins (2007) used data from the International Social Survey Programme from 2002. They distinguished five money management systems:

1. The **female whole wage system**, in which women manage all the money and men are given an allowance for personal spending.

2. The **male whole wage/housekeeping allowance system** in which men manage all the money or manage all apart from a housekeeping allowance they give to their partner.

3. The **joint pooling system** in which all money is pooled and in theory managed equally.

4. The **partial pooling system** in which some money is pooled but each partner keeps some money which is not pooled.

5. The **independent management system** in which no money is pooled.

Unlike previous studies, this study collected data on cohabiting couples as well as married couples.

As Table 5.5.3 shows, pooling systems were predominant in all groups, whether married or cohabiting, parents or non-parents. Overall, 54 per cent of couples used joint pooling and 73 per cent joint or partial pooling. Just 7 per cent used the housekeeping allowance system. This suggests a move towards greater sharing and greater equality between partners. However, there was considerably less sharing of money management among cohabiting couples, especially among those without children and those who had previously been married.

Vogler *et al.* note that Anthony Giddens (1992) has suggested that cohabitation will lead to more egalitarian relationships (see p. 292 for details of Giddens's ideas). Vogler, Brockmann and Wiggins,

Table 5.5.3 Household allocative systems used by cohabiting and married respondents (aged under 35) in Britain, in 2002

Allocative systems	Childless married respondents (%) (N = 50)	Childless cohabiting respondents (%) (N = 52)	Married parents (%) (N = 106)	Cohabiting parents (%) (N = 27)	All (%) (N = 235)
Female whole wage	8	–	9	11	7
Housekeeping allowance	4	–	12	4	7
Joint pool	58	39	59	52	54
Partial pool	20	40	9	15	19
Independent management	10	21	9	19	13
Total (%)	100	100	100	100	100

Source: Vogler, C., Brockmann, M. and Wiggins, R.D. (2007), 'Managing money in new heterosexual forms of intimate relationships', *Journal of Socio-Economics*, vol. 37, no. 2, April 2008.

however, conclude that the opposite was the case with cohabiting couples apparently having *less* egalitarian relationships than married couples.

Activity

What factors seem to influence money management systems?

Summary

1. Studies of power in households suggest that there has been some shift towards more shared decision-making but men tend to have the upper hand when they have a higher income.

2. Jan Pahl distinguishes systems of money-management based on pooling of resources or control by one partner. Women are more likely to have control in low-income households where money management is a burden.

3. Survey research suggests some move towards more egalitarian money management although there is greater inequality between cohabiting than married couples.

5.5.5 Domestic violence and abuse

Although there is some evidence of greater equality within personal relationships, a very different impression is provided by evidence on domestic violence and abuse. Domestic violence is one of the 'dark sides' of the family and may be closely linked to inequality in relationships. Domestic abuse is difficult to define and measure but research suggests that it may be more widespread than many people assume. The causes of abuse are varied but much research suggests that they are strongly linked to issues of power and the nature of masculinity and femininity.

Defining domestic abuse

The official Home Office definition of **domestic violence and abuse** is:

Any incident or pattern of incidents of controlling, coercive, threatening behaviour, violence or abuse between those aged 16 or over who are, or have been, intimate partners or family members regardless of gender or sexuality. ONS, 2016

This incorporates physical and sexual abuse but also less obvious forms of abuse which are psychological, emotional or financial. Most forms of domestic abuse

are illegal under general laws such as those governing assault, sexual offences and homicide, but a new offence of coercive and controlling behaviour was introduced in 2015 to cover some of the less physical types of abuse. Some less common, but still significant forms of abuse, include forced marriage and violent abuse of parents by adolescents (ONS, 2016).

The government's, and indeed any other definitions of domestic abuse, are open to interpretation, especially in relation to psychological, emotional and financial abuse. Different ways of collecting data on abuse therefore produces different statistics but there is no doubt about the extent of the harm that can result from abuse even when it does not involve violence or sexual crimes.

The extent and distribution of domestic violence and abuse

It is notoriously difficult to determine the amount of domestic abuse that takes place but there are several ways of estimating it. From 2015 the police started compiling information on whether crimes reported to them were related to domestic abuse and, as mentioned above, it was in the same year that offences of abuse which were not violent or sexual became illegal.

Police statistics

In the year to March 2016 there were over one million domestic abuse related incidents recorded by the police of which 41 per cent were deemed to involve criminal offences. A big majority, 78 per cent of these, were recorded as violent offences and just 3 per cent were sexual offences (criminal damage and arson were other significant categories). Around one in nine of all offences were related to domestic abuse as were around a third of violent offences.

The Home Office itself comments that despite efforts to encourage the reporting of domestic abuse by the police, such offences are seriously under-reported. Furthermore, it seems likely that the police themselves are still under-recording domestic abuse. A 2014 report by Her Majesty's Inspectorate of Constabulary (HMIC) found that about 19 per cent of crimes reported to the police were not recorded by them. Crimes of violence and sexual abuse were particularly likely to be unrecorded, raising questions about the accuracy of police crime statistics in general and domestic abuse statistics in particular.

Crime Survey for England and Wales statistics

Another very useful source of information on domestic abuse is the CSEW (Crime Survey for England and Wales), an ongoing major annual survey which asked people to report on whether they have been victims of crime or not. Although it has its limitations (it relies upon people being willing and able to report domestic abuse) it provides a useful indication of the extent of domestic abuse which has not been reported to the police. Figure 5.5.1 shows trends in domestic abuse over time based on CSEW data. Although it suggests a gradual decline, in 2015–2016 7.7 per cent of women and 4.4 per cent of men were victims of domestic abuse in that year alone. Overall, 6.1 per cent of the population were victims in this single year, nearly one in 16 of the population.

Activity

1. Outline the trends shown in Figure 5.5.1.

2. Suggest reasons why the data might not be entirely accurate.

The same survey (ONS, 2016) also produces data on victims of domestic violence and figures for 2016 show that:

> ❯ Those from routine and manual occupations are twice as likely to be victims of domestic violence as those from professional and managerial occupations.

> ❯ In 2016 only one in one thousand people who were married or in a civil partnership experienced domestic violence compared with

three per thousand who were cohabiting, five per thousand who were divorced and 15 per thousand who were separated (suggesting that the break-up of a relationship makes domestic violence more likely).

Source: https://www.gov.uk/government/publications/world-cup-2014-domestic-violence-campaign

Explanations for domestic abuse

Explanations for domestic abuse range from the psychological to those which explain it in terms of the overall structure of society. But how credible are these different explanations and how far do they complement each other rather than contradicting one another?

Psychological explanations

Some attempts to explain domestic abuse have focused on the characteristics of the abusers assuming that they are different from other members of the population. For example, research by Elizabeth Gilchrist, Rebecca Johnson, Rachel Takriti, Samantha Weston, Anthony Beech and Mark Kebbell (2003) for the Home Office studied records on 336 male perpetrators of various forms of domestic violence. They argued that there were two main types of offender but both had psychological problems which predisposed them to offending:

> ❯ **Anti-social/narcissistic offenders** had hostile attitudes towards women and tended to condone domestic violence as being acceptable in some circumstances. Emotional abuse often went

Figure 5.5.1 Proportion of adults aged 16 to 59 who experienced domestic abuse in the last year, by sex, CSEW

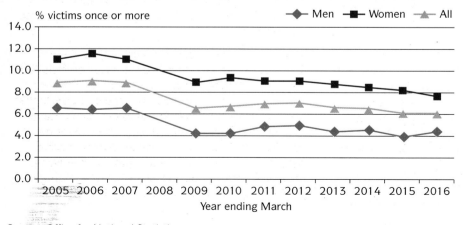

Source: Office for National Statistics.

hand-in-hand with domestic violence. These men could be very threatening in attempts to control women.

> **Borderline/emotionally volatile offenders** were less frequently emotionally abusive towards their partner but at the time of the physical abuse could make extreme threats. They tended to be controlling over money and to actively discourage their partner from going out to see other people.

Criticism of psychological explanations

Sandra Walklate (2004, cited in Newburn, 2013) argues that Gilchrist *et al.* are wrong to explain domestic violence simply in terms of the psychological characteristics of individuals. Domestic violence is not confined to a small group of men, because some studies suggest it is widespread (for example one study has found that a quarter of women experience domestic abuse at some time in their lives). Walklate therefore believes that male perpetrators are not completely atypical of other men and the root causes can be found in the patriarchal nature of society. From her viewpoint, male physical and sexual violence is one way of '**doing gender**' in a way that helps maintain patriarchal control.

Rebecca Dobash and Russell Dobash — structural and historical causes of domestic abuse

Walklate expresses views in line with a feminist interpretation of domestic abuse but her arguments are quite general and are not based on detailed evidence. A much more detailed feminist perspective on domestic violence has been developed by Rebecca Dobash and Russell Dobash (1979, 1998, 2011).

Culture, history and social structure

In a pioneering study of domestic violence Dobash and Dobash (1979) interviewed female victims of domestic violence and police officers and examined a range of secondary sources including police statistics and statements from victims. The focus of the study was 109 wives who had been assaulted by their husbands.

The Dobashes argued that domestic violence can only be understood in a broad historical and structural context and could not be seen as simply being a product of individual psychology. (Structural approaches emphasise the way that the overall organisation of society influences behaviour.) According to them, domestic violence is intimately linked with the existence of **patriarchy** and is essentially about the exercise of power by men over women in order to maintain that dominance.

Historically, there has been widespread acceptance of violence by husbands against their wives. For much of the 19th century, for example, it was considered acceptable to publicly criticise and punish wives who 'nagged or otherwise verbally abused their husbands'. This set of attitudes was reinforced by societal institutions which accepted physical 'punishments' of wives by husbands.

According to Dobash and Dobash, contemporary culture continues to accept that is appropriate and reasonable for husbands to use force to control their wives. Although public punishment of wives is no longer acceptable 'the imagery of the provoking wife' continues and acts as 'a powerful justification and rationalisation for the physical punishments and degradation meted out by husbands in private'. Husbands are still expected to be dominant in families, which remain patriarchal institutions. Domestic violence is used to maintain patriarchal control as men try to ensure that their wives carry out what they see as their 'duties' as wives and mothers. These attitudes are reinforced by a police force which is reluctant to intervene in domestic disputes and by a wider culture which tolerates domestic violence.

Specific causes of disputes and violence

From a study of 122 violent men and 134 female partners of those men, Dobash and Dobash (1998) identify several types of situation and issue which led to violence.

Conflicts of interest between husbands and wives were very important. Violence was often precipitated by situations in which the interests of the husband and wife diverged and the men wanted to ensure that their interests prevailed. For example, men became violent when they felt that their partners were not 'servicing their personal needs' such as preparing food that they approved of at a time of their liking. Women could even be 'punished for not anticipating, interpreting and fulfilling men's physical, emotional and sexual needs'. Conflicts of interest over money could also be important when men felt that they didn't have enough money left for their personal leisure.

Possessiveness and jealousy could be an important source of violence. Many of the men in the study were particularly possessive and could become violent if their wives had contact with other men or if they believed that their partners were being unfaithful. For many men, this was part of a wider view that women should not leave the home without their approval.

Similar issues of control were evident in disputes over sex, often involving men who believed that they should have control over the extent and nature of sexual activity. Furthermore, many of the men were so insistent upon the maintenance of their power and authority that they felt the women should not challenge this by disagreeing with them or arguing. Violence was often used to stop 'nagging' or to stop women 'going on and on'.

Masculinity and violence

The Dobashes accept that some women are violent, but argue that domestic violence is far more commonly used by men against their partners than by women against men. They see this as being part of masculine identity in which the use of force and intimidation are important signs of masculine worth. In violent encounters with other men, the willingness to use violence to defend yourself brings status regardless of whether you win a fight or not. In violent encounters against women, though, it is more important that men successfully assert their authority and control and do not allow themselves to be pushed around by a woman. This would challenge a man's sense of masculine identity. For these reasons, most male domestic abusers are not ashamed of their actions but rather they feel they were pushed into it and have no choice but to respond forcefully to challenges to their authority by women.

Then and now: Rebecca Dobash and Russell Dobash, *Violence against Women* (1979)

"Sociology has traditionally focused on social problems yet not all problems are widely recognised as such nor is it always possible to gain public and state recognition and support.

Then – At the outset of efforts to deal with intimate partner violence, in the US and UK some commentators rejected demands to deal with violence in the home dubbing it a family affair in which society and the state should not intervene. Women's Aid, the early battered women's movement, thought otherwise and we agreed. It was the early reports of this violence from Women's Aid that led us to embark on research on what is now widely recognized as serious social problem. In the late 1970s and 80s, there was a paucity of research on violence against women. The project we conducted involved the examination of over 34 000 police files revealing that 25 per cent of all assaults involved violence against a woman by an intimate male partner. This coupled with the results of intensive interviews of women who had been the victims of such an assault led us to conclude that violence against women in the home was a widespread problem resulting in serious physical injuries and emotional harm. Evidence from this study led to the publication of *Violence Against Wives*, in which we used the quantitative data to assess prevalence and main patterns and qualitative interviews to demonstrate the experiences of victimised women at the hands of their partners. This evidence reinforced the claims of the battered women's movement in the UK and USA.

That was then – what about **Now**? While it is difficult to assess the impact of research on any social problem, it is clear that in conjunction with the pressure of the women's movement, research has played an important role in bringing about change. National surveys conducted in many countries reveal that on average 35 per cent of women who have ever been in an intimate relationship have experienced domestic violence. The WHO describes the violence as a 'global pandemic' having 'devastating consequences'. Our latest research (*When Men Murder Women*) confirms these conclusions. Based on 866 casefiles and interviews of 180 men who have committed a murder, we found that when a woman is killed the murderer is most likely to be an intimate partner or ex-partner. The murders occurred in the context of the man's sense of entitlement, possessiveness, and women's attempts to escape. Internationally based research conducted by the UN, WHO, UNESCO and the Council of Europe reveals important developments, including: creation of 'restraining orders' for abusers; legislation making the violence a crime; increased arrest and prosecution, national and international legislation aimed at curbing the abuse of women; and identifying the abuse as an infringement of women's rights. Protection has developed and expanded. The shelter movement is now national and international and multitudes of women have benefited from the battered women's movement. A one-day survey in 2015 of thousands of shelters in 46 countries found that over 53 000 women and 35 000 children were being given safe housing and support. In the 1970s there were only three shelters in the UK, two in Scotland and one in England. The feminist inspired shelter movement has been an extraordinary development – demonstrating the importance and strength of feminism. **"**

Evaluation of Dobash and Dobash

Since some of the early research by Dobash and Dobash, attitudes towards domestic violence have changed, at least to some extent. Police forces make more effort to deal sympathetically with victims of domestic violence and government campaigns encourage the reporting of this type of offence. In part, these changes have taken place because the Dobashes and other researchers have brought the issue to public attention. Nevertheless, more recent research by Dobash and Dobash into men who murdered their intimate partners (Dobash and Dobash, 2011) has found that the assertion of male control continues to be important in male violence.

The research by the Dobashes is not always clear about why some men resort to violence and others do not. It has been argued that their research is not particularly sensitive to differences between groups of men and the different ways in which masculinity can be expressed. R.W. Connell (1995) argues that masculinity can take different forms and the dominant (or hegemonic masculinity) of professional and managerial men is less dependent on the use of violence than other forms of masculinity. The emphasis on masculinity does not explain the existence of domestic violence committed by women in heterosexual relationships or by women in lesbian relationships. The Dobashes have researched female domestic abuse against men (Dobash and Dobash, 2004) but conclude that most such violence tends to be much less harmful and less persistent than violence by men and, in any case, it is often a response to male violence and a form of self-defence. Nevertheless, they accept that there are a small number of serious, persistent female offenders who are not responding to violence or excessive control by men, but they don't offer a clear explanation for their behaviour.

The Dobashes also pay less attention than some theorists to material factors. The psychiatrist James Gilligan (2001) argues that much violence results from feelings of shame which often stem from material deprivation. In capitalist societies, material success is important for producing a sense of self-worth, and when inequality leaves many working class and minority ethnic men impoverished, it can lead to violence against their partners. Gilligan argues that there is strong correlation between rates of inequality and rates of violence in the UK.

Overall though, the pioneering research by the Dobashes has made an invaluable contribution to highlighting and explaining domestic violence, helping to introduce policies which have led to greater safety and more chance of redress for many victims.

Activity

A Home Office poster placed in men's washrooms in 2014 to coincide with the World Cup (football) tournament.

1. Why do you think the Home Office produced a poster reminding men that domestic abuse was not just about violence?

2. Suggest reasons why it was released to coincide with the World Cup.

Conclusion

Gilligan's work illustrates how a variety of social factors can help to explain domestic violence. While desire for patriarchal control might be central to male violence against women in domestic settings, the intersection of gender with class and ethnic inequality is also very important. However, whatever the relative importance of different social factors, sociological research certainly suggests that individual psychological reasons for domestic violence and abuse can only be fully understood in their wider social and structural context.

Key terms

Domestic violence and abuse Incidents or pattern of incidents of controlling, coercive, threatening behaviour, violence or abuse between family members. Domestic violence involves the use of physical force. Abuse can incorporate verbal or psychological intimidation as well as force.

Anti-social/narcissistic offenders Perpetrators of domestic abuse who are consistently hostile and abusive towards their partners.

Borderline/emotionally volatile offenders Perpetrators of domestic abuse who are consistently hostile and abusive towards their partners.

Hegemonic masculinity The dominant form of masculinity at a particular time in a particular place.

Patriarchy A pattern/structure of male dominance and control.

Summary

1. Domestic abuse includes psychological, emotional and financial abuse as well as physical and sexual abuse.

2. It is hard to be precise about the extent of abuse but statistics suggest women are considerably more likely to be victims than men; it is quite common, but there may have been some decline in recent years.

3. Psychological explanations of domestic abuse focus on the individual characteristics of the abusers.

4. Feminists argue that abuse is related to patriarchy.

5. Dobash and Dobash suggest there are cultural, historical and social structural causes of abuse and these are related to the nature of masculinity.

6. Much of the abuse by women is a response to abuse by men, but there are also some persistent female offenders who are not themselves victims of abuse.

PART 6 CHILDHOOD

Contents

Childhood is often seen as a fixed, biologically-based phase of life which inevitably shares universal characteristics regardless of time or place. From this point of view, children are biologically and mentally immature and because of this they occupy a distinctive role in all societies. The first unit of this part of the chapter critically examines such claims and considers evidence that childhood is socially constructed rather than natural. If this is the case, then the nature of childhood can change over time. But has this happened and if so why? Has the position of children improved or has it gone backwards? Are all children in a similar position or are they affected by inequality? Are children protected by adults or are they vulnerable because of adult control over them? These and other questions will be explored, focusing particularly on Britain, while also making comparisons with other cultures.

5.6.1 Childhood as a biological stage of life

Common-sense thinking sees childhood as a biological state through which everyone who becomes an adult must pass. From this common-sense perspective, the nature of childhood is seen as deriving from the physical and mental immaturity of children regardless of their culture. But is this really the case? Is childhood the same the world over and throughout history or does it vary depending on the culture of a society at a particular time?

The dominant framework

The assumption that childhood is a product of biology is part of what Alan Prout and Allison James (1997) referred to as the **dominant framework** within which children and childhood have been viewed in Western societies. Drawing on these ideas, Michael Wyness identifies the key features of the dominant framework (see Figure 5.6.1):

1. Childhood and adulthood are seen as dichotomous or as opposites. Figure 5.6.1 illustrates this dichotomous view. Children are seen as gradually acquiring culture, morality and the ability to take part in social life through a process of development and socialisation, but initially they are dominated by biological urges. Children are seen as simple because they have not yet developed the complex and sophisticated ways of acting and interacting with one another which are used by adults. For example, children only gradually develop the ability to understand and use complex language. Childhood is seen as a phase involving a process in which children, as incomplete persons, progress towards adulthood. Adulthood is seen as a state in which personhood has been attained. This approach therefore adopts a **deficit model of childhood** – children are defined in terms of their lack of adult attributes.

2. Children are not seen as entities in their own right but are seen as 'incomplete beings whereas adults are fully constituted social beings'. As a consequence of this approach, social scientists have generally studied children in terms of the sort of adults they will develop into and have been less concerned with children's experiences during childhood itself.

3. Children are seen as **proto-individuals** – primitive or early-stage unfinished individuals who need socialising before they can become complete members of society.

Alan Prout (2005) argues that the dominant framework, which sees the child as an incomplete individual, is an aspect of **modernity**. Modernity emphasises the importance of rationality (and becoming rational is an essential part of how the dominant perspective views growing up). According to Prout, the dominant perspective associates childhood with irrationality, incompetence and play, whereas adulthood is associated with rationality, competence and work.

Figure 5.6.1 The dominant framework

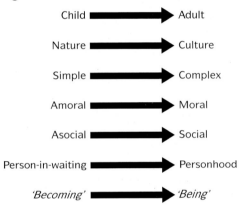

Source: A. Prout and A. James (1997) 'A new paradigm for the sociology of childhood?' in A. James and A. Prout (eds) *Constructing and Reconstructing Childhood*, 2nd edn, Falmer, London.

Ages and stages

According to Wyness (2006), the dominant framework has itself been dominated by psychological research using scientific methods. This approach has adopted what Wyness calls an **ages and stages** approach, which assumes that children develop through set stages at predictable ages. For example, Jean Piaget (1896–1980), a Swiss developmental psychologist, believed that children in all societies passed through fixed stages of development at roughly the same ages.

Evaluation of the dominant framework

1. Many social scientists have argued that childhood does not follow a series of fixed, predictable stages in all places at all times. They see the idea of childhood as a social construction that varies from

place to place and time to time (see the discussion of Ariès's work on pp. 323–325).

2. Stevi Jackson and Sue Scott (2006) point out that the experience of childhood is shaped by other social divisions such as class, gender and disability, which makes universal generalisations about children misleading.

3. Berry Mayall (2004) argues that developmental psychology tends to have a cultural bias towards Western, particularly Anglo-American, ideas about childhood and childrearing. While it claims to state universal truths about how children develop, in reality it simply describes Western views about how children *should* develop. For example, many other societies place much less emphasis on the development of rationality as one of the ultimate goals of child development.

4. Some critics raise more fundamental questions, arguing that the emphasis on the process of becoming an adult neglects any focus on children's own lives. Jackson and Scott believe it is important to recognise that children are active agents in their own lives and not just the passive recipients of socialisation.

5. Following on from the above, Mayall argues that the dominant framework emphasises the needs of children, needs which are met by adults, so that children can develop 'normally'. However, seeing children as competent social actors in their own right, shifts the emphasis towards children's rights, many of which are currently denied to them (see pp. 321–334).

6. According to Diana Gittins (1998) childhood is not a natural stage of life but a product of age patriarchy in which children's lives are structured and controlled by adults, particularly adult males.

Key terms

Dominant framework The common-sense view about children based on the assumption of their mental and physical immaturity.

Deficit model of childhood The view that the central characteristics of children involve children lacking the characteristics that adults have, making children inferior to adults.

Proto-individuals The earliest and most primitive form of individual; individuals not yet fully formed.

Modernity A phase in the development of society often seen as involving rational planning and the decline of religion and tradition.

Ages and stages The view that all children pass through different stages of development at roughly similar ages.

Social construction/social constructionism The view that things which appear to be natural are actually produced through social processes.

Age patriarchy A system of dominance involving adults, particularly adult males, exercising control over children.

Summary

1. Childhood is usually seen as an inevitable biological phase of life in which humans gradually mature as they progress towards adulthood.

2. The dominant framework sees children as incomplete human beings close to nature who lack rationality and the other capacities of adults.

3. The ages and stages approach suggests children pass through predictable developmental stages at particular ages.

4. The dominant framework has been criticised for ignoring variations in childhood between places and over time, which suggests that childhood is a social construct.

5. It has also been criticised for being based upon Western assumptions about childhood, ignoring the perspective of children and for allowing children to be dominated by adults.

5.6.2 Childhood as a social construction

Many sociologists have put forward the idea that childhood is a social construction. Despite some differences between advocates of this view, all agree that the idea of childhood, if it exists at all, varies from place to place and time to time.

Cross-cultural comparisons

Contemporary Western societies have distinctive ideas about childhood and it is often assumed that these ideas are normal and universal. From a social constructionist point of view they are not, as these examples illustrate:

1. In some societies it is still considered quite normal for children to do substantial amounts of work. According to the International Labour Organization (ILO, 2013) there were 168 million child workers in 2012. Wyness (2012) cites a study by Banks (2007) which found that in Bangladesh children as young as 11 or 12 work as sex workers using forged papers. The ILO (2013, cited in Wells, 2015) has found that many children are employed in hazardous occupations including construction, mining and quarrying. In sub-Saharan Africa and parts of Asia and the Pacific, children are expected to work to contribute to the household income.

2. In many societies, circumstances lead to children taking on roles which are typically thought to be ones which only adults can carry out. Michael Wyness (2012) points out that children often act as carers for their own parent or other adults. Around 175 000 children were acting as carers according to the 2001 census in the UK.

3. According to Wyness (2012) typical estimates put the number of child soldiers at around 300 000. They have been used in recent years in more than 30 countries including the Democratic Republic of the Congo, Syria and the Sudan. According to the UN (2007) the availability of light and cheap weapons means that children aged 10 or even younger are sometimes used to fight.

4. Ruth Benedict (1955, discussed in Pilcher, 1995) found wide cultural variations in the roles of children. In Samoa, children were not considered too young to do dangerous or physically demanding tasks. In Tikopia in the Western Pacific, children's individuality was respected and they were not expected to be obedient. Among Australian Aborigines in the 1920s, children were not discouraged from playing sexual games. Benedict concluded that compared to Western societies, some other societies differentiated much less between adulthood and childhood.

Social constructionist theories have also argued that contemporary Western ideas of childhood have only developed comparatively recently. The next section examines the historical development of ideas about childhood.

Activity

A child looking after her mother.

1. In what ways does this image challenge the conventional view of childhood?

2. Discuss the view that children in our society would be able to take on many more roles reserved for adults if they were allowed to do so.

The historical development of childhood

If childhood is a social construction, then it follows that it may have changed over time. There is certainly evidence of this taking place and several sociologists have researched historical changes in childhood and have sought to explain them.

Philippe Ariès: *Centuries of Childhood*

Philippe Ariès (1973, first published 1960) proposed one of the earliest and most influential theories of childhood as a social construction. Ariès argued that in Europe during medieval times (between roughly the 12th and 16th centuries) a modern conception of childhood did not exist. He said that, 'as soon as the child could live without the constant solicitude of his mother, his nanny or his cradlerocker, he belonged to adult society' (Ariès, 1973).

Early medieval childhood

In early medieval times, many people did not even know their chronological age since it had little social significance. At that time, many children died before reaching adulthood. Children were not therefore given the importance attached to them today. For example, parents did not get painters to do portraits of their children and mourning was kept to a minimum when a child died. It was only in the 16th century that portraits of children who had died began to appear, indicating that modern ideas of childhood had started to develop.

According to Ariès, at the start of the medieval period children were expected to help out and to take on what are now seen as adult roles as soon as they were physically able. However, work did not take up as much time as it does for adults today and a lot of time was spent on play and pastimes. There was little difference between children's and adults' pastimes; all ages joined in on an equal footing. There were also few specialist clothes for children and so children were dressed like miniature adults.

Today, children are regarded as innocent and in need of protection from adults and adult concerns, particularly in relation to sex. According to Ariès, this was not the case in the past. For example, he put forward evidence from accounts of French and Spanish royalty to suggest that it was not taboo to make sexual references to children or even to touch children's genitals.

In short, childhood was not viewed as a special time of innocence when children had to be sheltered. Children were simply seen as small adults.

The development of modern childhood

However, this gradually began to change towards the end of the medieval era. Children's toys and clothes were introduced, people started keeping paintings of children, children's deaths were mourned more and taboos about children and sexuality developed.

Ariès argued that these changed attitudes stemmed partly from churchmen who began to see children as 'fragile creatures of God who needed to be both safeguarded and reformed'. Most important of all, though, was the development of modern schools.

In medieval schools, all age groups were educated together. In France, in the 18th and 19th centuries, children started to be separated into age groups as age became the organising principle of education. As more children went to school, they became more segregated from the adult world as children were increasingly regarded as vulnerable and in need of protection. By this time, more children were surviving into adulthood and parents were investing more time and interest in their children. Children were increasingly kept apart from adults. The idea of childhood as a time of innocence and that children were an investment for the future became increasingly dominant.

Children were subject to hard discipline in schools and families to ensure that they were moulded into the correct shape, but society had become much more concerned with children, much more **child-centred** than it had ever been in medieval times. By the 20th century, specialist sciences such as psychology, psychoanalysis and paediatrics had developed to give further emphasis to the needs of children. Ariès concluded that now, 'Our world is obsessed by the physical, moral and sexual problems of childhood'.

Activity

Antoon Claeissens – A Family Saying Grace Before the Meal (1585).

What evidence does the painting provide to suggest that children were seen as 'little adults' and therefore part of adult society?

Evaluation of Ariès

The work of Ariès has generated considerable discussion and debate. Jane Pilcher (1995) notes a number of criticisms which have been put forward:

1. His work has been seen as value-laden. Ariès implies in his work that more recent child-centred views of childhood are superior to earlier views, which allowed children to be treated in ways that would be considered unacceptable today. Critics have argued that Ariès allows his own values to distort his work, leading him to be overcritical of medieval childrearing.

2. Ariès has also been criticised for arguing that there was no concept of childhood in medieval times. Others have suggested that it would be

more accurate to say that ideas on childhood were simply different at that time rather than absent altogether.

3. Ariès has also been criticised for generalising about modern childhood on the basis of data largely confined to French aristocratic families.

Explaining the development of modern childhood

Building on the ideas of Ariès, a number of reasons have been put forward for the emergence of the type of childhood that he described:

1. **Romantic love** Edward Shorter (1976) puts primary emphasis upon the development of ideas.

   He argues that from the 18th century, the idea of romantic love began to develop. People began to marry for love – rather than, for example, to have children or for financial security. As a result, children became seen as more important. As the products of a special relationship – that between a loving husband and wife – the children too were seen as special.

2. **Technological change** Postman (1982) argues that technological change explains the rise of modern ideas about childhood. In particular, he argues that the development of the printing press in the late 15th century meant that adults increasingly required children to learn to read. Learning to read is a gradual process in which skills are built up slowly, and this encouraged the idea that children were different from adults and needed educating gradually to become like adults.

3. **Policies** State policies have increasingly ensured that children are unable to take on many aspects of adult roles and have enshrined the idea of childhood as a special time of innocence in which children should be separated from the adult world. In the early stages of the Industrial Revolution in Britain the use of child labour, including some very young children, was widespread, for example in mines and in textile mills (Cunningham, 2006). However, in 1819 children under nine were banned from working in textile mills and older children were limited to a 12-hour day. Further legislation restricted the employment of children, including the 1889 Prevention of Cruelty to Children Act. The introduction and expansion of compulsory education has been particularly important in restricting the opportunity for children to work. Education was made compulsory between the ages of 5 and 10 in 1880. In 1918 the school leaving age was raised to 14 and to 16 in 1972, 17 in 2013 and 18 in 2015.

4. **The economics of children** The extension of the length of time that children were dependent on parents because they were prohibited from working gradually transformed children from a potential economic asset for their parents to an economic liability. This has reinforced the idea that children are projects in which parents invest rather than simply 'small adults'.

5. **Family size** This transformation in the economics of parenthood has contributed to a reduction in family size. Along with lower infant mortality, parents have arguably come to concentrate their efforts on the well-being of the small number of children they have, seeing them as needing nurturing and protection. Thus, Deborah Chambers (2012) believes there has been a shift from valuing children for their economic benefits to valuing them for emotional reasons.

6. **'Expert' knowledge** According to Donzelot (1977) the development of professionals who advocate theories of child development has influenced the nature of childhood 'Expert' knowledge, and parenting advice is now disseminated through popular media and through websites (for example *Mumsnet*).

Key term

Child-centred Focusing particularly on the well-being of children rather than adults.

Summary

1. There are wide variations in childhood between different societies and over time.

2. In some societies children are expected to work, some children act as carers for adults, some children become soldiers and in some societies there is relatively little differentiation between children and adults.

3. Philippe Ariès argues that in medieval times children were seen as little adults, chronological age was not seen as important and children were expected to take on adult tasks as soon as possible.

4. To Ariès, the development of schooling was important in creating modern childhood by separating children and adults and delaying the participation of children in adult activities.

5. Specialist professions such as paediatrics have helped to make society more child-centred.

6. Ariès has been criticised for misrepresenting medieval childhood and generalising on the basis of unrepresentative evidence.

7. Others have explained the emergence of modern childhood on a wide range of factors including the idea of romantic love in marriage, technological change, state policies, and children becoming an economic burden rather than an asset.

5.6.3 Contemporary debates on childhood

Contemporary debates on childhood are often framed in terms of fear. This fear takes many forms but broadly it tends to see childhood as being under threat, to see the experience of childhood deteriorating and/or the supposed 'innocence' of childhood being undermined. This unit examines several such claims but asks is the situation that simple? Is childhood really getting worse or even disappearing? Or is the picture more complex with social change occurring which cannot be seen as entirely negative, or, for that matter, entirely positive?

Neil Postman – the disappearance of childhood

Neil Postman suggested in 1994 that the distinction between childhood and adulthood was being eroded to such an extent that childhood was disappearing as a distinct life stage. The main reason for this was the development of the mass media.

In previous eras, there had been an **information hierarchy**: some adults could access much more information than others because they were literate – they could read and write. Children developed this ability only slowly. It was therefore possible to keep aspects of the adult world secret from children at least for a number of years.

According to Postman, media such as television had led to children seeing images (such as images of sex and violence) which had previously been largely inaccessible to them. Watching television does not require the development of the ability to read, and it can therefore be understood from an early age. Because children could now learn about virtually anything from the media, childhood was no longer a time of innocence.

A rather different view is taken by Jenks, however, (see the following page) and other studies of contemporary forms of media. These suggest that the impact of media today may be more varied than simply exposing children to adult content. In some ways, its impact may complement the ability of children to create their own social worlds and identities distinct from those of adults. However, it could also lead to the commercialisation of childhood – another possible threat to childhood which worries many people.

Contemporary issues: Online games and children's agency

As Postman's work shows, a common source of anxiety about children is that their innocence and autonomy are being undermined by the popular media of the day. However, Postman's view suggests that children are passive recipients of media messages. Children are seen as having little **agency**. Agency is the ability of individuals to make decisions and to act on the basis of those decisions in a way which enables them to have an impact on the world around them. In this context, children are regarded as lacking agency because it is assumed that they cannot interpret media messages for themselves and decide how they will respond to them.

This view is challenged by some studies of virtual worlds and online gaming. Research by Jackie Marsh (2010) involved group interviews with 17 English children aged five to seven who used the online virtual worlds of the commercial sites *Club*

Penguin and *Barbie Girls*. Marsh claims that the children were able to engage in forms of play which were creative and were not just shaped by the sites themselves. In *Club Penguin*, children engaged in fantasy play creating imaginary identities such as mermaids and pirates. The participants interacted with each other and constructed stories together using some of the virtual props (such as clothes) provided by the game.

A different view is taken by Sara Grimes (2015) who also studied children's use of *Club Penguin* and *Barbie Girls* along with four other virtual worlds aimed at young children. Grimes found that these sites had much more restricted opportunities for personalising elements of the game and controlling communications than adult-oriented MMOGs (massively multi-player online games). For example, much communication had to take place by selecting options from drop-down menus rather than typing in a text box. The sites also had strict codes of conduct specifying a wide range of unacceptable behaviours. Furthermore, according to Grimes, the games involved 'configuring the child as consumer', for example encouraging them to buy in-game currency with real money to gain advantages. According to Grimes, therefore, these games provided much less opportunity for young children to play creatively than conventional play in the material world, and instead their main effect was

to encourage children to become the consumers of commercial products.

What do children learn from online games?

Questions

1. To what extent are children likely be shielded from adult knowledge by the existence of online games designed for young children?

2. Do online games for

   a) younger children and

   b) older children

   encourage them to creatively develop their own cultures or to become the passive consumers of commercial products?

Christopher Jenks – the transition to late modern/postmodern childhood

Jenks (2005) agrees with Postman that there is concern about the death of childhood, or at least a loss of innocence among children. However, Jenks does not believe that childhood is disappearing. Society continues to impose rules on many aspects of childhood because of its symbolic importance. Children are still highly regulated and restricted by legal constraints governing their sexuality, education, behaviour in public places, alcohol consumption, political rights (or lack of them) and so on. Even though people are more aware that children can be violent, can misbehave, become sexually active and so on, society is still unwilling to accept that the idea of childhood is a social construction rather than a natural, biological category.

For these reasons Jenks puts forward a more complex view of childhood than the one offered by those who see it as under threat or even disappearing.

Childhood and modernity

Jenks characterises the development of modern childhood in terms of a shift from the Dionysian image of the child to the Apollonian image. The **Dionysian image of the child** is based upon Dionysus, the 'prince of wine, revelry and nature'. According to this image, children love pleasure and are curious and adventurous. In the pursuit of pleasure children can get themselves into all sorts of trouble and can, potentially, act in evil ways. Children are therefore in need of strict moral guidance and control if they are to grow up to be responsible adults.

There is little sentimentality in this image of children, and strict discipline can be used to control children.

327

According to Jenks, the Dionysian image was typical of pre-industrial societies, but it survived well into the modern era although it was gradually overtaken by an alternative **Apollonian image of the child** (from the Greek god Apollo).

According to this view, children are born good but are quite different from adults. Because they are different they cannot be treated like adults. They need more careful handling, and the good side of their nature must be coaxed out of them sympathetically. Each child is an individual and therefore special.

From such notions, the modern idea of the child developed. This in turn influenced ideas on child-centred education, the unsuitability of work for children, the avoidance of harsh or physical punishment, and the belief that children needed to be 'enabled, encouraged and facilitated' (Jenks, 2005).

Discipline and monitoring

Jenks does not believe that this resulted in children being left free to do whatever they wanted. Instead, new ways of monitoring and controlling children were introduced. These did not depend on hard physical violence but instead children were increasingly disciplined through the monitoring and control of space. They were restricted in where they could go at particular times and restricted in what they could do in different settings. At school, children spent more and more time sitting behind a desk and were expected to conform to school rules. Out of school, children were increasingly kept out of most public spaces unless accompanied by an adult. The modern family also monitored children and had become a rational institution designed to develop children so that they became productive and well-adapted adults. Childhood was increasingly concerned with **futurity** – what the child would become in the future – rather than the enjoyment and experience of childhood itself.

Late modern/postmodern childhood

Jenks believes that modernity has now been superseded by a new era. He refers to this new era both as **late modernity** and as postmodernity, using these terms interchangeably. Jenks, like many other sociologists, believes that the new era has resulted in a destabilisation of people's identities, so that they no longer have a secure, grounded sense of who they are. For example, family life is insecure with frequent divorce, and people change jobs more often than in the past. People develop a reflexive sense of self – they constantly monitor, revise, try to change their sense of who they are. This can make people anxious and unsure about their identity since it no longer has firm foundations.

Drawing heavily on the work of Ulrich Beck (1992), Jenks argues that children have become the final source of **primary relationships** – the most fulfilling and unconditional relationships, which last and from which people obtain the most satisfaction. Wives, husbands or partners used to be seen as the most important source of primary relationships, but an increasing proportion of such relationships break down through divorce, or separation. Because of this, parents now attach more importance to relationships with their children since unlike a marriage, the parent-child relationship is a permanent biological relationship. The relationship with children becomes the one thing on which adults can rely and they cling on to it in the uncertainty and instability of the postmodern world.

However, there is still some ambiguity about childhood. According to Jenks, we live in a society in which the independence of the individual is seen as a necessity, and it is also seen as necessary for children to develop this independence. Yet, as 'the symbolic refuge of ... trust, dependency and care in human relations', there is a strong sense that children need to be protected so that the last vestiges of the old society do not disappear.

Child abuse

In these circumstances, it is not surprising that there is considerable anxiety about childhood. Childhood is so precious and symbolic that there is great concern if it is seen as under threat. This sense of anxiety is revealed in attitudes towards child abuse.

Child abuse has become increasingly evident in contemporary society, with many more allegations of abuse than in the past and much more publicity given to the issue. People are therefore more aware of abuse and more fearful for their children. For example, many parents are worried about abduction and reluctant to let children go out without adult supervision. But however much parents want to protect their children from real or imagined threats, they ultimately feel that they cannot guarantee their safety. This is because they feel insecure themselves (see p. 332 for further discussion of child sexual abuse).

Conclusion

Given the ambiguity over childhood and the contradictory demands to protect children and to allow them to develop as independent individuals, Jenks suggests that it is now misleading to believe that such a thing as 'childhood' exists in reality. In contemporary society, the experiences and behaviour of children are extremely varied, and any single view of what childhood is will not do justice to the differences that exist between children.

Activity

Driving children to school.

Drawing on sociological ideas, suggest why so many parents drive their children to school rather than allowing them to walk by themselves.

Contemporary issues: Toxic childhood?

Sue Palmer is one of several commentators who have expressed concern about changes in childhood. In her book, *Toxic Childhood* (2015) Palmer argues that life is getting worse for children in Western countries such as the UK and in doing so she brings together many of the claims put forward in this section. She uses a range of evidence to support her view. For example, she notes that:

- by 2014 10 per cent of British children were believed to have a mental health condition

- this was reflected in statistics on problems such as drug use, eating disorders, suicide, self-harm and excessive alcohol consumption among children

- recorded rates of learning difficulties in childhood, such as ADHD (Attention Deficit Hyperactivity Disorder), autism, dyslexia and dyspraxia have risen rapidly. Some of these conditions have led to children taking prescribed drugs, for example Ritalin to treat ADHD.

Palmer believes that underlying these issues are three key problems. Conversations with long-serving teachers have convinced her that children increasingly:

1. have difficulty concentrating

2. find it hard to control their own behaviour

3. struggle to cooperate in groups.

Palmer attributes these problems to several factors. Technological developments have transformed homes so parents have less control over access to the media. Family life has become less stable and parents have less time to spend with their children because of the pressures of work in dual-earner families. At the same time religion has declined and cultural traditions have been swept away. All this has led to **toxic childhood syndrome** (a situation in which commercial and other pressures in the contemporary world make childhood increasingly harmful to children). Child rearing is rendered more and more difficult by 'TV and marketing messages, exercise and sleeping habits, childcare arrangements, parenting styles' (p. 16) and poor diet.

To detoxify childhood, parents need to reassert control, for example by controlling access to electronic media, imposing bedtimes and getting rid of junk food from children's diets. But children also need more freedom and time to learn to cooperate through being given time to play and exercise independently of adults and away from the pervasive influence of electronic media.

329

Evaluation

However, many sociologists regard this view of childhood as far too negative. Overall, the health of children has improved and far fewer children die before reaching adulthood than in Victorian times (Cunningham, 2006). Deborah Chambers (2012) believes that a shift to a more child-centred family has produced benefits for children who are no longer treated simply as the 'passive recipients of parental care and socialisation' but are given more say in their own upbringing. Chambers argues that exposure to new media is not simply negative because, for example, the use of mobile phones is now essential to peer group integration and development as adolescents. Similarly, the purchase and use of different brands is part of developing an independent identity.

However, the increasing centrality of children in family life along with concerns about child safety fuels parental anxiety about being 'good parents'. This in turn leads to some restrictions on children's freedom of movement outside the home. For these reasons, Chambers acknowledges that childhood is changing but with mixed effects which are neither wholly negative nor positive. Instead, childhood is characterised by tension between managing and protecting children and giving children more rights, and giving them opportunities to make choices for themselves.

Activity

1. Suggest ways in which the image above could be seen to illustrate toxic childhood.

2. Suggest ways in which the image could be used to suggest more positive aspects of contemporary childhood.

Key terms

Information hierarchy A situation in which some groups have superior access to information than others.

Agency The ability of individuals to make decisions and to act on the basis of those decisions in a way which enables them to have an impact on the world around them.

Apollonian image of the child The view that children are born good and are only corrupted through contact with the adult world.

Dionysian image of the child The view that children are amoral pleasure seekers.

Futurity A concern with the future rather than the present.

Late modernity To some sociologists, the current period of societal development in which identities become much more fluid and subject to the decisions of the individual.

Reflexive sense of self When individuals are very aware of their sense of who they are, they monitor it and often try to change it.

Primary relationships The longest-lasting and most significant personal relationships that individuals have in life.

Toxic childhood syndrome A situation in which commercial and other pressures in the contemporary world make childhood increasingly harmful to children.

Summary

1. Many commentators express fear about contemporary childhood.

2. Postman believes childhood is disappearing because the media give children access to adult information.

3. Jackie Marsh contradicts Postman's view by arguing that online gaming gives children more agency although Sara Grimes believes MMOGs for young children offer limited agency and are very commercialised.

4. Jenks believes there is an ongoing transition to late modern/postmodern childhood in which the unstable relationships and identities of adults lead to them investing even more in relationships with their children.

5. These changes heighten fears about childhood and increase anxiety, for example around the risks of child abuse.

6. Sue Palmer believes childhood has turned toxic but Deborah Chambers believes increasingly child-centred families have produced some positive as well as some negative effects.

5.6.4 Childhoods – differences and inequalities

Most of the theorists examined so far accept that childhood is socially constructed but they tend to believe that a particular version of childhood is dominant at any particular time. They also tend to follow this up with an assumption that this version of childhood is either an improvement on previous socially constructed versions of childhood or a step backwards. However, not all children experience childhood in the same way and this unit examines this issue.

Unequal childhoods

Alan Prout (2005) suggests that divisions within countries between different groups of children are important. In Britain, children from poorer backgrounds have higher rates of illness, do less well in education and probably suffer more neglect and abuse than children from richer backgrounds. Prout suggests that increasing family diversity (see Part 4) leads to greater variety in children's experience, as do factors such as class, ethnicity, disability and gender.

Prout's Ideas can be illustrated with a variety of evidence.

Poverty and social class

According to the Child Poverty Action Group (CPAG, 2017) there were 3.9 million children in poverty in 2014–2015 and this had a significant impact on their experience of childhood. For example, for some it meant going hungry and it could restrict their ability to join in activities along with other children because of costs. 60 per cent of children in the poorest quarter of families could not afford to go on holiday. Poverty also impacts on the health of children with the result that poor children are more likely to have their childhood blighted by illness as well as having a lower life expectancy.

Activity

Child poverty.

With reference to the image and your own knowledge, suggest ways in which poverty could have a negative impact on childhood.

Gender

Girls and boys are not socialised in the same way and therefore do not have the same experience of childhood. For example, Angela McRobbie (2000) argues that pre-teen girls are given considerably less freedom than pre-teen boys. They are believed to be more vulnerable to assault or even abduction than their male counterparts so they are less likely to spend time in public places without adult supervision. In terms of the balance between dependence on adults and independence, childhood is not the same for girls and boys. Karen Wells (2015) therefore argues that childhood is gendered in ways which affect 'the allocation of tasks' and 'the organisation of time and space' (Wells, 2015, p. 49). Girls and boys have different amounts of choice in what they can do, where they can go and how much free time they have, with girls often expected to do a great deal more unpaid domestic work than boys.

Ethnicity

As an earlier part of this chapter showed (see pp. 285–290) there are significant cultural variations between families from different ethnic backgrounds. For this reason, there are also significant variations in the experience of childhood for children from different ethnic groups. For example, Bhatti's research (1999) found that more emphasis was placed on family honour and family responsibilities in the socialisation of children in British Pakistani families than in White British families.

Intersections of class, gender and ethnicity

Differences and inequalities in the experience of childhood do not just stem from class, gender and ethnicity acting independently; they are also the result of how they intersect and interact. As Karen Wells (2015) points out, class, ethnicity and gender all affect access to resources. The experience of being a boy or girl will vary with ethnic group and social class so these major social divisions act together in shaping childhood.

Contemporary issues: The sexual abuse of children

Many of the issues and concerns raised by sociologists and other contemporary commentators are highlighted by recent cases revealing the sexual abuse of children. These cases raise questions about the vulnerability of children to exposure to the adult world, the possible 'disappearance of childhood' and issues of inequality between different groups of children.

Child sexual abuse allegations in the UK have been made against football coaches, teachers, religious leaders, media personalities and politicians as well as 'ordinary' members of the public. Historical allegations of abuse became so widespread that in February 2017 the head of the police operation to investigate historical allegations of abuse said that the police faced being overwhelmed by the volume of allegations (Johnston, 2017).

Some of the most publicised examples of child sexual abuse involved the abuse of White girls by predominantly British Asian men in Rochdale, Oldham and Rotherham (Perraudin, 2017).

In 2012, nine men from Rochdale and Oldham were found guilty of a range of offences including rape and sexual activity with a child. The offences took place between 2005 and 2008. During the trial, evidence showed that teenage girls, the youngest of whom was just 13, were given drink and drugs by the men and 'passed around' for sex. The victims were White girls from working-class backgrounds and many them had been brought up in care homes. Particularly concerning about the case was that police were aware of the allegations and had investigated them between 2008 and 2010 but had not brought charges and had chosen to drop the investigation despite having a great deal of evidence against alleged offenders. In some cases, the victims were regarded as having made a 'lifestyle choice' or as having chosen to be prostitutes despite being under 16, instead of being seen as victims of crime. Abuse continued after the investigation was dropped. Seven officers were eventually served with notices of misconduct but none were subject to any disciplinary action other than being given 'words of advice' by senior officers.

Similar cases of sexual abuse were also revealed in Rotherham (Tufail, 2015) and an independent report into these offences suggested that upwards of 1400 had probably been abused in that town alone. Five men were sent to prison for some of these offences in 2010. *The Times* newspaper (cited in Tufail, 2015) alleged that the Rotherham case was not initially pursued against the men because the police were concerned that they would make racial tensions worse and they might be seen as racist.

However, Waqas Tufail argues that the coverage of the crimes in the media has been racialised and has been influenced by widespread hostility to Muslims. He notes that sexual abuse of children by White offenders has not generally been seen in racial terms and coverage of a number of sexual abuse allegations against White police officers has been minimal. Tufail suggests that these cases can better be understood in terms of the powerless position of the girls who were the victims of the offences than in terms of the ethnicity of the offenders. He says, 'the unpalatable truth may be that the contempt police officers often hold for minority groups was trumped in these instances by their contempt for these vulnerable girls' (Tufail, 2015, p. 36).

Questions

1. What does child sexual abuse suggest about the credibility of different views on the changing nature of childhood?

2. In view of the cases described here, discuss the view that class, gender and ethnicity interact in shaping the experience of childhood.

3. Why do you think the accusations of the victims were not acted on for so long? What part might the age, class and ethnicity of the victims have played in this?

Summary

1. The experience of childhood is not the same for all children.

2. Class inequality and poverty affect the living standards and opportunities of different groups of children.

3. Childhood is gendered. For example, according to McRobbie, girls are given less freedom than boys.

4. There are ethnic variations in family life and the experience of childhood.

5. Class, gender and ethnicity intersect and interact in shaping childhood.

6. The sexual abuse of children in Rotherham, Rochdale and Oldham illustrates the intersection of class, gender and ethnicity and shows how some children are very vulnerable during childhood and can suffer extreme abuse.

5.6.5 Childhood and the social structure

The preceding section examined childhood in terms of inequalities between children. However, it failed to consider children as a social group in its own right with, potentially at least, different interests to adults. In short, it did not consider the position of children in the overall social structure. There have been some attempts to see children as a distinctive social group in terms of Marxist and feminist theory but some sociologists, such as Berry Mayall deny that these perspectives capture the nature of the relationship between adults and children. Instead they argue that a sociology of children is needed to replace the *sociology of childhood*.

Feminist and Marxist views

There are some parallels between the position of children and women in society: for example, both are prone to being victims of domestic abuse and both are generally subordinate to men (Wyness, 2013). Furthermore, both children and women lack or have lacked in the past full social status which has made it difficult for women and children to assert their rights.

Hood-Williams (1990, cited in Wyness, 2012) therefore argues that there are two types of patriarchy (or male dominance). **Marital patriarchy** involves the dominance of men over women. **Age patriarchy** involves the dominance of parents over children.

However, this approach does not explain why age-based dominance should be seen as a form of *patriarchy* which implies the dominance of *men* rather than the dominance of *adults*. Furthermore, Michael Wyness (2012) suggests that there are some elements of feminism which prioritise the interests of women over those of children. Some feminists have 'treated children as … a burden or obstacle to the realisation of women's interests' (p. 43). Wyness suggests that children are in a weaker position than women because they lack basic rights which women have now gained (such as property rights and the right to vote). Therefore, while feminism can help provide insights into the position of children in society, their position cannot be simply explained in terms of patriarchy.

Marxists have tended to see the position of children in terms of economic exploitation. For example, Marx and Engels (discussed in Wyness, 2012) saw children during the industrial revolution as a source of easily exploited, cheap labour which could be used in times of labour shortage and discarded when not needed. However, it is hard to see children in these terms in societies where child-labour is illegal and children make a limited economic contribution (even in terms of unpaid domestic labour).

For the above reasons, some sociologists have argued that existing perspectives on inequality and exploitation cannot fully explain the position of children in society. Instead they have developed a 'new sociology of children' which focuses on the disadvantaged position of children in the social structure without relying on theories designed to explain gender or social class inequalities.

Berry Mayall – sociology and children

Berry Mayall (2004) is critical of much of the sociology of childhood. She argues that it tends to see childhood in terms of the viewpoint and priorities of adults. It can therefore be accused of being **adultist**. Children are routinely portrayed as the passive recipients of socialisation (as Mayall puts it, as **socialisation projects**), or as simply the occupants of the social role of childhood. As in society, where children's views are rarely solicited or listened to, so it is in sociology. However, Mayall argues that several factors have led some sociologists to start to take children more seriously:

1. The women's movement led to the opening up of sociology to one disadvantaged group – women. This paved the way for children to be given more attention.

2. A children's rights movement has gained momentum in its own right since the Second World War. For example, the United Nations Convention on the Rights of the Child established the principle that children should be seen as having rights in the same way as adults.

3. Within sociology some writers began to question the way that children were portrayed. For example, Jens Qvortrup (1991) argued that the economic importance of children was seriously underestimated. Writing a report on an international study of childhood, he noted that children did a great deal of hidden work which made a significant contribution to the economy but which was largely ignored by economists.

The present tense of childhood

Because of such factors, Mayall has emphasised what she calls the **present tense of childhood**. Childhood should not be seen as preparation for adulthood. Instead, the sociology of childhood should concentrate on studying what it is like being a child and it should take children's point of view seriously.

Linked to this is a political stance that supports greater rights for children. Mayall believes that societies such as Britain give children far too few rights. Children are vulnerable up to a point because of their small physical size and biological immaturity. However, most of their vulnerability stems not from their chronological age, but from the way society treats them.

For example, children have found it difficult to get protection from adult abuse because children's claims are not taken as seriously as those of adults. Children lack the economic power to walk away from an abusive household and, because they cannot vote, they lack the political power to make the issue a priority. Similarly, children have little say in how the education system is run, and they have little freedom to participate in politics or to earn their own living.

Mayall argues that the powerlessness of children is not inevitable. In some countries children have greater rights than in Britain. In Norway and Sweden, children are recognised as citizens although they do not have the same rights as adults. Furthermore, children, in Britain and elsewhere, sometimes take on adult roles very competently when circumstances make this necessary. For example, older children sometimes end up caring for parents and younger siblings if their parents are ill or disabled.

The new sociology of children

Mayall believes that in order to explore and develop the potential for improving the position of children in society it is necessary to develop a **new sociology of children** rather than a sociology of childhood. A sociology of children recognises the competence of children as social actors and the crucial role children play in shaping their own lives:

> *Children are understood as agents in their learning from their earliest days. Children do things that make a difference to relationships and to their own lives. Children have knowledge about what matters to them. They make assessments of events and of relations. They have clear moral sense, learned from their earliest encounters with dilemmas in daily life.*
> Mayall, 2004, p. 43

Conclusion

Mayall concludes that the sociology of children should link with a children's rights movement, just as the sociology of gender linked with the women's rights movement. A prerequisite for this is that children are genuinely heard in research. In the past, most research on children involved observation. But Mayall believes that research based on interviews is better because it allows children to voice their own issues and concerns in a way that promotes more equal rights between adults and children.

Evaluation of Mayall

Mayall is just one of several sociologists advocating and developing the sociology of children. She makes important criticisms of sociologies of childhood and demonstrates how listening to children can enhance an understanding of the social world. Her views on increasing the rights of children go much further than most people would accept at present. However, demands for women's rights were widely thought to be fanciful at the start of the 20th century, but did gradually gain acceptance. Perhaps the same will happen with children's rights. Nevertheless, an important difference remains between the campaigns for women's rights and those for children's rights. Women campaigned for their own rights and female sociologists analysed their own situation. At the moment, it is still largely adults campaigning for children's rights and it is exclusively adults researching the sociology of children. When children lead campaigns for children's rights and child sociologists study children, then the role of children will truly have changed.

Activity

Teenagers in Lancaster protest after the Brexit vote that 16–18 year olds were not allowed to take part in the referendum.

1. Suggest ways in which this photograph illustrates the limited power that children have in shaping society.

2. Some political parties have advocated giving 16–18 year-olds full voting rights. Why do you think this has not yet happened?

Key terms

Age patriarchy The dominance of parents over children.

Marital patriarchy The dominance of husbands over wives.

Adultist Biased in favour of adults rather than children.

Socialisation projects The idea that children are seen by adults as the passive recipients of socialisation to be moulded to fit the preferences of adults.

New sociology of children A version of sociology which views social life in terms of the perspectives and interests of children.

Present tense of childhood Seeing childhood in terms of the experience of children rather than in terms of the process of becoming an adult.

Summary

1. Children can be seen as occupying a distinctive place in the social structure.

2. Feminists tend to see their place in terms of patriarchy but a problem with this is that children are dominated by women as well as men.

3. Marxists tend to see the place of children in terms of economic exploitation but this does not seem a useful approach in societies in which children do little work.

4. Berry Mayall and others believe a new sociology of children is needed which recognises children as social actors, acknowledges the distinctive interests of children and is linked to movements for children's rights.

PART 7 DEMOGRAPHY

Contents

This part of the chapter examines questions related to **demography** – the study of populations, their characteristics and how they change. Population change can be affected by three factors: births, deaths and migration. This part discusses questions such as why have both the birth rate and death rate declined in the United Kingdom? How has the population structure changed and what are the effects of an ageing population? How do you account for the fluctuations in migration to and from the UK and how has globalisation influenced this? The factors that shape demographic changes are linked both to individual decisions and to social structures. For example, lifestyle decisions (such as whether to smoke) affect the death rates, but factors outside the control of the individual (such as rates of poverty and the standard of healthcare) are crucial too. Sociologists therefore examine how these individual choices and structural factors interact in shaping demographic change and the impact this has on families and households.

5.7.1 Factors shaping demography

Logically, the size of a country's population can only change as a result of babies being born, people dying, and people leaving or entering a country (migration). Understanding demography requires an understanding of each of these factors, but also how they interact with one another.

Births, deaths and migration

The total population of any country is shaped by three factors:

1. The **birth rate**, which is defined as the number of live births per year per thousand of the population.

    The birth rate is affected by the number of women of childbearing age in the population (since only they can have children). Childbearing age is usually taken to be between 15 and 44. In different places at different times the likelihood of women of child bearing age having children varies and this is reflected in the fertility rate.

    The **fertility rate** is the number of live births per year per thousand women of childbearing age.

    Another useful concept for understanding population change is the **total fertility rate**, which is the average number of children women in a population will have during the lifetime of each woman.

2. The **death rate**, which is defined as the number of deaths per year per thousand of the population. This is partly affected by the age structure of the population, since older people are more likely to die than younger people.

    The **infant mortality rate** is the number of babies who die per thousand live births during the first year of their lives. Infant mortality rate has an important impact on population changes since only children who survive childhood can go on to have children themselves.

3. The third factor affecting population size is **migration**.

    Immigration (that is entry into a country) increases the size of the population while **emigration** (leaving a country) reduces the size of the population. There are different definitions of migration and political decisions affect who exactly is counted as a migrant. However, UK statistics use a United

Nations definition which defines a migrant as a person who changes country of 'normal residence' for at least a year.

The difference between immigration and emigration is known as **net migration** and it is this which determines the overall effect of migration on population size. When there is **positive net migration** more people are entering the country than leaving (so the population is growing), but when there **is negative net migration** more people are leaving than entering (so the population is falling).

Natural change in population growth takes place as a result of there being more births than deaths or vice versa, but overall change is clearly affected by net migration as well.

Overall population change since 1900

According to the Census, in 1901 the population of the UK stood at just over 38.3 million. By 1951 it had risen to 50.3 million and by 2001 to 59 million. Estimates for mid-2016 put the figure at 65.6 million (ONS, 2016).

Figure 5.7.1 shows annual population changes in the UK between 1944 and 2016. It demonstrates that in all but a handful of years between these dates the UK population has been growing by less than 1 per cent per year.

Figure 5.7.2 demonstrates that in the early 1990s, there was negative net migration (more emigrants than immigrants), but since then there has been positive net migration (more immigrants than emigrants) with immigration contributing more to population growth than natural change in most years. However, for much of the 20th century, the UK was a net exporter of people. Throughout the period there has been natural growth in the population, but the rate of growth has varied.

Jane Falkingham and Tony Champion (2016) note that in the last 50 years, population growth has been very uneven. For example, there was high growth in the 1960s fuelled by a 'baby boom' (a period when the birth rate was particularly high) but growth in the most recent years has come from a combination of net immigration and a significant rise in births, partly because immigration has boosted the number of women of childbearing age in the population. Immigration of young adults also helps to cut the death rate. This demonstrates that births, deaths and migration interact in complex ways.

Figure 5.7.1 Annual population change for the UK (mid-1944 to mid-2016)

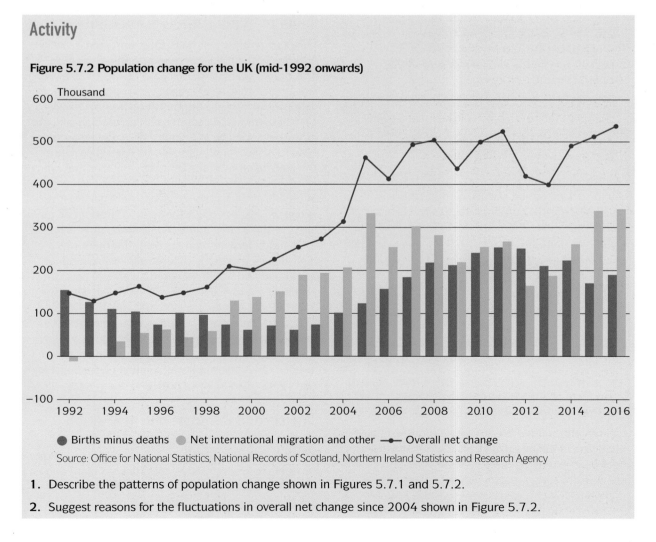

Source: Office for National Statistics, National Records of Scotland, Northern Ireland Statistics and Research Agency

Activity

Figure 5.7.2 Population change for the UK (mid-1992 onwards)

● Births minus deaths ● Net international migration and other ─●─ Overall net change

Source: Office for National Statistics, National Records of Scotland, Northern Ireland Statistics and Research Agency

1. Describe the patterns of population change shown in Figures 5.7.1 and 5.7.2.

2. Suggest reasons for the fluctuations in overall net change since 2004 shown in Figure 5.7.2.

Summary

1. Demography is the study of populations which change as a result of births, deaths and migration.

2. The British population has been consistently growing in recent decades.

3. Natural growth in population size has been one factor causing the rise in the UK but in recent years positive net migration has been the main factor.

Key terms

Demography The study of populations.

Birth rate The number of live births per year per thousand of the population.

Fertility rate The number of live births per year per thousand women of childbearing age.

Total fertility rate The average number of children women in a given population will have during their lifetime.

Death rate The number of deaths per year per thousand of the population.

Infant mortality rate The number of babies who die per thousand live births during the first year of their lives.

Natural change (in population growth) The change in population size which takes place as a result of there being more births than deaths or vice versa.

Migration (international) The movement of people from one country to another for a period of one year or more.

Immigration The movement of people into one country from another country for a period of one year or more.

Emigration The movement of people out of one country to another for a period of one year or more.

Net migration The differences between the number of immigrants and the number of emigrants resulting in a net loss or net gain of population.

Positive net migration A situation in which there are more immigrants to a country than emigrants from it.

Negative net migration A situation in which there are more emigrants from a country than immigrants to it.

7.2 Births

The House of Commons (1999) notes that the number of births in the UK declined in the 20th century with the exception of two baby booms which followed the two world wars, plus an additional peak in the 1960s. Much of the explanation for this overall decline rests in women typically having fewer children. This is closely linked to a falling total fertility rate. In 1900 this stood at 3.5 children but by 1997 it was less than half that, 1.7. It fell to a low of 1.63 in 2001 but then increased to a new peak of 1.94 in 2010 (ONS, 2013).

This raises two central questions. Why has the total fertility rate declined over the long term and why has it risen somewhat since the turn of the millennium?

The long-term decline in fertility rates — demographic transitions

Long-term trends in fertility rates are often explained in terms of the theory of **demographic transition**. This theory was first put forward as the 1920s when it was argued that demography was transformed when countries underwent the transition from relatively poor, less-developed societies to increasingly affluent industrial societies. In preindustrial societies women tend to have a large number of children because of the high infant mortality rate which meant that many children did not survive until adulthood. Furthermore, in preindustrial societies children were generally an economic asset because they started work at an early age. Having a large number of children (that is having a high total fertility rate) ensured that there was a high chance that some children would survive until adulthood and would therefore be able to provide economic insurance for parents. However, when the infant mortality rate started to fall due to a variety of factors, there was a period of adjustment before fertility rates fell. Eventually, though, adults cut the number of children they had and population growth levelled off. A transition was complete from high birth and death rates to lower birth and death rates.

The second demographic transition

A number of social scientists argue that in more developed societies a **second demographic transition** takes place in which birth rates fall even more and they can become lower than death rates (known as **sub-replacement population fertility**). As a result, advanced societies can have a falling population (assuming that immigration does not make up for this reduction in births). The replacement level for populations, i.e. the level at which populations do not fall or rise, is generally seen as being a total fertility rate of around 2.1 (since not all new-borns go on to have children themselves and men cannot have children) and after the second demographic transition the fertility rate can often be lower than this. After this transition, fertility rates eventually tend to stop falling and to stabilise, but at a very low level.

Nicholas Eberstadt (2015) argues that in the second demographic transition there is much greater instability in marriage, with people tending to marry later, higher rates of divorce and separation, increased likelihood of cohabitation but more short-lived relationships.

The causes of declining fertility rates

Nicoletta Balbo, Francesco Billari and Melinda Mills (2012) identify three types of factor which are important in explaining the decline in fertility rates that is associated with demographic transitions.

These are:

- Contraceptive and reproductive technology.
- Economic factors.
- Cultural factors.

Contraception

Balbo, Billari and Mills (2013) suggest that developments in contraception have been crucial in allowing people to control their fertility. Latex (rubber) condoms first became available in the early years of the 20th century, but it was only in the 1950s that they became more reliable and easy to use. The most significant development in contraception was the development of the hormonal contraceptive pill which was first approved for use in the UK in 1961. It was available on the NHS from 1961, but only for married women and only in 1974 could it be prescribed for single women (Coast and Freeman, 2016). Since then the range of available contraceptives has expanded providing more ways of controlling fertility and thereby playing a role in reducing fertility rates.

Economic factors

One of the most significant factors leading to falls in fertility rates has been the changing economic position of women in society. Female employment outside the home rose rapidly in the period following the Second World War. Growing dependence on two incomes to maintain family lifestyles discouraged families from having large numbers of children which would limit the ability of the family to have both parents in paid work (particularly full-time work).

Ann Buchanan and Anna Rotkirch (2013) argue that there is quite a strong relationship between female employment rates and fertility with fertility rates declining as female employment increased after the Second World War. This structural change in the labour market has been key to declining fertility rates. However, more recently there has been something of a reversal with women in employment being more likely to have children. Nevertheless, the age at first birth has been rising, partly due to more women in the UK progressing on to higher education and wishing to establish careers before having one or more children. Buchanan (2017) comments that 'in developing their careers, some women simply leave it too late' and she notes better educated women tend to have lower fertility rates than less well-educated women.

Research by Ann Buchanan and Anna Rotkirch (2013) based on informal interviews with young mothers contacted through the website *Mumsnet* found that many women mentioned the cost of raising children when explaining their decisions about whether to have children and how many children they would like. Several respondents argued that children had gone from being an economic asset (by providing work in family businesses) to being an economic cost. Many women were very cautious about the economic costs of childcare and of reducing their working hours given their mortgage commitments.

Cultural factors

Buchanan and Rotkirch (2013) argue that part of the shift towards smaller family size could be related to a greater child-centredness. Parents are increasingly concerned to give their children good opportunities in life and they believe that they can devote more time and attention to their children if their family is limited to a small number of children. This is particularly true of middle-class parents but similar attitudes may spread to all social classes.

Buchanan and Rotkirch (2013) also link declining fertility rates to changing values about how a woman's worth is judged in the UK. They argue that while in the past 'a woman's worth was based on her ability to provide numerous children, today other factors, such as having a good education and a career as well as a family, are valued.' (Roberts, Williams and Buchanan, 2013, p. 109). Clearly, economic and cultural factors overlap here, and the influence of feminist ideas can also be detected in such attitudes. Similarly, the research based on the sample identified through *Mumsnet* found that women were taking a more balanced approach to considering their own quality of life with the needs of family. As a result, new norms had developed about the ideal family size.

Births and fertility rates — conclusion

A range of factors have interacted to reduce total fertility rates ranging from those operating at a structural level (such as changes in the labour market) to the preferences of individuals. Many of these changes have tended to reinforce one another with, for example, economic change going hand-in-hand with changing attitudes making it hard to determine which factors have had the biggest impact.

There is general agreement that the trends in countries such as the UK have been towards lower birth rates and widespread agreement that there has been a second demographic revolution.

The effects of changes in fertility rates

Declining total fertility rates over the medium term has meant that with fewer children in the population, adults are less likely to live in households containing many, if any children. This has contributed to causing many of the changes in households and family life discussed in earlier parts of this chapter. These include:

> falling family size

> a reduction in the proportion of the population living in nuclear families

> the increase in single person households

> smaller average household size (Falkingham and Champion, 2016).

While declining fertility rates and a reduced burden of childcare have made it easier for women to stay in paid employment and progress their careers, it has contributed to wider economic problems.

Contemporary issues: Recent rises in the birth rate

Short-term trends are not always in line with this longer-term trend. As noted earlier, birth rates have increased in recent years such that in 2010 the total fertility rate was the highest since 1973 (ONS, 2013). The Office for National Statistics attributed this to the following factors:

> A rise in the fertility rate among women in their 20s with more women currently in their 20s having children.

> Women born in the 1960s and 1970s who had postponed having children doing so in middle age (sometimes with the help of new reproductive technologies).

> The higher fertility rates of foreign born-women and increased immigration of young women to the UK.

> The influence of government policy such as increased maternity and paternity leave and the impact of child tax credits.

However, with government cuts in tax credits and downward pressure on immigration since the Brexit vote in 2016, fertility rates may start to fall again.

'Taking back control' of borders with respect to immigration from the EU was one of the important issues in the campaign.

Questions

1. Suggest reasons why the Brexit vote might reduce immigration to the UK and increase short-term emigration from the UK.

2. What impact is Brexit likely to have on birth rates in the UK both in the short term and the long term?

One problem is the increase in the **dependency ratio**. The dependency ratio is the ratio of those who are not of working age (the young and elderly) to those of working age (19–64). **Youth dependency ratios** are based on the ratio of those aged under 19 to the working-age population, whereas **elderly dependency ratios** are the proportion of those aged over 64 to those of working age.

Youth dependency ratios declined between 1971 and 2011 (Norman, 2016) because of the falling birth rate, but adult dependency ratios increased as the population aged and death rates fell (see below). The falling youth dependency ratio can be good for public finances and the economy in the *short term*, because there are fewer children to support from the wages and taxes of those in work, but in the *long term* it leads to a relative shortage of people of working age on whom the dependent population relies for the creation of wealth.

The low birth rate also contributes to the rising average age of the population as the proportion of young people declines. As a result, elderly dependency ratios also increase. This has a number of significant consequences (see pp. 345–349) such as problems with the funding of pensions and care for the elderly.

One way to deal with the problems created by low fertility rates and the resulting ageing of the population is to allow or encourage increased immigration of people of working age to counteract shortages in the workforce and reduce the dependency ratio. However, large-scale positive net migration has proved politically controversial in the UK and may be a factor behind the vote to leave the EU (the Brexit vote).

Key terms

Demographic transition The change from one pattern of demography to another, particularly when both birth and death rates fall significantly over a period of time.

Second demographic transition A relatively recent shift in advanced societies to very low birth and death rates.

Sub-replacement population fertility A situation in which too few children are born in a society to replace the number of people dying.

Dependency ratio The ratio of those who are not of working age (the young and elderly) to those of working age (19–64).

Youth dependency ratio The ratio of those aged under 19 to the working-age population.

Elderly dependency ratio The proportion of those aged over 64 to those of working age.

Summary

1. The birth rate in the UK generally declined in the 20th century but there was a small rise between 2001 and 2010.

2. Long term, there has been a substantial fall in the fertility rate.

3. A declining fertility rate has been linked to demographic transitions in which the fertility rate goes down in response to declining infant mortality rates.

4. Developments in contraception have contributed to falling fertility rates.

5. The costs associated with raising children and greater female involvement in the Labour market underpin the economic causes of declining fertility rates.

6. Cultural changes have resulted in smaller family size being seen as more desirable.

7. Declining total fertility has affected family size and structure and increased the dependency ratio.

5.7.3 Deaths

There has been a remarkable transformation in the death rate since the 19th century and as a result, on average, people live much longer than in the past. The factors that have caused this are not particularly controversial, but what is more disputed is the relative importance of different factors. In particular, sociologists have debated how much of the fall in death rates is caused by medical advances and how much by other factors such as improved living standards. Some commentators have also begun to question whether death rates will continue to decline. Are we witnessing the beginning of a trend where death rates level off or actually start increasing?

Trends in the death rate and life expectancy

The **death rate** (or mortality rate) is the number of deaths per year per thousand of the population. The

Figure 5.7.3 Age-standardised mortality rates (ASMRs), 2001–2016, England and Wales

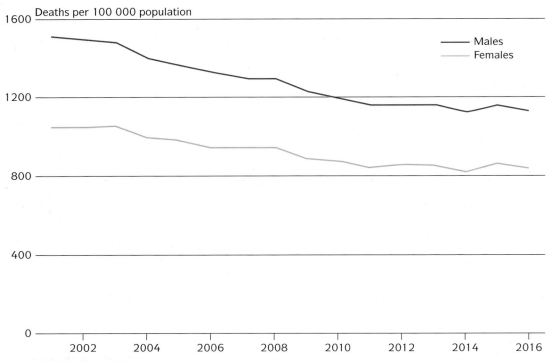

England and Wales

Source: Office for National Statistics

overall mortality rate has fallen over the long term in the UK and is now less than half the rate in 1901. Life expectancy is the average number of years a person can expect to live, either at birth or at a particular age.

A better measure of trends in mortality than simple mortality rates are **age-standardised mortality rates (ASMRs)** which adjust mortality rates to take account of the age structure of the population. Fairly obviously, mortality rates tend to be higher in elderly groups in the population than younger groups and ASMRs take account of this.

Between 1983 and 2013 the ASMR fell by 45 per cent for males and 36 per cent for females (ONS, 2014). Figure 5.7.3 shows trends in ASMRs between 2001 and 2016 and show a general decline over the period although there was an increase in 2014–2015.

There has been a corresponding increase in life expectancy. In 1901 in the UK, life expectancy at birth was just 45 for males and 49 for females but by 2001 it was 75.7 years for males and 80.4 years for females (Evandrou, Falkingham and Vlachantoni, 2016). By 2012–2014 it had increased further and in England stood at 79.5 years for males and 82.3 years for females (ONS, 2015).

Part of the rise is attributable to big declines in the **infant mortality rate** – that is the proportion of babies born alive that die before reaching one year old. The infant mortality rate was just 3.7 deaths per thousand live births in 2015 compared with 9.4 in 1985. However, Evandrou, Falkingham and Vlachantoni (2016) point out that mortality rates have fallen in all groups.

Reasons for the falling death rate

The range of factors responsible for the falling death rate is not particularly controversial, but the relative importance of different factors is more disputed.

Medical improvements

According to Stephen Moore (2013), the **biomedical model of health** assumes that the mind and body are separate entities and health is entirely shaped by

Figure 5.7.4 Death rates from specific diseases 2001–2016

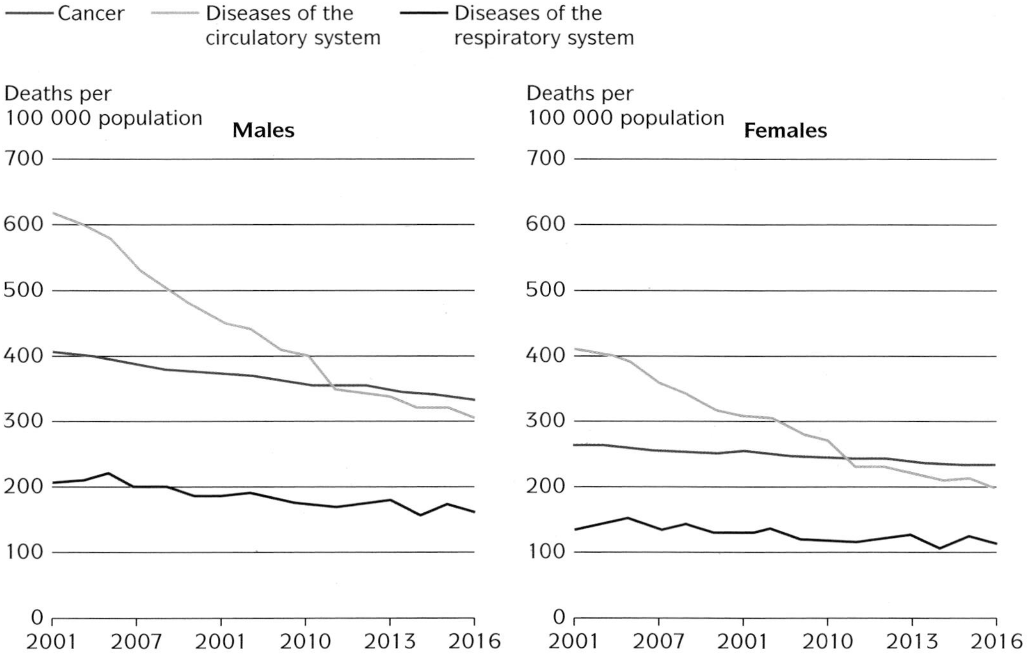

——— Cancer   ——— Diseases of the   ——— Diseases of the
                       circulatory system   respiratory system

Deaths per 100 000 population — **Males**

700, 600, 500, 400, 300, 200, 100, 0

2001, 2007, 2001, 2010, 2013, 2016

Deaths per 100 000 population — **Females**

700, 600, 500, 400, 300, 200, 100, 0

2001, 2007, 2001, 2010, 2013, 2016

Source: ONS (2017) 'Deaths registered in England and Wales, 2016' [online]

the biological functioning of the body. Consequently the causes of illness and ultimately death can be understod entirely in terms of a specific aetiology – that is a specific cause for disease. From this viewpoint, the death rate has been cut by treating diseases better or preventing them from occurring in the first place.

Activity

1. Decsribe the trends in deaths from different types of disease shown in Figure 5.7.4.

2. List all the reasons you can think of for the falling death rates for these diseases. Which do you think might have been most important?

In the UK in the late 19th and early 20th centuries infectious diseases were one of the main causes of premature death, but as the 20th century developed, antibiotics and immunisation helped to dramatically cut or even eliminate diseases such as tuberculosis, smallpox and polio. Similarly, diseases such as measles, mumps and rubella have been greatly reduced by vaccination programmes. Tranter (1996) argues that more that 75 per cent of the fall in the death rate between the mid-19th century and the 1970s was due to a fall in deaths from such diseases. However, there is more than one reason why this

decline took place and medical improvements are certainly not the whole story.

In 1948 the National Health Service (NHS) was introduced. This made treatment free at the point of use available to the whole population. The NHS has had a significant impact, for example it has helped to cut the infant mortality rate dramatically (see above) thus raising average life expectancy considerably.

As people have lived longer, infectious diseases have become less significant as causes of death while diseases of older age groups, particularly cancer, heart disease and strokes, have become major killers. However, medical improvements have helped to cut the death rate from these diseases considerably. The biggest falls have been in diseases of the circulatory system (heart disease and stroke) (ONS, 2017) which have been achieved partly through improvements in treatment. These include the wider availability of heart bypasses and treatments such as stents to deal with clogged arteries which can cause heart attacks. The widespread use of drugs such as beta blockers (which reduce blood pressure) and statins (which cut cholesterol in the blood) have been important as well. Death rates from some cancers, for example breast cancer, have also fallen significantly with improvements in drug treatments, radiotherapy and surgical techniques.

Improved nutrition, hygiene and public health

The importance of medical improvements has been questioned by Thomas McKeown (1979) who argued that from the 18th century right through to the 1960s improvements in nutrition and hygiene were much more important than medical improvements. He notes that diseases such as TB and polio declined steeply before immunisation was introduced. McKeown therefore argues that improvements in nutrition were more important than medical changes because they made people more resistant to disease. Similarly, improvements in hygiene reduced the risks of developing disease and accounted for about 20 per cent of the long-term fall in the death rate. More recently, various public health measures such as The Clean Air Act of 1956 (which helped to reduce deaths from air pollution) have reduced mortality and public health campaigns designed to discourage unhealthy lifestyles may also have had an impact.

Social, economic and environmental factors

There is a large body of evidence which suggests that social and environmental factors influence the death rate. For example, The Marmot Review (2010) confirmed earlier research showing a strong relationship between deprivation, social class and mortality. Sometimes the impact is direct, for example the decline of heavy industry and particularly dangerous occupations such as coal mining and fishing have cut deaths from accidents at work and industrial diseases (such as lung diseases contracted from mining). However, the benefits can be indirect as well. Marmot (2004) challenges the biomedical model rejecting the view that death rates can be explained simply in terms of the incidence of specific diseases. Marmot argues that psycho-social factors influence death rates with factors such as low income, low social status and stress increasing the likelihood of premature death. Wilkinson and Marmot (2003) argue that factors such as insecure employment, lack of pension provision, and working in dangerous jobs and jobs with no prospects all create 'psychological wear and tear' which increases mortality rates.

From this viewpoint, gradually rising living standards, improved housing and greater educational opportunities have reduced overall mortality. The development of the welfare state since the Beveridge Report in 1942 has increased general economic security, particularly for the least well-off and may therefore have contributed to falling death rates. Rising living standards can also have a more direct impact (for example by enabling people to improve nutrition). However, the reductions have been uneven with mortality remaining relatively high in the most deprived areas but dropping very low in the most affluent. In 2016 the age-standardised mortality rate was 12.8 in Blackpool but just 8.7 in Monmouthshire (ONS, 2017).

Changing lifestyles

The development of medical knowledge has made it possible to inform the public about how they can improve their own health through lifestyle changes. Examples include better information about the impact of diet, weight, alcohol consumption, exercise and smoking on longevity. Perhaps the most successful public health campaign has concerned smoking. The proportion of the adult population who smoke fell from 46 per cent in 1974 to 19 per cent in 2013 with a ban on smoking in places of work (including bars and restaurants) from 2007 helping to cut consumption. Campaigns to increase the consumption of fruit and vegetables and reduce the consumption of saturated fats have had some success. However, there has been less success in cutting deaths from alcohol consumption with rates of alcohol related deaths higher in 2015 than in 1994 (ONS, 2017) and rates of obesity and physical inactivity remain stubbornly high.

Rising living standards and other social and economic changes don't always have beneficial effects on health and death rates. For example, greater affluence has made alcohol more affordable and wider car ownership can cut rates of physical exercise.

Conclusion

A combination of factors has resulted in the falling death rate with different factors being more or less important in particular eras. In the long term, falling death rates from infectious diseases have been particularly important, but social and economic changes may have been more important than medical advances. The significance of psycho-social factors should not be underestimated as illustrated by class and regional differences in mortality. However, specific medical advances (for example in relation to heart disease) and lifestyle changes (particularly the reduction in smoking) have also been significant.

Contemporary issues: The end of falling death rates?

Joan Garrod (2017) notes that in 2015 there was an unexpected rise of over 5 per cent in death rates in England and Wales. This raised the possibility that the long-term decline in death rates was coming to an end. One reason that has been suggested for this was the decline in government spending resulting from austerity. Professor Dominic Harrison, an advisor to Public Health England, attributed this rise to cuts in the social care budgets of local authorities which limited their ability to care for the elderly. However, others argued that cold weather and flu were more likely to be responsible.

Questions

1. Suggest reasons why falling government expenditure in areas such as social care, social security payments, housing benefits and health might increase the death rate.

A protest against austerity and cuts to social care.

2. Do you think the long-term fall in death rates may be coming to an end? Give reasons for your answer.

Key terms

Age-standardised mortality rates (ASMRs) Death (or mortality rates) adjusted to take account of the age structure of the population.

Biomedical model of health A model of health and illness which assumes that the mind and body are separate entities and health is entirely shaped by the biological functioning of the body.

Summary

1. Age-standardised mortality rates have fallen substantially in recent decades and life expectancy has increased considerably.

2. The biomedical model of health attributes these changes to improving medical treatment and prevention of disease, particularly infectious diseases.

3. The introduction of the NHS has made medical treatment more widely available and has helped cut death rates, most recently particularly for circulatory diseases.

4. Thomas McKeown believes improvements in hygiene and nutrition are mainly responsible for falling death rates but social, economic and environmental factors are also very significant and changing lifestyles may have had some impact.

5.7.4 Ageing

The average age of the population in the UK is rising and a growing proportion of the population are over retirement age. But what are the consequences of this both for society as a whole and those in older age groups? And how have sociologists analysed the position of older age groups in the population?

The consequences of falling death rates – an ageing population

A combination of low birth rates and low death rates has resulted in an ageing population (a population in which the average age is rising). Falkingham and Champion (2016) note that the median age in the UK increased from 33.9 years in 1974 to 40.0 years in 2014. Furthermore, Maria Evandrou, Jane Falkingham and Athina Vlachantoni (2016) observe that in 1901 less than 5 per cent of the population was 65 or over, but by 2014 this had reached 17.7 per cent. The fastest growing age group in the UK has been the over 90s who made up just 0.4 per cent of the population in 1989 but 0.8 per cent in 2014 (Falkingham and Champion, 2016).

Figure 5.7.5 A population pyramid showing projected change in population age and sex structure in England between 2014 and 2024. The pyramid shows the number of people in different age groups.

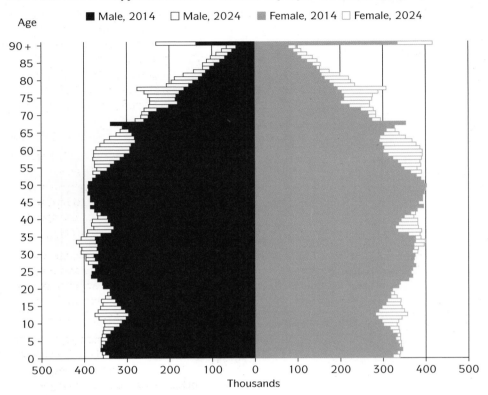

Source: ONS (2016) [online]

Activity

1. Describe the population structure in 2014.

2. Describe the projected population structure in 2024.

3. Analyse the effect these changes will have on the dependency ratio.

Of course, increasing life expectancy is a very welcome development and on average the chances of retaining good health into retirement are also increasing. However, Maria Evandrou, Jane Falkingham and Athina Vlachantoni (2016) argue that there have been a number of negative consequences of the ageing population.

Pensions

As more people reach retirement age and stop working, the dependency ratio increases and this creates problems for public finances.

Not only does revenue from income tax fall as older people withdraw from the workforce, but the burden of pensions increases both for the state (paying state pensions) and private pension schemes. As individuals survive longer beyond retirement, they tend to receive a greater total amount in pension payments. With low interest rates over recent years, the level of savings needed to pay for retirement pensions which are funded out of savings has increased considerably. This has put financial strain on both private and public providers of pensions and many private schemes have increased the contributions and/or reduced the benefits payable to future pensioners.

Another consequence is that successive governments have put up the age at which people receive state pensions. In the past men received their state pension at 65 and women at 60, but under the Pensions Acts of 2007 and 2014 this is due to rise to 68 for both groups.

Public services

The ageing population has placed an increasing strain upon public funding for social care costs. Evandrou, Falkingham and Vlachantoni (2016) note that restrictions on public spending have led to a reduction in the spending on social care costs for the elderly who cannot care for themselves. This has placed a strain on family members and charities who have sometimes helped to fill the gap left by inadequate public funding. It has also impacted on the NHS with the elderly sometimes being unable to leave hospital because of the lack of social care. This so-called 'bed blocking' has affected the ability of the NHS to provide care for other patients. Wesley Key (2016) notes that the average annual costs of hospital and community care are three times greater for those aged 85 and older than for 65–74 year olds, putting extra strain on an already over-stretched NHS.

Housing

Key (2016) suggests that the ageing population has led to an increase in single-person households as a result of widowhood. With a shortage of housing nationally and rising house prices, this creates pressure on the housing stock. The amount of sheltered housing has increased but it struggles to keep pace with the ageing population. Places in care homes have not expanded fast enough to cope with the rising elderly population requiring care. Some pensioners live on their own but occupy large houses, and an expansion of housing suitable for single retired people might help to ease housing shortages for younger age groups.

Ageing population and social policy

For all the above reasoins, the ageing of the population poses serious problems for policy-makers. Successive governments in the UK have not found a method of funding social care in a way that is politically acceptable and many commentators believe that NHS funding is inadequate to deal with rising demand from older age groups. Nevertheless, political parties remain keen to attract the support of older voters who are considerably more likely to vote than younger age groups. Partly for this reason, state pensions have risen faster than wages in recent years and pensioner poverty has declined considerably since the mid-1990s (Age UK, 2017). However, as Age UK points out, about one in seven pensioners still live below the poverty line and the position of individuals over retirement age varies greatly with some being very badly off.

Perspectives on ageing

Some perspectives on ageing simply see it in biological terms. From this viewpoint ageing involves physical deterioration. However, of course ageing does not affect individuals in the same way and the impact of ageing on individuals is closely tied up with the changing role of older age groups in society. This section examines sociological perspectives on ageing.

Functionalism and disengagement theory

Elaine Cumming and William E. Henry (1961) were unusual among sociological theorists of age in claiming that the marginalisation of old people was actually functional for society. They argued that the **disengagement (withdrawal)** of people from social roles was necessary and beneficial for society.

Cumming and Henry claim that, as people age, they lose vitality. Their health usually declines and they become more self-absorbed. These changes make the elderly less well equipped than they were to carry out important social roles such as paid employment.

If people continue in these roles into old age, then the roles will not be carried out particularly well, causing problems for the effective functioning of society. Older people will block opportunities for younger people by continuing to occupy key positions leading to stagnation in society. Furthermore, attempting to maintain previous roles beyond an age when they can comfortably perform them leads to frustration and fatigue for older people.

With more people remaining healthy and active beyond typical retirement ages, government increases in the pension age and the increasing proportion of the population in older age groups, disengagement theory is becoming less credible. However, there is some concern that pension and benefits changes are forcing some older people to continue in work beyond the age when they feel physically and mentally equipped to do so.

The interpretation of age – age as a social construct

Hockey and James (1993) do not see the social roles of the elderly as a product of a functional disengagement from society. Instead they argue that the role of the elderly results from a particular interpretation of old age in Western societies.

Age is to a considerable extent a **social construct**, meaning that it is dependent on the culture of a particular society at a particular time. Although biological changes do affect people as they age, it is the meaning attached to old age that can be more disabling than physiological changes.

In contemporary Britain, everyday talk, stereotypes and the media all serve to make old age appear similar to childhood. In the process, old age is **infantilised**. The elderly are made to seem childlike. As a result, they lose the status of being adults who have full personhood.

Individual and institutional ageism

There is plenty of evidence that discrimination against the elderly or ageism does exist and at least partly this results from the meaning attached to old age. For example, Lorraine Green (2010) argues that ageism significantly increases the problems faced by people as they age. She defines ageism as 'the systematic stereotyping of and discrimination against individuals on the basis of their age' (Green, 2010).

Green claims that there are many examples of routine ageism in the way the elderly are treated by individuals in everyday life. These include: 'using terms like "old dear" to refer to elderly ladies, talking in a patronising infantilistic manner to the elderly, sending ageist supposedly humorous birthday cards' (Green, 2010, p. 188).

Much more serious are examples of abuse of the elderly by individuals. Green refers to a study by Thobaben (2008) which estimated that between one in 10 and one in 50 of those aged over 65 in the UK have been harmed, mistreated or exploited by a carer or a member of their family.

However, Green does not believe that disadvantages faced by older people are entirely the result of individual meanings. Some disadvantages are systematic and result from the way society is organised and structured. **Institutional ageism** – systematic neglect of the needs of the elderly or outright discrimination against them by organisations – can have equally damaging effects.

Health care is an area where the elderly are particularly vulnerable to institutional ageism. For example, Green cites research that suggests that elderly women are less likely than younger women to be offered breast screening, despite a medical need for it, and that in accident and emergency departments older people are less likely to receive intensive attempts at resuscitation than younger people.

The existence of institutional ageism suggests that there could be structural factors to do with the organisation of society which disadvantage older people in addition to discriminatory beliefs and individual ageism. This has led some sociologists to develop more structural perspectives on ageing.

Structured dependency

John Vincent (1995) has developed an approach to analysing old age which attaches primary importance to issues of power. He sees the disadvantages of the elderly as linked to **structured dependency**. This approach has much in common with Marxist perspectives. From this viewpoint, the elderly tend to be dependent, disadvantaged and poor, not as a result of biological decline, but because society is structured in such a way as to make them dependent. Compulsory retirement ages and the provision of state pensions and welfare services for the elderly tend to make them dependent whether they like it or not.

Vincent also argues that dependency in old age is linked to other forms of socially structured inequality such as ethnicity, class and gender. Old age is often characterised by material deprivation – the elderly are more likely to be poor than other groups in the population. However, this is not true for all groups of the elderly. Women and those from working-class backgrounds and disadvantaged ethnic groups are most likely to experience poverty in old age. For these groups, low pay and/or part-time work during their working lives may have restricted their entitlement to pensions. For the rich, old age may be an entirely different and much more appealing prospect.

Postmodernism

Postmodern perspectives adopt a very different viewpoint. Blaikie (1999) argues that in a postmodern culture, old age need not be a time of dependency and decline, but can be a time of increased choice and opportunity. Although age eventually catches up with people, at least in the early years of retirement old age is much less of a barrier to living an active life than it once was. Blaikie even speculates that medical advances may eventually make decline and dependency in old age a thing of the past.

Among the supporters of postmodern views are Mike Featherstone and Mike Hepworth (1991) who believe that in recent times for some groups the life course has begun to be **deconstructed**, or broken down, making it less predictable.

The 'baby boomers' who were born after the Second World War, when there was a high birth rate, and who grew up in the 1960s and 1970s are taking with them into old age many of the values and cultural tastes of their youth. Unlike previous generations they try to maintain youthful lifestyles as they age. They increasingly reject chronological age – the number of years lived – as an indicator of their real selves. They regard chronological age as a mask which hides their more youthful essential, inner self. Featherstone and Hepworth quote research suggesting that many people see themselves as having a **personal age** different from their **chronological age**, usually seeing themselves as younger than their birth certificate indicates.

Activity

The Rolling Stones have continued touring into their 70s.

1. How does the example of the Rolling Stones illustrate the idea of the **deconstruction** of the life course?

2. Continuing to attend rock concerts is one way that baby boomers try to maintain a youthful lifestyle as they age. Suggest other ways in which they might do this.

Conclusion

Vincent's structured dependency approach can be accused of having an overly pessimistic view of old age, while postmodern perspectives can equally be accused of having an overly optimistic approach. However, both may be an advance over disengagement theory because they recognise that the nature of old age varies from society to society and that there is nothing inevitable about the social roles of the elderly in any one society at a particular time. Furthermore,

approaches such as that put forward by John Vincent demonstrate an awareness that the experience of ageing is also shaped by other inequalities in society.

Key terms

Disengagement The withdrawal of people from social roles.

Social construct Something which is thought to be natural but which is really produced by the culture of a particular society at a particular time.

Infantilised Making adults (particularly the elderly) appear child-like or treating them like children.

Institutional ageism Systematic neglect of the needs of the elderly or outright discrimination against them by organisations.

Structured dependency Structures in society which undermine the independence of social groups.

Deconstruction Breaking down societal structures such as age-related social roles.

Personal age How old a person regards themselves as being.

Chronological age The number of years somebody has lived.

Summary

1. The average age of the population has been increasing in the UK with rising life expectancy and falling birth rates.

2. The ageing of the population increases the dependency ratio and puts pressure on funding pensions and public services.

3. Increased life expectancy puts pressure on housing and makes increasing demands on family members.

4. Functionalists believe the disengagement of the elderly from social roles is beneficial for society but others see age as a social construct.

5. The elderly can be subject to discrimination by individuals who are ageist or by institutions which are institutionally ageist.

6. Structural approaches believe that the dependency of the elderly results from the social structure but postmodernists believe that the limitations imposed by ageing are breaking down.

7. The experience of ageing is affected by social inequalities such as those linked to class, gender and ethnicity.

5.7.5 Migration

Patterns of immigration to and emigration from the UK have changed significantly over recent decades. But what factors persuade people to move to another country and how do these movement affect the population of the UK? How is migration linked to the process of globalisation? How are people's identities affected by migration? These are some of the key questions that arise from studying migration and they will be addressed in this unit.

Immigration

Immigration has been a hot political topic in recent years in the UK where there has been much discussion about whether levels of immigration are a 'problem' or not. Emigration has received less attention. But how much immigration has there been and what causes this movement of people?

Patterns of UK immigration

In the earliest years of the 20th century most immigrants to the UK were from Ireland and in the 1930s a considerable number of refugees came to Britain fleeing war and persecution in Europe. After the Second World War, there was a labour shortage in the UK which led to immigration from the Commonwealth particularly the West Indies, Pakistan, India and Bangladesh. Much of this immigration took place in the 1960s and 1970s, but new legislation in 1970s and 1980s greatly restricted immigration from these areas.

Membership of the EU means that citizens in other EU countries have had an automatic right to move to the UK and work. The EU has gradually expanded and in 2004 Poland became a member while Romania and Bulgaria joined in 2007. The expansion of the EU into countries with relatively low wages has resulted in significant levels of migration to the UK from these countries. Partly because of this, since the early 1990s there has been substantial positive net migration (more immigration than emigration) into the UK.

In 2016 positive net migration was around 250 000, down from a peak of some 330,000 the previous year (ONS, 2017). About half of the immigration in 2015 came from EU countries with the rest coming from elsewhere. Although there has been political opposition to high rates of immigration, and this was partly responsible for the vote to leave the EU in 2016 (the Brexit vote), skill shortages and an ageing population have meant that the British economy has relied to some extent on immigration for economic growth.

Much of the immigration into the UK from the EU and from elsewhere has been driven by **pull factors** which make the UK an attractive destination. Some of the pull factors have been (comparative) economic prosperity with relatively high wages, and the relatively full employment compared with some other countries.

However, **push factors** have also been important with war conflict, and political instability creating large numbers of refugees (displaced people seeking refuge when their home country is not safe) leaving countries such as Iraq, Afghanistan and Syria. Economic and political problems have also created a flow of refugees and economic migrants (people seeking a better living standard) from parts of Africa.

Parvati Raghuram and Umut Erel (2014) suggest that migration cannot be understood simply in terms of push and pull factors. They point to the importance of **networks** as well. Much migration does not take place by individuals but involves groups. Often migration is linked to family and other social connections between places. Social networks make it easier for people to move from one country to another and become established in their new place of residence.

Activity

'The Jungle', a camp composed of migrants and refugees in Calais who were trying to cross the Channel to get to the UK. The camp was cleared by the French authorities in 2016 when at least 7000 people were living there in very poor conditions.

With reference to 'push' and 'pull' factors, suggest reasons why 'The Jungle' camp grew up in Calais.

Emigration

There has been less commentary in the UK on patterns of emigration, but it has had a major impact on population trends and in the aftermath of the 2016 Brexit vote, emigration from the UK rose.

Patterns of emigration from the UK

For most of the 20th century, the UK was a net exporter of people (negative net migration) and even in recent years there have been substantial numbers of emigrants from the UK. In 2016, 339 000 people left the UK as international migrants (ONS, 2017).

Emigration figures for the UK for recent decades include those leaving to start new lives in countries such as Australia, Canada, New Zealand and the USA, those moving to work or live in EU countries (including retired people going to live in France and Spain), and those studying abroad.

Much emigration involves people who have been temporary residents leaving the UK, for example those who came to the UK to work or to study without necessarily intending to stay permanently. The ONS (2017) noted a marked increase in emigration to the EU in 2016 as some immigrants from the EU decided to return to their countries of origin in response to the uncertainty resulting from the Brexit vote.

Migration and the population of the UK

Both immigration and emigration have had a significant impact on the population structure and size:

> Since the mid-1980s, net migration has contributed to population growth in the UK both because immigration has exceeded emigration and because of the age and fertility rates of immigrants.

> The age structure of the population has been affected by net migration with more people in their 20s and 30s than there would be without migration (Falkingham and Champion, 2016). This has helped to reduce the dependency ratio by increasing the proportion of the population which is of working age.

> Positive net migration has also pushed up the overall fertility rate and average family size since immigrants tend, on average, to have higher fertility rates than non-immigrants. This has also

slowed down the increase in the average age of the population.

> Migration has led to greater ethnic diversity in the UK. For example, between the 2001 and 2011 censuses the percentage of non-White residents in the UK rose from 8.7 per cent to 14 per cent (Haralambos and Holborn, 2013). Falkingham and Champion (2016) note that by 2014, 13 per cent of the UK population were born abroad (8.3 million people) with 3 million from the rest of the EU. India, Pakistan, Bangladesh and China were the largest contributors to the foreign-born population from outside the EU.

Based on migration patterns along with other changes in the population, Falkingham and Champion (2016) argue that 'Over the next twenty-five years we can say with a fair degree of certainty that the population will get larger … and the population will become more diverse both in terms of ethnic composition and family forms' (p. 12).

Globalisation and migration

Globalisation involves a growing inter-connectedness of different parts of the world with national boundaries becoming less and less significant. Increased international migration is both a cause and consequence of this process. A variety of factors have increased international migration including the collapse of the communist bloc in the Soviet Union and Eastern Europe, conflict in Africa, Syria, Afghanistan, Iraq and elsewhere, and growing economic inequalities in some parts of the world.

The 'age of migration'

According to Stephen Castles and Mark J. Miller (2009) we have entered an 'Age of migration' with the following characteristics:

1. There has been a **globalisation of migration**, with more countries becoming significantly affected by movements of people, and countries that experience positive net migration tending to receive immigrants from a wider range of countries than was the case in the past.

2. There has been an **acceleration of migration**, with increased flows of people in all the major regions.

3. Increasingly, there has been a **differentiation of migration** with many different types of migrants arriving in most countries. For example, the UK

receives refugees, temporary migrant workers and people arriving for permanent settlement.

4. A fourth trend is the **feminisation of migration**. In the past, migrants were mostly males, but this is no longer the case. Many female workers move from low wage economies to take on service sector jobs such as childcare and domestic labour in countries with higher wage rates.

5. Another trend is the **growing politicisation of migration**, with migration becoming a prominent and contested political issue in many places. Policies on migration have become tied up with national security issues. There is increasing awareness that international agreements may be necessary to regulate migration flows (such as refugee flows to Europe).

Migrant identities

The globalisation and acceleration of migration raises issues about migrant identities. Migrants may continue to identify with their country of origin or come to identify with the country to which they have emigrated. As Parvati Raghuram and Umut Erel (2014) argue, many countries encourage **assimilationist policies** which encourage immigrants to integrate into the culture of the society they have moved to. However, conversely, **multiculturalism** can encourage minority ethnic groups to retain their cultural distinctiveness.

With these contradictory pressures, Raghuram and Erel (2014) suggest that **translocalism** often develops – a situation in which migrants retain/develop links to more than one location. This in turn can lead to the development of **hybrid identities** in which individuals and groups see their identity as based on a combination of more than one identity. For example, Harriet Bradley (1997) suggests that groups may define themselves as being 'British-Indian' or 'Black-British' mixing together more than one source

of identity. The complexity of identities formed in response to migration can be illustrated by studies of ethnicity and family diversity (see pp. 285–290).

Activity

'Refugees welcome' banner displayed above the River Spree, Berlin.

In 2015 Germany allowed nearly 900 000 refugees to enter the country with many coming from Syria, Iraq and Afghanistan. The policy of allowing refugees to come to Germany in large number from crisis-hit areas was applauded by some as a humanitarian policy which would benefit the country. However, it proved controversial, with some Germans seeing it as harmful, and efforts were made by the government to cut numbers in subsequent years.

1. With some reference to the image, suggest reasons why some people might welcome refugees.

2. Suggest reasons why some people are hostile to immigration by refugees.

3. How does this example suggest that migration is increasingly politicised and globalised?

Key terms

Globalisation The growing inter-connectedness of different parts of the world with national boundaries becoming less and less significant.

Assimilationist policies Policies which encourage immigrants to integrate into the culture of the society they have moved to.

Multiculturalism Policies which encourage minority ethnic groups to retain their cultural distinctiveness or which celebrate that distinctiveness.

Translocalism A situation in which migrants have strong links to more than one place in the world.

Hybrid identities When individuals or groups see their identity as based on a combination of more than one source of identity (e.g. British-Indian).

Summary

1. A range of different groups have been immigrants to Britain with immigration from the West Indies, India, Pakistan and Bangladesh in the 1960s and 70s and more recent immigration from Eastern Europe being particularly notable.

2. Migration is influenced by push and pull factors but can also be linked to the social networks of migrants.

3. For most of the 20th century the UK was a net exporter of people but in recent years there has been positive net migration.

4. Migration has resulted in greater ethnic diversity in the UK, has counteracted the ageing of the population and increased the fertility rate.

5. Globalisation has increased the rate of migration and led to a greater variety of migrants.

6. With the globalisation of migration, more hybrid identities have developed.

EXAM PRACTICE QUESTIONS

AS-LEVEL PAPER 2
FAMILIES AND HOUSEHOLDS

0 1 Define the term 'symmetrical family'. **[2 marks]**

0 2 Using **one** example briefly explain one way in which families can be child-centred. **[2 marks]**

0 3 Outline **three** reasons for the decline in the death rate. **[6 marks]**

0 4 Outline and explain **two** ways in which the family can be seen as functional for society. **[10 marks]**

0 5 Read **Item A** and answer the question that follows.

Item A

Some sociologists used believe that the nuclear family was the dominant type of family in Britain. However, most sociologists today believe that there is growing family diversity and social acceptance of that diversity in Britain today. Changes in social attitudes coupled with changes in legislation mean that there is no longer one dominant family type today.

Applying material from **Item A** and your own knowledge, evaluate the reasons for increasing family diversity in Britain. **[20 marks]**

A-LEVEL PAPER 2
FAMILIES AND HOUSEHOLDS

0 1 Outline and explain **two** ways in which social policies might favour traditional nuclear families. **[10 marks]**

0 2 Read **Item A** and answer the question that follows.

> ### Item A
>
> In heterosexual families today, the roles of male and female partners tend to be very different from what they were in the past. Women are more likely now to have paid employment, even if the couple have young children. The change from having male breadwinners to dual worker families has affected relationships between men and women and may have made them less unequal than they were. However, there are still significant differences in conjugal roles.

Applying material from **Item A**, analyse **two** changes in conjugal roles that have taken place in the last hundred years. **[10 marks]**

0 3 Read **Item B** and answer the question that follows.

> ### Item B
>
> Some sociologists see the changing position of children within families as the 'march of progress' in which families are becoming more child-centred. Children are becoming better protected and better looked after within families due to both improved knowledge and legislation. However, other sociologists question this view, stressing inequalities between children and adults as well as among children themselves, highlighting the limited rights of children and their vulnerability to neglect and abuse.

Applying material from **Item B** and elsewhere, evaluate the view that the position of children in families has progressively improved. **[20 marks]**

6 EXAM PREPARATION AND PRACTICE

The sociology skills pyramid

AQA sociology requires you to demonstrate specified skills in order to be successful in the exam. These skills can be seen as being in a hierarchy, with some foundational skills which need to be demonstrated before you can go on to demonstrate the higher-level skills. Very often these skills are closely interconnected, and you demonstrate them simultaneously through the way you write about the subject.

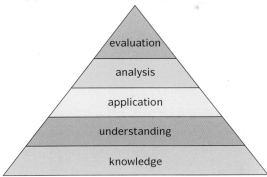

All five skills are examined in AS and A-level sociology. They are grouped into the three Assessment Objectives (AOs) as shown in the table below.

Table 6.1 Assessment Objectives

Assessment Objective	What they say
AO1	Demonstrate knowledge and understanding of: • sociological theories, concepts and evidence • sociological research methods.
AO2	Apply sociological theories, concepts, evidence and research methods to a range of issues.
AO3	Analyse and evaluate sociological theories, concepts, evidence and research methods in order to: • present arguments • make judgements • draw conclusions.

Using this chapter

Practice exam-style questions for each of the topics covered in this book have been provided in this chapter to help you develop your writing skills and test your knowledge and understanding.

Read each question carefully, taking note of the Remember tips which suggest how to respond effectively in the time available in the exam.

When you have written your own response to the question, read through the sample responses and commentaries and decide whether your answer could be improved.

Timing

As a rough guide, allow around 1.5 minutes for each mark allocated. For example, spend around 15 minutes answering a 10-mark question and about 45 minutes answering a 30-mark question. However, it is important to remember that these suggested timings include reading the questions (including the items, where relevant), so you will not have the full time for writing your response. For longer questions you should also allocate some of the time for planning your response.

AS-level Paper 1 Education exam practice questions

0 1 Define the term 'ethnocentric curriculum'. **[2 marks]**

Remember

> This is a short answer question; you should only spend a maximum of three minutes on it.

> You must define the term in the question.

> You can use an example which may support your definition.

> Even if you aren't sure of the term in the question it is worth having a go.

Response

An ethnocentric curriculum is one that gives priority to one ethnic group over others. This is usually the dominant culture of a particular society, for example, the UK curriculum being more focused on White culture than other ethnic groups.

Examiner's comments

This answer is awarded full marks as it is a clear explanation of the term. In the first instance it explains what an ethnocentric curriculum is and then develops this with a fully supported example which helps them to gain the second mark.

Mark 2/2

0 2 Using **one** example briefly explain how material factors can result in social class differences in educational achievement. **[2 marks]**

Remember

> This is a two-mark question. Your response should be clear and concise.

> You should spend no longer than three minutes on this question.

> The question requires you to use one example only.

> You are asked to provide a brief explanation. Therefore no analysis is required.

Response

Many working class children may not be able to afford materials such as a laptop or textbooks to help them with their homework and revision outside of school time. The middle and upper classes can usually afford these material resources and so they tend to get higher marks in exams and coursework.

Examiner's comments

This candidate is able to effectively describe material deprivation, such as the lack of learning aids. Examples are given of material deprivation and the candidate then goes on to explain why the lack of materials may impact students' achievement in education, linking this to different social class categories.

Mark 2/2

0 3 Outline **three** reasons why students may join anti-school subcultures. **[6 marks]**

Remember

» This is a short answer question; you should spend around nine minutes on it.

» You will need to outline three reasons. To make them clear, you could use sentence openers such as 'one reason is…'.

» Identify the reasons and briefly develop each one with further explanation or an example.

Response

Willis suggested that one reason working class boys may join a subculture is because they become fatalistic about school as they wish to pursue manual jobs in the future that often do not require formal qualifications.

Some students also form subcultures based on ethnicity, for example Shain studies how many Asian girls in the greater Manchester area form subcultures in relation to their faith or as part of a recognised gang. These gangs are usually hostile to schools and they don't value working hard at school.

Ward also notes how many boys from poorer backgrounds form a lad subculture in which they misbehave in school because they are going to go into manual jobs after they leave school and therefore show little interest in education.

Examiner's comments

This candidate offers three reasons which are clearly laid out. The first reason is awarded two marks as the concept of fatalism is identified and supported by a study. The second reason identifies the concept of ethnic subcultures and successfully explains how this can lead to people joining an anti-school subculture. No marks were awarded for the third reason as this repeats the first. The candidate again makes an attempt to explain some of the reasons why boys join anti-school subcultures.

Mark 4/6

0 4 Outline and explain **two** reasons for boys' educational underachievement. **[10 marks]**

Remember

» This is worth 10 marks and must be written in continuous prose.

» The question asks you for two reasons. You must make these clearly distinct. Do not be afraid to use sentence starters such as 'one reason is… a second reason is'.

» Spend approximately 15 minutes on this question.

» Out of the 10 marks awarded, you are not given five marks for each reason. You will be awarded marks for the overall quality of your response. Sometimes one of your reasons may be longer or you may remember more evidence, but there is no need to worry about that. Do not fixate on the fact they both have to be the same length. Your response will be marked in a holistic manner.

» To get into the top mark bands you need to show analysis and application.

» You might want to state which reason has made more impact, as this will help you to analyse.

» You should use examples to support your ideas.

Response

Statistics show that boys underperform in relation to girls particularly at both GCSE and A-level. This is most noticeable in subjects such as English and other language based subjects.

The candidate does display some awareness of the question.

One reason for this is the changes in the world of employment. Jackson discusses how there has been a decrease in manual jobs which has resulted in the education system becoming more feminised with a focus away from practical tasks to more academic work. Francis agrees with this theory and identifies that this has caused an increase in laddish behaviour where boys become disinterested in large parts of schooling.

The candidate could have outlined what laddish behaviour is, and given some examples of it, such as disobeying authority figures.

Another reason girls do better is because of the impact of feminism which has given rise to more girls becoming career minded and putting a huge amount of focus on their education. Sharpe found that girls now put career very high up in their priorities compared to 40 years ago when the priority for girls was marriage and children. Third wave feminism continues to influence females through more positive images of women in power throughout the media.

This point fails to address the demands of the question as it goes off on a tangent explaining why girls do better.

Therefore, the gap between boys and girls remains quite wide particularly in working class areas where boys often fail.

Examiner's comments

The candidate provides a sophisticated response. The first explanation identifies the idea that boys are underperforming in school because there are fewer jobs for them due to the feminisation of the workplace, which has impacted on the educational success and aspirations of boys. This is then developed using two relevant sociological studies which are applied accurately. There is a limited amount of analysis which could have been developed further.

The second reason given contains material which does not address the question and is therefore awarded no marks. The candidate gives a reason for rising female achievement rather than looking at why boys underachieve. It is very important to focus precisely on what the question is asking and in this case the focus should be on the underachievement of boys rather than the high levels of achievement by girls.

Mark 5/10

0 5   Read **Item A** below and answer the question that follows.

Item A

Functionalist sociologists would suggest the education system of societies such as Britain benefits everyone and helps society to run smoothly. Not only does education teach shared values, but it also helps to train the workforce and allows employers to select the people with the most appropriate skills for the most appropriate jobs. These views are, however, questioned by many sociologists who do not support functionalism, including feminists and Marxists.

Applying material from **Item A** and your own knowledge, evaluate the view that the education system is functional for society as a whole. **[20 marks]**

Remember

> This is an essay question and carries the most marks on AS Paper 1.

> Spend around 30 minutes on this question.

> You must write in continuous prose and there should be a short introduction.

> Each point you make must be developed with some sociological theory, a sociological study or some statistics.

> To get into the top mark bands you need to show analysis and evaluation.

> You may find it helpful to make a short plan in order to assist your essay writing.

> Keep referring back to the question so you don't lose relevance. Make sure you meet the demands of the question by referring to the item, applying your own knowledge and evaluating the view in the question.

> You must use the item. It will help form the basis of your answer, but you must explain and develop the material in the item and not just repeat the same words.

> A short conclusion is required. However, it must add some value. In the conclusion try to make a direct answer to the question based upon the arguments you have put forward.

Response

Functionalists are consensus theorists and they therefore tend to focus on the positives of the education system: they believe that schooling is of benefit to the individual but also helps society as a whole. However, other perspectives such as feminists and Marxists are conflict theorists and they disagree that education always helps everyone within society.

This introduction shows clear knowledge of the basics of functionalism. There is also a hint of analysis by bringing in Marxism as a counterpoint.

As Item A states, functionalists believe that education 'helps to train the workforce and allows employers to select the people with the most appropriate skills'. Durkheim referred to this as the specialised division of labour. What Durkheim meant by this is that education provides people with a wide range of skills to go into different occupations. Those who wish to go into professional jobs gain the relevant qualifications they need through the national curriculum and those that go into manual jobs gain skills such as timekeeping, uniform, respect for authority and so on through the hidden curriculum.

Parsons agrees with this theory by discussing the theory of role allocation. By this he means that schools select and filter different students into different groups and provide them with skills necessary for their employment, so at the end of school students all go off into a range of careers. This is also known as the organisation of human capital and as item A states 'helps society run smoothly'.

The candidate makes use of the item in this point and displays some knowledge. However, an opportunity is missed to analyse and evaluate. Marxists do not agree with the function of role allocation, as they believe that it is not based on skill but rather just reinforces the social class system. If you leave all the evaluation until the end, you can end up devoting too little space to demonstrating your ability to evaluate.

Davis and Moore state that the reason education is functional for society as a whole is that it maintains the system of stratification. By this they

361

mean that those with the most talent in education become rewarded with the higher status and higher paid jobs and those that did not succeed in education will fulfil other jobs that are lower paid but still need to be completed in order for a society to continue to function.

Functionalists believe that the reason education is beneficial to society is that it teaches individuals about meritocracy as hard work and talent are rewarded. For writers such as Durkheim this is an important message as it causes students to strive to improve themselves and acts as a motivator to work hard in school.

Therefore, functionalists believe that school brings consensus to society as it gives individuals a purpose and an aim. This is often referred to as social solidarity because schools act as an important institution in the socialisation of children into adults. Functionalists compare society to the human body whereby all the institutions play an important role just like an organ does, with education alongside the family as the most vital organs that keep a society alive.

However, not all sociologists agree with functionalists. Marxists believe that education is not fair for all and only benefits those with money and wealth. Likewise, feminists believe that the education system maintains patriarchy and sexism towards women.

In conclusion then, functionalists believe that education helps everyone in society as it acts as an important mechanism of socialisation by providing people with the skills they need to go out into the wide world and start employment and because it forms the key part of secondary socialisation following the role of primary socialisation played by the family.

The candidate fails to discuss meritocracy as a concept in this point, even though it is the essential point. This means they also miss out on including the Marxist claim that meritocracy is a myth.

This is a reasonable point but it could have been expressed more clearly.

Some of the information in this point fails to meet the demands of the question. For example, the organic analogy is not explicitly linked to the question.

Both Marxism and feminism are only mentioned briefly in this final statement. It would have been beneficial if the candidate had developed these points as this would have shown a deeper level of analysis and evaluation. For example, feminists do not think the education system is functional as it is patriarchal and reproduces gender inequalities.

Examiner's comments

This response displays broad knowledge of the functionalist perspective which places it in the 13–16-mark band. This candidate presents a wide range of functions of the education system. Yet the explanations of these functions all lack some depth. The candidate is able to effectively draw material from the item and build on it with relevant sociological evidence (as is evident in paragraphs 2, 3, 4 and 5). Application of the material is focused on the question. However, there is a distinct lack of evaluation which is only present towards the end of the response. The evaluation displayed is limited which prevents the response from being placed any higher in the 13–16-mark band. The response could have developed the discussion of Marxism and feminism further to provide some more specific evaluative points. For example, the Marxist view that the education system reproduces class inequalities could have been examined and some feminist research on patriarchy could have been referred to.

Mark 13/20

A–level Paper 1 Education exam practice questions

<u>0</u> <u>1</u> Outline **two** factors within school that may influence social class differences in academic
achievement **[4 marks]**

Remember

» Spend no longer than six minutes on this question. Your response should be short, clear and concise.

» You must present two clearly distinct factors.

» Identify each factor and then explain it.

» If it helps you can use the phrase, 'one in-school factor is', or 'a second in-school factor is'.

» You are awarded one mark for identifying a factor. You are then awarded another mark for developing or explaining it.

C grade response

One factor within school is teacher labelling. Teachers often label students by social class, with middle class students being seen as ideal, which helps motivate them to work hard and therefore do well.

Another reason is that working class students may have extra responsibilities at home such as looking after younger brothers and sisters or being expected to contribute financially to the family through a part-time job.

Examiner's comments

The first factor, labelling, is developed by stating that middle-class pupils are seen as ideal and is therefore awarded two marks. The second factor is not an in-school factor; it is an out-of-school factor and therefore it is not awarded any marks.

Mark 2/4

A grade response

One factor within school which affects social class differences in academic achievement is anti-school subcultures. Working class boys are more likely to join these to gain status. They often cannot get the status academically so join a group who do not value education and this leads to underachievement.

Another factor is that of teacher labelling. Interactionist sociologists believe that working class students are more likely to get negative labels from their teachers and are therefore likely to be placed in lower academic sets or streams, which holds back their academic progress.

Examiner's comments

This candidate clearly outlines two separate and distinct factors. Each factor is identified correctly and then explained with further development and therefore achieves full marks.

Mark 4/4

$\boxed{0}\ \boxed{2}$ Outline **three** ways in which the introduction of league tables has had an impact on schools.   **[6 marks]**

Remember

> This is a short answer question; you should spend around nine minutes on it.

> You will need to outline three clearly distinct ways. Do not be afraid to use sentence starters such as 'One way is…'.

> Identify the ways and briefly develop each one with further explanation or an example ensuring that the three points do not overlap.

C grade response

According to the New Right, league tables have a positive impact on the performance of schools as it makes them more competitive and thus pushes up standards. Schools are aware that they will be compared to other schools in the local area and will look to push up exam results in order to move up the league table.

The negative impact of league tables is that it causes some teachers to focus on the high achieving students, for example they may give them more time.

Teachers may also focus on those students who are performing at a D grade in order to try to raise their grade up to a C. They may give these students more focus than some of the other students as their results will be reflected in league table percentages.

Examiner's comments

The first point is correctly identified and then developed with a brief explanation. The second and third points are also relevant, however they make the same point by stating that teachers may only focus on teaching those students whose performance will improve the school's league table positions. What is essentially the same point cannot be credited twice.

Mark 4/6

A grade response

According to the New Right, league tables have a positive impact on the performance of schools as it makes them more competitive and thus pushes up standards. Schools are aware that they will be compared to other schools in the local area and will look to push up exam results in order to move up the league table and appear more attractive to parents.

A negative impact of league tables is that it causes some teachers to focus on either the high achieving students or those on the C/D borderline; they may give them more time, focus, resources and attention in order to help the student gain a grade that will help the school to improve its performance in the league tables.

Another criticism of league tables particularly from the social democratic perspective is that schools become completely exam focused which stifles creativity and enjoyment from lessons. Teachers are under pressure to simply teach students how to pass the exam rather than for the enjoyment or passion of learning.

Examiner's comments

This response shows three very clear and different impacts of the league tables and also notes both positives and negatives. Each reason is developed and therefore the response scores full marks.

Mark 6/6

0 3   Read **Item A** below and answer the question that follows.

> **Item A**
>
> In recent years, the A-level subjects with the highest proportions of female students were English, biology and psychology, whereas those with the highest proportions of male students were mathematics, physics and chemistry. When explaining these differences, some sociologists emphasise the image and nature of different subjects, the way they are taught, and the learning style associated with particular subjects. Others emphasise factors outside school such as gender differences in the way children are socialised.

Applying material from **Item A**, analyse **two** reasons for gender differences in subject choice. **[10 marks]**

Remember

» This question is worth 10 marks and your response must be written in continuous prose.

» The question asks you for two reasons and you must make these clearly distinct.

» Spend around 15 minutes on this question.

» Out of the 10 marks awarded, you are not given five marks for each reason. You will be awarded for the overall quality of your response. Do not worry if one of your points is stronger than the other as your response will be marked holistically.

» To get into the top mark bands you need to show analysis and evaluation.

» You might want to state which reason has made more impact, as this will help you to analyse.

» You can use examples to support your ideas.

C grade response

As mentioned in item A, males and females are likely to choose different subjects both in their options at GCSE and particularly in their choices for A-level. Evidence shows that females are more likely to choose language based subjects such as English and boys more mathematical subjects.

One such reason for this could be biological in that evidence suggests that males and females have different brains. Females are more likely to be creative and linguistic and boys are more likely to be practical and logical, therefore they pick different subjects. Many sociologists however believe that these differences are due to nurture more than natural biology.

In relation to this may be the way in which the subjects are taught by the teachers, for example English and Psychology are subjects which are often quite feminised with attention to language, detail, reading and written assessments in terms of essays. Conversely subjects such as physics and chemistry are more likely to have factual short answers and have a more practical element to the lessons which would appeal more to boys.

Despite this there have been efforts to get more students into certain subjects such as the girls into science and technology (GIST) campaign which seems to have worked in biology in particular.

The candidate could have developed this by stating why girls and boys choose certain subjects.

Although this point is worth crediting, it is weak. Biological arguments are seldom used in sociology and this one isn't explained well. The candidate could have introduced the concepts of spatial awareness and verbal reasoning which would have developed the point. An opportunity to analyse and evaluate with a feminist critique is missed. Feminists do not support biological arguments.

This point could have been developed further by addressing the fact that governments have made an attempt to combat these issues. Initiatives have seen changes in the way subjects are taught.

365

Examiner's comments

There are some good ideas and evidence within this answer, particularly the second reason explaining how subjects are taught, which uses the item. There is however a key 'hook' in the item about socialisation. The answer does not pick up on this hook, which would naturally lead into one of the reasons for subject choice.

Mark 6/10

A grade response

As mentioned in item A, males and females are likely to choose different subjects both in their options at GCSE and particularly in their choices for A-level. Evidence shows that females are more likely to choose language based subjects such as English and boys more mathematical subjects; reasons for this can be linked to both internal and external factors.

> The candidate uses the item and shows sound knowledge of the topic in question.

One such reason could be connected to primary socialisation which teaches us gender differences from an early age. The feminist Oakley identifies that parents use different verbal appellations on children and give them different toys through a process of canalisation. Boys' toys are likely to be more practical and active whereas girls' toys are likely to be domestic related or a book based learning tool. This early form of gender manipulation in socialisation could set the building blocks for the different ways in which boys and girls learn and ultimately the subject choices they make, though it could also be argued that these differences are biological rather than socialised.

> The candidate demonstrates good knowledge and understanding of relevant sociological concepts here.

> An opportunity to evaluate is missed here: gender socialisation is changing with some parents choosing gender neutral toys Also some children now challenge the process.

Inside school the different ways in which subjects are taught could be a reason for the subject choices boys and girls make. Science suggests that boys' brains are more logical and practical and therefore they may be attracted to maths and also the practical experiments of subjects such as chemistry. Females are more likely to have stronger linguistic and creative skills and they are therefore more attracted to subjects such as English and psychology due to the attention to language, detail, reading and written assessments in the form of essays. Feminists do criticise this idea and believe that these choices are not a result of biology but rather ideological conditioning.

> The second point is well made with relevant analysis and evaluation.

Despite these differences, there have been efforts to get more students into certain subjects such as the girls into science and technology (GIST) campaign which seems to have worked in biology in particular and likewise the 2005 breakthrough programme to help the exam performance of teenage boys.

> Further analysis is displayed in this conclusion.

Examiner's comments

This answer firstly identifies both of the key hooks in the item and builds on them, which shows the examiner clear evidence of understanding and application. The first point also introduces some theory in the form of feminism and the sociologist Oakley. The second point links teaching styles to biology and further theory could be used here to push the mark higher up the band. There is also some evaluation in the final concluding paragraph.

Mark 8/10

0 4   Read **Item B** below and answer the question that follows.

Item B

There are significant ethnic differences in educational achievement in Britain. British Chinese students are the highest attaining at GCSE with pupils of Indian ethnicity doing next best. White British students do less well than Bangladeshi and Black African students but better than Pakistani and Black Caribbean students. However, White British pupils are the lowest attaining ethnic group amongst pupils entitled to free school meals. Some sociologists see cultural differences between ethnic groups as the main factor explaining these differences in achievement.

Applying material from **Item B** and elsewhere, evaluate the view that ethnic differences in educational achievement are mainly the result of cultural factors   **[30 marks]**

Remember

> This question carries the most marks.

> You should spend around 45 minutes on this question.

> This question requires an essay style answer and must be written in continuous prose with an introduction and conclusion.

> You may want to make a quick plan to help you with your ideas.

> You must use the information in the item. Rather than simply repeating it, use it to help you develop one or more points and bring in ideas or examples which are not given in the item.

> You must also use your own sociological knowledge. Do not simply rely on the item. Your answer should contain relevant sociological theory, studies, evidence, statistics and examples.

> To get into the top mark bands you need to include substantial analysis and evaluation.

> You can use opposing sociological theories to help you gain analysis and evaluative marks.

> Use your conclusion to make an overall evaluation of your evidence and arguments.

> Keep referring to the question throughout, as this will help you to apply the relevant material for the question.

C grade response

As noted in Item B there are some very high achieving ethnic groups such as British Chinese pupils and some low achieving groups such as Black Caribbean and White working class pupils, and there are a variety of reasons for this.

One reason for these differing achievements is related to work ethic, for example in many Asian cultures education is very highly valued, and

Although the introduction uses the item, it has simply recycled it by stating some groups do better than others. To develop this the candidate could have suggested some reasons why ethnic differences in achievement exist or given a more developed explanation of these differences.

this may explain strong results amongst Chinese and Indian students. This view is supported by Basit who identified that many Indian families are dedicated to being socially mobile and their close knit families emphasise the importance of education and a strong work ethic. Archer agrees with this by noting how many male Muslim students see the importance of the male as the breadwinner and so there is a desire in school to succeed in order to be able to perform those instrumental roles to the best of their ability. Likewise, many White working class pupils may not look upon education favourably based on the occupations they wish to go into.

The paragraph does show some good knowledge. However, an opportunity is missed towards the end to develop the explanation of why working-class boys do not achieve highly in the education system. There is also a lack of analysis and evaluation, for example by arguing that the level of importance placed on educational success puts children under stress and pressure.

Family issues also have an impact. Driver and Ballard note that many Asian communities have extended families driving high parental expectations within education, and in many of these cultures there are also relatively low levels of divorce and single parenthood. This may also explain why there are some low levels of performance amongst Black Caribbean students as statistics show that there are higher levels of single parents and absent fathers amongst the cultural group. There is also likely to be a higher number of single parent families within White working class areas.

Knowledge shown is good but an opportunity for evaluation is missed. The candidate could have developed the point by bringing in the criticism made by feminists. Feminists are concerned this will demonise single mothers. The New Right would have some support for the point raised.

The interactionist view of labelling suggests that racism and discrimination may be an issue in education. For example, researchers such as Sewell have noted how Black pupils are likely to be negatively labelled by teachers and likewise Becker argues how working class pupils are less likely to be favoured by teachers too. The argument on discrimination in schools can also be linked to the idea that curriculums can be ethnocentric: this means that they tend to be focused and directed more towards the White majority. Tickly noted that the cultures of many ethnic minorities are invisible and schools tend to focus on White European cultures.

This point is not explicitly linked to the question, which asks for cultural factors. Labelling is an in-school factor which could lead to differing educational achievement among different groups, but it is not a cultural factor. The point is only marginally relevant to the question so does not gain marks. If this point had an analytical tone and the candidate had made a link back to the question, then it would have been more creditworthy.

Perhaps one of the most important factors to consider is that of the use of language. Bernstein noted that language can be divided into elaborated and restricted codes, and many ethnic groups would be judged to speak a restricted code which is then considered problematic in the educational setting because elaborated code language is far more valued. Driver also identified that certain groups such as Bangladeshi and Pakistani groups used to struggle with language as often their main language is used at home and so development and progression in the English language in school could be slow. Likewise, the language used by many Black Caribbean families or White working class students does not fit with the ideals of school.

The knowledge shown in this paragraph is good; however, it does lack analysis and evaluation. The candidate could have used Marxism to help support the discussion of language codes. Marxists argue this is just another tool to ensure class inequality is reproduced, as most of the formal curriculum, including exams, are in the elaborated code.

*Therefore, there are a range of reasons as to why students of different
ethnicities perform at different levels. These reasons are a combination
of external factors outside of school and internal factors inside of school.
Realistically both have an impact on the influence of overall grades rather
than just one particular reason.*

The conclusion sums up the main points again but does not add value. The candidate could have suggested which cultural factor has the most impact and why.

Examiner's comments

This answer displays a good range of knowledge most of which is supported by sociological evidence. It gives a broadly accurate basic account of three of the reasons for ethnic differences. Use of the item is limited and largely remains implicit. Analysis and evaluation is limited; there is an attempt at evaluation, using labelling theory, but it is not made clear that labelling is an alternative to cultural explanations and therefore can be used to criticise them.

Mark 18/30

A grade response

*Ethnicity refers to the shared culture of a social group which gives a
common identity. This is often based on factors such as race or religion.
Statistics show that ethnic groups have very different levels of educational
achievement. Many sociologists believe that it is the background and culture
of different ethnic groups that causes the differing levels of attainment whilst
others believe that factors inside the school also have an impact, as do
material and social factors.*

The opening of this essay is really good and displays not only good knowledge of ethnicity as a concept but also of educational achievement and ethnicity.

*There is strong evidence to suggest that cultural attitudes towards education
differ between ethnic groups, for example in many Asian cultures education
is very highly valued and this may explain strong results amongst Chinese
and Indian students as mentioned in Item B. This view is supported by Basit
who identified that many Indian families are dedicated to being socially
mobile and their close knit families emphasise the importance of education
and a strong work ethic. Archer agrees with this by noting how many male
Muslim students see the importance of the male as the breadwinner and
so there is a desire in school to succeed in order to be able to perform those
instrumental roles to the best of their ability. Modood has referred to this
strong work ethic amongst many Asian students as a 'desire of migrants'
in that they understand and appreciate the need to work really hard if they
wish to be socially mobile.*

A strong point is made which makes use of the item but then also develops it using the candidate's own knowledge. The use of contemporary sociology is good yet there is an opportunity missed to evaluate. For example, the pressure on some children to succeed educationally may not be good for their well-being, which in turn may affect long-term achievement.

*Driver and Ballard also support this argument by noting that many Asian
communities have extended families driving high parental expectations
within education; in many of these cultures there are also relatively low levels
of divorce and single parenthood. Conversely this may also explain why
there are some low levels of performance amongst Afro-Caribbean students
as statistics show that there are higher levels of single parents and absent*

fathers amongst the cultural group. Other sociologists, however, believe that the problem for many Afro-Caribbean students is actually material rather than cultural; the Swann report for example identified that these students are far more likely to be in low socio-economic positions compared to other ethnicities.

An opportunity is missed to analyse some of the low socio-economic positions parents are in, for example by referring to high unemployment figures and numbers in low paid jobs.

Sewell's research on Black underperformance also highlights the cultural issue of masculinity amongst some Black males. He noted that there is a certain amount of pressure to conform to a culture of dominant masculinity or street culture which often goes against the norms and expectations of the education system. Gilborn and Youdell however take a slightly different view to that of Black underperformance being caused by external cultural factors; they argue that it is actually the institutional racism and discrimination inside school that is the issue. For example, if teachers are more likely to negatively label young Black males then the issue is with the discrimination rather than the cultural behaviours of the individual. Law, Finney and Swann found in their research, however, that increasingly more ethnic minorities perform well despite the apparent obstacles that they face both culturally and within the school environment.

This point is well supported and evaluated.

The argument that differing ethnic performance may be internal can also be supported with evidence that shows the curriculum to be ethnocentric, which means that they tend to be focused and directed more towards the White majority. Tickly noted that the cultures of many ethnic minorities are invisible and the curriculum tends to focus on White European cultures. This however does not explain why 'White British pupils are the lowest attaining ethnic group amongst pupils entitled to free school meals' as noted in the item; this particular ethnic group is continuing to fall in levels of performance whilst others are improving. This again seems to be due to culture as it has been suggested that often there is a disruptive home-life, higher levels of single parenthood and a fatalistic attitude towards education.

This point is also well supported and evaluated. It is also applied very well to the question.

Perhaps one of the most important cultural factors to consider is that of language, dialect and accent. Bernstein noted that language can be divided into elaborated and restricted codes. Many ethnic groups would be judged to speak a restricted code which is then considered problematic in the educational setting because elaborated code language is far more valued. Driver also identified that certain groups such as Bangladeshi and Pakistani groups struggle with language as often the mother tongue is used at home and so development and progression in the English language at school can be slow. Post-modern theory suggests, however, that this pattern is changing as more ethnic groups assimilate with each generation and

English is more likely to become the dominant home language for many of these groups over time.

Therefore, it seems evident that cultural factors still play a huge role in the differing performances of ethnic groups. Bourdieu's cultural capital theory seems as relevant today as it has ever been, however it must also be noted that many cultures are changing dramatically due to globalisation and multiculturalism, and there appears to be a homogenisation of cultures rather than a continued separation.

The candidate integrates analysis and evaluation into the main body of the essay well.

It also seems that material factors are the dominant determining factor in relation to educational success. For many ethnic groups their attainment seems to be far more related to their wealth and standard of school than it does to their ethnicity or race. Marxists would argue that although ethnicity and culture of course play a role, it is ultimately social class that will have the biggest impact on educational success or failure.

The candidate reaches a fully supported and critical conclusion, and is also able to use sociological theory to develop the argument.

Examiner's comments

This is a well-structured essay. It demonstrates a wide range of knowledge which is in depth. Points are supported by sociological theory and the item is used and developed upon. The candidate also shows good analysis and evaluative skills using relevant evidence and theory. The conclusion is clear and has direction; it evaluates some of the different factors considered in the response. Note that it is not necessary to write such a lengthy response.

Mark 20/20

AS-level Paper 2 Research Methods exam practice questions

| 0 | 1 | Outline **two** problems of using questionnaires.   **[4 marks]**

Remember

- This is a short answer question. Spend around six minutes on it.

- You must present two clearly distinct problems.

- You could use theoretical, ethical or practical problems.

- You are awarded one mark for identifying a problem. You are then awarded another mark for developing or explaining it.

- Don't be afraid to word your answer as 'one problem would be… another problem would be…'. This makes it really easy for you and the examiner to see you have picked out two problems.

- As it won't take long to answer this question, it is worth having a go even if you aren't sure.

C grade response

One problem when using questionnaires is that they can often have relatively low response rates. In particular, postal questionnaires are often thrown away. People think they take up too much time.

Another problem is that questionnaires are not high in validity.

Examiner's comments

The first problem clearly uses the identifier of low response-rates which would score one mark. The candidate then develops the answer by explaining why questionnaires have low response rates, which gains another mark. A second problem is identified, which gains one mark; however, as there is no development the final mark cannot be awarded.

Mark 3/4

0 2 Evaluate some of the problems of using unstructured interviews when conducting sociological research.
[16 marks]

Remember

> This is worth 16 marks so you should spend around 24 minutes on it.

> This answer must be written in continuous prose.

> To make sure your answer has a good range of knowledge a minimum of three problems should be analysed.

> Each problem you present must be developed with some explanation as this is classed as depth in the mark scheme. For example, you could explain why the problem happens.

> To get into the top mark bands you need to show analysis and evaluation.

> To help you to analyse you could use theoretical, practical or ethical problems.

> To make sure you gain top marks for every problem you discuss, remember to evaluate the problem. Two possible ways to do this would be to either state how sociologists combat the problem, or provide the relevant strength which opposes the weakness.

C grade response

Unstructured interviews are interviews that are like a conversation. They flow and divert in all directions often led by the participant. There are often no pre-set questions, although the interviewer may have a rough guide of what they would like to find out. Unstructured interviews are favoured by interpretivist researchers, but positivist researchers note that there are many issues and problems with them as a research method.

One problem is that unstructured interviews can be very time consuming, both in terms of the time they take to conduct, but also in terms of writing up the findings. Analysing the results is also problematic as often the interviewee will go off on a tangent to the question and therefore much of the information may be irrelevant to the topic.

The candidate could have discussed how, even though findings may be difficult to analyse, the findings tend to have more depth than those produced using more quantitative methods such as questionnaires with fixed-choice questions. Although much of the interview may be off topic the candidate could have argued that, without this, new ideas may not be generated and that the interviewee has the freedom to say something the interviewer never expected.

Due to the fact that unstructured interviews are so time consuming this also means that they can only really be carried out on a small sample of people. This impacts on how representative they are. For example, if a sociologist only carried out three unstructured interviews then it would be difficult to make a generalisation of the findings for a larger section of a community or society.

Unstructured interviews are often problematic in terms of reliability too, as they do not rely on pre-set questions that are repeated to different interviewees. It is unlikely that the same set of questions are asked to people in unstructured interviews and therefore it becomes difficult to compare results.

Interpretivists however do see the benefits of using unstructured interviews and it is a common method for interactionists.

Here the candidate could have presented a contrasting method which generates large sample sizes such as a questionnaire to help analyse the results. Or the candidate could have developed the idea of something being representative of the topic. Often unstructured interviews are used for some of the most sensitive topic areas and without using this method we would have little knowledge of these areas. Although samples may be small and not representative of the whole population, they provide valuable insights into the groups in question, which are needed to make changes in social policy, for example unstructured interviews with the victims of domestic violence helped to change police practices in this area.

This conclusion is weak. The candidate could have explained why interpretivists prefer the use of unstructured interviews, perhaps by explaining the nature of the topics they research. For example, some sensitive topics may only be researched in this way. Or the candidate could have explained the human interaction side of interactionism, which explains why interactionists favour this research method.

The candidate identifies the issue of reliability, but fails to present the argument for validity which is a key strength of unstructured interviews. This would also display the candidate's ability to employ key research terminology.

Examiner's comments

The candidate begins with an explanation of what unstructured interviews are, which is also linked to sociological theory. This shows clear knowledge of the method in the question. The candidate correctly identifies three problems faced when using unstructured interviews. This means the range of the knowledge is good. Where the candidate lacks depth is in the description of these problems, and especially within the analysis of them. There is no discussion of how to overcome the problems. The candidate really needed to demonstrate some evaluative skills as this answer is really lacking in them. Each problem could have been contrasted with a strength. There is a conclusion which adds some value as it is linked to sociological methods but it is not developed and the candidate does not give a reason why the method is favoured by these theories.

Mark 9/16

A–level Paper 1 Theory and Methods exam practice questions

0 1 Outline and explain **two** arguments against the view that official statistics produce valid data. **[10 marks]**

Remember

❯ This answer must be written in continuous prose.

❯ Spend around 15 minutes on this question.

❯ This question can either be on a method or something from the theory section of the specification, so prepare for both in your revision.

❯ You must present two clearly distinct arguments against the view in the question.

❯ It is important to read the question more than once, to make sure you stay focused on the key words in the question (in this case 'arguments against').

❯ Out of the 10 marks awarded, you are not given five marks for each argument. You will be awarded marks for the overall quality of your response. Sometimes one of your arguments may be longer or you may remember more evidence, but there is no need to worry about that. Your response will be marked in a holistic manner.

❯ To get into the top mark bands you need to show analysis and evaluation.

❯ It would be advantageous to add a short conclusion, perhaps stating which argument has the most impact. This will help to show you can analyse and evaluate.

C grade response

Official statistics are numbers collected from various agencies.

One way in which official statistics do not produce valid data can be seen through crime statistics, which many sociologists argue do not show a true picture of the crime that is being committed. Crimes that are not reported or punished never make their way into the official statistics. This is often referred to as the dark figure of crime. What then occurs is an iceberg effect in that the only statistics the general public see in relation to crime is the tip of all crimes, while the vast majority are hidden underneath the surface. This means that we cannot really state that the crime statistics are a valid and truthful reflection of all crime.

These crime statistics may also be a problem because they are massaged and manipulated by the government. For example, if the government in power wants to portray an image that crime is being dealt with and is reducing, they may manipulate the statistics in order to show the results as being as low as possible.

The candidate could have further developed the introduction, perhaps stating some of the agencies responsible for collecting statistics. There could have been some discussion of how statistics are collected, such as through the use of the British Crime Survey.

There are no examples of which crimes are more likely to be in the dark figure such as domestic violence or white collar crime. If this had been done the candidate would have also been able to make a theoretical link with feminism or Marxism. This would have added further depth to the question along with some analysis of sociological theory.

An opportunity is missed here to discuss the Marxist perspective of power relationships within official statistics, which would have added more depth. To assist with evaluation, the candidate could have suggested measures to combat the issues, such as independent enquiries which look into government data, or they could have given illustrative examples.

Therefore, we cannot trust the validity of official statistics, and this is the reason why interpretivist sociologists often seek other methods such as interviews and observations in an attempt to gain more valid results.

The candidate has suggested two other methods which are not subject to the same validity issues, but could have explored this further. The candidate could also have stated which issue is the most problematic in relation to statistics. For example, the dark figure of crime is such a serious issue it means that the statistics will never be valid as not all crimes appear in them.

Examiner's comments

The introduction is brief but shows a limited understanding of what official statistics are. The candidate does present two clear problems with regard to the validity of official statistics. Both of the points raised display a good level of knowledge but only a limited level of analysis and evaluation. There is a brief attempt at evaluating the question at the end but again this is limited.

Mark 6/10

A grade response

Official statistics refers to those that are produced by the government on issues such as education, crime and population. Although sociologists should be able to trust the statistics available from the government there are many arguments to suggest these figures are not completely valid. Interpretivist sociologists in particular see it as problematic to use secondary data that was not compiled, researched and collected by the sociologist themselves.

There could be comparison of positivism, which favours the use of official statistics.

One such example of this issue can be seen through crime statistics which many sociologists argue do not show a true picture of the crime that is being committed. Crimes that are not reported or recorded never make their way into the official statistics, and this is often referred to as the dark figure of crime. What then occurs is an iceberg effect in that the only statistics the general public see in relation to crime are the tip of all crimes, while the vast majority are hidden underneath the surface. It has been argued by some sociologists such as Tombs that the government will often massage and manipulate statistics to support their political agenda, an example being when the party in power want to convince the general public that crime rates are reducing. Positivists argue, however, that crime statistics do give researchers a good starting point to begin to understand the issue of crime.

Marxism could have been used here to highlight the power relationship when considering the social construction of official statistics.

Another problem with the validity of official statistics can be demonstrated by the analysis of exam results which show the pass rate of a particular school or college. Neo-Marxists identify that private schools often maintain their high success rates by not entering students for exams or asking certain students to leave the school before the exam period. This questions the validity of the results as institutions can alter the statistics for their own benefit. It could of course be argued however that the results are still showing an accurate measure of those that actually took the exams.

Private schools and grammar schools have come under more scrutiny over recent years with their selective practices being publicised.

Therefore, we cannot trust the validity of official statistics and this is the reason why interpretivist sociologists often seek other methods such as interviews and observations in an attempt to gain more valid results. Positivists however feel that in order to gain macro data on a large scale then official statistics are a useful starting point from which to collect valid information and data.

Examiner's comments

This answer shows a good structure by clearly explaining what official statistics are, how we get them and the various areas of social life from which they can be collected. The candidate is also able to select appropriate theory such as interpretivism, positivism and Neo-Marxism. This further develops the answer and shows a good range of knowledge. Two separate problems of validity are raised which are clearly set out and they are from two different areas of sociology, which displays a good range of knowledge. At the end of the two main paragraphs there is also some analysis which directly discusses the statement in the question and makes an overall evaluation.

Mark 9/10

AS-level Paper 1 Methods in Context exam practice questions

0 1   Read **Item A** and answer the question that follows.

Item A

Investigating pupils' cultural background and educational achievement

Some sociologists believe that the cultural background of pupils has a significant impact upon the achievement of pupils in school. Differences in both class and ethnic background can affect whether children start their school careers with the skills and knowledge that will make it easy for them to succeed.

Sociologists may study the cultural background of pupils by using questionnaires to collect information from parents. Questionnaires can be seen as having practical, ethical and theoretical advantages for studying this topic. For example, it is easier and more convenient to access a sample of parents using questionnaires than using most other methods; it is clear that parents are giving consent if they are willing to fill in the questionnaires and this method may provide the best chance of getting a representative sample of parents. However, gaining access to a suitable sampling frame can be difficult, and getting parents to cooperate and ensuring that their answers give a true representation of cultural differences are further problems. Therefore, some sociologists prefer using qualitative methods to study the cultural background of pupils.

Applying material from **Item A**, and your own knowledge of research methods, evaluate the strengths and limitations of using questionnaires to study how the cultural background of pupils might influence educational achievement.   **[20 marks]**

Remember

❯ This question requires an essay response. You must write in continuous prose and there should be a short introduction.

❯ Spend around 30 minutes on this question.

❯ You must read the item carefully; it might be helpful to highlight or underline some of the key research themes within it.

❯ To get into the top mark bands you need to show analysis and evaluation.

❯ You may find it helpful to make a short plan in order to assist your essay writing.

❯ Keep referring back to the question so your response stays relevant. Make sure you meet the demands of the question, stick to the research method in question, keep linking your answer to the specific educational context and make sure your evaluation is relevant.

❯ You need to present the strengths and weaknesses of the method in the question. Think about theoretical, practical and ethical concerns.

❯ Make a reference to the sampling technique, including its strengths and weaknesses.

❯ Link your answer to the specific context mentioned in the item. Think about where the research takes place, the setting, the people involved, the topic and analyse whether questionnaires are really the best way to study the research question.

❯ A short conclusion is required. However, it must add some value. In the conclusion try to make a direct answer to the question. You could suggest an alternative research method which would also be beneficial for studying this topic area.

C grade answer

Questionnaires are a set of pre-set questions; they are given to the participant to complete. Item A states, like all methods, they also have some disadvantages.

With questionnaires, it is easy to access a sample of parents. Ethically there are no problems because parents are giving informed consent if they agree to complete a questionnaire. Questionnaires are also more likely than other methods to be representative and get a wide sample of parents. This is important because, without a sample that is representative of the wider population of parents, it would not be possible to generalise about this issue.

This is a brief introduction displaying some knowledge of the research process. The candidate could have suggested whether this method is preferred by positivists or interpretivists, and why. The item is simply recycled here with little added value.

This is a good paragraph which makes an attempt at providing the context. The candidate might have explained in more depth why questionnaires are suited to parents, perhaps stating that parents are busy and do not have much time. The concept of ethics could have been developed, for example the candidate could have explained what they are, and why it is so important to follow them during sociological research. Only one ethical concern is given, informed consent, but there are other ethical issues that could have been analysed such as confidentiality. Sampling is partially explored but again this issue could have been opened up further to gain additional marks for analysis and evaluation.

Other advantages of using questionnaires with parents to study how pupils' cultural backgrounds affects their achievements include the fact that they are quick and cheap to use. All respondents answer the same questions in exactly the same order so the questionnaires will provide quantitative data and the researcher can make links, for example statistical links between pupils' background and their achievements in exams.

Disadvantages include the fact that a researcher might not be able to access many parents in the first place (i.e. no access to a 'sampling frame' and also low response rate). Some parents might not actually bother to return the questionnaires if, for example, they see the questions about class and ethnicity as pointless or too personal, they might even throw them away. Questionnaires cannot provide a great deal of insight into the meaning of what the parents really think. Also, it would be difficult to measure complex concepts such as ethnicity or social class. In this case, more qualitative methods would be a better choice.

To conclude, questionnaires would be an appropriate method to use with this topic if the researcher wanted to gather a large amount of statistical data about it. However, if they wanted in-depth, detailed qualitative data on this topic, then methods such as unstructured interviews would be much more useful.

This paragraph highlights some of the practical issues of conducting questionnaires. However, there is a lack of analysis and evaluation. The candidate could have made a context link here: questionnaires may be quick and cheap but exams are complex and each student has their own experience of them, which suggests that a questionnaire might not be the most suitable method. The lack of qualitative data generated is also missed which would have been a good way to develop some evaluation.

Although the paragraph has an analytical tone, it does not have the depth required to push it any further into the next mark band. The analysis of questionnaires could have been developed by evaluating the validity of the use of questionnaires in researching this particular topic.

A reasonable conclusion which does offer an alternative method although it is not applied to the specific topic area identified in the question.

A-level Paper 1 Methods in Context exam practice questions

0 1 Read **Item A** and answer the question that follows.

> **Item A**
>
> **Investigating school subcultures**
>
> Pupils in schools often associate with other groups of pupils who they see as being similar to themselves. These groups can develop into distinct subcultures with their own norms and values which may complement or conflict with the values of the school and of its teachers. Class, gender and ethnicity can be important in subculture formation, but a wide range of other factors can be important too.
>
> Since subcultures are social groups, one way to gain information about them is to use group interviews or focus groups. These can allow researchers to explore the interaction between members of the same subculture. This interaction may also enable the researchers to obtain a more in-depth understanding of subcultures than they would be able to do in one-to-one interviews. However, the responses of pupils in a group interview might be influenced by the presence of their peers.

Applying material from **Item A** and your own knowledge of research methods, evaluate the strengths and limitations of group interviews for studying pupil subcultures. **[20 marks]**

Remember

> This is an essay-style question. You must write in continuous prose and there should be a short introduction.

> Spend around 30 minutes on this question.

> You must read the item carefully; it might be helpful to highlight or underline some of the key research themes within it.

> You may find it helpful to make a short plan in order to assist your essay writing.

> Keep referring back to the question so your response remains relevant. Ensure you meet the demands of the question.

> You need to present the strengths and weaknesses of the method in the question. Think about theoretical, practical and ethical concerns.

> To get into the top mark bands you need to show analysis and evaluation.

> Make a reference to the sampling technique and its strengths and weaknesses.

> Link your answer to the specific context mentioned in the item. Think about where the research takes place, the setting, the people involved, the topic and analyse whether group interviews are really the best way to study the research question.

> If you can think of any other sociological studies which have used this method for this topic you may want to mention them.

> A short conclusion is required. However, it must add some value. In the conclusion, try to make a direct answer to the question. You could suggest an alternative research method which would also be beneficial for studying this topic area.

C grade answer

Group interviews can be a useful method for studying pupil subcultures. For example, Paul Willis studied an anti-school subculture of twelve boys and included group discussions with the 'lads' in his study. The researcher can explore the way sub-cultural group members act together, as Item A indicates. By seeing group interaction at first hand, the researcher can get more depth. One-to-one interviews do not give the opportunity to observe the subculture in action, but this does. Group interviews are also cheaper and more data can be gathered in a limited amount of time.

Group interviews for studying pupils' subcultures have limitations as well as strengths. As Item A states, peer pressure might influence participants' responses. For example, members of an anti-school pupil subculture might refuse to participate in group interviews if they see the researcher as an authority figure or as on the side of the school or teachers. Pupils who don't belong to an anti-school subculture may feel intimidated about putting forward their views when there are other pupils who do belong to these sub-cultures.

Practical limitations include the fact that transcribing interviews can be time consuming when, for example, the group is made up of same-gender pupils who all sound alike. This makes it more expensive. One way round this would be to video record the group interview but this raises ethical concerns, particularly with younger pupils. Another ethical concern is that it can be difficult to obtain informed consent because neither the interviewer nor the participants know exactly how the discussions are likely to pan out beforehand. Some pupils may feel upset by the way the discussion unfolds. So a group interview will need a skilled and sensitive interviewer.

If the researcher was interested in factors such as class, gender and ethnicity, as referred to in Item A, then group interviews could be useful to some extent. However, it might be difficult to ask the pupils about their social class background in front of their peers and some pupils might not know much about their parents' occupations or incomes. It might also be insensitive to ask groups of pupils whether they receive free school meals if this is used as an alternative way of trying to measure social class.

There is no introduction. The candidate could have displayed knowledge by showing that they knew what a group interview was, for example by explaining what it involves and by stating that often interpretivists use them. There is a good link to Willis's study; however it could have been developed, for example by stating some of the main issues Willis found with group interviews. An opportunity has also been missed to develop how the method allows more depth to be gained, for example the candidate could have discussed the rapport that is built in group interviews. The style and setting of group interviews often means participants are more relaxed, so studying school children in this way would be beneficial.

The item is used in the paragraph but its relevance remains implicit; the candidate could have discussed why pupils feel under pressure in this setting. Further evaluation could be added by stating what researchers do to try to counteract this and prevent it from happening.

This paragraph addressed practical and ethical concerns raised by the use of group interviews but again it lacks depth. The candidate could have evaluated the limitations by suggesting some strengths, for example they may be time consuming but they are high in validity. Consent is gained before the interview and there are rules regarding things being said on and off the record. After the interview a debrief could take place or emotional support offered to the participants. Although this method may raise sensitive issues, it is one of the only ways to get pupils to open up about school subcultures.

This paragraph displays some more practical limitations of the method. However, again an opportunity is missed to evaluate; for example by suggesting that group interviews could be complemented by using other methods to collect quantitative data on sensitive issues.

Group interviews are a useful method for studying pupil subcultures and they have clear advantages. However, they also have limitations so it would probably be better to use them together with other methods rather than on their own.

> There is a conclusion, yet it adds no value. The candidate could have suggested the biggest strength or limitation and suggested an alternative method with reasoning as to why it is more suitable.

Examiner's comments

There is continuous use of the item throughout, however there is little attempt to develop this. Both range and depth are narrow; this answer offers a basic account of some of the limitations of using group interviews. Analysis and evaluation are limited with brief underdeveloped points made.

Mark 12/20

A grade answer

Group interviews with pupils, teachers or parents are becoming increasingly popular in qualitative sociological research on education and are often used in mixed methods research. As indicated in Item A, group interviews can be useful in gaining information about subcultures which are themselves social groups. Group interviews allow researchers to explore the way members of a particular subculture interact together. The researcher would thereby gain in-depth qualitative data based not only on what participants say about their values and norms and how far these conflict with those of the school but also how participants actually interact together as a group, express their values and describe their norms. This is a distinct advantage over the use of one-to-one interviews in which the researcher obviously would not observe group interaction.

> This introduction shows sound conceptually detailed knowledge both of group interviews and the topic in question.

Interpretivist sociologists are interested in gaining rich, detailed data. However, it is important to be aware that a group interview is an artificial situation and this may affect some pupils' behaviour, interaction and responses. For example, some students may take over the conversations or simply fabricate their answers as they think that's what the interviewer wants. This is known as the Hawthorne effect and it can affect the validity of the findings. The use of participant observation may generate more valid data if a student subculture is observed in naturally occurring settings such as classrooms or playgrounds over time and the researcher can build up good fieldwork relationships, rapport and trust. On the other hand, if participant observation is too costly and time consuming, group interviews may be a relatively cheap and quick alternative when investigating pupil subcultures.

> Both strengths and limitations are discussed in this paragraph with some evaluation through the discussion of participant observations. There is also a link to the context of the research, although the particular strengths and limitations for studying subcultures are not developed in the discussion.

If a researcher was on a limited budget or lacked time, group interviews would be useful as each one could include around six pupils. Practical limitations include the time and expense of transcription when several pupils are involved. Each interview must be transcribed; if the interviewer does this it is timely and each researcher is not free of bias, which could impact the results. Positivists dislike the nature of this as they think research should be value free. Plus, the participants are school children, so they may go off topic and the actual amount of valid data collected could be smaller than the researcher anticipated.

Practical strengths and weaknesses are given in this paragraph with some evaluation. To improve this answer and push it to full marks more practical elements could be discussed, such as employing a trained researcher to conduct the interviews.

Ethically, the limitations of group interviews when investigating pupil subcultures might outweigh the strengths. Getting informed consent may be problematic because the researcher can't anticipate in advance the direction the discussions may take. Nor can they guarantee that all participants will maintain confidentiality after the interview - the principle of confidentiality may be much more significant to the researcher than to some of the pupils. However, the participants do have the right to state some of the things they say should be kept confidential. Also they would have the right to withdraw at any time.

This paragraph effectively addresses some of the ethical strengths and weaknesses of the method and context.

If the focus was on anti-school rather than pro-school subcultures, members might be unwilling to participate in the research. They may suspect the researcher's motives, mistrust them or see them as part of the school's authority structure. They may agree to participate for a laugh but treat the group interview as a joke, particularly if they see the researcher as an outsider in terms of their class or accent. (However, girls in an anti-school subculture may be more open with a female researcher while boys may be more comfortable with a male researcher.) Such considerations are likely to reduce the validity of the data. By contrast, pupils who belong to subcultures whose norms and values complement those of the school and its teachers may be more likely to agree to participate, treat it seriously and provide truthful answers.

This paragraph makes strong content links; the candidate clearly has a sound understanding of the topic area.

Pupils who do not belong to an anti-school culture may refuse to participate in a group interview because the idea of talking in front of members of the subculture may be intimidating. As Item A states, their responses might be influenced by their peers' presence. They may censor what they say and, in this case, the group interview may not necessarily generate valid data about anti-school subcultures. Notoriously pupils who join anti-school subcultures are heavily influenced by their peers so perhaps a more individual approach to research could be used, like an unstructured interview. That way the pupils would not have their peers present.

Another strong paragraph which links the method and the context topic in question, with some good analytical skills displayed here.

When investigating the influence of class, gender and ethnicity in subcultural formation, the researcher must operationalise concepts such as social class. In educational research, pupils' social class is usually measured in terms of their parents' occupation. Where this data is missing, eligibility for free school meals may be used instead. During a group interview, it could be difficult to generate enough detailed data about participants' backgrounds to be able to assess their class position.

A clear understanding of key research considerations is shown here. The candidate uses the item but expands upon it by explaining what operationalising concepts are, and how they could be used.

In conclusion, group interviews are a better method for studying pupil subcultures than positivist methods such as questionnaires as too many pupils would not take these seriously or they might lie. However, participant observation would be more likely than group interviews to generate detailed, in-depth and valid data about pupil subcultures.

The candidate reaches a fully supported critical conclusion.

Examiner's comments

The response displays sound conceptually detailed knowledge. There is both range and depth in this response. Information from the item is present but it is developed and not just repeated. Relevant material is sensitively applied to the question. There is use of sociological theory, research concepts, and research design. Analysis and evaluation are present and are often linked to the topic area in context. A sound critical and fully supported conclusion is given.

Mark 17/20

AS-level Paper 2 Families and Households exam practice questions

0 1   Define the term 'symmetrical family'. **[2 marks]**

Remember

 > This is a short answer question; you should only spend three minutes on it.

 > You must define the term in the question.

 > You can use an example to support your definition.

 > Even if you aren't sure of the term in the question it is worth having a go.

C grade response

A symmetrical family is one in which the roles are likely to be shared between the man and the woman.

Examiner's comments

This is a partial definition of the term. The candidate suggests that roles are shared between the man and woman; however, there is no reference to what the important roles are. A little elaboration on the sharing of housework, childcare and paid employment would have enabled the candidate to gain both marks.

Mark 1/2

0 2   Using **one** example briefly explain one way in which families can be child-centred. **[2 marks]**

Remember

 > This is a short answer question; you should only spend three minutes on it.

 > Only use one example.

 > You will need to select one reason why families can be child-centred, and then develop it with an example.

C grade response

Families can be seen as being child-centred by spending more time and attention with their child.

Examiner's comments

This response it is accurate but it is only partial. The term child centredness is understood, however the application of the example is undeveloped. The candidate could have developed 'time' and how much more time is spent with the child.

Mark 1/2

| 0 | 3 |

Outline **three** reasons for the decline in the death rate. **[6 marks]**

Remember

» This is a short-answer question; you should spend around nine minutes on it.

» You will need to outline three clearly distinct reasons. Do not be afraid to use sentence starters such as 'one reason is…'.

» Identify the reasons and briefly develop each one with further explanation or an example.

C grade response

One reason for the fall in the death rate is due to improved nutrition. Societies have a better understanding of the content of their food and also the damage that certain foods can do such as too much sugar or saturated fats.

Another reason is the improvement in health care and medicine. As science and research improves there is a better understanding of dealing with and treating diseases.

There are also more hospitals compared with the past. They have better facilities and medicines to help those who are sick.

Examiner's comments

The first reason identified is the fall in death rate and develops this by using the example of improved knowledge of food nutrition. The second is improved healthcare, which is further developed by discussing improvements in science and knowledge. The final reason identified repeats the idea of improved medical services and therefore is not credited with marks.

Mark 4/6

| 0 | 4 |

Outline and explain **two** ways in which the family can be seen as functional for society. **[10 marks]**

Remember

» This question is worth 10 marks and your response must be written in continuous prose.

» This question asks you for two ways and you must make these clearly distinct. Do not be afraid to use sentence starters such as 'One way is… a second way is'.

» Spend around 15 minutes on this question.

» Out of the 10 marks awarded, you are not given five marks for each way. You will be awarded marks for the overall quality of your response. Sometimes one of your ways may be longer or you may remember more evidence, but there is no need to worry about that. Do not fixate on the fact they both have to be the same length. Your response will be marked in a holistic manner.

» To get into the top mark bands you need to show analysis.

» You might want to state which way has made more impact, as this will help you to analyse.

» You can use examples to support your ideas.

C grade response

Murdock argued that the family is functional for society as it serves an economic function. Functionalists believe that men play the instrumental role, which means being the breadwinner by earning the money and paying for the bills and paying to care for the children. In order for the man to perform this role then the mother must support the man through the expressive role of looking after the home and the children.

Murdock also said that the family performs the role of educating children through the process of socialisation. This means that parents teach their children norms and values of how to behave in a society installing positive and negative sanctions.

The economic function could be further explained.

The candidate could have suggested why other family types are able/unable to perform this role to the same standard. Feminism could have been used to critique the idea that women should play an expressive role. Postmodernism could have been used to highlight the idea that not all families in the contemporary UK have a male breadwinner.

The candidate does not explain what sanctions are.

An example of a norm or value could have been given, such as using a knife and fork when eating.

Examiner's comments

This response correctly identifies two of Murdock's functions of the family. There is limited explanation of both. The level of **analysis** is also limited, for example the candidate could have stated which function of the family is the most important, or has the most impact. The candidate could also have used other sociological theory to **evaluate** the function of the family.

Mark 6/10

0 5 Read **Item A** and answer the question that follows.

> **Item A**
>
> Some sociologists used to believe that the nuclear family was the dominant type of family in Britain. However, most sociologists today believe that there is growing family diversity and social acceptance of that diversity in Britain today. Changes in social attitudes coupled with changes in legislation mean that there is no longer one dominant family type today.

Applying material from **Item A** and your own knowledge, evaluate the reasons for increasing family diversity in Britain. **[20 marks]**

Remember

> This is an essay question and carries the most marks.

> Spend around 30 minutes on this question.

> You must write in continuous prose and there should be a short introduction and conclusion.

> Each point you make must be developed with some sociological theory, a sociological study or some evidence.

> To get into the top mark bands you need to show analysis and evaluation.

> You may find it helpful to make a short plan in order to assist your essay writing.

> Keep referring back to the question so your answer stays relevant. Make sure you meet the demands of the question.

> You must use the item. It will help form the basis of your ideas, but you must develop it and not simply repeat it.

> A short conclusion is required. However, it must add some value. In the conclusion try to make a direct answer to the question.

C grade response

Diversity refers to the idea that there are a range of different families in society now compared to in the past. As mentioned in the Item the most dominant family type was always the nuclear family but postmodernists now recognise that there is a much greater range of families now for a variety of reasons.

Firstly, there has been an increase in single parent families and this can be linked to a change in both social attitudes and legislation. For example, in the past society looked down on single parents. The numbers of single parent households were small. There has been an increasing acceptance, however, which is possibly due to the process of secularisation. Smart suggests that divorce has been normalised meaning that society is now more accepting of divorce compared to the 1950s, when it was a taboo. The increase in lone parents may also be related to the change in divorce law in 1969, which made the process of divorce both cheaper and quicker to carry out.

Another type of family that has increased as a result of divorce is the reconstituted family which is where people remarry and form a new family. Rapoport and Rapoport suggest this is now a common part of the life cycle for many people, and statistics show there has been an increase in this type of family. They also argue that there has been an increase in culturally diverse families such as people from different nationalities or ethnicities forming a relationship and therefore having dual heritage children.

Chambers suggests that there has also been an increase in cohabitation, this is couples living together as a partnership but not actually being married. In some cases, Chambers also notes an increase in living apart together (LATs) couples who are couples that do not share their residence but maintain their own home even though they are a partnership. These examples show an increase in independence for many people.

The candidate could have defined a single parent family, giving examples of how a person may end up living in this type of family.

There is no explanation of what secularisation means and why secularisation has produced greater acceptance of lone parent families. This would have helped the candidate develop the idea of how divorce is more socially acceptable.

An opportunity is missed to analyse the impact of the Divorce Reform Act in terms of increasing family diversity. Sociological theory could have also been used such as the support the Divorce Reform Act gained from feminism. The role of feminism as a factor in its own right could have been discussed.

The first point in this paragraph is linked to the growth of reconstituted families; an opportunity is missed to evaluate how co-parenting adds further to family diversity. The candidate may have also discussed the popularity of this family type as it is the fastest growing family type in the UK. The point about cultural diversity is not explicitly linked to the question.

This paragraph describes LAT yet it does not explore the reasons for the growth in LATS. This would have focused the paragraph on the question set. LATS have become popular because of social attitudes, expectations and individualistic ideas as well as globalisation and increased geographical mobility.

The argument of independence can also be seen by the increase of solo-living. Jamieson notes that there are more single person households now due to divorce but also as a result of personal choice as people are seeing the benefit of financial independence and personal freedom away from a traditional relationship.

There could have been a deeper discussion of solo-living with exploration of more of the reasons for the rise in it, and this would have addressed the question set in more focused way.

Therefore, in contemporary society there is far more choice in terms of how to live rather than just being in a traditional nuclear family. Sociologists suggest that many families now are patchwork families in that they are made up of all different people from a range of places and so the traditional nuclear family is still present but is now not considered the only way to live.

Examiner's comments

The concept of diversity is defined in the introduction showing a clear idea of the demands of the question. This response displays a good range of knowledge. There are four ideas which relate to the topic of family diversity. The answer does lack depth in places and could have been further developed. There is some use of relevant sociological material and this is accurately applied to the question. Material is supported through the use of relevant sociologists and there is a basic use of sociological theory. However, the answer tends to focus on presenting different family types rather than exploring in depth the reasons for the rise in such family types. Analysis and evaluation is also limited. There could have been discussion of theorists such as Stacey, Giddens, and Beck and Beck-Gernsheim to add theoretical depth.

Mark 13/20

A-level Paper 2 Families and Households exam practice questions

0 1 Outline and explain **two** ways in which social policies might favour traditional nuclear families.

[10 marks]

Remember

» This is worth 10 marks and must be written in continuous prose.

» This question asks you for two ways and you must make these clearly distinct. Do not be afraid to use sentence starters such as 'One way is... a second way is...'.

» Spend around 15 minutes on this question.

» Out of the 10 marks awarded, you are not given five marks for each way. You will be awarded marks for the overall quality of your response. Sometimes one of your ways may be longer or you may remember more evidence, but there is no need to worry about that as your response will be marked in a holistic manner.

» To get into the top mark bands you need to show analysis.

» You might want to state which way has made more impact. This will help you to analyse.

» You can use examples to support your ideas.

C grade response

One way in which policies may favour the traditional nuclear family is through tax and benefits. New Right thinkers, such as Murray, believe that the traditional married nuclear family is the ideal family unit for society. He believes that this is the ideal way to have a family, as two parents can support a child and each has a specific gender role to play. The mother is the primary care giver for the child and therefore child benefit should be paid to her. This still happens today.

The Conservative government in 2015 under David Cameron also extended the benefits to married couples by offering tax breaks to the traditional family. Those who benefited most were the couples with a main breadwinner and one partner staying at home. This further demonstrated a favouritism to those married couples.

The candidate could have analysed this by addressing the concept of diversity within the family. Some feminists criticise this policy for assuming that women will be the main carer for children although others believe it is essential for mothers to be paid this benefit so male partners do not waste the money on personal consumption.

The candidate ends the question abruptly and doesn't state which policy may have more impact or be more important. A brief discussion of how government policy supports all family types could have been used.

Examiner's comments

The candidate clearly outlines two different ways which are credit worthy. The first way addresses benefits being paid to the mother as she plays an expressive role in terms of being the primary care giver. The idea is supported with Murray's New Right perspective, which displays good knowledge. The second way — tax breaks for married couples — is also credit worthy. The candidate develops the idea by highlighting which government implemented the policy. Both points do lack some depth in terms of analysis and because of this score no higher.

Mark 6/10

0 2 Read **Item A** and answer the question that follows.

> **Item A**
>
> In heterosexual families today, the roles of male and female partners tend to be very different from what they were in the past. Women now are more likely to have paid employment even if the couple have young children. The change from having male breadwinners to dual worker families has affected relationships between men and women and may have made them less unequal than they were. However, there are still significant differences in conjugal roles.

Applying material from **Item A**, analyse **two** changes in conjugal roles that have taken place in the last hundred years.

[10 marks]

Remember

❯ Spend no longer than 15 minutes on this question.

❯ You must apply material from the item and then develop it; do not simply repeat it.

❯ Use the item as a hook. It will give you some clues to possible answers, which you could highlight as you read the item.

❯ You need to present two clearly distinct changes.

» This answer must be written in continuous prose.

» You need to develop each change focusing on why they are significant. You could use sociologists, studies, statistics and theory to aid you with this.

» Out of the 10 marks awarded, you are not given five marks for each change. You will be awarded marks for the overall quality of your response. Sometimes one of your changes may be longer or you may remember more evidence, but there is no need to worry about that. Do not fixate on the fact they both have to be the same length. Your response will be marked in a holistic manner.

» To get into the top mark bands you need to show analysis and evaluation.

» You might want to state which change has made more impact. This will help you to analyse.

A grade response

Conjugal roles refers to the relationships and responsibilities that partners take on as a couple and in general these conjugal roles are far more likely to be joint or shared than they were 100 years ago. This is also referred to as symmetrical roles whereby the tasks carried out by the mother and father are equal rather than separated based on their sex.

> A clear understanding of the term in the question is displayed.

These changes are often referred to as the march of progress by Young and Willmott. One such example as noted in Item A is that women are far more likely to be in paid employment now and therefore form a dual income family rather than one with just the father as the breadwinner. Much of this can be attributed to second wave feminism which influenced the change in employment laws such as the Equal Pay Act and the Sex Discrimination Act. Females are now also more likely to go to university than males, leading them into increased employment. Despite the increase in working mothers, Crompton and Lyonette believe that women are still more likely to do the majority of housework within a dual-worker family.

> The item is used and expanded upon.

> Analysis and evaluation using feminism is included.

The male role has also changed as many fathers are much more likely to take on housework and childcare duties; this is often referred to as the new man or complicit masculinity. Research by Miller shows that fathers now have increased the amount of housework they complete and tasks such as the cooking are more likely to be shared. Likewise, fathers are more involved in childcare duties by spending more time playing, reading and interacting with their children especially in what is termed as more child-centred society. Miller did find, however, that in families with joint conjugal roles couples often fall back into traditional roles over a period of time.

> Analysis and evaluation using Miller is developed.

Therefore, although there has undoubtedly been a move towards increased joint conjugal roles, there are still some roles that are more likely to be traditional and segregated amongst partners even in a postmodern, child-centred society.

> This offers a clear critical conclusion.

Examiner's comments

The candidate has a clear understanding of the term conjugal roles. The level of knowledge is in depth and ideas are supported by sociological ideas and research. This answer shows a good use of terminology and language throughout. Each point also displays some analysis and evaluation; the candidate is able to conclude at the end giving a reason to support and critique joint conjugal roles.

Mark 10/10

0 3   Read **Item B** and answer the question that follows.

Item B

Some sociologists see the changing position of children within families as the 'march of progress' in which families are becoming more child-centred. Children are becoming better protected and better looked after within families due to both improved knowledge and legislation. However, other sociologists question this view, stressing inequalities between children and adults as well as among children themselves, by highlighting the limited rights of children and their vulnerability to neglect and abuse.

Applying material from **Item B** and elsewhere, evaluate the view that the position of children in families has progressively improved.

[20 marks]

Remember

▸ This is an essay question and carries the most marks.

▸ Spend around 30 minutes on this question.

▸ You must write in continuous prose and there should be a short introduction.

▸ Each point you make must be developed with some sociological theory, a sociological study or some statistics.

▸ To get into the top mark bands you need to show analysis and evaluation.

▸ You may find it helpful to make a short plan in order to assist your essay writing.

▸ Keep referring back to the question so you don't lose track. Make sure you meet the demands of the question.

▸ You must use the item. It will help form the basis of your ideas. However, you must develop it and not simply repeat it.

▸ A short conclusion is required. However, it must add some value. In the conclusion try to give a direct answer to the question.

C grade response

Many sociologists believe that we are increasingly living in a child-centred society, which means one that is focused on the needs of children.

The sociologist Ariès used historical research of paintings and pictures to show how childhood has changed and improved since medieval times when children were simply seen and treated as mini adults, including working in difficult, labour intensive jobs from a young age. Today, there is legislation

The candidate could have stated how children are having their needs met, perhaps through the use of better knowledge of child welfare or increased educational opportunities.

to protect children from working in such conditions and being exploited for money and therefore this shows an improvement in the health and regulations for children.

Donzelat discusses how there are now far more laws to protect children such as the Children Act and also the introduction of services such as the NSPCC and Childline, which serve to protect children and also help children who are in dangerous or vulnerable families. This again is further evidence of an improved society for children.

Likewise, Postman argues that we are now more child-centred in terms of education in that we devote a lot of focus and attention to educating our children and supporting them in their learning. Chambers supports this idea by stating that parents now have children for love rather than simply as an economic benefit to bring money into the family.

Jenks also believes that the position of children has improved because there is less physical punishment than there used to be. In many countries such as the UK parents are not allowed to use excessive force in the discipline of their children, while in the past of course this was considered to be a normal practice.

However, not all of childhood is positive and many believe that there are still lots of issues and problems for children in the world today. Palmer suggests that there is toxic childhood and by this she means that children are exposed to a lot of negative images and sexualised images on TV and in other forms of the media. Palmer believes that children see sexual images presented in the media and also have access to pornography and violence on the internet.

Marxists also believe that children are becoming obsessed with consumerism from a young age and so their childhood seems to be more about what they own than enjoyment or play. This relates to the term pester power where children are always nagging their parents for the next must-have item especially around Christmas time.

In conclusion there is plenty of evidence to show that society is more child-centred than it used to be.

The work of Ariès could be evaluated here, for example his work was partly based on paintings which carry various weaknesses in terms of a secondary research method.

Sociological theory could have been used here to assist with analysis. For example, the New Right supports the use of legislation to monitor so-called problem families. Evaluation could have also been added; despite the higher levels of protection for children there have still been high profile cases which have uncovered prolific abuse.

An opportunity to evaluate is missed: it can be argued that children are now under too much pressure and stress from the education system and the constant testing that is in place.

A link to the question would help keep this paragraph focused at the end and prove that the lives of children have improved.

The response identifies a negative aspect of childhood and displays good evaluative skills.

More evaluative skills displayed.

A brief conclusion which could have been developed, for example by commenting on which piece of evidence is the strongest to support the view that society is child-centred.

Examiner's comments

This is a fairly good answer which includes a good range of sociologists and some important ideas on the question of childhood. The essay does show both sides of the debate but these are in juxtaposition rather than being woven into an argument with points for and against, which can make the essay look a little list like rather than demonstrating a fluent argument. The paragraphs are accurate but also brief; the points could be explained in more detail in order to display analytical skills and give more specific examples. The item is only touched on briefly.

Mark 13/20

A grade response

Postmodern sociologists often argue that we are increasingly living in a child-centred society, which means one which is focused on the needs of children with more care, policies, compassion and protection. However, there is also evidence to suggest that children are now living in an increasingly dangerous world whereby they are vulnerable to a range of concerns that did not exist in the past and that their position in society has not necessarily improved.

A developed introduction which shows a clear knowledge of the topic area.

The sociologist Ariès used historical research of paintings and pictures to show how childhood has changed and improved since medieval times when children were simply seen and treated as mini adults, including working in difficult, labour intensive jobs from a young age. Today there is employment legislation to protect children from working in such conditions and being exploited for money and therefore this shows an improvement in the health and well-being of children. Prout, however, argues that these laws are not enforced in all countries: in many parts of the world children are still working under unhealthy and dangerous conditions such as the mining for minerals in the Democratic Republic of Congo.

A good display of evaluation in the final sentence, although evaluation of Ariès's research method could have also been included as his argument was based on secondary data.

Donzelat discusses how there are now far more laws to protect children such as the 1989 and 2004 Children's Act and also the introduction of services such as the NSPCC and Childline, which serve to protect children and also help children who are in dangerous or vulnerable families. This supports the idea of what Young and Willmott called the 'march of progress' as mentioned in the item. Once again, however, these laws and agencies are not in all societies where hitting or smacking a child is seen as an acceptable form of discipline or sanction within primary socialisation and practices such as FGM exist in countries such as Egypt.

There is use of the item which is then developed.

Chambers suggests that couples now have children as a result of romantic love whereas in the past children were often seen as a necessity for economic gain, as the children could work and bring money into the family. This idea is supported by Postman who notes how child-centredness can be evidenced through the fact that families now devote a lot of focus and attention to educating children and supporting them in terms of college and university. Postman, however, also does believe that there have been some negative implications of this movement by stating that there has been a slow erosion of childhood.

Some development could have been added to this paragraph, for example comparing average family sizes past and present.

One such example of this erosion of childhood can be seen in the theory of toxic childhood by Palmer. She states that children are now being exposed to the likes of violence and pornography at such a young age that they are often victims of over-sexualisation, which means that they view sexually explicit images as the norm. This concern links to Bandura's theory that children will mimic or copy what they are often exposed to. However, there is an increase in awareness of trying to protect children from these issues through safeguarding programmes which try to restrict access to such images. Parents can also add child locks and codes to home-based media so that children cannot log into such websites.

A good display of evaluative skills.

Postmodernists such as Baudillard take a slightly different approach to understanding child improvements by saying that children now have more freedom, choice and diversity than they used to, for example in terms of targeted child products they can purchase, child centred services, choice of education and freedom to speak out or contribute to family decisions. Neo-Marxists however argue that this can be negative as children use pester power to keep on demanding more items. Grimes notes that the life of a child has become related to consumerism and what they own and that children become obsessed with capitalism and purchasing from a young age in a media saturated world.

Jenks points to another example of child improvements through the fact that children are now more protected and are less likely to be punished especially physically. In countries such as the UK it is illegal for parents to use excessive force on their child. Beck believes however that there are still risks but these risks have simply changed to issues in wider society such as the risk of global war or economic disaster. Likewise, Johnson states that despite the policies of protection we are still seeing in the media huge cases of sexual offences towards children all the time, and as the item states there seems to be 'limited rights of children and their vulnerability to neglect and abuse'.

There is some repetition in this paragraph but there are some good evaluative skills shown towards the end.

It therefore becomes very difficult to judge to what extent the position of children has improved. There has certainly been an attempt to protect children more than in the past though this can often result in over protection in what Gittins calls age patriarchy whereby the parent has too much control over every aspect of the child. There is also no doubt that there are more laws to try to protect children but evidence shows that these laws do not always act to protect children as much as they are designed to.

Finally, it is difficult to judge the statement because as Wyness says, childhood is socially constructed and means different things in different societies even to the extent of what age we consider childhood to end at. There is evidence to show that childhood has improved significantly in many western, developed societies but in many parts of the world the issues of child cruelty, punishment and oppression are still very much in evidence.

The essay reaches a critical and fully supported conclusion.

Examiner's comments

This a strong essay; it displays a wide range of in-depth knowledge. Points are supported by sociological theory and evidence. The candidate makes good use of the item and develops the ideas contained within it from their own knowledge. The essay has an analytical tone throughout and has some strong evaluative statements. The candidate is also able to reach a fully supported and critical conclusion.

Mark 20/20

GLOSSARY OF KEY TERMS

Ability groups   Groups in which students are placed on the basis of their perceived ability.

Academies   Under Labour, academies were designed to replace 'failing' schools and drive up standards.

Academy chains   A number of academies which join together to share policy and expertise.

Academy trusts   Charitable trusts which provide the overall policy and direction for academies.

Achieved status   Status or position in society based on achievement.

Adultist   Biased in favour of adults rather than children.

Age patriarchy   A system of dominance involving adults, particularly adult males, exercising control over children.

Age-standardised mortality rates   (ASMRs) Death (or mortality rates) adjusted to take account of the age structure of the population.

Agency   The ability of individuals to make decisions and to act on the basis of those decisions in a way which enables them to have an impact on the world around them.

Ages and stages   The view that all children pass through different stages of development at roughly similar ages.

Alienation   A process in which people come to feel detached from themselves, from other people or from things.

Anti-social/narcissistic offenders/ borderline/emotionally volatile offenders   Perpetrators of domestic abuse who are consistently hostile and abusive towards their partners.

Apollonian image of the child   The view that children are born good and are only corrupted through contact with the adult world.

Ascribed status   Status or position in society fixed by birth.

Assimilate   Become part of, and develop the culture of, the wider community.

Assimilationist policies   Policies which encourage immigrants to integrate into the culture of the society they have moved to.

Attainment gap   The percentage point gap in educational attainment between different social groups.

Audience analysis   Examining how audiences respond to and interpret documentary material.

Beanpole family   A family in which there are strong intergenerational links between children, parents and grandparents, but weaker intragenerational links.

Biomedical model of health   A model of health and illness which assumes that the mind and body are separate entities and health is entirely shaped by the biological functioning of the body.

Birth rate   The number of live births per year per thousand of the population.

Branch campus   A campus which is a branch of the main university

Case study   A study of a particular instance of something.

Chosen families   The group of people an individual regards as family members. It can include friends aswell as relatives and kin.

Chronological age   The number of years somebody has lived.

City technology colleges   Funded directly by central government and private industry. Specialised in maths, science and technology.

Civil partnerships   Legally recognised relationships for same-sex couples which became possible in the UK in 2004.

Closed questions   Questions in which the range of responses is fixed by the researcher.

Coding   Classifying answers into various categories.

Cola-isation   The entry of private companies promoting their goods into schools and colleges.

Collectivism   Emphasis on the group rather than the individual.

Commodification   A process in which more and more things become available for sale and purchase.

Commodity   Something that can be bought and sold.

Common-law family   In the context of Black Caribbean families an unmarried couple who live together and look after children who may or may not be their biological offspring.

Compensatory education   Making up for or compensating for the supposed deficiencies of so-called culturally deprived groups.

Compulsory heterosexuality   A situation in which alternatives to heterosexuality are considered socially unacceptable.

Confluent love   Love which only lasts as long as it provides satisfaction.

Conjugal bond   The relationship between husband and wife or other intimate partners.

Connectedness thesis   The theory that it is important to understand individuals through the networks of personal relationships they are involved in rather than simply as isolated individuals.

Conventional family   A nuclear, heterosexual family consisting of a married couple and one or two (but not too many) children.

Conversion   The process by which one form of capital reinforces another.

Converter academies   Schools which accept an invitation from the Department for Education to 'convert' to an academy. Usually high performing schools.

Correlation   A statistical link between two or more variables or factors.

Correspondence theory   A theory that states that there is a similarity between two things.

Counter-school culture/ anti-school culture   Student subcultures which reject the norms and values of the school.

Couple penalty   A situation in which couples are better-off living apart than they are living together as a result of tax and benefits rules.

Covert research   Hidden research where the researcher's true identity and the purpose of the research is hidden from participants.

Creaming   Selecting students who appear most likely to succeed for entry to educational institutions.

Cultural capital   The manners, tastes, interests and language of the 'dominant classes'.

Cultural deprivation theory   The idea that certain groups are deprived of or deficient in things seen as necessary for high educational attainment.

Cultural diversity   Variations in the lifestyle of families, for example variations in the lifestyle of families of different ethnic origins.

Culture   (of a school) The norms and values of a particular school as reflected in, for example, its teaching and learning styles and behaviour management.

Culture   The learned, shared behaviour of members of society.

Data   Information used in and/or produced by a research project.

Dating LATs   A couple who are living apart together and who are developing their relationship prior to possible cohabitation.

De-standardisation of the life course   A process in which the timing and order of the different stages in life become less predictable.

Death rate   The number of deaths per year per thousand of the population.

Deconstruction   Breaking down societal structures such as age-related social roles.

Deficit model of childhood   The view that the central characteristics of children involve children lacking the characteristics that adults have making children inferior to adults.

Definition of the situation   Defining and giving meaning to situations.

Demographic transition   The change from one pattern of demography to another, particularly when both birth and death rates fall significantly over a period of time.

Demography   The study of populations.

Dependency ratio   The ratio of those who are not of working age (the young and elderly) to those of working age (19-64).

Differential educational attainment   The different attainment levels of different groups – for example, class, gender and ethnic groups.

Dionysian image of the child   The view that children are amoral pleasure seekers.

Discourse analysis   Examining how words and images illustrate ways of knowing and thinking.

Disengagement   The withdrawal of people from social roles.

Divorce   The legal ending of marriage.

Divorce rate   The number of divorces per thousand married couples.

Documents   Secondary, mainly qualitative, data in written, visual and broadcast form.

Doing gender   Acting in ways which follow traditional socially constructed expectations of the behaviour of men and women and thereby reinforce those expectations.

Domestic division of labour   The way that tasks are divided up between members of a household.

Domestic labour   Work done within the home such as housework and childcare, it may be unpaid but it creates value just as paid work does.

Domestic violence and abuse   Incidents or pattern of incidents of controlling, coercive, threatening behaviour, violence or abuse between family members. Domestic violence involves the use of physical force. Abuse can incorporate verbal or psychological intimidation as well as force.

Dominant framework   The common-sense view about children based on the assumption of their mental and physical immaturity.

Dual earner/worker family   A family in which both partners do paid employment.

EBacc   The English Baccalaureate. A GCSE programme of five core subjects for all students. Also used to measure school performance.

Economic capital   Financial resources – income and wealth.

Economistic/material theories   Theories which explain the domestic division of labour in terms of the financial interests of the household.

Education Action Zones (EAZs)   A programme to raise the attainment of students in low-income, inner-city areas.

Education Maintenance Allowance (EMA)   A cash allowance payable to students aged 16–19 from low-income families in further education.

Educational Priority Areas   Low-income areas given additional resources for education.

Educational triage   The division of students into three groups in terms of their expected GCSE grades.

Elaborated code   Speech in which meanings are made explicit, spelled out.

Elderly dependency ratio   The proportion of those aged over 64 to those of working age.

Elimination   The elimination of members of the working class from higher levels of education.

Email survey   Questionnaire sent by email to the respondent.

Emigration   The movement of people out of one country to another for a period of one year or more.

Emotion work/labour   The work involved in trying to influence the emotions of other people.

Empirical   based on experience or observation.

Empty-shell marriage   A marriage in which the relationship between the spouses has broken down.

Epistemological   relating to how knowledge of a given subject is obtained.

Equality of opportunity   A system in which every person has an equal chance of success.

Ethical guidelines for research   The rights and wrongs of conducting research provided by social science organisations and university departments.

Ethics   Moral principles stating what is right and wrong.

Ethnic group   A group in society who are seen by themselves and/or by others to have their own subculture – their own norms and values. Ethnic group members often share a group identity and a sense of belonging.

Ethnicity   Cultural differences based on membership of groups which define themselves in terms of a relationship with a homeland.

Ethnocentrism   A belief that your own ethnic group or culture is superior to others.

Ethnography   The study of the way of life of a group of people in order to see their world from their perspective.

Ethos   (of a school) The distinctive values and character of a particular school.

Excellence in Cities   A programme which replaced EAZs with similar aims.

Experimental effect   Any unintended effect of the experiment on the participants.

Experimenter bias   The unintended effect of the experimenter on the participant.

Expressive role   A family role in which caring and emotion are important.

Extended family   Any family containing relatives other than parents and children, for example, aunts, uncles and grandparents.

Extra-curricular activities   Activities undertaken outside lessons at school such as clubs and debating societies or hobbies undertaken outside school such as swimming or rumba.

Falling back into gender   Reverting back to following traditional socially constructed expectations of the behaviour of men and women after becoming a parent.

False class consciousness   A false picture of society which disguises the exploitation of the subject class.

Fatalism   Accepting a situation rather than making efforts to improve it.

Feeling rules   Informal rules (norms) in society about what you should feel in different circumstances.

Female carer-core   Mothers and children, sometimes seen as the most basic family unit.

Fertility rate   The number of live births per year per thousand women of childbearing age.

Field experiment   An experiment conducted in everyday social settings.

Focus groups   A group discussion guided by a moderator.

Forces of production   Those things required to produce goods such as land, machinery, capital, technical knowledge and workers.

Formal content analysis   Counting how often particular words, phrases and images occur.

Formal school curriculum   The stated knowledge and skills which students are expected to acquire.

Formal-learning-type skills   The kind of skills used in formal learning such as counting, speaking and writing.

Formula funding   Schools are financed mainly on the basis of the number of students enrolled in the school.

Free schools   Non-profit making, state-funded schools set up by a variety of groups and approved by the Department for Education.

FSM students   Those receiving free school meals.

Function   The contribution a part of society makes to society as a whole.

Futurity   A concern with the future rather than the present.

Gatekeeper   The person or group in a particular setting such as a school with responsibility for allowing (or otherwise) a researcher to undertake research in that site.

Gender education gap   The difference in the educational attainments and examination results of female and male students.

Gender group   A group composed of males or females.

Gender pay gap   The gap in the average wage of men and women.

Generalisation   A statement based on a relatively small group which is then applied to a larger group.

Global educational league tables   Rankings based on international comparisons of educational attainment.

Globalisation   The increasing interconnection of parts of the world.

Going native   The researcher actually becomes a part of the group they are studying and does not return to their previous life.

Grammar schools   Secondary schools seen as suitable for academic students.

Grant maintained schools   Schools funded directly by the government and allowed to opt out of local authority control.

Habitus   The dispositions, expectations, attitudes and values held by particular groups.

Hawthorne effect   Changes in the behaviour of participants resulting from an awareness that they are taking part in an experiment.

Hegemonic masculinity   The dominant form of masculinity at a particular time in a particular place.

Heteronorm   The belief that intimate relationships between heterosexual couples are the normal form that intimate relationships take.

Hidden curriculum   The messages schools transmit which are not part of the standard taught curriculum and which are largely hidden from staff and students.

Historical documents   Documents from the past.

Hybrid identities   When individuals or groups see their identity as based on a combination of more than one source of identity (e.g. British-Indian).

Hypothesis   A statement that can be tested about the relationship between two or more variables.

Ideological conditioning   The process by which people are taught distorted beliefs which serve the interests of powerful groups in society, particularly capitalists.

Ideological State Apparatuses   Institutions, including the education system which transmit ruling class ideology.

Immediate gratification   Focusing on pleasures of the moment rather than putting them off for future reward.

Immigration   The movement of people into one country from another country for a period of one year or more.

Impression management   Managing the impression of self given to others.

***In vitro* fertilisation**   Fertilising an egg with a sperm in a test-tube.

Independent Commission on Fees   An independent organisation set up in 2011 to measure the impact of the increase in university fees.

Individualisation   An increasing emphasis on the individual rather than the group.

Infantilised   Making adults (particularly the elderly) appear child-like or treating them like children.

Information hierarchy   A situation in which some groups have superior access to information than others.

Infrastructure   The economic base of society.

Insider   A researcher who shares social characteristics such as gender or ethnicity with the research participants.

Institutional ageism   Systematic neglect of the needs of the elderly or outright discrimination against them by organisations.

Institutional racism   Racial prejudice and discrimination which form part of the taken-for-granted assumptions and operations of institutions.

Instrumental role   A family role in which achieving particular objectives is important.

Integrate   As used in this unit, to become part of the wider community while retaining a distinctive subculture.

Interactionism   A sociological theory which examines interaction – the action between members of small social groups.

Intergenerational links   Links between family members of different generations, for example grandparents and grandchildren.

Interpretivism   An approach focusing on meanings which are seen to direct human action. It favours qualitative data.

Interviewer bias   The effect that the interviewer has on the participant's answers.

Intragenerational links   Links between family members of the same generation, for example brothers and sisters.

Joint conjugal roles   Conjugal roles where the partners share responsibility for domestic tasks and both do paid employment.

Key informant   A member of the group being studied who provides important information and often sponsors the researcher.

Label   A definition of a person placed on them by others.

Laboratory experiment   An experiment conducted in a specially designed setting.

Late modernity   According to Giddens, the most recent phase of modernity.

LATs   People who are 'living apart together' that is partners who maintain separate households.

League tables   The ranking of schools in terms of their test and exam results.

LGBTI   Lesbian, gay, transgender, bisexual and intersex groups and individuals.

Liberal feminism   A version of feminism which is relatively

moderate and believes that the position of women in society can be improved through reform rather than radical or revolutionary change.

Life course   The process of moving through the different stages of life such as birth, adulthood, marriage, retirement and so on.

Life cycle   The different stages of life. The concept of life cycle treats these stages as more predictable than the idea of life course.

Life history   A case study of an individual's life.

Longitudinal study   A study of the same group of people over time.

Looking-glass self   A person's perception of the way others see them.

March of progress theory   A theory of the family which assumes that it develops in a progressive way responding and adapting to wider social changes.

Marital breakdown   The ending of a meaningful relationship between a married couple.

Marital patriarchy   The dominance of husbands over wives.

Marketisation   The process where organisations compete in the market.

Marketisation of schools   The introduction of market principles such as competition into the education system.

Marriage and partner LATs   A couple who are 'living apart together, and who see their relationship as long-term but do not anticipate cohabiting.

Material deprivation   A lack of material resources.

Matrimonial offence   In divorce, the idea that a spouse has acted

in such a way that their partner is entitled to seek a divorce.

Means of production   The things used to produce goods and services, for example raw materials.

Meritocracy   A system in which a person's position is based on merit- for example, talent and hard work.

Migration   (international) The movement of people from one country to another for a period of one year or more.

Mixed methods   Using two or more methods in the same research project.

Mixed-ability groups   Groups in which students are randomly placed or intentionally mixed in terms of their perceived ability.

Mobilising capitals   Using capitals to advance your position. Building on existing advantages.

Moderator   An interviewer who guides focus group discussions.

Modern individualism   To Berthoud the prioritizing of individual self-interest over the interests of families.

Modernity   A phase in the development of society often seen as involving rational planning and the decline of religion and tradition.

Monogamous nuclear family   A family of parents and children where the adult partners only have sex with each other.

Moral panic   An exaggerated and illogical concern about supposed social problems which is often the result of media sensationalism.

Mother household   In the context of Black Caribbean families a household in which the mother or grandmother of the children is head of the household and, for most of the time at least, the household contains no adult males.

Multi-academy trust   A charitable organisation which governs academy chains.

Multicultural education   Teaching based on a curriculum which includes the history and perspectives of the various ethnic groups in society.

Multiculturalism   Policies which encourage minority ethnic groups to retain their cultural distinctiveness or which celebrate that distinctiveness.

Multinational education businesses   Private education companies which have branches in two or more countries.

National curriculum   A curriculum which instructed all state schools what to teach.

Natural change   (in population growth) The change in population size which takes place as a result of there being more births than deaths or vice versa.

Negative net migration   A situation in which there are more emigrants from a country than immigrants to it.

Neoliberal feminism   According to McRobbie a version of feminism which is pro-capitalist.

Neoliberalism   The latest stage of capitalism which supports free markets and a minimal role for the state.

Net migration   The differences between the number immigrants and the number of emigrants resulting in a net loss or net gain of population.

New Deal for Young People   A programme designed to reduce youth unemployment.

New individualism   A renewed emphasis upon the needs and interests of individuals rather than the collective well-being of the family or community.

New reproductive technologies   Technological methods of allowing individuals and couples to have children when they would not otherwise be able to do so.

New Right   Politicians, academics and commentators who see traditional heterosexual nuclear families with the man as main breadwinner as the ideal and who believe that state intervention in economic and social life should be minimised -except in 'dysfunctional' families. They support free market economics.

New sociology of children   A version of sociology which views social life in terms of the perspectives and interests of children.

Non-directive interviewing   An interviewing technique which seeks to avoid leading participants to answer in particular ways.

Non-participant observation   Observation in which the researcher does not join those they are observing.

Normative/gender construction theory   Theories which explain the domestic division of labour in terms of socially constructed gender roles

Norms   Guides to appropriate behaviour in particular situations.

Nuclear family   A family of two generations (parents and children) related by blood or marriage who live together.

Observation schedule   Instructions which tell the observer what to look for and how to record it.

Official documents   Documents produced by government organisations and departments.

Old-fashioned values   To Berthoud a belief in the importance of traditional, stable, family life based on heterosexual (opposite sex) marriage.

Open enrolment   Parents have the right to send their children to the school of their choice.

Open-ended/open questions   Questions which allow the respondent to answer in their own words.

Operation Head Start   A programme of pre-school compensatory education in the USA.

Operationalise   Translating concepts into a form which can be measured.

Oppositional groups   Groups that oppose the status quo or resist authority such ascounter-school cultures.

Oppression   Keeping people in a state in which they are disadvantaged, exploited, and denied opportunity and freedom.

Organisational diversity   The range of different structures that families can have.

Overt research   Open research where the researcher's true identity and the purpose of the research is revealed to participants.

Parenting order   A 2003 policy which allowed the authorities to require the parents of children in trouble with the law to undergo education or counselling.

Parity of esteem   Equal status

Particularistic meanings   Meanings which are tied to a particular social context and not readily available to outsiders.

Particularistic standards   Standards which apply to particular people.

Patch-work family   A family made up of a variety of current and former partners and your own or their relatives. There is choice about who an individual sees as belonging to the patch-work family.

Patriarchal   A patriarchy is a society or group that is dominated by and run in the interests of men.

Patriarchal ideology   The idea that male dominance in society is reasonable and acceptable.

Patriarchy   A pattern/structure of male dominance and control.

Peer group   A group in which members share similar circumstances.

Penetrations   Insights into the false pictures presented by ruling class ideology.

Performance   The way people act in front of anaudience.

Performativity   How well an individual or organisation performs.

Personal age   How old a person regards themselves as being.

Personal documents   Letters, diaries, photographs and social media communications.

Personal life   The most meaningful parts of people's lives which involve relationships with other people they are close to.

Pilot study   A small-scale study to check on the suitability of the methods used in the main study.

PISA   Programme for International Student Assessment.

Plastic Sexuality   A form of sexuality in which the purpose of sex is not primarily to conceive children but is more about self-fulfilment.

Polygyny   When men are permitted to have more than one wife at the same time.

Positive discrimination   Discriminating in favour of a particular group.

Positive net migration   A situation in which there are more immigrants to a country than emigrants from it.

Positivism   An approach partly based on the methods used in the natural sciences. It favours quantitative data.

Postmodern   A term used by some sociologists for what they a see as a new period after modernity from the late 20th century onwards.

Postmodern family   The family under postmodernity which changes rapidly and has no fixed structure.

Postmodernity   According to some sociologists, a phase in the development of society in which there is no longer a belief in a single best way of organising social life and in which the idea of progress Is rejected.

Present tense of childhood   Seeing childhood in terms of the experience of children rather than in terms of the process of becoming an adult.

Present-time orientation   A focus on the present rather than the future.

Primary data   New data produced by the researcher during the research process.

Primary relationships   The longest-lasting and most significant personal relationships that individuals have in life.

Primary socialisation   The earliest and probably the most important part of socialisation.

Primitive communism   Very early societies in which no surplus was produced and no classes existed. Because of this there was no need for families.

Privatisation   A process where 1) services are subcontracted to private companies, 2) where

private companies compete with public organisations which previously held a monopoly of the services.

Privatise   Move from state ownership to private ownership.

Progress 8   A measure of school performancebased on the progress students have made from the end of primary school to GCSE.

Promiscuous horde   A situation in which there are no taboos on having multiple sexual partners from within the same society.

Props   The clothes and objects used in performances.

Proto-individuals   The earliest and most primitive form of individual; individuals not yet fully formed.

Provider ideology   The belief that it is right that men should be the main income earner for families.

Pure relationship   A relationship in which people stay together because the relationship is mutually rewarding rather than out of a sense of duty.

Qualitative data   All data that are not in the form of numbers.

Qualitative interviews   Semi-structured and unstructured interviews that generate data in the form of verbatim (or word-for-word) quotations.

Quantitative data   Numerical data – data in the form of numbers.

Quota sample   A stratified sample in which selection from the strata is not random.

Radical feminism   The most extreme version of feminism which tends to see society as being completely dominated by men and which sees the interests of men and women as being very different.

Random sample   A sample which gives every member of the sampling frame an equal chance of being selected.

Rapport   A friendly, trusting and understanding relationship.

Reconstituted family   A family formed after divorce and remarriage or cohabitation with a new partner which may include one or more children of either or both partners.

Reflexive sense of self   When individuals are very aware of their sense of who they are, they monitor it and often try to change it.

Reflexivity   The ability to reflect upon your life and make choices about the best way forward.

Relations of production   The relationships people enter into to produce food and material objects.

Reliability   Data are reliable when different researchers using the same methods obtain the same results.

Replication   Repeating an experiment or research study under the same conditions.

Representative group   A smaller group which has the same characteristics as a larger group.

Representative sample   A sample which is typical of the group in the wider society.

Repressive State Apparatuses   Institutions, such as the army and the police, which keep the subject class in its place.

Research characteristics   The key features of a field of sociological investigation (such as education) including the research settings (such as primary school classrooms) and research participants (such as primary school pupils).

Research ethics committee   A body in a university that scrutinises research proposals.

Research participants   Those who take part in research projects and are studied by researchers.

Resilience factors   Things which encourage high attainment, for example, completing homework every evening.

Response rate   The percentage of the sample that participates in the research.

Restricted code   A kind of shorthand speech in which meanings are not spelled out.

Risk factors   Things which reduce attainment, for example, extended absence form school.

Role   A set of norms which defines appropriate behaviour for a particular status.

Role allocation   A system of allocating people to roles which best suit their aptitudes and capabilities.

Role-taking   Putting yourself in the position of another person

Romantic love   A form of love in which you idealise the one you love and believe they are necessary for a fulfilling life.

Ruling class   The class who own the forces of production.

Ruling class ideology   A set of beliefs which present a false picture of society and justify the position of the ruling class.

Same-sex marriage   Legally recognised marriage for same-sex couples which became possible in the UK in 2014.

Sample   A selection of research participants from the larger group to be studied.

Sample attrition   The reduction of the original sample when it is used again.

Sampling frame   A list of members of the research population.

Sampling unit   A member of the research population.

School census   A survey that collects data from state schools in England about individual pupils (such as eligibility to FSM and attendance) and the schools themselves (for example, their educational provision).

Second demographic transition   A relatively recent shift in advanced societies to very low birth and death rates.

Secondary data   Data that already exist which may be used by the researcher.

Secondary modern schools   Schools seen as suitable for students best suited to practical tasks.

Secondary socialisation   The socialisation received in later life.

Secondary technical schools   Schools seen as suitable for students with an aptitude for technical subjects

Section 28   Part of *The Local Government Act 1988* which banned councils from promoting homosexual relationships as being similar or equivalent to heterosexual family relationships.

Segregated conjugal roles   Conjugal roles when partners tend to have different roles within their marriage, for example with one doing most of the housework and childcare and the other concentrating on paid employment.

Selective schools   Schools which select their pupils – for example, grammar schools who select on the basis of 'ability'.

Self-completion questionnaire   A questionnaire completed by the research participant.

Self-concept   An individual's picture or view of themselves.

Self-fulfilling prophecy   A prediction that comes to pass simply because it has been made.

Semi-structured interview   Similar to a structured interview, but the interviewer is allowed to probe with additional questions.

Semiotic analysis   The study of signs and symbols and how they combine to create meaning.

Separation   Married couples living apart because their relationship has broken down.

Setting   Placing students in ability groups for particular subjects.

Shop-floor culture   The culture of low-skill workers which has similarities to the counter-school culture.

Sites of ideological struggle   Places where there are conflicts based on different beliefs and values.

Snowball sample   Members of the sample select each other.

Social capital   A social network that can be used as a resource.

Social class   A system of social inequality in which people are grouped in terms of income, wealth, power and prestige.

Social construct   Something which is thought to be natural but which is really produced by the culture of a particular society at a particular time.

Social construction   A feature of society that most people take to be natural but which has actually been produced through social processes.

Social construction/social constructionism   The view that things which appear to be natural are actually produced through social processes.

Social desirability effect   The desire of the interview participant to reflect in their responses what is generally considered to be the right way to behave.

Social liberalism   Policies or views supportive of diverse family forms and greater equality within families.

Social mobility   Movement from one social class to another.

Social mobility strategy   A government strategy to measure the effect of social class on social mobility and to improve the chances of upward mobility for students from low-income families.

Social reproduction   The reproduction of social inequality from one generation to the next.

Social solidarity   Social unity, social cohesion, sticking together.

Social stratification   A system of social inequality such as the class system.

Social survey   The systematic collection of the same type of data from a relatively large number of people.

Socialisation   The process through which a person learns the culture of their society.

Socialisation projects   The idea that children are seen by adults as the passive recipients of socialisation to be moulded to fit the preferences of adults.

Sociological analysis   In terms of documentary research, examining the meanings social groups give to documentary material.

Specialist schools   Secondary schools specialising in particular subject areas.

Sponsored academies   Underperforming schools instructed by the Department for Education to become an academy. Run by sponsors – individuals or organisations.

Stabilisation of adult personalities   To Parsons, the role of the family in maintaining the psychological health of adults by providing warmth and security and allowing them to act out childish elements in their personality.

Status   A position in society.

Stratified random sample   A sample which attempts to reflect particular characteristics of the research population. The population is divided into strata in terms of age, gender etc., and the sample is randomly drawn from each stratum.

Streaming   Placing students in ability groups for all subjects. The whole class becomes an ability group.

Structured dependency   Structures in society which undermine the independence of social groups.

Structured interview   A questionnaire read out by the interviewer who also records the answers.

Structured/systematic observation   Observation which follows specific instructions.

Student premium   An additional payment to schools based on the number of their students with free school meals. Intended to raise the attainment of students from low-income families.

Sub-replacement population fertility   A situation in which too few children are born in a society to replace the number of people dying.

Subculture   The distinctive norms and values of a group which shares many of the aspects of the mainstream culture.

Subject class   The class who are exploited by the ruling class.

Superstructure   The rest of society which is largely shaped by infrastructure

Sure Start   A programme to improve the health and education of the under-fives and their families in the most deprived areas of England.

Symbolic capital   Honour, prestige and reputation.

Symbolic interactionism   A theory which argues that people interact in terms of meanings.

Symmetrical family   A family in which both husband and wife are in employment and both do some housework and provide childcare.

Textual analysis   Examining how words and phrases encourage a particular reading of a document.

The infant mortality rate   The number of babies who die per thousand live births during the first year of their lives.

The second modernity   The most recent phase of modernity according to Beck and Beck Gernsheim involving individualisation.

Thematic analysis   Interpreting the meanings, motives and ideologies which underlie documents.

Theory   A set of ideas which claims to explain something.

Total fertility rate   The average number of children women in a given population will have during their lifetime.

Toxic childhood syndrome   A situation in which commercial and other pressures in the contemporary world make childhood increasingly harmful to children.

Translocalism   A situation in which migrants have strong links to more than one place in the world.

Triangulation   Using mixed methods to check the validity of research findings.

Tripartite system   A three-part system of secondary education.

Triple shift   The three types of work that women are required to do – paid employment, housework and emotion work.

Tuition fees   Fees that most students in England are required to pay for a university education.

Tutor-proof tests   Tests in which results cannot be improved by tutors.

Underclass   According to Charles Murray a group at the bottom of society characterised by lone parenthood, unemployment and criminality which is dependent on welfare and which undermines traditional nuclear family life while encouraging irresponsible behaviour.

Undoing gender   Acting in ways which do not follow traditional socially constructed expectations of the behaviour of men and women and thereby undermine those expectations.

Universalistic meanings   Meanings which are not tied to a particular context or situation.

Universalistic standards   Standards which apply to everybody.

Unstructured interview   Few, if any, pre-set questions, though researchers usually have certain topics they wish to cover.

Unstructured observation   A description of behaviour as seen by the researcher.

Validity   Data are valid if they represent a true and accurate description or measurement.

Value   A belief that something is important and worthwhile, right or wrong.

Value consensus   An agreement about the main values of society.

Values   Beliefs that something is important and worthwhile.

Variables   Factors which affect behaviour. Variables can vary, for example temperature can increase or decrease.

Visiting relationship   In the context of Black Caribbean households a situation where the female head of household may still have a male partner, who does not live with her but visits frequently. The visiting man may play a full and active role as a parent.

Vocational education and training   An education and training system designed to teach work skills to meet the needs of industry.

Vocational GCSEs and vocational A-levels   New exams introduced in the hope of raising the status of vocational courses to the same level as academic qualifications.

Volunteer sample   Members of the sample are self-selected.

Web survey   Questionnaire answered on the researcher's website.

Welfare dependency   To New Right thinkers a situation in which individuals come to rely on 'hand outs' from the state preventing them from taking responsibility for themselves and their own family.

Youth dependency ratio   The ratio of those aged under 19 to the working-age population.

REFERENCES

Abbott, P. and Wallace, C. (1992) *The Family and the New Right*, Pluto Press, London.

Abraham, J. (1995) *Divide and School: Gender and Class Dynamics in Comprehensive Education*, Falmer, London.

Adam, S. and Brewer, M. (2010) *Couple Penalties and Premiums in the UK Tax and Benefits System*, Institute for Fiscal Studies, London.

Adams, R. (2016) 'Progress 8 and GCSEs: will the new way to judge schools be fairer?' *The Guardian*, 23 August.

Age UK (2017) 'Money matters' [online] Available at http://www.ageuk.org.uk/ professional-resources-home/policy/money-matters/ poverty-and-inequality/ Accessed 1/08/2017

Alderson, P. and Morrow, V. (2011) *The Ethics of Research with Children and Young People: A Practical Handbook*, 2nd edn, Sage, London.

Allan, A. J. (2010) 'Picturing success: young femininities and the (im)possibilities of academic achievement in selective, single-sex schooling', *International Studies in Sociology of Education*, vol. 20, no. 1.

Allan, G. (1985) *Family Life: Domestic Roles and Social Organization*, Blackwell, London.

Allan, G. and Crow, G. (2001) *Families, Households and Society*, Palgrave Macmillan, Basingstoke.

Allen, K. (2016) 'UK women still adrift on salary and promotion as gender pay gap remains a gulf', *The Guardian*, 23 August.

Allen, R. (2015) *Missing Talent*, Sutton Trust.

Allen, R. and Thompson, D. (2016) *How are the EBacc and Attainment 8 Reforms Changing Results?* Sutton Trust.

Allmark, P.J. *et al.* (2009) 'Ethical issues in the use of in-depth interviews: literature review and discussion', *Research Ethics*, vol. 5, no. 2.

Almond, B. (2006) *The Fragmenting Family*, Oxford University Press, Oxford.

Althusser, L. (1972) 'Ideology and ideological state apparatus: notes towards an investigation' in B.R. Cosin (ed.) *Education, Structure and Society*, Penguin, Harmondsworth.

Anderson, M. (1980) *Approaches to the History of the Western Family 1500–1914*, Macmillan, London.

Andrews, J. (2016) *School Performance in Multi-Academy Trusts and Local Authorities*, Education Policy Institute, 7 July.

Annese, L. (2016) 'Dispelling the myths: why the gender pay gap does not reflect the "choices" women make', *The Guardian*, 8 November.

Archer, L. (2003) *Race, Masculinity and Schooling: Muslim Boys and Education*, Open University Press, Maidenhead.

Archer, L. and Francis, B. (2007) *Understanding Minority Ethnic Achievement: Race, Gender, Class and 'Success'*, Routledge, London.

Ariès, P. (1973, first published 1960) *Centuries of Childhood*, Penguin, Harmondsworth.

Arnot, M. (2004) 'Male working-class identities and social justice: a reconsideration of Paul Willis's *Learning to Labour* in light of contemporary research' in N. Dolby and G. Dimitriadis with P. Willis (eds) *Learning to Labour in New Times*, RoutledgeFalmer, London.

Baidoun, A. (2014) *Ideologies of Israeli and Palestinian Media in Covering Conflict: Discourse Analysis on the Gaza Conflict 2013*, Lap Lambert Academic Publishing, Saarbrücken, Germany.

Balbo, N., Billari, F.C. and Mills, M. (2013) 'Fertility in advanced societies: a review of research', *European Journal of Population*, vol. 29, no. 1.

Ball, S.J. (2003) *Class Strategies and the Education Market: The Middle Classes and Social Advantage*, RoutledgeFalmer, London.

(2007) *Education PLC: Understanding Private Sector Participation in Public Sector Education*, Routledge, Abingdon.

(2012) *Global Education Inc. New Policy Networks and the Neo-Liberal Imaginary*, Routledge, London.

(2013) *The Education Debate* (2nd edn) The Policy Press, University of Bristol, Bristol.

Ball, S.J., Bowe, R. and Gewirtz, S. (1994) 'Market forces and parental choice' in S. Tomlinson (ed.) *Educational Reform and its Consequences*, IPPR/ Rivers Oram Press, London.

Ball, S.J., Maguire, M. and Braun, A. (2012) *How Schools Do Policy: Policy Enactments in Secondary Schools*, Routledge, London.

Ball, S.J., Maguire, M. and Macrae, S. (2000) *Choice, Pathways and Transitions Post-16: New youth, new economies in the global city*, Routledge Falmer, London.

Barlow, A., Burgoyne, C., Clery, E. and Smithson, J. (2008) 'Cohabitation and the law: myths, money and the media' in A. Park, J. Curtice, K. Thompson, M. Phillips, M. Johnson and E. Clery (eds) *The British Social Attitudes Survey: 24th Annual Report*, Sage, London.

Barlow, A., Duncan, S. and James, G. (2002) 'New Labour, the rationality mistake and family policy in Britain', in A. Carling *et al.* (eds) (2002).

Barlow, A., Duncan, S., James, G. and Park, A. (2001) 'Just a piece of paper? Marriage and cohabitation', in A. Park *et al.* (eds.) (2001).

Barrow, J. (1982) 'West Indian families: an insider's perspective' in R. Rapoport *et al.* (eds) (1982).

Bartlett, W. and Le Grand, J. (1993) 'Quasi markets and educational reform' in J. Le Grand and W. Bartlett (eds) *Quasi Markets and Social Policy*, Macmillan, London.

Basit, T.M. (2013) 'Educational capital as a catalyst for upward social mobility amongst British Asians: a three generational analysis', *British Educational Research Journal*, vol. 39, no. 4.

Bathmaker, A., Ingram, N. and Waller, R. (2013) 'Higher education, social class and the mobilisation of capitals: recognising and playing the game', *British Journal of Sociology of Education*, vol. 34, nos. 5–6.

Bauman, Z. (2003) *Liquid Love*, Polity Press, Cambridge.

(2007) *Liquid Times*, Polity Press, Cambridge.

(2012) *Liquid Modernity*, 2nd edn, Polity Press, Cambridge.

Beatty, C., Fothergill, S. and Gore, T. (2012) *The Real Level of Unemployment 2012*, Centre for Regional Economic and Social Research, Sheffield Hallam University, Sheffield.

Beaujouan, E. and Bhrolcháin, M.N. (2011) 'Cohabitation and marriage in Britain since the 1970s', *Population Trends*, no. 145, Autumn.

Beck, U. (1992) *Risk Society: Towards a New Modernity*, Sage, London.

(2009) *World at Risk*, Polity Press, Cambridge.

Beck, U. and Beck-Gernsheim, E. (1995) *The Normal Chaos of Love*, Polity Press, Cambridge.

Beck, U. and Beck-Gernsheim, E. (2001) *Individualisation*, Sage, London.

Becker, H.S. (1970) *Sociological Work*, Transaction Books, New Brunswick.

Beck-Gernsheim (2002) *Reinventing the Family: In Search of Lifestyles*, Polity Press, Cambridge.

Behnke, S. (2009) 'A classic study, revisited', *Monitor on Psychology*, vol. 40, no. 5.

Behrendt, L. (2016) 'Indigenous kids are still being removed from their families, more than ever before', *The Guardian*, 12 February.

Bennett, T. *et al.* (2009) *Culture, Class, Distinction*, Routledge, Abingdon.

Benston, M. (1972) 'The political economy of women's liberation', in N. Glazer-Malbin and H.Y. Waehrer (eds) *Woman in a Man-Made World*, Rand-McNally, Chicago.

Bernard, J. (1976) *The Future of Marriage*, Penguin, Harmondsworth.

Bernardes, J. (1997) *Family Studies: An Introduction*, Routledge, London.

Bernstein, B. (1970) 'A socio-linguistic approach to social learning' in P. Worsley (ed) *Modern Sociology: Introductory Readings*, Penguin, Harmondsworth.

(1972) 'Language and social context' in P.P. Giglioli (ed) *Language and Social Context*, Penguin, Harmondsworth.

Berrington, A. (2014) *The Changing Demography of Lone Parenthood in the UK*, ESRC Centre for Population Change Working Paper 48 [online] Available at https://www.understandingsociety. ac.uk/research/publications/522469 Accessed 30/05/2017.

Berthoud, R. (2000) *Family Formation in Multi-Cultural Britain: Three Patterns of Diversity* Institute for Social and Economic Research, University of Essex.

Best, L. (1993) ' "Dragons, dinner ladies and ferrets": sex roles in children's books', *Sociology Review*, vol. 2, no. 3.

Bhatti, G. (1999) *Asian Children at Home and at School: An Ethnographic Study*. Routledge, London.

Blackstone, T. and Mortimore, J. (1994) 'Cultural factors in child-rearing and attitudes to education' in B. Moon and A.S. Mayes (eds) *Teaching and Learning in the Secondary School,* Routledge, London.

Blaikie, A. (1999) *Ageing and Popular Culture*, Cambridge University Press, Cambridge.

Blatchford, P. (2003) *The Class Size Debate: is Smaller Better?* Open University Press, Maidenhead.

Boaler, Jo (2005) 'The "psychological prisons" from which they never escaped: the role of ability grouping in reproducing social class inequalities', *Forum*, vol. 47, nos. 2 and 3.

Boelstorff, T., Nardi, B., Pearce, C. and Taylor, T.L. (2012) *Ethnography and Virtual worlds: A Handbook of Method,* Princeton University Press, Princeton.

Boland, S. (2017) 'What will happen to women's rights now that Donald Trump is President?', *New Statesman*, 26 January.

Boliver, V. and Swift, A. (2012) 'Schools and social mobility', *Sociology Review*, vol. 22, no. 2.

Boulton, M.G. (1983) *On Being a Mother*, Tavistock, London.

Bourdieu, P. (1973) 'Cultural reproduction and social reproduction' in R. Brown (ed.) *Knowledge, Education and Cultural Change*, Tavistock, London.

(1974) 'The school as a conservative force: scholastic and cultural inequalities' in J. Eggleston (ed.) *Contemporary Research in the Sociology of Education,* Methuen, London.

(1984) *Distinction: A Social Critique of the Judgement of Taste*, Routledge & Kegan Paul, London.

(2016) 'The forms of capital' in A. R. Sadovnik and R. W. Coughlan (eds) *Sociology of Education: A Critical Reader* 3rd edn, Routledge, Abingdon.

Bourdieu, P. and Passeron, J. (1977) *Reproduction in Education, Society and Culture*, Sage, London.

Bowles, S. and Gintis, H. (1976) *Schooling in Capitalist America*, Routledge & Kegan Paul, London.

Brannen, J. (2003) 'The age of beanpole families', *Sociology Review*, vol. 13, no. 1.

Brannan, J., Heptinstall, E. and Bhopal, K. (2000) *Connecting Children: Care and Family Life in Later Childhood*, Routledge, London.

Braun, A., Vincent, C. and Ball, S. (2011) 'Working-class fathers and childcare: the economic and family contexts of fathering in the UK', *Community, Work and Family*, vol. 14, no. 1.

British Social Attitudes (2013) 'Attitudes have changed but have behaviours?' [online] Available at http://www.bsa.natcen.ac.uk/latest-report/

british-social-attitudes-30/gender-roles/attitudes-have-changed-but-have-behaviours.aspx Accessed 28/06/2017.

British Social Attitudes (2016) *NatCen Social Research* 33rd edn.

British Sociological Association. (1996). *Statement of Ethical Practice,* British Sociological Association, Durham.

Browne, J. and Elming, W., (2015) *The effect of the coalition's tax and benefits changes on household income and work incentives*, Institute for Fiscal Studies, London [online] Available at https://www.ifs.org.uk/uploads/publications/bns/BN159.pdf Accessed 15/4/2017.

Bruce, S. (1995) 'Religion and the sociology of religion' in M. Haralambos (ed.) *Developments in Sociology*, vol. 11, Causeway Press, Ormskirk.

Bruce, S. (2011) *Secularization*, Oxford University Press, Oxford.

Bryman, A. (1988) *Quantity and Quality in Social Research,* Unwin Hyman, London.

Bryman, A. (2016) *Social Research Methods*, 5th edn, Oxford University Press, Oxford.

Buchanan, A. (2017) 'Grandparents and the rise of beanpole families: ageing population and childcare', *Sociology Review* , vol. 27, no. 2.

Buchanan, A. and Rotkirch, A. (eds) (2014) *Fertility Rates and Population Decline: No Time for Children*, Oxford University Press, Oxford.

Buchanan, A. and Rotkirch, A. (2013) 'No time for children? The key questions' in A. Buchanan and A. Rotkirch (eds) (2013) *Fertility Rates and Population Decline; No Time for Children?*, Palgrave Macmillan, London.

Buchanan, A. (2017) 'Why are families smaller today?' *Sociology Review*, vol. 27, no. 3.

Burton, N, Brundrett, M. and Jones, M. (2014) *Doing Your Education Research Project*, 2nd edn, Sage, London.

Carling, A., Duncan, S. and Edwards, R. (eds) (2002) *Analysing Families: Morality and Rationality in Policy and Practice*, Routledge, London.

Cassen, R. and Kindon, G. (2007) *Tackling Low Educational Achievement*, Joseph Rowntree Foundation, York.

Castles, S. and Miller, M.J. (2009) *The Age of Migration: International Population Movements in the Modern World*, 4th edn, Palgrave Macmillan, Basingstoke.

Chambers, D. (2001) *Representing the Family*, Sage, London.

Chambers, D. (2012) *A Sociology of Family Life*, Polity Press, Cambridge.

Chambers, D. (2012) *A Sociology of Family Life*, Polity Press, Cambridge.

Champion, T. and Falkingham, J. (2016) 'Population change in the UK: what can the last twenty-five years tell us about the next twenty-five years?' in T. Champion and J. Falkingham (eds.) *Population Change in the United Kingdom*, Rowman and Littlefield, London.

Chandler. J. (1993) 'Women outside marriage', *Sociology Review*, vol. 2, no. 4.

Chapman, J. (2015) 'PM hails tax break for married couples', *Mail Online*, 20 February 2015 [online] Available at http://www.dailymail.co.uk/news/article-2960980/PM-hails-tax-break-married-couples-Long-awaited-help-arrives-stay-home-mothers.html Accessed 14/04/2017

Chapman, S., Holborn, M., Moore, S. and Aiken, D. (2015) *Sociology: AQA A-Level Year 1 and AS Student Book*, Collins, London.

Chester, R. (1985) 'The rise of the neo-conventional family', *New Society*, 9 May.

Chitty, C. (2002) *Understanding Schools and Schooling*, RoutledgeFalmer, London.

Cicourel, A.V. and Kitsuse, J.I. (1963) *The Educational Decision-Makers*, Bobbs-Merrill, Indianapolis.

Cingano, F. (2014) 'Trends in income inequality and its impact on economic growth', *OECD Social, Employment and Migration Working Papers*, no. 163 OECD Publishing.

Clegg, N. (2012) *Delivering Education's Progressive Promise: Using Pupil Premium to Change Lives*, Cabinet Office, London.

Coast, E. and Freeman, E. (2016) 'Reproductive and sexual behaviour and health', in T. Champion and J. Falkingham (eds.) *Population Change in the United Kingdom*, Rowman & Littlefield, London.

Coffield, F. and Williamson, B. (2011) *From Exam Factories to Communities of Discovery: The Democratic Route,* Institute of Education, University of London, London.

Cohen, L., Manion, L. and Morrison, K. (2011) *Research Methods in Education*, 7th edn, Routledge, London.

Colquhoun, R. (1976) 'Values, socialisation and achievement' in J. Beck *et al*. (eds) *Worlds Apart: Readings for a Sociology of Education*, Collier-Macmillan, London.

Connell, R.W. (1995) *Masculinities*, Polity Press, Cambridge.

Connolly, P. (1998) *Racism, Gender Identities and Young Children*, Routledge, London.

Cook, L.P. & Gash, V. (2010) Wives' Part-time Employment and Marital Stability in Great Britain, West Germany and the United States, *Sociology*, vol. 44, no. 2.

Cooper, D. (1972) *The Death of the Family*, Penguin, Harmondsworth.

CPAG (2017) 'Child Poverty: Facts and Figures' [online] Available at http://www.cpag.org.uk/child-poverty-facts-and-figures Accessed 4/07/2017.

Crompton, R. and Lyonette, C. (2008) 'Who does the housework? The division of labour within the home' in Park *et al*. (eds) (2008).

Cumming, E. and Henry, W.E. (1961) *Growing Old: The Process of Disengagement*, Basic Books, New York.

Cunningham, H. (2006) *The Invention of Childhood*, BBC Books, London.

Daubney, M. (2015) 'Is feminism destroying the institution of marriage?' *The Telegraph* 30 May 2017 [online] Available at http://www.telegraph.co.uk/men/thinking-man/11824814/Is-feminism-destroying-the-institution-of-marriage.html Accessed 4/06/2017.

David, M.E. (2016) *A Feminist Manifesto for Education*, Polity Press, Cambridge.

Davis, K. and Moore, W.E. (1967, first published 1945) 'Some principles of stratification' in R. Bendix and S. M. Lipset (eds) *Class, Status and Power*, 2nd edn, Routledge & Kegan Paul, London.

DCSF (26 June 2008) *Youth Cohort Study and Longitudinal Study of Young People in England: The Activities and Experiences of 16 Year Olds: England 2007*, Department for Children, Schools and Families, London.

(14 January 2009) *GCE/VCE/Applied A/AS and Equivalent Examinations Results in England, 2007/08 (Revised)*, Department for Children, Schools and Families, London.

De Laine, M. (2000) *Fieldwork, Participation and Practice*, Sage, London.

Deevy, M. and Beals, M. (2013) *The Scope of the Problem: An Overview of Fraud Prevalence Measurement*, Financial Fraud Research Center, Stanford.

Dench, G., Gavron, K. and Young, M. (2006) *The New East End: Kinship, Race and Conflict*, Profile Books, London.

Denscombe, M. (1994) *Sociology Update*, Leicester: Olympus Books.

Dermott, E. and Pomati, M. (2016) 'The parenting and economising practices of lone parents: policy and evidence' *Critical Social Policy*, vol. 36, no. 1.

Dex, S. and Ward, K. (2007) *Parental Care and Employment in Early Childhood*, Equal Opportunities Commission, London.

DfE (22 July 2010) *Youth Cohort Study and Longitudinal Study of Young People in England: The Activities and Experiences of 18 Year Olds: England 2009*, Department for Education, London.

(25 November 2010) *The Impact of Sure Start Programmes on Five Year Olds and their Families*, Department for Education, London.

(16 December 2010) *GCSE and Equivalent Attainment by Pupil Characteristics in England 2009/10*, Department for Education, London.

(26 January 2012) *GCE/Applied GCSE A/AS and Equivalent Examination Results in England, 2010/11 (Revised)*, Department for Education, London.

(22 June 2012) *Academies Annual Report 2010/11*, Department for Education, London.

(21 February 2013) *Participation in Education, Training and Employment by 16-18 Year Olds in England, 2012/13*, Department for Education, London.

(22 January 2014) *GCSE and Equivalent Attainment by Pupil Characteristics in England 2012/13*, Department for Education, London.

(29 January 2015) *Revised GCSE and Equivalent Results in England, 2013 to 2014*, Department for Education, London.

(10 December 2015) *National Curriculum Assessments at Key Stage 2 in England, 2015 (Revised)*, Department for Education, London.

(21 January 2016) *Revised GCSE and Equivalent Results in England, 2014 to 2015*, Department for Education, London.

(7 April 2016) *Level 2 and 3 Attainment in England: Attainment by Age 19 in 2015*, Department for Education, London.

(3 August 2016) *Widening Participation in Higher Education, England, 2013/14 Age Cohort*, Department for Education, London.

(1 September 2016) *National Curriculum Assessments at Key Stage 2 in England, 2016 (provisional)*, Department for Education, London.

DFES (2003) *Widening Participation in Higher Education*, HMSO, London.

(25 November 2004) *Youth Cohort Study: The Activities and Experiences of 18 Year Olds: England and Wales 2004*, Department for Education and Skills, London.

(24 February 2005) *Youth Cohort Study: The Activities and Experiences of 16 Year Olds: England and Wales 2004*, Department for Education and Skills, London.

(18 January 2006) *GCS/VCE A/AS Examination Results for Young People In England, 2004/05 (Revised)*, Department for Education and Skills, London.

(28 November 2006) *Youth Cohort Study: The Activities and Experiences of 18 Year Olds: England and Wales 2006*, Department for Education and Skills, London.

Ditton, J. (1977) *Part-time Crime*, Macmillan, London.

Dobash, R.E. and Dobash, R.P. (1979) *Violence Against Wives: A Case Against the Patriarchy*, The Free Press, New York.

Dobash, R.E. and Dobash, R.P. (2004) 'Women's violence towards men in intimate relationships' *British Journal of Criminology*, vol. 44, no. 3.

Dobash, R.E. and Dobash, R.P. (1998) 'Violent men and violent contexts' in R.E. Dobash and R.P. Dobash (eds) *Rethinking Violence Against Women*, Sage, London.

Dobash, R.E. and Dobash, R.P. (2011) 'What were they thinking? Men who murder their intimate partner', *Violence Against Women*, vol. 17, no. 1.

Donzelot, J. (1977) *The Policing of Families*, Pantheon Books, New York.

Douglas, J.W.B. (1964) *The Home and the School*, MacGibbon & Kee, London.

Douglas, J.W.B., Ross, J.M. and Simpson, H.R. (1970) *Natural Symbols*, Barrie & Jenkins, London.

Duncombe, J. and Marsden, D. (1995) 'Women's "triple shift": paid employment, domestic labour and "emotion work"', *Sociology Review*, vol. 4, no. 4.

Durkheim, E. (1938) *The Rules of Sociological Method*, Free Press, New York. (1961) *Moral Education*, Free Press, Glencoe.

Earlham Sociology (2017) *Gender and Subject Choice*.

Eberstadt, N, (2015) 'The Global Flight from the Family'. *Wall Street Journal, Eastern edition*; New York, 21 Feb 2015 [online] https://search-proquest-com.libezproxy.open.ac.uk/docview/1656549103?rfr_id=info%3Axri%2Fsid%3Aprimo https://www.wsj.com/articles/nicholas-eberstadt-the-global-flight-from-the-family-1424476179 Accessed 15/08/2017.

Edwards, K. (2013) 'Gove's history curriculum needs to do more to teach equality', *The Guardian*, 29 April.

Edwards, R. and Holland, J. (2013) *What is Qualitative Interviewing?* Bloomsbury, London.

Elgot, J. (2017) 'Labour would reverse £500 million of Sure Start cuts says Angela Rayner', *The Guardian*, 26 September, 2017 [online] Available at https://www.theguardian.com/politics/2017/sep/26/labours-angela-rayner-to-pledge-500m-of-sure-start-funding Accessed 01/10/2017.

Elliot, J. and Vaitilingam, R. (eds) (2008) *Now We Are 50: Key Findings from the National Child Development Study, Summary Report*, Institute of Education, University of London, London.

Elliott, A. (2009) *Contemporary Social Theory: An Introduction*, Routledge, Abingdon.

Engels, F. (1972) *The Origin of the Family, Private Property and the State*, Lawrence & Wishart, London.

Evandrou, M., Falkingham, J. and Vlachcanoti, A. (2016) 'The ageing population: implications for health and social care' in T. Champion and J. Falkingham (eds.) *Population Change in the United Kingdom*, Rowman and Littlefield, London.

Evans, G. (2006) *Educational Failure and Working Class White Children in Britain*, Palgrave Macmillan, Basingstoke.

Evans, G. (2007) *Educational Failure and Working Class White Children in Britain*, Palgrave Macmillan, Basingstoke.

Featherstone, M. and Hepworth, M. (1991) 'The mask of ageing and the postmodern life course' in Featherstone *et al.* (eds) (1991) *The Body, Social Process and Cultural Theory*, Sage, London.

Featherstone, M., Hepworth, M. and Turner, B.B. (eds) (1991) *The Body, Social Process and Cultural Theory*, Sage, London.

Feinstein, L. (2003) 'Very early evidence: how early can we predict future educational achievement?' *Centrepiece*, vol. 8, no. 2.

Fenton, S. (2017) 'Trump's abortion legislation is terrifying and shameful, but the UK isn't much better', *The Independent*, 12 February.

Fitzpatrick, T. (2011) *Welfare Theory: An Introduction to the Theoretical Debates*, 2nd edn, Palgrave Macmillan, Basingstoke.

Flanders, N.A. (1970) *Analyzing Teaching Behaviour*, Addison-Wesley Publishing Company, Reading, Mass.

Fletcher, R. (1966) *The Family and Marriage in Britain*, Penguin, Harmondsworth.

Fox Harding, L. (1996) *Family, State and Social Policy*, Macmillan, Basingstoke.

Francis, B. (2000) *Boys, Girls and Achievement: Addressing the Classroom Issues*, Routledge-Falmer, London.

Friedman, N.L. (1976) 'Cultural deprivation: a commentary on the sociology of knowledge' in J. Beck *et al. Worlds Apart: Readings for a Sociology of Education*, Collier-Macmillan, London.

Fuller, M. (1984) 'Black girls in a London comprehensive school' in M. Hammersley and P. Woods (eds) *Life in School, the Sociology of Pupil Culture*, Open University Press, Milton Keynes.

Gabb, J. (2008) in Redman, P. (ed.) 'Affective Attachment in Families' in *Attachment: Sociology and Social Worlds*, Manchester University Press, Manchester.

Gabb, J. (2008) *Researching Intimacy in Families*, Palgrave Macmillan, Basingstoke.

Galindo-Rueda, F., Marcenaro-Gutierrez, O. and Vignoles, A. (2004) 'The widening socio-economic gap in UK higher education', *Centre for the Economics of Education Discussion Paper*, London School of Economics and Political Science, London.

Gamoran, A. (2010) 'Tracking and inequality: new directions for research and practice', in M.W. Apple, S.J. Ball and L.A. Gandin *The Routledge International Handbook of the Sociology of Education*, Routledge, London.

Garrod, J. (2017) 'Life expectancy', *Sociology Review*, vol. 26, no. 4.

Garrod, Joan (2016) 'Education and the white working class', *Sociology Review*, vol. 26, no. 2

Geertz, C. (1973) *The Interpretation of Cultures*, Basic Books, New York.

Gewirtz, S. (2001) 'Cloning the Blairs: New Labour's programme for the resocialisation of working-class parents', *Journal of Education Policy*, vol. 16, no. 4.

Gewirtz, S., Ball, S.J. and Bowe, R. (1995) *Markets, Choice and Equality in Education*, Open University Press, Buckingham.

Gibson, C. (1994) *Dissolving Wedlock*, Routledge, London.

Gibson, L. (2010) *Using Email Interviews*, National Centre for Research Methods, Manchester.

Giddens, A. (1973) *The Class Structure of the Advanced Societies*, Hutchinson, London.

(1991) *Modernity and Self-Identity: Self and Society in the Late Modern Age*, Polity Press, Cambridge.

Giddens, A. (1990) *The Consequences of Modernity*, Polity Press, Cambridge.

Giddens, A. (1992) *The Transformation of Intimacy: Sexuality, Love and Eroticism in Modern Societies*, Polity Press, Cambridge.

Giddens, A. (2009) *Sociology*, 6th edn, Polity Press, Cambridge.

Gilchrist, E., Johnson, R., Takriti, R., Weston, S., Beech, A and Kebbell M. (2003) *Domestic violence offenders: characteristics and offending related needs* HMSO findings 217 [online] Available at http://webarchive.nationalarchives.gov.uk/20110218135832/http://rds.homeoffice.gov.uk/rds/pdfs2/r217.pdf Accessed 30/11/2017.

Gillborn, D. and Mirza, H.S. (2000) *Educational Inequality: Mapping Race, Class and Gender*, London: OFSTED.

Gillborn, D. and Youdell, D. (2000) *Rationing Education: Policy, Practice, Reform and Equity*, Open University Press, Buckingham.

(2001) 'The new IQism: intelligence, "ability" and the rationing of education' in J. Demaine (ed) *Sociology of Education Today*, Palgrave Macmillan, Basingstoke.

Gilligan, J. (2001) *Preventing Violence*, Thames and Hudson, London.

Gingerbread (2017) 'Statistics' [online] Available at https://gingerbread.org.uk/content/365/Statistics Accessed 30/05/2017.

Giroux, H. (1984) 'Ideology, agency and the process of schooling' in L. Barton and S. Walker (eds) *Social Crisis and Educational Research*, Croom Helm, London.

(2011) *On Critical Pedagogy (Critical Pedagogy Today)*, Bloomsbury, London.

Gittins, D. (1998) *The Child in Question*, Palgrave, Basingstoke.

Giulianotti, R. (1995) 'Participant observation and research into football hooliganism: reflections on the problems of entrée and everyday risks', *Sociology of Sport Journal*, vol. 12, no. 1.

Glasgow University Media Group (1976) *Bad news*, Routledge & Kegan Paul, London. Global Drug Survey (2014) *Methodology*.

(2016) *Findings*.

Global Media Monitoring Project (2016) www.whomakesthenews.org.

Goffman, E. (1959) *The Presentation of Self in Everyday Life*, Doubleday Anchor, New York.

(1968) *Asylums*, Penguin, Harmondsworth.

Goldthorpe, J. (2016) 'Decades of investment in education have not improved social mobility', *Observer*, 13 March.

Gordon, L. (1984) 'Paul Willis – education, cultural production and social reproduction', *British Journal of Sociology of Education*, vol. 5, no. 2.

Gough, K. (1972) 'An anthropologist looks at Engels' in N. Glazer Malbin and H.Y. Waehrer (eds) *Woman in a Man-Made World*, Rand McNally, Chicago.

Green, F., Allen, R. and Jenkins, A. (2014) *The Social Composition of Free School after Three Years*, Institute of Education, University of London, London.

Green, L. (2010) *Understanding the Life Course: Sociological and Psychological Perspectives*, Polity Press, Cambridge.

Green, L. (2015) 'Age and the life course: continuity, change and the modern mirage of infinite choice' in M. Holborn (ed.) *Contemporary Sociology*, Polity Press, Cambridge.

Greer, G. (2000) *The Whole Woman*, Anchor, London.

Grey, T. (2015) 'Najat Valland-Belkacem is the youthful new face of France', *Vogue*, 1 April.

Griffin, J.H. (1960) *Black Like Me*, Signet, New York.

Grimes, S. M. (2015) 'Configuring the child player' *Science, Technology and Human Values*, vol. 40, no. 1.

Grogan, S. and Richards, H. (2002) Body image: focus groups with boys and men, *Men and Masculinities*, vol. 4, no. 3.

Hall, E.T. (1973) *The Silent Language*, Doubleday, New York.

Hallam, S. and Parsons, S. (2014) 'Streaming six-year-olds by ability only benefits the brightest', *The Conversation* [online] Available at http://theconversation.com/streaming-six-year-olds-by-ability-only-benefits-the-brightest-32065 Accessed 19/12/2017.

Halsey, A.H., Floud, J. and Anderson, C.A. (1961) *Education, Economy and Society*, Free Press, New York.

Halsey, A.H., Heath, A. and Ridge, J.M. (eds) (1980) *Origins and Destinations*, Clarendon Press, Oxford.

Hannay, T. (2016) *Examining Academies, Part 1 and 2*, SchoolDash.com, 12 April.

Haralambos, M. (1994) *Right On: From Blues to Soul in Black America*, Causeway Press, Ormskirk.

Haralambos, M. (ed.) (1994) *Developments in Sociology*, vol. 10, Causeway Press, Ormskirk.

Haralambos, M. and Holborn, M. (2013) *Sociology Themes and Perspectives*, Collins, London.

Hardill, I., Green, A., Dudlestone, A. and Owen, D.W. (1997) 'Who decides what? Decision making in dual career households', *Work, Employment and Society*, vol. 11, no. 2.

Hargreaves, A. (1982) 'Resistance and relative autonomy theories: problems of distortion and incoherence in recent Marxist analyses of education', *British Journal of Sociology of Education*, vol. 3, no. 2.

Hargreaves, D.H. (1967) *Social Relations in a Secondary School*, Routledge, Abingdon.

Hart, N. (1976) *When Marriage Ends: A Study in Status Passage*, Tavistock, London.

Harvey, D. (2010) *The Enigma of Capital and the Crises of Capitalism*, Profile Books, London.

Harvey, D.G. and Slatin, G.T. (1975) 'The relationship between child's SES and teacher expectations: a test of the middle-class bias hypothesis', *Social Forces*, vol. 54, no. 1.

Heelas, P. and Woodhead, L. (2005) *The Spiritual Revolution: Why Religion is Giving Way to Spirituality*, Blackwell, Oxford.

Henricson, C. (2012) *A Revolution in Family Policy*, The Policy Press, Bristol.

HESA (Higher Education Statistics Agency) (2016) www.hesa.ac.uk.

Hey, V. (1997) *The Company She Keeps: an Ethnography of Girls' Friendships*, Open University Press, Buckingham.

Hill, M. (2005) 'Ethical considerations in researching children's experiences' in S. Greene and D. Hogan (eds) *Researching Children's Experience: Approaches and Methods*, Sage, London.

Hirsch, D. (2007) *Experiences of Poverty and Educational Disadvantage*, Joseph Rowntree Foundation, York.

Hirsch, D. (2012) *Does the tax and benefit system create a 'couple penalty'?* IFS, London.

Hite, Shere (1994) *The Hite Report on the Family: Growing up under Patriarchy*, Grove Press, New York.

HMIC (2014) *Crime-recording: Making the Victim Count*, HMIC, London.

Hobbs, D. (1988) *Doing the Business*, Oxford University Press, Oxford.

Hochschild, A. (1983) *The Managed Heart: Commercialization of Human Feeling*, University of California Press, CA.

Hochschild, A. (2011) 'Emotional life on the market frontier', *Annual Review of Sociology*, vol. 37.

Hockey, J. and James, A. (1993) *Growing Up and Growing Old: Ageing and Dependency in the Life Course*, Sage, London.

Hodkinson, P. (2002) *Goth: Identity, Style and Subculture*, Berg, Oxford.

Holborn, M. (ed.) (2015) *Contemporary Sociology*, Polity Press, Cambridge.

Holborn, M. (ed.) (2004) *Developments in Sociology*, vol. 20, Causeway Press, Ormskirk.

Homan, R. (1991) *The Ethics of Social Research*, Longman, London.

Hughes, M. (1994) 'Researching Parents after the 1988 Education Reform Act' in D. Halpin and B. Troyna (eds) *Researching Education Policy: Ethical and methodological issues*, Falmer Press, London.

Human Rights and Equal Opportunities Commission (1997) *Bringing Them Home*, Commonwealth of Australia, Sydney.

Humphreys, L. (1970) *Tearoom Trade: Impersonal Sex in Public Places*, Duckworth, London.

Hutchings, M. (2015) *Exam Factories? The Impact of Accountability Measures on Children and Young People*, NUT teachers.org.uk.

The House of Commons (1999) 'A Century of Change: Trends in UK Statistics Since 1900', The House of Commons, London.

IFS (2017) *Spending on Adult Social Care Per Adult*, IFS, London.

ILO (2013) *Marking progress against child labour – Global estimates and trends 2000–2012* [online] Available at http://www.ilo.org/ipec/Informationresources/WCMS_221513/lang--en/index.htm Accessed 03/07/2017.

Independent Commission on Fees (2015) *2015 Final Report.*

Iniesta-Martinez, S. and Evans, H. (2012) *Pupils Not Claiming Free School Meals*, Department for Education, London.

Institute for Fiscal Studies (2015) *Ethnic Minorities Substantially More Likely to go to University then their White British Peers*, www.ifs.org.uk/publications/8042

(2016) *The Distribution of Household Wealth in the UK*, 19 April.

Ireson, J., Hallam, S. and Hurley, C. (2001) *Ability Groupings in the Secondary School: Effects on Key Stage 4*, Institute of Education, University of London, London.

Jackson, C. (2006) *Lads and Ladettes in School: Gender and a Fear of Failure*, Open University Press, Maidenhead.

Jackson, S. and Scott, S. (2006) 'Childhood' in G. Payne (ed.) (2006).

James, A. and Prout, A. (eds) (1997) *Constructing and Reconstructing Childhood*, 2nd edn, Falmer, London.

Jamieson, L. (1997) *Intimacy: Personal Relationships in Modern Societies*, Polity Press, Cambridge.

Jamieson, L. (1999) 'Solo-living, demographic and family change: the need to know more about men', *Sociological Research Online*, vol. 14, no. 2.

Jamieson, L., Stewart, R., Li, Y., Anderson, M., Bechhofer F. and McCrone, D. (2002). 'Single, 20 something and seeking?' in Allan, G. & Jones, G. (eds.) *Social Relations and the Life Course*, Palgrave, London.

Jamieson, L. (2005) 'Boundaries of intimacy' in L. McKie and S. Cunningham Burley (eds).

Jamieson, L., Wasoff, F. and Simpson, R. (2009) 'Solo living, demographic and family change: the need to know more about men', *Sociological Research Online*, vol. 14, no. 5. [online] Available at http://www.socresonline.org.uk/14/2/5.html Accessed 5/04/2012.

Jay-Z (2010) *Decoded*, Virgin Books, London.

Jenks, C. (2005) *Childhood*, 2nd edn, Routledge, London.

Johnston, C. (2017) 'Number of child sexual abuse claims overwhelming police says lead officer', *The Guardian*, 28 February 2017 [online] https://www.theguardian.com/society/2017/feb/28/child-sexual-abuse-claims-overwhelming-police-says-lead-officer Accessed 5/07/2017.

Josephy Jr, A.M. (1984) *Now that the Buffalo's Gone*, University of Oklahoma Press, Norman. (1995) *500 Nations*, Hutchinson, London.

Kan, Man-Yee and Laurie, H. (2016) 'Who is doing the housework in multi-cultural Britain', *Sociology*, December 2016.

Karabel, J. and Halsey, A.H. (1977) *Power and Ideology in Education*, Oxford University Press, Oxford.

Keddie, N. (1973) *Tinker, Tailor... The Myth of Cultural Deprivation*, Penguin, Harmondsworth.

Key, W. (2016) 'The "oldest old": The UK's over-85 population', *Sociology Review*, vol. 25, no. 4.

Kirby, P. (2016) *Leading People 2016: The Educational Backgrounds of the UK Professional Elite*, Sutton Trust, February.

Klineberg, O. (1971) Race and IQ, *Courier*, vol. 24, no. 10.

Kruk, K.E. (2013) 'Parental income and the dynamics of health inequality in early childhood — evidence from the UK', *Health Economics*, vol. 22, no. 10.

Labov, W. (1973) 'The logic of nonstandard English' in N. Keddie (1973).

Lader, D., Short, S. and Gershuny, J. (2006) *The Time Use Survey 2005*, Office for National Statistics, London.

Lampl, P. (2016) 'Foreword' to P. Kirby, *Leading People, 2016*, Sutton Trust, February.

Laslett, P.K. (1965) *The World We Have Lost*, Methuen, London. (1977) *Family Life and Illicit Love in Earlier Generations*, Methuen, London.

Lauder, H., Brown, P., Dillabough, J. and Halsey, A.H. (eds) (2006) *Education, Globalisation, and Social Change*, Oxford University Press, Oxford.

Lauder, H., Hughes, D. *et al.* (1999) *Trading in Futures: Why Markets in Education Don't Work*, Open University Press, Buckingham.

Law, I. and Swann, S. (2011) *Ethnicity and Education in England and Europe: Gangstas, Geeks and Gorjas*, Ashgate, Farnham.

Law, I., Finney, S. and Swann, S.J. (2014) 'Searching for autonomy: young black men, schooling and aspirations', *Race Ethnicity and Education*, vol. 17, no. 4.

Lawson, A. (1988) *Adultery: An Analysis of Love and Betrayal*, Blackwell, Oxford.

Lee, D. and Newby, H. (1983) *The Problem of Sociology*, Hutchinson, London.

Lesthaeghe, R. (2014) 'The second demographic transition: A concise overview of its development', Royal Flemish Academy of Arts and Sciences [online] Available at http://www.pnas.org.libezproxy.open.ac.uk/content/111/51/18112.full.pdf Accessed 04/07/17.

Let Toys Be Toys (2016) *Annual Survey*, 15 December, lettoysbetoys.org.uk.

Levin, H.M. and Belfield, C.R. (2006) 'The marketplace in education' in Lauder *et al.* (eds) (2006).

Licht, B.G. and Dweck, C.S. (1987) 'Some differences in achievement orientations' in M. Arnot and G. Weiner *Gender under Scrutiny*, Hutchinson, London.

Liebow, E. (1967) *Tally's Corner*, Little Brown, Boston.

Lobban, G. (1974) 'Data report on British reading schemes', *Times Educational Supplement*, 1 March.

Long, R. and Bolton, P. (2015) *Faith Schools: FAQs*, Briefing paper, House of Commons Library, London.

Lupton, R. (2004) *Schools in Disadvantaged Areas: Recognising Context and Raising Quality*, London School of Economics and Political Science, London.

Mac an Ghaill, M. (1994) *The Making of Men: Masculinities, Sexualities and Schooling*, Open University Press, Milton Keynes.

Machin, S. and McNally, S. (2006) *Gender and School Achievement in English Schools*, Centre for the Economics of Education, London.

Machin, S. and Vernoit, J. (2010) 'Academy schools: who benefits?', *CentrePiece*, Autumn.

Macionis, J.J. and Plummer, K. (1997) *Sociology: A Global Introduction*, Prentice-Hall, NJ.

Maguire, M. (2000) 'Researching "street criminals": a neglected art' in R.D. King and E. Wincup (eds), *Doing Research on Crime and Justice*, Oxford University Press, Oxford.

Malinowski, B. (1922) *Argonauts of the Western Pacific*, George Routledge & Sons, London.

Marmot, M. (2015) 'The richer you are, the better your health – and how this can be changed', *The Guardian*, 11 September.

Marmott Review (2010) *Fair Society: Healthy Lives* [online] Available at ww.ucl.ac.uk/marmotreview Accessed 31/07/2017.

Marmott, M. (2004) *Status Syndrome*, Bloomsbury Publishing, London.

Marsh, J. (2010) 'Young children's play in online virtual worlds', *Journal of Early Childhood Research*, vol. 8, no. 1.

May, V. (2011) 'Introducing a sociology of personal life' in V. May (ed.) (2011) *Sociology of Personal Life*, Palgrave Macmillan, Basingstoke.

May, V. (2015) *Families and Personal Life: All Change?* In M. Holborn (ed.) *Contemporary Sociology*, Polity Press, Cambridge.

Mayall, B. (2004) 'Sociologies of childhood' in M. Holborn (ed.) (2004).

McKenzie, L. (2010) 'Being looked down on: fear of stigma and its impact upon the participation in local services by working-class mothers'. Social Policy Association Conference Paper, University of Lincoln, 5 July 2010 [online] Available at http://www.social-policy.org.uk/lincoln/McKensie.pdf Accessed 01/10/2017.

McKeown, T. (1979) *The Role of Medicine*, Blackwell, Oxford.

McKie, L. and Callan, S. (2012) *Understanding Families: A Global Introduction*, Sage, London.

McKie, L. and Cunningham-Burley, S. (eds) (2005) *Families in Society: Boundaries and Relationships*, Policy Press, Bristol.

McKnight, A., Glennerster, H. and Lupton, R. (2005) 'Education, education, education…: an assessment of Labour's success in tackling educational inequalities', in J. Hills and K. Stewart (eds) *A More Equal Society? New Labour, Poverty, Inequality and Exclusion*, Policy Press, Bristol.

McLanahan, S. and Booth, K. (1991) 'Mother-only families' in A. Booth (ed.) *Contemporary Families*, National Council on Family Relations, Minneapolis, MN.

McRobbie, A. (2000) *Feminism and Youth Culture*, 2nd edn, London, Routledge.

McRobbie, A. (2013) 'Feminism, the family and the new mediated maternalism', *New Formations*, Winter 2013, issues 80–81.

Milgram, S. (1963) 'A behavioural study of obedience', *Journal of Abnormal and Social Psychology*, vol. 67, no. 4.

Millar, F. (2016) '"Tutor-proof" 11-plus professor admits grammar school test doesn't work', *The Guardian*, 12 September.

Miller, T. (2011) 'Falling back into gender? Men's narratives and practices around first-time fatherhood', *Sociology*, vol. 45, no. 6.

Mills, C.W. (1959) *The Sociological Imagination*, Oxford University Press, Oxford.

Modood, T. (2004) 'Capitals, ethnic identity and educational qualifications', *Cultural Trends*, vol. 13, no. 2.

Moore, S. (2013) 'Health, medicine and the body' in M. Haralambos and M. Holborn, *Sociology Themes and Perspectives*, 8th edn, Collins, London.

Morgan, D. (1996) *Family Connections*, Polity: Cambridge.

Morgan, D. (2006) 'Focus groups' in V. Jupp (ed.) *The Sage Dictionary of Social Research Methods*, Sage, London.

Morgan, D. (2011) *Rethinking Family Practices*, Palgrave Macmillan: Basingstoke.

Morgan, D.H.J. (1975) *Social Theory and the Family*, Routledge & Kegan Paul, London.

Morgan, D.H.J. (1994) 'The family' in M. Haralambos (ed.) (1994).

Morgan, P. (2007) *The War Between the State and the Family*, Institute of Economic Affairs [online] Available at https://papers.ssrn.com/sol3/papers.cfm?abstract_id = 977911 Accessed 9/4/2017.

Morgan, P. (2014) 'Cameron's family test is a charade. His policies crucify the one-earner couple with children', *The Conservative Woman* [online] Available at http://www.conservativewoman.co.uk/dr-patricia-morgan-camerons-family-test-charade-policies-crucify-one-earner-couple-children/ Accessed, 4/9/2017.

Murdock, G.P. (1949) *Social Structure*, Macmillan, New York.

Murray, C. (1984) *Losing Ground*, Basic Books, New York.

NatCen (2016) *British Social Attitudes Survey*. (2016) *British Social Attitudes 33, Technical Details*.

National Audit Office (2013) *Establishing Free Schools*, The Stationery Office, London.

National Child Development Study (2016) Institute of Education, University of London, London.

National Family Mediation (2013) 'Divorce no longer a social taboo in Britain as two-thirds say collapse of a marriage has no stigma attached' [online] http://www.nfm.org.uk/index.php/about-nfm/news/213-divorce-no-longer-a-social-taboo-in-britain-as-two-thirds-say-collapse-of-a-marriage-has-no-stigma-attached Accessed 7/06/2017.

National Union of Teachers (2016) *Free Schools*, EduFacts.

Ndaji, F., Little, J. and Coe, R. (2016) 'A comparison of academic achievement in independent and state schools', *Centre for Evaluation and Monitoring*, Durham University.

Nead, L. (1988) *Myths of Sexuality: Representations of Women in Victorian Britain*, Oxford, Blackwell.

Newburn, T. (2013) *Criminology*, 2nd edn, Routledge, London.

Norman, F., Turner, S., Granados, J., Schwarez, H., Green, H. and Harris, J. (1988) 'Look, Jane, look: anti-sexist initiatives in primary schools' in G. Weiner (eds) *Just a Bunch of Girls*, Open University Press, Milton Keynes.

Norman, P. (2016) 'The changing geography of deprivation in Great Britain, 1971–2011 and Beyond' in T. Champion and J. Falkingham, (eds) *Population Change in the United Kingdom*, Rowman and Littlefield, London.

Nuffield Foundation (2015) *High Take-up of Private Tuition by Primary School Pupils Revealed*, www.nuffieldfoundation.org.

Oakley, A. (1974) *Housewife*, Allen Lane, London.

Oakley, A. (1982) 'Conventional families' in Rapoport *et al.* (eds) (1982).

Oxfam (2016) 'Women spend two days a month more than men on housework and childcare in UK, survey finds' [online] Available at http://www.oxfam.org.uk/media-centre/press-releases/2016/03/women-spend-two-days-a-month-more-than-men-on-housework-and-childcare Accessed 8/07/2017.

ONS (2013) *Families and Households 2013* [online] Available at https://www.ons.gov.uk/peoplepopulationandcommunity/birthsdeathsandmarriages/families/bulletins/familiesandhouseholds/2013-10-31#living-alone

ONS (2013) 'Why has the fertility rate risen over the last decade in England and Wales?' [online] Available at http://webarchive.nationalarchives.gov.uk/20160106055455/http://www.gov.uk/ons/rel/vsob1/birth-summary-tables--england-and-wales/2011--final-/sty-fertility.html Accessed 9/07/17

ONS (2013) 'Cohort fertility' [online] Available at https://www.ons.gov.uk/peoplepopulationandcommunity/birthsdeathsandmarriages/conceptionandfertilityrates/bulletins/cohortfertility/2013-12-05#what-is-cohort-fertility Accessed 9/07/2017.

ONS (2014) 'Marriage statistics, cohabitation and cohort analyses [online] Available at https://www.ons.gov.uk/peoplepopulationandcommunity/birthsdeathsandmarriages/marriagecohabitationandcivilpartnerships/datasets/marriagestatisticscohabitationandcohortanalyses Accessed 2/06/2017.

ONS (2014) 'Adult smoking habits in Great Britain' [online] Available at https://www.ons.gov.uk/peoplepopulationandcommunity/healthandsocialcare/healthandlifeexpectancies/compendium/opinionsandlifestylesurvey/2015-03-19/adultsmokinghabitsingreatbritain2013 Accessed 01/08/2017.

ONS (2014) 'Mortality in the United Kingdom: 1983≠2013' [online] available at https://cy.ons.gov.uk/peoplepopulationandcommunity/birthsdeathsandmarriages/deaths/articles/mortalityintheunitedkingdom/19832013 Accessed 31/07/2017.

ONS (2015) 'Conception and fertility rates' [online] Available at https://www.ons.gov.uk/peoplepopulationandcommunity/birthsdeathsandmarriages/conceptionandfertilityrates Accessed 27/07/2017.

ONS (2015) 'Life expectancy at birth and aged 65' [online] Available at https://www.ons.gov.uk/peoplepopulationandcommunity/birthsdeathsandmarriages/lifeexpectancies/bulletins/lifeexpectancyatbirthandatage65bylocalareasinenglandandwales/2015-11-04 Accessed 31/07/2017.

ONS (2016) 'Annual survey of hours and earnings: 2016 provisional results' [online] Available at https://www.ons.gov.uk/employmentandlabour

market/peopleinwork/earningsandworkinghours/bulletins/annualsurveyofhoursandearnings/2016provisionalresults#gender-pay-differences Accessed 20/06/2017.

ONS (2016) 'Appendix tables: focus on violent crime and sexual offences' [online] Available at https://www.ons.gov.uk/peoplepopulationandcommunity/crimeandjustice/datasets/appendixtablesfocusonviolentcrimeandsexualoffences Accessed 25/06/2017.

ONS (2016) 'Civil partnerships in England and Wales, 2015' [online] Available at https://www.ons.gov.uk/peoplepopulationandcommunity/birthsdeathsandmarriages/marriagecohabitationandcivilpartnerships/bulletins/civilpartnershipsinenglandandwales/2015#main-points Accessed, 11/04/2017.

ONS (2016) 'Divorces in England and Wales 2014' [online] Available at https://www.ons.gov.uk/peoplepopulationandcommunity/birthsdeathsandmarriages/divorce/bulletins/divorcesinenglandandwales/2014 Accessed 3/6/2017.

ONS (2016) 'Domestic violence and abuse' [online] Available at https://www.gov.uk/guidance/domestic-violence-and-abuse Accessed 25/06/2017).

ONS (2016) 'Population estimates', [online] Available at https://www.ons.gov.uk/peoplepopulationandcommunity/populationandmigration/populationestimates Accessed 3/7/2017.

ONS (2016) 'Statistical bulletin: domestic abuse in England and Wales: year ending March 2016' [online] Available at https://www.ons.gov.uk/peoplepopulationandcommunity/crimeandjustice/bulletins/domesticabuseinenglandandwales/yearendingmarch2016#prevalence-of-domestic-abuse-from-the-crime-survey-for-england-and-wales Accessed 25/06/2017.

ONS (2016) 'Families and households in the UK' [online] Available at https://www.ons.gov.uk/peoplepopulationandcommunity/birthsdeathsandmarriages/families/bulletins/familiesandhouseholds/2016 Accessed 4/10/2017.

ONS (2016) 'Women shoulder the responsibility of unpaid work' [online] Available at http://visual.ons.gov.uk/the-valueof-your-unpaid-work/#calculator Accessed 28/06/2017.

ONS (2017) 'Deaths registered in England and Wales 2016' [online] Available at https://www.ons.gov.uk/peoplepopulationandcommunity/birthsdeathsandmarriages/deaths/bulletins/deathsregistrationsummarytables/2016 Accessed 31/07/2017.

ONS (2017) 'Marriages in England and Wales' 2014' [online] Available at https://www.ons.gov.uk/peoplepopulationandcommunity/birthsdeathsandmarriages/marriagecohabitationandcivilpartnerships/bulletins/marriagesinenglandandwalesprovisional/2014#marriages-between-opposite-sex-couples-rise-in-2014 Accessed 11/4/2017.

ONS (2017) 'Migration in the UK' [online] Available at https://www.ons.gov.uk/releases/migrationintheukfeb2017 Accessed 15/07/2017.

ONS (2017) 'Population estimates for UK: mid 2016' [online] Available at https://www.ons.gov.uk/peoplepopulationandcommunity/populationandmigration/populationestimates/bulletins/annualmidyearpopulation estimates/mid2016#uk-population-continues-to-grow-at-08-per-year Accessed 9/07/2017.

Oxfam (2016) 'Women spend two days a month more than men on housework and childcare in UK, survey finds' [online] Available at http://www.oxfam.org.uk/media-centre/press-releases/2016/03/women-spend-two-days-a-month-more-than-men-on-housework-and-childcare Accessed 8/07/3017.

Oakley, A. (1972) Sex, Gender and Society, Temple Smith, London. (1974) The Sociology of Housework, Martin Robertson, Oxford.

Oliver, P. (2010) The Student's Guide to Research Ethics, Open University Press, Maidenhead.

O'Connell Davidson, J. and Layder, D. (1994) Methods, Sex and Madness, Routledge, London.

O'Connor, H. and Madge, C. (2001) 'Cyber-mothers: Online synchronous interviewing using conferencing software', Sociological Research Online, vol. 5, no. 4.

Ofsted (2015) Annual Report.

ONS (Office for National Statistics) (2005) The National Statistics Socio-economic Classification: User Manual, Palgrave Macmillan, Basingstoke.

ONS (Office for National Statistics) (2017) Crime in England and Wales: Year Ending 2016, Office for National Statistics, London, 20 October.

ONS (Office for National Statistics) (2017) Household Disposable Income and Inequality in the UK: Financial Year Ending 2016, Office for National Statistics, London, 10 January.

Orgad, S. (2005) Storytelling Online: Talking Breast Cancer on the Internet, Peter Lang Publishing, Oxford.

Pahl, J. (1989) Money and Marriage, Macmillan, Basingstoke.

Pahl, J. (1993) 'Money, marriage and ideology: holding the purse strings', Sociology Review, vol. 3, no. 1.

Palmer, S. (2015) Toxic Childhood, How The Modern World is Damaging Our Children and What We Can do About It, Orion, London.

Papapolydorou, M. (2014) '"When you see a normal person …": social class and friendship networks among teenage students', British Journal of Sociology of Education, vol. 35, no. 4.

Park, A., Curtice, J., Thompson, K., Jarvis, L., and Bromley, C. (eds) (2001) British Social Attitudes: The 18th Report, Public Policy, Social Ties, Sage, London.

Park, A., Curtice, J., Thompson, K., Phillips, M., Johnson, M. and Clery, E. (eds) (2008) The British Social Attitudes Survey: 24th Annual Report, Sage, London.

Parker, M. (2000) Organisational Culture and Identity, Sage, London.

Parsons, T. (1951) The Social System, Free Press, New York. (1961) 'The school class as a social system' in Halsey et al. (eds).

Parsons, T. (1959) 'The social structure of the family' in R.N. Anshen (ed.) The Family: Its Functions and Destiny, Harper & Row, New York.

Parsons, T. (1965b) 'The normal American family' in S.M. Farber (ed.) Man and Civilization: The Family's Search for Survival, McGraw-Hill, New York.

Paton, G. (2012) 'Pupil premium "making little difference", say heads', The Telegraph, 1 May.

Pawson, R. (1989) 'Methodology' in M. Haralambos (ed), Developments in Sociology, vol. 5, Causeway Press, Ormskirk.

(1995) 'Methods of content/document/media analysis' in M. Haralambos (ed.), Developments in Sociology, vol. 11, Causeway Press, Ormskirk.

Payne, G. (2006) (ed.) (2006) Social Divisions, 2nd edn, Palgrave Macmillan, Basingstoke.

Pearce, C. (2006) Playing Ethnography: A Study of Emergent Behaviour in Online Games and Virtual Worlds, SMARTlab Centre, London.

(2009) Communities of Play: Emergent Cultures in Online Games and Virtual Worlds, MIT Press, Cambridge, MA.

Perraudin, F. (2017) 'Offenders in Rochdale child sexual abuse scandal "remain at large"'. The Guardian 16 May, 2017 [online] Available at https://www.theguardian.com/uk-news/2017/may/16/offenders-in-rochdale-child-sexual-abuse-scandal-remain-at-large Accessed 05/07/2017

Philo, G. and Miller, D. (2002) 'Circuits of communication and power: recent developments in media sociology' in M. Holborn (ed), Developments in Sociology, vol. 18, Causeway Press, Ormskirk.

Piff, K.P. et al. (2012) 'Higher social class predicts increased unethical behaviour', Proceedings of the National Academy of Sciences, vol. 109.

Pilcher, J. (1995) Age and Generation in Modern Britain, Oxford University Press, Oxford.

Pilger, J. (2014) 'Indigenous Australian families', The Guardian, 21 March.

Pilkington, A. (2003) Racial Disadvantage and Ethnic Diversity in Britain, Palgrave Macmillan, Basingstoke.

Platt, J. (1976) Realities of Social Research, Chatto & Windus, London.

Platt, L. (2009) Ethnicity and Family: Relationships within and between Ethnic Groups. An Analysis Using the Labour Force Survey, Equality and Human Rights Commission, London.

Postman, N. (1982) The Disappearance of Childhood, W.H. Allen, London.

Power, S., Edwards, T., Whitty, G. and Wigfall, V. (2003) Education and the Middle Class, Open University Press, Buckingham.

Prout, A. (2005) The Future of Childhood, Routledge Falmer, London.

Prout, A. and James, A. (1990) 'A new paradigm for the sociology of childhood?' in A. James and A. Prout (eds) (1990).

Pugsley, L. (2002) 'It's a white knuckle ride: reflections from the PhD experience' in G. Walford, (ed). Doing a Doctorate in Educational Ethnography, JAI, Amsterdam.

Punch, K.F. (2009) Introduction to Research Methods in Education, Sage, London.

Qureshi, K., Charsley, S. and Shaw, A. (2015) 'British Asians and Family Structure', Sociology Review, November.

Qvortrup, J. (1991) *Childhood as a Social Phenomenon: An Introduction to a Series of National Reports*, 2nd edn, European Centre for Social Welfare Policy and Research, Vienna.

Raghuram, P. and Erel, U. (2014) 'Migration: changing and connecting places' in J. Clarke and K. Woodward (eds) *Understanding Social Lives 2* The Open University, Milton Keynes.

Rampino, T. and Taylor, M. (2013) *Gender Differences in Educational Aspirations and Attitudes*, Institute for Social and Economic Research. (2015) 'The education gender gap', *Sociology Review*, vol. 24, no. 4.

Randall, V. (1987) *Women and Politics*, Palgrave Macmillan, Basingstoke.

Ranson, S. (1996) 'Markets or democracy for education' in J. Ahier, B. Cosin and M. Hales (eds) *Diversity and Change,* Routledge, London.

Rapoport, R. (1989) 'Ideologies about family forms – towards diversity' in K. Boh *et al.* (eds) *Changing Patterns of European Family Life*, Routledge, London.

Rapoport, R.N., Fogarty, M.P. and Rapoport, R. (eds) (1982) *Families in Britain*, Routledge & Kegan, London.

Reay, D. (1998) *Class Work: Mothers' Involvement in their Children's Primary Schooling*, UCL Press, London.

(2001) ' "Spice Girls", "Nice Girls", "Girlies" and "Tomboys": gender discourses, girls' cultures and femininities in the primary 'classroom', *Gender and Education*, vol. 13, no. 2.

(2006) 'The zombie stalking English schools: social class and educational inequality', *British Journal of Educational Studies*, vol. 54, no. 3. (2013) 'Social mobility, a panacea for austere times: tales of emperors, frogs and tadpoles', *British Journal of Sociology of Education*, vol. 34, no. 5–6.

Reay, D., David, M.E. and Ball, S.J. (2005) *Degrees of Choice: Class, Race, Gender and Higher Education*, Trentham Books, Stoke-on-Trent.

Reclaiming Schools (2017) *Progress 8 – Another Attack on Working-Class Schools,* Reclaiming Schools, 21 January.

Research Ethics Guidebook (2017) Institute of Education, University of London, London.

Resolution (2012) Census figures highlight risk to cohabiting couples [online] Available at http://www.resolution.org.uk/news-list.asp?page_id = 228&n_id = 192 Accessed 2/06/2017.

Reynolds, T. (2002) 'Re-analysing the Black family' in Carling *et al.* (eds) (2002).

Richardson, H. (2016) *Heads Hit Out over English Bacc 'League Tables'*, BBC News online, 4 February.

Rikowski, G. (2002) 'Globalisation and education: a paper prepared for the House of Lords Select Committee on Economic Affairs, Inquiry in the Global Economy', www.leeds.ac.uk/educol/documents/00001941.htm

(2005) 'In the dentist's chair: a response to Richard Hatcher's critique of *Habituation of the Nation* – Part One'. www.flowideas.co.uk/print.php?page = 147

Rist, R. (1970) 'Student social class and teacher expectations: the self-fulfilling prophecy in ghetto education', *Harvard Educational Review*, vol. 40, no. 3.

(2016) 'On understanding the processes of schooling: the contributions of labelling theory' in A. R. Sadovnik and R. W. Coughlan (eds).

Roberts, J, Williams, K. and Buchanan, A. (2013) 'Why are Women Having Fewer Babies? The Views of *Mumsnet* Users' in A. Buchanan and A. Rotkirch (eds) (2013) *Fertility Rates and Population Decline; No Time for Children?* Palgrave Macmillan, London.

Rollock, N., Gillborn, D., Vincent, C. and Ball, S.J. (2015) *The Colour of Class: The Educational Strategies of the Black Middle Classes*, Routledge, London.

Rose, G. (2012) *Visual Methodologies: An Introduction to Researching with Visual Materials* 3rd edn, Sage, London.

Rosen, H. (1974) *Language and Class*, 3rd edn, Falling Wall Press, Bristol.

Roseneil, S. (2005) 'Living and loving beyond the boundaries of the heteronorm: personal relationships in the 21st century' in McKie and Cunningham-Burley (eds) (2005).

Roseneil, S. (2016) 'Couples who live apart', *Sociology Review*, vol. 25, no. 3.

Rosenthal, R. and Jacobson, L. (1968) *Pygmalion in the Classroom: Teacher Expectation and Pupils' Intellectual Development*, Holt, Rinehart and Winston, Inc., New York.

Rosenthal, R. and Jacobson, L. (1968) *Pygmalion in the Classroom*, Holt, Rinehart & Winston, New York.

Ruppanner, L. (2012) 'Housework conflict and divorce: A multi-level analysis', *Work, Employment and Society,* vol. 26 no. 4.

Ruspini, E. (2015) *Gender, Relationships and Social Change,* Policy Press, Bristol.

(2002) 'Bourdieu and education: how useful is Bourdieu's theory for researchers? *The Netherlands' Journal of Social Sciences*, vol. 38, no. 2.

Sadovnik, A.R. and Coughlan, R.W. (eds) (2016) *Sociology of Education: A Critical Reader*, 3rd edn, Routledge, London.

Savage, M. (2015) *Social Class in the 21st Century*, Penguin Random House, UK.

Scholes, L. (2015) 'Clandestine Readers: boys and girls going "undercover" in school spaces', *British Journal of Sociology of Education*, vol. 36, no. 3.

Schools Network, *Specialist Schools and Academic Trust,* www.ssatrust.org.uk.

Seale, C. (2012) 'Sampling' in C. Seale (ed.) *Researching Society and Culture*, Sage, London.

Sewell, T. (1997) *Black Masculinities and Schooling*, Trentham Books, Stoke-on-Trent.

(2008) 'Racism is not the problem', *The Guardian*, 5 September.

Shain, F. (2010) 'Refusing to integrate: Asian girls and the experience of schooling' in C. Jackson, C. Paechter and E. Renold (eds) *Girls and Education 3–16: Continuing Concerns, New Agendas*, Open University Press, Maidenhead.

Sharpe, S. (1976) *'Just Like a Girl': How Girls Learn to be Women*, 2nd edn, Penguin, London.

Shaw, A. (2014) 'Ethnic diversity in the United Kingdom: family forms and conjugality' in. Treas, in J. Treas and J. Scott Richards (eds) *The Wiley-Blackwell Companion to the Sociology of the Family*, John Wiley, Oxford.

Sheeran, Y. (1993) 'The role of women and family structure', *Sociology Review*, April.

Shepherd, J. (2007) 'League tables', *The Guardian*, 11 January.

Shorter, E. (1976) *The Making of the Modern Family*, Penguin, Harmondsworth.

Silva E. and Smart C. (eds) (1999). (eds) (1999) *The New Family?* Sage, London.

Slack, A.K., Mangan, J., Hughes, A. and Davies, P. (2014) ' "Hot", "cold" and "warm" information and higher education decision-making', *British Journal of Sociology of Education*, vol. 35, no. 2.

Smart, C. (2007) *Personal Life*, Polity Press, Cambridge.

Smart, C. (2011) 'Close relationships and personal life', in May (ed.) (2011).

Smart, S. (2012) Feeling uncomfortable: young people's emotional responses to neo-liberal explanations for economic inequality, *Sociological Research Online*, 17(3). Accessed 16/5/17

Smith, T. and Noble, M. (1995) *Education Divides: Poverty and Schooling in the 1990s*, CPAG, London.

Social Mobility & Child Poverty Commission (2013) *State of the Nation 2013: Social Mobility and Child Poverty in Great Britain*, The Stationery Office, London.

Social Trends, Office for National Statistics, London.

Somerville, J. (2000) *Feminism and the Family: Politics and Society in the UK and USA*, Macmillan, Basingstoke.

Spender, D. (1982) *Invisible Women: The Schooling Scandal*, Writers and Readers Ltd, New York.

Stacey, J. (1996) *In the Name of the Family: Rethinking Family Values in the Postmodern Age*, Beacon Press, Boston, MA.

Stacey, J. (2011) *Unhitched: Love, Marriage and Family Values from West Hollywood to Western China*, New York University Press, New York.

Stands in Timber, J. and Liberty, M. (1967) *Cheyenne Memories*, Yale University Press, New Haven.

Stanko, E.A. (1988) 'Keeping women in and out of line: sexual harassment and occupational segregation' in S. Walby (ed.) *Gender Segregation at Work*, Open University Press, Milton Keynes.

Stanley, L. (2010) 'To the letter: Thomas and Znaniecki's *The Polish Peasant* and writing a life, sociologically speaking', *Life Writing*, vol. 7.

Stannard, K. (2013) 'Teach girls to disrupt, subvert and challenge authority – don't always praise their attentiveness', *Times Educational Supplement Online*, 13 June.

Stanworth, M. (1983) *Gender and Schooling*, Hutchinson, London.

(1984) 'Women and class analysis: a reply to John Goldthorpe', *Sociology*, vol. 18, no. 2.

Stewart, H. (2012) 'Fullfact confirms LSN analysis on academies', *Local Schools Network*, www.localschoolsnetwork.org.uk.

Stonewall (2016) 'Key dates for lesbian, gay, bi and trans equality' [online] Available at http://www.stonewall.org.uk/about-us/key-dates-lesbian-gay-bi-and-trans-equality Accessed 16/04/2017.

Strand, S. (2008) 'Minority ethnic pupils in the longitudinal study of young people in England: extension report on performance in public examinations at age 16', *DCSF Research Report*, DCSF-RR029.

(2014) 'Ethnicity, gender, social class and achievement gaps at age 16: intersectionality and "getting it" for the white working class', *Research Papers in Education*, vol. 29.

(2015) *Ethnicity, Deprivation and Educational Achievement at Age 16 in England: Trends Over Time*, Department for Education, London.

Sugarman, B. (1970) 'Social class, values and behaviour in schools' in M. Craft (ed.) *Family, Class and Education*, Longman, London.

Sullivan, A. (2001) 'Cultural capital and educational attainment', *Sociology*, vol. 35, no. 4.

Sutton Trust (2014) *Research Brief: Extra-curricular Inequality*, 4 September.

Swartz, D.L. (2003) 'From correspondence to contradiction and change: *Schooling in Capitalist America* revisited', *Sociological Forum*, vol. 18, no. 1.

Taylor, M. (2006) 'Guidelines ban covert pupil selection', *The Guardian*, 9 September.

Taylor, T.L. (2002), 'Living digitally: embodiment in virtual worlds' in R. Schroeder (ed.) *The Social Life of Avatars: Presence and Interaction in Shared Virtual Environments*, Springer-Verlag, London.

Temple-Malt, E. (2017) 'Civil partnerships and changing family relationships', *Sociology Review*, vol. 26, no. 3.

The Conservative Party Manifesto 2015 [online] Available at https://www.conservatives.com/manifesto2015 Accessed 20/12/2017.

The Telegraph (2014) 'Gay marriage will undermine family life sociologist warns', *The Telegraph* 4 March 2013 [online] Available at http://www.telegraph.co.uk/news/politics/9908951/Gay-marriage-will-destabilise-family-life-sociologist-warns.html Accessed 15/04/2017.

Thomas, W.I. and Znaniecki, F. (1958) *The Polish Peasant in Europe and America*, Dover, New York.

Thrupp, M. and Hursh, D. (2006) 'The limits of managerialist school reform: the case of target-setting in England and the USA' in H. Lauder *et al.* (eds) *Education, Globalisation and Social Change*, Oxford University Press, Oxford.

Tikly, L., Haynes, J., Caballero, C., Hill, J. and Gillborn, D. (2006) 'Evaluation of Aiming High: African Caribbean Achievement Project', *DFES Research Report RR801*.

Tong, R. (2016) *Feminist Thought: A More Comprehensive Introduction*, 4th edn, Westview Press, North Carolina.

Torrance, H. (2006) 'Globalising empiricism: what, if anything, can be learned from international comparisons of educational achievement?' in H. Lauder *et al.* (eds), *Education, Globalisation and Social Change*, Oxford University Press, Oxford.

Tranter, N.L. (1996) *British Population in the Twentieth Century*, Macmillan, London.

Treas, J. and Tsui-o T. (2011) 'How couples manage the household: work and power in cross-national perspective', *Journal of Family Issues*, 4 December, 2011.

Trowler, P. (2003) *Education Policy*, 2nd edn, Routledge, London.

Tufail, W. (2015) 'Rotherham, Rochdale, and the racialised threat of the "Muslim Grooming Gang"' *International Journal for Crime, Justice and Social Democracy*, vol. 4, no. 3.

Vaughan, R. (2016) 'GCSE results: pioneering free schools report promising scores', *Times Educational Supplement*, 25 August.

Venkatesh, S. (2009) *Gang Leader for a Day*, Penguin, London.

Vincent, J.A. (1995) *Inequality and Old Age*, UCL Press, London.

Vogler, C., Brockmann, M. and Wiggins, R.D. (2007) 'Managing money in new heterosexual forms of intimate relationships', *Journal of Socio-Economics*, vol. 37, no. 2.

Walby, S. (1990) *Theorizing Patriarchy*, Blackwell, Oxford.

Waldfogel, J. and Washbrook, E. (2010) *Low Income and Early Cognitive Development in the U.K.*, Sutton Trust, London.

Walford, G. (1993) 'Researching the City Technology College Kingshurst' in R. Burgess (ed.) *Research Methods*, Nelson, London.

Walford, G. (2001) *Doing Qualitative Educational Research: A Personal Guide to the Research Process*, Continuum, London.

Walklate, S. (2000) 'Researching victims' in R.D. King and E. Wincup (eds), *Doing Research on Crime and Justice*, Oxford University Press, Oxford.

Wallace, G., Rudduck, J. and Harris, S. (1994) 'Students' secondary school careers: research in a climate of "Moving perspectives"', in D. Halpin and B. Troyna, (eds) *Researching Education Policy: Ethical and methodological issues*, The Falmer Press, London.

Walters, S. (2012) *Ethnicity, Race and Education: An Introduction*, Continuum, London.

Ward, M.R.M. (2015) *From Labouring to Learning: Working-class Masculinities, Education and De-industrialization*, Palgrave Macmillan, Basingstoke.

Ward, M.R.M. (2015) *From Labouring to Learning: Working-Class Masculinities, Education and De-industrialisation*, Palgrave Macmillan, Basingstoke.

Weale, S. (2016) 'Teachers in deprived schools "more likely to be inexperienced"', *The Guardian*, 9 March.

Weber, M. (1958) *The Protestant Ethic and the Spirit of Capitalism*, The Free Press, New York.

Weeks, J., Donovan, C. and Heaphey, B. (1999) 'Everyday experiments: narratives of non-heterosexual relationships' in Silva and Smart (eds) (1999).

Wells, K. (2015) *Childhood in Global Perspective*, 2nd edn, Polity Press, Cambridge.

Whitty, G. (2002) *Making Sense of Education Policy*, Sage, London.

Whyte, W.F. (1955) *Street Corner Society*, 2nd edn, University of Chicago Press, Chicago.

Wiliam, D. (2016) *Wales Pisa Results: Little will be Learned*, BBC News online, 4 December.

Wilkinson, R. and Marmot, M. (2003) *Social Determinants of Health*, 2nd edn, WHO, Copenhagen.

Williams, D. *et al.* (2009) 'The virtual census: representations of gender, race and age in video games', *New Media & Society*, vol. 11, no. 5.

Williams, J. (2016) 'Adults not leaving home', *Sociology Review*, vol. 26, no. 1.

Williams, W.L. (1991) *The Spirit and the Flesh: Sexual Diversity in American Indian Culture*, Beacon Press, Boston.

Willis, P. (1977) *Learning to Labour*, Saxon House, Farnborough.

Willmott, P. (1988) 'Urban kinship past and present', *Social Studies Review*, November.

Wintour, P. (2011) 'David Cameron unveils £448 million plan to help "problem families"', *The Guardian*, 5 December 2011 [online] Available at https://www.theguardian.com/politics/2011/dec/15/david-cameron-plan-problem-families Accessed 15/04/2017.

Wintour, P. (2012) 'Coalition's child poverty advisor: bring back EMA', *The Guardian*, 18 October.

WISE (2016) *Annual Report, 2015–2016*, www.wisecampaign.org.uk.

Wyness, M. (2006) *Childhood and Society*, Palgrave Macmillan, Basingstoke.

Wyness, M. (2012) *Childhood and Society: An Introduction to the Sociology of Childhood*, 2nd edn, Palgrave Macmillan, Basingstoke.

Young, M. and Willmott, P. (1961) *Family and Kinship in East London*, Penguin, Harmondsworth.

Young, M. and Willmott, P. (1973) *The Symmetrical Family*, Penguin, Harmondsworth.

Younger, M. (2014) 'The gender and education agenda in the United Kingdom, 1988–2013 – the ever-turning wheel' in Dhar, D. (ed.) *Education and Gender* Bloomsbury Academic, London.

Zaretsky, E. (1976) *Capitalism, the Family and Personal Life*, Pluto Press, London.

Zwysen, W. and Longhi, S. (2016) *Labour Market Disadvantage of Ethnic Minority British Graduates: Univeristy Choice, Parental Background or Neighbourhood?* Institute for Social and Economic Research.

INDEX

PERMISSIONS ACKNOWLEDGEMENTS

The publishers gratefully acknowledge the permission granted to reproduce the copyright material in this book. Every effort has been made to trace copyright holders and to obtain their permission for the use of copyright material. The publishers will gladly receive any information enabling them to rectify any error or omission at the first opportunity.

Images: (l = left, r = right, t = top, b = bottom)

Cover weedezign/Shutterstock, p.1 Michele Burgess/Alamy Stock Photo, p.2 Matt Timson, p.3 Michele Burgess/Alamy Stock Photo, p.4(r) National Anthropological Archives/Smithsonian Institution, p.4(l) Indian Photo Agency/REX/Shutterstock, p.5 BBC Photo Library, p.7(l) National Anthropological Archives/Smithsonian Institution, p.7(r) National Anthropological Archives/Smithsonian Institution, p.11(t) Matt Timson, p.11(b) Matt Timson, p.13 Matt Timson, p.14(t) Matt Timson, p.14(b) Anyka/Alamy Stock Photo, p.15 Ron Sachs-Pool/ Getty Images, p.18(t) Matt Timson, p.18(b) Matt Timson, p.20 Barry Diomede/Alamy Stock Photo, p.22 David Handschuh/NY Daily News Archive/Getty Images, p.23 Barry Diomede/Alamy Stock Photo, p.24(l) Photofusion/ REX/Shutterstock, p.24(r) Jamie Jones/REX/Shutterstock, p.27 Photo 12/Alamy Stock Photo, p.28 Jonathan Goldberg/Alamy Stock Photo, p.30 Trinity Mirror/Mirrorpix/Alamy Stock Photo, p.34 Public domain, p.36(t) Andrew Parsons/REX/Shutterstock, p.36(l) BasPhoto/Shutterstock, p.36(r) Featureflash Photo Agency / Shutterstock.com, p.40 Robert Daemmrich Photography/Corbis/Getty Images, p.41 The World Bank, p.42 Quinton Winter, p.46 Matt Timson, p.51 Matt Timson, p.56 GeoPic/Alamy Stock Photo, p.59 Mark Smith-Belt/Alamy Stock Photo, p.64 Matt Timson, p.65 Matt Timson, p.72 Alexey Fedorenko/Shutterstock, p.72 Edmund/ Shutterstock, p.76(l) Matt Timson, p.76(r) Matt Timson, p.82 Matt Timson, p.84 Matt Timson, p.86 Matt Timson, p.86 Matt Timson, p.87 Creative Lab/Shutterstock, p.90(l) Matt Timson, p.90(r) Matt Timson, p.92 Matt Timson, p.97 The Arran Alexander Collection, p.100 Matt Timson, p.102(l) Catchlight Visual Services/ Alamy Stock Photo, p.102(r) Rades/Shutterstock, p.106 Solis Images/Shutterstock, p.111 Kzwnon/Alamy Stock Photo, p.113 JGI/Tom Grill, p.117 Matt Timson, p.121 rawpixel.com/Shutterstock, p.125 Matt Timson, p.126 Matt Timson, p.133 GaudiLab/Shutterstock, p.135(t) Philip Oldman/BPI/REX/Shutterstock, p.135(b) Matt Timson, p.137(l) Matt Timson, p.137(r) Matt Timson, p.138 Matt Timson, p.141 Matt Timson, p.144 Matt Timson, p.145 Matt Timson, p.146(l) Matt Timson, p.146(r) Matt Timson, p.147(l) Matt Timson, p.147(r) Matt Timson, p.150(l) Matt Timson, p.150(r) Matt Timson, p.153 Matt Timson, p.154 Matt Timson, p.156 Matt Timson, p.160 Matt Timson, p.161 Matt Timson, p.162 Matt Timson, p.163 Matt Timson, p.165 Matt Timson, p.165 Matt Timson, p.169(t) Matt Timson, p.169(b) Matt Timson, p.174 Matt Timson, p.176 By John Taylor (1578–1653) [Public domain], via Wikimedia Commons, p.177 Image courtesy of The Advertising Archives, p.178(l) Matt Timson, p.178(r) Matt Timson, p.178(b) Matt Timson, p.180(l) World History Archive/ Alamy Stock Photo, p.180(r) World History Archive/Alamy Stock Photo, p.181(t) Tribune Content Agency LLC/ Alamy Stock Photo, p.181(b) Debby Wong/Shutterstock, p.184 Matt Timson, p.185 Matt Timson, p.187 Matt Timson, p.190 MonkeyBusiness Images/Shutterstock, p.192 Matt Timson, p.195 MonkeyBusiness Images/ Shutterstock, p.196 MonkeyBusiness Images/Shutterstock, p.200 Matt Timson, p.203 DGImages/Shutterstock, p.204 Matt Timson, p.207 Matt Timson, p.211 Uber Images/Shutterstock, p.214 Matt Timson, p.217 Matt Timson, p.218 kilukilu/Shutterstock, p.220 wavebreakmedia/Shutterstock, p.222 Matt Timson, p.225 Matt Timson, p.227 bipiphoto/Shutterstock, p.232 Monkey Business Images/Shutterstock, p.235 Hemis/ Alamy Stock Photo, p.236 wong sze yuen/Shutterstock, p.238 Print Collector/Contributor, p.239 Daxiao Productions/Shutterstock, p.240 Ateam/Shutterstock, p.243 Hindustan Times/Contributor, p.245 Peter Marshall/ Alamy Stock Photo, p.246 Matt Timson, p.247 Ateam/Shutterstock, p.248 Women in Economic Decision Making/Wikimedia Commons, p.249 Lopolo/Shutterstock, p.252(l) BushaPhoto/Shutterstock, p.252(r) Matt Timson, p.254 Dan Kosmayer/Shutterstock, p.256 Uladzik Kryhin/Shutterstock, p.258 Michael Kovac/Contributor, p.259(l) Monkey Business Images/Shutterstock, p.259(r) C. Smart, p.263 Pictures Ltd/Corbis/Getty Images, p.264 Photofusion Picture Library/Alamy Stock Photo, p.267 Trinity Mirror/Mirrorpix/Alamy Stock Photo, p.269 Mark Richardson/Alamy Stock Photo, p.272 Photographee.eu/Shutterstock, p.273(r) Guy Bell/Alamy, p.273(l) Traditional Family Property, p.275 Stockfour/Shutterstock, p.276 Pressmaster/Shutterstock, p.278

Elizabeth Beck Gernsheim, p.280(l) Frank Chmura/Alamy Stock Photo, p.280(r) keith morris/Alamy Stock Photo, p.283 ONS, p.284 Photographee.eu/Shutterstock, p.286 Luke Peters/Alamy Stock Photo, p.289 Monkey Business Images/Shutterstock, p.292 ONS, p.295 Dmytro Zinkevych/Shutterstock, p.296 ONS, p.297 ONS, p.300 Vgstockstudio/Shutterstock, p.304 Slaven Vlasic/Contributor, p.308 Ekaterina Iatcenko/Shutterstock, p.310 Jamie Wilson/Shutterstock, p.311 Monkey Business Images/Shutterstock, p.312 bbernard/Shutterstock, p.313 Drpixel/Shutterstock, p.316 ONS, p.319 Licensed under the Open Government Licence v3.0, p.321 A. Prout and A. James , p.323 Image Source/Alamy Stock Photo, p.324 By Anthonius or Antoon Claeissins (www. weissgallery.com) [Public domain], via Wikimedia Commons, p.327 Corepics VOF/Shutterstock, p.329 Monkey Business Images/Shutterstock, p.330 p_ponomarera/Shutterstock, p.331 Jeff J Mitchel/Getty, p.335 Oliver Clarke, p.337(t) ONS, p.337(b) ONS, p.340 Clifford Norton/Alamy Stock Photo, p.342 ONS, p.343 ONS, p.345 Mary Turner/Stringer, p.346 ONS, p.349 MICHAEL CAMPANELLA/Contributor, p.350 YuG/Shutterstock, p.352 Philip Game/Alamy Stock Photo, p.356 bipiphoto/Shutterstock.

Text:

Extracts on pp.27, 28 from *Schooling in Capitalist America* by Samuel Bowles and Herbert Gintis, Haymarket Books, 2011, pp.9, 12, 137. First published by Basic Books, NY. Republished with permission of Hachette Books Group, and conveyed through Copyright Clearance Center, Inc.; Extracts on pp.29–31, 201 from *Learning to Labour: How working class kids get working class jobs* by Paul Willis, Columbia University Press, copyright © Paul Willis 1977. Reproduced by permission of Taylor & Francis Books UK; An extract on p.33 about Nord Anglia Education, www.nordangliaeducation.com; Extracts on pp.35, 81, 82 from 'The forms of capital' by Pierre Bourdieu published in *Sociology of Education: A Critical Reader 3rd edn*, eds. A. R. Sadovnik and R. W. Coughlan, Routledge, 2016, pp.83–96. Reproduced by permission of Taylor and Francis Group LLC, a division of Informa plc; Extracts on p.37 from "Is it right that public schools have charitable status?" by Carole Cadwalladr and Charlotte Vere, *The Guardian*, 29/11/2014, copyright © Guardian News and Media Ltd, 2017; An extract on p.56 from "Stop whingeing you spoilt little brats – and get a paper round!" by Jan Moir, *The Daily Mail*, 21/01/2011, http://www.dailymail.co.uk, copyright © Solo Syndication, 2011; Extracts on p.63 from "Decades of investment in education have not improved social mobility" by Prof John Goldthorpe, *The Observer*, 13/03/2016, copyright © Guardian News and Media Ltd, 2017; An extract on p.64 from "Theresa May's speech on grammar schools" *New Statesman*, 09/09/2016, http://www.newstatesman.com/, copyright © New Statesman Limited; An extract on p.64 adapted from "Grammar school plans are divisive and stupid, says Michael Morpurgo" by Michael Morpurgo, *The Guardian*, 14/09/2016, copyright © Guardian News and Media Ltd, 2017; An extract on p.64 from "John Prescott: Theresa May wants to go back to telling 11-year-olds they're failures and I'm bloody angry", *The Mirror*, 10/09/2016, copyright © Mirrorpix 2016; Extracts on p.85 from *Class Strategies and the Education Market: The Middle Classes and Social Advantage* by Stephen J. Ball, Routledge, 2003, pp.64, 168. Reproduced with permission; Extracts on pp.91, 92 from 'The Zombie Stalking English Schools: Social Class and Educational Inequality' by Diane Reay in *British Journal of Educational Studies*, 2006 pp.288–307, Taylor & Francis. Reproduced with permission of Taylor & Francis Ltd, http://www.tandfonline.com; Extracts on pp.245, 246 from *The Whole Woman* by Germaine Greer, Doubleday 1999, Anchor Books 2000, copyright © Germaine Greer, 1999. Reproduced with permission from Aitken Alexander Associates, Random House Group Limited and Alfred A. Knopf, an imprint of the Knopf Doubleday Publishing Group, a division of Penguin Random House LLC. All rights reserved; Extracts on pp.98, 207 from *Boys, Girls and Achievement: Addressing the Classroom Issues* by Becky Francis, Routledge, 2000, pp.11, 27–28. Reproduced with permission; An extract on p.101 about the WISE Campaign, https://www.wisecampaign.org.uk. Reproduced with permission; An extract on p.102 from a Facebook post by Rheann MacLaren on 28/04/2016, https://www.facebook.com. Reproduced with kind permission of Rheann MacLaren; Table 2.5.3 on p.108 'HE participation at age 18 or 19 amongst the cohorts taking their GCSEs 2003 to 2008, by ethnic group' in *Ethnic Minorities Substantially More Likely to go to University then their White British Peers* by Claire Crawford and Ellen Greaves, Institute for Fiscal Studies, November 2015, Fig. 18, www.ifs.org.uk/publications/8042. Reproduced with permission; An extract on p.112 from "Racism is not the problem" by Tony Sewell, *The Guardian*, 05/09/2008, copyright © Guardian News and Media Ltd, 2017; An extract on p.118 from 'Educational capital as a catalyst for upward social mobility amongst British Asians: a three generational analysis' by Tehmina N. Basit in *British Educational Research Journal*, Vol. 39 (4), 2013, pp.714–732, John Wiley & Sons, copyright © 2012 British Educational Research Association; An extract on p.121 from *The Making of*